S0-AVB-893

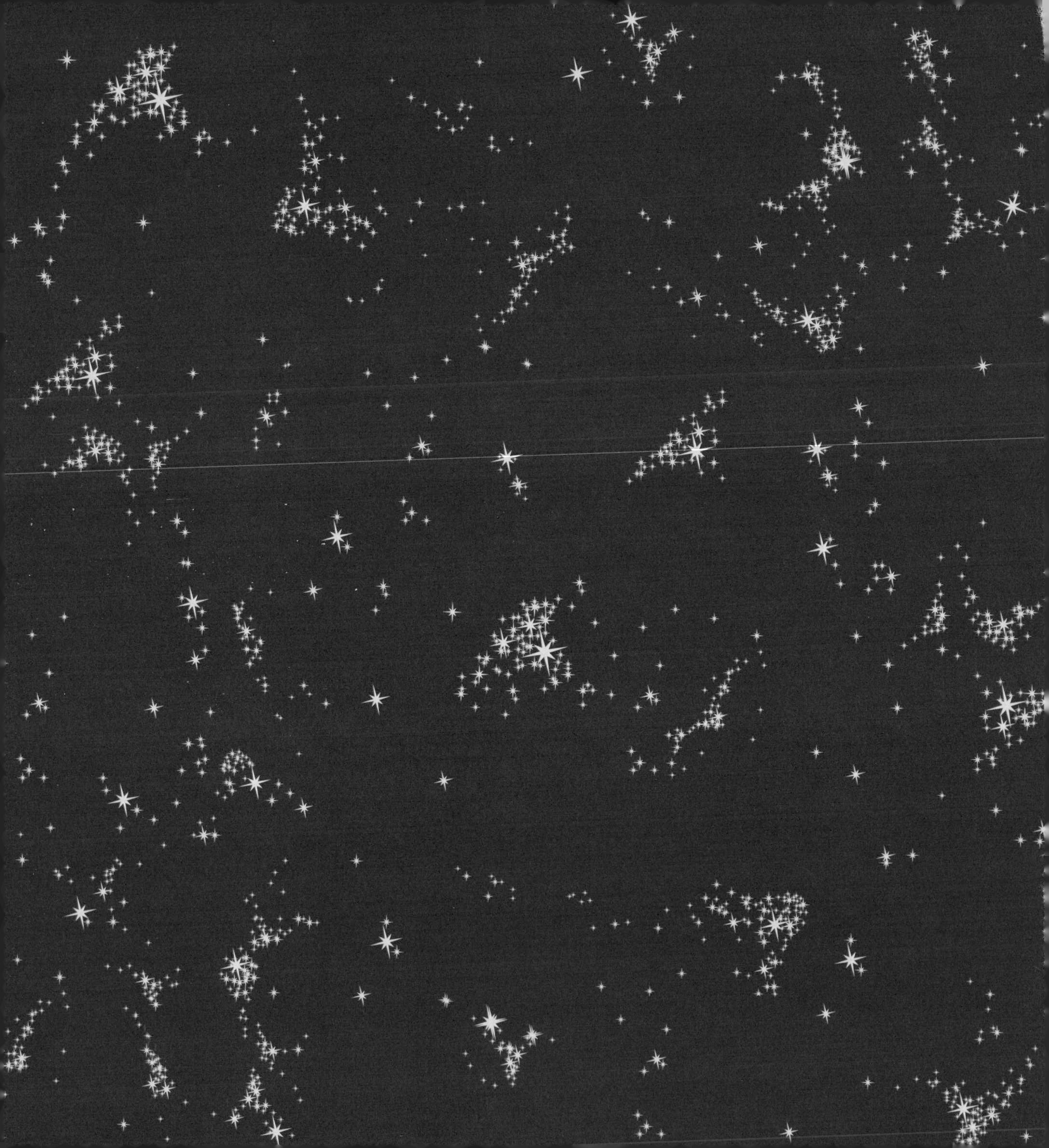

1001 SPELLS

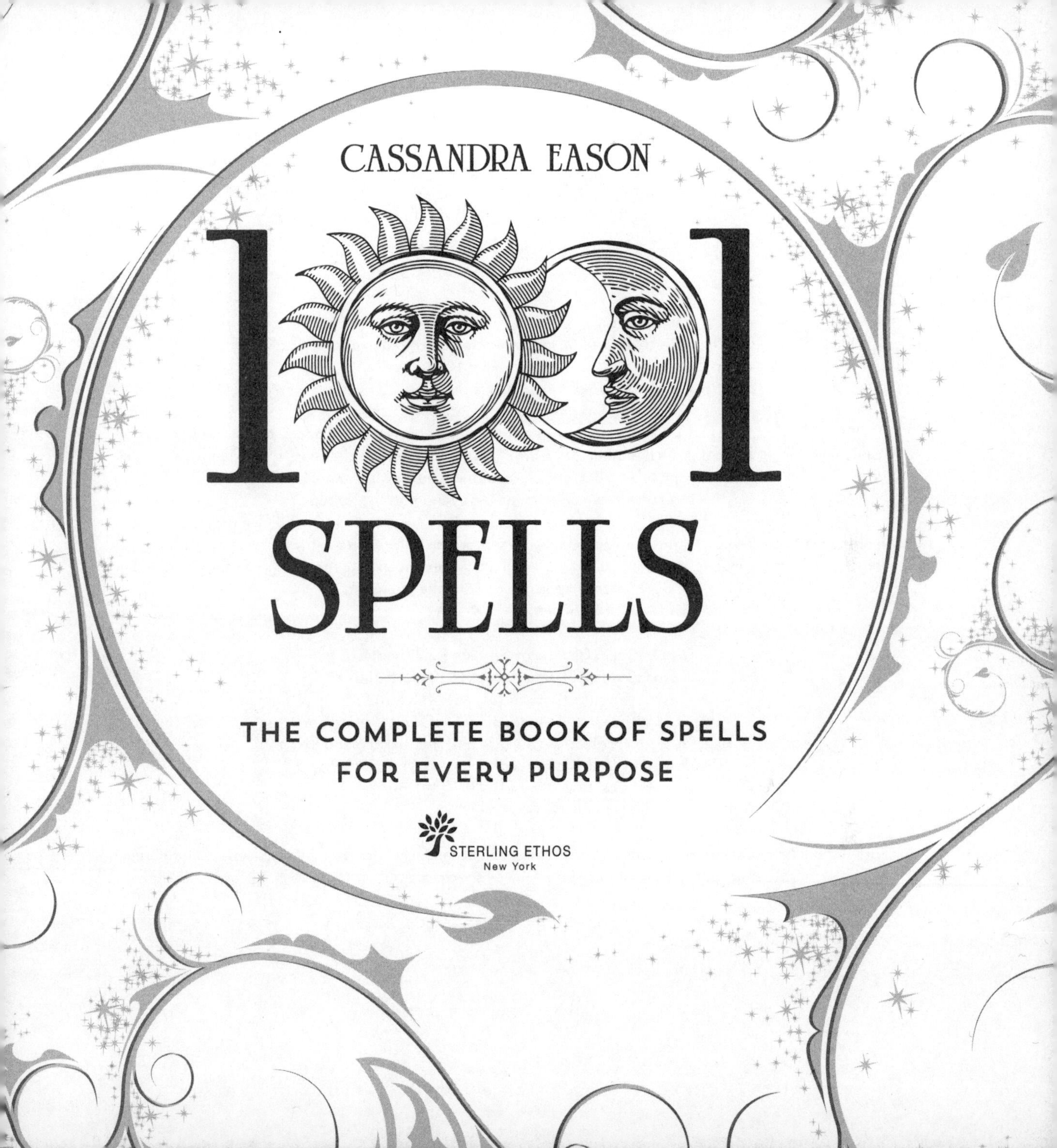

CASSANDRA EASON

101 SPELLS

THE COMPLETE BOOK OF SPELLS FOR EVERY PURPOSE

STERLING ETHOS
New York

STERLING ETHOS
New York

An Imprint of Sterling Publishing Co., Inc.
1166 Avenue of the Americas
New York, NY 10036

Photo Credits: Courtesy the author: 521; Dreamstime.com: © Lestyan (sun/moon): cover, throughout; Shutterstock: 519 bottom, © Architecteur: 30, © art_of_sun: 204, © Fejas: 13, 519 top, © JARADIgyula: cover, © Kenshi991: 520 bottom, © pixeldreams.eu: cover, © tan_tan: 4; Courtesy Wikimedia Foundation: AnonMoos: 520 top

ISBN 978-1-4549-1741-0

Distributed in Canada by Sterling Publishing Co., Inc.
c/o Canadian Manda Group, 664 Annette Street
Toronto, Ontario, Canada M6S 2C8
Distributed in the United Kingdom by GMC Distribution Services
Castle Place, 166 High Street, Lewes, East Sussex, England BN7 1XU
Distributed in Australia by Capricorn Link (Australia) Pty. Ltd.
P.O. Box 704, Windsor, NSW 2756, Australia

For information about custom editions, special sales, and premium and corporate purchases, please contact Sterling Special Sales at 800-805-5489 or specialsales@sterlingpublishing.com.

Manufactured in the United States of America

16

www.sterlingpublishing.com

DEDICATION

To my beloved children Tom, Jade, Jack, Miranda, and Bill, and my grandchildren, Freya and Holly, who have all helped me through serious illness this year to finish this book. To John Gold, my subeditor, protector, and mentor; and Konnie Gold, my inspiration and wonderful friend; to dearest Debbie, my website guru; and my Goddess daughter Caitlin Waller, with whom I tried out many of the spells; and, not least, to Kate Zimmermann, my editor who has kept faith with me as I have written my way back to health.

CONTENTS

INTRODUCTION

Welcome to *1001 Spells*, the culmination of forty years of research and spell casting. The book contains a few of my old tried-and-tested spells, which cannot be changed without losing their essence. But by far the majority of the spells in this book are brand-new or total rewrites of earlier spells in new formats that have worked far better than the originals.

Here you will find everything from love rituals to spells to combat those who play mind games at work, from selling your home fast and profitably to making money from your long-hidden creative talents, from removing nasty spirits to countering the intentions of those who are jealous of you and wish you ill, from old Egyptian rites made new to modern computer spells. The terms *rituals* and *spells* are used interchangeably, since both, in essence, mean following a formula to achieve a particular aim.

Each spell will tell you what you will need to carry it out or cast it—all simple materials you'll find in your kitchen cupboards, the garden, the supermarket, or online; the best time to cast the spell; and step-by-step instructions to guide you from the beginning to the days and weeks after the spell to ensure that the spell's effects last.

If a spell does not feel quite right for your circumstances or you cannot get a particular ingredient, crystal, or candle color, then make substitutes to fit with your lifestyle and needs. Spells are templates, formats to guide you; they are not written in stone. So change the words and actions until they feel right for you. We all possess the innate powers to work magick. If in doubt, white will substitute for any color, clear quartz for any crystal, and lavender for any fragrance.

Each spell follows sound magical practices, harms no one, and if it is banishing something or someone destructive from your life or the life of a loved one, will remove or bind the bad behavior or danger caused to you or your loved ones without hurting the perpetrator. Such justice is for karma, though, sometimes by showing people in their true light, earthly justice will swiftly follow.

If you want to know more about how magick works or why I have chosen particular days or times for a spell, read my *Book of Shadows*, published by Sterling Ethos, which has plenty of blank pages for you to write your own adaptations of your favorite spells. If you want to delve even more deeply into the realms of magick, take one of my step-by-step magick or psychic development online courses, available at my website: www.cassandraeason.com.

Use the index as well as the different sections to find exactly the right spell, and after a short time you will notice that your personally created spells, based on mine, come quite naturally into your mind, and you are creating your own magick.

Above all, enjoy magick and don't worry if you go counterclockwise instead of clockwise or a candle won't light. True magick comes from the heart, soul, and mind, and if you work with good intentions and the spell really matters to you, there is no wizard in the sky to mark you on a scale of 1 to 10.

This book has been a huge undertaking for me because in the middle of writing it I became seriously ill and needed major surgery. But as I inched my way back to health, I had a notebook and a pen smuggled into the hospital (I was banned from using my computer) and my darkest hours were illuminated by creating beautiful spells filled with hope and promise. Here I am, six months later, having completed the culmination of my research as well as a major step on my life's journey.

So enjoy the book and you will hear me in every word, teaching you what I love so passionately—magick—the power to make a difference in our lives and the world.

Cassandra Eason

CHAPTER 1

LOVE MAGICK

Here are spells for attracting new love; rebuilding trust if you have been betrayed; finding your twin soul; increasing love and commitment; sustaining marriage; living together with lasting love; ensuring fidelity; restoring passion; reconciling; and ending love peacefully.

SECTION 1: FINDING NEW LOVE

1

A LOVE-CALLING SPELL

You will need:

One green candle
Your favorite piece of jewelry
One rose or lavender incense stick in a holder

Timing:
Fridays

The Spell

- Put the jewelry in front of the candle.
- Light the candle, look into the flame, and say: *I call my love to find me and stay with me faithfully and lovingly as long as the sun shines and the waters of the earth flow.*
- If you already know who the person is, refer to him or her by name throughout the spell.
- Light the incense stick from the candle and write the same words in the air over the candle and jewelry, using the incense stick as a smoke pen.
- Pass the jewelry in a clockwise direction three times above the candle flame and repeat the same words.
- Blow out the candle, repeating the same words once more.
- Wear the jewelry whenever you go on a date or to a place where you hope to meet someone new.
- Cast the spell again any Friday you wish to keep the energies flowing.

2

FOR CALLING YOUR TWIN SOUL, KNOWN OR UNKNOWN

You will need:

Six pink candles in a circle
A pink or red rose
A heatproof dish half filled with soil

Timing:
Fridays

The Spell

- Before lighting, trace the following sentence with the index finger of your dominant hand on one side of each candle: *Come to me, my twin soul, come swiftly and stay with me everlastingly and faithfully.*
- Light the candle you wrote on first, repeating the words aloud.
- Light each candle in turn, repeating the words at each lighting.
- Take a petal from the rose, holding it briefly in the flame of the first candle you lit. As it singes, repeat the words again.
- Drop the singed petal into the dish.
- Burn another petal in each candle in turn, repeating the words and actions.
- Drop each singed petal in the dish of soil.
- Hold the dish of burned petals above the center of the circle of candles, repeating the words once more.
- Blow out the candle circle as fast as you can.
- Bury the singed petals outdoors and scatter the remaining petals plucked from the rose.

3

A VICTORIAN MIRROR SPELL

You will need:

A mirror large enough to see yourself in
A floral-scented candle
A hairbrush

Timing:
Midnight

The Spell

- Just before midnight, light the candle. Make sure the light is reflecting in the mirror.
- At midnight, gaze into the mirror, brushing your hair gently and rhythmically. Count silently to 100.
- At 100, continue brushing, whispering continuously these age-old words: *Come my lover, come to me, over river, over sea, over mountains, far or near, in this looking glass appear.*
- When you are in a dream state, put down the brush, touch the mirror with your lips, and close your eyes.
- Open your eyes slowly and blink. Behind you, reflected in the glass, you may momentarily see the face of the one who will love you in the future or someone you have met already.
- If you see nothing, shut your eyes again, count to 100 quickly, and imagine the candlelit mirror in your mind.
- Blow out the candle. Your lover's image will come into your mind.

4

A TRADITIONAL CRESCENT MOON SPELL TO ATTRACT NEW LOVE

You will need:

A map of your city or country or of the world for a cosmopolitan lover
One box of pins
One magnet

Timing:
Any night from crescent moon until full moon

The Spell

- Scatter the pins over the map, saying, *Near and far o'er land and sea, a lover true, I call to me.*
- Circle the magnet clockwise over the map, collecting all the pins.
- Say continuously, *So do I draw love to me, as pin to magnet joined are we. So I call my lover true, come before the next moon is new.*
- Put the pins in the unlidded box with the magnet inside on top of the unfolded map near a window.
- On the night of the full moon, leave a silver candle to burn so that candlelight and moonlight shine on the box.
- Leave everything in place until love comes or repeat at the next new moon, whichever comes sooner.

5

AN ANCIENT EGYPTIAN SEVEN DAUGHTERS OF HATHOR LOVE-KNOT RITUAL TO ATTRACT AND KEEP LASTING LOVE

You will need:

Seven red ribbons of equal length, one for each daughter of the love goddess Hathor
A red candle

Timing:
The hour before sunset

The Spell

- Light the candle, placing the ribbons one in front of the other next to it.
- Tie the nearest two ribbons (ribbons 1 and 2) together with a knot. As you do so, say: *Daughters of Hathor, I ask that my true love may find me and stay with me lovingly. Mother Hathor, guide the way.*
- Tie the third ribbon to the second, repeating the words.
- Do this for each ribbon, tying the fourth to the third, the fifth to the fourth, the sixth to the fifth, and finally the seventh to the sixth. Each time, repeat the words.
- Let the candle burn through. Set the chain of ribbons on your bedroom window overnight.
- In the morning, tie it to a tree and repeat the chant seven times.

6

TO FIND NEW LOVE, ESPECIALLY AFTER BETRAYAL OR IF YOU HAVE LOST CONFIDENCE IN YOURSELF

You will need:

Two green, pink, or white candles
Your favorite fragrance

Timing:
Before going out socially or logging on to a dating site

The Spell

- Place the fragrance between the candles.
- Light the left candle, saying: *I call my love to find me this night.*
- Light the right candle, repeating the words once more.
- Pass the fragrance bottle around each candle, left first, nine times: three times clockwise, three times counterclockwise, and three times clockwise again.
- As you do this, say three times: *I call my love in fragrance and in fire to find me this night.*
- Put a drop of the fragrance in the center of your brow, on the base of your throat, and on each inner wrist. Repeat the words, *I call my love in fragrance and in fire to find me this night.*
- Return the bottle to its place, blow softly into each flame, and whisper, *Come, love, and find me this night.* Do not blow the candles out while doing this.
- Blow out each candle in turn, repeating, Come, *love, find me and stay with me.*

7

A ROSE QUARTZ HEART TWIN-SOUL RITUAL IF YOU NEVER SEEM TO MEET THE RIGHT PERSON

You will need:

One pink candle
Matching rose quartz hearts set in front of a candle
Dried or fresh rose petals in a bowl
One pink drawstring bag

Timing:
Any Friday

The Spell

- Light the candle, and say, *My willing heart I give to you, a heart so gentle, heart so true, come love and find me.*
- Scatter rose petals in a heart shape around the candle and quartz hearts, saying continuously, *Like moth to flame, butterfly to flower, I call true love now at this hour.*
- Put the crystals and some rose petals in the drawstring bag, repeating both chants.
- Close the bag and pass it nine times clockwise over the candle, still chanting. When you finish the final chant, blow out the candle.
- Carry the bag with you when you go out on dates or to meet new people.

8

A SLAVIC LOVE WISH RITUAL TO BRING THE RIGHT LOVE IF YOU HAVE BEEN ALONE FOR A WHILE

You will need:

A large silver-colored bucket or glass bowl half filled with water
Seven small moonstones or small pure white stones

Timing:
A bright full moon night or the nights before or after the full moon

The Spell

- Position the bucket or glass bowl to catch the image of the moon or moonlight within it.
- Gaze into the silver light, and say: *Father Moon, I would not hold you captive a moment longer than I need. Send to me my lasting gentle love and go on your way with blessings.*
- Drop the moonstones into the water one at a time, repeating the words for each stone.
- Thank Father Moon and leave the water all night in the moonlight.
- In the morning, pour the water into small glass bottles to use in love baths and showers in the month ahead before socializing.
- Carry the moonstones as a love token in a silver bag.

9

TO CALL YOUR TWIN SOUL, KNOWN OR UNKNOWN, TO FIND YOU

You will need:

Nine silver coins
Nine white flowers
Nine small fruits
One small basket

Timing:
Early morning

The Spell

- Carry your basket of coins, flowers, and fruits to the edge of a lake, pool, ocean, or pond.
- Call out across the water: *I seek my true twin soul and no other, by the power of the flowing waters, to find me, that instantly we may know each other.*
- Cast the coins, flowers, and fruit into the water one by one, chanting softly and continuously: *Twin soul, this morn I call to thee. Find your way home to me. From far off shores or nearer lands, come, love, swiftly and take my hands.*
- Hold your hands high above your head and then outstretched toward the water to touch your twin soul magically across the waves or the next street.
- Collect small offerings from the shore, placing them in the basket, and repeat all the chants.

10

FOR NEW LOVE AND TRUST IF YOU HAVE BEEN HURT BY A PREVIOUS LOVER; CAN ALSO BE APPLIED AFTER A DIVORCE

You will need:

A thin silver ring that fits on your wedding finger. Treat yourself.

Timing:
The crescent moon in the sky or, if cloudy, the first day it is visible

The Spell

- Face the moon. Place the ring in the palm of your nondominant hand, circling over it six times with the other hand, repeating six times: *One for love, you moon above, send love to me. Two for love, you moon above, fidelity. Three for love, you moon above, eternally. This ring I wear secure in self until new love shall find me.*
- Place the ring on your wedding finger and repeat the words.
- When you marry or if your new love buys you a ring, you can change the moon love ring to the other hand.

11

A KNOT RITUAL TO INCREASE LOVE BETWEEN YOU AND SOMEONE YOU WOULD LIKE TO KNOW BETTER

You will need:

Two small dolls or two tiny featureless figures crafted from modeling clay
A pink ribbon and a green ribbon

Timing:

Monday

The Spell

- Give one doll your name and the other doll your would-be lover's name.
- Hold a doll in each hand, closing your hands with the dolls inside, saying: *I seek to become closer in love with* [name].
- Tie the two dolls face to face with the ribbons, making three knots, saying for each knot: *Three times the lover's knot secures, firm be the knots, long the love endures.*
- Keep the knotted dolls under your pillow for three nights. On the fourth morning undo the knots one by one, shaking each ribbon free, saying: *Three times the lover's knot flies free, the love is bound with him/her and me.*
- Join the ribbons loosely at the top with a single knot. Hang the ribbons behind the bedroom door. Keep the dolls face to face near the bed.

12

A CHEEKY ENCHANTMENT WORKPLACE SPELL TO INCREASE THE LOVE VIBES WITH SOMEONE WHO SEEMS NOT TO NOTICE YOU

You will need:

A mug for your would-be beloved
Tea bag, herbal tea, or coffee
A long metal spoon

Timing:

Any natural break (you may have to make coffee for everyone, but enchant only one)

The Spell

- Add the tea or coffee and hot water to the mug to be enchanted.
- Begin stirring clockwise with the spoon in your dominant hand, moving the other hand counterclockwise above the mug (not too close), chanting softly: *Look on me with eyes of love, let lasting bonds between us grow. I bind and wind connection in, that lasting love we may soon know.*
- Make your words (even in your head) become softer and stir more slowly until all ends in silence and stillness.
- Offer the drink to your would-be beloved and say in your mind: *With growing love from me to you.*

13

AN INSTANT WORKPLACE CONNECTION SPELL

You will need:

Any food on a plate: a cake, biscuit, a pile of files, a computer disk, keys, or a tool you hand over to the person you would like to connect with romantically.

Timing:

As often as possible

The Spell

- The essence is speed. Offer the object slowly, passing the other hand around it, and say in your head nine times faster and faster:

Love grows with every touch,
Love knows there can be much,
Between us, desire flare and flame
Meet my eyes, touch my heart,
Passion starts as I speak your name.

- As you hand over the item, unobtrusively brush against him or her with your hand and say the person's name aloud conversationally, meeting his or her eyes.

14

A WHITE FLOWER AND MOON SPELL TO HAVE YOU NOTICED BY SOMEONE YOU LIKE

You will need:

A clear glass or silver-colored bowl half filled with water
Nine white flowers
A smooth stick or pointed crystal quartz
A pink ribbon

Timing:

A later waxing moon; if it is dull, add silver candles to reflect in the water

The Spell

- Go outdoors if possible. Moving clockwise, encircle the bowl with the white flowers.
- Stir the water nine times clockwise with the stick or crystal, saying,

Moon of increase, let love grow,
That [name of person] may love show,
Moon shine down your beauteous light,
Make me beloved to his/her sight.

- Leave the water outside overnight.
- In the morning, sprinkle nine drops of moon water over the ribbon, repeating the chant three times.
- Wear or carry the ribbon for nine days and thereafter on any occasion when you know the person you like will be present.
- Bottle the remainder of the water to splash on your wrists when your love is near.

15

A TRADITIONAL THREE-NIGHT CANDLE AND MIRROR RITUAL TO STRENGTHEN LOVE

You will need:

One pink candle
One green candle
One round or oval mirror

Timing:
Three nights before the night of the full moon, after dark

The Spell

- On the first night, light the two candles, pink first and then green.
- Place the mirror on a flat surface, reflective side up. Place the candles near the edges of the mirror.
- Say: *Flame and flare, connect us lovingly and everlastingly, myself and* [name love].
- Gaze between the candles into the mirror, calling your love's name softly.
- Move the candles closer, saying: *So do we move nearer to each other's heart and soul.*
- Blow out the green candle and then the pink, looking into the afterglow in the mirror and calling your love again.
- On night 2, repeat the spell exactly but move the candles even closer.
- On night 3, follow the spell words and actions as before and move the candles so close that they touch.
- As you look in the glass through the candles, say: *Our hearts entwine and we are one.* Picture yourself and your love on your wedding day.
- Let the candles burn down.

16

A SEVEN-DAY MAGNET SPELL TO INCREASE ROMANTIC COMMITMENT, ESPECIALLY LONG DISTANCE OR OVER THE INTERNET

You will need:

Two black magnets with positive/negative poles at the ends
A red candle
Patchouli or any fiery essential oil, such as dragon's blood
A small red drawstring bag

Timing:
The hour after sunset for seven days, beginning on a Friday

The Spell

- Light the red candle behind the magnets with the poles repelling.
- Burn the candle until one-seventh of it has melted down, saying: *Friday is the day of love; may my lover ever closer move.*
- Turn the magnets so that they jump together. Blow out the candle, repeating the words.
- Do exactly the same for the next six evenings, separating and then joining the magnets but changing the name to the appropriate day of the week.
- On the next Friday put the joined magnets in the drawstring bag, adding three drops of oil, saying: *May we never be parted by time, space, or circumstance.*
- Take the magnets out of the bag every Friday and repeat the spell, anointing them with one drop of oil.

17

A HAIR AND RIBBON BRAIDING SPELL TO INCREASE COMMITMENT IN A SLOW BUT LOVING RELATIONSHIP

You will need:

Seven red ribbons
Seven strands of hair from your love's head (you can get them from a hairbrush or comb)
Seven strands of hair from your head

Timing:

Friday early morning

The Spell

- Hold the seven ribbons together in your nondominant hand, allowing them to blow free.
- Pass your other hand over the ribbons seven times clockwise and say: *Seven by seven the power I raise, calling love and joyous days, days of lasting love and bliss, sealing love with one sweet kiss.*
- Braid the ribbons together and wind in the hairs, one of yours knotted with one from your love, repeating the words softly and continuously as you wind and weave.
- When you are finished, kiss the ribbon braid and pin it near your heart where it cannot be seen. Repeat the words as you do this.

18

A VENUS MEDITERRANEAN LOVE-JOINING RITE

You will need:

A bunch of ripened grapes

Timing:

At noon, in sunlight

The Spell

- Pick a grape, saying: *The vine it binds and twines our love.*
- Eat the grape.
- Pick another grape and recite: *Your heart to mine.*
- Eat the grape.
- Pick and recite: *The vine it winds and finds us one.*
- Eat the grape.
- Pick another grape and say: *Our hearts entwine and you are mine.*
- Continue the cycle until you have eaten all the grapes or can eat no more.
- If possible, share the grapes with your love and say the words in your mind.

19

A WINDY NIGHT LOVE-CALLING RITUAL

You will need:

Nothing

Timing:

A windy night

The Spell

- Open your bedroom window and stand directly in front of it, facing the direction of your beloved's home no matter how far away.
- Whisper his or her name three times into the wind and then say:

Winds from the sea,
Bring to me,
This love that will last,
Until time is past.
Hear, love, and return me this sign.

- Wait and you will feel the link. Make actual contact with your love by phone or mail as soon as possible.

20

AN APPLE SPELL TO GET A LONG-TERM LOVER TO SHOW COMMITMENT

You will need:

An apple divided almost exactly in half. If your lover does not like apples, find another fruit you can divide in half.

A silver-colored knife

Timing:

During the waning moon (also a good time for picking fruit)

The Spell

- Wash the fruit under running water, saying:

Fruit sweet, as he/she does eat,
move [name] to lasting state.

Fruit sweet, as he/she does eat,
let him/her not hesitate.

Fruit sweet, as we do eat, no longer wait to say I do,
Me and you, our lifetime through.

- At an opportune time, cut the fruit in half and share it with your lover, reciting the words in your mind three times.
- Retrieve any leftovers you can and bury them with other fruit either in the ground or in a pot, reciting the words again.

21

A TWIN-RING SPELL FOR A LONG-TERM COMMITMENT OR MARRIAGE, ESPECIALLY IF THERE ARE OBSTACLES OR OUTSIDE INTERFERENCE

You will need:

Two matching thin gold or silver rings
One green candle
One bowl of dried basil
One green drawstring bag or purse

Timing:

The night before the full moon

The Spell

- Light the candle, circling the flame three times clockwise with each of the rings in turn, holding them above the flame, saying:

Around and around the ring of truth,
love in age and love in youth,

Love in sickness and in health,
love in hardship, love in wealth.

Come, my love, and with me stay,
stay forever and a day.

- *Let none come between us.*
- Blow out the candle and send the light to your love, picturing yourselves exchanging rings.
- Keep the rings in the bag under your mattress until your commitment, betrothal, or wedding, when you can wear them on a chain around your neck.

22

A UNITY CANDLE MARRIAGE OR COMMITMENT SPELL

You will need:

One large white pillar candle
Two smaller white candles in separate holders

Timing:

Before or during a commitment or marriage ceremony. Alternatively, you can cast the spell yourself before you move in together or marry, in which case say both sets of words and do both sets of actions.

The Spell

- You and your lover light a white candle, and as you do so, each of you says: *My love and faithfulness I give to you, fidelity my whole life through.*
- Both simultaneously light the pillar candle from each other's candle and say: *No more two but one, one light, one inspiration, one heart.*
- Extinguish the separate candles one after the other, and as you do so, say in turn or twice if alone: *No longer two but one, willingly united in love and fidelity, in trust and in harmony, in unity to remain eternally.*
- Let the pillar candle to burn down.
- Have separate small candles for children and light the central candle from their flames.

23

TO KEEP OR RESTORE PASSION IN A COMMITTED RELATIONSHIP

You will need:

A red candle
A strawberry, rose, or musk incense stick
Dried rose petals or rose potpourri in a bowl

Timing:
Fridays

The Spell

- In the bedroom, light first the candle and then the incense from the candle; as you do so, say: *Candle of love, incense of desire, I call my love in fragrance and in fire.*
- Take a handful of rose petals with your dominant hand.
- Pass the closed hand containing the petals three times over the flame, then three times over the incense smoke, saying: *In flower and fragrance, in fragrance and in fire, three times I call my love's desire.*
- Scatter the handful of petals, first in a clockwise circle around the incense and then in the same direction around the candle. Use all of them, saying: *I call my lover, with fragrance and with flower. At this hour my beloved, in passion and in fire.*
- Extinguish the candle and let the incense burn through. Scoop up the rose petals and hide them beneath the mattress.
- Burn the candle during lovemaking.

24

A SOLO LASTING ANCIENT EGYPTIAN COMMITMENT RITUAL

You will need:

Two red candles
Two incense sticks of cedar, frankincense, or myrrh
A pot of sand

Timing:
Sundays

The Spell

- Etch invisibly with the index finger of the hand you write with on each candle the Ankh, the Egyptian lasting love hieroglyph of Osiris and Isis, the divine Egyptian couple.
- Light one candle and then light the other from the flame of the first and say: *I dedicate these candles to our Ankh love that will endure like the sun shimmering perpetually over the oasis waters.*
- Light each incense stick, holding one in each hand, from each candle in turn, repeating the words.
- Draw the Ankh symbol in the air first with the left incense over both candles and then with the right, repeating the words.
- Draw spirals with both incenses over the candles simultaneously, reciting the words, making the Ankhs larger and the words louder and faster. With a final burst of power on the final *waters* (you will know when the power is ready), plunge both incenses into the sand and blow out the candles together.
- Say, *Our love is sealed perpetually by the power of the Ankh.*

25

A WEDDING CEREMONY DREAM RITUAL TO TURN A COMMITTED RELATIONSHIP OR LONG-LASTING BETROTHAL INTO A MARRIAGE

You will need:

A prayer book containing the wedding ceremony (the traditional version is best)
Two red and white ribbons
A sprig of lavender or fresh rosemary or a long-stemmed rose
Any ring that fits your wedding finger

Timing:

Before you go to bed, especially the last day of the month

The Spell

- Open the prayer book at the marriage ceremony at the place where it says, *With this ring I thee wed.*
- Repeat these words six times and put the ring on your wedding finger.
- Place the rose, lavender, or rosemary in the prayer book to mark the place; close the book; and bind the books with the knotted ribbons to signify union in marriage.
- Put the prayer book by the side of your bed and go to sleep picturing your wedding and calling your love.
- If you do not dream of the wedding, repeat the spell when you wake.

26

A TWIN CANDLE SPELL TO KEEP LOVE STRONG THROUGH THE YEARS

You will need:

Two beeswax or real wax candles
A flat metal tray
A paper knife

Timing:

Friday, as evening falls

The Spell

- Light the first candle, melting a little wax on to the tray to secure the candles as they stand side by side.
- Light the second candle from the first and say: *As this wax melts, so melts his/her heart. As the candles burn, so burns his/her love for me, inflames and kindles desire and fidelity from year to year.*
- When both candles have burned and melted, as the remaining pool of wax cools, before it is solid, use the knife to draw a large heart in the wax.
- Write both your and your love's initials within the heart and say, *May love grow stronger and endure from year to year.*
- When the wax is almost solid, cut around the edges of the heart so that you can lift it.
- Keep the heart wrapped in silk in a drawer until it crumbles.
- Replace the heart and bury the crumbled one.

27

A FIDELITY RITUAL FOR A MARRIAGE IN LATER LIFE OR ONE IN WHICH YOU HAVE COME TOGETHER WITH ONGOING DIFFICULTIES

You will need:

A pot of trailing ivy (or, as noted, honeysuckle or vine)
A bowl of water
Your engagement or wedding ring or any ring to symbolize unending love

Timing:
Thursday or any anniversary

The Spell

- Pick off nine ivy leaves, starting at the top of the frond, and as you pick each one, say: *Ivy, ivy, I love you, keep my lover true, though I would not bind him/her, I now our vows renew.*
- Surround the ring with the nine leaves, one at a time, and say for each one: *Our hands and hearts with one consent, have tied this knot until time does end.*
- Add the leaves to the water one at a time, saying for each: *Ivy, ivy, I love you, keep my lover true. Though I would not bind him/her, I now our vows renew.*
- Swirl the water nine times clockwise and bind the two leaves that move closest together with some of the ivy frond.
- Cast them into flowing water, repeating all the spell words.
- Bury the other seven leaves.
- If you cannot obtain ivy, substitute honeysuckle or vine.

28

MAKING A FIDELITY HERB CHARM

You will need:

Three of four of the following lasting fidelity herbs, dried, the kind you buy in supermarkets: yarrow, rosemary, sage, basil, caraway seeds, or thyme
A small bowl of salt
A blue drawstring bag
A bowl and spoon

Timing:
Thursday

The Spell

- Slowly mix a small quantity of your chosen herbs in the bowl with three pinches of salt, saying softly and continuously: *Earth, air, water, fire, for me alone my love's desire. Fire, water, earth, and air, may he only for me care.*
- Continue mixing and chanting faster. When you feel the power in the herbs pulsating, mix more slowly and chant more softly until your words fall into silence and the mixing is still.
- Put the mixture into the bag, close it, and hold it, repeating the words nine times.
- Wash away any spare herbs under running water.
- Hang the bag over the marital bed until it loses its fragrance and then renew it.
- Tip the old herbs to the four winds.

29

FOR BRINGING A SECRET LOVE INTO THE WORLD SO THAT YOU MAY BE TOGETHER FOREVER

You will need:

Dried or fresh chopped rosemary leaves
A bowl

Timing:
Wednesday morning

The Spell

- Go outdoors.
- Scatter a quarter of the rosemary to the winds, saying: *By the power of rosemary, bring this love now hidden in the shadows into the light of glorious day that we may be together openly forever.*
- Cast a quarter of the rosemary onto open ground or soil, repeating the words.
- Throw a quarter of rosemary into running water, a stream, a river, or the sea or under a cold tap, repeating the words.
- Sprinkle a little rosemary into the flame of a large red candle, saving just a few grains in the bowl. Or cast it into a bonfire or on barbecue coals, saying the words again.
- Put the remaining grains on your finger and eat them. If you are pregnant, tie it in a small cloth, saying the words three more times.

30

A BASIL CELL PHONE FIDELITY SPELL

You will need:

Your partner's cell phone (if you are the one going away and your partner will be at home, you can empower the home phone as well)
A jar of dried basil
A small lidded jar

Timing:
The night or early morning before you or your partner goes away on a trip

The Spell

- Sprinkle a clockwise circle of basil around the phone(s), saying nine times: *Be only for me, think only of me, and when we speak let it be lovingly, until you/I return faithfully.*
- Sweep up with a small broom and pan and keep the basil in the lidded jar.
- Every morning and night, add another pinch of basil, shake the jar nine times, and repeat the words.
- When you or your partner returns, tip all the basil to the four winds.

31

TO KEEP YOUR PARTNER FAITHFUL UNDER TEMPTATION IF YOUR PARTNER HAS A ROVING EYE

You will need:

A rich blue candle and a red candle, side by side

A silver paper knife or engraving tool

Timing:

Midnight

The Spell

- Etch on the blue fidelity candle, love forever, and on the red roving eye candle, temptation be gone.
- Light the blue candle, saying, *May love burn eternal between me and you. May none come between us, blaze faithful flame true. None ever have, nor ever will do.*
- Light the red candle from the blue one and say, *Be as a shield against all false fire, burn only for me, make me your desire.*
- Extinguish the red candle with a snuffer or cup and throw it away.
- Let the blue candle burn out. Collect any wax and engrave your own and your partner's entwined initials on it, placing it in a sealed glass jar in the kitchen.

32

TO STOP SOMEONE SPECIFIC FROM TRYING TO STEAL YOUR PARTNER

You will need:

A red candle and a blue candle, the blue candle to the right

Timing:

Preferably midnight or whenever you know temptation will arise from the other person

The Spell

- In this stronger version of the spell above, using the index fingernail of the hand you write with, lightly scratch on one side of the blue candle, BANISHED BE, and on one side of the red candle, YOU WHO WOULD DESTROY OUR LOVE.
- Light the blue candle and say: *As this wax melts, united ever shall we be. Let none come between us or take your love from me.*
- Light the red candle from the blue one and say: *False passion burn, burn away. Temptation turn away, you shall not stray. Grow cold like this flame I now let die.*
- Extinguish the red candle.
- Blow softly three times into the blue flame and say your lover's name after each breath.
- Blow out the blue candle and say: *Be only for me. Look only on me. Think only of me with love and fidelity. So must it be, banished be all others.*
- Clap over the blue candle.

33

AN ANTIEMOTIONAL VAMPIRE SPELL IF A RELATIVE, EX-PARTNER, OR CHILD FROM A PREVIOUS LIAISON IS INTERFERING IN YOUR CURRENT RELATIONSHIP

You will need:

A ball of red children's play clay
A red candle
A bowl of garlic salt

Timing:
Tuesday

The Spell

- Form the clay into a featureless figure to represent the person who is destroying the relationship deliberately or unconsciously. Create one figure for each individual source of interference.
- Set the figure(s) in front of the candle.
- Light the red candle, hold the figure(s) in your hands, and say: *By this flame, I burn away your power to drain our life, love, and energies.*
- Return the figure.
- Drop into the flame a pinch of garlic salt and say: [name of interference] *drain our life, love, and energies no more by thought, word, and deed.*
- Let the candle burn, saying: *Burn away, turn away, fever of intensity, your power over our love is gone.*
- Roll the figure back into a ball and bury it with any leftover candle wax, saying: *So is your power over us through, no more of you.*

34

A WHITE ROSE AND CANDLE SPELL FOR A TWIN-SOUL LOVE THAT CANNOT BE REVEALED BECAUSE OF RACE, RELIGION, OR PRIOR UNBREAKABLE COMMITMENTS

You will need:

Two white candles
A long thorn to engrave the candle
A white rosebud
A vase filled partway with water

Timing:
Any cloudy night

The Spell

- With the thorn, inscribe your initials and those of your secret love on the first candle. Draw a rose shape around them. Light it.
- Light the second candle from the first, extinguishing the first candle, saying, *Within the secrecy of the white rose must we live, under the secrecy of the white rose must we love.*
- Pick up the rosebud and whisper, *Yet will our love endure within the white rose.*
- Blow out the candle and in the darkness hold the rose, repeating all the spell words softly.
- Place your rosebud in the vase, between the candles.
- Every evening, relight both candles for five minutes.
- Hold the rose in the light and repeat the spell words three times.
- When the rose has died, cast the petals into flowing water. You will find that opportunities to be together increase.

35

TO INCREASE THE DEVOTION OF A PARTNER WHO IS FREQUENTLY ABSENT AS A RESULT OF WORK, FRIENDS, HOBBIES, OR OTHER COMMITMENTS

You will need:

A box with a lid
Some earth on which you have treaded
Some earth on which your beloved has treaded
A spoonful of sugar
Marigolds or other fast-growing flowers

Timing:
Thursday

The Spell

- Scoop up both types of soil into the box, sprinkling the sugar over both items.
- Close the box and shake six times, saying: *Our busy lives they barely touch, but deep within our hearts so much love connects us. May love daily grow in sweetness and mingle as togetherness.*
- Place the mingled soil in a plant pot or the garden. In it, plant the flowers, saying: *As these flowers grow and flourish may our mingled love daily grow in sweetness.*

36

IF A PARTNER'S BAD HABIT, ADDICTION, OR EXTRAVAGANCE IS DAMAGING THE RELATIONSHIP

You will need:

A soft wax candle
Two long, strong pins
Dried sage

Timing:
Every Saturday evening until the problem improves

The Spell

- Light the candle and say, *As this candle burns, so burns away* [name problem] *that mars our happy union.*
- As the candle begins to soften, insert the two pins, pushing gently but firmly through the center of the wick to form a cross.
- Say, *Within these pins do I bind* [name problem] *that mars our happy union.*
- Sprinkle a pinch of sage in the flame and say: *'Tis not these pins I wish to burn, but my lover's weakness turn. Into the wisdom of wise sage, that* [name problem] *as pins fall, banished be what mars our happy union.*
- When the pins fall, extinguish the candle, disposing of candle and pins.

37

TO BURY THE BONE OF CONTENTION, ISSUE, OR TABOO SUBJECTS THAT CAN BE MAJOR FLASH POINTS IN A RELATIONSHIP

You will need:

A small spade
A matching bone or stone for every major issue affecting either of you
A permanent marker or sharp knife
Flowers or flowering herbs, such as lavender

Timing:
Just before dusk

The Spell

- Dig a hole in the earth, saying: *So do I lay to rest [name all the issues] that cause seemingly irreconcilable differences in our relationship.*
- Write or scratch on each bone or stone a word or symbol to represent the main problems you are burying on behalf of both of you. They may include people who cause trouble.
- Set the bones or stones in the ground one at a time, saying for each, *Rest in tranquility, no more to trouble thee or me, but grow and flourish as new love and life.*
- Cover the hole with earth and in the soil set your flowers, saying: *New love from old sorrow, and so a new tomorrow.*

38

TO OVERCOME UNREASONABLE JEALOUSY OR POSSESSIVENESS BY A PARTNER

You will need:

A doll for the jealous partner, relative, or ex; you can make it from modeling dough
Red wool
Scissors

Timing:
Saturday morning

The Spell

- Loop three pieces of red wool around the figure representing the jealous person and around three fingers of your nondominant hand.
- Cut the loops one by one from your fingers, and as you do so say:

Jealousy binds,
Cut, unwind,
Leave me free,
So must it be.

- Tie the same three pieces of wool around the figure, making nine knots to secure the three pieces to the figure, saying: *Bound is jealousy, setting us free, may pangs of fire cease, possessiveness decrease, bringing us peace, the weaving is spun, the stranglehold gone.*
- Bury the figure on the banks of a river or lake.
- Repeat the ritual when necessary, making the loops on your fingers looser and the knots tighter each time.

39

TO RESTORE FUN, PASSION, AND LAUGHTER TO A RELATIONSHIP THAT HAS HIT A DULL OR DOWNBEAT PATCH

You will need:

A ceramic bowl
Dried mint
Powdered cinnamon
Dried ginger
Lavender
A red bag

Timing:
Sunday

The Spell

- Add all the ingredients to the bowl in the order given above, saying, *Mint for excitement and surprises, ginger for passion for life and for love. Cinnamon to make our hearts glad and our eyes sparkle. Lavender for laughter and childlike fun and all that is spontaneous.*
- Swirl the bowl faster and faster, reciting the words louder and faster until they jumble.
- With a final swirl and *fun,* scoop some of the mix into the bag, close it, and toss it nine times higher and faster, repeating the words and then slowing them down to silence and stillness
- Plan a trip or weekend away and keep the bag with a picture of the two of you in natural sunlight.

40

TO REKINDLE WHAT BROUGHT YOU TOGETHER IN TIMES OF TROUBLE

You will need:

A wedding, betrothal, or special occasion picture
Twin red roses
Twine or red wool
Rose essential oil in a lighted burner or diffuser or a lighted rose incense cone

Timing:
Friday

The Spell

- Set the roses so that they cross over the picture and say: *Roses of eternity, together can we overcome adversity.*
- Bind the roses loosely with three knots so that they are still crossed on the picture, repeating the words.
- Pass the bound roses through the vapor or incense smoke three times, saying: *For better for worse, our vows are strong, in spite of adversity, our love will be long.*
- Then do the same with the picture, repeating the second set of spell words.
- Take the roses outdoors, still bound, and hang them upside down on a tree, repeating the first set of spell words and allowing the wind to carry away the petals in its own time.
- Let the incense or oil burn through and each night hold the picture and repeat all the spell words.

41

AN ANCIENT SEA SPELL FOR THE RETURN OF A LOVER WHO HAS LEFT YOU

You will need:

The sea, a tidal river, or any flowing water
A gold earring, thin gold ring, or gold-colored coin
An empty glass bottle with a screw-top lid or cork

Timing:

Mondays

The Spell

- Visit the water source before twilight. Cast the gold into the water as an offering to the benign guardian essences of the water.
- Scoop some water in the bottle, and as you do so, say: *Lady Ocean, Mother Sea, I take of yours not willingly, but as a token of what I lack. I ask your help to bring him/her back.*
- (Use *sea* even if you're using a stream, for ultimately all water ends in the sea.) Hold it and call your true love's name nine times and say, *Lady Ocean, Mother Sea, carry him/her home in love to me.*
- Tip the water back into the water source, saying: *Lady Ocean, Mother Sea, I return what is yours; return mine to me.*
- Go home and make contact.

42

FOR RECONCILIATION AFTER A QUARREL OR PARTING

You will need:

A bowl with mixed small fruits, such as berries, grapes, and edible seeds

Timing:

Outdoors, Friday evening as the light fades

The Spell

- Hold the bowl and say: *What has been lost can grow again even stronger than before.*
- Eat a fruit and say, *Return to my heart and my life without blame or reproach.*
- Scatter a seed on the ground and say, *What has been lost will grow again even stronger than before.*
- Continue eating fruits and scattering seeds, repeating the words.
- When all the fruit is gone or you have eaten enough, tip the rest of the fruit and seeds on the ground, saying, *Return to me willingly, come back to me lovingly, without blame or reproach, for what has been lost must and shall return stronger than before.*
- Let the fruit and seeds take root in the earth or leave them for the birds to carry away and germinate.

43

A POTPOURRI SPELL FOR THE RENEWAL OF LOVE WHEN ONE OF YOU HAS RETURNED TO THE MARITAL HOME AFTER A SEPARATION

You will need:

A large bowl of lavender- or rose-based potpourri
Three or four small bowls
A feather or fan

Timing:

Soon after the return

The Spell

- Pass the feather or fan in your dominant hand in clockwise circles over the bowl of potpourri and your other hand in counterclockwise circles a few inches above it.
- Chant softly, slowly, and mesmerically: *My love, I give my love to you, a love more precious once renewed. Once more we join our hearts as one, willingly until time is run. You are my love and ever will be. I call you, love, in love back to me.*
- Divide the potpourri between the four bowls and set them around the home, especially in rooms in which you have quarreled.
- Repeat the movements with feather, hand, and words weekly over each bowl.
- When the potpourri loses its fragrance, scatter it outdoors and repeat.

44

A PARSLEY, SAGE, ROSEMARY, AND THYME SPELL TO CALL A LOST LOVE BACK WHEN ALL ELSE HAS FAILED

You will need:

A fast-burning deep red candle
Old photos and mementos from happier times with your love, including music you both enjoy
A deep-lipped or flat metal tray to collect candle wax
Mix of dried rosemary, parsley, sage, and thyme
A piece of white silk

Timing:

Midnight

The Spell

- Light the red candle. As it burns, look at the old mementos, listening to the music.
- After the candle burns out, sprinkle the dried herbs in the shape of a heart into the pool of melted wax, repeating until you have finished. Say: *By parsley, sage, rosemary, thyme, call back, I ask, this love of mine.*
- Gently wrap the heart in silk with a picture of you and your love, adding a few more loose herbs, tying it with white ribbon, saying: *By parsley, sage, rosemary, and thyme, I hold your heart entwined in mine.*
- Each week unwrap the picture, add a few more herbs, and repeat the spell words until your love returns.

45

A BUBBLE RITUAL FOR SENDING LOVE IF YOU PARTED IN ANGER OR BITTERNESS AND YOUR PARTNER IS BEING STUBBORN

You will need:
A child's large bubble blower and soapy water or a ready-made bubble set

Timing:
Wednesday, best of all on a windy day

The Spell

- Face the direction in which your true love currently is.
- Blow a bubble, holding it on the bubble blower, saying: *Return in love, to my heart and my arms, let once more laughter rise. I send only love and welcome to you through the skies.*
- Blow the bubble gently and repeat the words.
- Send five more bubbles skyward, waiting until each bubble has dispersed before creating the next and repeating the chant each time.
- As the last bubble flies away, call your love's name six times and say: *We will know joy once more; I will never close the door.*
- Make a loving gesture; if you have heard nothing after six days, repeat the spell, using twelve bubbles.

TO RID YOURSELF OF AN UNWANTED ADMIRER OR EX-LOVER WHO WILL NOT TAKE NO FOR AN ANSWER

You will need:
A gray candle and a white candle close together

Timing:
Three nights, beginning on Saturday

The Spell

- Light the gray candle for yourself and say: *No more notice me. I am free, surrounded by the mists of invisibility.*
- Move the unlit white candle away from yours, saying: *No longer desire me or seek connection. My rejection though kindly is clear. Find love and life new, the binding is through, and you shall no longer be near.*
- Blow out the candle.
- On night 2, light the gray candle, repeat the first words, and move the unlit white candle farther away from yours, repeating the second words.
- Again blow out the candle.
- On night 3, move the unlit white candle as far away as possible from yours, saying: *Follow your own path in joy; no longer walk along mine.*
- Light the white candle and let it burn through and then light the gray candle, saying: *May the mists of invisibility remain between us perpetually as you go your way and I mine.*
- Extinguish the gray candle and dispose of it and any wax from the white candle.

47

FOR CUTTING THE TIES OF A DESTRUCTIVE RELATIONSHIP OR ONE THAT IS GOING NOWHERE

You will need:

A dark blue pillar candle
A length of thin red curtain cord or strong thread
A container of soil

Timing:

Saturday after dark

The Spell

- Light the candle and say: *By the power of fire, I am set free.*
- Tie a knot in the center of the cord and say: *Tie and wind and seek to find freedom from* [name the destructive person or situation].
- Hold the knot over the flame with the cord taut in both hands.
- Say:

The cord between us was long.
The cord between us was strong.
But now it is decaying, fraying,
Burning, breaking.

- Drop both burned halves into the pot of soil, letting the flame burn out, saying: *The link is broken, and I am free.*
- Bury the charred cords where nothing grows, still in the soil from the spell.

48

AN ANCIENT SCOTTISH STONE OR CAIRN (STONE PILE) SPELL FOR LEAVING A LOVER WHO NEVER CAN BE YOURS

You will need:

A plot of dirt or a very large plant pot if necessary
A stone for every day of the month ahead
A packet of flower or herb seeds or small seedlings

Timing:

The beginning of a calendar month

The Spell

- Each day place a stone so that they make a circle and plant a few seeds around or beside each stone or start your stone pile (cairn).
- Scratch a symbol with meaning for you and your love on each stone, saying: *Today I walk without you, talk no more to you nor speak your name. I place my stone and plant my seeds in memory of what we shared.*
- Make a small positive plan to be fulfilled by the next day when you place the next stone. Whenever doubts creep in, walk your stone cairn or border and touch each of the stones, saying, *May you and I walk in happiness apart.*

49

A HAND-PARTING SPELL

You will need:

A dark red cord about three to six and a half yards long
A tree

Timing:
The hour before sunset

The Spell

- Wind the cord around a tree nine times, securing it with a very loose knot, looping the other end over your hands.
- Slowly unwind the cord from the tree, moving in circles farther and farther from the tether, chanting: *Hand part, my heart; hand fast, not last; let go, unwind, unbind, untie, release, too tight bonds now must cease.*
- With a final tug, pull the knot free, unloop your hand, and as you do so, say: *Unbound, unwound, hand parted, and so life begins anew; the ties are through.*
- Loop the cord over the tree so that it will decay naturally.

A CANDLE RITUAL TO MARK A DIVORCE OR OFFICIAL SEPARATION

You will need:

A large white candle
Two smaller white candles
A small square white candle (if there are children or a continuing joint business venture)

Timing:
The time of the decree nisi, decree absolute, or final break

The Spell

- In silence, light the large white candle, saying: *The unity between us now is ended peacefully.*
- From the large candle, light the two smaller ones, saying: *So you and I go our separate ways without bitterness or recrimination.*
- When you feel able, extinguish the marriage candle, saying: *The flame of love grows dim, and so we part, with thanks for happy times we shared.*
- If you have children or a business, light the square candle from both small candles in turn, saying: *That we will always be united in the love of our children/business.*
- Let the candles burn through.

CHAPTER 2

MONEY MAGICK

This chapter contains spells for short-term and urgent fiscal circumstances; for the gradual growth of prosperity and to stop the draining of resources; for savings and long-term prosperity to fulfill your dreams; for restoring fortunes after loss; and for overcoming debt, speculation, and money-spinning ventures.

51

AN INSTANT MONEY SPELL

You will need:

A money candle, a lucky square Chinese candle with a coin pressed into the wax, or a soft wax candle with a coin pressed into the wax about three-quarters of the way down (if necessary, prelight to soften the wax and secure the coin)

Timing:

As soon as you discover the urgent need

The Spell

- Light the candle and gaze into the flame, saying six times (nine times if things are really dire) in rapid succession:
- *One thousand dollars* [or however much you need, be precise], *it surrounds, it compounds, it astounds ME!*
- On *ME*, blow out the candle and call out the amount of money you need and add *Now*!
- Avoid thinking about the money problem. If nothing has happened within twelve hours, repeat the spell.

52

A GOLD AND SPICE SEVEN-DAY SPELL FOR A FAST INFUSION OF MONEY

You will need:

A small piece of gold, such as an earring
A small jar of powdered ginger
A gold or white purse

Timing:

Noon

The Spell

- Add the gold in the purse with three pinches of ginger, saying: *Gold and silver I have none, into my life good fortune comes and swiftly.*
- Add three more pinches of ginger, saying the same words.
- Close the purse and shake it three times; as you do so, say, *The wolf is howling at the door; good fortune I can wait no more. Gold and silver must I have some; into my life good fortune comes swiftly.*
- Keep the purse with urgent financial demands.
- Repeat the spell daily for seven days in total (unless the results come sooner), leaving the gold in the purse and adding three pinches more of ginger each day as you recite the words, shaking the purse three times.

53

ANOTHER SPELL FOR SPECIFIC MONEY WITHIN A WEEK AND A CONTINUING INFLOW

You will need:

Seven white or red tea lights set in a circle
Bills or demands that require settling within a week or a representative sum written in red ink in the center of the circle

Timing:

Seven days, including the day the money is needed

The Spell

- Light the first tea light farthest away from you, saying: *Spell of increase, money grow, that by* [name the day you need the money] *increase shows.*
- Holding the bills or the paper between your hands, blow out the tea light. Say: *Money comes by* [name day]. *I send light to make all right.*
- On the second day repeat these three steps, blow out the tea lights in reverse order of lighting, and repeat the final chant after blowing out each light.
- Each day light an extra tea light so that by the seventh day all seven are burning.

54

A FOUR-ELEMENTS MONEY SPELL TO STOP YOU FROM PANICKING ABOUT SMALL URGENT DEMANDS FOR MONEY

You will need:

A mix of four dried money herbs: basil, sage, rose, rosemary, patchouli, thyme, or mint
A small bowl to hold the herbs
A yellow candle

Timing:

Early Wednesday

The Spell

- Light the candle.
- Add the herbs to the bowl, swirling the bowl nine times clockwise.
- Hold the bowl over the flame, saying: *I release these money-bringing powers in perfect trust and perfect love, knowing I will be given the resources I need when most I need them.*
- Drop a pinch of herbs into the candle for the power of fire, repeating the words.
- Blow out the candle, saying: *In perfect trust and perfect love.*
- Outdoors, scatter a few pinches to the winds for the power of air, repeating: *In perfect trust and perfect love.*
- Bury some herb for the element of earth, repeating: *In perfect trust and perfect love.*
- Cast the rest into running water, saying again: *In perfect trust and perfect love.*

55

A RUNIC FIRE SPELL TO ATTRACT FAST MONEY IN THE SHORT TERM

You will need:

A red candle
A thin-bladed paper knife

Timing:

Whenever the need is urgent or you need an inflow of money in the short term

The Spell

- On the front and back of the unlit candle, etch the magical Viking rune Fehu that releases as well as symbolizes fast money:

- Light the candle, saying nine times in rapid succession the precise amount you need:

[Amount], *no delay*
On the way
To me

- At the end of the final chant, blow out the candle and call out the amount of money you need and add, *Now!*
- If nothing has happened within twenty-four hours, repeat the spell.

56

AN INSTANT MONEY SPELL IF YOU ARE BEING PRESSURED FROM ALL DIRECTIONS FOR MONEY

You will need:

A small pot of salt
A small pot of coins of any denomination
A yellow or gold candle

Timing:

Sunday

The Spell

- Light the candle so that it shines on the money.
- Scatter a circle of salt around the candle and money, saying: *Money grow, money flow, bring me swift prosperity.*
- Repeat the words eight more times and on the ninth chant of *prosperity,* clap nine times, blowing out the candle.
- Scoop up the salt, tipping it and the rest of the salt in the pot under flowing water (a kitchen tap will do), saying: *Go from me, flow from me, to the rivers and the sea, return as swift prosperity.*
- Give the coins to a charity.

57

A NINE-DAY FAST-WORKING CRYSTAL MONEY SPELL

You will need:

A large money crystal and eight smaller ones using any of the following crystals or a mix of them
Yellow citrine
Green aventurine
Jade, olivine, or peridot, bloodstone, or golden tiger's eye, or yellow and green glass nuggets or shiny beads

Timing:
Sunday

The Spell

- Each morning, surround the large stone with two smaller one on each side to create a square. Use approximate directions if you want.
- Place the crystals in sunlight or near a heat source, saying: *Incubate fast wealth, grow, sparkle hastily, that I may be free of money worries imminently.*
- Each evening, unmake the square, repeating the spell words.
- Put each stone in turn in a brown bag or purse and leave it at night near the center of the home, surrounded by a ring of salt sprinkled clockwise.
- In the morning re-create your square with the same words.
- On the ninth evening, arrange the crystals as a display where light will shine on them.

58

A SALT AND WATER FAST AND SHORT-TERM FINANCES SPELL

You will need:

A bowl of salt
A piece of paper or card on which to collect the salt
A bowl of water

Timing:
Before sunset

The Spell

- Run your fingers through the salt in the bowl and say: *This is instant prosperity. May my prosperity likewise grow instantly and keep flowing.*
- Pour a pile of salt onto the paper or card, heaping it into a cone shape, saying the words again.
- Tip the salt into the bowl of water and say the words, *This is instant prosperity. May my prosperity likewise flow and flow.*
- Swirl the bowl of water nine times clockwise, repeating these words.
- Pour the bowl of salt water into flowing water, saying: *Prosperity now, will flow to me, now and continually, so I ask and it shall be.*

59

A BASIL PATHWAY SPELL FOR MONEY NEEDED URGENTLY THAT WILL CONTINUE FOR THE FORESEEABLE FUTURE

You will need:

Two jars of dried basil, a money herb

Timing:

When you need an urgent infusion of cash

The Spell

- Take five paces from your front door. If there are flower beds or earth on either side of the path, scatter some of the basil there as you walk. Improvise with flowerpots for an apartment.
- When you have taken five paces, turn and walk back along the same path, scattering a basil trail along the path and saying continuously: *Create a pathway to my door, bringing wealth and so much more. Wealth and joy, prosperity, but first send money swift to me.*
- Sweep up the basil and scatter it outdoors, repeating the words.

60

A CRESCENT MOON SPELL FOR IMPROVING FINANCES IN THE MONTH AND THREE MONTHS AHEAD

You will need:

A bunch of white flowers
A silver-colored coin

Timing:

The crescent moon or a day or two later, after sunset

The Spell

- Stand in an open space, facing the moon, holding the coin in your nondominant hand. Put the flowers on the ground.
- Bow three times to the moon and turn the money over in your hand three times.
- Whisper the financial help you need, bow three times more, turn over the money three more times, toss and catch it three times, and say: *Three by three so this shall be.*
- Throw the coin over your left shoulder, still looking at the moon.
- Pick up the flowers, saying softly, *Moon I know, as you do grow, increase shall be, in you and in me.*
- Moving toward the moon, separate the flowers and form them into a crescent shape on the ground.
- Walk away in the direction of the moon.
- Repeat the spell on the crescent moon for the next two months.

61

A MIRROR, MOON, AND MONEY SPELL FOR THE GROWTH OF MONEY OVER THE YEAR AHEAD

You will need:

A mirror, preferably a Chinese hexagonal mirror
A golden coin

Timing:

The night of the full moon every month for a year

The Spell

- Go outdoors.
- Tilt the mirror so that you can catch the image of the moon or golden moonlight in it.
- In front of the moon image or light in the mirror, hold a golden coin and say: *Full moon, moon power, I ask this hour, silver and gold, on me shower, before this moon is old.*
- Cast the coin as far as you can ahead of you. Holding the mirror so that you can see your reflection in it, turn slowly around nine times counterclockwise, saying the same words continuously.
- Then hold the mirror flat so that it reflects the sky and say: *And so I am filled with the light of growing prosperity.*
- Hang the mirror at home so that it faces the front door and each night touch it and say, *And so I am filled with the light of growing prosperity.*
- Repeat the spell at every full moon.

62

MAKING A MONEY TREE TO INCREASE THE INFLOW OF MONEY OVER THE MONTHS AHEAD

You will need:

A miniature tree or a bonsai
Nine silver or gold ribbons
Nine small silver or gold coins with holes in them

Timing:

Any time close to the full moon night

The Spell

- Tie the nine coins to the branches with the nine ribbons, saying as you attach each: *As I bind you to the money tree, may you grow, multiply, and bear fruit that my needs may be met and my moneymaking potential may likewise grow.*
- Water the money tree, saying: *Water inflow that I may know my finances likewise increase show.*
- Water the tree daily, repeating both sets of words.

63

A SPELL FOR CONSERVING AND GROWING FINANCIAL RESOURCES

You will need:

A green plant or herb, such as basil or rosemary
Six small green candles
Six coins

Timing:
During the waxing moon

The Spell

- Light a circle of the candles around the plant. In front of each, set a small coin to make a larger circle around the circle of candles.
- Pick up the first coin and say: *Grow and increase, do not cease, increase and grow, let it be so.*
- Blow out the first candle and bury the coin in the flowerpot, repeating: *Increase and grow, let it be so.*
- Continue to chant as you hold each coin in turn, blow out its candle, and bury the coin in the pot. The coins should form a circle in the soil.
- When all six coins are buried, relight the candles, leaving them to burn through.
- Water the plant regularly, repeating all the spell words.
- When the plant gets big, transplant it to the garden and replant the coins beneath it in the earth for continuing prosperity.

64

A MONEY POT OR JAR SPELL FOR CONTINUING GRADUAL MONEY INFLOW

You will need:

A supply of coins in any denomination with which you can purchase things
A brown pottery jar with a lid
Dried bay leaves from the supermarket or any green leaves

Timing:
Ongoing

The Spell

- Each morning hold a coin and say: *May money accumulate and incubate through the days and weeks and month and years.*
- Drop the first coin in the pot, add a bay leaf, and repeat the words.
- Replace the lid and keep the pot in the kitchen or a warm place (traditionally the family hearth).
- Each day repeat the same words and actions.
- When the pot is almost full, scatter the leaves to the winds, repeating the words, and use the coins to buy something small that will bring pleasure, leaving one coin in the pot.

65

A SPELL TO STOP MONEY FROM FLOWING OUT TOO QUICKLY

You will need:

A sink or washbasin

Timing:

Saturday, after dusk

The Spell

- Turn on the cold tap, leaving the plug out.
- As the water flows away, say: *Flowing and going, going and flowing, stop the outgoing tide.*
- Slow the flow of water and put in the plug; as you do so, say: *Slowing the flowing, slowing the going, slowing outgoing tide. Stay money, stay, flow inward and not flow away.*
- Pull out the plug, letting the water flow away.
- Turn the tap on again even more slowly and leave the plug in, saying: *Money flow slowly, inward and stay. Money flow slowly; in, not away*
- When the sink is half full, turn off the tap, leaving the water with the plug in for at least ten minutes before letting out the water
- Repeat weekly, each time leaving the final water an extra five minutes before emptying.

66

A SPELL TO STOP ONGOING DEMANDS FROM DRAINING YOUR RESOURCES

You will need:

A blue cord or ribbon
A small padlock and chain (an old one will do)
An old box

Timing:

During the waning moon period

The Spell

- Tie a knot about a quarter of the way down the cord, saying: *Knot one I make; the flow I break. Outgoings bind, money find, within this knot.*
- Tie a second knot about halfway down the cord; as you do so, say: *Knot two I make; the flow I break. Outgoings bind, money find, within this knot.*
- Tie a third knot about three-quarters of the way down the cord; as you do so, say: *Knot three I make; the flow I break. Outgoings bind, money find, within this knot.*
- Tie the two ends of the cord together; as you do so, say: *Knot four, the last; outgoings past. Money bound; solvency found.*
- Place the knotted cord inside the box, securing the box with the padlock and chain. Throw away the key.
- Keep the box in the place where you usually work out your finances.

67

A TRADITIONAL FOLK SPELL FOR ENSURING ONGOING AND LONG-TERM FINANCIAL SECURITY

You will need:

A tub of sunflower seeds or seeds from any golden flower
A large plant pot with soil
A small trowel or spade

Timing:
The beginning of a month

The Spell

- Put a few seeds in the pot.
- Hold your hands around the pot and say: *May I always have enough for my needs and a little more.*
- Dig in the seeds and pass your hands over the pot three times, with your right hand moving clockwise and your left hand counterclockwise, saying three times: *Grow golden in my life, grow tall that there will be enough for all.*
- Add a sprinkling of seeds each day in the same way for four weeks.
- Then set the pot outdoors in a sheltered sunny spot and pass your hands again over the pot three times, saying this time: *Abundance gives and abundance receives. May I always have enough for my needs and a little more that there will be enough for all.*
- As the seeds grow, so will prosperity.

68

A WEEKLY SPELL TO ATTRACT ENOUGH FOR YOUR FINANCIAL NEEDS THROUGHOUT THE YEAR

You will need:

A red drawstring bag
Two bar magnets
Cloves
Salt
A red candle

Timing:
Sunday morning

The Spell

- Hold a magnet in each hand, poles attracting but not touching, and name all the months starting with the current month, then add: *drawing prosperity the whole year through*
- Let the magnets join, repeating the words.
- Tip some cloves in the bag, saying: *Cloves of prosperity, your wealth I seek, enough for my needs from week to week.*
- Add nine pinches of salt to the bag, saying: *Three by three, salt bring twelve-month-long prosperity.*
- Set the joined magnets in the bag and close it, saying: *Attract to me by week and month and year prosperity*
- Carry the bag with you.
- Each Sunday light a red candle, hold the bag in front of it, and ask for enough for the week ahead. Blow the candle out. Replace the bag after a year and a day.

69

A GOLD OR BRASS RUBBING SPELL FOR BUILDING UP RESOURCES AND TURNING THE CORNER FINANCIALLY

You will need:
A large brass or gold-colored dish (or substitute glass)
A soft yellow cloth
Shiny necklaces, bracelets, yellow flowers, crystals, gold coins, yellow fruit

Timing:
In sunlight or the light of a yellow candle

The Spell

- Polish the dish clockwise. As you do so, slowly and continuously whisper: *Gold/ brass/glass, restore all; let me not fall, let gold abundant be, that I may see, slowly increasing security, as I do turn the corner from poverty.*
- When the dish is gleaming, fill it with the shiny objects and golden fruit and set it where air will circulate all the way around.
- Replace the flowers when they fade, scattering them to the winds; eat a piece of the fruit daily to absorb the prosperity, in both cases after reciting the spell chant three times.
- Keep the dish topped up and repolish it on the first day of each new month.

70

A CLOVES SPELL TO RIGHT THE FINANCIAL BALANCE IN YOUR LIFE

You will need:
A large tub of cloves
A large clear glass storage jar

Timing:
Tuesday

The Spell

- Shake the unopened cloves seven times and say seven times: *Cloves, cloves, money bringer, bring gain, not loss, into my life.*
- Open the tub, add two cloves to the jar, and take out one, shaking the open container seven times, saying: *One loss, two gain, and so fortunes begin to rise again.*
- Seal both jars and leave the storage jar where light shines.
- Repeat on the second day exactly but add three cloves and take out two, adapting the words accordingly. Put the discarded cloves each day back into the original tub.
- Each day, add one more clove. On day 3, you will add four cloves, take away three, and adapt the words.
- When the storage jar is full, tip the contents outdoors and save one clove in the jar and start again.

71

A SPELL FOR FINANCIAL GROWTH TO BUILD LASTING PROSPERITY

You will need:

A ball of children's green play clay
A few small green plants
A plant pot of soil or a garden

Timing:
At twilight

The Spell

- Roll the ball until it is round, saying over and over softly, *May my life bear fruit and prosperity, continue to flourish ever more richly as it grows in its own unique ways.*
- With the index finger of your dominant hand, draw dollar signs (or your own currency sign) all over the ball and repeat the words as you do so.
- Make a hole in the earth and place the clay inside it, saying: *May my life bear fruit and prosperity, continue to flourish ever more richly as it grows in its own unique way.*
- Put the plants in the same hole and cover it over, repeating the words.
- As the plants grow, water them, each time repeating the same words.

72

MAKING A PROSPERITY SPELL BAG TO KEEP YOUR FINANCIAL PAPERS IN

You will need:

A bowl and a wooden or ceramic spoon
Two spices: ginger, saffron, cinnamon, nutmeg, allspice, or turmeric
Two money-growing herbs or dried flowers: chamomile, lavender, patchouli, mint, sage, rosemary, or thyme, or use a herbal tea mix
Three gold-, silver-, or copper-color coins or green money notes of any denomination
A few drops of orange, patchouli, or frankincense essential oil or sunflower cooking oil
A fabric purse or drawstring bag

Timing:
Thursday morning

The Spell

- Shake the spice and herbs in the bag or purse, mixing them together, saying faster as you mix faster: *Money grows, abundance flows, light grows, abundance knows no bounds.*
- Add two or three drops of oil, repeating the words, continuing to chant and mix faster, until you plunge the spoon into the bowl, saying, *Abundance knows no bounds.*
- Add money, repeating the words.
- Keep the bag with financial papers for a year and a day and then throw it into water and replace.

73

AN INCENSE SPELL FOR ACQUIRING MONEY FOR SOMETHING SPECIAL

You will need:

A brochure or paper on which you have written the target with its price
A money herb incense stick such as sage, frankincense, or cedar

Timing:

Noon

The Spell

- Light the incense stick and in the air around the edges of the paper, draw dollar signs (or your local currency signs) clockwise in spirals, saying: *Cosmos, I call, enough for this need,* [name what you want], *is all I seek, precisely, no more, I will repay in kindness and kind, enough and no more by* [date] *may I find.*
- Finish by writing the precise amount, the need, and the date in large smoke letters and numbers over the center of the paper, repeating the spell words.
- Take the incense outdoors to burn away.
- Cover the brochure or paper with currency signs drawn in the air with the index finger of your dominant hand and repeat the spell words for the final time.

74

AN ONGOING WEALTH ACCUMULATION SPELL

You will need:

A solid gold-colored wax candle
A large flat metal tray
Three silver coins
A paper knife

Timing:

On the full moon

The Spell

- Light the candle and, looking into the flame, say: *Burn, flame, burn; turn Dame Fortune's smile to me, for I will use prosperity wisely and well.*
- When the candle is melted, press the three silver coins into the pool of wax in a triangle shape on the tray.
- With the paper knife draw a clockwise circle of dollar signs (or your own currency signs) in the wax. Cut a circle of wax to include the coins and the currency signs and gently lift it out.
- Leave the wax and coins where moonlight will fill them overnight and then until noon.
- Wrap it in soft cloth and hide it where you do your finances.
- Replace when it crumbles.

75

A MOON WATER MONEY SPELL TO CALL IN MONEY MONTH AFTER MONTH

You will need:

A deep glass bowl half filled with water
Seven silver coins
If it is a dark night, place silver candles around the bowl

Timing:
The night of the full moon or the nights immediately before or after one

The Spell

- Outdoors, position the bowl so that light shines into the water.
- Drop all seven coins into the water and then plunge your hands three times into the silver water. Say: *Fill my hands with magic gold. I gather all that I can hold. Come, lasting prosperity; give to me all I can see.*
- Hold your hands above the bowl and allow the water to drip from your fingers.
- Leave the moon water outside overnight and then fill three small bottles with it, placing a coin in each. Sprinkle a few drops on your doorstep throughout the month to draw in money.

76

A FUN BUT HIGHLY EFFECTIVE SUNSHINE AND RAIN PROSPERITY SPELL

You will need:

Six coins
Puddles in sunlight

Timing:
After the rain

The Spell

- Drop a coin in the first six puddles, each time saying three times very fast: *Sun be sunny; water in sunlight, bring me money and all shall be right.*
- When you have cast the final coin, splash in the puddles in reverse order of casting, reciting the chant just once as you stamp in each one.
- Leave the coins in the puddles and go have some pleasure.

77

A RUSSIAN GOLDEN FLOWER SPELL TO INCREASE YOUR SAVINGS

You will need:

Small, slightly dry yellow flowers (traditionally golden-colored dried fern).

Timing:

Midsummer's Eve or any Sunday sunset

The Spell

- Holding a golden flower, climb up a hill or stand in an open place at sunset.
- Break off the petals and cast them toward the sunset, saying: *Golden flower/fern, bring to me, savings increasing day by day, that my fortunes growing may accumulate and stay secure from week to month and month to year.*
- Take a small quantity of the flower home and keep in a sachet with your savings books or dividend certificates and replace it when it crumbles, repeating the spell.

78

AN OLIVE OIL SPELL TO INCREASE SAVING POSSIBILITIES

You will need:

A bottle of virgin olive oil
Ten olives
Small cherry tomatoes

Timing:

Noon

The Spell

- Lay the bottle down, then make a triangle of olives around the bottle, with the highest point of the triangle at the top of the bottle.
- Enclose the triangle in a circle of cherry tomatoes (natural prosperity bringers).
- Gently shake the bottle within the triangle nine times, saying: *As olives ripen abundantly, money stays, grows triumphantly, savings grow rich as this oil, in countless ways through many days.*
- Leave the bottle of oil surrounded by the olives and tomatoes until sunset.
- Wash the olives and tomatoes and use them and some oil in a meal. Every time you use the oil, hold it and say the spell words.

79

A THREE-DAY CANDLE SPELL FOR GROWTH OF SAVINGS, DIVIDENDS, AND PROFITABLE RETURNS

You will need:

Three gold-colored candles of ascending height
Raw sweet corn or any golden vegetables
Three gold-colored fruits
Two handfuls of nuts
A few seeds
A pottery jar

Timing:
Dusk

The Spell

- Place candles in ascending order, left to right, and surround them with the vegetables, fruits, nuts, and seeds. Light the smallest gold candle and say three times: *Living light, grow and bear fruit.* Then eat one of the golden fruits, and blow out the candle.
- At dusk on the second day, relight the smallest candle; repeat three times what you said above.
- Light the second candle, saying six times, *Living light grow, increase show and bear fruit.* Then eat a golden-colored fruit and a handful of nuts and blow out both candles.
- At dusk on the third day, light the smallest golden candle, saying three times: *Living light grow and bear fruit.* As you light the second, say six times: *Living light grow, increase show and bear fruit.*
- Light the third candle, saying nine times: *Living light grow, increase show and bear fruit, prosperity know.* Then eat the remaining golden-colored fruit, the second handful of nuts, and the seeds. Let the three candles burn through, and use leftover food in cooking.

80

A WEEKLY GREEN OLIVE INCREASE SPELL TO KEEP MONEY FLOWING INTO YOUR HOME AND YOUR LIFE

You will need:

A dish full of golden-green olives with stones
A small lidded pot for the stones
A green crystal, green glass nugget, or green glass bead inside the pot

Timing:
Thursday morning

The Spell

- Hold your hands palms down about six inches above the dish and circle them together clockwise. As you do so, say nine times: *Ripen slow, unfold the growing gold, for I do know, the stones inside, your ever increasing potential hides.*
- Put the dish of olives near the center of your home where visitors and family may eat them in passing, with the pot for the stones next to it.
- When the dish is empty, top it up and repeat the enchantment.
- When the pot is full, tip the stones into a hole but leave it open, repeating all the spell words.

81

A TIGER'S EYE SPELL TO RESTORE PROSPERITY AFTER LOSS AND PREVENT FURTHER FINANCIAL SETBACKS

You will need:

A golden-brown candle
A golden tiger's eye crystal, any gleaming brown or gold crystal, a gold bead, a shiny brown natural stone, or a gold button
Three frankincense or sandalwood incense sticks
A brown purse or drawstring bag

Timing:
Three consecutive days

The Spell

- When you wake, light the candle and then light the first incense stick from the candle.
- Pass the crystal around the candle flame three times clockwise, saying three times: *I call upon the power of flame, to turn this loss into gain. Prosperity return once more, even better than before.*
- Blow out the candle, leaving the incense to burn.
- On the second morning, light the candle and the second incense stick and repeat the spell exactly.
- On the third morning, light the candle and the third incense stick.
- Repeat the spell but let the candle burn.
- Using the incense stick like a smoke pen, write in the air over the crystal and candle, PROSPERITY RETURNS ONCE MORE, EVEN BETTER THAN BEFORE.
- Carry the crystal in the purse.

82

A SEVEN-DAY CANDLE SPELL TO REDUCE DEBT

You will need:

Seven blue tea lights or small candles
A paper listing the debts or total amount you owe
A red pen

Timing:
Saturday after dark

The Spell

- On night 1, put all the tea lights in a circle, with the debt paper in the center. Light all seven tea lights, saying for each one, *Debt, melt away, no longer stay to blight my life. May solvency restore the light.*
- Blow out the candles.
- On night 2, light only six candles and repeat the spell.
- Continue until on night 7 only one candle is lit. Repeat the spell but leave it burning.
- On the debt paper draw a red cross and write across it, DEBT, YOU ARE BOUND FROM TROUBLING ME OR INCREASING FURTHER.
- Fold the paper up small and put it in the freezer.
- On night 8, burn any unfinished candles, repeating the spell words just once.

83

A SPELL TO TAKE AWAY A PARALYZING FEAR OF DEBT THAT STOPS YOU FROM SEEKING SYMPATHETIC HELP

You will need:

A child's blackboard or thick colored paper
White and red chalk

Timing:

A rainy day; if you are in a dry area, use a bucket of water

The Spell

- Write the amount owed and your fears and difficulties from unsympathetic debt collectors in white chalk and then draw a cross through it all in red chalk.
- Take it out in the rain and leave it, saying: *Rain, rain, wash away, fear of debts I cannot pay. Rain, rain, wash away, worries that haunt me night and day. Rain, rain, take from me this misery and set me free.*
- When the paper has dissolved, scoop it up and throw it away. Scrub the area clean or wash out the bucket, adding a little lemon juice.
- If you are using a chalkboard, leave it to dry.

84

A HAIR SPELL FOR BINDING WHAT SEEMS AN IMPOSSIBLE FINANCIAL SITUATION SO THAT YOU HAVE TIME TO REGROUP BEFORE ANYONE PULLS THE PLUG ON YOUR LIFE

You will need:

Eight of your hairs, cut from your head or from a hairbrush, plus eight hairs from a partner if the partner also is involved in the problem
A dark blue cord or ribbon

Timing:

Friday sunset

The Spell

- Bind the hairs around the cord, knotting them firmly. If necessary, use thread to fix them. Say: *I bind my strength, I wind my strength, for I must, for I trust I will win through. I bind my strength, I wind my strength and power to fight again renewed.*
- Hold both ends of the cord tight and repeat the words seven times.
- Hang the cord in your hallway or inside your front door, and every time you face a threat or difficulty, touch each of the hairs in turn and repeat the words.

85

TO ENSURE MONEY OR VALUABLE ITEMS YOU LEND TO A FRIEND OR FAMILY MEMBER ARE RETURNED IF THIS IS FREQUENTLY AN ISSUE

You will need:

A paper on which you have written the amount lent and the payback date
Two bar magnets
Two yellow bags
A photo of the person to whom you are lending the money
Dried lavender, *a come back to me* herb

Timing:

Before lending the money or item

The Spell

- Place a bar magnet, poles repelling, on either side of the paper and place the photo on top of the paper.
- Hold the magnets over the paper, poles attracting so that they join, and say: *This is a willing loan, not a gift, between* [name yourself and the other person]. *Return to me at the due time/in good condition* (if family members are careless with your possessions).
- Put a magnet in each bag and add a little lavender, repeating the words. Hide the bags with photo and paper in a drawer.
- On any interim payment date or weekly, repeat the spell, adding lavender to each bag.
- On the due date, repeat the spell, leaving the magnets joined on top of the paper and photo in bright light.
- Scatter lavender outdoors.

86

TO RECOVER OVERDUE REBATES, COMPENSATION, OR MONEY OWED TO YOU BY PEOPLE FOR WHOM YOU HAVE WORKED

You will need:

Seven banknotes of any denomination
Dried tarragon, the dragon's herb
A green candle
A small open pot

Timing:

Seven consecutive days, starting Saturday

The Spell

- Light the candle. Put a folded currency note in the pot, in front of the candle.
- Scatter three circles of basil around the candle and pot, saying, [name of debtor], *please pay my money* [name amount] *now. This is an urgent reminder. For I can wait no longer.*
- Blow out the candle.
- Each day repeat the spell, adding a new currency note to the pot, scattering basil over the same circles. Each day strengthen the request, using your own words.
- On day 7, let the candle burn through.
- On day 8, if you have not been paid, scatter the basil outdoors, saying: *Pay me instantly, now it must be.*
- Send a very strongly worded reminder to the most senior person connected with the money owed and repeat the spell cycle.

87

A TRADITIONAL KELP (SEAWEED) AND WHISKEY SPELL FOR HALTING AND REVERSING THE TIDE OR THE THREAT OF LOSS

You will need:

Powdered kelp (available from health food stores) or a piece of seaweed
A lidded glass jar
Whiskey

Timing:

The night before a full moon

The Spell

- Add the kelp to the jar and cover with whiskey.
- Seal the jar and say: *Tide of increase, flow to me, carry away all that threatens me. May I keep what is so dear and better fortunes soon appear.*
- Place the jar on a window ledge, shake it weekly, and repeat the chant.
- Every New Year's Eve, bury the unopened jar near your home before midnight and replace it on New Year's Day.

88

A CANDLE SPELL FOR BALANCING THE BOOKS IF YOU NEVER SEEM TO BE ABLE TO CATCH UP FINANCIALLY

You will need:

A soft wax or beeswax yellow candle on a tray
A paper knife
Dried thyme or parsley
A dark-lidded glass jar

Timing:

Wednesday evening

The Spell

- Etch on one side of the candle your approximate monthly or annual total expenditures.
- On the other side etch your total monthly or annual income.
- Light the candle and say: *Wax as you flow and fall, blend and reconcile all, that gain will outweigh loss*
- When all the wax has melted on the tray and cooled, chop or grate the wax into fine pieces, put it in the dark jar, and add a thick layer of thyme or parsley on top, saying: *Loss sink, do not rise, profit grow up to the skies.*
- Keep the jar in the highest part of the house so that your fortunes will rise and your debts sink.

89

A SPELL TO CURB THE DESIRE TO SPEND WHAT YOU DO NOT HAVE

You will need:

Credit and debit cards
A purple ribbon
A dish of salt
A dish of pepper

Timing:
The night before you shop

The Spell

- Make a square of credit cards
- Create four alternating circles outward of salt and pepper around the cards, saying four times: *Limits shall there be, not to curtail pleasure, but to wisely, moderately spend, conserve, and not waste treasure.*
- Tie the ribbon in three bows around the cards, saying: *I bind myself willingly, to spend of necessity, no longer compelled randomly, impulsively, unthinkingly.*
- Leave the cards in the circles overnight.
- Before shopping, unbind the cards, saying: *I unbind myself willingly, to spend of necessity, no longer compelled randomly, impulsively, unthinkingly.*
- Tie the ribbon inside your bag, touching it if you are about to make an impulse buy, repeating the words in your mind.

90

TO HELP YOURSELF, A FAMILY MEMBER, OR A FRIEND THROUGH BANKRUPTCY

You will need:

A child's blackboard or thick colored paper
Colored chalks, including white
A soft cloth

Timing:
The waning moon

The Spell

- Write on the board in large letters in white, *insolvency be gone.*
- Rub out *be gone* and *in* to leave only *solvency and* then cover every bit of the board, writing the word *solvency* over and over in colored chalk.
- Decorate the edges with the person's name in rainbow colors, drawing rainbows, flowers, flags, and butterflies, chanting, *Insolvency turns to solvency, defeat into victory, and you [name] shall flourish and flower, now, for from this very hour, insolvency is gone.*
- Keep the board where light shines on it and each week redraw, writing *insolvency* smaller and *solvency* larger until it fills the board.

SPECULATION AND MONEY-SPINNING VENTURES

91

A CRESCENT AND FULL MOON SPELL FOR TURNING A SMALL MONEY-SPINNING VENTURE INTO SOMETHING PROFITABLE IN THE LONGER TERM AND ON A LARGER SCALE

You will need:

A symbol of your venture, such as an earring you have made if designing jewelry or a spade if you are starting a gardening business

Timing:

During a crescent moon night and again during a full moon night

The Spell

- Stand somewhere secluded outside, facing the crescent moon.
- Turn over the symbol three times, saying each time: *New moon, true moon, moon in the sky, make my venture grow as you ride high.*
- Hide the symbol under a rock or in a tree hollow.
- On a full moon night return to the same place.
- Retrieve the symbol (take a spare in case it has been moved) and hold it facing the moon, saying: *Mother Moon in your full power, I ask success on me you shower, by the time the moon is once more new, make my venture blossom too.*
- Return the symbol to its place. Continue the cycle on subsequent crescent and full moons.

92

FOR ANY FORM OF SPECULATION OR LAUNCHING A MAJOR MONEYMAKING VENTURE IN WHICH INVESTMENT BY OTHERS IS ESSENTIAL

You will need:

A tub of sea salt
A piece of stiff card
A glass bowl half filled with water

Timing:

Wednesday

The Spell

- Form a pile of salt on the piece of card in the center of a table and carefully shake it seven times, saying: *Accumulate, make more; let money inward pour; accumulate and speculate; no time to wait, and so I call on Lady Luck to smile on my endeavor.*
- Fold up the ends of the card and tip the salt cone into the water, rapidly repeating the words seven more times.
- Stir the water fast with the index finger of your dominant hand seven times so that the water swirls and then lick your finger.
- Go outdoors and hold the bowl up to the sky seven times, repeating the words seven more times even faster, then pour the water on the ground in a cascade (not on plants it may harm), saying: *I accumulate, I speculate, I can make more, and so money pours and pours inward by the score.*
- Do something daring to further your endeavor.

93

ACCUMULATION SPELL BEFORE A PROPERTY DEAL OR INVESTMENT IN WHICH THERE ARE UNKNOWN FACTORS

You will need:

Six dice
Any papers connected with the transactions
A small purse or drawstring bag

Timing:

Midday

The Spell

- Toss the dice in your closed hands higher and faster, saying: *Roll the dice, shake the dice, twice the luck, twice the spice, as a* maybe *becomes a* take all.
- Allow the dice to fall on the papers. The numbers do not matter, but six is especially lucky.
- Pick up the dice and repeat the shaking, chanting and throwing six times.
- Transfer the dice to the bag and toss the bag six times over the papers, throwing it higher and higher as you chant faster. On the sixth high throw catch the bag and end the chant with a shout.
- Keep the bag of dice on the papers and repeat the spell at crucial points.

94

A MONTHLONG SPELL FOR A CRUCIAL PERIOD OF ACQUIRING OR RELEASING NECESSARY FUNDS TO MAKE A VENTURE POSSIBLE

You will need:

A blue candle
Twenty-eight to thirty-one squares of blue paper for each day of the month
A silver or gold writing pen

Timing:

The first of the month or whenever needed

The Spell

- On day 1, write your venture on the first piece of paper, saying: *Day by day shall you grow, and my venture fulfillment know, day by day.*
- Light the candle and put the paper around it facedown, repeating the words.
- Blow out the candle after ten minutes.
- Each day write the venture on a new paper, repeating the spell and placing it facedown in a circle around the candle.
- By the end of the month, all the papers are facedown around the candle (replace if necessary).
- On the first day of the next month cycle, singe each paper in the candle flame after reading it aloud, dropping it in the soil to burn or go out.
- Let the candle burn, burying the papers or ash in the soil in an open space, repeating the spell words, adding: *So shall the dream flourish day by day, month by month, year by year, day by day.*

95

A PEARL AND INCENSE SPELL TO STIMULATE ACTIVITY IN A STAGNANT FINANCIAL MARKET OR DEADLOCK TO BRING THE RIGHT BREAK

You will need:

Six incense sticks in a fast-bringing money fragrance: cinnamon, ginger, mint, or sage
A vase for the incense sticks
Twelve pearls (from a broken necklace or the kind you buy in packets or pearl buttons)

Timing:
Monday

The Spell

- Surround the incense with pearls at approximately clock face positions.
- Light the incense; as you do so, say: *Spice bring life, move on this stagnation that all hesitation may fly like the wind*
- Make smoke circles around the pearls with each separate incense stick, repeating the words, so that the circles radiate outward.
- Return each to the vase and take them all outside to release the energies.
- Keep the pearls in a glass jar where you have your financial papers and shake daily, saying the spell words.

96

A HERB-ROLLING SPELL TO DRAW TO YOU THE RIGHT INFORMATION AND RESOURCES AT THE RIGHT TIME FOR ACCUMULATING FUNDS.

You will need:

A small, rough-textured natural beeswax or grainy red candle
Kitchen paper or a plate
Dried parsley and/or mint

Timing:
3 p.m. or when the sun is high

The Spell

- Sprinkle plenty of herbs on the paper or plate, rolling the candle back and forth, saying: *Roll, roll, roll, hold tight, cling right, draw universal blessings, kindled by this light.*
- When some herbs have stuck to the candle (it need not be many), light the candle and say: *Burn, burn, burn, hold tight, cling right, draw universal blessings, kindled by this light.*
- Blow out the candle and say: *Spread, spread, spread, hold tight, cling right, draw universal blessings, kindled by this light.*
- Repeat the spell weekly, rolling the candle in more herbs, as long as the candle lasts.

97

A VIKING RUNIC SPELL FOR WHEN YOU ARE INVOLVED IN OVERSEAS INVESTMENTS OR HAVE FINANCIAL DEALINGS ABROAD

You will need:

Grass, sand, or soil on which you can you can mark your Gebo rune

Timing:

As it gets light

The Spell

- Draw the Gebo rune in the earth with a stick, enclosing it in a circle. Alternatively, make the Gebo and the circle from stones. Gebo is symbol of expansion, with what is sent out returning threefold.
- Walk around the Gebo circle clockwise and then walk to the center of the Gebo down any of its arms.
- Face the direction of the rising light, saying: *The way is open, the path is clear, I call success from far and near. No obstacles remain in sight, I reach for success as I follow the light.*
- Rub out the circle or remove the stones, walking toward the light while repeating the words.
- Leave the Gebo sign, ancient symbol of Mother Earth, and make connections with your overseas interests.

98

A SPELL TO DOUBLE YOUR MONEY OR INVESTMENTS

You will need:

A red or green banknote of any denomination or currency and a second worth double the first

A white large resealable envelope and green ink pen

Dried white sage, basil, mint, or vetivert

Timing:

The day before the full moon

The Spell

- Put the smaller-value banknote in the envelope and write on the front: *double your money.*
- Say: *Double your money, double your money, double your money, it's your lucky day, double your money and take it away.*
- Add a little herb to the envelope before sealing, repeating the words, shaking the envelope twice.
- The next morning add the second banknote to the envelope, add more herb, repeat the words twice, seal, and shake four times.
- Weekly shake the envelope four times and repeat the words four times.

99

AN INNER SUN SPELL TO ENSURE THAT ANYTHING YOU NEED TO SELL, LARGE OR SMALL, BRINGS A SWIFT GOOD RETURN

You will need:
Nothing

Timing:
Before releasing the item onto the open market or auction and any key sale potential moments

The Spell

- Face the item(s) to be sold or a picture if a house and land or a holiday home.
- Putting your hands in the center of your upper stomach, fill them with your personal inner sun power that links you directly with the sun.
- Extend your hands horizontally, palms down, fingers tucked in so that only the index fingers are extending. Jab simultaneously toward the target, saying: *I fill you with my inner sun to shine glorious, impress that there will be no duress at selling you swiftly, profitably, and satisfactorily.*
- Touch your upper stomach again and then, palms outward, vertical, fingers together, push nine times hard to transfer your inner sun power to the item, repeating the words for each push.
- Clap nine times over your head, repeating the words after each clap.
- Take the item to be sold or call the agent.

100

AN ONGOING SPICE RACK SPELL IF YOU SPECULATE IN STOCKS OR INFORMAL INVESTMENTS

You will need:
A spice rack with six different spices, such as saffron, chili, curry, ginger, allspice, cinnamon, cloves, turmeric, and nutmeg
A small red candle for each spice jar

Timing:
Before cooking

The Spell

- Put a candle behind each spice jar and set in a circle.
- Light the candle farthest away, saying: *Spices hot, candle fire, increase profitability higher and higher. Spices burn, blaze to prosperous days, no doubt, no fear, the right decisions flare up here.*
- Do the same thing for each spice and candle, repeating the words.
- When all the candles are alight, quickly swap the places of each spice around the circle so that they end in their original places while chanting the words faster and faster.
- When all are in their original places, blow out the candles in one blow if you can, saying: *Accumulation through speculation, success, no stress, I gain, no pain.*
- Return the spices to the rack and regularly use them in cooking, repeating the spell before any major deals.

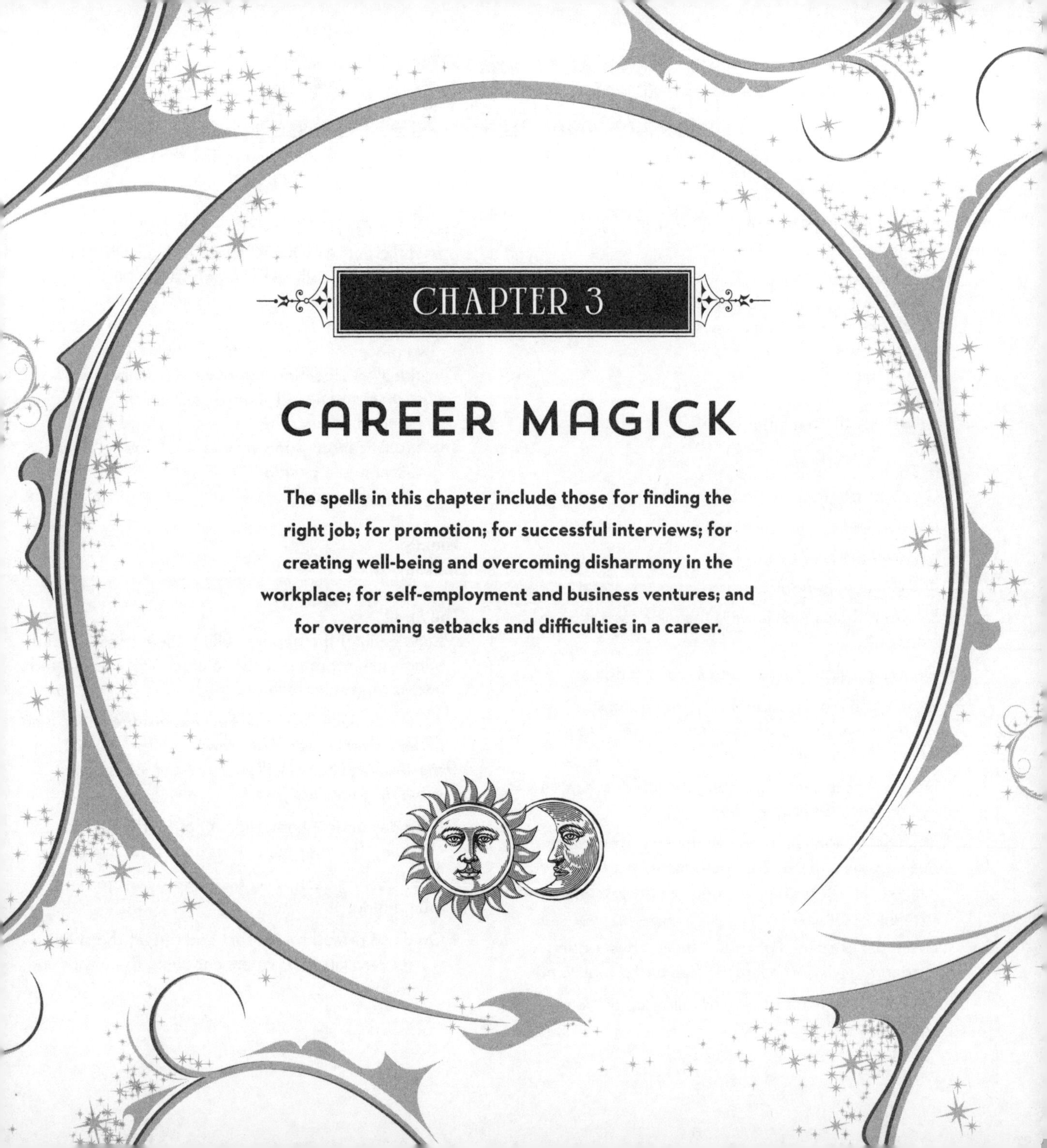

CHAPTER 3

CAREER MAGICK

The spells in this chapter include those for finding the right job; for promotion; for successful interviews; for creating well-being and overcoming disharmony in the workplace; for self-employment and business ventures; and for overcoming setbacks and difficulties in a career.

101

A THREE-DAY SPELL TO GET A JOB

You will need:

Three blue candles in a row
A job description from a newspaper, or write your own

Timing:
Thursday for three nights

The Spell

- On night 1, light the leftmost candle.
- Read aloud your job description.
- Say: *This job is mine, this job is for me, ever closer and closer shall it be.*
- Blow out the candle, leaving the job description in front of it.
- On night 2, light the first and second candles.
- Reread the job description, repeating the spell words and adding, *So close that I can see, the job will very soon belong to me.*
- Blow out both candles, setting the job description in front of and between them.
- On night 3, light all three candles, read the job description, and say: *This job is mine, this job is for me, ever closer and closer can I see the job that now belongs to me.*
- Leave the candles alight. Burn the job description outdoors, saying: *The job flies free and comes to me.*
- On day 4, apply for the job or follow up on your application.

102

TO GET THE RIGHT JOB IF IT IS A FIRST JOB OR YOU ARE RETURNING TO WORK AFTER AN ABSENCE.

You will need:

Two pieces of paper, on the first written the ideal job, location, approximate salary, organization, and so forth, and on the second your strengths, qualities, and qualifications and why you would be an asset in the position.
A long red cord

Timing:
Tuesday

The Spell

- Read each of the papers, rolling them together and tying them together with the cord, which is knotted into seven separate knots.
- As you tie each knot, say: *Seven times the knots, bind in the power, power that grows hour by hour. Within these seven knots, I will succeed, the job is mine when the knots are freed.*
- Each day undo a knot, repeating the rhyme and changing the knot number as each one is released.
- After untying each knot, take a step toward job hunting.
- On day 8 reread the papers and repeat the spell words, rerolling the papers and tying them with one loose bow.

103

TO OVERCOME A LACK OF CONFIDENCE IF YOU ARE NEW TO JOB HUNTING OR ARE UNCERTAIN OF YOUR ABILITIES

You will need:

A feather you have found or bought
White thread

Timing:

A windy day

The Spell

- Tie the feather very loosely to the end of a high branch of a tree or bush on top of a hill or in an exposed space.
- As you do so, say: *Fly high, let me be likewise free from doubt and fear, that as you reach the sky, I too may success see so near.*
- Walk away without looking back.
- Go to the tree weekly with another feather.

104

A FAST SPELL FOR GETTING THE RIGHT JOB IF YOU ARE LOSING HOPE AFTER UNSUCCESSFUL APPLICATIONS

You will need:

Five flat black or dark-colored stones
Five flat white stones
A basket or bag to carry them
A lake, pool, river, or pond or the ocean

Timing:

Wednesdays

The Spell:

- Say aloud the kind of the job you want, being as specific as possible.
- One at a time, skim the black stones fast over the water, saying: *Away doubts, away rejections, my projection is success.*
- Taking the white stones in the same hand, skim them even faster, saying: *Opportunity comes to me swiftly and indubitably, and so the next job I see will definitely be mine.*
- When you apply or have an interview, picture the white stones skimming and recall the spell words.

105

A TRADITIONAL ARCHANGEL SACHIEL SPELL TO OBTAIN A PERMANENT JOB IF YOU CAN GET ONLY TEMPORARY WORK

You will need:

A bright blue candle, Sachiel's color
A tub of dried sage, Sachiel's herb
A paper knife

Timing:

Seven nights starting Thursday, Sachiel's day

The Spell

- Light the blue candle, saying seven times: *Wise Sachiel, who brings permanent employment, May a permanent job be mine.*
- On a white plate spread the herbs thinly, writing with the knife the same words in the herbs even if it is not clear.
- Put a pinch of the herbs in the candle, repeating the words.
- Raise your hands high over the candle and plate and clap seven times to release the power of the spell.
- Blow out the candle and say softly and very slowly seven times: *A permanent job shall be mine.*
- Scatter the herbs on the plate outdoors.
- Repeat this spell for six more days.
- On day 7, let the candle burn all the way through.

106

AN AFRO-CARIBBEAN SALT SPELL TO DO WELL IN AN INTERVIEW WHEN THERE IS FIERCE COMPETITION

You will need:

Sea salt in a dish
A string of bells (toy ones or a Tibetan string)
Silver cooking foil

Timing:

Five, ten, fifteen, or twenty hours before the interview

The Spell

- Hold the silver bells over the salt, ringing them five, ten, fifteen, and then twenty times, afterward saying: *Silver bells, for me ring, success in interviews to me bring. Salt of wealth, words of power, bring persuasion to me at this hour* [name the interview hour].
- An hour before you leave for the interview, make three twists of salt in foil.
- Hide one foil twist in the hall or entrance of your home and another in your favorite sitting place in the house, taking the third to the interview.
- If possible, surreptitiously deposit this in the building either in the bathroom or in a bin in the waiting room, repeating the spell words.

107

A CANDLE SPELL TO SPEAK TO THE RIGHT PERSON WHEN PHONING TO INQUIRE ABOUT A VACANCY OR GET AN INTERVIEW

You will need:

Three yellow candles in a row
The phone number and, if you know it, the name of the right person on paper

Timing:

Before phoning

The Spell

- Light the first candle close to the phone, gently blowing in the flame.
- Say aloud as if you were speaking to the right person even if you do not know the name, *May I speak with you urgently about this job. I am just the person you are looking for.*
- Blow out the candle and say: *I will call soon. Please answer me.*
- Light the first two candles and repeat the spell exactly. Then light all three and let them burn.
- Phone as soon as you can after the spell. Persist until you reach the person you need to talk to.

108

A FIRE SPELL FOR QUITTING A BORING JOB AND TAKING A LEAP INTO THE UNKNOWN FOR CAREER ADVANCEMENT

You will need:

A bonfire, a fire pit, a dish, or a barbecue without the grill on top (cook on it afterward to absorb the magick) or a huge candle embedded in a bucket of sand or soil
A tub of mixed dried rosemary and thyme

Timing:

If you are hesitant about making a change but an opportunity arises

The Spell

- Light a fire in the receptacle.
- When the fire is burning well, shake the tub nine times, saying: *Fire and light, from certainty and limitation to freedom and delight. Flare to endless possibility, for I can see the future bright and clear for me.*
- Walk around the fire three times clockwise, three times counterclockwise, and three times clockwise again, throwing herbs into the fire until they are all gone.
- When the fire dies down and is cool, dig some ashes into the ground and plant a tree or small bush on top, repeating the spell words.

109

A BALLOON SPELL FOR GETTING YOUR JOB APPLICATION NOTICED AMONG A PILE OF OTHERS

You will need:

A balloon

A luggage label on which you have written, MAY MY APPLICATION RIDE HIGH AND BE NOTICED.

Timing:

Before or immediately after sending your personal profile/application

The Spell

- Climb halfway up a hill or across an open space, affix the label to the balloon, and say ten times, *Find me, notice me favorably, hire me; I am right for your vacancy.*
- Go to the top and repeat the words ten times before releasing the balloon.
- Run or walk down the hill as fast as you can, repeating both sets of words.

110

TO GET AN INTERVIEW IN AN AREA OR FIELD WITH HIGH UNEMPLOYMENT

You will need:

A copy of your résumé or profile

A triangle of three blue soft wax candles, with your résumé in the center

Timing:

Weekly until you get an interview or offer

The Spell

- Light all three candles and say, *I light this fire to raise my profile higher. Think highly of me. Speak well of me, that you [name company] may see, how right I will be, in this job I so greatly desire.*
- Carefully drip wax on each of the four corners of the résumé.
- When the wax is set, fold the corners inward, dripping wax to seal the paper together. Say, *Set a seal to reveal the break that I will take with all my zeal and so my fortunes wake.*
- Blow out the candle; as you do so, repeat: *So does my light shine forth.*
- Keep the wax-sealed copy where daylight can shine on it until your lucky break comes.

111

TO BOOST YOUR CONFIDENCE BEFORE A MAJOR PROMOTION OR INTERVIEW FOR A BETTER JOB

You will need:

Children's play clay
Salt
Any tree or fruit incense
A bowl of water
Clear and gold glass nuggets, glass beads, or buttons

Timing:

Outdoors, the brightest time of the day

The Spell

- Shape the clay into a featureless image of yourself. Sprinkle it with salt for the earth, spiral the lighted incense stick over it for air, hold it to the light for fire, and sprinkle it with water. Say: Within me, earth, air, water, fire, calls the job I most desire.
- Press the nuggets into the figure, saying: *May I shine bright as the sun, my gifts find expression without repression, and my true worth be manifest.*
- Keep the figure where natural light shines.
- For your interview, take it in a little pouch or bag. Hold it before the interview, repeating both sets of words. As you go in, say in your mind four times: *May I shine bright as the sun.*

112

FOR OVERDUE PROMOTION OR A RAISE

You will need:

A mirror
Six golden candles
A favorite piece of jewelry

Timing:

In morning light close to the full moon

The Spell

- Around the mirror, light golden candles unless moonlight is shining on the glass.
- Put on the jewelry.
- Stand in front of the shimmering mirror and, with your arms outstretched, make an arch over your head and in front of your body in spirals.
- Say softly and continuously, I am pure gold. *I am gold within, gold shines from me, golden light and golden moon—deserved gold will come soon.*
- Touch the jewelry and repeat the words.
- Blow out the candles and repeat the spell words.
- Wear the jewelry when you ask for promotion or a raise, touching it while reciting the words in your mind.

113

A SUN WATER SPELL TO OPEN THE DOOR TO ADVANCEMENT, ESPECIALLY IF THERE IS A GLASS CEILING OR PREJUDICE

You will need:

A clear glass bowl half filled with water

Five small yellow citrine crystals, golden glass nuggets, or yellow glass beads

Timing:

From dawn until noon on a Sunday. Midsummer is best of all.

The Spell

- At dawn, add the crystals to the bowl one at a time, outdoors if possible, saying for each: *Gold of sunlight, break through the dawn, that my golden future may soon be born. Glorious noon, shine, bring growing days, burn. Sun bright, open golden new ways.*
- At noon, remove the crystals and leave them in a circle on the ground.
- Tip half the water on the ground, repeating the words. Let the rest filter into clear glass bottles to splash on pulse points at times when you have a chance to shine, again repeating the words.

114

TO OBTAIN A LEADERSHIP POSITION

You will need:

A road with streetlights, a garden with solar lights, or string lights on a tree

A tube of gold glitter

Timing:

Thursday after dark

The Spell

- Stand where there is no light, saying: *I do not like the shadows of obscurity. I reject the shades of anonymity, and so I claim my place in the light.*
- Move to where the lights shine and say: *I embrace this opportunity to shine. And so I seize this leadership as mine.*
- Sprinkle glitter all around you as you twirl faster and faster until you become slightly dizzy. Say: *Let the light shine all around me, on me, and within me. I seize this leadership as mine.*
- The next morning, go all out for the position.

115

AN ORIENTAL SUCCESS CORD SPELL TO RAISE YOUR PROFILE SO THAT PEOPLE SEE YOU AS A NATURAL LEADER

You will need:

A string of silver- or gold-colored bells on a cord (Tibetan ones are ideal)

Red ribbon in five equal pieces, each long enough to tie into a bow

Timing:

The first day of the week, month, or year

The Spell

- Starting at the top and working down to the bottom of the cord, tie five red bows at regular intervals, saying: *Notice me positively and see my leadership potential powerfully as I increase my profile and prospects of promotion.*
- Ring each bell, repeating the chant.
- Hang the bells where natural light shines.
- When you have hung the bells, ring each one separately and recite the words twice for each ring. Then ring the bells together, repeating the words once more.
- Leave the bells hanging on the wall. Ring them and chant each day before work.

116

A BINOCULARS OR TELESCOPE SPELL TO ACHIEVE A MAJOR CAREER AMBITION THAT SEEMS FAR AWAY

You will need:

A telescope or binoculars (you can use children's toy ones).

Timing:

Early morning daily

The Spell

- Look through the wrong end of the telescope and say: *Promotion/advancement seems far away, yet they are mine if the course I can stay.*
- Turn the telescope around and look through the right end. Say: *Promotion/advancement I see them so clear. Just to reach out and results are so near. The way it is open, plain is to see. I look for advantage, and success welcomes me.*
- Each morning look through the right end of the telescope and say the second set of words.

117

AN ORANGE AND LEMON SPELL FOR A MAJOR LEAP OR CAREER MOVE TO A SENIOR POST

You will need:

Bergamot, lemon, lemon verbena, or lemongrass essential oil (or fragrance burning oil)
Neroli (orange blossom) or orange essential oil or fragrance burning oil
An oil burner or a diffuser
Alternatively, light orange and lemon incense sticks

Timing:
Sunday

The Spell

- Fill the oil burner a third full with water, adding five drops of lemon essential oil and five drops of orange essential oil to the water. (If using fragrance oils, just fill one-third with the oils.)
- Light the burner. As fragrance or vapor spreads, waft sweet-smelling air with your hands. Do the same with incense smoke. Say ten times: *Stir energies and upward carry me. To where I rightfully should be. My influence pervading all I see. In roles of seniority.*
- Let the burner or incense burn through.
- Take the orange and lemon oils to work every day, adding a few drops to a cup of hot water to inhale as you work. Alternatively crumble orange and lemon incense sticks, keeping them in a dish in your workspace.

118

A TRADITIONAL VIKING HIGH-FLYING SPELL TO FACILITATE MAJOR CAREER AMBITIONS OR GET THE JOB OF YOUR DREAMS

You will need:

Three gold-colored coins
Ideally a seashore or tidal river before high tide; if not, any water source
Dried thyme and rosemary

Timing:
Tuesday

The Spell

- Build a small fire close to the water's edge.
- Sprinkle thyme and rosemary into the flames, saying: *Burn bright that the height of my ambition I achieve. Leap high, do not deny, my speedy rise. Flame that I may swiftly attain what must be mine sooner to gain.*
- Cast the gold coins into the water, naming your urgent ambition, saying: *Lady of the Ocean, Mother of the Sea, I bring you gold, give power to me.*
- Wait until high tide meets the fire, carrying the fire away.
- Repeat your wish, casting a second tiny piece of gold into the sea, repeating the second chant.
- If you are working with nontidal water, scoop a bucket of the water to douse the fire, using the same words.
- Make the final offering before leaving the shore, repeating the words.

119

A STEPPING-STONE SPELL IF YOU ARE FOLLOWING A SET PATH OR TRAINING TO ENSURE EACH STEP IS SUCCESSFUL

You will need:

Stepping-stones over water if possible; if not, set seven flat large stones at intervals on grass or soil.

A round white stone

A feather

Timing:

Before any career transitions

The Spell

- Hold the white stone in your dominant hand and the feather in the other hand and cross the stepping-stones, stopping on each one, saying: *Step by step I move toward greater fulfillment, step by step move up the ladder of attainment, step by step follow the pathway toward the top, I shall not stop.*
- When you reach the middle stone, cast the white stone into the water or as far as you can on the ground, saying: *I reach out far and wide, my own path I decide—and now.*
- Continue to walk across the stepping-stones, saying the stepping-stone words continuously.
- On the last stone, cast the feather free, repeating all the spell words.

120

TO GET HIDDEN POWERS FOR ADVANTAGE IN YOUR WORKPLACE

You will need:

A small item used daily that is associated with your trade or career in the center of a circle

A dish of salt farthest away in the circle

An incense stick in a tree fragrance to the right

A red candle nearest to you

A bowl of water to the left

Timing:

Wednesdays

The Spell

- Light the candle and then light the incense from the candle.
- Sprinkle a circle of salt clockwise around the item, saying: *By the power of earth do I call my secret power at this hour to bring me rapid advantage and advancement.*
- Waft a clockwise circle of incense, saying: *By the power of air* (add the rest of the chant).
- Pass the candle around the item and say, *By the power of fire* (add the rest of the chant).
- Sprinkle a clockwise circle of water drops over the salt circle, saying: *By the power of water* (add the rest of the chant).
- Hold the item between open cupped hands, saying nine times as you gently toss it: *By earth, air, water, fire, enter here my secret power at my desire.*
- On nine, toss it high and catch it.
- Touch the item at work to release the secret power.

HARMONY AND DISHARMONY IN THE WORKPLACE

121

FOR A HAPPY AND HARMONIOUS WORKPLACE

You will need:

A square of paper to draw a detailed plan of the workplace
Colored marker pens
Three floral incense sticks
A blue candle
A green plant

Timing:

Any waxing moon day

The Spell

- Draw a plan of the workplace. For a second floor, draw a second plan, repeating the spell.
- Mark circles where people sit and small squares for equipment or socializing and meeting areas.
- At the four corners of the plan, place the incense sticks. Place the green plant in the center.
- Light the candle, saying: *Light of calm, light of peace, spread across this workplace without cease, bring harmony and unity that contented we shall be.*
- Blow softly into the candle three times, repeating the words.
- Light the incense sticks from the candle, repeating the words for each and then blowing softly into each three times.
- Let the candle and incense burn.
- The next day, set the plant in your workspace.
- When things seem fraught or tensions are set to rise, say the spell words three times and touch the plant.

122

A SPELL FOR CREATING A RAINBOW OF HARMONY IN YOUR SPACE IN A LARGE, IMPERSONAL ORGANIZATION

You will need:

Seven small round crystals in red, orange, yellow, green, blue, purple, and white or clear glass nuggets, beads, or buttons
A glass bowl half filled with water

Timing:

Ideally a rainbow in the sky or sunshine after rain

The Spell

- Drop each crystal, in any order, into the bowl of water; as you do so, say: *Rainbow, rainbow, magic measure, sparkle and glisten with your treasure. Rainbow of joy make my workplace like home that safe I feel until day is done.*
- When the sun fades, dry the crystals. Put them in a bag and bottle the rainbow water.
- Set the crystals in a circle in your workspace, touching them when you feel overwhelmed by company policy or the impersonal atmosphere.
- Sprinkle a little of the water on any plants in your area.

123

A FULL MOON OIL HARMONY SPELL FOR DRAMA KINGS AND QUEENS IN YOUR WORK LIFE

You will need:

A bottle of essential or fragrance oil in lavender, rose, or any floral fragrance
A silver candle (optional)

Timing:

Full moon

The Spell

- Outdoors, or indoors by candlelight if the weather is dull, hold the unopened oil in the hand you do not write with.
- With your other outstretched hand, arm raised and fingers together, point to the moon (or the ceiling), swirling your hand through the candlelight with the index and middle fingers.
- Say: *Lady Moon, grant us your peace and with it fill this oil.*
- Touch the bottle lid with the same two fingers.
- Point again to the moon, saying: *Lady Moon, grant us your harmony and with it fill this oil.*
- Point to the moon a third time and say: *Lady Moon, grant us your tranquillity and with it fill this oil.*
- Tap the bottle lid three times, repeating one chant for each tap.
- Leave the sealed bottle in moonlight.
- Next morning, at work, add a couple of drops of oil to a cup of warm water on your desk or workbench or soak a cotton wool ball in oil and put it on the radiator.

124

A TRADITIONAL HERB SPELL TO CREATE A HAPPY WORKPLACE IF THERE HAVE BEEN MAJOR CHANGES OR THERE IS UNCERTAINTY AHEAD

You will need:

A white candle
Four tablespoons of unscented baby powder
Rosewood or any floral essential or fragrance oil
Two or three teaspoons of dried crushed lavender heads, vervain, or valerian
A wooden or ceramic bowl and spoon
A strong envelope

Timing:

Late Sunday night

The Spell

- Light the candle and work by its light.
- Put the powder and flowers in the bowl and then add eight to ten drops of oil, mixing until they are blended in a smooth powder, saying continuously: *Light of calm, spread harmony, peace to overcome uncertainty, may changes blend, anxiety end, as this mix draws new unity.*
- Put the mix in the envelope, passing it six times over the candle, repeating the chant six times.
- Each morning put a pinch outside the entrance to the workplace, hiding another in the bathroom or a plant pot in a communal area.

125

AN INSTANT TAPPING SPELL FOR RESTORING BALANCE IF WORKPLACE TEMPERS RUN HIGH OR IMPOSSIBLE DEADLINES ARE CAUSING TENSION

You will need:
A pen to be used only for tapping

Timing:
Friday evening initially at home and then whenever needed at work

The Spell

- Tap the pen on a surface gently, building up a slow regular rhythm, one and two and three—one, two, three, four or whatever rhythm feels right.
- When you have established your rhythm, chant softly aloud in time, *May peace embrace this entire place, tranquillity too, flowing through, calmness now enfolds all as I do call this tapping into being.*
- Keep the pen in your workspace, and whenever tensions rise, start tapping the rhythm with the pen softly. If tensions run high, chant in your head the spell words along with the tapping.

126

TO STOP VICIOUS GOSSIP OR TROUBLEMAKERS IN THE WORKPLACE

You will need:
A small lidded bottle
Sour milk
Dried ginger powder or allspice
Eucalyptus essential oil or a bath foam or shampoo containing eucalyptus

Timing:
The waning moon

The Spell

- Half fill the bottle with sour milk, saying: *Venom and viciousness, sourness and spite, begone and trouble me no more.*
- Add a few pinches of ginger or allspice, repeating the words.
- Add eucalyptus, saying the same words.
- Put on the lid, shaking the bottle vigorously, repeating the words ten times.
- Turn the bottle ten times counterclockwise, saying, *Turn away malice, malevolence, mischievous utterings, your unkind muttering, shall be undone. And so your power to hurt is gone.*
- Tip the contents away under a running tap, saying, *Transformed be from negativity to gentleness, malice to kindness and positivity, as rivers flow to sea.*
- Wash out the bottle with hot water and eucalyptus.
- Repeat as necessary.

127

A CRYSTAL OR DARK STONE SHIELD TO PREVENT INTRUSION IN YOUR WORKSPACE AND COUNTER CRITICAL PEOPLE WHO RUIN YOUR CONCENTRATION AND PEACE

You will need:

A smallish dark oval crystal, crystal egg or dark oval stone found near your home or workplace

Timing:

Every year and a day

The Spell

- Hold the crystal between your open cupped hands, up to sunlight, breathing on it three times softly and then saying, *Be protection for me against negativity, intrusion, interruption, and hostility. Be as a shield for me, letting only positivity pass though.*
- Set the crystal in your workspace, facing a door or area through which people pass. Holding it, name anyone who is disruptive and intrusive, repeating the spell words.
- Wash the crystal weekly under running water. Replace after a year and a day, returning the stone where you found it and burying the crystal.

128

A SPELL TO SOFTEN SOUR WORKPLACE MEMBERS, MANAGERS, OR FACTIONS

You will need:

Boiling water
A jug
Sugar, honey, or sweetener
A teaspoon

Timing:

At drinks break in the workplace's kitchen (alternatively, do the spell at home in advance)

The Spell

- Pour a small quantity of boiling water into the jug. Add a teaspoonful of sugar for each difficult person, naming them all and saying for each one: *May you sweeter daily be.*
- Stir nine times counterclockwise, repeating the words nine times as you do so (or say them in your mind).
- Continue to stir until the sugar is dissolved.
- Pour the sugar water down the drain; as you do so, repeat the words nine times.
- If the difficult people take sugar, stir their drinks counterclockwise as you add sugar or sweetener, reciting the chant. If they do not take sugar, briefly touch the outer base of their mugs before filling with the unwashed spoon you used for the spell.

129

A HAND-WASHING RITUAL WHEN THINGS GET FRAUGHT AT WORK

What you need:
Nothing

Timing:
Whenever you are under pressure or a decision is demanded before you are ready

The Spell

- Go to the workplace's bathroom and wash your hands, using soap; as you do so, say in your head over and over: *You do not do, you do not do, pressure and disruption you are through, desist at once from constant interruption.*
- Rinse your hands under running water, repeating the words.
- Splash water in the center of your brow, at the base of your neck, and on your inner wrists, saying for each body area: *This will I do, this I will do, regain my own center that none may pursue, disrupt, or break through my harmony.*
- Dip both hands once more under the tap and then shake your hands dry and return to work totally in control and ready for anything.

130

A HAPPY POSITIVE OFFICE PARTY, WORK OUTING, OR TRAINING INITIATIVE

You will need:
A packet of large dried beans
A strong fabric drawstring bag

Timing:
The evening before the event

The Spell

- Add a bean for each person attending the event, including yourself. Approximate if there will be a lot of people.
- Say for each person: *May we mingle and mix joyously, may we blend as a team harmoniously as friends, enjoy good company that there may be no disharmony.*
- If you know certain people are potentially confrontational or may behave inappropriately, name them as you hold their beans and say the chant three times, ending with and merge peacefully.
- When you have added all the beans, close the bag tightly, shaking it ten times; as you do so, say: *Merge and mix, mingle and blend, may competitiveness and differences find an end. Happy shall we be in one another's company.*
- Take the bag with you, and just before you leave, shake it ten more times and repeat both chants.

SELF-EMPLOYMENT AND BUSINESS VENTURES

131

A COMPUTER SPELL FOR LAUNCHING A NEW BUSINESS VENTURE

You will need:
A computer

Timing:
Daily, a week before the launch

The Spell

- In the center of the computer screen, write a word or phrase or draw an image to represent the new venture, such as your company logo or a photo of you and any company members.
- Say: *May this business/venture grow and flourish as I do nourish the seeds of enterprise that I will rise through days and months and years.*
- As you chant, gradually increase the size of the image or word on the screen until it fills the whole screen.
- When you cannot enlarge the word or image any further, end the spell by saying: *The launch takes on its full power, and as I count to three, so expansion is free, limitless, boundless, one, two, and three, the power is in me.*
- On the count of three, press the print button so that the image will emerge in a tangible form that you can pin on the wall as a reminder of your progress.

132

TO TURN AN INTEREST OR TALENT INTO A LUCRATIVE CAREER

You will need:
A stream, a lake, a canal, or a river with a bridge
Five twigs with growing leaves
A gold-colored coin and a silver-colored coin

Timing:
When the sun and moon are both in the sky

The Spell

- With the twigs in the hand you write with and the coins in the other hand, standing on the bridge, turn to first to the sun and then to the moon, raising your hands and saying: *Sun power, moon power, at this hour, make my talents shine, bring moon silver, sunshine gold, that I may generate wealth untold through my endeavors.*
- Cast the twigs one at a time from the bridge upstream into the flow, saying: *Flow and grow, unobstructed be, that I may see results as this the water reaches sea.*
- Watch your wishes float under the bridge. Throw the coins off the down side, repeating all the spell words.
- Contact a potential outlet for your talents.

133

FOR ESTABLISHING A WORK BASE AT HOME

You will need:

A soft blue wax candle in the center of the room on a tray
Twelve unused coins of any denomination (from a bank or post office)
Allspice or cinnamon in a jar

Timing:

After dusk in your projected workspace, every night for a week

The Spell

- Light the candle, saying, *Make this sanctuary, a hive of productivity, let me establish my working haven at home that both may be in harmony and creativity, but the workspace is just for me.*
- Drop a few grains of spice into the flame, repeating the words.
- As the wax begins to fall on the coins, say: *Increase and grow, flow that my work sanctuary may be for me a hive of productivity.*
- When the wax is cool but not hard, cut a circle from the wax containing the coins. Keep this circle wrapped in blue silk in your workspace drawer.

134

A SPELL FOR MAKING UNSATISFACTORY BUSINESS PREMISES YOUR OWN, ESPECIALLY IF THEY HAVE A HISTORY OF FAILED BUSINESSES

You will need:

A new broom
A bucket of hot water
A scrubbing brush
Pine, juniper, or tea tree essential oil
A string of silver bells
A mirror
Nine white flower heads in a bowl of water

Timing:

The morning you move into the premises

The Spell

- Starting at the back of the premises, sweep dust and litter out the front door, saying: *Sweep, scrub, and rub away the old, sweep, scrub, and rub in new gold.*
- Scrub the main areas from back to front, adding nine drops of oil to the water bucket. Keep saying the same words.
- When you get to the front door, scrub the front step, repeating the words, then tip the water outside, saying, *Away with the old, in comes new gold.*
- Go to the center of the premises and ring the bells nine times, then sprinkle flower water around the entire premises from back to front.
- Standing again in the center, swivel the mirror clockwise around you to catch the light and then hang it on a wall facing the front door.

135

A SPELL FOR CLEANSING ANY EQUIPMENT YOU INHERIT OR BUY TO MAKE IT WORK FOR YOU

You will need:

Dried hyssop or mint or green tea bags
A cup, jug, or teapot
A teaspoon

Timing:

Whenever you buy or hire equipment

The Spell

- Make a hyssop infusion with one teaspoon of dried herbs, pouring on almost a cupful of boiling water. For larger amounts, mix one ounce of the dried herb to a pint and a quarter of water. Or use tea bags.
- Stir the infusion, saying continuously, *Hyssop, hyssop* [or name herb], *cleanse and purify. Bless and sanctify that this* [name equipment] *will serve me well, giving birth to new resources and sources of income.*
- Let the mix stand for five to ten minutes, stirring occasionally, then strain the infusion or the remove tea bag.
- Sprinkle three counterclockwise circles of the infusion around the item, groups of small items, or a photograph, repeating the chant.
- Pour any remaining mix outdoors on soil.

136

A TRADITIONAL CHINESE METAL AND WIND SPELL FOR LONG-TERM GROWTH, ESPECIALLY OVERSEAS AND ON THE INTERNET

You will need:

Three coins with holes in the center (Chinese divinatory coins or gold disks or washers)
A long thin red cord
Metal wind chimes (ones with dragons are good).

Timing:

Wednesdays

The Spell

- Tie the coins at regular intervals to the cord, saying for each, *Far and wide, o'er land and sea, new business flies direct to me.*
- Knot the cord top and bottom with three knots, at each one saying, Threefold increase shall there be over land and over sea.
- Attach the cord to the wind chimes, putting both chants together.
- Hang the wind chimes near a window or the entrance to the room or rooms where you work.
- Each morning before starting work, blow on the chimes three times, saying both chants again.
- If you are seeking worldwide recognition, hang the cord outdoors on a sheltered bush or tree.

137

A MEDIEVAL HANDSEL SPELL TO MAKE YOUR BUSINESS PROFITABLE IN THE EARLY DAYS

You will need:

The first check, receipt of payment, or currency note you receive (the Anglo-Saxon term *handsel*)

Timing:

The evening after you receive your first income

The Spell

- Hold the payment in the hand you write with and say five times very fast: *The first is always sweetest, but then pours in much more, money flowing inward, payments by the score, handsel is as handsel does, flowing, growing, pouring, flooding through the door.*
- Keep the payment in a display case on your workspace wall.

138

A SMOKE SPELL FOR BREAKING INTO MARKET, FAIR, AND FESTIVAL SALES

You will need:

Three or four incense cones in any tree or fruit fragrance on a heatproof dish with a handle for carrying

A large feather or fan

Timing:

After you set up your stall

The Spell

- Light the incense cones and blow each one gently until it releases smoke, saying for each, *This is my territory, this my sanctuary to draw to me, those who bring profitability for my creativity. Enter all in noncompetitiveness, sharing, and complete friendliness that we may offer our gifts for pleasure, not just for treasure, and make this day a joy for all.*
- Hold the incense plate in the hand you write with and, using the feather, the fan, or your other hand, waft spirals of smoke over the stall and around the artifacts, repeating the chant softly and continuously until you feel calm and confident.
- Put out the incense by inverting it on the plate.

139

A CELTIC SPELL FOR GRADUALLY MOVING TO SELF-EMPLOYMENT OR STARTING FROM SCRATCH

You will need:

A glass dish
A tub of gold glass nuggets, loose pearls, buttons, beads, or small yellow crystals
A clear cookware jar

Timing:
Any time you start any self-employed activities

The Spell

- Face the morning sun, outdoors if possible. Say: *May there always be work enough for my hands, strength to achieve my daily round. At the end of each day, may there be satisfaction in work well done and money honestly earned and rewarded.*
- Every time you make a sale or order, place a nugget in the dish.
- When the dish is full, transfer all the nuggets except one to the jar and start again.
- Leave the dish and jar in an area of the workspace where light will shine on them.
- On Sunday and at midsummer leave outdoors all day.

140

A HONEY POT RITUAL TO INCREASE PROFITABILITY IF CUSTOMERS ARE SLOW TO COMMIT

You will need:

A jar of honey
A spoon
A beeswax candle or yellow wax candle

Timing:
In sunshine or extra candlelight

The Spell

- Light the candle, saying, *Lady Mother, honeybee, shine your sweetness down on me. As bee to nectar, butterfly to flower, will customers be drawn to me by my new selling power, and persuasively with honeyed words will orders on me shower.*
- Put some honey on the spoon. Hold it up to the light and say: *Lady Mother, honeybee, I offer you your own that your sweetness on me shower.*
- Eat a little honey from the spoon, repeating both chants.
- Return the lid to the honey and wash the spoon in hot water, as you do so saying both sets of words.
- Let the candle burn down next to the honey pot.
- Eat some honey before taking or offering goods or services for sale.

SECTION 5:

OVERCOMING CHANGES AND SETBACKS TO A CAREER

141

TO RECOVER FROM FIRING OR UNFAIR DISMISSAL

You will need:

Damp soil
Thick-soled shoes or boots
A deep plant pot
Growing herb or flower seedlings, especially thyme, chamomile, or coriander

Timing:
Early morning

The Spell

- Stand in the soil with legs apart, pressing down with your feet hard until you have imprinted the soil. Say: *I am myself, successful, complete, failure is earth beneath my feet. I will rise again, higher and higher, rise as high as I aspire.*
- Repeat the words three times, continuing to stamp your impressions on the same spot in the earth.
- Fill the plant pot with the imprinted soil and plant the herbs or flowers, saying: *From dark to light, grow to great height, so I shall rise and touch the skies, though the way seems dark, new life will grow, as the seeds of my great future now I sow.*
- Repeat the words of the spell as you water the plant and if you ever despair.

142

A SPELL TO BREAK INTO A DIFFICULT MARKET OR CAREER IF YOU HAVE SUFFERED MANY SETBACKS

You will need:

Children's colored building blocks

Timing:
Saturdays

The Spell

- Make a foundation with six bricks, near the center building a pile of three bricks, saying: *Step by step, stage by stage, I rejoice in every small advantage, push by push, there is no rush, I climb each step, each step is higher for patience and perseverance will me inspire.*
- Start a second pile of three bricks to the right so that the two piles touch, repeating the words.
- Add three more bricks to first the left-hand and then the right-hand pile carefully, again saying the words.
- Keep adding a brick at a time until the towers topple, saying, *I have the power to persevere, never to give in, so I will win. If it takes months or years, so shall I persist, for I will taste sweet victory.*
- Rebuild the towers to the point where they are stable, leaving them as a reminder.

143

A RELAXING SPELL FOR LEARNING NEW TECHNOLOGY OR NEW SKILLS THAT ARE ESSENTIAL FOR WORKPLACE CHANGES

You will need:

A triangle of three yellow candles
The manual, book, or paperwork connected with the new process inside the triangle
A small purse
Dried parsley, sage, rosemary, and thyme (memory herbs)
A deep ceramic dish and wooden spoon

Timing:
Before sleep

The Spell

- Light the candles, open the manual at the beginning, and read a page or two.
- Then say: *Parsley, sage, rosemary, thyme, hard this does seem to this mind of mine, but cut through the jargon, the techno mixed speech, and in a very short time competency I easily will reach.*
- Grind the herbs in the bowl with the spoon faster and faster, chanting, *Parsley, sage, rosemary, thyme, make this techno jargon mine.*
- Blow out the three candles, place the manual next to your bed, and when you wake, read the same section again.
- Before work scatter the herbs outside.
- Each night and morning add more knowledge.

144

A SPELL TO HELP PARENTS COMBINE A FAMILY WITH PAID WORK OR STUDY

You will need:

A white candle
A dish of nine marbles or glass beads
A bag

Timing:
After a hard day juggling priorities

The Spell

- Light the candle, adding the marbles to the bag.
- Shake the bag nine times, saying, *I am not Superwoman/man, the world turns without me, too much to do, let's cut to priority.*
- Remove a marble from the dish and shake the bag eight times, repeating the words and removing another marble.
- Continue until you have only one marble left in the bag, shake once, and say: *This is all about me, for my strength, you see, keeps the wheel turning* [you can add the name of a supportive partner if you have one. *I am priority. And so to myself will kinder be.*
- Tip the final marble into the dish. Plan how you can cut corners to give yourself more time.

145

A SUN SYMBOL SPELL FOR WHEN YOU HAVE HAD AN OPPORTUNITY TAKEN FROM YOU

You will need:

A circle of yellow or orange paper
A black pen
An orange, red, or gold candle

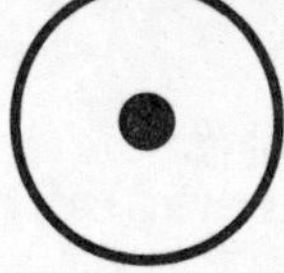

Timing:
Midday

The Spell

- Draw a large black dot in the center of the paper circle to represent the astrological glyph for the sun.
- Light the candle and say, *Light shine on me, I deserve it, you see, my sun has been dimmed, unfairly you know unjustly and so, I reclaim my place in the sun, now, anyhow, anywhere, sun get me there.*
- Write all around the sun circle until it is filled precisely with what you deserve and when and the obstacles or people in the way.
- Set the sun in front of the candle and repeat the spell words.
- Let the candle burn through.
- Every Sunday, light another candle and repeat the spell words as you hold the sun circle.

146

TO HELP CAREERS OR THOSE IN CARING PROFESSIONS SURVIVE CHALLENGES AND PRESSURES

You will need:

A white candle
Seven green ribbons
Seven white flowers
A dish

Timing:
Sunday evening and the next six days

The Spell

- Light the candle, saying: *Help me tomorrow and every day of the week, compassion and kindness is what I do seek. Light the way for me.*
- Pass the first ribbon over the flame, tying a loose knot in it, saying: *I tie up reserves of strength for tomorrow that it may be filled with joy, not sorrow.*
- Place it in front of the candle and pluck each petal from the first flower, placing the petals in the dish
- Blow out the candle. In the morning release the petals outdoors, saying, *Now strength is free, fly back to me when needed.*
- Carry the ribbon in your bag; if you become tired or dispirited, release the knot, saying, *Strength flies to me.*
- Repeat the spell daily with a new flower and ribbon, starting a new cycle when all seven have been used.

147

A SPELL FOR ANYONE WHO MAKES HOMEMAKING A FULL-TIME CAREER

You will need:

Old-fashioned lavender polish

A favorite family ornament or piece of furniture

Timing:

Any quiet time at home

The Spell

- Begin to polish the chosen item slowly and rhythmically saying as a continuous chant, *May this home be the heart and hearth of peace, sanctuary, a source of strength, harmony without cease. That my endeavors create a home, not just a shell. May I work well to benefit my family now and through future ages. The home the heart and hearth of peace, through all the stages of our lives, never shall it cease.*
- Touch your heart with the hand you write with and then the chosen furniture or artifact with the same hand. Say once more, The home the heart and hearth of peace, never to cease.
- Repeat weekly if you ever doubt the importance of what you do in keeping the home and family together.

148

IF A LOVED ONE FACES PHYSICAL DANGERS OR HARDSHIP IN HIS OR HER CAREER

You will need:

A photograph or printout of the family member or friend

Four large round dark stones or rocks in a square around the picture

Four dark blue or purple candles, one set between each rock

Timing:

A few days before departure to a dangerous place or mission

The Spell

- Hold the picture, saying, *May the strong walls of love enclose you, may the mighty rocks of my protection enfold you and the god/goddess hold you in the palm of his/her hand until you return safe to me/your family.*
- Light the candles clockwise around the square, repeating the words for each one.
- Touch each rock in turn, again saying the spell words.
- Let the candles burn. Keep the rocks around the picture. Once a week light candles around the picture and say, *I light the way home for you. May the god/goddess hold you in the palm of his/her hand until you return safe to me/your family.*

149

TO OVERCOME BEING PASSED OVER BECAUSE OF AGE, FAVORITISM, OR SEX BUT YOU CAN'T PROVE IT

You will need:

Two matching shells that fit together (you can use the shells from seafood)
Blue thread
A pearl or pearl button
Any body of water, ideally the sea

Timing:
Tuesday

The Spell

- Hold one shell in each hand, saying, *Though I fit in every way, my prospects weaken by the day, prejudice hard to prove, unfairness even slower to move.*
- Put the pearl inside one half of the shell and say, *My treasure upon the waters will I cast to justly bring promotion fast.*
- Enclose the pearl with the second shell, binding the shells together tightly with three knots, saying, *Bind up prejudice, banish words, for I seek merit rewarded, recognition accorded. I ask I may be heard.*
- Cast the joined shells into water, saying, *Lady of the Waters, this tribute is your own. I ask only of you in my best light I am shown.*

150

A SPELL FOR SURVIVING A TAKEOVER OR THREATENED JOB CUTS

You will need:

A stopwatch

Timing:
Whenever rumors start or changes seem unwelcome

The Spell

- Start the watch in a park or open space.
- Move in circles, saying three times as it ticks away, *Rumors and gossip, fears and tears, changes unwelcome looming so near. A backward stage, a backward step, no, I will embrace it and forward leap.*
- Stop the clock. Say, *I will hear no more. Balance and security must be restored.*
- Start the clock again and walk forward saying, *I will not walk in circles but straight toward my goal. I will survive, I will thrive, change, you are welcome, I embrace you soon, time will not hinder me but dance to my tune.*
- Let the watch tick. As you walk, plan how you can turn any changes to your advantage.

CHAPTER 4

HEALTH AND HEALING SPELLS

This chapter includes ten all-purpose spells for health and healing; spells for overcoming fears, phobias, and bad habits; spells for healing children and older people; spells for planetary and global healing and preventing natural disasters; spells for reducing pain; and spells for relieving suffering when all seems hopeless,

151

THE WORLD'S SIMPLEST, MOST SECRET, AND MAYBE MOST EFFECTIVE HEALTH AND HEALING SPELL

You will need:
A glass of water
Alternatively, a plastic bottle of mineral water.
If necessary, empower any available drink

Timing:
Any health or healing purpose, any place

The Spell

- Hold a glass of water between your hands. Because water is pure, you can use it as a magical space and imprint it with whatever you need.
- For a specific health or healing purpose, say what you most need. For example, say: *My headache is lifting and I am full of energy.*
- Empower the water for health, vitality, and strength for the days or hours ahead.
- Keep your hands cupped around the glass for about two minutes and then slowly sip the water, thinking the empowerment.
- If you always feel tired in the morning, fill a glass of water before sleep, endowing it with energy and enthusiasm for the day ahead. Drink the water as soon as you wake, saying: *I fill myself with the enthusiasm and joy for the day ahead.*

152

A TRADITIONAL SPELL TO RECOVER FROM AN ILLNESS OR DEPRESSION IF PROGRESS IS SLOW

You will need:
Three white candles of ascending sizes set in a row, the smallest to the left
A pot of salt

Timing:
Every morning

The Spell

You can carry out this spell for someone else, naming that person at the beginning of the spell and throughout it.

- Light the smallest candle, saying, *Each day I feel new strength to me.*
- Light the second candle from the first, saying, *Each day greater vitality.*
- Light the third candle from the second, saying, *Each day better I will be.*
- Sprinkle a pinch of salt into each flame, saying for the first candle, *Cleansed be.*
- For the second candle say, *That I may see,*
- For the third candle say, *Recovery.*
- Hold your hands toward the candles, palms down, fingers together, then touch your heart, saying, *So do I take within me strength, health, vitality.*
- Blow out the candles in reverse order, saying, *I receive this healing light with thanks, blessings be on my swift recovery.*
- Leave the salt to absorb sickness and throw it away the same night before bed.

153

A VERY ANCIENT WATER SPELL TO REMOVE VIRUSES AND INFECTIONS, GALLSTONES AND KIDNEY STONES, TUMORS, BLOCKAGES, FUNGAL INFECTIONS, WARTS, AND VERRUCAS

You will need:

A single golden-colored coin or, if the affliction is in the form of stones or little growths, three or four coins

A flowing water source

Timing:

Saturdays

The Spell

- Stand by the water source, rubbing the coin(s) nine times counterclockwise, either directly on the affected part of your body or over your clothes above the relevant area. For a widespread debility or a virus, choose a token part of the body.
- As you rub, say nine times for each coin: *Leave me, affliction. Pass into this coin as token of my need to part from you. Our connection must be through.*
- Cast the coins one at a time into the water, saying: *I sell this affliction willingly to the healing waters to be transformed to fertilizing rain. I ask no return.*
- As you leave the water source, do not look back.

154

AN ABSENT HEALING SPELL FOR EVERY PURPOSE

You will need:

A large piece of uncut, unpolished calcite in any color, rose quartz, or amethyst; alternatively, you can use a crystal sphere or pyramid

A pink or a lilac- or rose-scented candle

Timing:

Twilight

The Spell

- Light the candle so that the crystal glows. Call the person or animal or name the place to be healed.
- Say, *Pain and sorrow, sickness and distress, be transformed and blessed by the power of this crystal and this flame.*
- Place the crystal on the table, holding your hands over it but not quite touching it. Repeat the words softly and mesmerically.
- When the power buzzes through your fingers, hold your hands vertically, palms outward, waist height, and say the words again. Ask any favorite archangel to help you,
- Return the hand you do not write with to the crystal and with the other hand push toward the healing target.
- When you feel the power diminishing, change hands until you feel the power of the crystal slowing down and your energies ebbing. The healing is now complete.
- Wash the crystal in running water and leave it to dry naturally.

155

A HEART-TO-HEART ABSENT HEALING SPELL FOR A PERSON OR ANIMAL WITH WHOM YOU HAVE A CLOSE EMOTIONAL CONNECTION

You will need:
Your healing crystal
A green candle (optional)

Timing:
Fridays

The Spell
- Polish the crystal with a soft white cloth, saying, *My love for you as healing I send my care for you. And so I send from my heart to yours the cord of healing willing, true.*
- Hold the crystal to your heart with both hands.
- Say the same words.
- Call the person's name three times softly. When you feel the energy flowing freely between your heart and the crystal in a two-way direction, hold the crystal outstretched to a natural source of light or green candle, repeating the words softly and continuously.
- When you sense healing is complete, allow the connection to fade and put the crystal down on the table to break the connection between you, but very gently. Healing is complete. Polish the crystal gently.

156

FOR BURNING AWAY AN ILLNESS, FEVER, OR PROGRESSIVE CONDITION THAT IS CAUSING DEGENERATION

You will need:
A dark red candle
A thin-bladed paper knife

Timing:
The waning moon or Tuesday

The Spell
- Write on one side of the candle, using the paper knife, BURN AWAY AFFLICTION, and on the other, TURN AWAY AFFLICTION (substitute the name of the person you are helping).
- Light the candle, look into the flame, and say nine times, going faster and faster, *Burn away, turn away, fever of intensity. Set me free that I may be, strong again and so remain* [or name the person].
- Blow out the candle, as you do so saying: *Burn no more in me* [or name person]. *But set me* [name] *free that I may be strong again and so remain.*
- When you repeat the spell, trace the words on the candle with your index finger instead of etching them with the knife.

157

A SELF-HEALING RITUAL IF YOU FEEL UNWELL OR EXHAUSTED BUT THE CAUSE CANNOT BE FOUND

You will need:

A semicircle of six pink candles
A dying purple or blue flower
A blossoming pink or white flower
A pot of soil

Timing:
Sunset

The Spell

- Light the candles from left to right, saying once, *Flame of hope, flame of power, restore my strength hour by hour. That I may flare with life like you, and health and light in me renew.*
- In each candle burn a dying petal, saying, *Into the fire, sickness burn, burn away, restore and transform with each new day.*
- Drop the singed petals into the pot of soil.
- Pass the blossoming flower six times around the candles in a circle, saying, *Rise, rise to the skies, new health thrive.*
- Let the candles burn.
- Bury the burned petals, still in the soil, and scatter the living flower petals outdoors.

158

A GARLIC SPELL TO REDUCE A CHRONIC CONDITION THAT FREQUENTLY FLARES UP

You will need:

A clove of garlic or garlic powder
A dish of salt
An area of earth

Timing:
Saturday late

The Spell

- Crush the garlic clove into the salt or sprinkle the powder, saying: *Cleansed from me, buried be, that new growth I shall see [or name person]. May new health blossom, flourish, the old obliterated, decimated, expurgated, deep in Mother Earth so new growth will give birth to healthy me.*
- Bury the mix in a deep hole in the earth, repeating: *May new health blossom. Flourish, the old obliterated decimated, expurgated, deep in Mother Earth so new growth will give birth to healthy me.*

159

AN ONION SPELL TO PREVENT A CONDITION FROM SPREADING AND MAKE ITS EFFECTS GRADUALLY DIMINISH

You will need:

A large onion
A vegetable knife

Timing:

Saturday near midnight

The Spell

- Take the outer skin off the onion, saying, *Shred and shed all that keeps my illness growing. As it is going, diminishing, fading, so do I thrive, not just survive.*
- With the knife, scratch a representative name or image for the condition on the onion, repeating the words three times.
- Bury the onion deep outdoors and on it scatter herb or flower seeds, digging some in and letting the rest take root or be taken by the birds. Say, *New life from old, as growth unfolds, the old fades away, the new will now stay.*
- If the transformed onion also forms shoots, that is a bonus.

160

A SPELL FOR SENDING CONCENTRATED HEALING TO A FAMILY MEMBER OR FRIEND MANY MILES AWAY

You will need:

Four white candles in a square
A photograph of the person to be healed in the middle of the square
A floral incense stick
A bowl of salt
A bowl of water

Timing:

Sunset nightly until things improve

The Spell

- Light the candles and say, *I send to you* [name] *the power of fire, your healing to quicken and inspire.*
- Light the incense, passing it nine times around the candles and photograph, saying nine times: *I send to you* [name] *the power of air, your healing to restore and repair.*
- Add six pinches of salt to the water, swirl six times, and sprinkle a circle of drops around the candles, saying, *Here in healing four powers unite, healing powerful, golden, bright, water, earth, air, and fire, bring the healing I desire.*
- Let the candles and incense burn through and tip the water away into earth.
- Leave the photo where natural light will shine on it.

161

TO RESTORE BALANCE IF AN OBSESSION OR PHOBIA IS SPOILING YOUR LIFE

You will need:

Cooking scales, the kind with balancing pans
A jar of grains (you can use nonallergenic grains if you have food intolerances)
A spoon

Timing:
Monday, especially just after the full moon

The Spell

- Pile one pan with grains and leave the other empty.
- Say continuously, *Grain by grain shall balance be restored in my life.*
- Begin spoon by spoon to transfer the grains to the empty pan, saying, *Grain by grain, obsession goes [name issue] and harmony grows.*
- Once the pans are even, stop saying the words. If you want to lose the obsession completely, continue until the new pan is full and adapt the words.
- Tip the grain into a new cooking jar and use in baking or cereals in the days ahead, repeating the words as you spoon out the mix for use.

162

TO OVERCOME A BAD HABIT THAT HAS BOTHERED YOU FOR YEARS

You will need:

An old pair of worn or too tight shoes
A bowl of salt and pepper mix
White vinegar

Timing:
Tuesday

The Spell

- Go outdoors and dig a hole. Take off the old shoes.
- Drop the shoes into the hole, followed by salt and pepper and vinegar, saying, *You no longer fit, you no longer do, you are worn out and finished, finished old shoes.*
- Fill in the hole, naming what you no longer need in your life.
- Put on a pair of newer shoes and say, *You will do, you will do, new shoes carry me forward to adventures new. The past is through.*
- When tempted in future, scatter flower seeds in the earth above the shoes and say, *The past is through. You will do, you will do, new shoes carry me forward to adventures new.*

163

A RED RIBBON SPELL TO HELP FACILITATE A LONGER-TERM RECOVERY OR HEALTHY LIVING PLAN WHEN EMOTIONS GET IN THE WAY

You will need:

A sturdy bush or small tree indoors or out

A quantity of red ribbons, enough for one a day for the program

Timing:

Saturday or a significant weekday for the plan

The Spell

- Go to the bush or plant a special one with the first red ribbon and say as you attach it, *This is me, growing stronger week by week, healthier than before, more and more.*
- Touch the ribbon and say, *The power of the earth makes me stronger week by week, healthier than before, more and more.*
- Do something positive for the new regime.
- Each week or if you waver, repeat until the bush is full of ribbons and you are on the way to the new world. Each time touch the added ribbon and repeat the words.

164

TO BREAK THE SMOKING HABIT

You will need:

A pack of playing cards, just the spades, ace to king, to represent the smoking, and the diamonds, ace to king, for giving up plus the money saved

A pot of lavender or any fragrant flower

Timing:

Ongoing

The Spell

- Lay out the spades in ascending order, ace to king.
- Surround them with a circle of the ace to king of diamonds in ascending order.
- When you are tempted to smoke, crush the cigarette in the pot of lavender.
- Cover the ace of spades with the ace of diamonds, *saying, From high to low does craving grow. Freedom grows with the sweet flowers, and I say no.*
- Give yourself a small nonoral treat.
- When the cards are all covered, start again, plant the flower, and use a new pot.

165

TO OVERCOME GAMBLING PROBLEMS

You will need:

Six dice and a shaking pot
A box of old gambling slips or casino receipts

Timing:

Whenever tempted to gamble

The Spell

- Shake the dice six times in the pot and say six times, *Luck of the draw, lose and not win, gambling I shake away, no need to play, urgency gone away, forever and a day.*
- Make a final shake and then burn an old slip in a pot of soil, saying, *Gambling burns a hole in my pocket, and so of course I stop it.*
- Scatter the ashes.
- When you have used all the slips, write red paper ones with GAMBLING AWAY, NO MORE STAY, GONE FOREVER AND A DAY.

166

TO BEAT CLAUSTROPHOBIA

You will need:

A cell phone
Lavender oil or your favorite fragrance

Timing:

Weekly and whenever you know a situation may arise

The Spell

- Every Sunday night touch the center of your brow, the base of your throat, and your inner wrist points with a drop of the fragrance, saying, *Space and fragrance are all around me, walls disappear,* I *can breathe and am free, nothing to fear.*
- Before entering an elevator, inhale the fragrance on a tissue and repeat the words in your mind three times.
- In the confined space act as if you were making a phone call to your favorite person, repeating the spell words in your mind while listening to the imagined answers.
- If you panic, inhale again.

167

A SPELL AGAINST EATING DISORDERS

You will need:

A small quantity of raisins
A tangerine or similar small tasty food

Timing:

Whenever the food issue arises

The Spell

- Savor the food item regardless of what is being craved by smell, touch, and taste, slowly focusing only on the food, saying in your mind nine times, *Always enough for my needs, whenever my needs, within the temple of my body, I eat at my leisure and so take pleasure.*
- When you have finished eating, repeat the words until you are calm.
- Then decide what would give you pleasure to eat, if anything, and enjoy it slowly, saying the words in your mind if necessary.
- Eat and focus solely on the pleasure of the food and, rather than eating mindlessly, stop and repeat the words before continuing to eat.

168

TO OVERCOME PHOBIAS OF ANIMALS, OBJECTS, OR SITUATIONS

You will need:

A picture of what you fear (if necessary, blank side uppermost).
Red string
A sharp knife or scissors
An old box

Timing:

The beginning of any month

The Spell

- Bind the paper in the string, securing it with ten knots, saying ten times, *I bind you from terrifying, frightening, and troubling me. For you see your reign is done and I have won, and so I cut the ties between us one by one.*
- Cut the knots and then the paper into ten pieces and put in the box.
- Repeat weekly with a smaller image until you can look at it before cutting.
- If you fill the box, empty the contents in a hole dug where nothing grows.

169

A GENTLE SPELL TO REDUCE THE EFFECTS OF PANIC ATTACKS, HYPERVENTILATION, AND SOCIAL PHOBIAS

You will need:

A favorite piece of jewelry
Rose hip, chamomile, or valerian herbal tea mix or tea bags
A small bowl in which to make the tea

Timing:

Fridays weekly or when you fear something will panic you

The Spell

- Make the tea as usual and begin stirring three times clockwise, three times counterclockwise, and three times clockwise as long as you wish in a rhythm, saying, *Nought harm, peace calm, fears flow from me, leaving harmony, inwardly feel, outwardly reveal as peace without cease.*
- Pass the jewelry over the cooled tea nine times clockwise, repeating the words nine times.
- Pour away the tea outdoors and wear the jewelry whenever you know a panic situation might arise, touching it and saying the words in your mind if you feel panic rising.

170

TO HELP A LOVED ONE OVERCOME ALCOHOL OR SUBSTANCE ABUSE

You will need:

A picture of the person before the problem arose or became acute, however young
Four feathers
A white candle

Timing:

Sunday mornings

The Spell

- For the week before the first spell, put the feathers in a square around the picture and have them remain there between subsequent spells.
- Each night light the white candle and waft each feather in turn over the picture, saying, *May freedom be restored, more joyous than before. I blow away what destroys you that you will feel anew life and hope supported by those of us who love you.*
- Extinguish the candle.
- On the actual spell morning, repeat the words and actions but let the candle burn.
- Carry the feathers to a windy place and release them, saying the same words for each one.
- Replace with new feathers and a new candle.

171

TO HEAL A CHILD WHO HAS A CHRONIC ALLERGY OR CONDITION

You will need:

A piece of white paper
A pen that writes in white
A green ink pen
A helium balloon

Timing:
Mondays during the waxing moon

The Spell

- Write all over the paper in white ink on both sides so that it is invisible the name of the child and *illness* BE GONE. You also can use this spell for an adult.
- Draw in green, all over the writing, trees, plants, birds, and butterflies, saying as you do so, *Grow strong, tall as the trees, be free as a bird.*
- Punch holes in the paper so that you can attach it as a taper to the balloon string.
- Hold the balloon in an open space so that the wind tugs it and repeat the spell words faster until you can say them no faster. Then release the balloon with the words *Fly free as the birds.*

172

TO HELP A CHILD WITH COMMUNICATION OR SOCIAL DIFFICULTIES SUCH AS AUTISM, ASPERGER'S, OR ADHD

You will need:

A favorite book or toy
A piece of music or song the child likes
Children's paints and a big piece of paper

Timing:
Thursday mornings

The Spell

- Play the music while holding the toy and saying over and over, *Open the way to the world for my beloved* [name].
- When the music ends, begin to paint in bold colors doorways and windows all over the paper, saying continuously, *Be a doorway into the world for my beloved* [name]. *Open the window to others that he or she may know the joy of social connections.*
- When the painting is dry, hold the toy over it as you replay the music and repeat all the spell words.
- When the music ends, hang the picture somewhere bright.
- Each morning, hold the toy and repeat the spell words.

173

TO HELP A CHILD IN THE HOSPITAL OR RESPITE CARE

You will need:

A picture of the family together
Four trailing plants whose fronds are long enough to be knotted together
Four pink candles

Timing:

Daily for a week before the child leaves home.

The Spell

- Light the four candles around the picture clockwise after the child is in bed, saying for each one, *Surrounded be with the love of your family, enclosed in the light of care whether with us or far away.*
- Place a pot in each corner of the picture and knot a frond to the next pot, saying, *United is the family, far or near, joined by the love that grows in our hearts more dear when we are apart.*
- Blow out the candles. Each night of the week, repeat the spell, relight the candles, and do the spell again, touching each tied frond and if possible joining more.
- Take the photo to the hospital.

174

WHEN A CHILD GETS ONE MINOR ILLNESS AFTER ANOTHER

You will need:

A bell
Small worry dolls or featureless clay figures to represent the child's illness cycle (you can do this for more than one child by using extra dolls)
Green ribbons

Timing:

Mondays

The Spell

- Beginning with the children's room(s), ring the bell all around the room(s), saying, *Clear be of lingering sickness, malaise, and all the old ways of unwellness, virus, or infection.*
- Tie a ribbon around the middle of each figure, saying, *Well shall you be, totally, lastingly. The winds and waters shall carry all sickness from this place and embrace a healthy future permanently.*
- Hang each figure away from the home on a bush or tree to be blown or washed away.
- Put a vase of fresh flowers next to the children's picture.

175

TO ENCOURAGE A CHILD WITH DISABILITIES TO REACH HIS OR HER FULL POTENTIAL

You will need:

A flower coming into bud in a pot
Twelve tiny green crystals, glass nuggets, or beads set in a circle around the pot
Twelve small white or green tea lights in a circle around the crystals

Timing:

The start of every month

The Spell

- Light each candle clockwise, designating a month for each, starting with the current one.
- Say for each one, *The light shines on all, the years grow tall, and you too* [name child] *will flourish and flower and bloom every day in your unique way.*
- Plant the twelve crystals in a circle in the soil, repeating the spell words, and then pass your hands slowly above the plant, naming the months. Let the candles burn.
- When the flower fades, plant it outdoors and repeat the spell with a new budding plant.

176

TO STRENGTHEN AN OLDER PERSON WHOSE MEMORY IS FADING

You will need:

An up-to-date picture of the person on top of a pile of older photos
Three dishes of any floral potpourri, two small and one large, each half full
Six white tea lights

Timing:

Saturday afternoon

The Spell

- Put some potpourri from the first small bowl into the large one, saying, *The past is rich still, memories of a life that makes you what you are. May your star never fade.*
- Place some potpourri from the second bowl into the large one, saying, *Present days shall be rich still, small gems, glittering joys as the light still shines, though intermittently. May your star never fade.*
- Make a pathway of the pictures, oldest first, and light candles on either side, saying, *So shall the future be rich with diamond moments as the bridge of light extends through months and years. May your star never fade or laughter turn to tears.*
- Let the candles burn and show the photos and place the potpourri from all three bowls in the older person's room or home.

177

FOR AN OLDER PERSON UNDERGOING SURGERY OR INVASIVE TREATMENT

You will need:

A small fabric worry doll or make a children's pink play clay one
Dried mint, lavender, or chamomile
A soft silk scarf

Timing:

Before the treatment in early light

The Spell

- Lay the doll on the cloth and say, *May you lie gently in the arms of love, grow strong again, free from pain, for there are good years ahead just over the horizon.*
- Sprinkle half the herbs or petals over the doll, repeating the words.
- Wrap the scarf tightly around the doll and sprinkled herbs and knot it, saying the words again.
- The day of the operation and in the days until recovery, open the scarf and add a few more herbs or petals, repeat the words, and retie the scarf.
- If any herbs are left afterward, throw them into running water.

178

TO MAINTAIN HEALTH IN AN AGING PARENT OR GRANDPARENT FAR AWAY

You will need:

A packet of sunflower seeds or any golden flower seeds

Timing:

Sunday mornings

The Spell

- Hold the dish of seeds up to the light, saying, *May the sun that shines on all warm and fill you with vitality.*
- Bury a third, saying, *Life grows anew strong and clear.*
- Cast a third into running water, saying, *Life flows anew strong and clear.*
- Throw a third into the air, saying, *Life flies free anew strong and clear.*
- Send the faraway person some yellow flowers and every night repeat the spell words as you hold that person's picture.

179

A TRADITIONAL EVERGREEN SPELL FOR ANY AGING FAMILY MEMBER TO PROLONG A GOOD INDEPENDENT QUALITY OF LIFE

You will need:

A large evergreen plant or tree, indoors or out

Twinkling electric or solar lights (at one time candles were used)

Timing:

At twilight

The Spell

- As darkness falls, switch on the lights on the tree or the solar lights.
- Extend your hands so that they are covered in light, palms down, fingers outstretched in the direction the person lives, and say, *I send you light that you may flourish bright as the evergreen and as long living.*
- Repeat the actions, saying, *I send you health that you may flourish strong as the evergreen and as long living.*
- Repeat once more and send any special messages of support, clap six times, and say, *Health, wealth, strength, joy, harmony, and well-being.*
- Leave the tree illuminated for a while if the lights are electric.

180

TO RESTORE ENTHUSIASM FOR LIFE IN AN OLDER PERSON AFTER AN ILLNESS OR LOSS

You will need:

A play clay featureless figure

A small box of clear crystals, glass nuggets, beads, or pearl buttons

A bowl of mixed dried sage and thyme

A chopping board

Timing:

Any bright morning, especially Sunday

The Spell

- Roll the figure in the herbs on the chopping board.
- Say as you do so, *By thyme and sage, be renewed with the strength of youth in later age that you will smile again and feel joy in each new day once more.*
- Shake excess herbs off the figure and cover it with shining crystals, saying, *Shine as the sun, glow as the stars and moon as vitality and hope flow back soon into your life.*
- Set the figure where it will catch sun and moonlight indoors, and on dark evenings light a purple candle next to it.

181

A SEVEN-DAY SPELL FOR RESTORING GREENNESS AND REFORESTATION TO THE WORLD

You will need:

Seven small green plants and an empty tub of soil or a garden area

Water, if possible rainwater or water from a natural source

Seven moss or tree agates, the gardener's crystal, or any small green crystals or glass beads

Timing:

Friday for seven days

The Spell

- On Friday, plant the first seedling and plant the crystal beneath it, saying, *Friday, bring back greenness, regenerate the fertile places anew, forests, fields, and wildernesses too. Restore the lungs of Mother Earth. For one tree planted, grow five, for five, ten, and then a hundred. Thus shall the earth be green again and breathe anew.*
- On Saturday, say, *Friday, Saturday* and continue the words above as you plant the second seedling and crystal in a circle.
- Continue until you have planted all seven seedlings and crystals, adding a day to the chant each time. On day 7, name all seven days; you have planted all the seedlings and crystals.
- Water weekly, naming all the days of the week in the chant. If any plant dies, replace it on the appropriate day of the week.

182

TO HEAL POLLUTED OCEANS, RIVERS, LAKES, AND STREAMS

You will need:

A small bottle of pure mineral or filtered water

A clear quartz crystal or a pure well-washed shiny white stone small enough to fit in the bottle

Your favorite flower remedy, such as the Bach remedies (optional)

A white candle

Timing:

Any transition: the beginning of a week, month, or, best of all, year

The Spell

- Light the candle and open the bottle of water, dropping the crystal into it, saying, *Cleansed be, river, lakes, and sea, flow clean once more that the store of fish and wondrous creatures may multiply, flow pure and wholesome; you, the source of life, live once more.*
- Place the crystal in the bottle of water and add a drop of the flower remedy you are using. Say, *May fresh water flow from mountains, over plains, be clear, near and far, that the waters of the world may be blessed and healed and so bring blessings by the score.*
- Put the lid on the bottle, shake nine times, repeating all the spell words once, and leave the bottle next to the candle while it burns down.
- As soon as possible after noon, pour the water into a stream, a river, or the sea, keeping the crystal in the bottle for the next time. Repeat all the words as you pour.

183

FOR REVERSING GLOBAL WARMING, AIR POLLUTION, AND DAMAGE TO THE OZONE LAYER

You will need:

A globe of the world (available at toy stores)
A bowl of pure sparkling mineral water

Timing:

When the light is bright

The Spell

- Stand the globe either near a window or, if the weather is fine, in the open air, spinning it clockwise until it stops, saying, *The world turns, sustaining life, the birds in the air, the fish in the sea, the plants of the earth, and all creatures who walk or run or crawl over the land. We are the caretakers of all, borrowing the earth from our descendants.*
- Dip the index finger of the hand you write with into the water and spin the globe counterclockwise, saying, *So shall destruction be halted, humankind's toxicity no longer pour toward the stars and all harm reversed. May the skies be healed and purified.*
- Dip your finger and turn the globe five more times counterclockwise; as you do so, repeat the second chant.
- Let the globe spin freely clockwise and repeat the first chant.
- Repeat monthly or whenever you hear of an ecological disaster.

184

TO RESTORE LIFE TO LITTERED OR ABANDONED URBAN WASTELAND

You will need:

A pot of your favorite cooking herb
Any floral incense stick
A photo of the area with the pot in the center

Timing:

If possible, after morning rain

The Spell

- Light the incense stick and circle the picture nine times, making clockwise smoke spirals, saying softly, *May beauty be restored, what is abandoned cared for, and the waste-littered lands grow lovely with flowers once more.*
- Write the same words while saying them slowly in incense smoke in the air over the pot of herbs and the picture.
- Let the incense burn through.
- When you have time, plant the pot of herbs in or near the unloved place, and using gloves and a stick, pick up some litter, repeating the words.

185

SAFETY FROM CYCLONES, WHIRLWINDS, HURRICANES, AND TORNADOES

You will need:

A long scarf
A box with a padlock

Timing:
When danger is imminent or you hear a severe cyclone warning in another part of the world

The Spell

- Hold the scarf up to the wind. Tie the ends of the scarf quickly in three knots, saying for each one: *You are bound from wreaking devastation. Let there be no hesitation in turning your force away.*
- Place the scarf in the box, saying, *Danger be contained within that my beloved home/ neighborhood/land/ specific area may be unscathed until this peril passes.*
- Put the box in a sheltered dark place.
- When danger passes, free the scarf and hold it to the air, saying, *Pass on your way in peace and tranquillity to blow harmlessly away from where you can wreak harm and negativity.*

186

TO CALM FOREST FIRES AND DIVERT LIGHTNING STRIKES AND ELECTRIC STORMS

You will need:

Four blue candles in left-to-right ascending height

Timing:
In very dry hot times or when you hear news of an impending fire threat

The Spell

- Light all four candles in descending order, right to left, saying, *Burn not fiercely, cease your trail of destruction, with the dimming of this light.*
- Extinguish the tallest candle.
- Repeat for each of the candles still in descending order, with words and actions, until all four are extinguished.
- End the spell by saying, *So shall the flames be dwindled, no more kindled, dimming, fire dying, extinguishing that all may be preserved.*

187

TO PROVIDE RELIEF FROM FLOODS, DESTRUCTIVELY HIGH TIDES, AND TSUNAMIS

You will need:

A large glass or ceramic bowl
A jug of water
A bowl of soil of similar size

Timing:
To minimize bad effects when disaster is impending or has occurred

The Spell

- Outdoors, fill the bowl three-quarters with water and say, *May the waters recede, be absorbed, and life be restored as it was before.*
- Tip a third of the water onto the ground, repeating the words.
- Tip a third of the soil onto the damp earth, repeating the words.
- Continue alternately tipping water and soil until the water is absorbed and say, So have the waters receded, been absorbed, and life will be restored as it was before.
- Use the damp earth for planting herbs or vegetables.

188

TO PROVIDE RELIEF FROM DROUGHT

You will need:

A chalkboard or flat stone
Children's chalks

Timing:
When there is bad drought in an area

The Spell

- Draw a desert, dead trees, and withered plants all over the board in chalk and say, *Drought, drought, you must go away, hardship you will cause so you must not stay. The clouds I call, filled with rain that life may grow and flourish again.*
- Rub out the desert and replace it with clouds, saying the words as you draw.
- Say, *Rain, rain, fall from the air, fill the rivers everywhere, water for people, animals, and crops, and refresh the parched earth before you stop.*
- Rub out the clouds and draw rain falling from the sky, green grass, flowers, animals, crops, and tall trees, repeating the second set of words.
- Thoroughly soak the board with a jug of water.
- Do the spell weekly until rain comes.

189

TO PREVENT THE ADVERSE EFFECTS OF EXTREME COLD AND AVALANCHES

You will need:

A small block of ice or some ice cubes
A jar of hot spice such as ginger or chili
A wooden spoon
An old saucepan

Timing:

At the beginning of a cold snap or when you hear news of areas hit by very cold temperatures

The Spell

- Working in a warm room, sprinkle a little of the spice on top of the ice and say: *Your icy grip turn away, warm the bitter cold, bring warmth again, take from us the perils of ice, snow, biting winds, and avalanche and milder days unfold.*
- Transfer the saucepan to the stove, and as the ice begins to melt, stir into it clockwise the spice you added so that it colors the water, all the time repeating the words and adding the names of any adversely affected places.
- Stir until the ice has gone and the mixture has become warm, chanting continuously as you do so.
- When steam appears, turn off the heat and, if possible, pour the hot liquid onto an icy area outdoors or pour it down the sink, turning on the cold tap so that the mixture hisses as it disappears.

190

FOR THE ANGEL SUIEL'S PROTECTION AGAINST VOLCANOES AND EARTHQUAKES

You will need:

A purse filled with any edible seeds, such as sunflower, pumpkin, or coriander
A red candle

Timing:

Every three months in an earthquake zone, when there are warnings of an earthquake in an area you will be visiting, or for relief if you hear of a disaster

The Spell

- Light the candle and set the purse of herbs in front of it.
- Look into the flame and say, *Wise Suiel (Sooiel), angel of earthquakes, let the land not shake too violently. Pass gently that the earth may remain firm beneath my feet and homes and property, people, and animals may see no danger.*
- Pick up the purse and shake it above the candle flame slowly ten times, repeating the words for each shake.
- Return the purse to the front of the candle and let the candle burn down.
- When the candle has burned down, place the purse above a door or window lintel at home, pack it in your suitcase, or keep it on top of a picture of a disaster.
- If you live in an area with earthquake activity, replace the herbs in the purse every three months, scattering the old herbs onto earth.

191

TO REMOVE CHRONIC PAIN

You will need:
A bowl of water
A silver candle

Timing:
Any time during the waning moon period

The Spell

- If there is no moonlight (the moon rises later each night and is smaller and paler), light the candle and hold the bowl of water so that either moonlight or candlelight shines in the water.
- Say, *Grandmother Moon I ask that you take away this pain/affliction, sorrow* (word it as you wish) *from* (name the focus of the healing, which may be yourself).
- Wash your hands in the water and say softly: *I wash my hands in your waning light, kind Grandmother Moon. Bring the healing that I ask and wrap me* [name] *in your deep cloak of comfort.*
- If you are using a candle, blow it out and tip the water away outdoors or under a running tap.

192

TO REPLACE ACUTE OR CHRONIC PAIN WITH HEALING

You will need:
A deep red candle
A blue candle
A small purple amethyst or a purple glass bead
A pink rose quartz crystal or blue lace agate or a pink or blue glass bead
A small purse

Timing:
Before bed

The Spell

- Light the red candle and hold the amethyst in the closed hand you do not write with, saying, Take away all pain, absorbed be in this stone that I may be free again.
- Light the blue candle from the red one and hold the rose quartz in the open hand you write with, saying, I absorb the gentle light of healing, and I am free again.
- Continue alternating the spell words as you gaze first into the red and then into the blue flame.
- When you sense the amethyst becoming heavier, extinguish the red candle.
- Wash the amethyst under running water.
- Let the blue candle burn, and when it is fully burned, put both crystals in the bag.
- If you experience pain, hold the crystals as before and repeat the words, again washing the amethyst.
- Recharge them once a month by repeating the spell.

193

TO FIND THE RIGHT TREATMENT FOR ONESELF OR A LOVED ONE FOR A CHRONIC OR DEBILITATING CONDITION IF MEDICAL PRACTITIONERS HAVE NOT FOUND THE SOLUTION

You will need:

An orange candle
Three orange or red stones or crystals in a triangle around the candle
Three sticks of any tree or fruit incense in separate holders in a triangle around the stones

Timing:

Wednesday, if possible at 10 p.m., the healing hour.

The Spell

- Light the candle and say, *Light your way to me, you who know the answer.* I will find those who know the answer to open up the way.
- Light the first incense and write in incense smoke over the stones and candle, GUIDE ME TO YOU, YOU WHO KNOW THE ANSWER.
- Repeat the words and actions as you light the second and then the third incense.
- Blow out the candle, repeating both sets of words, and let the incense burn outdoors.
- Take the stones outdoors, bury one in the ground, and say, *Over land and over seas, through the skies, there comes to me, the one who knows the answer.*
- Take the second stone into an open space and throw it as far as you can, repeating the spell words.
- Cast the final stone into water and say the words once more.
- Check the Internet and support groups for updates, repeating all the words before you use the web browser.

194

TO BRING MOON HEALING FOR EMOTIONAL PAIN AFTER ABUSE OR TRAUMA

You will need:

A small clear crystal sphere or a clear glass goblet to reflect the moon's image
A fiber-optic lamp or one that changes color if there is no moonlight
A dark silk cloth (optional)

Timing:

At the full moon or the three days before it when the moon is bright

The Spell

- Outdoors, hold the crystal sphere or glass goblet so that the moon is reflected within it. If there is no moonlight, work indoors, using the light of the lamp to illuminate the sphere. Say, *Mother Moon, I ask tonight, fill this sphere with healing light, take with you this heartfelt pain, that I may laugh and live/love again.*
- Cover the sphere with the cloth or switch off the lamp, saying, *Mother Moon, absorb my sorrow that I may laugh and live tomorrow.*
- Repeat the spell monthly.

195

TO HALT THE PROGRESS OF OR ACHIEVE REMISSION FROM A DEBILITATING ILLNESS THAT IS GETTING WORSE RAPIDLY

You will need:

A ball of black thread

Timing:

When you or the person for whom you cast the spell is having a good day

The Spell

- Tangle the thread into webs and knots, saying, *You* [name illness] *are no longer welcome in my life* [or name sick person], *for you bring strife, tangle up my life, but no more, go out the door.*
- Go to an external door, open it, and say, *You are no longer welcome here* (or name sick person). *Visit me no more, for I shall not answer the door.*
- Pick up the black thread and put it in an outside garbage can. Close the door firmly, repeating the spell words.
- When you feel the onset or warning signs of an attack, touch your navel and say, *I close the door on my unwanted visitor. You no longer have house room.*

196

TO HELP CLEAR THE BODY OF A CONDITION THAT IS MALIGNANT OR IS ATTACKING THE IMMUNE SYSTEM

You will need:

Six small pink or blue candles

A small round or oval mirror propped up so that you can see into it

Timing:

Any time you (the sick person) are despairing

The Spell

- Arrange and light the candles in a semicircle around the mirror, sitting behind them facing the mirror so that your face is illuminated.
- Recite six times in a whisper, *Fade with the light from here. Pain be contained, absorbed, diminished within the glass, a pale reflection, soon to cease.*
- Blow out all the candles in rapid succession, saying as you do so, *Pain fade, rest in the darkness, flow from the body into the darkened glass and let pain pass.*

197

FOR RAISING THE THRESHOLD OF PAIN OR COPING WITH INVASIVE LONG-TERM TREATMENT

You will need:

A deep blue candle
A piece of paper and a blue pen
A small leafy twig

Timing:
Any waning moon day (or Saturday)

The Spell:

- Light the candle and say, *I take this light to fill me with the power to resist pain/to respond favorably and powerfully to my treatment.*
- Write the words on the paper and say them again.
- Breathe softly three times into the candle and repeat the words three times, once after each breath.
- Let the candle burn in a safe place.
- Wrap the paper firmly around the twig, if necessary securing it with string, and burn the twig and paper outdoors in a metal container such as a bucket and scatter the ashes.
- As you do so, repeat the words five times.
- Cast the spell again during each waning moon or on Saturdays until the treatment is over.

198

WHEN THINGS LOOK BAD, A BARIEL ANGEL OF SMALL MIRACLES CALLING

You will need:

A supply of small white tea lights set in three circles around a central white larger candle.

Timing:
When extra help is needed in an uncertain medical situation over three days

The Spell

- Light the central candle and say, *Bariel, angel of small miracles, bring the small miracle I do desire* (name what you need and for whom) *and I will do good in the world.*
- From the candle, light clockwise the inner ring of candles, repeating the words for each one.
- Blow out the central candle, saying the same words again, and let the candle ring burn.
- Replace the inner candle ring.
- On day 2, relight the central candle and from it relight clockwise the innermost and middle circles of tea lights, saying the same words for each one.
- Blow out the central candle, repeating the words, and let the two tea light rings burn.
- Replace the burned out candle rings.
- On day 3, relight the central candle, saying the same words, and from it relight the innermost, middle, and outer tea light rings, saying the same words for each light.
- Let all the candles burn through.

199

WHEN THINGS SEEM HOPELESS, A HAMIED ANGEL OF BIG MIRACLES INVOCATION

You will need:

Three tall white candles in a row

Timing:

In total darkness after midnight

The Spell

- Light the left-hand candle and say, *May the dazzling light of Hamied, angel who makes the impossible possible and what seems hopeless filled with promise, bless* [name] *and bring the miracle so urgently needed at this hour.*
- Light the central candle from the first one and repeat the words.
- Light the right-hand candle, touching its flame to first the left and then the central candle, saying the words for each one.
- Leave all three candles to burn in a safe place, saying, *Hamied, angel who brings comfort to what seems lost, blaze your light and restore brightness and healing in this darkest hour.*

TO HELP A FRIEND OR FAMILY MEMBER LET GO OF LIFE PEACEFULLY, ESPECIALLY IF HE OR SHE IS AFRAID

You will need:

Three brown or dark golden flowers in a vase
Three purple candles in descending order of size, left to right
A candlesnuffer or cup
A bowl of soil

Timing:

When it feels right

The Spell

- Light the tallest candle and burn a single petal from one of the flowers in it, saying, *Dear* [name], *do not be afraid to let go. When you are ready to move on, we let you go willingly from our love to the love hereafter. You will pass from our arms to those who are waiting in love to welcome you.*
- Burn the petal in the candle and drop it into the soil.
- Light the second candle from the first and burn a petal from the second flower in it, extinguishing the first candle and dropping the burned petal to the earth, repeating the words.
- Light the third candle from the second. Take a petal from the third flower and again burn it, saying the words once more. Extinguish the second candle.
- Let the final candle burn.
- Release the remaining petals on the flowers one by one to the winds.

CHAPTER 5

HOLIDAY AND TRAVELING MAGICK

This chapter contains spells for happy holidays; days and weekends away; safety while traveling and on vacation; long distance travel and backpacking; traveling for a specific purpose and relocation; and commuting and work-related travel.

201

FOR FINDING THE RIGHT VACATION AT THE RIGHT PRICE

You will need:

A brochure or Internet holiday printout
A favorite pendant or a crystal pendulum

Timing:

When choosing a hotel or location for your vacation

The Spell

- If you have not chosen the location, run your pendulum down a list of possible locations one by one as you say over and over, *Find for me what is best to be, that I may see, the perfect choice for my/our holiday,* until you feel a tingling in your hand or a pulling down of the pendulum over a specific location.
- Pass the pendulum slowly over each hotel or resort, saying the same words repeatedly until you get a response. If you get more than one, you can pass the pendulum over those places again until you get a definite swing or *know* any of them would be right.
- Quickly plunge the pendulum into water three times or make three water droplet circles around a delicate gem.

202

FOR A PERFECT DAY OUT OR BECAUSE YOU WANT A PERFECT DAY

You will need:

Two long, brightly colored scarves in a light fabric

Timing:

Around sunrise, outdoors

The Spell

- Open your arms wide and hold one scarf loosely in each hand so that any breeze catches it.
- Say slowly nine times as you wave both scarves slowly and rhythmically, *This is my perfect day.*
- Repeat the words nine more times faster and start to move so that you are twirling in a spiral and waving the scarves faster.
- Keep repeating the words and movements until you are speaking very quickly and the scarves are almost flying.
- When you can move no faster, throw the scarves in the air, clap, catch them, and say, *This is my perfect day.*
- Knot the scarves so that you are wearing one long scarf and twirl the ends throughout the day, saying nine times, either in your mind or aloud, *This is a perfect day.*

203

FOR A HAPPY WEEKEND OR SHORT BREAK AT HOME OR OVERSEAS

You will need:

Four green candles
A long green cord or ribbon
Four travel incense sticks: fern, fennel, frankincense, sage, or lavender

Timing:

The day before your minibreak, in the morning if possible

The Spell

- Make a circle with the four candles at the main direction points, with the incense sticks equidistant between them.
- Place the ribbon or cord in the center of the circle.
- Light each of the candles in turn, beginning with the one to the north, and say as you do so, *Light of laughter, travel with me, brief though this break may be, this I ask and it shall be.*
- Light the incense, beginning with the one in the northeast, saying for each, *Breath of tranquillity, travel with me, brief though this break may be, this I ask and it shall be.*
- Pass the ribbon or cord around each candle, repeating the spell words.
- Pass the ribbon or cord through the smoke of each incense stick in turn, again saying all the spell words.
- Tie a knot in the ribbon or cord for every day of the break, taking it in your luggage and undoing a knot for every day, making a wish.

204

FOR HAPPY, HARMONIOUS RELATIONSHIPS ON VACATION IF THERE ARE POTENTIAL CONFLICTS OR PERSONALITY CLASHES AMONG MEMBERS OF THE PARTY

You will need:

A picture of the people together or individual photos on top of one another
A pink flower head for each person
A glass bowl of water
Growing plants

Timing:

Friday

The Spell

- Hold a pink flower for each person in turn, saying for each one, *May there be peace and harmony on our holiday, happy days and fun-filled nights, keep all right.*
- One at a time, drop the flower heads into the bowl of water, repeating the same words.
- Sprinkle water drops in the shape of a heart around the photo(s), saying the words again.
- Tip the rest of the water onto growing plants, saying, Let harmony grow between us day by day on this precious holiday.
- Leave the flower heads around the picture until they fade, then scatter the petals outdoors, saying, *All dissension go and conflict cease, for this will be a time of peace.*

205

COUNTING DOWN TO A SPECIAL TRIP IF YOU ARE ANXIOUS

You will need:

A paper divided into calendar squares, days, weeks, or months according to the time scale with the last one being the trip date

Two dice

Timing:

Ongoing until the date of your trip

The Spell

- Lay the calendar flat and go to the first date square.
- Shake the two dice over the square and let them fall on the calendar where they will, saying, *Good luck shall be mine, closer do I move to my adventure, lucky, lucky, lucky will I be, as this wonderful opportunity comes to me.*
- Cross out that square and make a bold step toward planning the next stage of your venture.
- Continue until you reach the square representing the date of your trip.
- Between spells, keep the calendar with the dice on top in a place that catches daylight.

206

FOR A FAMILY REUNION OR LARGE-SCALE FAMILY HOLIDAY

You will need:

A tub of small, brightly colored wrapped candies or chocolates

Timing:

Any Friday

The Spell

- Take out a candy to represent each person.
- Touch each candy in turn, name the person, and say, *May we blend and harmonize, join and synchronize, on this our joyous reunion.*
- Return each candy to the tub.
- Cover the tub with its lid and shake ten times, naming all the people, and repeat the spell words.
- Take the candies on holiday to share, shaking the tub ten times and repeating the words before offering.

207

FOR A HAPPY JOURNEY IF YOU ARE TRAVELING WITH YOUNG OR MUCH OLDER FAMILY MEMBERS OR PETS

You will need:

A large yellow candle
A large orange candle
Eight smaller blue candles set in two parallel rows like a pathway
A bowl of mixed salt and pepper

Timing:

Wednesday evening

The Spell

- Set the yellow candle at the farthest end of the candle pathway and the orange candle nearest to you.
- Light the orange and yellow candles, naming all the travelers, including pets, and say, *May this journey be stress-free, let it progress easily, that we may arrive harmoniously.*
- Light the left-hand and then the right-hand blue candle, then continue up the row from the orange, but do not light the yellow, repeating the words for each one.
- Sprinkle salt and pepper in the orange candle, saying, *So do I burn away all hazards, obstacles, and delays before me that we may arrive harmoniously.*
- Extinguish the orange candle.
- Light the yellow candle, repeating all the words.
- Blow out each of the blue candles and finally the yellow one, saying all the words for each.
- Repeat the spell words immediately before traveling and if problems loom.

208

FOR A HAPPY HOLIDAY ALONE

You will need:

Two circles drawn one inside the other in pencil on white paper
An eraser
A smiley face drawn inside the inner ring
Three incense sticks in a triangle around the outer ring

Timing:

Sunday

The Spell

- Light the farthest incense, swirling the smoke over the inner ring, saying, *A perfect holiday just for me, exploring new places in new company. Lonely is different from being alone, by myself the world will become my home. I am free as a bird in a world full of friends, the horizons are endless, and my path never ends.*
- Repeat the words as you light and swirl each incense.
- Spiral incenses 1 and 2, one in each hand, then 2 and 3, and finally 1 and 3, still saying the words.
- Rub out the circles, smile, and say, *I am complete in myself and my own company; I go into the world, world welcome me.*

209

A FIRST GROWN-UP VACATION WITHOUT THE FAMILY

You will need:
Nothing

Timing:
Morning

The Spell

- Establish a clapping rhythm and then chant over and over, *No more burgers, no more zoos, sophistication, recreation for me and for you. Freedom beckons, don't you see? Not as Mom and Dad but you and me.*
- Start to stamp instead of clapping, and when you have the rhythm, continue chanting.
- Chant faster and start clapping again as well and end with a final clap and stamp, saying, *And so we will travel, just you and me, and for a while we are childlike but free.*

210

FOR ANY KIND OF HAPPY TRAVEL OR HOLIDAY

You will need:
Basic ingredients to make pastry or dough
A mixing bowl and rolling pin
Salt
Dried mint or basil
A small tub of clear glass nuggets, tiny clear crystals, clear buttons, beads, or small white stones

Timing:
Afternoon, in sunshine if possible

The Spell

- Add three pinches of salt to the mixing bowl, turning the bowl three times clockwise for each pinch, saying, *Salt, clear the pathway for me, three by three, that I may travel easily.*
- Add all the ingredients to the bowl, stir, and knead them, saying over and over, *Smooth my journeys, swift and sure, this spell, once cast, long shall endure.*
- Roll out a long thin strip of pastry or dough, joining it in a circle and repeating the words as you work.
- Sprinkle mint on the circle, saying, *Travel safe and reach the end, no hazards on my road to send, smooth my pathways, safe and sure, this spell, once cast, long shall endure.*
- Press glass nuggets into the circle, saying, *The road is light, the path is clear, my journey safe and without fear.*
- Leave the pastry until dusk, then squeeze it into a ball. Bury beneath a tree.

SAFETY WHILE TRAVELING AND ON VACATION

211

A SAFE TRAVEL AND ARRIVAL SPELL, ESPECIALLY IF THERE HAS BEEN PREVIOUS UNREST IN THE HOLIDAY AREA OR A PLANE CRASH

You will need:

A Saint Christopher medallion or a turquoise, moonstone, or a pearl, either on its own or as part of a necklace or bracelet, or a lucky pendant
A paper knife
A bowl of water
A bowl of salt

Timing:

Two or three times in the week before you travel

The Spell

- Add three pinches of salt to the water and draw a cross on the surface with the paper knife, saying, *Blessings be on this water, preserve me/us from all danger, accidents, crashes, harmful situations, and ill-intentioned strangers.*
- Scatter water drops over the medallion/gems (empower one for each family member; you can even attach them to pet collars), repeating the words.
- With the paper knife, draw a cross in the air above the medallion(s) and then add a circle around that, saying, *With gates of steel, so am I/are we bound, that safety around me/us will be found.*
- Wear the medallion(s) while traveling and on vacation.

212

AN ALTERNATIVE ANGEL PROTECTION FOR YOU, YOUR FAMILY, OR A LOVED ONE ON ANY JOURNEY OR TIME AWAY

You will need:

Three silver candles arranged in a triangle
A silver ribbon
A drawstring bag

Timing:

The night before travel, after dusk

The Spell

- Set the ribbon on top of the bag.
- Light the candles, beginning with the single one at the top, saying for each, *Guardian angels three, Raphael, Ambriel, and Damabiah, let no harm befall me* [or name].
- Tie three knots in the ribbon, naming Raphael for the first, Ambriel for the second, and Damabiah for the third, adding for each, *Let no harm befall me* [or name], and put it in the bag.
- Let the candles burn down around the bag and then take the bag with you or give it to a loved one.

213

IF YOU MEET SOMEONE ON HOLIDAY YOU DON'T GET ALONG WITH WHO WON'T LEAVE YOU ALONE

You will need:

A printout picture of you all together; make sure the person or people are on the outside to the right
A pair of nail scissors
A sealed envelope
Flower petals

Timing:
Any early morning

The Spell

- Hold the picture and say, *You* [name] *are really nice, sugar and spice, but you're getting under our/my feet, much less often I'd like to meet.*
- Carefully cut the person's side of the picture off and pop it in the envelope with the flower petals, saying, *You can have fun under the sun; you're not our appendage; your presence we/I gauge a little intrusive and much too effusive.*
- Seal the envelope and put it in a drawer until the end of the holiday.
- Keep the rest of the picture in light.
- At the end of the holiday, print out the full photo and give it to the person (but without your address).

214

TO COUNTERACT FEARS AND THREATS OF TERRORISM WHILE TRAVELING AND ON VACATION

You will need:

A pink scarf
A map showing your departure place and destination (you can draw a sketch map)
Four dark red candles, one at each corner of the map
Seven dark red ribbons
A bowl of salt

Timing:
Tuesday

The Spell

- Light each candle counterclockwise, saying for each, *Stand vigil for me/us that I/we may travel/vacation without fear of terrorist attack and return home in safety.*
- Sprinkle salt into each flame and repeat the words for each.
- Fold the map and tie it with seven ribbons, making seven knots, saying, *I banish all hatred and attack as we travel and stay, keep violence, destruction, and violence away.*
- Return the map to the center of the candle square until the candles are burned.
- Wrap it in the scarf and include in luggage.

215

FOR TRAVELING ALONE LATE AT NIGHT, RETURNING TO A DARK CAR GARAGE OR SUBWAY, PASSING THROUGH A CROWDED AREA WHERE THERE ARE DRUNKS, OR WAITING FOR A TAXI IN A LONELY PLACE

You will need:

A small sagebrush or cedar smudge stick or incense stick

A circle of red candles large enough to stand in safely

Timing:

Before a potential hazard or monthly if these situations are a regular occurrence

The Spell

- Light each candle counterclockwise, saying, *I call around me this circle of fiery guardians, to keep me unmolested, unharassed, neither threatened, intimidated, nor menaced, in places dangerous, lonely, or unprotected.*
- Hold the smudge in each candle in turn, blowing the tip so that it glows.
- Draw a waist-high circle of smoke around yourself as you turn counterclockwise, repeating the words.
- Quickly blow out the candles counterclockwise around the circle, saying, *None may harm me within this guardianship of fire.*
- Go outdoors and smudge again, repeating the words, and leave the smudge to go out.
- Carry a small bag of the unburned smudge leaves in uncertain places, or, if you used incense, crumble two fresh sticks and carry the incense herbs in the bag.

216

IF YOU HAVE RELATIVES OR FRIENDS WORKING OVERSEAS IN CONFLICT AREAS

You will need:

A picture of the person in uniform if in the armed forces or in typical traveling or working clothes if a civilian

Nine bright red candles in a circle

Nine new metal nails in a circle around the candles

A bowl of salt

Timing:

Before your bedtime

The Spell

- Place the photo in the center of the circle of nine candles.
- Light the candles counterclockwise, and for each naming of the person say, *Candle flame and flare that you may walk through perilous places unscathed.*
- Touch each of the nails clockwise, saying for each, [name], *defense of impenetrable iron I send, that you may walk through the perilous places unscathed.*
- Add a pinch of salt to each candle, moving clockwise, saying, *The salt of life sustain you that you may walk unscathed through the perilous places.*
- Blow out the candles, saying for each three times, *Fire, iron and salt, salt, iron and fire, with these three I enclose you that you will walk unscathed in perilous places.*
- Leave the picture within the circles until the next spell.

217

TO OVERCOME FEAR OF FLYING

You will need:
A sodalite, malachite, turquoise, or lapis crystal; a small crystal angel; or a favorite piece of jewelry

Timing:
Nightly, the week before flying

The Spell

- Hold the crystal or jewelry in the open hand you write with and pass the other hand, palms down and fingers together, above the crystals. Moving your hand slowly and rhythmically, say, *On the wings of angel Damabiah, angel of the sky, carry me high. I fear nothing, safe in your care, I can fly anywhere knowing I will be unharmed. I am calm with no anxiety. So I ask and it shall be.*
- Take the crystal in your cabin luggage and before takeoff do the spell subtly, holding the crystal or jewelry in the same hand and again during turbulence and before landing.
- If you panic, keep saying the words, picturing Damabiah supporting the plane with his blue wings.

218

TO PROTECT YOUR LUGGAGE, DOCUMENTS, PETS, AND CHILDREN FROM BEING SEPARATED FROM YOU DURING TRAVEL

You will need:
Travel documents, wallets, money belts, credit cards, luggage, pictures of children and pets

Timing:
The night before you travel

The Spell

- Set the small items in the circle in the center of a square made by the luggage.
- Around each piece of luggage, draw a clockwise circle with the first and second fingers together of the hand you write with, then draw an invisible square around the outside of the visible square of luggage and a triangle around any pictures, repeating as you do so, *Safe from harm, loss, or theft, do not stray, stay with me, until we reach our destination and all come home with me.*
- At the airport, say the words in your mind as you stand with the luggage before checkout, drawing a small circle and square subtly with your hand in their direction.
- Repeat the spell before the homeward journey.

219

FOR OVERCOMING CHILDREN'S TRAVEL SICKNESS

You will need:

Dried lavender and/or powdered ginger and mint

An animal or a novelty-shaped purse (on a string so that the child can wear it) featuring the child's favorite character

Rose essential oil, rose water, or fragrance

A bowl and spoon

Timing:

Wednesday

The Spell

- Place the herbs in the bowl. If the child is old enough, allow her or him to mix faster and faster while you say faster and faster, *Sickness, sickness go away, don't come back any day.*
- After saying the word *day*, add three drops of rose oil/rose water/fragrance.
- Stir again, saying, *As I count now to three, travel sickness you must flee, three, two, one, travel sickness now is gone forever, Shooo.*
- Add the herbs to the purse.
- Give the child the purse to hold or wear on the journey or hang it up over the car seat for a small child.

220

A KNOT SPELL FOR SAFE TRAVEL

You will need:

Three strands of thick wool, each large enough to fit comfortably around your wrist: one yellow, one blue, one green. You can make them for other family members as well

A red candle

Timing:

The night before the trip

The Spell

- Light the candle and hold the ends of each piece of wool in the flame so that it slightly singes, saying for each, Safe be from malice, threat, and danger.
- Weave or plait together the three cords or pieces of wool, saying continuously and softly, *Bind and wind protection in, safe from malice, secure from danger, from accident or threat of stranger.*
- Tie the ends together with seven knots, one after the other, saying: *Seven times the sacred knot I tie, be safe on earth, on sea and sky.*
- Let the candle burn.
- Wear the bracelet until the end of the holiday. If it breaks, retie the knots at the place where the cord has snapped, saying the chants as you make the seven knots once more.

221

FOR THE DREAM HOLIDAY OF A LIFETIME

You will need:

A map ringed with your ultimate destination, departures, stopovers, and planned major excursions
A row of four yellow candles in front of the map
A bowl of salt

Timing:

Thursdays, ongoing

The Spell

- Light each candle left to right, saying for the first, *A hazard-free journey on the way*, for the second, *The right accommodation wherever I/we stay*, for the third, *New scenes and experiences that we see*, and for the fourth, *Good weather and fine company*.
- Carry the candles in turn to the same positions at the back of the map, sprinkling salt in each flame so that it sparkles, saying for each, *I will achieve this desire by the quadruple power of fire*.
- Blow all four out together, saying, *I will achieve my desire in this quadruple power of fire*.
- Leave the map and candles in place until the next spell, saying, *This will be the best holiday ever*. When you have used all four candles, replace them.

222

BEFORE A LONG JOURNEY OR HOLIDAY

You will need:

A tube of glitter
A piece of paper and a blue pen
Pictures of where you will be going and/or photos of you (and anyone you will be traveling with) on previous happy holidays
Glue

Timing:

The beginning of a week or month

The Spell

- Make a collage of your journey with images and photos, between the spaces writing BON VOYAGE, HAPPY HOLIDAY, HAVE A MAGICAL TIME, LOTS OF LAUGHTER, WHAT A BIG ADVENTURE, or whatever you want.
- Spread a little glue thinly on the collage, then scatter glitter all over the collage, saying, *A golden journey, I/we venture far, following moon and sun and star, new lands to explore, new customs, people, and more, the horizon never runs out, I/we follow without doubt*.
- Take the picture outdoors, shaking off any excess glitter while repeating the words.
- Hang your collage in the kitchen or a warm place, adding to it whenever you wish.
- Take a picture of it with you on your travels and leave the original hanging until your return.

223

FOR GETTING THE LONG-DISTANCE HOLIDAY YOU WANT

You will need:

Four frankincense or any tree fragrance incense sticks in the four corners of a photo of the destination taken from the Internet or a brochure

A small toy model for each mode of travel (boat, plane, etc.) set in the middle of the picture

Timing:

Early morning

The Spell

- Light the farthest incense clockwise, saying for each, *I span the globe instantly and blow away successfully, all barriers to my journey to* [destination].
- Take the first incense you lit and pass it around the outside of the photo, saying, *Power of air carry me, to where it is I wish to be* [destination].
- Repeat for the other incense sticks.
- Pick up the most representative model plane, boat, or train and set it in the center of the desired destination, saying, *Carry me by land and sea, where it is I wish to be* [destination].
- Let the incense burn.

224

TO HAVE YOUR DREAM VACATION SOON IF PLANS SEEM NEVER TO COME TO FRUITION

You will need:

Four dandelions with white spores or four thistles with spores (if you can't get either, substitute bubbles)

A purse to hold the dandelions or thistles

Timing:

Wednesday

The Spell

- Stand on a hill, facing the direction you would most like to travel.
- Spin three times clockwise, three times counter-clockwise, and three times clockwise again, saying nine times, *North, south, east, west, take me where I love the best. East, south, west, north, soon may I venture forth.*
- Spin around clockwise nine times, saying, *Far from home may I roam, far to fly, o'er sea and sky, far to cross dear Mother Earth, bring I ask my plans to birth.*
- Open the purse and blow the dandelion spores (one dandelion for each direction, beginning with your chosen one), saying for each, *Fly far, fly free, cross sky, earth, and sea, with you I go, let it be so.*
- Run or walk fast down the hill, repeating the final chant until you reach the bottom.
- When you get home, take a step toward planning your trip.

225

TO FACILITATE A LONG-DISTANCE TRIP IF PEOPLE ARE GETTING IN THE WAY OF YOUR PLANS

You will need:

A small bowl of rose petals or any perfumed petals (fresh, not dried)

Timing:

Dawn or early mornings after sunrise on a windy day

The Spell

- Go to an open space and fill your writing hand with petals as you hold the bowl in the other hand.
- Scatter rose petals in the air, not worrying if some fall on you. Say faster and faster as you scatter them, *Carry me from here to there, how it happens I don't care, remove all obstacles in my way, for here I would no longer stay, make it soon, within one/two/three moon(s).*
- Keep dipping into the bowl, scattering and chanting.
- Turn around and around in circles, repeating the chant and scattering the petals faster until you start to feel dizzy.
- Release the final petals and shout the words at the top of your voice.
- Remove the first obstacle and repeat until you are on your way.

226

TO PROTECT A BACKPACKING ADULT CHILD WHILE SHE OR HE IS AWAY

You will need:

A large ball of red thread
A garment she or he will be wearing
A green candle
A fruit fragrance incense

Timing:

Monday evening

The Spell

- Pass the ball of thread seven times through the smoke of the lighted incense and seven times around the flame of the lighted candle, saying each time, *May your travels be filled with fun and laughter, adventure, and so much more, for you travel safe in my protection until victorious you return to this shore.*
- Sew a loop of red thread into the lining of the garment, repeating the words softly as you sew. Blow out the candle and let the incense burn.
- Each Monday, cut a piece of thread, again passing it through the incense smoke and around a lighted candle, repeating the spell words once. Knot it seven times, saying, *You travel safe in my protection until victorious you return to this shore.*
- Put the knotted thread in a special box. Continue until the wanderer returns.

227

TO CONNECT IF YOU LOSE TOUCH WITH A BACKPACKING CHILD, RELATIVE, OR FRIEND

You will need:

The most recent picture of the person (use a printout from a social media site)

The name of the last known contact place written on a slip of paper on top of the photo

In a circle around these items, alternating, candle first, four incense sticks, either floral or sandalwood, and four white candles

A bowl of water

Timing:

When you start to feel worried

The Spell

- Light first the candles clockwise, saying, [Name], *call me, reach me, connect with me once more. I ask the angels keep you safe until you reach familiar home shores.*
- Light each incense from the candle to its right and spiral each in turn over the picture, saying the same words, getting faster with each, then plunge all four in turn in the water so that they hiss, saying, *Call me now.*
- Let the candles burn.
- Repeat daily until you have contact.

228

A SAINT JULIAN THE HOSPITALLER PRAYER FOR BACKPACKERS OR THOSE TRAVELING FAR FROM HOME ON A BUDGET

You will need:

A photo of the traveler

A lamp

Timing:

Nightly, using your local time zone

The Spell

- As twilight falls, light the lamp next to the photo.
- Holding it between your hands so that the light still reflects on it, recite the ancient prayer of Saint Julian, patron saint of ferrymen, impoverished and long-distance travelers, innkeepers, and adventurers: *My child/brother/sister sleeps this night I know not where. Grant them kind lodging or if they are under the stars make their bed soft, their sleep peaceful, and watch them until the morning.*
- Return the photo in front of the lamp and let the lamp burn for an hour.

229

TO GET HOME FROM A DISTANT LOCATION WHEN RESOURCES ARE TIGHT OR THINGS ARE GOING WRONG

You will need:

A roll of paper strong enough to walk on
Brightly colored marking pens
A torch

Timing:

Friday, when it would be dark back home

The Spell

- On one end of the paper, write the name of your current location in red and then draw a red cross through it.
- At the other end, draw a house and then write in blue, THERE'S NO PLACE LIKE HOME within it.
- Draw a set of red and yellow footprints the size of your shoe in a spiral pathway leading from the house to the cross.
- Stand on the first footprints and shine a torch at your feet (close curtains if necessary), saying six times, *There's no place like home.*
- Continue until you have reached the step before your home, using the same words.
- Shine the torch on your home and say, *There's no place like home and home is where I will be, may the way be opened soon for me.*
- Roll up the paper and repeat weekly until return is possible.

230

FOR A HAPPY AND HAZARD-FREE LONG-DISTANCE CRUISE

You will need:

A double-lidded shell such as a mussel or oyster shell
A pearl, moonstone, silver button, or bead or any small silver item such as a thin ring
Twine or string in silver or white

Timing:

Friday afternoon

The Spell

- Set the pearl inside the shell and say, *So will I see the world, so will new sights unfurl while I am safe in luxury, cocooned in my palace of the sea.*
- Close the shell and bind it tightly with seven knots, repeating the words and adding, *Sevenfold, sevenfold, new joys to behold.*
- Cast the shell into water and say, *Sail far, to places uncharted, magical lands beyond measure, each moment of my voyage will bring a fresh treasure. And so I venture on the adventure of a lifetime.*

TRAVELING FOR A SPECIFIC PURPOSE AND RELOCATION

231

FOR A SPECIAL VACATION SUCH AS A BEACH WEDDING, HONEYMOON, OR ANNIVERSARY

You will need:
Fifteen green balloons

Timing:
Weekly for five weeks before the vacation

The Spell

- On week 1, launch the first balloon, saying, *May happiness ride high that this* [name occasion] *will be all I/we dream of and more.*
- On week 2, launch two balloons, repeating the words; on week 3, fly three; on week 4, launch four; and on week 5, fly five balloons, each time repeating the spell words.
- On week/day 5, add, *This will be the best* [name occasion] *ever.*

232

A SPELL FOR AN ADVENTURE OR ACTIVITY HOLIDAY FOR YOU AND/ OR A FAMILY MEMBER

You will need:
Two large feathers or an old-fashioned fan
Three yellow candles alternating with three tree-fragrance incense sticks set in a triangle formation
Pictures of the sports or a brochure for the holiday
A picture of you or person for whom you are casting the spell side by side with the adventure pictures, inside the triangle

Timing:
Any Wednesday before the trip

The Spell

- Light each candle and incense in turn from its own candle to the left of it, saying, *Excitement, thrills, adventure, speed, this holiday is what I need* [or name activity].
- With a feather in each hand or the fan, spiral air over the pictures, saying the same words faster and faster as you move the feathers faster. End by saying, *Fire of excitement flare, danger be not there, and so I/we/* [name] *seize(s) the moment of adventure.*
- Plunge the incense sticks, lighted end down, into a bowl of sand or soil.
- Let the candles burn, saying, *Fire flare high, excitement rise to the skies. Adventure awaits me.*

233

FOR A MUCH-NEEDED LUXURY SUCH AS A LONG HOT BATH OR SHOWER WHEN YOU ARE EXHAUSTED OR OUT OF SORTS

You will need:

A natural herbal bath or shower product
Small candles to illuminate the bathroom

Timing:

If you are hesitating about treating yourself

The Spell

- Light the candles so that they will illuminate the water, saying, *May this break restore body, soul, and mind that I will find rest, relaxation, and rejuvenation, for I do deserve and need such consolation.*
- Turn on the bath or shower, adding the product to the water.
- Sit or stand in the candlelit water, swirling the light pools, repeating the words over and over softly and rhythmically.
- When you feel restored, pull out the plug or switch off the shower, saying the words as the water swirls away.
- Carry the candles to the bedroom. If you were hesitating about doing something for yourself because of your busy schedule or a tight budget, book your appointment or make the purchase now before enjoying a relaxing evening.

234

A TRIP TO FIND OR RETURN TO YOUR FAMILY ROOTS

You will need:

A purple candle
A memento or photo of the ancestral family back home or of the place if you have not traced the family
Lilac or vanilla oil or fragrance

Timing:

Before the trip, when you first arrive and when visiting a records office, parish church, or former family home

The Spell

- Light the candle and say, *Illumine the path to the old lands that I may stand where once my ancestors lived and loved and cried that I may see and know and feel the roots I bear inside.*
- Hold the memento and repeat the words.
- Put a drop of fragrance in the center of your brow and say, *I reach out to you to guide me home that we once more may be as one.*
- Let the candle burn while you do online research.
- When you arrive, put a drop of fragrance on your brow each morning, repeating all the spell words before you research or visit old relatives you have never met.

235

FOR A HOLIDAY TO BRING TWO PEOPLE CLOSER AGAIN

You will need:

A basket of dead leaves or petals
A basket of fresh leaves or petals
A tree or bush in an open space

Timing:

Friday

The Spell

- Scatter dead leaves around the tree counterclockwise, naming a previous happy memory of a holiday or day out together for each one.
- When you can think of no more memories, tip the remaining dead leaves onto the ground, saying, *This holiday will bring us close once more, open for us a loving door.*
- Take the basket of thriving leaves to a pond, lake, or river or the sea. Cast them into the water, naming for each a wish for your future.
- When you can think of no more hopes, tip the remaining leaves into the water, saying, *This holiday marks the beginning of a future of gold, peace between us as joys unfold. I welcome the holiday and the future.*

236

FOR SAYING BON VOYAGE TO A FAMILY MEMBER RELOCATING ABROAD OR TO A DISTANT STATE

You will need:

A photograph of the person or people relocating
White ribbon
Dried rose petals or rose potpourri

Timing:

Dawn a day or two before the departure

The Spell

- Outdoors if possible, facing the direction the person will relocate, hold the photo in front of you, saying, [Name], *though I may no longer share the days with you, yet will my love, constantly with the morning light, daily be renewed.*
- Scatter a circle of rose petals or potpourri all around you, turning until you face the same direction in which you started, repeating the words.
- Wrap the white ribbon with three loose knots around the photo, saying, *I let you go willingly to your world excitingly new, yet will my love, constantly with the morning light, daily be renewed.*
- Place the photo with some of the rose petals or potpourri in a dish next to the photo and set in a window facing the direction of the new land.

237

A KITE RITUAL FOR A DESIRED RELOCATION

You will need:

A kite
Three luggage labels or strip of papers with a hole punched in them

Timing:

Monday, Tuesday, and Wednesday if possible

The Spell

- Write on the first label the place to which you wish to relocate. Say, *Wishes fly free, go from me so I can be where I most wish to see* [name place].
- On day 2, write the time frame for your relocation on the second label, saying the same words, changing *where* to *when*.
- On day 3, write the same words but substitute *how* for *when* on the third label. Describe what will make the relocation happy.
- Tie the labels to the kite and, repeating all the words, go to an open place.
- Let the kite fly free, and as you watch it disappear, say, *Wishes flown free, gone from me, soon I can be free*.

238

A FOUR-FEATHER SPELL FOR A SUCCESSFUL EMIGRATION

You will need:

Four white or gray feathers
A child's sandbox or tray
Two green-leafed twigs

Timing:

Thursday, outdoors

The Spell

- Make a pile of sand and push two feathers into it, saying, *As birds follow the sun through the sky, so shall I/we to our new land fly high, and there see a home from home, filled with endless possibility*.
- Make a second pile of sand on the other side of the box. Hold the other two feathers in turn, repeating the words, putting each feather on the new pile.
- Take each feather from the sandbox in turn. Attach it with string to a tree as the wind blows, repeating the words.
- Stick a small green-leafed twig into the first pile, saying, *We will never forget our old home*.
- Do the same for the second pile, saying, *Our new home*.
- Smooth the sand and leave the twigs in place.

239

TO DOWNSIZE YOUR PROPERTY SO THAT YOU CAN HAVE A SIMPLER, MORE NATURAL LIFE

You will need:

Two golden-brown candles
A brown drawstring bag
Three dried leaves or petals from your present garden or a potted plant
Three brown crystals or pebbles from your garden or near your home
A small bowl of salt

Timing:
The evening before you move

The Spell

- Light the first candle.
- Place three pinches of salt, leaves, and stones in the bag and close it, saying, *My home has been a special place for me, a haven and a sanctuary.*
- Pass the bag three times around the candle flame, saying three times, *I will travel light to my new life of simplicity and harmony, to a fresh special place for me, a haven and a sanctuary.*
- Let the candle burn. Take the bag and the second candle with you.
- In your new home, light the second candle and pass the bag around it three times clockwise, saying, *I make my new home a special place, a haven of simplicity.*
- Keep the bag in the kitchen or near a hearth.

240

TO FIND A VACATION APARTMENT OR A SECOND HOME OVERSEAS

You will need:

Four incense sticks in citrus fragrances, large ones if outdoors, in a square formation
Incense holders big enough to stand on the floor or in the ground
A bowl of water in the center of the square

Timing:
A cloudy afternoon

The Spell

- Make space indoors or out so that you can move inside the square.
- Set an incense stick in a holder in a square, midway along each wall.
- Light the incense sticks, starting with the one farthest away, saying for each, *May the winds carry me across land and sea, where waits the right apartment/house just for me.*
- Take the first incense stick you lit out of the holder and plunge it into the bowl of water in the center of the room so that it hisses, saying, *Power flow free, carry me across land and sea, where waits the right apartment/house just for me.*
- Repeat for the other three incenses. Remove the incense sticks from the water, let them dry, and crumble or break them so you can scatter them outdoors.
- Wash the water bowl under running water, repeating, *Power flow free, carry me across land and sea, where waits the right apartment/house just for me.*

SECTION 5:

COMMUTING AND WORK-RELATED TRAVEL

241

FOR SAFE COMMUTING

You will need:

A green candle
Small home-related items such as miniature pictures of family and pets, a favorite lucky charm, a Saint Christopher medallion, or a tiny crystal angel
Dried lavender or sandalwood or rose potpourri you have used at home
A green drawstring bag

Timing:

The night before your weekly or regular commute

The Spell

- Light the green candle, saying, *Angel Elemiah, who shields all commuters from harm, bring protection on my daily/weekly travels.*
- Fill the bag by its light, saying the same words softly over and over.
- Blow three times into the candle and three times into the bag, saying after each breath, *Elemiah, bring protection on my daily weekly/travels.*
- Leave the bag in front of the candle until it burns through.
- Keep the bag in the glove compartment of the vehicle.
- Each morning hold it and repeat, *Elemiah, bring protection on my daily weekly/travels.*
- Re-empower monthly by burning a green candle, holding the bag, and saying all the spell words, again, leaving the candles to burn.

242

TO GUARD AGAINST ROAD RAGE, MUGGINGS, AND ATTACKS ON TRAINS AND BUSES

You will need:

A small toy vehicle to represent your most common mode of travel in which there are potential regular hazards
A cup or vase large enough when inverted to cover the toy
A mint, lavender, frankincense, dragon's blood, or other spicy incense stick

Timing:

Monthly or before a trip alone that worries you

The Spell

- Light the incense and draw protective squares in smoke in the air around and over the vehicle, saying, *In times of danger, give me invisibility, shield me with invulnerability, that I may be unnoticed and unnoticeable until I reach safety.*
- Cover the vehicle with the cup or vase and repeat the words, passing the incense smoke, again in squares, around the inverted vase or cup.
- Let the incense burn and leave the toy inside the inverted vase or cup.
- Say the spell words whenever you feel afraid.

243

FOR PEACEFUL TRIPS TO SCHOOL, SHOPPING TRIPS, OR WHEN FERRYING DIFFICULT FAMILY OR COLLEAGUES

You will need:

A drawstring bag
Dried rose petals or rose potpourri
A copper coin, ring, or small item
A drop or two of lavender, chamomile, lemon, or vervain fragrance oil
A pink candle
A bowl and spoon

Timing:
Sunday evening

The Spell

- Light the candle and say, *I seek peaceful journeys, smiles, and soft words that no dissension may be heard.*
- Add the potpourri and oil to the bowl and mix slowly, repeating the words over and over more softly, and mix more slowly until you end in silence and stillness.
- Add it to the bag with the copper.
- Let the candle burn next to the closed bag and keep the bag in the car, saying the words three times before the journey.
- Each week, hold the closed bag in front of a pink lighted candle, repeating the words three times, and then blow the candle out. When the fragrance goes, replace the bag contents and repeat the spell.

244

IF YOU DRIVE FOR A LIVING OR IF IT IS PART OF YOUR JOB

You will need:

Your car, van, or bus keys

Timing:
Weekly, the night before your workweek begins

The Spell

- Toss the keys slowly in your open cupped hands, repeating, *Make my work a pleasure, may each day bring treasure. Guard me from fatigue and others' error, difficult passengers, and demanding time pressures that a satisfactory end to each journey shall there be.*
- Keep tossing the keys higher and chanting faster and louder until with a final open-handed toss you catch the keys and say, *This week will be filled with harmony.*
- Toss the keys three times each morning or evening before starting work, saying all the words once.

245

TO MAKE AN ANCIENT ROMAN PROTECTION AMULET FOR LONG-TERM OR DISTANCE COMMUTING AND WORK-RELATED DRIVING

You will need:

A long narrow strip of high-quality paper
Red wool
A red fabric bag to carry or a small silver tube with a neck chain in which to roll the amulet and wear around your neck
A pen, if possible a fountain pen, and black ink

Timing:

In natural light

The Spell

- Make the following word square for yourself or someone close to you.
- Write in silence:

SATOR
AREPO
TENET
OPERA
ROTAS

- Make all the letters the same size, working from left to right.
- Roll the finished amulet into a scroll and secure it with three knots of red wool, still in silence.
- Place it in the bag or tube and carry it or wear it when you travel.
- Replace every Midsummer Eve.

246

TO AVOID COMMUTING ACCIDENTS OR WHEN DRIVING IN CONNECTION WITH WORK

You will need:

A turquoise, kunzite, sugilite, jet, smoky quartz, garnet, or bloodstone crystal; a moonstone if you travel at night; or a silver good luck charm
A large bowl of water

Timing:

Monthly, the first Saturday evening of the month

The Spell

- Work by lamplight.
- Drop the crystal or charm into the bowl, saying: *This is my token of safety to protect me against breakdown, accidents caused by others' carelessness, my own inattention, or hazardous weather.*
- Ripple the water with both hands, saying, *So flows my journey, safely, uneventfully, and hazard-free.*
- Put drops of water on the base of your throat and both of your inner wrist points, saying, *So I take within me the protection of the waters.*
- Take the crystal from the water and pass it around the purple candle flame clockwise, saying, *The power of fire inspires my journey, safely, uneventfully, and hazard-free.*
- Tip the water into flowing water.
- Keep the crystal or charm with you as you drive.

247

WHEN UNEXPECTED DELAYS OR PROBLEMS ARISE WHILE YOU ARE COMMUTING OR TRAVELING FOR BUSINESS

You will need:
A watch

Timing:
When things start to go wrong

The Spell

- Stop the watch and say in your mind, *Time stand still. I will backtrack to restore my smooth-running journey once more.*
- Put the watch back to the approximate time when things started to go wrong, saying, *And now in quick succession we will put this lack of progression back on track again.*
- Return the watch to the current time, saying, *Continue now, anyhow, for life is back on track to stay, and so I must be on my way.*
- Explore options. If any official is dismissive or makes excuses, touch your watch and recall the spell, and doors will open.

248

TO SLEEP IN AN IMPERSONAL MOTEL ROOM OR ONE WHERE YOU FEEL UNSAFE WHEN WORKING AWAY FROM HOME

You will need:
A softly shaded lamp
A picture of loved ones or a memento of home

Timing:
Before you go to bed

The Spell

- Put the lamp near the middle of the room. Holding the picture or memento in the hand you do not write with, walk around the sphere of light clockwise, spiraling the other hand to enclose yourself in light, saying, *Lamp bright, shine your light, enfolding me safely through the night, safe until dawn, to greet the morn, renewed by sleep's tranquillity.*
- Picture the circle of light as a force field around the bed, the room, or, if in an unsafe area, the building.
- Set the memento next to your bed and switch off the lamp, saying, *Light within me, safe until dawn, to greet the morn, renewed by sleep's tranquillity.*

249

TO KEEP IN CONTACT WITH A PARTNER OR FAMILY MEMBER WORKING AWAY FROM HOME IF HE OR SHE IS EASILY DISTRACTED AND DOES NOT STAY IN TOUCH

You will need:

Whatever form of communication you will be using, such as phone, computer, or tablet

Timing:

When you know the person will be free to talk or at a prearranged time

The Spell

- Switch on the computer or video messaging service or call up the number on the phone but do not dial it.
- Call your partner's name slowly and softly nine times.
- Setting the phone flat on the table or sitting in front of the computer, tap your hands softly and rhythmically on the table, chanting continuously, *Think of me, me only see, that we may be connected lovingly this day/night.*
- Call your love's name nine more times, returning to chanting and tapping, then calling the name again, for five or ten minutes.
- If your love has not connected, make contact. If there is no response, return to calling the name and tapping for five minutes and contact again.

TO SEND STRENGTH TO YOUR PARTNER IF HE OR SHE IS UNHAPPY WORKING AWAY FROM HOME AND MISSES YOU OR THE FAMILY

You will need:

A circle of family photographs or photographs of you and your partner

Ten white tea lights or small candles encircling the photos

Timing:

A time when the family or you and your partner normally would be together

The Spell

- Light the first candle, saying, *I/we reach out to you this night though far away. Never from our thoughts you stray, for within our hearts you always stay. Feel our love as we send it in this light.*
- Light each candle, moving clockwise, repeating the words until only the tenth candle remains unlit.
- Light the tenth candle, saying, *With ten flames we send you light, for you are with us on this night, for you will never be alone, we count the days until you come home.*
- Take the photo and let any family member(s) present send a silent blessing as you pass it around.

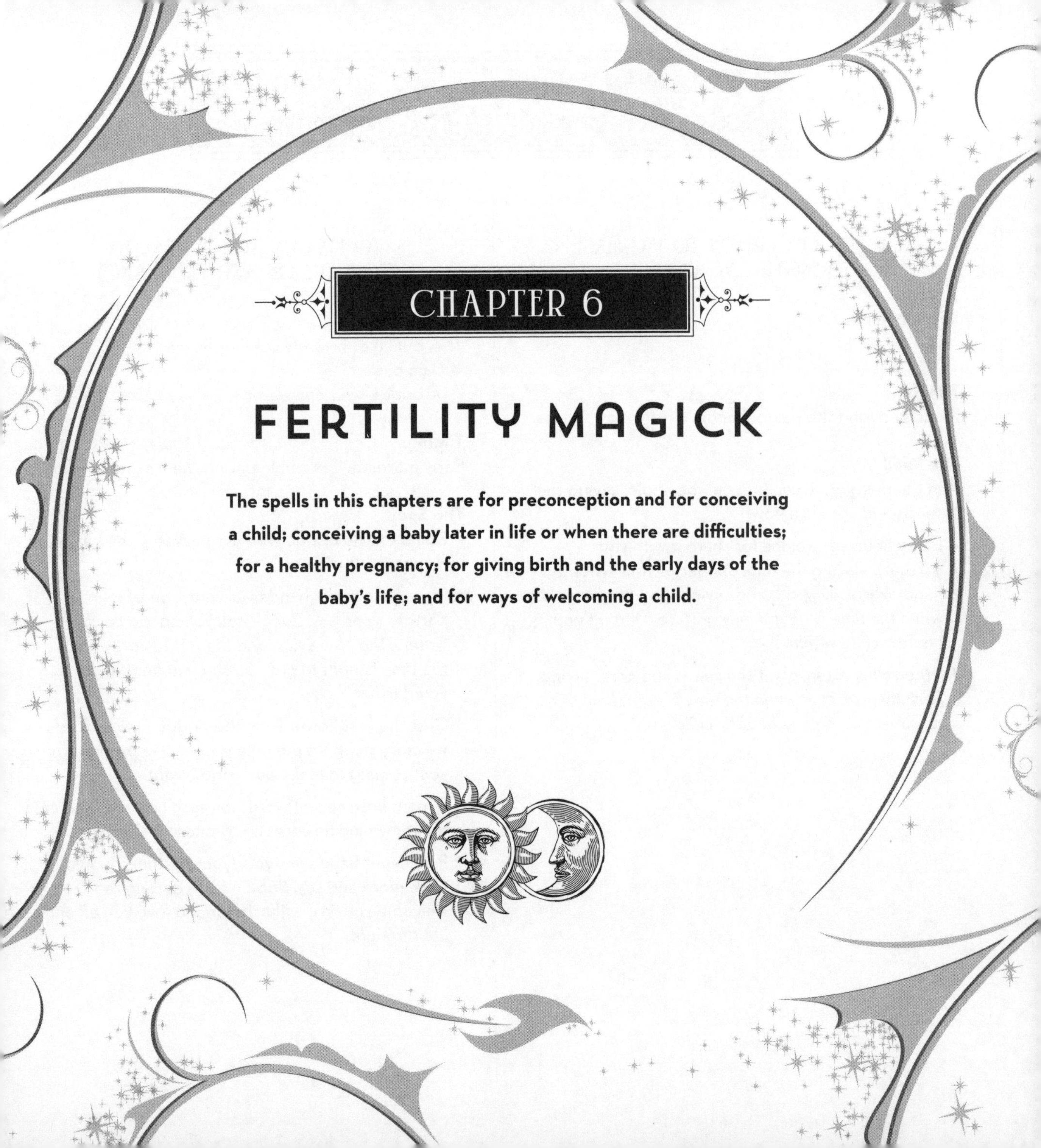

CHAPTER 6

FERTILITY MAGICK

The spells in this chapters are for preconception and for conceiving a child; conceiving a baby later in life or when there are difficulties; for a healthy pregnancy; for giving birth and the early days of the baby's life; and for ways of welcoming a child.

PRECONCEPTION SPELLS AND SPELLS TO CONCEIVE A CHILD

251

FOR PRECONCEPTION TO INCREASE STRENGTH AND HEALTH

You will need:
A ripe apple

Timing:
Monday during the waxing moon

The Spell

- In the morning, slice and peel the apple, saving the seeds and core in a bowl.
- Every hour, eat a piece (or share it with your partner), placing the index finger of your writing hand over your womb and saying, *Fertility grow that when the time is right, I may nurture a strong and healthy child within.*
- When all is eaten, plant the seeds and core, saying, *Fertility grow that when the time is right, I may nurture a strong and healthy child within.*

252

TO PREPARE FOR A HEALTHY CONCEPTION AND PREGNANCY

You will need:
A bunch of brightly colored flowers in a basket
A bridge over any water

Timing:
Early morning, if possible during the waxing moon

The Spell

- Stand on the bridge with the basket in the hand you do not write with.
- Place your other hand over your womb/your partner's and say, *Baby, I call you on the flowing waters, the blue skies, and the fertile earth when the time is right to grow strong and healthy for your birth.*
- Cast the first flower from the bridge saying, *So do we call you, when the time is right. We prepare for your coming to make our world bright.*
- Repeat both sets of words for each flower as you cast the remaining flowers one by one into the water.
- Place your hand over your/your partner's womb once more and say, *Baby, we are getting ready to welcome you. We will care for and love you all our life through.*

253

TO INCREASE PRECONCEPTION ENERGIES, ESPECIALLY IF YOU HAVE USED CONTRACEPTION FOR A LONG TIME

You will need:

A silver-colored bowl, half filled with water
Seven small white flowers
Silver candles (if indoors)

Timing:

When the moon is bright, full, or nearly full, a few months before you start trying for a baby

The Spell

- Go outdoors and face the moon, or if it is dark, light silver candles indoors near an uncurtained window.
- Set the flowers around the bowl where the moon or candlelight shines in the water, saying, *Lady Moon, I call your fertility within this water that you will grant me/us a healthy son or daughter. Bright as your light, gentle as your glow, that I may know when right it is to be, and joys of conception and pregnancy.*
- Leave the water overnight, mesh-covered if necessary, and in the morning filter it into small glass bottles and refrigerate.
- Each morning and night, massage a few drops of moon water over your womb, repeating the words.
- Continue the ritual monthly until you start trying for a baby. If you wish, you can continue until conception.

254

TO WELCOME A BABY INTO YOUR LIFE, ESPECIALLY IF IT IS YOUR FIRST

You will need:

Fourteen perfectly round hazelnuts or other small smooth round nuts
A small piece of silver cloth or silver paper/foil

Timing:

The first day of your menstrual cycle even if it is irregular

The Spell

- On day 1, as near to sunset as possible, lay the first nut on the silver cloth or paper near the window in your bedroom, or near the door if you don't have a window, saying, *Beloved infant, this symbol of fertility, calls you enter me, that we will become a happy family.*
- Each subsequent evening, unless you have a nut allergy, eat the nut from the previous night and add a new one to the silver paper, repeating the words.
- On the fifteenth morning, wrap the last nut in the silver and plant the nuts in a sheltered spot outdoors or in a deep pot. If you have a nut allergy, persuade your partner to eat one each night; if he or she will not eat them, wrap them all in the silver and bury them.
- Repeat the cycle if necessary until you relax into its rhythm.

255

TO CONCEIVE A CHILD

You will need:

A pink rose quartz crystal, a pearl, or a pink glass bead
A long silver pin, long needle, or thin paper knife
A pink scarf

Timing:

The three nights before the full moon and the full moon itself

The Spell

- On night 1, hold the crystal in the hand you do not write with and the pin in the other hand, saying as you move them close together, not touching, *So shall two become three, baby, we ask you to join our loving family.*
- Leave them on an indoor window ledge in your bedroom and repeat on days 2 and 3.
- On the full moon night, touch the crystal with the sharp point of the pin and say the words again.
- If possible, make love.
- The next morning, wrap the crystal and pin in the scarf and keep in a bedroom drawer until conception is confirmed or for the next month.

256

A FULL MOON AND MOTHER EARTH RITUAL TO CONCEIVE A CHILD

You will need:

An area of earth outdoors or a large pot of soil indoors
Two larger green plants and a smaller one

Timing:

Full or nearly full moon

The Spell

- Go into the moonlight or where you can see the moon (if it is too cloudy, work indoors, lighting silver candles around the pot).
- Open your hands wide and high toward the light, palms flat and uppermost, saying, *Mother Moon, I would be a mother/parent like you. I ask you this night, fill me with your fertile light.*
- Plant the two larger plants next to each other, separated by a small amount of space. Say, *Welcome, little one, for we will be there as you flourish and grow in our care.*
- Plant the smaller plant between the two larger ones, saying, *Flourish and grow in our care, we will be there until you come safely in our arms and our life.*

257

TO CONCEIVE NATURALLY IF YOU DO NOT WANT TO USE OVULATION CHARTS

You will need:

A fresh egg
Children's brightly colored pens
A white candle

Timing:

Late on Friday

The Spell

- Light the candle and say, *Mother Earth, I call my little one to birth, to thrive and grow. May this be so within three moons or very soon.*
- Decorate the egg with flowers, butterflies, spirals, and circles, saying the spell words as a soft chant.
- Dig a hole outdoors or in a deep pot and bury the egg, saying, *Mother Earth, quicken life within me and bring birth.*

258

A TRADITIONAL CONCEPTION RITUAL FROM INDIA

You will need:

A whole coconut
A hammer or implement to break open the coconut
Five different kinds of seeds

Timing:

When the moon is full, outdoors

The Spell

- Facing the moon, hold the coconut in your outstretched hands and say, *The fruit is sweet with fecundity, the shell the womb, the milk new life, Mother Moon, by your bright light, I offer this symbol of fertility.*
- Break open the coconut (or do this beforehand). Drink a little milk, eat some of the fruit, and dig a small mound in the earth or deep in a pot of soil.
- Repeat the words and bury the rest of the coconut in the soil, first tipping the milk into the hole.
- Plant five different kinds of seeds in the mound and tend them regularly.

259

IF YOU WANT A BOY

You will need:

A tiny basket lined with fresh leaves (if possible from a fruit- or nut-bearing tree)
Tiny blue objects, such as buttons, candies, and/or blue fruits
A small boy doll or male worry doll or craft one from modeling clay or dough

Timing:
Sunday

The Spell

- Place the baby in the basket and add tiny blue objects, saying eight times, *Any healthy child we welcome, that is true, but blue for a boy would bring us such joy.*
- Let the basket float free on any water source, repeating eight more times, *Blue for a boy will bring us such joy, if right to be, so shall we see our little son.*

260

TO HAVE A GIRL

You will need:

A jar of honey
A pink candle
An undergarment
Three pink ribbons

Timing:
Monday

The Spell

- Light the candle so that it shines on the honey.
- Take a spoonful of light-filled honey, eat it, and say, *All babies are welcome, but this prayer I unfurl, to complete our happiness/family we wish for a girl.*
- Tie the ribbons together and pin them to an undergarment.
- Blow out the candle and then instantly relight it, repeating the words and eating another spoon of honey.
- Let the candle burn.
- Each day until you conceive, wear the ribbons and eat a small quantity of honey or add it to cooking.

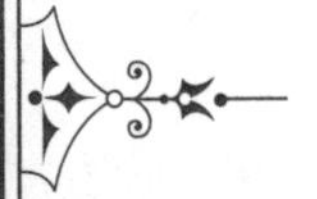

261

TO CONCEIVE A CHILD IF YOU ARE AN OLDER PARENT AND WORRY ABOUT FERTILITY OR HEALTH ISSUES

You will need:

Seven pears in a bowl so that there will be a ripe one every day

Timing:

Seven consecutive days

The Spell

- Each morning, take a ripe pear and cut it into equal pieces, preserving the core and seeds.
- Eat it or share with your partner, after each piece saying, *The fruit is sweeter for its maturity, ripe with sunset fertility, I eat the fruit in its later fecundity, and so I/we will soon conceive a healthy child, raised in security and harmony.*
- When you have eaten the pear, cast the seeds and core into flowing water just before sunset and say, *Late-blooming fertility is sweet, child of mine, I wait eagerly until we can meet.*
- Repeat until all seven pears are gone.

262

BRINGING FERTILITY TO A NEW RELATIONSHIP IN LATER LIFE OR ONE IN WHICH AFTER HAVING CHILDREN YOU ARE UNABLE TO CONCEIVE ANOTHER

You will need:

Colorless or light brown self-hardening modeling clay

Three yellow candles

Nuts, grains, olives, and/or edible seeds in a bowl

Timing:

In the morning, if possible outdoors in sunlight (if not, light yellow candles)

The Spell

- From a large ball of clay, create a simple pot of coils with a flat base and smooth the coils, saying softly as a repetitive chant, *Mother Earth, though old as time, daily you give birth. As I make this vessel of fertility, grant a new child will come to me.*
- Leave your pot to dry, in the sun if possible.
- When the pot is dry, place the grains in it, saying, *Mother Earth, may this fertile offering bring fertility.*
- Let the candle burn next to the pot.
- Each day add seeds to the pot for six more days, repeating all the spell words.
- On the seventh day, bury the pot and its contents in the earth.

263

TO WELCOME A LATE UNEXPECTED PREGNANCY TO AN EXISTING FAMILY OR TO START A SECOND FAMILY

You will need:

Colored beads of different sizes and a string on which to thread them

Timing:

When the pregnancy occurs or is planned

The Spell

- In the center of the string, thread a large bead for the parents, a medium-size one for existing children (even if adult), and a smaller one for the anticipated or desired arrival.
- Say as you thread, *We are one family, we are a unity, but now we welcome new life and new vitality, always together, but adding new harmony.*
- Add an even number of tiny beads on each side of the others, naming for each one the benefits and blessings an increasing family will bring.
- Wear the necklace or bracelet or hang it behind the front door.
- Touch each bead weekly and repeat the spell words until the birth.

264

TO PERSIST IF ATTEMPTS TO CONCEIVE ARE UNSUCCESSFUL

You will need:

An old scarf
A packet of edible seeds

Timing:

Sunday morning

The Spell

- Carefully knot the scarf around the seeds so that you can carry them.
- Open the scarf, preferably in a windblown place, saying, *Winds of fertility, blow warm on me, take stagnation away and bring fecundity.*
- Tie the scarf to the first tree you see, or if no trees are available, secure it anywhere outdoors.

265

IF THE MEDICAL PROFESSION IS DISMISSIVE OR NEGATIVE ABOUT YOUR OR YOUR PARTNER'S CHANCES OF CONCEIVING

You will need:

A large shiny bauble on a long loop of string or a sun catcher (a crystal on a chain that is meant to hang in windows and catch the light)

Timing:

Friday

The Spell

- Hold the bauble or sun catcher in the hand you write with and spin it seven times in each direction, saying, *Sun of fertility, reflected be, shine life and light on all you see.*
- Hang the bauble or sun catcher from a window where it will catch the morning light, saying, *As you shine bright as the sun, prove all wrong, we will have our own baby before long. Fill us with fertility, this I ask and it must be.*
- Every morning twirl the bauble or sun catcher seven times again in each direction, repeating the spell words.

266

TO RESTORE PASSION AND ENTHUSIASM TO LOVEMAKING IF IT HAS BEEN RULED BY OVULATION CHARTS AND IMPOSED CONSTRAINTS

You will need:

A red candle

Any dried petals or dried tarragon or rosemary in a bowl

An orange, frankincense, or any spicy incense

A floral essence or cologne in a spray bottle

A heart shaped locket or heart-shaped rose quartz, or cut out a red heart drawn on paper

Timing:

Tuesday

The Spell

- Light the candle where it shines on the heart, saying three times, *I call fertility with the power of fire that we may experience desire once more.*
- Light the incense from the candle and draw smoke hearts in the air over the heart, saying three times, *I call fertility with the power of air that passion once more we will share.*
- Make a circle of petals or herbs clockwise around the heart, saying three times, *I call fertility with the power of earth that joy in our love will experience rebirth.*
- Spray the fragrance over the heart, saying, *I call fertility with the power of water that spontaneity will bring our son or our daughter.*
- Blow out the candle, let the incense burn, and try to arrange a fun weekend away, making love when you want. Take the heart with you.

267

TO HASTEN CONCEPTION IF YOU FEAR TIME IS RUNNING OUT OR ONE OR BOTH OF YOU HAS A FERTILITY OR POTENCY ISSUE

You will need:

An egg
A bowl and a whisk
A lighted oil burner or electric diffuser containing a floral fragrance

Timing:

Friday

The Spell

- Pass the egg through the fragrant smoke three times in each direction, saying, *Three by three, a baby comes to me/us, fertility returns, increases, grows as each week turns.*
- Blow out the oil burner or switch off the diffuser, crack open the egg, whisk it in the bowl faster and faster as you say the words faster and faster, and with the final turns, push the whisk firmly into the bottom of the bowl, saying, *Three by three, so it shall be.*
- Use the egg in a meal or cake; if you are allergic, feed it to an animal.

268

FOR A PREGNANCY WHEN YOU HAVE TRIED EVERYTHING AND ALMOST GIVEN UP HOPE

You will need:

An oval or round crystal quartz and a pointed one
A glass bowl half filled with water

Timing:

Sunday, when light breaks through

The Spell

- Drop the oval quartz into the water, stirring the water in all directions with the pointed quartz, saying, *Barbelo, wise angel who brings us gifts most needed and desired, fill my womb with your fertilizing fire, that we may be inspired with the gift of a child, for we will be the most loving parents.*
- Leave the bowl in the light until noon.
- Touch the round crystal still in the water with the pointed one, saying, *So are we joined in love. Barbelo, bring forth our child; we ask, for we will be the most loving parents.*
- Filter the sun water into clear glass bottles and every morning and evening add to bathwater or splash on your breasts and womb, repeating all the spell words.
- Tip any left on the following Sunday onto growing plants and, if you wish, repeat the spell, making new water.

269

A SECOND SPELL TO BRING HOPE AFTER TRYING IN VAIN

You will need:

Ingredients to make pastry or dough

Timing:

A bright dry day

The Spell

- Sit on fresh green grass with your hands and feet firmly planted on the ground and say, *Mother Earth, I take in your fertility, I absorb your loving power that granted this infant will be.*
- Return indoors and make a small pastry or dough roll, decorating the top with three figures, with the smallest in the middle. As you make it, say the same words three times.
- Eat the bread or pastry while sitting on the grass and say, *Mother Earth, I have taken within myself your fertility, I ask only that you grant me/us a healthy baby soon.*
- Scatter the crumbs for the birds and if possible spend the day close to nature.

270

IF YOU OR YOUR PARTNER HAS A GYNECOLOGICAL CONDITION THAT MAKES CONCEPTION DIFFICULT

You will need:

A bar magnet
Straight shiny pins
Children's drawing pen and paper
A lidded box

Timing:

Monday weekly and around the full moon

The Spell

- Draw a house with rainbow colors that contains you and your partner and any existing children, plus the new baby in a cradle, with a rainbow over the top of the house. Write, LITTLE ONE, WELCOME TO OUR FAMILY, TWICE AS PRECIOUS BECAUSE HARD WON.
- Scatter the pins on the picture and say, *Anything can be overcome, any obstacle removed, I call you with devotion and pure love, twice as precious because hard won.*
- Gather all the pins with a magnet, put them and the magnet in a lidded box, and keep them in a drawer until the next spell.
- Hang the picture in the brightest place in the house and read the words every time you pass it.

271

SAFE WITHIN THE WOMB OF THE MOTHER

You will need:

A long green thread
A green candle
A bowl of salt

Timing:

As often as you wish, especially in the early weeks of pregnancy if you feel anxious

The Spell

- Light the candle and pass the ends of the thread three times close to the flame; do it quickly so that you do not set it alight.
- Begin tying nine knots in the thread. For knot 1, say, *Stay safe within the womb of the mother, day and night, until the time is right to pass into the waiting arms of those who love you.*
- Repeat for the next eight knots and then tie a tenth to join the two ends, saying, *Rest safe, little baby, within this circle of love.*
- Hang the circle in the future baby's room, and whenever you feel anxious, touch each knot, repeating all the spell words.

272

FOR A SAFE AND HEALTHY PREGNANCY AND DELIVERY

You will need:

Seven crystals of different colors, choosing ones you like. If you cannot obtain crystals, substitute pearls
A white drawstring bag for the crystals
Seven small pink candles in a circle

Timing:

Once your own pregnancy or that of someone close to you is confirmed

The Spell

- Set the candles in a circle and the crystals on top of the bag in the center.
- As you light each candle clockwise, say, *Seven lights, you baby of love, I bring that safe you grow and strong within; seven lights to your safe birth will guide, dear baby of love, rest warm inside.*
- Hold each of the crystals in turn, and for each crystal, make a wish for the baby's future life. Set each crystal in front of a candle to make an inner circle.
- Repeat the same words, adding, *You, baby of love, I promise true, through all my days to cherish you.*
- Blow out the candles and send the light to the little one silently asking for a safe pregnancy and delivery.
- Give the crystals in the bag to the mother.

273

FOR A HAPPY PREGNANCY IF YOU ARE NOT WITH THE FATHER OF THE CHILD

You will need:

A picture of yourself with the baby's father if he is in the child's life, otherwise a family member or friend who has been supporting you
A scan picture
Four pink roses in a vase

Timing:
If you are feeling emotionally low

The Spell

- Place the pictures with the scan on top, next to the vase.
- Take the first rose, putting a single petal on top of the pictures, saying, *You will always be beloved, your life through, even if just me and you.*
- Add a petal from the second rose, saying, *You will always know security with me, even if just me and you.*
- Add one from the third rose, saying, *You will have a carefree childhood, your life through, even if just me and you.*
- Add one from the fourth rose, saying, *You will always have a happy family, your life through, even if just me and you.*
- Release four rose petals outdoors, saying all four sets of words.
- When the roses fade, add the petals to a potpourri or dried lavender in a bowl in the infant's future room.

274

BEFORE A SCAN OR TESTS, ESPECIALLY IF YOU FEEL WORRIED

You will need:

A small doll (a worry or toy one)
A round purse
Dried lavender, hibiscus, or chamomile flowers; dried vervain herbs; or vanilla pods
A white candle

Timing:
The day or night before the scan or tests

The Spell

- Light the candle and pass it nine times around the doll, saying each time, *Little one, filled be with vitality, that I may see life growing strong and sure within me.*
- Add the doll and flowers or herbs to the purse and close it, passing the candle nine times around it, repeating the words nine times.
- Take the purse to the scan, saying the words in your head beforehand.
- Keep the purse with the scan picture or any test results.

275

FOR A CALM PREGNANCY IF CLOSE RELATIVES ARE INTERFERING

You will need:

A very gentle bath product such as chamomile or lavender

Candles for the bathroom

Timing:

An evening when you need some space

The Spell

- Light the candles and run the bath or shower, adding the bath foam to the water or a washcloth in the shower.
- Swirl the light pools, saying, *Spirit of the waters, power of the light, may all be tranquil in my sight. You,* [name], *interfere in love but far too much; step back and do not make so much intrusion, it leads only to confusion. We,* [your name] *and* [name partner], *reclaim our power, we do know best, so let it rest.*
- Empty the bath or shower, put all phones and electronic devices on silent, do not answer the door, and spend a relaxing evening with your partner, making plans for what you want for the baby.
- Say the spell words in your mind when the next interference begins.

276

TO CONNECT WITH AN UNBORN INFANT

You will need:

A special piece of music you love

A rose quartz, pink mangano calcite, or small crystal angel

A soft blanket

Timing:

Once the baby is kicking

The Spell

- Sit quietly, with your partner if you wish, and put on the music.
- Place your hands (and your partner's) over the womb and say softly, *Child of mine/ours, safe inside, we are as one safe within the womb, and so I/we send you love as life begins.*
- Place the crystal over your womb and gently massage the womb (or ask your partner to), saying the words again.
- Wrap yourself in the blanket and repeat the words, adding any special blessings.
- When the music finishes, keep making contact with your hand(s) and talking softly to the baby within.
- When the baby is born, the music, crystal massage, and blanket will prove soothing to the little one.

277

FOR A SUCCESSFUL AND HAPPY TWIN/ MULTIPLE INFANT PREGNANCY AND BIRTH

You will need:

A bowl of small fruits
A bowl of grains or edible seeds
A bowl of nuts (omit if you have an allergy)
A large bowl

Timing:

When the twin/multiple birth is confirmed

The Spell

- Take some fruits in the hand you do not write with and eat them one by one, saying, *Double/triple pleasure brings double/triple treasure. Within me strength I take, that you may thrive, and daily make progress until the time we laugh and run together under the sun.*
- Repeat for the grains and nuts.
- Tip each bowl in turn into the large bowl and swirl to mix, saying, *Double/triple pleasure brings double/triple treasure, friends forever will you be, sharing life devotedly, my double/triple blessings.*
- Outdoors, scatter half the mix to be eaten by birds or absorbed by the earth and keep the other half in a sealed container for eating, repeating all the spell words.
- Place your hand over your womb and say, *My double/triple treasure thrive and daily grow, until the time it shall be so, we laugh and run together under the sun.*

278

TO KEEP A PREGNANCY STABLE AND HELP IT RUN TO FULL TERM IF YOU ARE ANXIOUS OR EXPERIENCED PROBLEMS IN EARLIER PREGNANCIES

You will need:

A dark ball of thread
A soft scarf
A small hoop or a circle of wire
A box with a lid large enough to hold the hoop

Timing:

When you feel anxious or at the time a problem occurred in an earlier pregnancy

The Spell

- From the ball of thread, cut or break long pieces, tying knots in them, wrapping or attaching them with short pieces of thread to the hoop, and knotting them together to make a crisscross pattern like a web, saying softly over and over, *Gabriel, archangel of as yet unborn children, keep my little one safe within, until the time is right to enter the world.*
- Wrap the hoop in the scarf and put it in the box, securing the lid with nine knots, saying the words for the last time.
- Keep the box in a safe dark place until your due date.

279

TO KEEP THE INFANT SAFE WITHIN IF YOU HAVE HAD LOTS OF FALSE ALARMS FOR LABOR

You will need:

A soft green scarf
One green ribbon for each month left or each week if it is not long to the due date

Timing:
Saturday

The Spell

- Tie a knot between the first and second ribbons, continuing until they are all joined in a circle, all the while saying softly, *Sleep sweet, sleep tight, rest snug, by day and night, do not come into the world until the time is right.*
- Wrap the ribbon circle in the scarf, knot it firmly, and keep it in a drawer by your bed.
- Each month or week, undo one of the knots and repeat the words.
- When all are undone by the due date, put the ribbons in a purse and say, *Baby, the time is near, for you to join us, welcome here.*

280

IF THE BABY IS LATE COMING AND YOU ARE GETTING IMPATIENT

You will need:

A long red ribbon
An electric fan

Timing:
When you are overdue

The Spell

- Stand in front of an electric fan, holding the ribbon in one hand and saying nine times, *Winds of fertility, I let you blow free, asking only that it be, you release my infant to enter the world soon and easily.*
- Switch off the fan and say, *Winds of fertility, I release you to be totally free, asking only that it be, you release my infant to enter the world soon and easily.*
- Hang the ribbon from the outside of a front-facing window.
- Each day, if baby is too comfortable inside, repeat the spell, adding a new ribbon until action takes place.

281

FOR A SAFE AND EASY DELIVERY AT FULL TERM

You will need:

A long red ribbon
A green trailing plant

Timing:
In late pregnancy

The Spell

- Tie two fronds of the plant together, saying, *Stay safe, little one, and when the time is right, may the gateway to the world open easily and gradually that labor will flow naturally and your birth will be filled with harmony.*
- Tie six loose knots in the ribbon, saying the same words for each one.
- Around the due date, untie or cut the plant fronds, repeating the words.
- When labor begins, untie or get someone present to untie every knot in the ribbon, saying for each, *Baby of my heart, come into the world easily and gradually, that you may flow naturally from your secure sanctuary to be greeted by my/our love.*

282

FOR RELATIVES TO SEND STRENGTH IN CHILDBIRTH

You will need:

A closed padlock and its key
A cupful of water
A knotted ribbon or a trailing plant

Timing:
When labor is taking place, especially if it is slow

The Spell

- Hold the padlock, undo it with the key, and say, *Open the door and be bound no more.*
- Cut through a frond of the plant or untie the knotted ribbon, saying, *I cut through the bonds. I release the mother and child. Come into the world, little one, where we wait to greet you.*
- Collect a cupful of water and pour it as slowly as possible into the earth in a potted plant or down a washbasin, saying, *Mother Earth, bring easy birth to* [name mother] *as the waters flow.*
- Repeat the spell after a couple of hours if necessary, continuing the sequence after relocking or tying a frond/knot as long as necessary. You can adapt the stages to a hospital waiting area.

283

IF YOU KNOW YOU ARE HAVING A CESAREAN BIRTH

You will need:

A red cord
A red soft purse or drawstring bag
A red crystal

Timing:
Any Wednesday before the birth date

The Spell

- Hold the crystal between your cupped hands and say, *May your entry into the world be gentle, may your passage be smooth and uneventful; soon you will be securely in my arms, assisted by those who will help me move you safely into life and me to speedy recovery. So shall it be.*
- Tie just one loose knot in the center of the cord, repeat the words, and put the cord and crystal safely into the bag.
- Before the cesarean, open the bag, untie the cord, and say, *Soon you will be securely in my arms, assisted by those who will help me move you safely into life and me to speedy recovery. So shall it be.*
- Hold the crystal and say the same words.
- Put both back in the bag, and just before you go to meet your baby, touch the bag and say, *Baby, we are one.*
- Afterward, keep the crystal near the baby's cradle and throw the cord into water when you are recovered.

284

TO HELP FIRST-TIME MOTHERS AND FATHERS TRUST THEIR ABILITY TO DO THE BEST FOR THEIR CHILD

You will need:

A comfortable chair or bed

Timing:
When you have a few minutes in the hospital or at home and the baby is sleeping

The Spell

- Lie or sit, resting, cradling your hands around the baby. Say, *You are new to being my child. I am new to being your mother/father. Together will we grow in love and tenderness. I will always do my best for you.*
- Enclose the baby's hands in yours and say, *I will teach you and you will teach me what loving unity can be. One day we will recall when we first touched in love and the angels above gave you to me. Know this bond will always be between us.*
- Repeat the spell whenever you worry about your parenting skills.

285

FOR A CHRISTENING OR NAMING CEREMONY

You will need:

A small round polished crystal
A jug of water

Timing:

The morning of the christening or naming ceremony

The Spell

- Anyone connected with the child can do this.
- Take the crystal and jug of water into the garden or to anywhere you have a large green plant.
- Hold the crystal over the earth or the plant and pour a little water on it. Name a gift or blessing you wish for the baby.
- As the water falls on the earth, say: *Mother Earth bless and protect my/this child that he/she may walk safely and happily the pathways of beauty all through life.*
- Continue to pour and ask for blessings. Ask for the things you consider important as well as for worldly success, and each time you pour, repeat the blessing of Mother Earth.
- When the jug is empty, go indoors, dry the crystal, and use it to begin a collection of crystals you will give to the child on a milestone birthday.
- Each birthday or anniversary of the christening/naming ceremony, buy a new crystal and repeat the spell.

286

TO WELCOME A NEW BABY INTO THE FAMILY

You will need:

Three white good-quality candles
Ten small pearls in a circle around the candles

Timing:

After hearing the good news

The Spell

- Light the first candle and say, *I/we welcome you into the world/our family. This candle burns for your golden future. May you always walk with the protection and guidance of those who will grow to know and love you.*
- Light the second candle from the first and say, *This candle burns for your naming/christening day* [or the day the little one comes home]. *May you always walk with the protection and guidance of those who will grow to know and love you.*
- Light the third candle from the second and say, *This candle burns for your going into the world* [kindergarten, first day at school]. *May you always walk with the protection and guidance of those who will grow to know and love you.*

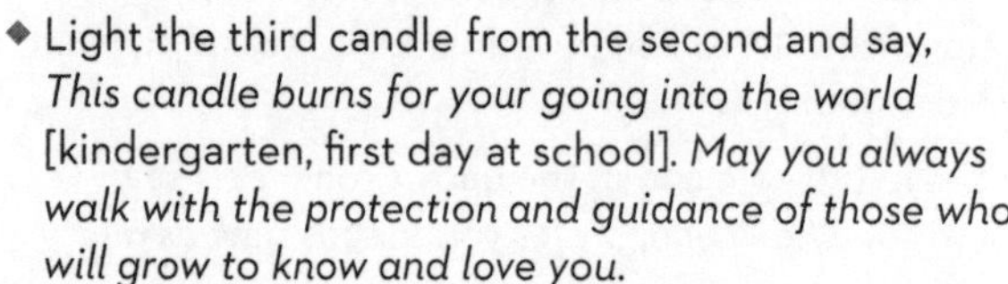

- Let the first candle burn. Blow out the other two, relighting on the suggested milestone or other important days.
- Keep the pearls in an ornamental jar to be placed in the baby's bedroom or next to a picture of the baby.

287

A TRADITIONAL SPELL FOR BRINGING A BABY HOME

You will need:
Three gold coins in a bag

Timing:
When you bring your new baby home

The Spell

- As soon as you enter your home, say, *Baby, welcome home.*
- Carry the baby through every room downstairs, and if you have stairs, take the baby to the top, saying in each room and on the stairs, *So shall you rise in joy and prosperity, successfully and healthily. May your life be golden, filled with the love of the family to whom you bring unity.*
- Carry the baby through each upstairs room, repeating the words.
- If you do not have stairs, gently lift the baby upward, still cradled in your arms, as you enter the front door.
- Leave the coin bag in the baby's room and say, *May you have enough for your needs always and a little more.*
- Sit with the baby in the main room of the home and say, *May the angels guard you always and may you never be without the love of we who will care for you devotedly.*

288

FOR THE BIRTH OF A NEW GRANDCHILD, CLOSE RELATIVE, OR FRIEND'S CHILD OR YOUR GODCHILD

You will need:
Nine small green candles in a circle
Nine pearls or crystals, forming an outer circle, one in front of each candle
A small lidded jar in the center of the candles

Timing:
When you hear the good news

The Spell

- Light the first candle and, if you know the chosen name, use that or say, *Beloved baby, welcome to the world of love and infinite possibility.*
- Put the first pearl or crystal into the jar and say, *May you always have the gift of health and strength.* Do this for each pearl or crystal in turn.
- For pearl or crystal 2, say, *May you always know love, laughter, and happiness.*
- For pearl or crystal 3, say, *May you be generous and openhearted.* For pearl or crystal 4, say, *May you be quick-minded and eager to learn.* For pearl or crystal 5, say, *May you be kind to people and respectful to all creatures on the earth.*
- For pearl or crystal 6, say, *May you be open-minded and tolerant of all who are different.* For pearl or crystal 7, say, *May you love nature and make the earth beautiful.* For pearl or crystal 8, say, *May you have rich creative talents.*
- For pearl or crystal 9, say, *May you be independent and eager for new adventure.*
- Let the candles burn and afterward give or send the jar of pearls or crystals to the parents for the child's room.

289

A TREE PLANTING FOR A NEW BABY

You will need:

A small tree or bush

An area to grow it where the child will see it through the years

Timing:

This can be part of a naming ceremony in the garden or after a christening or can be carried out independently by parents or relatives

The Spell

- Name the baby and say, *As this tree grows, you will strength and health know, as this tree flourishes, so will you be nourished by the love and care of those around you.*
- Dig a hole, adding to it a special small nonperishable treasure in a waterproof sealed metal box. Plant the tree, watering the roots and saying, *As this tree grows tall, may you fill the lives of others with your unique gifts and blessings.*
- As the child grows, measure him or her against the tree, and when the child turns eighteen, dig up the treasure as a special present.

290

A BABY BLESSING IF YOU ARE FAR AWAY OR ESTRANGED FROM THE PARENTS/A PARENT, PERHAPS BECAUSE OF DIVORCE OR REMARRIAGE

You will need:

A basket of six yellow and orange flowers, three of each

Timing:

When you hear news of the birth

The Spell

- Carry the flowers to a fast-moving water source, a tidal river, or the ocean.
- Cast the flowers one by one into the water, saying for each, [Estranged or distant family members], *I send your baby love upon the waters and to you who still are dear. Even though I may not see you often, my blessings to you fill my home. May this be the year we are reunited.*
- Find six stones, three dark and three light, near the water source and skim each in turn, first the dark and then the light, saying for each, *May this be the year we are reunited, but until then, I send you blessings.*

291

FOR CONCEPTION BY IN VITRO FERTILIZATION, WHETHER YOUR FIRST TRY OR A SUBSEQUENT TREATMENT

You will need:

A fragrance oil burner with the bowl one-third filled with water and a tea light or an electric diffuser to heat it

Orange, neroli, lemon balm, or ylang ylang fragrance or essential oil

Timing:

Three evenings before a course of treatment begins

The Spell

- Gently heat the water and add a few drops of oil to the water or the required amount to the diffuser, saying, *May our love mix and mingle and that united love burrow deeply and securely inside that you flower and flourish and one day dance through the world, our little miracle unfurled.*
- Keep adding drops of oil, repeating the words.
- When there is just a little liquid left in the burner, blow out the tea light or switch off the diffuser.
- On night 2, repeat the spell, adding to what is left in the burner or diffuser. Do the same thing on night 3, but this time wait until all the oil has gone or the tea light goes out. End by saying, *Welcome our little miracle to the world.*

292

FOR A SUCCESSFUL LAST TRY IVF SPELL IF ONE OR BOTH PARTNERS IS GETTING DISHEARTENED

You will need:

Three small crystal eggs such as agate, soapstone, or rose quartz

A small bowl to hold them

A paper knife

A soft bag

Timing:

If you or your partner is hesitating to try again

The Spell

- Touch the first egg and say, *In spite of expertise and our best care, we could not keep you in our family, and yet we know that it will be.*
- Return the egg to the bowl, doing and saying the same for the second.
- Hold the third in one hand and touch it with the knife in the other hand and say, *And so in hope that flows from me, I ask, come join our family.*
- Put the third egg in the bag and leave it with the knife beside it, just touching the bag. Repeat the words each evening as you hold the bag in one hand and touch it with the knife once more.
- Take the crystal egg in the bag for any treatment, touch it, and repeat the words.
- Leave the knife wrapped in a scarf in a bedside drawer with the other two eggs.

293

A SPELL FOR SUCCESSFUL SURROGACY

You will need:

Three candles of differing sizes: the first, medium-size, to the left; a small one in the middle; and a large one to the right.

Timing:

Any time during the surrogacy for reassurance

The Spell

- Light the left-hand candle and say, *I/we send my blessings to* [name], *who shelters and nurtures so lovingly my/our child.*
- Light the small candle from the first one and say, *Welcome to my/our lives, beloved child, doubly welcome there, because you have twice the love and care.*
- Join the flame of the small candle to the right-hand one, and as that candle burns, say, *Soon we shall be a family, but grateful eternally to she who carries our precious treasure. We promise you, child of my/our heart, love without measure from the start.* Leave all candles to burn through.

294

BEFORE ARTIFICIAL INSEMINATION WHETHER THE DONOR IS KNOWN OR UNKNOWN

You will need:

A small container, not too deep
Cotton wool or soil
Fast-growing cress seeds or another edible fast-growing seed

Timing:

One to two weeks before the implantation

The Spell

- Scatter the seeds in the container, embedded on cotton wool or shallow soil, saying, *I take willingly and thankfully the seed of he who quickens life within me. May we join together within my womb, that my baby may grow and flourish safe, strong, and healthy, a joy to me and legacy of he who helped me willingly.*
- Water the seeds daily, repeating the words, and when the cress is grown, cut and eat it, saying, *May the baby grow and flourish safe strong and healthy, a joy to me and legacy of he who helped me willingly.*
- Do not worry if it does not thrive; just repeat the spell.
- After treatment, eat the final cress if any is left and bury the container outdoors, saying, *Rest deep within me, secure in love, flourish healthily until I meet my precious gift and hold you in my arms.*

295

TO HELP A PARTNER WHO IS NOT THE BIOLOGICAL FATHER BECAUSE OF INFERTILITY TO BOND CLOSELY WITH AN INFANT CONCEIVED WITH DONOR SPERM

You will need:

A picture of you and the soul father who will help care for your child
A small bear or cuddly toy

Timing:

During pregnancy and the weeks after the birth

The Spell

- Hold the picture, touch your partner's image, and say, *You will be father of our child through every milestone met in life, in joy and strife.*
- Put the toy on top of the picture and touch the toy. With the index finger of the hand you write with, draw in the air over them spirals and knots, repeating the words.
- Then say, *Now we are bound as one family, in unity and love daily and perpetually.*
- Keep the picture and toy together between spells. When baby is born, substitute a picture of the three of you.

TO HELP A MOTHER WHO IS DEPRESSED CONNECT WITH THE INFANT

You will need:

A supply of small white candles
A picture of the mother and baby together

Timing:

Daily as long as necessary.

The Spell

- On day 1, light a white candle next to the picture, touching the mother and infant, and say, *May light flood back into your life that you may know the joys of motherhood and that you are the best mother to your child.*
- Touch your heart and the picture and say, *I send you love and strength from my heart.*
- Let the candle burn.
- On day 2, light two candles next to the picture and begin a clockwise circle of candles, repeating the spell and leaving the candles to burn.
- On day 3, light the candles and continue the spell until on day 10 you light ten and let them burn.
- If you need to continue the spell, start with one candle and build up again.

297

FOR THE ADOPTION OF A BABY OR YOUNG CHILD

You will need:

A box with a lid
Legal papers relating to the birth and any small memento sent by the birth mother
Papers relating to the adoption and a small memento of the adoption to be given to the child later in life
A green ribbon

Timing:
Soon after the adoption

The Spell

- Hold the birth papers and any memento, saying, *I/we give thanks to she,* [name], *who gave you birth. You will always be as precious to me/us as though I/we brought you to earth. I/we offer devoted parenting through good times and ill, knowing one day you may seek to find your birth mother, for she will be that still.*
- Place the papers in the box with any memento and add the adoption papers and your gift, placing both by your heart and saying the same words.
- Tie the ribbon loosely in a bow around the box, saying the words again. When the child is old enough, show him or her the contents of the box and offer both mementos.

298

FOR LOVING SHORT-TERM AND RESPITE CARE FOSTERING

You will need:

Small white candles for the new family member and for the existing ones, in a circle
Any dried scented flower petals or floral potpourri
A kitchen storage jar
Orange, neroli, rose, or lavender essential or fragrance oil

Timing:
After the infant or child arrives

The Spell

- Light each candle clockwise, naming a family member aloud with each lighting, beginning with yourself and ending with the child who will be joining you temporarily.
- Say for each, *Though our new family member may stay a short while, we will offer care as though our own child.*
- Add a handful of flowers to the jar for each family member.
- Add three drops of oil to the jar, saying, *You are welcome,* [name], *to our family circle until you return with our love to your own/new family when it is right to be.*
- Keep the petals in a bowl in the main living room.
- After the child has left, release the petals outdoors, saying, *Go free to your own/new family, knowing you carry our love in your heart.*
- Repeat when your next foster baby or child arrives.

299

FOR HAPPY LONG-TERM FOSTERING

You will need:

A large white candle and a small one to its left. Add candles if you are fostering more than one child

Timing:

When the infant or child comes

The Spell

- Light the small candle for the child and from it the large one, saying, [Name], *we rejoice as you join our family, whether forever or temporarily. We do not seek to replace your birth family but offer our care additionally.*
- Blow out the small candle and say, *Welcome to our hearts without hesitation or limitation.*
- If the child does leave you, whether in months or years, replace the large candle and light the small candle from it, saying, *You are ready to rejoin/join your own/new family. But as kindred in our hearts you will always be.*
- If the child stays, burn the small candle (or a replacement if it has crumbled), giving blessings for the future, on the child's eighteenth birthday.

300

FOR ADOPTING AN INFANT OR YOUNG CHILD FROM ANOTHER CULTURE

You will need:

A book containing pictures and information about the infant's birth culture

An artifact or memento from the child's root culture

A picture of the child with the new family

A vase of flowers, all identical, one for each member of the family, including the new arrival

Timing:

When the child arrives

The Spell

- Set the items on a small table with a colorful cloth.
- Pass your right hand in clockwise circles and at the same time your left hand in counterclockwise circles, saying softly and repeatedly, *We will never deprive you of your heritage or roots, yet day by day you will grow new shoots as we offer you the finest of both worlds.*
- Take a single flower from the vase and hold it, saying, *We do not seek to uproot you but give you diversity so you can see a multicultured life unfurl and be at home everywhere and anywhere in the world.*
- Return the flower to the vase.
- Keep the items on the table. As the child gets older, read the book together and add more artifacts from both cultures.

CHAPTER 7

GOOD LUCK MAGICK

The spells in this chapter includes spells for creating instant good luck and lasting good fortune in all areas of your life, including games of chance and success at garage sales and auctions; creating lucky charms to carry with you; and reversing runs of misfortune.

301

TO ATTRACT INSTANT GOOD LUCK

You will need:
A stopwatch or a digital timer on an electronic device

Timing:
Whenever you need good luck fast

The Spell

- Set the timer to a minute and say very fast, *Good luck hurry, good luck scurry, to my door, more and more.*
- Set it for two minutes and say the words even faster as many times as possible before the timer beeps.
- Then set it for three minutes and chant even faster.
- End by saying, *Three by three, good fortune hurries, three by three, good fortune scurries, to my door, more and more.*
- Whenever you need good fortune quickly, say the second set of words three times in your mind if necessary and make some external gesture, such as a tap on the table, a toss of your head, or a foot shuffle and a subtle stamp to transfer the power to you.

302

TO ATTRACT GOOD FORTUNE FAST

You will need:
A white candle
Nine small shiny objects such as coins, jewels, crystals, or a mixture surrounding the candle
A small bowl of salt

Timing:
When you need a fast infusion of resources

The Spell

- Light the candle and say fast, *Good luck be mine as I count nine: 1, 2, 3, 4, 5, 6, 7, 8, 9.*
- Then, as you touch each object clockwise, say fast, *9 for the first, 8 for the second,* and so on, until you get to *1*; then say, *Good luck has come instantly, 3, 2, 1, the spell is done.*
- On *done*, quickly blow out the candle.
- Relight it and leave it to burn, transferring the objects to a dish to catch the morning light to ensure that luck continues.

303

TO CALL FAST GOOD LUCK IN THE FORM OF HELP FROM AN UNEXPECTED SOURCE

You will need:

A circular path or track, perhaps in a park for walking or jogging

Timing:

When you have done everything you can and need good luck soon

The Spell

- Start walking or jogging, saying in your mind over and over, *From all around, from sky to ground, good fortune is following, easy to see, I just reach out, and it finds me.*
- When you return to where you started, stretch out your arms and pull good fortune toward you, turning on the spot through all four directions, saying, *From east, north, south, and west, I call the best good luck, find me, fate do the rest.*

304

WHEN YOU NEED GOOD LUCK THE NEXT DAY FOR A SPECIFIC PURPOSE SUCH AS AN INTERVIEW, DRIVING TEST, EXAM, OR SPECIAL DATE

You will need:

Three green candles of ascending height, arranged left to right

Any three crystals: green chrysoprase, sunstone, green jade, or staurolite (or use a favorite pendant)

Timing:

Around sunset the day before the event

The Spell

- Light the shortest candle and shake the crystals or pendant in your closed hands, saying, *Luck grows with the morning light, I know it's right, tomorrow will be lucky indeed, that is agreed.*
- Use the first candle to light the middle candle, blow out the first, then repeat the words and actions.
- Light the largest candle from the second, blow out the second candle, then repeat the same words and actions.
- Blow out the third candle.
- Relight in reverse order; shake the crystals once more, saying the same words. Leave them or the pendant in front of the largest candle while the candles burn out.
- In the morning, carry the crystals in a bag or wear the pendant to bring you good luck.

305

TO STIR THE ENERGIES TO SPEED A BONUS, REBATE, OR GOOD NEWS YOU ARE EXPECTING

You will need:

A round red stone found near your home or a red crystal

Timing:

Early Friday morning

The Spell

- Throw the stone in the air three times and catch it, saying, *More haste, more speed, for what I need,* [purpose], *is urgent indeed.*
- Throw and then catch the stone three more times a little faster, saying the words more rapidly each time.
- Repeat three more times, making the last throw the highest, and as you catch it, say, *Good luck, you are caught, faster than I thought, please deliver from reluctant giver, come now, I ask, complete this task—and very soon.*
- Go to a water source, even a pond. Throw the stone or crystal as far as you can into the water, saying, *You must deliver from reluctant giver, come now, I ask, complete this task—and very soon.*
- If you cannot find water outdoors, drop it in a bucket and tip the stone and water away outside your premises.

306

IF YOU ARE IN THE RUNNING FOR A SPECIAL OPPORTUNITY OR OFFER AND NEED A DECISION IN YOUR FAVOR SOON

You will need:

A circle of gold candles

A picture of yourself smiling in the middle of the candles

A medium-size mirror to hold and later prop up on a flat surface

Timing:

After dark

The Spell

- Light each candle clockwise, one from the other, saying for each, *Extra good luck with each candle glow, extra good luck that all may be so:* [name urgent need or desire]. *So will I shine when good fortune is mine.*
- Prop the mirror so that you can see the candle circle within it and say, *Twice the luck with twice the light, this chance of mine will turn out right.*
- Let the candles burn, with the mirror still reflecting the light.
- In the morning, polish the mirror, repeating all the spell words. Hang it where morning light is reflected in it.
- Every time you pass the mirror, look into it, smile, and say, *So will I shine when good fortune is mine.*

307

FOR INSTANT GOOD LUCK IF YOU NEED TO THINK AND ACT FAST IN A CHANGING SITUATION

You will need:

A tree or bush outdoors or an ornamental potted one indoors

Ten shiny baubles (the Christmas kind) or glittery decorations

Timing:

Friday

The Spell

- Hold the first bauble saying, *Lucky me that I can get from A to Z instantly and not a trip or slip, but slide and glide effortlessly to fortune.*
- Tie the bauble to the tree, saying the words again, and repeat for the next nine baubles in the same way.
- Spin each bauble on the tree in turn, saying for each, *Turn and spin, spin and turn, for I am in good luck mode, think fast, act faster, and so I win the day.*
- Say all the spell words fast three times, spin around ten times clockwise, and use the momentum to think on your feet and quickly resolve the problem.

308

TO HELP A FRIEND OR RELATIVE DESPERATELY IN NEED OF INSTANT GOOD LUCK

You will need:

A long green ribbon

An electric fan

Timing:

Sunday morning

The Spell

- You can, if you wish, carry this spell out for yourself for instant luck.
- Hold the ribbon in the airstream of an electric fan, saying, [Name], *with good fortune now be filled, so is it willed, your needs fulfilled that you will possess the success you deserve.* (Name any particular areas/ events in which good luck is needed fast.)
- Switch off the fan and tie nine loose knots in the ribbon, saying for each one, *With nine knots, for you,* [name], *luck be secure, long be good fortune, firm may your luck endure.*
- Hold the knotted ribbon in the fan's airstream, repeating the words.
- Hang the ribbon on an indoor window ledge. Next morning, undo the knots, saying, *The knots are free, good luck will you see.*

309

TO ENDOW A SECRET GOOD LUCK TOKEN TO USE AT WORK OR IN YOUR WORKPLACE FOR AN INFUSION OF GOOD FORTUNE

You will need:

A small item you use every day, such as a pen, flash drive, tool, or keys

A small box with a lid

Timing:

Sunday evening

The Spell

- Place the item in the box and put on the lid.
- Clap seven times over the box, saying each time, *Luck I call you secretly inside, for your power do I wish to hide, to be summoned when I am most in need, luck I keep you safe indeed.*
- Take off the lid, say the words fast, put the lid back on, and continue doing this seven times in total.
- Remove the item, saying the words seven more times. Keep it with you at work, holding it when you need to release your good luck fast.

310

TO GENERATE GOOD LUCK IN A STAGNANT SITUATION AND MOVE THINGS FORWARD FAST AND POSITIVELY

You will need:

A string of small bells, such as Tibetan

Timing:

Sunday morning

The Spell

- Jingle the bells nine times and say nine times, *Jingle bells, jingle bells, jingle through the day, ring and chime good fortune in, send stagnation away.*
- Hang the bells where the air will ring them spontaneously, such as near a front door, but so that you still can reach them.
- Ring them nine times more, saying each time, *Jingle bells, jingle bells, jingle through the day, ring and chime good fortune in, good luck's here to stay.*
- Whenever things seem to be moving slowly in the days ahead, ring the bells nine times and repeat both sets of words each time.

311

TO CHANGE BAD LUCK INTO GOOD BY USING THE WANING MOON

You will need:

A small purple candle
A larger white one, with the purple candle to the left
A small bowl of salt
A paper knife

Timing:
Three times during the waning moon

The Spell

- Scratch the purple candle with the knife, writing vertically (from top to bottom), BAD LUCK AWAY, AND THEN WRITE ON THE WHITE CANDLE, GOOD LUCK STAY.
- Light the purple candle, saying, *Take away sorrow with the dying of the moon.*
- Light the white candle from the purple one, saying, *Good luck, bright luck, come to me,* [areas of life where you need good luck most].
- Add a pinch of salt to the white candle's flame, saying, *Burn bright and light the way to good fortune* [name areas where you most need luck].
- Extinguish the purple candle, saying, *Take bad luck away with the dying of the moon.*
- Let the white candle burn a few minutes, then blow it out, saying, *I am lucky and will even luckier be.*
- Leave the candles in place until the next spell. You do not need to write the words again on the candle in subsequent spells.

312

TO RESTORE GOOD LUCK IF UNFAIR PEOPLE OR SITUATIONS HAVE TAKEN IT FROM YOU

You will need:

Two candles, one gray and one green
A charm or favorite piece of jewelry, placed in front of the green candle
A dish of salt
A piece of gray thread
A dish of soil

Timing:
Saturday

The Spell

- Light the gray candle, sprinkling salt in the flame, saying, *May misfortune be gone and good luck won.*
- Tie a knot in the center of the thread and hold the ends of the thread so that the knot is in the gray candle flame. When it breaks, drop the burning ends in soil, saying, *So do I break the ties to those who have/what has brought me misfortune.*
- Light the green candle from the gray, saying, *May good luck be won and misfortune gone.*
- Sprinkle salt into the green candle, saying, *Burn bright and light the way to amazing good fortune. May none/nothing stand in the way.*
- Extinguish the gray candle, saying, *Misfortune be gone with the dimming of the light.*
- Burn the green candle.
- Wear or carry the charm or piece of jewelry in the days ahead.

313

FOR TURNING BAD LUCK INTO GOOD IF YOU FEEL YOUR HOME IS UNLUCKY

You will need:

Five yellow or white flower heads in a bowl of water
Two candles, one purple and one white

Timing:

Sunday morning, when the home is quiet

The Spell

- In the center of your home, light the purple candle, saying, *Bad luck I no longer fear, for it may not linger here.*
- Use the purple candle to light the white one and then extinguish the purple one, saying, *As the light dims, so fades misfortune.*
- Sprinkle flower water around the house, saying in each room and area, *May every corner of this home be filled with light, laughter, love, and loveliness.*
- Take the water outdoors and tip it onto the earth.
- Carry the white candle through every room and area, repeating for each, *May every corner of this home be filled with light, laughter, love, and loveliness.*
- Leave it to burn in the center of the home.

314

TO RESTORE GOOD LUCK IF YOU BREAK OR LOSE A LUCKY CHARM OR ITEM

You will need:

A replacement lucky charm
A soft silk scarf
The pieces of the broken charm; if it is lost, draw an image of it on a piece of paper and cut it into large pieces

Timing:

As dusk falls, ideally on the last day of the month

The Spell

- Set a piece of the old charm on the scarf next to the new one so that they are touching, saying, *Luck cannot be lost, and so with trust I transfer good fortune, so luck is renewed with no further ado.*
- Knot the scarf and leave the old and new charms together for twenty-four hours in a dark place.
- Unwrap the scarf, repeating the words seven times.
- Bury the paper pieces or the broken charm (secured in a box so that it will not hurt any wildlife if it is sharp) under a tree.

315

A GOOD LUCK SHELL AND MOON SPELL IF OTHER PEOPLE ALWAYS SEEM TO GET THE GOOD FORTUNE

You will need:

A smooth, round white shell or white stone

A green permanent marker

Timing:

Any of the three nights before the full moon or a full moon night whenever the moon is bright

The Spell

- Write GOOD LUCK COMES TO ME all over the shell inside and out.
- Take it into the moonlight, saying, *Lady of the Moon, Lady of the Moon, come to me, stay with me, Lady of the Moon.*
- Begin to turn around very fast, holding the shell between your hands while chanting the spell words.
- When you get dizzy and see the moon rushing toward you, sit down on the ground and, still holding the shell, whisper, *So good fortune rushes to meet me, I thank you, Lady of the Moon, for blessings soon to be received.*
- Sleep with the shell beside you until the writing fades.
- On the next full moon night or just before it, cast the shell into water and make a new shell good luck charm by repeating the spell.

316

TO REVERSE A RUN OF BAD LUCK IN LOVE OR LIFE

You will need:

A tall white candle, a medium-size gray one, and a short black or brown one

Two paper bags

A white scarf

Timing:

On the last day of the month

The Spell

- Light the black candle and say, *Bad luck, misfortune, burn away; ill luck, you can no longer stay.*
- Use the black candle to light the gray candle and say, *Misfortune be absorbed in gray, bad luck you now must melt away.*
- Use the gray candle to light the white candle and say, *Good luck, bright luck, come to me, happier days ahead to see.*
- When the black candle has burned, let it cool and break it into pieces, saying, *Bad luck and misfortune have left my life, no more sorrow, no more strife.*
- Put the wax in a paper bag and throw it away.
- When the gray candle has burned, do the same thing.
- When the white candle has burned, replace it and burn a white candle in your home every night for the next six days.

317

TO CUT THE THREAD OF MISFORTUNE BY USING KNOTS

You will need:

A purple or brown strong thread long enough for nine knots
A longer piece of white thread
A pair of scissors

Timing:

Sunday around sunrise or when you wake up.

The Spell

- Tie nine knots in the dark thread, saying for each, *I bind and wind misfortune in; no longer linger at my door, ill fortune, trouble me no more.*
- Cut each knot in turn, saying, *I cut the link with misfortunes old, sorrows, you have lost your hold.*
- After the spell, throw the pieces in an outside garbage bin.
- Tie nine knots in the white thread, saying, *I bind and wind good fortune here, my luck will grow through months and years.*
- Keep the white thread in a little pouch or purse and renew the white thread every year and a day. Repeat the white thread words and throw the old one in running water.

318

FOR A LUCKY NEW BEGINNING IN ANY AND EVERY AREA OF YOUR LIFE

You will need:

Two rattles or lidded jars half filled with dried peas or lentils

Timing:

Sunday, midmorning

The Spell

- Holding a rattle in each hand, standing in the center of the room, face in turn each of the directions approximately: north, east, south, west. Shake the rattles softly and say in each direction, *Misfortune, misfortune, go away, do not return any day.*
- Turn clockwise faster, nine times through all the directions, rattling more and more rapidly, and say faster, *Life starts anew, past sorrows through. Bad luck cannot stay, misfortune away.*
- When you can rattle and speak no faster, stand in the center facing north and slow the words and rattling until they fade into silence.
- Go outdoors, shake the rattles just once softly, and say, *I welcome my new beginnings.*

319

TO TAKE AWAY BAD FORTUNE AND BRING GOOD LUCK IF YOU FEEL THINGS ARE HOPELESS

You will need:

One small black or dark brown candle (to the left)
One large white candle (to the right)
One small black stone or small snowflake obsidian
One small white stone or clear crystal
One small pot of fragrant flowers

Timing:

As darkness falls on Saturday

The Spell

- Place the black stone in front of the dark candle and the white stone in front of the white one.
- Light the dark candle, saying, *Darkness burn out of sight, carried away by the night.*
- Use the dark candle to light the white one and blow softly into the white candle flame, saying, *My luck will change with this new light, wrongs will cease and all be right.*
- Extinguish the dark candle.
- Bury the black stone in the soil around the plant, saying, *I bury the past with blessings.*
- Leave the white stone in front of the white candle until it has burned.
- In the morning, throw the white stone high and far in an open place, saying, *My luck has changed, as I can tell, good fortune's mine, all shall be well.*

320

TO REMOVE BAD LUCK FROM ALL AREAS OF YOUR LIFE

You will need:

A piece of paper
A blue pen and a red pen
A small plastic recyclable lidded container

Timing:

Right at the end of the waning moon cycle

The Spell

- Write in blue all over both sides of the paper, in all directions, vertically, horizontally, and diagonally so that the words overlap, BAD LUCK BE GONE FOREVER, RETURN TO ME NEVER.
- Draw a big red diagonal cross through both sides, saying, *You are banned from my life, you trouble and strife, forever; return to me never.*
- Fold the paper as small as possible and place it in the container, saying all the spell words. Add water and close the lid firmly.
- Keep it in the freezer for a month.
- After the month, dispose of it well away from your home in a recycling bin.

321

FOR IMMENSE GOOD FORTUNE IN GAMES OF CHANCE

You will need:

A large green candle of natural wax that will melt or a beeswax candle

Three green crystals, such as amazonite, jade, chrysoprase, or aventurine, mixed if you wish

A green bag or purse

Timing:

Saturday, around noon

The Spell

- Light the candle.
- As the wax melts, push each crystal into the wax near the base of the candle, saying, *Much haste, no waste, no time, the win is mine. As I chance my arm, keep me calm to speculate and calculate the hand of fate.*
- Clap as you move around the table clockwise, moving faster and faster, say, *Much haste, more speed, win I shall, win indeed. Burn bright, success is in sight.*
- Keep chanting and spiraling with a final clap over your head, saying, *Success will shine, the win is mine.*
- Let the candle burn.
- Put the crystals and the attached wax into the bag.
- Take the bag when you enter a game of chance and put it on top of tickets or betting slips.

322

TO WIN MONEY AND COMPETITIONS BY USING LUCKY CRYSTALS

You will need:

A green aventurine, amazonite, chrysoprase, or snowflake obsidian

A pine, patchouli, or rose incense stick

A green scarf

Timing:

Wednesday, after dawn

The Spell

- Put the crystal in the center of the scarf.
- Light the incense stick. Using the stick like a pen, write in smoke in the air seven times over the scarf, WIN, WITH NO SPACES BETWEEN THE WORDS.
- Pick up the crystal in the hand you do not write with, drawing seven times over it in incense smoke, WIN.
- Write in the air in front of yourself at brow level, still holding the crystal, seven times, WIN.
- Let the incense burn.
- Place the crystal on top of competition entries or by the phone or computer.
- Between uses, keep the crystal knotted in the scarf tied with seven knots.
- After seven uses, re-empower the scarf and crystal with a new incense stick, repeating the spell.

323

TO SPIN THE WHEEL OF FORTUNE IN YOUR FAVOR

You will need:

A small tarot pack containing the wheel of fortune card or a miniature playing card pack with a joker
Dried fennel or thyme
Salt
A piece of foil with the card on top
A small wallet or pouch

Timing:

The day before taking part in a game of chance

The Spell

- Scatter a little salt and thyme or fennel on the card, saying, *Wheel of fortune, upward turn, bring the win that I do yearn. Salt and thyme/fennel use your power to draw good fortune at this hour.*
- Wrap the foil over the card and herbs like a parcel and put it in the wallet, saying, *Whenever I touch you, wheel within, I will activate a win.*
- Immediately before a game or bet, touch the wallet.

324

TO WIN COMPETITIONS OR RAFFLES

You will need:

A lucky gold-colored charm or a golden tiger eye or iron pyrites
Three gold candles
A small glass dish filled with cloves or dried juniper berries

Timing:

The day of the full moon, if possible around noon

The Spell

- Make a triangle of candles around the dish of cloves/juniper.
- Light each one, saying, *Gold of fortune increased be, Lady Luck, smile down on me.*
- Circle the crystal/charm seven times clockwise around each candle flame, repeating the chant for each one.
- Place the crystal/charm in the center of the dish, saying, *Lady Luck, this crystal shower, with overflowing winning power.*
- Taking a candle in each hand (the ones nearest to you) and pass them around the dish seven times, saying, *Light of gold, intensify; nothing now can me deny the right answers and right numbers, for Lady Luck no longer slumbers.*
- Blow out the candles and place the crystal in the wallet with seven cloves or berries on any entry or ticket.

325

POPCORN POPPING FOR MAKING FAST DECISIONS IN GAMING

You will need:

Uncooked popcorn
An airtight container

Timing:

The night before you need to make snap decisions in a game of chance

The Spell

- Cook the popcorn or heat it in a microwave, chanting, *Pop, pop, pop, pop, and never stop; make a lot and eat a pot, and you will win your corn.*
- Eat some of the hot corn to absorb good luck, keeping the rest in an airtight container.
- Before going to make a bid or play a game of chance, eat some empowered popcorn, chanting the rhyme ten times fast in your mind.

326

TO HAVE LUCK IN AUCTIONS OR BIDDING ON THE INTERNET

You will need:

Three Chinese lucky coins or three gold-colored coins
Three gold candles in a row with a coin in front of each

Timing:

A few hours beforehand

The Spell

- Light the first candle, shake the coin in front of it three times, and place the coin in front of the second candle.
- Light the second candle, shake the two coins in front of it, and put them in front of the third candle.
- Light the third candle and then shake the three coins, saying, *Make a bid, low not high, luck is rising to the skies, stake your claim, keep your nerve, the coins help you not to swerve, get rid of opposition and you soon gain the top position.*
- Move the coins back to their own candles and let the candles burn.
- Shake all three coins before any bid or claim and keep them in your pocket or close to your computer if you are making an Internet bid.

327

TO DOUBLE YOUR MONEY IN GAMES OF CHANCE

You will need:

A new banknote and another new note worth double the first
A white resealable envelope
Dried sage, thyme, fennel, basil, or vetiver
A red pen

Timing:

Around the full moon

The Spell

- Put the smaller-value banknote in the envelope, writing on the front, DOUBLE MY MONEY AND TRY TO GET RICH, DOUBLE MY MONEY WITH NO SLIPS OR HITCH.
- Sprinkle a little herb on the front of the envelope, saying, *Double my money in a flash, double my money, needn't be rash. The will is good, the spell is right, double my money overnight.*
- In the morning, open the envelope and take out the money, repeating all the chants.
- Replace the banknote in the envelope, adding the larger one, and reseal the envelope. Write on the back, DOUBLE MY MONEY, TRY TO GET RICH, DOUBLE MY MONEY WITH NO SLIPS OR HITCH.
- The next morning, open the envelope and take out the money, using it in the gaming and saying the words in your mind.

328

TO REVERSE A SERIES OF LOSSES AND REPLACE THEM WITH WINS

You will need:

Beads you have threaded on a string, but do not tie the ends
A big bowl

Timing:

Friday near the beginning of the month

The Spell

- Holding the necklace over the bowl, slide the beads off the string and shake the bowl of beads seven times, saying, *The links to ill fortune now are broken, the words bad luck will not be spoken, the dice will roll, the wheel will turn, and unbreakable fortune now return.*
- Restring them and this time knot the string tightly with seven small knots, repeating the words.
- Wear or carry the beads in a bag on your next gaming venture, touching each in turn before beginning, repeating the words.

329

TO FIND UNEXPECTED TREASURE AT AN ANTIQUE FAIR, GARAGE SALE, OR TRUNK SHOW OR ONLINE

You will need:

A flashlight

A small precious item you own, such as inherited jewelry

Timing:

The night before the sale, after dark

The Spell

- Before switching off the light in a darkened room, hold the item and say, *Like attracts like, good luck draws more, may I find treasure no one else saw.*
- Put the treasure on a small table, turn off the light, and switch on the flashlight so that it illuminates the darkness.
- Turn in all directions on the spot, clockwise and counterclockwise, swirling the flashlight and repeating the words.
- Continue sweeping the darkness with the beam until it focuses on the item so that it is caught within the concentrated beam.
- Say, *Treasure attracts treasure, good luck draws more, may I find treasure by the score.*
- In the morning, touch the item, repeating all the spell words.
- At the sale or online, trust your instincts, imagining the flashlight beam guiding you to the treasure.

330

MAKING A LUCKY GAME OF CHANCE MAGICK BAG

You will need:

A lucky hand root (obtainable online but toxic and thus optional)

A miniature ten of diamonds playing card

Dried sage in a tiny bag

A silver dollar or coin

A token from a games arcade or a gambling chip

A green aventurine or amazonite crystal

A white drawstring or leather bag

A white cord

A little whiskey, sherry, port, or malt wine

Timing:

After sunset on Wednesday, working just by candlelight

The Spell

- Place all the items in the bag or purse in silence. Add a drop or two of alcohol.
- Close the bag or purse with the cord, tying it with three knots and saying, *Rich I'll be, for luck's with me. Fortune, I ask, favor me in all my speculation, that there will be no hesitation in reaching out for all I see.*
- Re-empower on Midsummer Eve, using the same ingredients and bag.

331

FOR LASTING GOOD FORTUNE BY USING A RING

You will need:

A ring you already wear or a new silver or copper one
Five small green candles in a circle around it

Timing:
Thursday for the next seven days

The Spell

- Light candle 1 and pass the ring once clockwise around it, saying, *Ring of flame, so I do name, ring without end, lasting luck you will send.*
- Light candle 2 from candle 1 and pass the ring around it twice, repeating the words twice.
- Continue to light the candles, passing the ring three times around the third, saying the words three times, right up to five, when you will pass it five times around the fifth candle and say the words five times.
- Return the ring to the center, blowing out the candles.
- Repeat the spell for seven days. On day 7, let the candles burn.
- Wear the ring as your good luck token.
- Cast the spell every three months to keep up the power.

332

SEVEN KNOTS TO BIND IN LASTING GOOD FORTUNE

You will need:

A long green cord or ribbon

Timing:
Friday for the next seven days

The Spell

- On day 1, tie the first knot, saying, *Today I bind good fortune in.*
- On day 2, tie the second knot, saying, *That I will have the power to win.*
- On day 3, tie the third knot, saying, *That I will always win the day in every way.*
- On day 4, tie the fourth knot, saying, *That good luck knocks upon my door.*
- On day 5, tie the fifth knot, saying, *That every venture prospers more.*
- On day 6, tie the sixth knot, saying, *That success follows as I strive.*
- On day 7, tie the seventh knot, saying, *And good luck always stays alive.*
- Hang the cord behind a door, and when you need luck, touch each knot, saying its words.
- Every Midsummer Eve, cast the old cord in water. On Midsummer Day, make a new one.

333

TO BRING GOOD LUCK FOR NINE MONTHS

You will need:

A floral incense stick
A green candle
A lucky charm, medallion, favorite jewelry, or crystal
A dish of soil

Timing:
Saturday

The Spell

- Light the candle, saying, *Good luck be mine as I count nine: 1, 2, 3, 4, 5, 6, 7, 8, 9.*
- Light the incense from the candle and with the smoke pen write in circles in the air around the charm, saying, *Good luck be mine as I count nine: 1, 2, 3, 4, 5, 6, 7, 8, 9.*
- Write and speak faster and faster until letters and numbers jumble.
- Plunge the burning end of the incense into the soil, saying, *Mother Earth, give fortune birth. Nine months of good fortune comes to me.*
- Burn the candle, crush the incense stick, and bury it in the garden or a plant pot, saying, *Mother Earth, give fortune birth.*
- Wear or carry the charm for nine months, after which repeat the spell using the same charm.
- Do this every nine months.

334

SEVEN-YEAR CHARM EMPOWERMENT

You will need:

A charm or jewelry with personal significance
Seven small candies, fruits, or chocolates in a circle around the charm

Timing:
Seven days, starting Sunday

The Spell

- On Sunday, hold the charm or put on the jewelry and eat the first chocolate or candy, saying, *Sunday and every day, so the sweetness enters me, knowing life will sweeter be.*
- On Monday, do the same thing and say, *Monday and every day, so the sweetness enters me, knowing life will sweeter be.*
- Continue adding the name of a day and eating a candy each day.
- On day 7, put the charm in a little bag or touch the jewelry, saying, *Be filled with sweet fortune that increases day by day, month by month, and year by year, and so good luck shall remain here.*
- Repeat every three months.

335

AN IRISH LEPRECHAUN RITUAL TO KEEP GOOD FORTUNE FLOWING INTO YOUR LIFE

You will need:

A ceramic or toy leprechaun
Two pouches, one containing a silver-colored coin and the other a gold-colored coin, one on either side of the leprechaun
A small hammer (leprechauns are shoemakers)
A pot of coins in front of the leprechaun

Timing:

Friday or if you see a rainbow

The Spell

- Hammer softly in front of the leprechaun, saying continuously, *Lucky leprechaun, bring to me, good fortune over land and sea, that daily luckier I will be.*
- Add the silver coin from the pouch to the pot, hammering and saying, *May what I give return to me, that daily luckier will I be.*
- Put the gold coin in the pot, hammer, and say, *No tricks today, the luck is real, and so your crock of gold reveal.*
- Shake the pot seven times and return the silver and gold coins to the pouches, saying, *So I return what is yours by right, but the crock of gold for me shines bright.*
- Place the pot of coins, leprechaun, hammer, and magick pouches where light shines, saying, *My dues are paid and fortune stays.*

336

HOW TO TURN THE TRADITIONAL BELIEF OF SEVEN YEARS OF BAD LUCK INTO GOOD IF YOU BREAK A MIRROR

You will need:

The pieces of the broken mirror
A white cloth
A green cord
Seven beautiful flowers

Timing:

After breaking the mirror

The Spell

- Carefully wrap the mirror in the scarf, saying, *Seven years of misfortune now are bound, seven years of good luck will be found.*
- Knot the green cord seven times around the cloth, saying, *So I wind ill fortune in, seven years of good luck will I win.*
- Throw away or bury (safely in a secure box) the mirror shards in the cloth and buy a replacement mirror. Set seven beautiful flowers in front of it, saying, *Seven times seven, good fortune's mine. This mirror with best luck shall shine.*

337

A CASSIEL ARCHANGEL BLESSING TO ENSURE LUCK ENTERS AND REMAINS IN YOUR LIFE IF YOU ARE IN A DOWN PERIOD

You will need:

An indigo or purple candle
A piece of white paper
A purple pen
Purple ribbon

Timing:

Saturday, Cassiel's day

The Spell

- At bedtime, light the candle. By its light, copy the following blessing: WISE CASSIEL, ARCHANGEL WHO TURNS THE WHEEL OF FORTUNE, GRANT ME GOOD LUCK—[say how you need it most]—AND A WINDFALL, HOWEVER MODEST, TO BOOST MY FORTUNES. I WAIT WITH TRUST THAT YOU WILL BRING A NEW BEGINNING WITH THE MORNING AND THAT THE TIDE OF GOOD FORTUNE WILL AT LAST TURN IN MY FAVOR AND REMAIN IN MY LIFE.
- Read this aloud very softly, facing the candle so that your words fade into silence.
- Roll the message into a scroll and tie it once with the ribbon. Keep it in a secret place.
- Let the candle burn.
- Every month on crescent moon, carry the scroll outdoors.
- Do not unroll it. Ask that Cassiel make your fortunes grow.
- Once a year, burn the old blessing and rewrite it.

338

TO MAKE YOUR OWN GOOD FORTUNE

You will need:

Five candles of ascending size
Five paper footprints of your right foot in a row from hall to front door

Timing:

Thursday

The Spell

- Set the candles in ascending size next to each footprint in the hallway, leading toward the front door and the largest candle.
- Light the smallest candle, candle 1, and step on the first footprint, saying, *Step 1, good luck I make anew, within five years, I will win through.*
- Light candle 2 and step on the second footprint, saying, *Step 2, a natural expression of what will be my due progression to lasting good fortune.*
- Light candle 3 and step on the third footprint, saying, *Step 3, Why should I hesitate? The future now is looking great.*
- Light candle 4 and step on the fourth footprint, saying, *Each step I take, my fortune makes.*
- Light candle 5 and step on the fifth footprint, saying, *Step 5, I acknowledge my potentiality, grasping the infinite possibility of making my own fortune.*
- Open the front door and step outside, saying, *The world is mine. I make my own good fortune.*
- Come in and close the door, blowing out each candle in reverse order, making a wish for each.

339

A LUCKY BAMBOO RITUAL FOR ALL THE LUCK IN THE WORLD IF YOU ALWAYS HAVE TO DO THINGS THE HARD WAY

You will need:

A very long strip of paper with a large hole punched into it
Three red pieces of string
A lucky bamboo plant, either indoors or out
A green pen

Timing:
Sunday morning

The Spell

- Write on the paper in green pen on both sides, GOOD LUCK, ALES GUTEL, BONNE CHANCE, BUONA FORTUNA, LYKE TIL, BOA SORTE, BUENA SUERTE, [add or substitute GOOD LUCK in languages from your own part of the world].
- Attach the paper with all three strings through the hole, each knotted once, to the lucky bamboo, saying three times, *May all the luck in the world come and stay with me, lucky, luckier, luckiest will I be.*
- Water the bamboo, repeating three times, *May all the luck in the world come and stay with me, lucky, luckier, luckiest will I be. Lucky bamboo, this is my plea.*

340

TO DRAW LASTING GOOD FORTUNE BY USING A MAGNET

You will need:

A magnet and seven shiny nails
A silver ring and a gold-colored or brass ring
Dried allspice, ginger, or saffron in a little bag
A red bag

Timing:
Sunday around noon, if possible in bright sunlight

The Spell

- Put the nails around the magnet and turn the magnet until all are attached, saying, *Magnet, magnet, draw to me, good fortune soon and permanently, that I may attract wherever I go the means to live comfortably.*
- Put the magnet and attached nails into the bag.
- Add the rings and say, *Around and around, wheel's fortune turns, bringing me what I do yearn* [name the areas of luck you most seek].
- Add the spice, saying, *Gold and silver, now the fire, the strength of iron draws my desire* [again name the areas where you seek luck most].
- Carry your little bag with you whenever you need special luck.
- On Midsummer Eve dispose of nails and spice, and on Midsummer Day renew the bag with new nails, new spice, and the same rings, bag, and magnet.

341

A TRADITIONAL ELEPHANT GOOD LUCK RITUAL TO KEEP THE FORTUNES OF YOUR HOUSEHOLD RISING

You will need:

A small model elephant for each external door, plus one to stand at the bottom of the stairs (if you have stairs) and one at the top

A gold-colored coin to go under each elephant

Timing:

Thursday

The Spell

- Set an elephant inside each entrance to the right as you enter. Hold a gold coin for each in turn, saying, *Good luck I call, elephant increase this gold for me that I may see a golden future every day in every way.*
- Place the coin under the elephant, repeating the words.
- If you have stairs, set elephants at the top and bottom, putting a coin underneath each one, repeating the spell words.
- Touch the elephant at the bottom of the stairs, saying, *Lucky elephant, may my fortunes rise, so the only limit is the skies.*
- Touch the elephant at the top, saying, *So does good fortune grow, higher and higher, as to new luck I daily inspire.*
- If you do not have stairs, set the elephants in the main living area, one on the floor and one high up.

342

A KWAN YIN BLESSING FOR GOOD LUCK WHERE IT IS MOST NEEDED IN YOUR LIFE

You will need:

A statue of Kwan Yin, the Tibetan/Buddhist and Chinese goddess of compassion and good fortune, now a folk icon

Two floral incense sticks in a double holder in front of the statue

A small dish also in front of the statue

Timing:

When you need a boost of good fortune

The Spell

- Light the incense sticks, saying, *Wise mother who has vowed to stay on earth until all are happy, I ask for good fortune for myself* [or name another person] *in* [specify the area of life in which good luck is needed]. *Thank you for blessings soon to be received.*
- Spiral an incense stick in each hand, writing in the air in incense smoke over the statue the name of recipient and the type of fortune needed.
- Return the incense sticks to the holder to burn.
- Place a small offering in the dish, such as a flower, a crystal, or some grains in a bag.
- Add an offering daily, repeating the spell words until the request is granted.

343

A MONEY PIG RITUAL FOR GOOD LUCK, ESPECIALLY IN FINANCES

You will need:

A piggy bank
A coin (one each day)
A green candle

Timing:
Every evening

The Spell

- Light the green candle, saying, *Three by three, luck comes to me, can't you see, I soon shall be filled with prosperity in every way. Good luck comes and good luck stays.*
- Shake the pig three times, repeating the words.
- Keep the pig in a warm place in the house. Every day, add a coin and repeat all the words and actions.
- When it's full, start a piggy savings account for something special.
- Always leave one coin in the piggy bank to keep good luck rolling.

344

A LUCKY FROG OR TOAD CHARM

You will need:

A Chinese three-legged toad with a coin in its mouth or a ceramic frog plus a gold coin
Dried thyme, cloves, chamomile flowers, fennel, dried rose petals, or potpourri

Timing:
Ongoing

The Spell

- Set the toad or frog in the traditional feng shui good fortune/wealth area of your home, the southeastern part of your main room, or the southeast of your home. If you use a frog, put the coin in front of it.
- Place a small handful of herbs, flowers, or cloves in a bowl next to the toad or frog, saying, *So good fortune accumulates in every way, day by day.*
- Repeat every day.
- When the bowl is full, transfer the contents to a large one in the center of your home, saying, *So good luck grows and I do know, this will go on, shine like the sun as fortune flows constantly into my life.*
- Refill the small bowl day by day.

345

A MONTHLY LUCKY WHITE RABBIT CHARM

You will need:

A white ceramic rabbit

Timing:

Every first day of the month, with March being the luckiest of all

The Spell

- Hold the rabbit between your open cupped hands, saying, *Lucky rabbit, lucky days, this month brings luck in every way, good luck comes and good luck stays.*
- Turn around twelve times clockwise, naming the months, beginning with the current one, and then counterclockwise, saying them again.
- Turn, holding the rabbit with your arms outstretched, to face the four directions and then hold it toward the earth and upward to the sky.
- Say, *North, south, east, west, earth, and sky, so each month luck rises high, I embrace the very best.*
- Keep the rabbit in a sunny part of the home.

346

A SAINT DUNSTAN LUCKY HORSESHOE CHARM

You will need:

A real horseshoe or an ornamental one to be set over the front door outside or over a fireplace, either with points up to keep the luck in or points down to draw luck from the earth

A hammer and nails to fix the horseshoe to the lintel or wall

Salt

Timing:

The first of the month

The Spell

- Sprinkle salt around the horseshoe, saying, *By the power of Saint Dunstan, who nailed the Devil to the wall and said none might enter where the horseshoe stood tall, bring immense good fortune to my home and good luck to me/my family wherever I/we roam.*
- Hammer the horseshoe to the wall or over the door, saying over and over, *Power of the horseshoe charm, protect me/us from all harm, bring us/me fortune through the year, secure in life and with no fear.*
- Each May 19, Dunstan the blacksmith bishop's day, light a red candle near the center of your home, repeating all the spell words.

347

A LUCKY BUDDHA RITUAL

You will need:

A laughing wooden or metal Buddha
A small dish in front of him

Timing:

Whenever you need good luck and/or good news

The Spell

- Rub the tummy of the Buddha three times clockwise and ask for any good fortune you need in any area of your life, especially luck in financial affairs.
- If you need good news, name where you need the good news and rub the Buddha's right ear clockwise. It is said you will receive good news before the week is over.
- Place a crystal, coin, or flower in the dish as an offering (keep the flowers fresh).
- Add something small every day, rubbing the Buddha's tummy just once, again asking for any special good luck you need.
- When the dish is full, put the nonperishable items in a big bowl near the Buddha to attract abundance to your home.

348

TO BRING LASTING GOOD FORTUNE BY USING A LEMON PIG CHARM FROM THE CHILEAN TRADITION

You will need:

A lemon
Four silver-colored long pins (sometimes lucky pigs have only three; your choice)
A dish of salt

Timing:

Saturday evening, the waning moon

The Spell

- Using the lemon as the body of the pig, roll it in salt, sticking the pins in as the legs.
- If you wish, draw the features and tail.
- Say five times, *Lemon pig, take misfortune away, release good luck in my life to stay.*
- Burn the pig in a metal bucket half filled with sand outside the front door or on a bonfire, removing the pins beforehand.
- Wrap the pins securely in cloth. Make lemon pigs monthly if you have a lot of misfortune to replace.

349

A GNOME SPELL TO BRING GOOD LUCK, HEALTH, AND PROSPERITY TO YOUR HOME AND ALL WITHIN IT

You will need:

A gnome statue in your garden or in a large plant pot in greenery, if possible a plain brown or gray pottery gnome
A gold-colored coin and a silver-colored coin
A small-lidded pot

Timing:
Around sunset

The Spell

- Place the coins beneath the gnome and say, *It is not your treasure I wish to possess, but great good fortune and success. I make this offering now to you that daily you my luck renew.*
- Leave it for three weeks (gnome magick is slow but lasting, and gnomes do not like to be rushed).
- After three weeks at sunset, set the pot in front of the gnome.
- Each sunset put a coin in the pot, saying the spell words, and replace the lid.
- When it is full, leave one coin in and use the money to buy a plant or something beautiful for the garden. Continue the offerings.

350

AN ANCIENT ABRACADABRA LUCKY CHARM

You will need:

A small triangular piece of paper or a circle cut from soft clay or from the wax of a melted beeswax candle (mark while still soft)
A red pen or small paper knife
A small red bag to hold the charm

Timing:
Around sunrise or when you wake

The Spell

- Beginning at the bottom, draw or etch the single letter A, writing upward from left to right and adding a letter each time (see below) until the full word is written at the top.
- Recite the word *abracadabra* nine times.
- Hide the charm in your bedroom facedown in the bag so that the letters cannot be seen.
- Whenever you need an extra infusion of luck, hold the closed bag, reciting *abracadabra* nine times before returning it to its hiding place.
- Replace on Midsummer or New Year's Day, casting the old one in running water unless it crumbles, in which case replace it at any sunrise.

ABRACADABRA
ABRACADABR
ABRACADAB
ABRACADA
ABRACAD
ABRACA
ABRAC
ABRA
ABR
AB
A

351

TO CREATE A HAPPY, RELAXED HOME WHETHER YOU LIVE ALONE OR SHARE YOUR HOME

You will need:

Six soft pastel-colored candles, such as pink, green, or blue

Timing:

Whenever you expect challenging visitors or noisy family members or arrive home feeling tense

The Spell

- Hold each candle in turn and say for each, *I fill you with happiness, I fill you with harmony, that your light will bring total tranquillity to my home and me/all therein.*
- Light each candle in turn, one from the other, and place one in the hall and five around the room where you relax, saying, *Blessings on my home, and may peace flow without cease as these candles burn and tensions turn to happiness.*
- Relax by candlelight until the candles burn through or you go to bed and blow them out.

352

TO KEEP YOUR HOME HAPPY AND HARMONIOUS IF YOU HAVE A BUSY LIFE OR PEOPLE CONSTANTLY RUSH IN AND OUT

You will need:

A small leafy branch
Six long-stemmed yellow or blue flowers
Twine or string
A small bowl of water

Timing:

Sunday morning

The Spell

This also works well if you have had sorrow or quarrels at home.

- Tie the flowers at regular intervals along the branch, saying, *Peace in my home is what I seek, every day of the week.*
- Dip the pointed end into the water. Beginning at the front door, waft the branch an inch or two above the floor, moving from front of the house to the back, bottom to top and down again, saying the spell words softly and continuously.
- Take the branch out of the front/main door, standing it upright in the garden or a plant pot for the flowers to blow away.
- Tip the water outside the front door, saying, *Harmony is restored, tranquillity once more.*

353

FOR SHUTTING OUT THE WORLD AFTER A HARD DAY, ESPECIALLY IF YOU LIVE ALONE

You will need:

Candies or small fruits
A large scented candle
A small bowl of salt

Timing:

When you get home after a bad day or if you find it hard to let go of work issues

The Spell

- Switch your cell phone to silent and play soft music.
- Light the candle, saying, *This is my sanctuary, my haven of tranquillity, safe cocooned within my peace, all beyond this place shall cease.*
- Put grains of salt in the candle flame, naming any cares or irritations from the day. Repeat the spell words.
- Sit comfortably, choosing a candy or fruit. Before you eat it, say, *I take within myself all pleasure, my own company will I treasure.*
- As you eat it, say, *Safe cocooned within my peace. All beyond this place has ceased. This then is my sanctuary, my haven of tranquillity.*
- Eat as many or few candies or fruits as you want.
- Forget all ideas of reconnecting with the world. Life will still be there in the morning.

354

A FIVE-HERB ABUNDANCE BAG

You will need:

Five small dishes, each containing one of dried basil, bay leaves, coriander seeds, cloves, juniper berries, mint, rosemary, sage, or thyme
A drawstring bag
A golden brown candle
A small dish of soil
A small dish of salt

Timing:

The evening of the new moon

The Spell

- Place the seven dishes in a circle with the candle in the center.
- Light the candle, saying, *I offer light to Mother Earth that she will bring abundance to birth to this home and all who live herein.*
- Add a small quantity of each herb to the bag, naming for each a blessing that your home life brings and one you seek.
- Add three pinches of salt, saying, *I offer salt to Mother Earth that there will be enough for my/our needs and tranquillity.*
- Sprinkle soil into the bag, saying, *I offer her own to Mother Earth for a safe, peaceful, and happy home.*
- Close the bag, hiding it on the floor behind furniture that is rarely moved.

355

A LIGHTING OF THE LAMPS EVENING RITUAL

You will need:

Any electric lamps you have in your home
Six small white candles set around a larger white candle in the room where you relax

Timing:

At dusk

The Spell

- Switch on each lamp upstairs and down rather than the main lights, saying for each, *This is the time of the lighting of the lamps, when birds return to their nest and the world slowly moves to rest.*
- Light each candle, blowing softly in the flame once, saying, *At this time of the lighting of lamp, may this flame burn steadily until night falls and sleep enfolds all in her soft cocoon.*
- At bedtime, blow out any candles that still are burning. Switch off the lights one by one, saying, *May the light of love and tranquillity continue in my/our home and life 'til the lighting of lamps on the morrow.*

356

CALLING YOUR HOUSEHOLD ANGEL TO BRING HAPPINESS AND ABUNDANCE TO YOUR HOME

You will need:

An orange candle
A small ceramic or crystal angel statue in front of the candle near the center or heart of your home

Timing:

When you return home in the evening or are ending your day

The Spell

- Each evening, light the household angel candle, saying, *I call on Mother Derdekea to care for my home and family/pets and enfold me/us in her soft green cloak as I/we sleep.*
- Hold the angel statue and repeat the words, asking Derdekea for any special blessings you need for your home life.
- Carry the candle through every room, transferring it to the meal table, saying, *Derdekea, I thank you for the abundance you bring. May I always have enough for my needs and a little more.*
- After eating, blow out the candle. Relight it for a few minutes in your bedroom, asking Derdekea for quiet sleep and safety until the morning.

357

TO INVITE A LAND GUARDIAN TO BRING PROTECTION AND BLESSINGS TO YOUR HOME

You will need:

A rounded rock the size of a small fist, found close to your home

Timing:

Every year and a day

The Spell

- Pass your hands, palms down and flat, over the stone nine times in circles, saying softly, *Wise guardian of the land, I ask you to rest within this stone a year or more and bring blessings and protection by the score.*
- Set the stone by your hearth or near the front door.
- After a year and a day, return it to its former home and select a new guardian rock.
- Weekly, sprinkle around it a circle of water droplets in which you have dissolved a pinch of salt, asking for any help you need with the week ahead.
- Whenever there is any planned redecoration, people coming to stay, renovations, or family news, tell the guardian about the plans and all will go well.

358

A SCANDINAVIAN WAY OF BRINGING GOOD LUCK TO YOUR HOME

You will need:

Panpipes, a tin whistle, or a recording of fiddle music

A dish full of shiny items

Timing:

Sunset on six days (skipping Thursday, the traditional day of rest for luck, bringing elves/essences)

The Spell

- As darkness falls, stand at the open door. Play the recording, panpipes, or whistle (even inexpertly).
- Place the dish of shiny objects near the stove and turn off the lights, leaving the kitchen, saying, *You are welcome here with your good fortune, prosperity, and great good cheer.*
- If you are experiencing accidents or bad luck at home, leave a small bowl of sugared or honeyed porridge or rice pudding with cinnamon and a pat of butter on top, asking for your luck to be changed. Do the same thing on Christmas morning.
- In the morning, give the porridge to an animal or empty it into long grass.
- Again, warn the house elves/essences in advance about changes with your family or home and add another shiny object to the dish.

359

AN ALTERNATIVE MAGICK BAG FOR HAPPINESS, HEALTH, AND ABUNDANCE IN YOUR HOME

You will need:

A red bag
Dried bay leaves or juniper berries
Oats or grains in a tiny sealed bag
Three silver coins
A small twig
Knotted sewing silk
A twist of salt in foil
An orange candle

Timing:

Any transition evening just before the beginning of a week, month, or year

The Spell

- Add the items one by one to the bag by the light of an orange candle, saying for each, *Enough for my needs, food, fuel, clothes, money, health, and good fortune, these I ask and I will share my abundance.*
- Close the bag and shake it seven times, saying each time, *Abundance in all ways comes to me, a year of fortune will I see in my beloved home.*
- Blow out the candle. In the morning, hold the bag, repeat all the spell words, and hide it in a high, dark place at home.
- Make a new bag on the nearest transition date to a year and bury the old one.

360

CREATING A SOUTH AMERICAN ABUNDANCE BASKET FOR YOUR HOME

You will need:

A wicker or straw basket with a yellow cloth inside and enough golden items to fill it, such as the following:
Small orange crystals or orange and yellow glass beads
Gold, orange, and red ribbons
Inexpensive fashion jewelry of all kinds
Wrapped candies and chocolate in colored foil
Tiny fun items wrapped in shiny paper
Individual packs of nuts, dried golden fruits, and seeds

Timing:

Every month to six weeks

The Spell

- Add a selection of items to the basket, saying softly and continuously, working either in sunlight or in yellow candlelight, *Abundance give and abundance receive, spreading abundance for all to share, increasing abundance and loving care.*
- Keep the basket in your hallway.
- Once a month or every six weeks invite friends, family, and colleagues to bring and share supper.
- Shake the basket onto a large yellow tablecloth, giving everyone a small party bag to fill.
- Afterward, return leftover nonperishable items to the basket and top it up again, repeating the words.

361

CINNAMON, OAT, AND GINGER CAKES TO BRING WHAT YOU MOST NEED INTO YOUR HOME AND LIFE

You will need:

Cinnamon or ginger oat biscuits or cakes, either homemade or bought
A biscuit jar or cake tin

Timing:

The first of the month, in the morning

The Spell

- Take the cakes or biscuits into the garden or an open space, crumbling the first one into the earth or onto a bird table, saying, *Earth Mother, accept my tribute willingly that you will in return offer me/us what I/we do yearn:* [name what is needed most].
- Put the rest of the biscuits or cakes in the jar or tin, saying the words aloud or in your mind each time you eat before offering them to others. You can alter or add in accordance with the need.
- When the jar or tin is empty, bake or buy fresh biscuits or cakes whenever you have a request or the matter is ongoing.
- Repeat the spell.

362

BLESSING SPICE JARS TO SPREAD ONGOING HAPPINESS, PEACE, AND PROSPERITY IN THE HOME IN CHALLENGING TIMES

You will need:

Two orange candles on either side of an herb or spice rack containing your favorite herbs or spice jars

Timing:

Whenever needed

The Spell

- Light the candles, one from the other, saying, *May this kitchen be filled with harmony and good fortune and become a sanctuary and repository of all that is good and healing.*
- Carry the candles to each corner of the kitchen, repeating the words.
- Set one on either side of the spice rack. Gazing into each flame in turn with your hands outstretched, say, *I take in your light, I take in your radiance, that all may be filled with illumination.*
- Gently shake your hands over every jar in turn, saying for each, *Be filled with light, be filled with radiance, that all may be illuminated with blessings.*
- Blow out the candles. Use the herbs or spices in cooking, and when they are gone, re-empower more.

363

AN APPLE BOWL SPELL FOR BRINGING RENEWED ENTHUSIASM AND VITALITY TO YOU AND YOUR HOME

You will need:

A bowl of seven golden or red apples
A paring knife

Timing:

Wednesday at lunchtime, ongoing

The Spell

- Peel an apple, and as you do so, say, *Apple of vitality, give to me/us new energy that I/we may embrace life enthusiastically, and health and joy unfolding be.*
- Quarter the apple and eat each quarter, sending a blessing to yourself and loved ones for health and vitality.
- Bury the peel and seeds in the garden or in a deep tub, as you do so repeating the chant, this time asking for your own health, energy, and vitality to continue or grow stronger.
- Give the other apples away to children, friends, or family members or eat one a day yourself. Replenish the bowl, repeating the spell weekly if you wish.

364

ABSORBING THE POWER OF THE RAINBOW FOR INCREASED GOOD FORTUNE IN YOUR LIFE AND HOME

You will need:

Fresh raw or lightly cooked foods from each of the six color groups below (combining indigo and purple); examples include:
Red: apples, red currants, strawberries, red peppers
Orange: carrots, oranges, melons, pumpkins
Yellow: bananas, sweet corn, grapefruit, yellow peppers
Green: cucumber, pears, lettuce, spinach, grapes
Blue: plums, blueberries, damsons
Purple: black currants, grapes, eggplant

Timing:

Early morning

The Spell

- Going out into the open air if possible, eat a little of the food from each color group in turn. Say before you eat each one, *Rainbow, rainbow, shining bright, fill my heart and soul with light. As your iridescence grows, rainbow within me, so your radiance glows.*
- Use any remaining rainbow food in cooking.

365

A TRADITIONAL ITALIAN TOMATO SPELL FOR SPREADING ABUNDANCE, HEALTH, LOVE, FERTILITY, AND WELL-BEING THROUGH THE HOME AND ALL THEREIN

You will need:
A dish of tomatoes, some ripe and some ripening, in the center of the kitchen table

Timing:
Ongoing

The Spell

- Hold a ripening tomato in the hand you do not write with, saying, *Ripen to your full maturity, bring health and love, prosperity, and fertility* [name any area where you or loved ones need these qualities].
- Take a ripe tomato in the other hand and say, *Your ripeness brings me sweetness, your richness offers happiness* [name anyone else who needs happiness].
- Return the ripening tomato to the bowl and eat the others or put it in salad or a meal, saying, *I take within your sweetness, I absorb in me your ripeness, that happiness will daily grow; it shall be so. In every way within this home, love comes to stay.*
- Replace the tomatoes regularly to keep love and good fortune flowing.

366

A FAR EASTERN HONEY SPELL TO ENSURE ENOUGH RESOURCES FOR YOU, YOUR HOME, AND YOUR LOVED ONES FOR THE LONG TERM

You will need:
A jar of honey
A spoon
A yellow candle

Timing:
Sunset

The Spell

- Light the candle and hold the honey jar up so that light shines into it, saying, *May I/we have enough resources for our needs in my/our home and life for a hundred springtimes.*
- Remove the lid from the jar of honey and again hold it up so that light shines into it, saying, *May I/we have enough resources for our needs in our home for a hundred summers.*
- Dip the spoon into the honey, saying, *May I/we,* [name(s)], *have enough resources for our needs in my/our home and life for a hundred leaf falls.*
- Eat the honey, saying, *May I /we,* [name(s)], *have enough resources for our needs in my/our home and life for a hundred winters.*
- Blow out the candle, saying, *May none within these walls ever be hungry or thirsty and never may the sun set on anger.*

367

USING MINT TO BRING PROSPERITY, LUCK, HEALTH, AND HAPPINESS INTO YOUR HOME AND LIFE IN THE SHORT AND LONG TERM

You will need:

A mint tea bag
A cup or mug of hot water
Mint plants

Timing:

Any morning you feel jaded, need a boost in luck, or have an unexpectedly high household bill

The Spell

- Pour the water on top of the tea bag and stir it with a spoon three times in each direction, starting clockwise, saying with each stir, *Fortune, health, enter quickly here, the future I need never fear. Lucky mint flows in my home and me, and this day brings prosperity.*
- Sip the mint tea slowly, leaving a little in the bottom, and then repeat the words.
- Sprinkle a few drops outside the front door to draw fortune in.
- Plant fresh mint in pots in your kitchen or garden that you can use in cooking and teas to attract lasting good fortune. Say as you plant, *Fortune, health, remain lastingly, that happy time ahead at home shall be, lucky mint flows in lastingly, and the future brings prosperity.*

368

GARLIC KITCHEN PROTECTION TO KEEP ILLNESS AWAY FROM THE HOME AND DRAW RESOURCES AND POSITIVE PEOPLE INTO IT

You will need:

A string of garlic bulbs or hang them along a string before the spell
A green candle
A dish of salt

Timing:

Ongoing, starting on Wednesday evening

The Spell

- Light the candle and say, *Keep away sickness, misfortune, and sorrow, may abundance and health greet every morrow.*
- Holding the garlic string by the ends, pass each bulb over, in front of, and behind the candle, repeating the words.
- Sprinkle a pinch of salt in the candle so that it sparkles.
- Lay the garlic string flat and scatter salt on each garlic bulb, saying the words over each bulb as you sprinkle the salt on it.
- Shake off excess salt from the garlic, saying, *Bring to my home abundance, health, good fortune, good people, and just enough wealth.*
- Hang the garlic string in the kitchen where air circulates around it until it shrivels. Replace it but do not use this garlic for cooking.

369

A TRADITIONAL CHINESE CENTER OF WELL-BEING IN THE KITCHEN TO PREVENT ACCIDENTS AND SPREAD HARMONY THROUGH THE HOME

You will need:

A picture of the Chinese kitchen god Tsao-Wang, god of the stove and hearth, and his wife, Tsao-Wang Nai-Nai, or a small jade or wooden Buddha
A small kitchen shelf to hold all the items
A small offerings dish
Three incense sticks in front of the picture
A small green fern or feathery plant for fresh energies

Timing:
Monday morning and ongoing

The Spell

- Light the incense sticks one from the other, saying for the first, *I ask the wise guardian(s) to keep safe this kitchen and my home from accidents and disasters.*
- For the second incense say, *I ask the wise guardian(s) to bring blessings and harmony for all who live or enter here.*
- For the third say, *I ask the wise guardian(s) that there will always be sufficient food, fuel, clothing, and money within this home.*
- Fill the offerings dish with tiny fruits, crystals, seeds, or flowers.
- Light three incense sticks whenever you have time, repeating the words.
- On New Year's Eve and the beginning of the Chinese New Year, burn a red candle.

370

A KITCHEN ANGEL RITUAL FOR HEALTH, PROTECTION, ABUNDANCE, AND HAPPINESS

You will need:

A dish of salt
A loaf of bread
A dish of butter
A pot of honey
An orange candle

Timing:
Wednesday morning

The Spell

- Place the items in a square around the candle with the salt farthest away, the bread to the left, the butter nearest you, and the honey to the right.
- Place a sprinkle of salt on your tongue, saying, *Mother Isma, kind angel of the kitchen, bring to birth the health, happiness, and prosperity of the earth.*
- Take a piece of bread. Holding it to the candlelight, say, *Mother Isma, kind angel of the kitchen, let me share protection and abundance of the air.*
- Put butter on the bread, saying, *Mother Isma, kind angel of the kitchen, inspire me with well-being of the fire.*
- Add honey and eat the bread, saying, *Mother Isma, kind angel of the kitchen, fill my home with love flowing like the water.*
- Let the candle burn before removing the food.
- Leave the salt dish in the kitchen to absorb any negativity; throw it away and replace it each morning.

371

TO TURN THE TINIEST INDOOR OR BALCONY PLANT DISPLAY INTO A GARDEN OF POWER AND HEALING

You will need:
Six small moss or tree (dendritic) agate crystals, jade, amethyst, or green glass beads

Timing:
Friday morning

The Spell

- Leave the crystals open from early morning to noon, saying, *Be filled with power, be filled with light, that you will grow in loving might, though small my garden, hardly land, in nature's richness I do stand.*
- Plant a small crystal in your favorite five plants, repeating the spell words. Save the sixth crystal.
- Whenever you water your plants, use water in which you have soaked the sixth crystal overnight. Remove the crystal afterward and leave it where light will shine on it.

372

A HEALTH AND ABUNDANCE TREE TO EMPOWER YOUR HOME, ITS BOUNDARIES, AND ALL WITHIN

You will need:
A tree or bush outdoors or a smaller one indoors in a large pot
A stone fruit that should read A FRUIT WITH A STONE INSIDE.

Timing:
Thursday afternoon during the waxing moon

The Spell

- Hold the fruit in your open cupped hands and say, *May health, wealth, abundance, and plenty grow. May my larder/food store never empty and my home be filled with peace and sanctity.*
- Eat the fruit and repeat the words.
- Plant the stone beneath the tree or bush, saying, *Abundance spread, abundance shed on every boundary and room, that there will be enough and more when next* [add month] *I see the waxing moon.*

373

A SOLAR LIGHT GARDEN SPELL TO SPREAD HAPPINESS IN AND PROTECTION AROUND YOUR HOME AND KEEP AWAY ALL DANGER

You will need:

Solar lights outside your home or fairy lights on indoor greenery in a pot of soil

Timing:

When the solar lights shine or you switch on the fairy lights after dusk

The Spell

- Shake your hands within the light.
- Point your index fingers, palms down and outstretched, toward your home from the garden or from the door into the room, saying, *Spread the light and luck within, in every corner be protection that joy will grow in all directions.*
- Return your hands to the light, shake again, and repeat the words and actions, saying, *Abundance gives and light receives, all fear from my home recedes.*
- If you are using fairy lights, sit in their light or go indoors and look through the window at your solar lights, picturing the energies flowing through you and your home.

374

MARKING THE BOUNDARIES OF YOUR HOME MAGICALLY TO KEEP YOUR HOME AND LAND SAFE FROM ALL HARM

You will need:

A small silver bell, Tibetan bells, wind chimes, or a recording of bell music and headphones

Protective plants, bushes, or trees such as basil, bamboo tied with red string, bay tree, cactus, eucalyptus, hawthorn, juniper, mint, myrtle, palm, pine, rosemary, roses, rowan, or sage

Timing:

Just before nightfall

The Spell

- Begin inside the home, walking the four external walls on every floor and ringing the bell; repeat for the boundaries of your garden and front path or balcony.
- Place a protective flower, shrub, or herb pot at each of the farthest four corners of home and garden (eight in total), saying for each, *Be as protection for me against all negativity, be guardian and shed positivity within my boundaries.* (If you do not have a garden, put two plants at each corner inside the property.)
- Visit each of the corners again inside and outside, saying at each, *One from theft, two from storm, three from sickness and from harm, four from fire and careless stranger, five from foe and unseen danger, six from malice, seven from pain, eight from flood, nine may joy remain. May this spell last through moon and sun.*

375

TO REVIVE A DYING TREE, PLANTS THAT ARE NOT THRIVING, OR A NEGLECTED GARDEN

You will need:

Sun water (a bowl of water that has been left outdoors from dawn until noon)

Timing:

Sunday, around noon

The Spell

- Collect the sun water and put your hands around the bowl, saying, *Sunlight healing, light revealing, bring new life and growing power; sunlight healing, light revealing, on these plants/tree/garden your goodness shower.*
- Sprinkle the plants/tree/garden with the water, saying, *Root deep in Mother Earth, that you may live long, and when you are done, bring new seeds to birth.*
- Each week, make new sun water. As you sprinkle it on the tree/plant/area of garden, say, *Grow from earth to the sky, breathe new green life to beautify.*

376

A GARDEN RITUAL TO RECONNECT WITH LIFE IF YOU ARE SPACED OUT OR DISENCHANTED

You will need:

A small round brown pebble found in the garden

A small brown drawstring bag

Timing:

Around sunrise

The Spell

- Stand barefoot in your garden, holding the stone in the hand you write with.
- Press down hard with your feet and point your hands downward, still holding the stone, saying, *I feel life flowing upward into my body.*
- Still holding the stone in your hand, upwardly extending your arms, say, *I feel life flowing downward into my heart and soul.*
- Hold your hands close to a thriving green bush or large plant.
- Circle the stone clockwise over or around the bush or plant, saying, *I feel life flowing within my body, mind, and soul, and I am whole again.*
- Place the stone in the bag, saying, *Be filled with life and light of the garden that I too may reach the heights of energy and enthusiasm once again.*
- Whenever you feel jaded, hold the stone, repeating all the spell words.
- Leave the stone under full moonlight to reempower it.

377

MAKING A PROTECTIVE MAGICAL GARDEN

You will need:

Nine bamboo canes or plants
Nine red strings
In hotter climates, four cactus, orange, or lemon trees or four hawthorn, sage, or rosemary bushes; use lilac or honeysuckle in cooler areas

Timing:
Saturday afternoon

The Spell

- Plant a cactus or cool weather bush at each corner of the house outdoors (as near as possible if you are attached to another house), saying, *Stand sentinel for me against all danger, from malevolent foe or malicious stranger.*
- Inside put cacti in the indoor corners, including the balcony and just outside your apartment's entrance.
- Insert nine bamboo cane/bamboo plants along your perimeter fence.
- Tie scarlet string from each of the bamboo, knotted nine times, saying the same words.
- If you do not have a garden, plant a protective window box outside your apartment with basil, catnip (very lucky), chamomile, cumin, dill, parsley, rosemary, sage, thyme, vetiver, or wild garlic. Use the same spell words.

378

A WITCH BALL RITUAL TO KEEP HARM AWAY FROM A GARDEN AND HOME

You will need:

A witch ball (large silver, green, or blue Christmas bauble or a glass fishing float) or a large convex mirror (miniature if indoors)
A large citronella, cedar, or pine outdoor incense stick or a sagebrush or cedar smudge stick (if you do not have a garden, use a smaller incense stick indoors)

Timing:
In sunlight

The Spell

- Hang the witch ball on a tree branch near the center of the garden or on an ornamental branch indoors, saying: *Protect all with your brightness, fill everything with lightness, bless all who shelter here with health, wealth, and love, to live in harmony without fear.*
- Swirl the ball nine times clockwise, nine times counterclockwise, and nine more times clockwise, saying softly and continuously, *Three by three, nine by nine, drive darkness away and brilliance shine.*
- Light the incense or smudge stick, moving around the tree nine times as before, repeating the second chant.
- Every week, polish the ball, repeating the first chant.
- Each time you pass the ball, swirl it, saying, *Reflect in your radiance, moon and sun from above, safe will we be, enclosed in love.*

379

TO DRAW BIRDS, BUTTERFLIES, AND WILDLIFE TO YOUR GARDEN

You will need:

Birdseed
Wildflower seeds

Timing:

Saturday, early

The Spell

- Stand in the center of the garden, turn around seven times in both directions, clockwise first, saying with arms outstretched, *You creatures of the air, birds, butterflies, and benign winged creatures, you are welcome here. Small creatures who scurry and hurry, find refuge in this sanctuary.*
- Go to fragrant flowers or those which will blossom fragrantly, extending your hands toward them. Turn in both directions seven times, clockwise first, saying, *Butterflies and bees, here you will see welcome.*
- Plant wildflower seeds in a flower bed or uncultivated area, afterward turning seven times in both directions, clockwise first, saying, *You small creatures who scurry and hurry, here is welcome and sanctuary.*
- Scatter birdseed or fill a feeder, turning seven times in both directions, clockwise first, saying, *Birds of the air, shed your cares, for here you will find welcome.*
- Every time you put out food for the birds or tend the garden, go to the center and turn seven times clockwise and then counterclockwise, repeating the first chant.

380

USING A BONFIRE TO BRING HEALING AND FERTILITY TO YOUR GARDEN AND HOME

You will need:

A bonfire, a barbecue without the grid, a fire dish, or a small fire in a brazier
A new thriving green plant

Timing:

Tuesday evening or a significant date in your seasonal or family calendar

The Spell

- When the bonfire is burning, hold a long stick so that it singes and then throw it onto the fire, saying, *From old life comes new. From ashes rises rebirth, life flames anew, fed by Mother Earth.*
- Burn two more sticks or more if needed, repeating the spell words and asking what is needed for your home, self, and loved ones.
- Allow the fire to burn down and leave the ashes overnight.
- In the morning, scoop up the ashes.
- Plant the new plant, adding the ashes to the soil and repeating the chant.

CHAPTER 8

MAGICK FOR THE HEARTH AND HOME

This chapter includes spells for bringing happiness and blessings into your home; spells for successful accident-free home improvements; spells for removing bad energies from your home; and spells for finding the property that is right for you.

381

FINDING THE RIGHT LOCATION BY USING A MAGNET AND PINS

You will need:

A map covering the entire area that interests you
More detailed maps of the area, either a road map or one printed from the Internet
A box of pins
A magnet

Timing:
Wednesday

The Spell

- Spread out the area map on the floor and say, *North, south, east, west, show me where I will love the best. East, west, south, north, show me where to venture forth.*
- Kneeling close to the map, close your eyes, repeat the words, and scatter the pins.
- Look where the largest concentration of pins has fallen, and if they are scattered, repeat until you get a clear result.
- Gather all the pins with the magnet and return them to the box.
- Take a detailed map of the area where there are most pins and repeat the words and actions until you have an even closer idea of the right location.
- Even if the location is unexpected, arrange to visit the area, and, as you explore, you will find the ideal home.

382

IF YOU HAVE MANY TIES TO AN OLD HOME AND FIND IT HARD TO LET GO BUT MUST MOVE

You will need:

A large storage jar
Small items associated with the happiness of the home
A red candle
Nine long red threads
A dish of soil

Timing:
If your home is not selling and you suspect you are holding on to it too long

The Spell

- Light the candle and say, *Happiness has been mine/ours in this beloved home, sorrows too, but now my/our time here must be through.*
- Tie a knot in the first thread. Holding the ends, let the knot burn in the flame, saying, *I let go with thanks to this old life and move on gratefully with joy, not strife.*
- Drop the ends in the soil. Repeat for the next eight threads.
- Fill the jar with memorable items, saying for each, *Thank you for the memories that will always stay with me.*
- Put the jar inside a packing box for the future move so that you can take it to your new home.
- Let the candle burn.
- Bury the threads still in the soil.

383

A FOUR WINDS SPELL TO FIND THE PROPERTY THAT IS RIGHT FOR YOU IN THE AREA YOU WANT

You will need:

Paper on which you have drawn a detailed plan of the chosen area
A small red candle in each corner of the plan
A spicy incense stick to the right of the plan

Timing:

Wednesday

The Spell

- Light the candles in turn clockwise, starting with the one farthest away, saying, *I call Boreas, the wind of the north, to guide me to the home that is right for me, that the move will occur happily and soon, within three moons* (choose your time scale).
- For the second candle, say, *I call Eurus, the wind of the east,* adding the rest of the words.
- Light the third candle saying, *I call Notus, the wind of the south,* adding the rest of the words.
- Light the fourth candle, saying, *I call to Zephyrus, the wind of the west,* adding the rest of the words.
- Light the incense from each candle and make spirals over the plan, saying, *North, south, east, west, winds guide me to which home will be the best.*
- Leave incense and candles to burn.

384

TO BRING HAPPINESS AND BLESSINGS INTO A TEMPORARY HOME OR IF IT IS NOT WHERE YOU WANT TO BE

You will need:

A long piece of twine
Nine wild or white cultivated flowers
A basket

Timing:

During the waxing moon

The Spell

- Place the nine flower heads, each with a little of the stem still on each flower, in the basket.
- Walk around your home with them, saying, *Though not from choice, my home is dear, harmonious days and happy nights, make this right while we are here.*
- Attach the flowers to the twine, knotting them along it, repeating the words for each one.
- Suspend the flower twine by both ends near the front door, saying, *So will I settle here temporarily and will live happily until I see the right home for me.*
- When the petals fade or fall, cast the twine in water, saying, *Bring me the right home I desire so much, until then contentment is enough.*

385

TO SECURE A PROPERTY, WHETHER TO BE PURCHASED OR RENTED, WHEN THERE IS FIERCE COMPETITION

You will need:

A newspaper or real estate agent's details of the property you really want
A blue candle behind the details

Timing:
Before you make an appointment to view

The Spell

- Light the candle and blow into the flame three times, saying, *Bring to me this property, keep for me this property, for me and no other do I draw it to me.*
- Hold your hands toward the flame and shake them vigorously over the specific property three times, repeating the words three times.
- Say, *I will live there happily, for it must be mine and mine alone.*
- Blow out the candle, saying, *Light enter this property that it will be for me, immediately, instantly, easily, for it must be mine and mine alone.*
- Relight the candle and make the appointment to view or put in your offer, saying all the spell words very fast beforehand.
- Blow out the candle again and relight it briefly before further negotiations.

386

MOVING INTO A TEMPORARY OR RENTED ACCOMMODATION TO MAKE IT FEEL LIKE YOURS

You will need:

A medium-size ceramic bowl half filled with water
A white candle

Timing:
Sunday

The Spell

- Stand on the front doorstep, facing inward, saying, *Become mine, a haven of security that my home life is filled with unity.*
- Sprinkle water along the doorstep, saying, *Blessings on my borrowed home and all who enter here, become as dear, borrowed home, as though you were my own.*
- Move around each room, sprinkling water around the door, window ledges, and four corners, repeating all the words.
- Open any back door and, facing outward, sprinkle water on that doorstep, saying the words again.
- Go to the main table of the house, sprinkling drops of water all around it on the floor.
- Light a white candle in the center of the table, saying the words again.
- Let the candle burn. Throw the water out of the front door, saying, *Within these walls I rest contentedly until I move to permanency.*

387

MOVING INTO A NEW HOUSE TO TRANSFER THE GOOD FORTUNE AND LEAVE BEHIND ANY BAD MEMORIES

You will need:

Something small, with happy memories from the old home, such as a pot of soil with a favorite small garden plant

A small old object that no longer works or is rusty

A small plant for the new owners

Timing:

Before you leave the old home for the new

The Spell

- The day before leaving, dispose of the broken item in a garbage can away from the home, saying, *You are gone, you are done, and with you the sad memories and regrets for what could never be.*
- Pack the item to be taken in hand luggage. When you reach the new home, make sure it is the first item unpacked, saying, *Good fortune and happy memories transferred be, that good times in my/our new home I/we shall see.*
- In the evening situate your transferred item in its chosen place, saying, *Rest here awhile that I/we will smile each day in our new home.*

388

BRING LUCK AND PROTECTION TO A NEW HOME

You will need:

A small dark glass jar with a lid

Any key from your old house and one from your new

Nine metal nails

Salt

Dried rosemary

Old red wine or vinegar

Timing:

The week after moving

The Spell

- Tie together with the cord, using three knots, the old and new keys.
- Add them to the jar, saying, *New and old bring days of gold and nights of harmony in this my sanctuary.*
- Add next the nails, salt, and rosemary, saying for each, *Keep safe these walls, good fortune send, but from my door keep all who malice intend in this my sanctuary.*
- Add enough wine until the items are covered, seal, and shake seven times, saying seven times, *Stand sentinel, admitting only those who speak and mean well to this my sanctuary.*
- Bury the bottle as near to the front door as you can or keep it in on a dark high shelf where it will not be disturbed.

389

FOR SUCCESSFUL AND ACCIDENT-FREE HOME IMPROVEMENTS OR BUILDING WORKS

You will need:

Paint, tools, and materials in a circle in a room you will be transforming
A pale-colored pen
A sage or any tree-fragrance incense stick

Timing:
The night before renovations or redecorations begin

The Spell

- Light the incense stick and walk around the outside of the circle of items, writing in the air in a continuous smoke circle, shoulder high, BLESS THIS HOME AND OUR ENDEAVORS AND KEEP US SAFE FROM HARM.
- In pen, write on an area to be painted, using small letters, the date of the beginning of renovations and the names of the family members who live there.
- Just before finishing, seal a small domestic item in a fireplace or under plaster in an alcove.
- When the work is completed, walk around each room and area, writing BLESSINGS AND THANKS FOR SUCCESSFUL COMPLETION in incense stick smoke in the air.
- Find a hidden place in the home to write the completion date and BLESS THIS HOME.

390

A BLESSING OF THE EARTH ON YOUR NEW HOME WHETHER IT IS YOUR OWN OR RENTED

You will need:

Ingredients to make bread or a packet mix if you are in a hurry

Timing:
The first free Friday in your new home

The Spell

- Mix the ingredients or packet, kneading the dough and saying softly over and over, *Bless this home, Mother Earth, and all who live within, that it may be a place of love and unity herein.*
- Let the dough rise, covered with a cloth, while you make an area of the home as you want it with your unique touches.
- When the dough has doubled in size, say, *May happiness increase and multiply daily in this home.*
- Shape the loaf, repeating all the words, and with the index finger of the hand you write with, invisibly draw the infinity sign an inch or two above it.

- Crumble the first slice of baked bread for the birds and eat the rest with family or friends while it is still warm.

SECTION 2:

CREATING THE RIGHT ENERGIES AT HOME

391

A TRADITIONAL RITUAL TO REMOVE BAD ATMOSPHERE AND FEELINGS FROM YOUR HOME

You will need:
A round black stone and a white one

Timing:
Full moon, day and night

The Spell

- Hold the black stone in your open cupped hands, naming whatever you want to lose: quarreling, sickness, or lethargy. Say over and over, *Be filled with negativity I seek to lose, grow heavy with the* [name] *I no longer choose; linger no longer in my home, become a stranger, far to roam.*
- When the stone seems heavier, cast it into water or bury it in earth where nothing grows, saying, *You are gone, you are done, I have no more of you. Your power is through.*
- Leave the white stone outdoors for a full sunlit day and a full moon.
- Set it in a bright spot in your home, saying, *Attract positivity, happiness, and peace. Stone of hope, stone of light, may your power never cease.*
- Every full moon, leave the stone for a full twenty-four hours outdoors.

392

A CELTIC ELEMENTS RITUAL FOR WHEN YOUR HOME FEELS OUT OF BALANCE

You will need:
An herbal incense cone for sky
A red candle in a deep heatproof holder for fire
A dish of potpourri or dried sage for earth and one of lavender or rose water or fragrance for sea
A square slate, stone, or chalkboard (draw on it with white chalk a triskele, the Celtic sacred symbol of protection and harmony)

Timing:
At first light

The Spell

- Indoors, light the candle in the center of the triskele, the incense cone on the upper left coil, the fragrance on the upper right, and the rose or lavender water on the lower coil.
- Light the incense from the candle.
- Say, *By the power of the earth,* scattering potpourri around the outside of the slate, *By the power of sky,* passing incense around it, and *By the power of the sea,* scattering rose water around it, all clockwise.
- Lift the candle above the center of the triskele, saying, *By the power of fire so do I call, earth, sea, and sky, elements all, banish disharmony that I may know unity.*
- Rub out the triskele.

393

A MONTHLY RITUAL TO CLEAR OUT STAGNATION OR DISCORDANT ENERGIES FROM THE HOME

You will need:

Individual bowls of dried mint, salt, pepper, juniper berries, dried cloves, or dried cranberries and coriander, cumin, or sunflower seeds

A larger empty bowl

Timing:

The last day of the month, before sunset

The Spell

- Add salt to the larger bowl, saying, *Never let the sun go down in anger, nor slumber while stagnation lingers; the month is nearly gone, and so new life must come.*
- Add pepper, berries, and seeds, repeating the same words for each.
- Swirl the bowl nine times clockwise, nine counterclockwise, and nine clockwise, speaking the words faster as you swirl the bowl faster.
- Put the bowl down with a bang, saying, *The month is nearly done, new energies will come. Staleness begone.*
- Go outside early the next morning, scattering the mix.
- Fill the larger bowl with flower petals and the dried mint, saying, *New month with every hour, continuing goodness on me shower.*

394

A SPRING CLEANING RITUAL FOR ANY TIME OF THE YEAR

You will need:

A vacuum cleaner

Small lavender heads, fragranced carpet-freshening powder, or talcum powder

Timing:

Whenever there has been a quarrel or bad atmosphere in your home

The Spell

- Sprinkle the lavender heads or powder around the floors, starting with the gloomiest, saying continuously, *Out with sorrow, out with pain, joyous things alone remain.*
- Vacuum in ever widening counterclockwise circles, alternating with clockwise circles, saying all the time, *Three times three, the power I raise, bringing with it happier days; dust to dust, away you must. New life bring, welcome spring.*
- Empty the vacuum cleaner.

395

FOR CHANGING THE FORTUNES OF THE HOME IF THERE HAS BEEN A RUN OF BAD LUCK, NEGATIVE SITUATIONS, OR TROUBLESOME VISITORS

You will need:

Pine or lemon floor cleaner dissolved in a bucket of warm water or nine drops of lemon, geranium, pine, or tea tree essential oil added to the water

A scrubbing brush and mop

Timing:

Any Monday morning

The Spell

- Stir the water in the bucket clockwise nine times with the mop, saying, *One for joy, two for gladness, three and four to banish sadness, five and six flee useless anger, seven eight nine remain no longer.*
- Begin to scrub or mop paved, tiled, or uncarpeted areas, indoors and out, including doorsteps, repeating the spell words.
- On the final scrub or mopping, say nine times, *Nine, eight, seven, six, five, four, three, two, one; the spell is done, sorrow/sickness, bad luck/anger now be gone.*
- Throw leftover water out the front door.

396

A FAR EASTERN CLEANSING TO KEEP THE ENERGIES OF YOUR HOME FLOWING TO ENSURE POSITIVE PROGRESS IN EVERY AREA OF YOUR LIFE

You will need:

A scented candle

A small bell or wind chimes

Tree fragrance incense

A tray to carry items from room to room

Timing:

Sunday morning

The Spell

- Light the candle in the room nearest the center of the home, saying, *May all flow with grace and beauty, stirring good fortune and harmony.*
- Carry the candle into the four corners, beginning with the one nearest the door, moving counterclockwise and saying the words as you walk.
- Repeat the actions and words clockwise.
- Ring the bell softly three times, following exactly the same order, words, and actions.
- Light the incense from the candle, continuing all words and actions exactly, making smoke spirals.
- Do exactly the same thing in every room and area.
- Let the candle burn in the first room, setting the incense outside the front door.
- Set the bell near the candle and ring it once, saying the words for the final time.

397

REBALANCING THE HOME BY USING THE FOUR ELEMENTS (WESTERNIZED STYLE)

You will need:

For earth: potpourri, salt, dried sage or thyme, fruit, flowers, or a pottery dish

For air: an oil burner or incense, dried lavender, a silver knife, a box of pins, feathers, or a wind chime

For fire: a mirror, clear crystals, or beads threaded on cord (or a sun catcher), golden candles, sun symbols, spices, or bright metal objects

For water: rose or perfumed water, a fish tank, a coffee machine, water bowls with colored stones or crystals, moon symbols, or a small water feature (a small indoor electric fountain or plants set around a mini-pool in a large pot).

Timing:

The beginning of a week or month

The Spell

- Place one of each elemental item in every room or area, saying for each, *Blend and harmonize, mix and synchronize, to make all right.*
- In bedroom, add an extra water element, saying, *Peaceful rest and happy dreams are best.*
- In living and eating areas, add extra water and earth, saying, *Joyous conversation, security, and relaxation.*
- In working areas or hallways, add extra fire and air, saying, *Protection, achievement, and clear direction.*
- Pass through all areas once more, saying, *Balanced be, calm and happy, empowered by elemental powers, every hour.*

398

A HOME CLEARING IF THINGS ARE NOT RIGHT

You will need:

A small sagebrush or cedar smudge stick or tree incense stick

A compass to identify in advance the four main directions as you stand in the center of the home

Timing:

The brightest part of the day

The Spell

- Open all windows and inner doors.
- Light the smudge stick and face north, making waist-high clockwise circles of smoke using your extended arm, saying, *May there be peace in the north.*
- Turn east, spiraling the smudge stick, saying, *May there be peace in the east.*
- Turn south, again spiraling the smudge stick, saying, *May there be peace in the south.*
- Face west, spiraling the smudge stick, saying, *May there be peace in the west.*
- Open the front door and face outward, making smoke spirals. Say, *May only peace enter, remain, and fill my whole home with blessings.*
- Leave the smudge stick outside the door.

399

AN ANOINTING RITUAL IF THERE HAS BEEN SICKNESS OR SORROW IN THE HOME

You will need:

A bowl of lavender, lilac, or rose water or a floral fragrance diluted in a little water

Timing:

Saturday mornings and then every first day of spring

The Spell

- Anoint each door knob or handle with a few drops of fragrance, starting from outside the front door and sprinkling a few drops on each external window ledge, saying for each, *Blessings on all, may sickness and sorrow call here no more, henceforth do I bar every door. Let there be laughter, health, and good cheer, misfortune and sadness depart now from here.*
- Go indoors, again anointing door handles, starting inside the front door and ledges in every room, repeating the words.
- Pour any fragrance that is left down a bathroom drain, saying, *Now only goodness remains.*

400

AN ANTINEGATIVITY HOME SPRAY

You will need:

A pump action spray, the kind used for watering plants

One or more of chamomile, jasmine, lavender, lemon balm, neroli, rose, rosewood, or ylang ylang essential oil

Timing:

Ongoing

The Spell

- Add ten to fifteen drops of essential oil to half a liter of water in the spray bottle.
- Shake the mixture, saying, *Spread joy around, peace abound, with this spray I open the way to light, health, and happiness all around.*
- If sadness, resentment, or lethargy has penetrated the house, mix three drops of neroli essential oil, two drops of lemon oil, three drops of lemongrass oil, and three drops of lemon balm oil with the water.
- Whenever the home or particular rooms feel dark or sad or there has been a quarrel, spray the mist finely into the air, repeating the words as you spray.

CHAPTER 9

WISH MAGICK

This chapter includes wish spells for dream fulfilment; spells for achieving your goals in the arts or media; spells for attracting life-changing opportunities; and spells for fighting injustices, launching creative ventures, removing illness and misfortune, turning major loss into major gain, and attaining your wildest dreams.

401

A CANDLE WISH SPELL

You will need:

A large white candle in a deep wide holder
A thin strip of white paper
A blue pen
A pot of soil

Timing:
Midnight as the week, month, or year turns from old to new

The Spell

- Light the candle and say, *This is what I wish,* [desire], *and I ask that it will be fulfilled within* [number] *moons.*
- Write the wish and time scale on the paper, saying it aloud as you write.
- Hold the end of the paper in the flame until it catches alight, again saying the wish and time scale.
- Drop the burning paper into the soil.
- Blow out the candle flame, saying, *May this wish come true within* [number] *moons.*
- Bury the ash and any remaining paper under a tree, repeating the wish and time scale, saying, *May this wish come true.*

402

FOR A CRESCENT MOON WISH, IDEALLY FULFILLED BY THE FULL MOON

You will need:

Seven white flower heads in a basket

Timing:
When you first see the crescent moon, even if it is not the first night

The Spell

- Face the crescent moon, holding the basket outstretched.
- Say softly, *I see the moon, the moon sees me, I bless the crescent moon, may the moon bless me, that when you are full once more, granted my wish may be.*
- Whisper your wish, daring to reach out for what you most want.
- One by one, arrange the flowers into a crescent shape on the ground, repeating the words and whispering the wish for each one.
- When you have done this, add, *Crescent moon, take my offering, that my wish by full moon you will bring.*
- Leave the flowers to blow away or fade, in which case dig them back into the earth.

403

KNOT WISHES OVER NINE DAYS

You will need:
A long piece of green cord

Timing:
Between noon and 3 p.m. on the first day and thereafter when you have time

The Spell

- Summarize your wish in a few words, saying it nine times.
- Tie the first knot, working left to right, saying, *By the power of one, the spell's begun.*
- Do the same thing every day but add a line to the chant.
- On day 2, add, *By the knot of two, may my wish come true.*
- On day 3, add, *By the knot of three, the power I see.*
- On day 4, add *By the knot of four, the power grows more.*
- On day 5, add, *By the knot of five, the wish will thrive.*
- On day 6, add, *By the knot of six, the spell is fixed.*
- On day 7, add, *By the knot of seven, my cause is leaven.*
- On day 8, add, *By the knot of eight, not long to wait.*
- By day 9, you have tied all nine knots; say all nine chants nine times, having added, *By the knot of nine, the wish is mine.*
- Hang the wish cord where the air flows freely.

404

AN ANCIENT LATE-WAXING MOON THREE-WISH RITUAL

You will need:
A body of water: a stream, a river, or a pond or a bowl of water outdoors in which you can see moonlight; if not, set a torch angled in the ground so that it shines on the water

Timing:
The three days before the full moon

The Spell

- On night 1, gaze into the water and say three times, *Bright moon, true moon, moon in the stream, grant the wishes of which I do dream.*
- Make the first wish, or you can repeat the same wish each night.
- Go to bed early. Even if you cannot see the moon, say the words again three times through the open window.
- On nights 2 and 3, repeat the spell.
- On night 3, after the spell, cast a small moonstone, selenite, or pearl into the water and say, *Moon, your own I return. Grant these wishes for which I yearn.*

405

A KITE WISH

You will need:

A children's kite
A long strip of paper with a hole in it or a luggage label
A green pen
Five green ribbons
Green string

Timing:

Any windy day

The Spell

- Write your wishes, as many as you can fit on both sides, or the same wish repeated on the strip of paper. Speak the words as you write.
- Attach the paper to the kite tails with string, using five knots, saying five times, *This knot I tie that you will fly and carry my wishes to the sky.*
- Now affix each ribbon to the tail again, using five knots, repeating the words five times for each.
- Fly the kite in an open space, and when you feel it tugging, let it go, saying five times, *By the power of five, my wish is alive, fly free and send it back to me:* [shout your wish into the wind].
- Watch the kite until it is out of sight, turn away, and repeat the second chant.

406

A BALLOON WISH FOR A SECRET DESIRE

You will need:

A helium balloon with a design linked to your wish, for example, a heart for love

Timing:

An open space in wind

The Spell

- Hold the balloon and whisper the wish nine times faster and faster.
- Let the balloon tug in your hand and say nine times, *None may my secret know, to none my inner dreams I show, carry it high into the sky, with you my wish and I do fly.*
- Let the balloon go, calling, *The wish is free, so shall it be, return in joy and openly.*
- Turn around and do not watch the balloon.

407

A WEEKLY WISHING WELL RITUAL AT HOME

You will need:

A large glass bowl or goblet (smoky if possible) half filled with water you keep as your wishing well
Three gold-colored floating candles on the surface of the bowl
Three silver coins
A pointed clear crystal or silver-colored paper knife

Timing:

Morning, just as it is getting light

The Spell

- Light the candles in turn and push them gently over the water, saying for each one a wish or the same wish for all, adding, *Wishing well, I ask of you, make this/these wish(es) soon come true.*
- Drop the first coin into a light pool, saying your first wish again and adding, *Wish I ask flow now to me, may my wish soon granted be.*
- Drop the other two coins into different pools of light, making a wish for each one or the same wish for all, repeating the second chant.
- Stir the water three times clockwise with the crystal or knife; as you do so, say three times, *One for silver, two for gold, wishes soon for me unfold.*
- Blow out each candle in order of lighting, repeating its wish and the first set of words.
- If the wish(es) are urgent, repeat the spell daily for a week.

408

BUBBLE WISHES FOR URGENT NEEDS

You will need:

A bubble blower and bubbles, either purchased or homemade
Wildflower or edible seeds

Timing:

Late Wednesday or Thursday afternoon

The Spell

- Shake the bubble mixture ten times, reciting your wish ten times; take off the lid and stir clockwise ten times, saying ten times, *Bubbles, work your magick for me, that my wish(es) are granted urgently.*
- Blow the first bubble, and as it floats away, say: *Wish(es) fly free, carrying my hopes from thought to actuality.*
- Continue blowing and wishing (more than one wish if you like), for each wish repeating the second wish chant as you release each bubble, until the bubble jar is empty.
- Scatter seeds in thanks.
- Repeat the spell weekly for four weeks in total for a longer-term wish, if possible on a Wednesday or Thursday afternoon in the same location.

409

WISH BOX MAGICK FOR ONGOING WISHES

You will need:

A wooden or metal box with a lid and key
A red candle
Paper and a red pen
A ball of red thread

Timing:
Sunday evenings, weekly

The Spell

- Light the red candle and in red pen write what you most wish for in the week ahead.
- Fold your wish as small as possible. Burn a length of thread from the ball in the candle flame and then tie three knots around the wish.
- Say, *Wish maker, wish maker, this do I yearn. And a kindness I offer in return. Wish maker, wish maker, let it come true—and I will repay it, I promise you.*
- Put the folded wish into the box, repeating the words; close and lock the box and blow out the candle.
- Repeat weekly, changing the wish whenever necessary and adding to the box.
- When the wish box is full, tie the bundle of wishes with red thread in three knots and then burn them, burying the ashes under a tree or bush.
- Keep the most recent wish in the box.

410

A SHELL WISH

You will need:

An open double shell
Any white small crystal or round white stone
Twine or seaweed

Timing:
Ideally the sea or tidal water near full tide, otherwise any flowing water

The Spell

- Hold the stone in your open cupped hands, blowing on it three times softly, whispering your wish between breaths.
- Put the crystal or stone in the bottom half of the shell and, holding the shell and stone in open cupped hands, blow softly three times over them, repeating the wish again between breaths.
- Tie the two sides of the shell together with the seaweed or twine. Gently set the shell afloat, saying, *May the waters carry you over oceans deep and blue that when the tide does turn, my granted wish may return.*

411

A KNOT WISH TO BRING A LONG-CHERISHED DREAM TO REALITY

You will need:

A red candle
A long blue cord

Timing:

Thursday after dark for nine weeks

The Spell

- Light the candle, saying, *This is my long-cherished dream*—[name dream]—*and week by week, what I seek,* [dream], *comes closer.*
- Tie the first knot loosely and recite the whole chant each time you add a knot: *Knot one renew, my power in two, in courage be within knot three. The power is more; I make knot four. And so I strive within knot five. With fate not fixed, I tie knot six. My strength is leaven, I tie knot seven. I master fate, and so knot eight. The wish is mine within knot nine.*
- Blow out the candle.
- Leave the candle and cord in place.
- Each Thursday, add a new knot, repeating the chant, and on week 9, let the candle burn.
- On Friday morning, undo the knots very fast, saying, *The wish is mine within knot nine. The power is free, so I decree and it shall be.*
- Cast the untied cord into running water or leave it tied on a tree branch.

412

A THIRTEEN-MONTH FULL MOON WISH TO FULFILL A MAJOR DREAM WITHIN THE YEAR

You will need:

Silver bells on a string
A twig or clear crystal point

Timing:

Outdoors on a full moon night or any night around then when the moon is bright. If necessary, do the spell indoors with seven silver candles in a ring and stand in the middle.

The Spell

- Face the moon, standing within the reflected moonlight with the twig in the hand you write with and the bells in the other hand, saying, *Moon light, moon bright, as you do reach your fullness, in thirteen moons or even less, may this my dream be manifest.*
- Ring the bells seven times slowly, repeating the words after each ring, and then make your wish.
- Walk in a counterclockwise circle seven times within the pool of light, circling the twig in clockwise circles, repeating the words seven times. Then, facing the moon, repeat the wish.
- Ring the bells again once, repeating the words.
- Bury the twig or crystal point in the center of the light.
- Do the spell every full moon. Between spells, hang the bells just inside your front door.

413

A BREAD WISH TO BRING A CREATIVE ENTERPRISE INTO BEING

You will need:

A bread mix, or make your own from a standard recipe using fast-rising yeast

Timing:

When you wake

The Spell

- Work in silence, keeping a little dough aside. When you have shaped your loaf, say, *This is my wish,* [name wish], *that creative success I shall see, expressing outwardly, what slumbers still within me.*
- While the dough is rising, draw up your master plan and the minimum time needed, plus possible outlets.
- When the bread has risen, make a symbol of your future venture with the dough and add your initials on top.
- Repeat the words, followed by your master plan, and bake the bread.
- When the bread is ready, eat some while it is warm.
- Afterward, scatter crumbs outdoors, repeating the spell words.
- Come indoors and read your master plan aloud. Do something practical to further the dream.

414

A MAGICK WISH BOTTLE TO CALL NECESSARY RESOURCES AND SUPPORT FOR YOUR BIG DREAM

You will need:

A red candle or oil lamp
A dark glass bottle with a cork or screw-top lid
Salt

Timing:

Late Tuesday evening

The Spell

- Light the candle, holding the open bottle in front of it so that the flame shines through it, saying aloud, *May my wish come true* [say the wish in your mind] *and I may be guided to resources and people new to further this endeavor.*
- Add a pinch of salt to the bottle, saying aloud, *May my wish come true* [repeat the wish silently] *that all obstacles and opposition melt like this candle away and I stay on track for this endeavor.*
- Holding the bottle to your lips, whisper the wish into the bottle.
- Screw on the top.
- Hold the bottle again in front of the flame, repeating the first set of spell words.
- Let the candle burn.
- Keep the magick bottle in a secret place; once a week, hold it and recite your wish in your mind three times.

415

A MONTHLY WISH BOX RITUAL FOR A DREAM THAT REQUIRES STEP-BY-STEP FULFILLMENT

You will need:

A medium-size wood or metal box
A small plain paper notebook with removable pages
A pen kept for wishes
A blue ribbon to tie around the box

Timing:

The first day of each month for twelve months

The Spell

- On the first piece of paper, write your wish on one side, and step 1 that you intend/hope to take in the month ahead on the other. Say, *Month by month, step by step, I will achieve my dreams, hard though it seems.*
- Fold the paper and place it in the box, naming the month and repeating the spell words.
- Close the box and tie it with four loose knots, saying, *The power I tie to multiply, month by month, step by step, until I reach the sky.*

416

A DRAGON FIRE MAGICK SPELL FOR WHEN YOU ARE ALMOST THERE

You will need:

A small red candle in front of you at the top of an imaginary triangle
A small dish of dried tarragon herbs, the dragon's herb, or dried parsley at the left bottom point of the triangle
A dragon's blood incense stick or any spicy incense at the bottom right point.
A dragon model or picture or one crafted from clay in the center

Timing:

Tuesday

The Spell

- Light the candle, saying, *I call upon you, wondrous golden dragon; I kindle your flame to fire and inspire my wish into reality.*
- Light the incense from the candle, saying, *I call upon you, wondrous golden dragon; I kindle your fragrance to carry through the air everywhere my wish to reality.*
- Draw the outline of a dragon in incense smoke around the imagined triangle, saying, *I invoke your shimmering presence, wondrous golden dragon, drawing on your power at this hour to bring my wish to fruition.*
- Let the candle and incense burn, scooping up and scattering the remaining herbs outdoors.
- Set the dragon where you will see it upon waking.

417

BIRDSEED WISHES FOR A DREAM THAT WILL INVOLVE BIG CHANGES

You will need:
A container of birdseed

Timing:
Mornings in which you can feed wild birds

The Spell

- Holding the birdseed container in both hands, face the four directions, starting with north. Turning clockwise, scatter seeds on the ground in each direction, saying for each, *I will be free as wild birds, follow my dreams, Carry my wishes, for change welcome seems, No limitation, no boundaries, no hesitation, I fly on the breeze.*
- When the birdseed is gone, wait until some of the birds fly away and then repeat the words as you turn again in all four directions.
- As you walk away, say, *North, east, south, west, change fulfill my wishes wherever best.*
- Only now whisper your wish and say, *Fly free, return as fulfillment, bringing good change to me.*

418

A SAND OR EARTH RITUAL TO REGAIN YOUR BELIEF IN A DREAM THAT IS SLOW IN COMING

You will need:
Sand or earth close to the ocean or a tidal river or firm earth or sand near water, such as an artificial beach or a lake
A child's spade (optional)
A long stick
A gold-colored coin

Timing:
Just before the tide turns near tidal waters or at a day transition: dawn, noon, or sunset

The Spell

- Write your name, your star sign, and your wish in the sand or earth close to the water with the stick, enclosing the writing in a square.
- Rub out the square, saying, *I accept no limits. I cannot wait, I need fulfillment, do not hesitate. Bring me my wish with tide turn, for world you must learn I have waited too long, and it is wrong just to yearn, please bring fulfillment now, anyway, anyhow.*
- If the water is tidal, let the wish or name wash away. If it is not, use the spade to throw sand or earth into the water, rubbing out the rest, in both cases repeating the words.
- Throw the coin into the water as tribute.

419

A STAMPING SPELL IF PEOPLE LAUGH AT YOUR DREAM

You will need:
A raincoat and rain boots or sturdy shoes

Timing:
A rainy day or just after rain when there are puddles

The Spell

- Find a muddy area and stamp in circles first counterclockwise and then clockwise so that the footsteps blur. Say, *This is my dream, this my wish, this is my plan. I will finish it.*
- Jump in three puddles one after the other, stamping in each, saying, *Laugh all you will, my wish I fulfill, my dreams they are big, I care not a fig, whatever you say, I will have my day.*
- Repeat the cycle of mud and puddles until you feel confident and then show those who doubt you that you can attain your wish.

420

A PICTURE BOARD RITUAL TO FOCUS ON A WISH IF YOU FEEL LIKE GIVING UP

You will need:
A picture board
Images printed from the Internet and cut from magazines showing people fulfilling the dream or places and items connected with it

Timing:
Ongoing

The Spell

- Set the picture board flat. Write your wish and time frame over and over invisibly on the whole board in large letters with the index finger of the hand you write with.
- Add the first picture, saying, *This is my wish manifest in actuality, with courage I shall bring it to reality.*
- Clap your hands after affixing each picture, saying, *I call my wish into being.*
- Continue to add pictures, saying the words and clapping until you have covered half the board.
- Hang the board somewhere warm, such as the kitchen.
- Whenever you doubt your dream, add more pictures, repeating the words and actions until the board is full and your wish begins moving toward actuality.

421

STAR MAGICK FOR A LUCKY BREAK IN THE PERFORMING ARTS OR MEDIA

You will need:
A silver charm or silver jewelry

Timing:
As the stars are coming out

The Spell

- Focus on the first star to appear in the sky, or if you see a number of stars, pick one that seems especially bright.
- Hold the charm up to the stars with the hand you do not write with and point the other hand toward the star.
- Say three times aloud, *Star light, star bright, first star I see tonight, I wish I may, I wish I might, fulfill the wish I make tonight*.
- Enclose the charm in your hands and then open them and, holding the charm close to your mouth, silently wish for the lucky break you need.
- Carry the charm or wear the jewelry to any auditions, screen tests, or interviews.

422

MODERN STAR MAGICK TO STAND OUT FROM THE CROWD IF THE COMPETITION IS FIERCE

You will need:
Small glittery foil stars in a bowl

Timing:
When the sky is full of stars

The Spell

- Hold the bowl of stars and, looking at them, say, *When you wish upon a star, makes no difference who you are, when you wish upon a star, your dreams will find you.*
- Make your wish continuously as you turn around clockwise faster and faster, holding the bowl, until you have to steady yourself and the stars seem to rush toward you.
- Sit on the ground and look up at the stars, saying, *My wish will come true. I too will become a star.*
- Whenever you see an opportunity, scatter some of your empowered stars on any paperwork (print out mail or write down offers made by phone), repeating all the spell words.

423

A POLESTAR OR SOUTHERN CROSS RITUAL FOR GETTING TO THE TOP, ESPECIALLY IN THE CREATIVE WORLD

You will need:

Ideally, a place where there is a tree through whose branches you can look up and see the polestar or the Southern Cross or somewhere you can see it clearly above you

Timing:

Whenever the polestar or Southern Cross is visible

The Spell

- Look upward at the polestar through the tree or overhead, saying, *Guiding star, as you climb the shining sky, carry my dream wish so high, I will not doubt any more but know my talents will soar and make me shine like you my whole life through.*
- Ask for any specific ways you wish to attain success and inspiration and then say, *Dreams are many, days are few, and so my wish I give to you that you will make me shimmering too.*
- When you are ready, go home and create as you never have before.

424

A METEORITE RITUAL TO ATTRACT A LIFE-CHANGING OPPORTUNITY TO ATTAIN FAME AND FORTUNE

You will need:

A small meteorite obtained from a crystal store or online
A bright red candle
A drawstring bag
Parsley, basil, tarragon, or a spice

Timing:

A starlit sky; especially lucky if a meteor shower or shooting stars are predicted

The Spell

- Holding the meteorite in the hand you write with, focus on the brightest patch of stars.
- Make your wish and then say three times: *Shower me with your fiery power and make my wish come true, that I may one day blaze as glorious as you.*
- Go indoors and light the red candle; holding the meteorite in the opposite hand, repeat the words three times more as you pass it three times clockwise around the flame.
- Leave the meteorite with the candle until the candle has burned.
- Put the meteorite in the bag, adding a little herb or spice.
- Carry the meteorite as a lucky charm and say the spell words whenever you see an opening for you.

425

WISHING POWDER MAGICK IF YOU WANT TO GET TO THE TOP IN A BIG ORGANIZATION BUT HAVE BEEN OVERLOOKED

You will need:

Dried powdered cinnamon, allspice, and ginger
Lavender, rose, or lemongrass fragrance oil
A bowl and wooden spoon
A paper bag

Timing:
The evening before your workweek

The Spell

- Add a small quantity of all the spices to the bowl, saying for each, *Success I seek within this company, a rise in fortunes to fulfill me, better terms, lots more money, so every day will be more sunny.*
- Add a drop or two of oil to bind the mix.
- As you mix clockwise, repeat the words more rapidly as you stir faster until you can mix and speak no faster.
- With a final strong movement down with the spoon in the center of the bowl, say, *Success is mine.*
- Place the mix in the paper bag.
- Go early to work and sprinkle the mix near the front entrance, repeating all the spell words in your mind.
- On the way home, scatter any remaining mix outside the building.

426

TO SUCCEED IN A TALENT CONTEST OR REALITY SHOW

You will need:

A prerecorded episode of a similar show
Gold glitter

Timing:
Before applying and again before the audition

The Spell

- Turn on the show and watch until you see an act similar to yours or a person resembling you in some way.
- Turn the volume right down and spin around nine times clockwise faster and faster, repeating, *I am a star, and this will be my lucky break.*
- Sing at the top of your voice, dance, or sell yourself in an interview until the silent figure on screen takes a bow or no longer is featured.
- Turn around nine times more counterclockwise and then state your precise wish and add, *And so I will never stop until I reach the very top.*

427

TO GAIN ENTRY TO A PRESTIGIOUS MUSIC SCHOOL, STAGE SCHOOL, OR CREATIVE ARTS COLLEGE

You will need:
A gold candle
White paper and a gold or yellow pen

Timing:
Sundays when the sun is at its height

The Spell

- Write your talent and where and when you wish to study all over the candle invisibly with your index finger. Then write invisibly on top of that, MAY THE RIGHT DOORS OPEN TO ME AND ALL SEE MY POTENTIAL THROUGH MY TALENTS.
- Light the candle and say, *May the right doors open to me and all see my potential through my talents, for I wish to study at* [name the school or college]. *It is meant.*
- On the paper, write the name of the establishment to which you wish to gain entry, any scholarships, and the time frame, adding, *May the right doors open for me swiftly that I may gain entry and so achieve my potential through my talents.*
- Tear a corner off the paper, burn it in the candle, and cut the rest into pieces, burying it under a thriving plant to release the power and keep it growing.

428

ANOTHER STAR RITUAL TO MAKE SERIOUS MONEY FROM A HIGH-PROFILE CAREER

You will need:
A starry night
Three small pieces of jewelry, if possible real gold or gold-plated; if not, a shiny gold substitute
A sparkly purse

Timing:
As the stars come out (and the moon if possible)

The Spell

- Hold the gold in the open hand that you write with and the purse in the other hand upward to the stars, saying, *Star of fortune, shine on me, famous I would wish to be. Star like you, I would shine, star of fortune, make fortune mine.*
- Place the gold in the sparkly purse and, before closing it, whisper into it, *I am a star and will achieve fame and fortune. Hold my power.*
- Toss and catch the purse seven times, repeating all the spell words seven times, getting softer and slower.
- Cradle the purse and say, *Make me a star. I will go far.*
- Whenever you further your ambitions, take the purse and hold it, saying in your mind over and over, *Make me a star. I have come far.*

429

TO WIN A PLACE IN A TOP SPORTING TEAM OR TRAINING OPPORTUNITY OVERSEAS

You will need:

A video of yourself playing sports
A video of a world-famous player

Timing:

When a major chance appears and you will be on trial

The Spell

- Play a short extract of the film of the world champion, but chanting and cheering yourself as she or he wins, saying, *Come on,* [substituting your name for his or hers] *over and over.*
- Play a longer extract of yourself, continuing the chant, and when it ends, clap ten times fast, saying, *I am a champion, I take all on and win. My new life begins.*
- Before the trial, clap or stamp ten times and repeat the second set of words in your mind.

430

TO BECOME AN ACKNOWLEDGED EXPERT IN TRADITIONAL ARTS, CRAFTS, OR A SPECIALITY AREA

You will need:

A brown candle
Small symbols of your chosen expertise, whether charms or actual items used, in a small basket

Timing:

Saturday

The Spell

- Light the candle, blow softly once into the flame, and say, *Weave and wind the older ways, weave and bind the golden days, that I become a treasury of wisdom, knowledge, expertise.*
- Close your eyes, say the words, and select one item from the basket to be your special talisman.
- Set this item down and move your hands, one on either side, so that you almost touch it, then move your hands apart, still saying the words, until as you move your hands nearer each time and less far apart, you end up holding it firmly.
- Take this item along hidden in a bag to shows, exhibitions, and festivals; when selling your work, touch the bag and repeat the words.

431

A CANDLE CIRCLE WITH FRIENDS TO SEND HEALING WISHES TO SOMEONE IN DISTRESS

You will need:

A candle in an open box or basket for each person
A central candle

Timing:

After dark

The Spell

- Light the central candle saying, *We create this circle of light that we might send relief and healing to* [name person or people suffering and the circumstances].
- Each person takes a candle, lighting it from the central candle, before taking his or her place in the circle, saying, *We create this circle of light that we might send love to* [name person or people] *in their time of distress.*
- Standing around the circle, each person in turn clockwise blows softly into his or her candle flame, saying, *Blessings,* [naming a blessing they want to send].
- Each blows softly in his or her flame once more, saying, *Wishes,* [naming a wish for the future for the person/people]. Then each person then blows out his or her candle in turn clockwise, saying, *Light.*
- In the darkness, one person says, *May there be light in the darkness, hope in despair, and may peace come.*
- Let the central candle burn and share food, talk, or sing.

432

A COLLECTIVE FIRE CEREMONY TO GENERATE POWER TO FIGHT AN INJUSTICE OR UNWELCOME DEVELOPMENT FACING YOU ALL OR THE LOCAL AREA

You will need:

A bonfire or fire dish
Granular incense in packets, one for each person
A tiny bowl of salt for each person

Timing:

Around the full moon

The Spell

- Each person circles the fire in a continuing ring of people, casting incense in the fire for each circuit, chanting collectively over and over, *Fire grow, fire glow. It shall be so by the power of the fire.*
- When the incense is gone, each person in turn throws salt in the fire three times, saying, *Salt sparkle, fire crackle, carry this wish ever higher that we will gain our desire:* [name your wish concerning the issue].
- Circle the fire in a continuous circle, clapping and stamping faster and faster, until one person calls out, *The wish is free, the power you see, it shall be so as we desire, by the blazing power of fire.*
- Let the fire burn, enjoying supper and discussing plans.

433

A COLLECTIVE INCENSE WISH RITE FOR RAISING MONEY FOR A LARGE-SCALE EMERGENCY AT HOME OR OVERSEAS

You will need:

A long incense stick for each person present
A central candle or a small fire to light the incense

Timing:

When it is really dark; outdoors for safety

The Spell

- Light the central candle, naming the purpose of the rite and those who need aid, saying, *May those in need swiftly receive that they can succeed rebuilding their lives.*
- Each person lights his or her incense and begins to whirl it fast. If it is swirled fast enough, it makes light trails against the dark sky.
- When all the incense is alight, everyone chants faster, swirling the incense faster, saying continuously, *Send aid this night that all may be right.*
- When everyone can chant no faster, plunge the incense sticks one after the other into a large bucket of soil, lighted end down, saying one after the other, *Send aid.*
- Go indoors and plan a fund-raising event.
- If you cannot get the light trails effect (it will come with practice), incense smoke is equally powerful.

434

FIRE OFFERINGS TO BRING BLESSINGS AND RELIEF TO OTHERS SICK OR IN NEED (OR YOURSELF)

You will need:

A selection of flower petals for love, harmony, and happiness; nuts for prosperity and career; seeds for prosperity, health, and travel; and fruits for fertility, creativity, and family
Salt
An offerings dish
A green candle
A Buddha, Kwan Yin, angel, fairy, god or goddess, or Mother Mary statue

Timing:

Weekly, after dark

The Spell

- Light the candle in front of the statue and say, *May the light of* [name statue or say *the benign light of the universe*] *grant these blessings to* [recipient(s)].
- Place nine small offerings, the same or mixed, in the dish and hold it toward the candle, saying, *I make this offering in gratitude for blessings soon to be received.*
- Leave the offerings in front of the candle and statue.
- Blow out the candle, sending light to where it is needed, and after a week scatter the offerings outdoors and repeat for the same person or people or for someone else.

435

A COLLECTIVE WATER RITUAL TO LAUNCH CREATIVE VENTURES OR POSITIVE LIFE CHANGES

You will need:

A small square piece of wood for everyone present
A small beeswax or organic candle for everyone
Flowers in bright colors for everyone
Small fruits

Timing:

Any seasonal change point or close to the full moon

The Spell

- Go to a lake, river, a pool, or the sea, standing close to the waterline.
- Each person holds his or her wooden raft, in turn saying, *Carry for me,* and silently naming his or her wishes, unless it is a joint venture, in which case devise the words in advance and speak them aloud in turn.
- Each person lights a candle, setting it on the raft, naming the wish again silently unless it is a joint wish.
- Add a flower and fruit to each boat and on a prearranged signal launch the boats gently at the same time, saying together softly, *Mother Sea, carry for me this wish swiftly and powerfully to return successfully. So shall it be.*

436

COLLECTIVE CANDLE WEB WISHES SENT FROM DIFFERENT PLACES TO STRENGTHEN A DISASTER AREA OR DANGER ZONE OR WHERE THERE IS FAMINE, FLOOD, OR FIRE

You will need:

A pure white candle for each person, wherever those people are

Timing:

At 10 p.m. Wednesday wherever you are

The Spell

- At a prearranged time, allowing for time zone differences and using a prearranged format, each participant lights his or her candle near a window.
- Looking through the candle flame into the darkness, each person says three times softly, *The web of light illumines the world, and so we add our blessings that* [name disaster or danger] *may be relieved, all conflict cease, and there be peace. May peace prevail on earth.*
- Let the candle burn and sit quietly for fifteen minutes, allowing blessings to flow through your mind and then letting your thoughts roam free.
- Blow out the candle and send the light to where it is needed.
- Repeat weekly if necessary.

437

A CRESCENT MOON CANDLE WISH PARTY

You will need:

Two silver candles for each person present
A large silver central candle
An empty pot
A large pot of soil in the center
Slips of paper and a blue pen for each person

Timing:

When the crescent moon can be seen in the sky

The Spell

- All the people sit in a circle, surrounding their candles with coins, jewelry, and glittery items.
- On the first candle each traces invisibly his or her zodiac sign (as a glyph if you know it) and lights the candle, saying, *Crescent moon, as you do grow, bring the dream I wish for so, within three moons* [or another time frame].
- Each then lights his or her second candle, repeats the words, and on a slip of paper writes the wish anonymously, putting it in the empty pot.
- Each person then chooses a wish from the pot by feel to read aloud and then singes it in the candle and drops it into the pot of soil.
- When this is done, all the people recite their own wishes in their minds nine times.
- On a prearranged signal, the candles are blown out, except for the central one, which is left burning for the rest of the evening.

438

A FAMILY MAGICK WISH TREE

You will need:

A tall uprooted branch with several smaller branches secured in the ground
Biodegradable paper slips with a hole and colored pens
String

Timing:

Whenever the family has wishes or needs or you need to send healing to an absent or estranged family member.

The Spell

- Starting with the youngest member of the family, each draws an image or writes a wish on a slip of paper, closes his or her eyes, and recites it silently three times.
- The wishes are mixed up facedown, and each person takes one and does not read it but adds a wish for the whole family on the other side of the paper, hanging that wish on the tree, saying, *Winds of the earth, winds of the sky, carry our wishes, so away they may fly.*
- The oldest person writes on a slip, *May* [family member or friend who is absent or estranged] *know the love and strength of the family.*
- Let the papers blow away or fade, adding more at any time.

439

A DYING LEAF RITE TO REMOVE SORROW, ILLNESS, OR MISFORTUNE FROM YOUR HOME, LOVED ONES, OR WORKPLACE

You will need:

A branch from a tree or a dying bush that has fallen, with leaves that are dying that you can secure in the ground
A small thriving green plant
A large empty pot

Timing:
Saturday at sunset

The Spell

- Stand facing the sunset and begin one by one to pluck the leaves, naming for each a sorrow you wish to lose and the people or person most concerned, adding, *May this sorrow/sickness/misfortune fade with the dying of the leaves.*
- Drop each in the pot saying, *It is gone, it is done, peace comes.*
- Continue until you have mentioned every issue and then plant the new greenery nearby, saying, *From old comes new, new life, new hope, fresh beginnings.*
- Tip away the pot of dying leaves in an open space.

440

A TREE RITUAL WITH A FRIEND, PARTNER, OR FAMILY MEMBER

You will need:

Two thick environmentally friendly cords or ropes long enough to wrap around a tree

Timing:
Any bright morning

The Spell

- Stand on either side of the tree and begin winding the ropes clockwise around the tree so that they overlap, looping them together in a loose knot on the trunk.
- Leave sufficient length so that you can each move away from the tree and hold your rope taut.
- As you wind, say, *Empowering tree, rise into me, knot binding, knot finding, knot winding. Powerful we'll be, success we'll see.*
- Very quickly, slip the knot and unloop the cords counterclockwise, yelling, *The power is free, the power's in me, and so you see, my/our wish* [your wish at the same time whether a joint wish such as healing an absent person or preserving a threatened area of land or wildlife habitat or separate personal wishes] *shall be.*
- Let go of the ropes so that they fall on the ground, shouting, *As we count three, two, one, the wish is won.*
- Knot the wish cords side by side on the tree.

441

FIRE FEY WISHES FOR A DESIRED OPPORTUNITY OR OFFER WHEN THE ODDS ARE STACKED AGAINST YOU

You will need:

An area lit by faery lights where the colors constantly change
Alternatively, two torches, one for each hand
Gold glitter

Timing:
Friday after dark

The Spell

- Stand in darkness, saying, *I do not welcome shadows of obscurity. Fire feys come alive that I will thrive and achieve the nearly impossible.*
- Switch on the lights or torches, swirling around clockwise so that you are bathed in light, or whirl the torches around your head and shoulders, saying, *I welcome the chance to shine. Success be mine to achieve the nearly impossible.*
- Turn the lights off or switch off and put down the torches, scattering glitter and turning counterclockwise on the spot, saying, *Though others may obscure my light, yet will I win the fight; fire feys, grant my nearly impossible dream.*
- Switch on the lights or torch, turning fast near the faery lights, or swirl your torches faster and faster, saying, *I am pure light and fire, fire feys, thank you for fulfilling my desire.*

442

WATER SPRITES WISHING WELL MAGICK FOR HEALING OR FERTILITY WHEN EFFORTS SEEM IN VAIN

You will need:

A wishing well
Three coins

Timing:
Early morning on the first of the month

The Spell

- Throw the first coin down the well, saying, *You water sprites who guard this well, you are my last hope, truth to tell; grant this day* [say what you need and for whom if not yourself] *or when it's right that these dark times may turn to light.*
- Cast the second coin into the well, repeating the words.
- Throw the third coin down into the water and say the same words.
- In return, offer help to a water project, a dolphin charity, or clean water projects overseas or support for local wetlands.
- If possible, return on the first day of each month until all is resolved.

443

A FAERY DUST WISH

You will need:

A tiny bottle of faery dust, available from New Age stores or online, or silver glitter

A circle of trees or bushes or a faery ring, a natural circle of toadstools or mushrooms

Paper, a red pen and glue

Timing:

Early morning

The Spell

- Holding the tube of faery dust or glitter in the hand you write with, walk around the edge of the circle (inside) nine times clockwise, saying your wish nine times in your mind.
- In the center, call your wish once as you scatter a little faery dust.
- Thank the nature spirits and walk out of the circle. Do not look back.
- When you get home, write your wish in waterproof red pen across a piece of paper, spread glue thinly, and sprinkle the rest of the faery dust or glitter on it.
- Pin it blank side up behind a cupboard.

444

A RAINBOW FAERY RITUAL FOR GETTING BACK ON THE RIGHT PATH AFTER SOMEONE OR SOMETHING HAS WRECKED YOUR DREAMS

You will need:

A small box filled with gold stars (the sticky kind)

Children's marker pens or paints

A piece of white paper

Colored chalks (optional)

Timing:

When you see a rainbow through the window of your home

The Spell

- Go outdoors and, with a stick in the earth, small stones or leaves on grass, or chalk on a paved area, make a curved rainbow shape eighteen footsteps long.
- Stand at the beginning of the rainbow and walk it (on a paved area, draw one in colored chalks), saying continuously, *Rainbow faeries, rainbow faeries, on your path I wend, let me find the treasure at the rainbow's end.*
- Make your wish. When the rainbow fades, say, *So I reclaim my dreams.*
- Indoors, paint a rainbow and stick gold stars all over it, repeating the words and the wish in your mind as you work.
- Keep your picture where only you can see it. Whenever things get hard, trace your hand over the painted rainbow, repeating the words, and add more stars.

445

ANOTHER RAINBOW FAERY RITUAL FOR ATTAINING YOUR WILDEST DREAMS

You will need:
Four silver and three gold coins

Timing:
When you see a rainbow

The Spell

- Whenever you see a rainbow, go outdoors and say, *Rainbow magick, bring to me, what it is that now I see.*
- Say your wish and picture its fulfillment.
- Walk three times in circles faster and faster, once clockwise and once counterclockwise and then once clockwise again, saying continuously, *By the treasure in the crock of gold, so my wildest dreams unfold, spirits of the rainbow, make it so.*
- Open your arms toward the rainbow, saying, *I am the rainbow, and my wishes will come true, spirits of the rainbow, this I ask of you.*
- When the rainbow fades, bury the coins, saying, *Spirits of the rainbow, bring me wonders untold, and in return I offer you tributes of silver and gold.*

446

BRINGING WISHES INTO ACTUALITY BY USING DANDELION OR BUTTERFLY FAERY ENERGY

You will need:
A dandelion clock with spores or butterflies

Timing:
Wednesday

The Spell

- Pick a dandelion and blow softly three times so that you do not dislodge any spores.
- Make your wish after each breath.
- Turn three times clockwise, three times counterclockwise, and three times clockwise again, saying nine times, *Dandelion faery, flying high, carry my wishes to the sky.*
- Blow harder as the spores fly away, repeating the words after each breath.
- When all are flown, whisper, *Dandelion faery, I give you my wishes in hope and in trust and ask you return with my dreams fulfilled.*
- Count the number of times you blow the spores as an indication of days, weeks, or months, depending on the nature of the wishes, before fulfillment.
- If there are no dandelion spores nearby, visit a butterfly farm, choosing a settled butterfly each time you make a wish.
- Blow softly three times toward each butterfly, whispering the wish three times for each butterfly as they fly away.
- When all have flown, say, *Butterfly faeries, carry my wishes and return with my dreams fulfilled.*

447

A GALADRIEL ELVEN QUEEN RITUAL FOR THAT SPECIAL DREAM

You will need:

A picture of Galadriel from Tolkien's *Lord of the Rings* or a small faery or elf statue

Small silver bells on a string

Timing:

A clear day

The Spell

- Stand near a tree with a hollow in it and ring the bells seven times, saying, *Seven by seven, seven by seven, I call the elven queen. Wise Galadriel, I feel you close though you are not seen.*
- Ring the bell seven times more, whispering your wish seven times into the hollow of the tree seven times, repeating the spell words.
- Pick wild flowers or greenery to take home. If this is not permitted, buy flowers, keeping them near the picture or statue.
- Ring the bells, saying the words every evening for the next six days.

448

A CLIODNA, SEA GODDESS OF THE GOLDEN HAIR, WISH IF YOUR LOVE SEEMS UNATTAINABLE OR HAS GONE AWAY

You will need:

Two separate halves of a shell, two matching white stones, or two tiny identical aquamarines

A body of water, whether sea, lake, or wide river

Timing:

Just before sunset

The Spell

- Standing on the shore, name your lost or unattainable love as you hold half of the shell in each hand.
- Bring them together in your open cupped hands, saying nine times, *Cliodna of the golden hair, may the waters bring* [name] *and me together when it's right to be. I ask this of you, for you lost your love and called him over the sea.*
- With one shell or stone in each hand, cast them at the same time on the ninth wave as it moves into shore. Repeat the words nine times more.
- Collect the stones or shells and take them home, saying the words whenever you hold them.

449

A FAERY RING WISH SPELL FOR REKINDLING AN ABANDONED DREAM OR WHAT HAS BEEN LOST

You will need:

Ideally, a circle of mushroom or toadstools
If not, create a circle of sticks or stones large enough to walk inside
Three shiny crystals or beads

Timing:

Before sunset, after which you should not walk in faery rings

The Spell

- Walk (or run) three times counterclockwise around the faery ring, then three times clockwise, and then three times counterclockwise again.
- Toss three shiny crystals or gold or silver earrings into the center after completing the circuits, making your wish.
- Say, *Around and around and around the ring, faery magick will it bring, faery folk my wish can't wait, for I know it's not too late. I ask you my lost dream to bring, and so I make my offering.*
- Leave the crystals or beads in the center and walk just once clockwise around the circle, reciting the words three times.

450

A FAERY GODMOTHER MAGICK SPELL TO TURN MAJOR LOSS INTO MAJOR GAIN

You will need:

A pointed stick or crystal as your wand
A pumpkin
A sharp knife
A dish and a bowl

Timing:

Between 11 p.m. and midnight

The Spell

- Tap the pumpkin seven times with the crystal or stick, saying, *Faery godmother, bring to me, no golden coach with horses three, but turn my loss into gain, that I may know success again.*
- Cut the top off the pumpkin, scooping out the flesh and seeds as though making a jack-o'-lantern.
- Keep the flesh for cooking and put the seeds in a dish.
- Cut seven large holes around the pumpkin and light a candle inside.
- Gently revolve the pumpkin clockwise, reciting the days of the week, starting with the present one, then tap the pumpkin seven times again, saying, *Faery godmother, turn my fate, week by week, to what I seek, not a prince or fancy ball, but I ask you, restore all.*
- Blow out the candle, bury the pumpkin seeds, and cook the pumpkin flesh.
- Each night, tap the pumpkin, turning it seven times and repeating all the words.
- Continue until the pumpkin loses its freshness.

CHAPTER 10

MAGICK FOR ALL SEASONS AND CELEBRATIONS

The spells in this chapter include blessings for special occasions and family harmony spells for children; spells for rites of passage; and spells for overcoming estrangements, ending bad relationships, and reuniting family members.

451

TO BRING AND KEEP HAPPINESS AND HARMONY AMONG THE FAMILY

You will need:

Photographs of family members, including those not living at home, in a circle, yourself in the center
A circle of small white round stones, small crystals, glass nuggets, or shells to enclose the photos
A lavender, rose, lilac, or orange incense stick

Timing:
The beginning of a week or month

The Spell

- Hold each photograph in turn including your own, naming each, saying, *We are the circle of unity, may we always live in harmony.*
- Light the incense stick and, using it like a smoke pen, make clockwise circles above the photos.
- Above each picture make a smoke knot, repeating the words softly.
- Let the incense burn away.
- Leave the photographs with the circle around them.
- Redraw the smoke web and say the words before a family gathering.

452

A BLESSING FOR A SPECIAL MEAL

You will need:

A small silver- or gold-colored bell
A dish of still mineral water
A white candle in the middle of the dining table

Timing:
After setting the table for a meal

The Spell

- Ring the bell three times in each of the four corners of the table, saying at each corner, *Bless all who gather here, bring laughter and good cheer. May disharmony remain outside, and only love and peace abide.*
- Sprinkle three drops of water at each of the corners, repeating the spell words.
- As the meal begins, light the white candle and say the spell words in your mind, unless you think those gathered would appreciate hearing them as a blessing.

453

A THREE-CANDLE BLESSING BEFORE A LARGER GATHERING IF YOU KNOW SOME CHALLENGING PEOPLE ARE COMING

You will need:

Three large white candles set in a triangle in the center of the table

A small ornamental bowl of sugar

Timing:

Before people arrive

The Spell

- Light the candles clockwise, saying for each one, *Shine light, shine bright on all my kin, let only peace enter within. May the gathered company bring warmth and care, that laughter and happiness all will share.*
- Dissolve five teaspoons of sugar under a flowing warm water faucet, saying five times, *May each of you in kinship meet, mix and blend as sugar sweet. May conversation easily flow, and each to all hospitality show.*
- Set the bowl of sugar near the candles and if any is left after the meal, dissolve the remaining sugar under warm water afterwards.
- Let the candles burn through.

454

TO MAKE NEW FAMILY MEMBERS, SUCH AS NEW PARTNERS AND THEIR CHILDREN OR IN-LAWS, WELCOME

You will need:

A circle of small white candles, one for every member of the existing family and in the center a single white candle to represent the new family members

A small potted plant for each family member old and new and, for each child, a tiny pack of shiny wrapped candies or a small toy

Timing:

Before the arrival of new family members

The Spell

- Light first the new family members' candles, naming each one and then saying, *You are welcome within the unity of the family.*
- Now name each of the existing family members and light their candles from the central candle clockwise, saying afterwards, *May the new light add to the brightness of our family, that you will spread new unity.*
- When the family arrives, say to each one, old and new, *You are welcome.*
- Give each of them their plant or gift when they leave.
- Blow out the circle of candles counterclockwise and then the central one, saying afterwards, *Thank you for this unity. May our family grow harmoniously.*
- Relight the candles around the home the following evening.

455

FOR HARMONIOUS FAMILIES, IF THERE IS TENSION RESULTING FROM DIVORCE OR REMARRIAGE AND NEW FAMILY ADDITIONS

You will need:

A sagebrush or cedar smudge stick or a tree fragrance incense stick

Small flowering plants in pots of the same kind, arranged in a square outdoors, one plant for each existing family member, ex-spouses and ex-grandparents, and new adults and children or in-laws

An area of the garden or a very large planter, filled with earth

Timing:

Daytime, during the waxing moon, when it appears faintly in the sky

The Spell

- Light the smudge or incense stick and, following the square created by the plants, draw four clockwise smoke squares above the plants, saying four times, *This is the security of the family, parts may break away but the unity will stay. Let all dissension melt away, for we are still one family, come what may.*
- Let the incense or smudge stick burn away.
- Plant the flowers as close together as practical, saying, *There need be no differences if we can grow together, for families may change but love goes on forever.*
- Repeat the spell words whenever you water or prune the plants.

456

HOSPITALITY MAGICK TO ENCOURAGE FAMILY MEMBERS TO SHARE FAMILY LIFE IF THEY ARE INDIFFERENT OR TOO BUSY TO COMMUNICATE

You will need:

A dried bay leaf for each family member or any dried savory leaf used in cooking

A sharp knife

Timing:

While you are cooking

The Spell

- On each leaf, scratch the initial of the first name of each family member, including those who rarely communicate.
- As you do so, say, *Come into my life once more,* [name], *I have an open door. I offer hospitality and request the pleasure of your company, that and nothing more.*
- When you have etched all the names; add the leaves, one by one, to a casserole, stew, or vegetables. Stir them nine times in both directions, and let the mixture cook.
- When you eat the meal, whether alone or with immediate family, repeat the spell words in your mind.
- If you do not want to cook, burn the bay leaves, one by one, repeating the spell words for each one.
- Invite *all* the family and include bay leaves and the bay spell while cooking.

457

TELEPHONE, TABLET, OR COMPUTER MAGICK FOR LOVING COMMUNICATIONS WITH FRIENDS, PARTNER, OR FAMILY WHO ARE FAR AWAY

You will need:
A pendant, a chain necklace, or a bracelet with a clasp
Sugar
A glass of hot water

Timing:
Wednesday, before you are due to communicate by phone, tablet, or computer

The Spell

- Hold the jewelry with the clasp unfastened and say, *Though we are far,* [name person or people you will be speaking to], *yet can we join in love across the miles. For smiles can travel and nothing mar this sweet communication.*
- Put on the jewelry and fasten the clasp, saying the spell words again.
- Stir five teaspoons of sugar in the water, stirring five times clockwise and saying, *Words be sweet, words of care, for we are joined in love anywhere and in my spirit I am there with you.*
- Place the water next to the phone, tablet, or computer, and call, email, or use a VoIP program, touching the jewelry if words seem stilted or won't come.
- Afterwards, pour the water away under running water, and say, *Follow the rivers to the sea, I send love 'til you come home to me,* [name].

458

TO REUNITE FAMILY DIVIDED BY A POINTLESS QUARREL, WHEN EVERYONE IS TOO STUBBORN TO MAKE UP

You will need:
A large ball of green or pink children's modeling clay

Timing:
Friday, just before sunset

The Spell

- Make and name one small round ball for everyone involved, with larger ones for the people most unwilling to compromise, saying for each, *May words be softer, actions kinder, let not the sun go down in anger. But let us be reunited in love again.*
- Make a large round piece of clay for the united family, add your ball to it, and smooth it in, saying, *So shall all be mended and dissension ended.*
- Add each ball, in turn, to the family one, naming the person and saying for each the second set of spell words.
- Once the smaller balls have been rolled into the larger one, bury the family ball under a fragrant bush, saying, *Disharmony to unity, so shall it be.*
- Invite everyone to a fun event, forbidding anyone from bringing up the subject of the quarrel.

459

CREATING A TOGETHERNESS CAKE

You will need:

A mixing bowl and spoon
Ingredients for a large cake or a cake mix
Cake icing (optional)A tub of sugar hearts or flowers

Timing:

Before a meal when family or close friends will be present

The Spell

- Mix the cake ingredients clockwise, saying continuously, *Love cannot be measured but kinship/friendship must be treasured. Within this mix, I do fix, days of joy and pleasure, and memories to treasure.*
- Name nine happy family/friend memories as you pour the batter into the baking tin, adding as you put it in the oven, *There shall be many more, good times by the score. I bind this wish within this dish as I do make my togetherness cake to share.*
- Ice the cake, if you wish, and add a sugar heart or flower for each family member, and then nine more, making nine wishes for future happiness.
- Share the cake and get out old photo albums, recalling memories and making new plans.

460

FOR HAPPY MEALTIMES, WHETHER FOR ONE OR A FAMILY, IF YOU ARE ON A BUDGET OR RUNNING SHORT AT THE END OF THE MONTH

You will need:

Two matching green candles

Timing:

Any day, before preparing a meal

The Spell

- Light one of the candles in the kitchen, and pass your hands an inch or so above the food being prepared six times. Circle the right hand clockwise and the left counterclockwise at the same time.
- Say softly six times, *I/We kindle this flame in thanks, I/we have enough for my/our needs this day. For hard though times may seem, love is here to stay.*
- Before setting the table, carry the candle to the center of the table, repeating the spell words six times as you pass your hands six times over the table and the candle.
- When the food is on the table, light the second candle from the first, so they are side by side on the table, saying in your mind, *Love gives and love receives, blessings by the score. Harmony, tranquillity, what need I/we anything more?*

461

TO HELP A CHILD OR A TEENAGER MAKE GOOD FRIENDS AND REMOVE OR IGNORE BAD INFLUENCES WHO ARE CAUSING PROBLEMS

You will need:

Two bright-red and two white candles, set alternately in a square around the photograph
A box of pins
A magnet
A photograph of your child having a good time

Timing:

Wednesday, after dark

The Spell

- Light the red candles, saying for each one, *Take away the attraction of negative influences from my child's life*—[name child and negative influences]—*and help my child to see them in their true light.*
- Light the two white candles, saying for each one, *Draw to my child good friends and good influences, that he may value them and see them in their true light.*
- Scatter half the pins over the picture and collect them on the magnet, discarding them, saying the spell words you uttered for the red candles.
- Scatter the other half over the picture, collect them on the magnet, and put them in a box in natural light, repeating the spell words you uttered for the white candles.
- Extinguish the red candles, but leave the white ones burning.

462

POWER ANIMAL PROTECTION FOR OLDER CHILDREN AND TEENAGERS WITH PROBLEMS AT SCHOOL OR AT HOME

You will need:

A small model, crystal animal, or silver charm appropriate to the problem: a dolphin for learning or attention-span difficulties, a bear if the child is at boarding school or has issues with visits by an estranged parent, a bird if the child is sick or physically limited, a lion or tiger to resist bullying, an owl for study and examinations, a wolf for a school phobia or eating problems, a butterfly for popularity (or use your own ideas)

Timing:

Night and morning

The Spell

- Ask the child to hold the animal in her closed hands, picturing the animal conferring strength or protection.
- Choose a single word to activate the animal's power, repeating it aloud nine times while the child shakes the animal nine times in her closed hands.
- Last thing at night and first thing in the morning, ask the child to hold the animal, shaking it and repeating the chosen word nine times.
- If possible, put a silver animal charm on a chain for the child to touch at times of crisis. If not, ask the child to say the word nine times in her mind for instant power.

463

ASKING MURIEL, ANGEL OF DREAMS, TO BANISH A CHILD'S NIGHTMARES OR FEARS OF THE DARK

You will need:

A small crystal angel, an iridescent opalite, a moonstone, an amethyst, or a rose quartz symbolizing Muriel, the angel of dreams

A softly colored nightlight or safe rainbow-colored fiber-optic lamp

Timing:

At bedtime

The Spell

- The first time you show the angel to the child, hold Muriel in front of the light source on a bedside table, telling your child, *This is Muriel, angel of beautiful dreams.*
- Explain that Muriel has a magick carpet and if the child wakes up from a bad dream or is scared of the dark, to look up, call out to Muriel, and say, *Muriel, take me on your magick carpet* to see *your angel friends.*
- Hold the angel with your hands around the child's. Into it, put your blessings and protection.
- Set Muriel on a high shelf with the light behind her.
- Every night at bedtime, take her down for the child to hold and to say, *Muriel take me on your magick carpet to see your angel friends.*
- Again, hold the angel while the child does, sending your blessings for the night ahead.

464

FAIRY MAGICK FOR HAPPY, PEACEFUL BEDTIMES, IF A CHILD FINDS IT HARD TO SETTLE AFTER THE DAY

You will need:

Five small candles (pink, green, blue, yellow, and purple), each enclosed in a glass container

Timing:

Five nights before bedtime, when you read the child a bedtime story

The Spell

- Light all five candles and turn off the lights.
- Tell a story about the fairy of the pink candle. Then, one by one, blow out the other candles, allowing the child to make a wish for each.
- Carry the pink candle to the bedroom and blow it out, telling the child to shut his eyes and follow the pink fairy to her magical place with her rainbow sisters.
- Each night, tell a story about a different candle fairy after relighting all the candles. Afterwards, blow them out until they will light no more.
- Repeat the same words and actions.
- On day 6, buy a small fairy statue.
- Put the statue in the child's bedroom and say that if he closes his eyes, the fairy will take him on an adventure.

465

A MOTHER OF PEARL RITUAL TO PROTECT YOUR CHILD DAY AND NIGHT WHEN SHE IS AWAY FROM YOU OR YOU ARE ABSENT

You will need:

A silver candle
A small lidded jar
Seven mother of pearl buttons or beads

Timing:

The first Monday after a full moon, and whenever you apart

The Spell

- Light the candle, placing the jar where candlelight shines on it.
- Pass each button or bead around the flame once, saying for each one, *Be filled with my love, be filled with my blessings, be filled with my protection, that though apart, we are together in our hearts.*
- After empowering it, place each one in the jar.
- Put on the lid, shake it seven times, saying for each shake, *Monday, Tuesday, every day, guard my precious child for me. So I ask and so I say, with these pearls protected be.*
- Let the candle burn, then put the jar on a high shelf in the child's bedroom.
- Before she must be away, perhaps because you share joint custody or you are absent overnight, shake the jar seven times, repeating all the spell words seven times, once for each shake
- If you are home, do the same every night during her absence.

466

A TRADITIONAL MOTHER EARTH RITUAL WHEN YOU KNOW A CHILD OR TEENAGER HAS A DIFFICULT DAY AHEAD OR IS GOING ON A TRIP WITHOUT YOU

You will need:

Soil from the garden or in a planter near the front door

Timing:

When the child of any age leaves the house for a challenging day

The Spell

- As the child walks down the path/the steps/through the front gate, throw a handful of earth after him (subtly), saying, *May Mother Earth protect you until safely you return. My shield of care guards you everywhere. Blessed may you be.*
- Brush the soil off your hands over the ground or planter, repeating the words and say, *Mother Earth, protect my child who is your own.*

467

COMPUTER ANTIBULLYING MAGICK FOR CHILDREN OF ALL AGES

You will need:

A computer with a graphics program

Timing:

When the child has bullying issues, but is scared to complain

The Spell

- On the screen, ask the child to draw a large outline of a bully or bullies, as ugly and funny as she can.
- In the figure(s), she can type/dictate the nasty things the bully does and says.
- Enclose the bully and the words in a circle, expanding their size until the circle fills the screen.
- Say with the child, *You do not frighten me at all. I will cut you down to size until you are very small.*
- Reduce the size of the bully and the circle, gradually saying, *You are small. I am tall. So disappear. Now you are the one who feels the fear.*
- When the figure and circle are tiny, ask the child to press the DELETE button, saying together, *You I can't see, don't mess with me, your power is through. I don't fear you.*
- Tell the child to say the words in her mind whenever the bully or bullies approach or make remarks, as she will then give off "Don't mess with me" vibes.

468

A GOLD THREAD AND SILVER NEEDLE RITUAL FOR TRANSITION POINTS IN A CHILD'S OR TEENAGER'S LIFE

You will need:

Gold metallic thread for the power of the sun

A silver-colored needle for the protection of the moon

A garment the child or teenager will wear at the transition

Timing:

Noon, on Sunday

The Spell

- Sit in sunlight or bright daylight.
- Thread the needle and make nine stitches hidden inside the lining of the garment, on a tag, or hem.
- As you sew the nine stitches, say softly nine times, *I sew for you stability, I make for you security, that this change will bring you harmony. May you be protected by gold, sewn in love as life unfolds.*
- Leave the garment outside until the light fades.
- Say the spell words in your mind nine times as your child leaves for kindergarten or school for the first time, changes schools, goes to college, or enters his first home, and give him, or pack, the empowered garment.

469

TO STOP AN OLDER CHILD OR TEENAGER FROM OBSESSING OVER COMPUTER GAMES OR SOCIAL NETWORKS

You will need:

Access to the offending computer, tablet, or smartphone

Four green crystals (green and black malachite are best), one set at each corner of the device

A small bag with a drawstring or a purse

Timing:

When the young owner is not present

The Spell

- Hold your hands so that your fingers are pointing upward and your palms inward toward the screen. Move them from about an extended arm's length away to an inch or two from the screen, in and out in a slow, regular motion, saying, *May there be limitations, sensible reservations, lose your power, hour after hour, to fascinate and dominate.*
- Clap your hands three times, saying three times, *Wait, please dedicate your time to better use. The power of the machine is now defused.*
- Shake your fingers in front of the screen, repeating the second chant.
- Hide the crystals in a small closed bag or purse high in the room where the young person mainly uses the device.

470

A TOY SPELL TO PROTECT A LITTLE ONE AT DAY CARE OR AFTER-SCHOOL CARE, IF YOU HAVE TO WORK LONG HOURS

You will need:

Your child's favorite toy or security blanket

Timing:

While the child is sleeping holding the toy, and in the early days if the child is reluctant to leave you

The Spell

- Hold both the child and the toy in your arms so all three are linked.
- Free your dominant hand and touch first your heart, then the child's, finally drawing a heart with your finger on the toy or blanket.
- Say, *Three hearts are one, one heart serves three. Though I cannot be with you physically, yet I will be in your heart and you with me.*
- When you leave the child, hand him the toy and hold it between you as you cuddle him, saying the spell words in your mind and briefly touching your hearts and then the toy.

471

TO PROTECT ADULT FAMILY MEMBERS WHO ARE BEING BULLIED IN THE WORKPLACE, BY PARTNERS, OR BY OTHER FAMILY MEMBERS

You will need:

A piece of white paper and a black pen
A gold pen
Garlic salt
Dried sage
Dried or powdered nettles or parsley
A lidded pot

Timing:
Tuesday

The Spell

- In the center of the paper, write in black the bullied person's name, drawing a gold square around it.
- Outside the square write the bully's or bullies' name(s), crossed through in black, saying, *May* [name] *be protected from the nastiness of* [name of bullying person/people/organization]. *They may not enter this barrier of gold.*
- Place garlic, sage, and nettles in the pot, swirling it nine times counterclockwise.
- Scatter some of this mix on the paper over the bully's or bullies' name(s), repeating the spell words.
- Pour the scattered herbs back into the pot, fold the paper, and put that in the pot, saying, *Now you can do no harm. You are disarmed.*
- Place the lid on the pot, keeping it somewhere dark, but accessible.
- Each morning shake the pot, saying, *[*Name of person to be protected], *walk safe, work/live freely, speak freely without interference from any.*

472

TO PROTECT TEENAGERS AND ADULT FAMILY MEMBERS WHO ARE INTERACTING WITH DRUG TAKERS AND DRUG PUSHERS

You will need:

A photograph of the person under threat
Two small flashlights

Timing:
After dark, when you can be alone

The Spell

- Set the photograph on a table with a flashlight on either side of it.
- Switch off the lights and, with a flashlight in each hand, say, [Name], *may you not be drawn into the darkness of depravity, be surrounded by light, so against this you can fight. Please listen to me.*
- Switch on the flashlights, holding one in each hand, simultaneously spiraling over and around the photograph, repeating the spell words softly and continuously for two or three minutes.
- Switch off the flashlight in your nondominant hand, saying, *May those who draw you to darkness, in your life have no part, may the light of my love illumine your heart.*
- Continue to swing the flashlight in your dominant hand over the picture, then turn off this flashlight too and sit in darkness, whispering, *Blessed and protected be. Please listen to me.*

473

TO HELP AN ADULT CHILD OR A FAMILY MEMBER NOT TO REOFFEND OR SLIP BACK INTO OLD WAYS AFTER HAVING GOTTEN INTO TROUBLE

You will need:

A purple candle
A purple cord

Timing:
Three consecutive Saturdays

The Spell

- Light the candle and say, *Together we will see this through, for good or ill. I care for you.*
- Pass the ends of the cord through the flame so they are singed, repeating the spell words.
- Tie a knot in the cord, saying, *I bind those who lead you into wrongful ways. I bind you from the weakness that makes you stray.*
- Blow out the candle, hanging the cord outdoors.
- On week 2, repeat the spell and tie a second knot in the cord.
- Blow out the candle, returning the cord to the same place.
- On week 3, repeat everything, but, instead of tying another knot, release the two existing knots, saying, *I free you from those who lead you into wrongful ways. I bind you from the weakness that makes you stray.*
- Let the candle burn through.
- Take the cord to water and throw it in, saying, *From trouble go free and free remain. May trouble return not here again.*

474

TO STRENGTHEN A FAMILY MEMBER WHOSE ADDICTION OR LIFESTYLE AFFECTS THE FAMILY IN A NEGATIVE WAY

You will need:

A spool of thread
Scissors
A pot without a lid
A small bowl of salt

Timing:
Ongoing

The Spell

- Unravel a length of thread and cut it off the spool, saying, *I cut the ties that hold us all in thrall. May the addiction diminish, fade, fall, that we may at last be free of it all.*
- Tie the piece of thread in knots and drop it in the pot.
- Add a pinch of salt to the pot, saying, *Cleansed be of what holds us in thrall, diminish, fade, and finally fall.*
- Put the pot where light will shine on it.
- Continue each day, if possible, adding pieces of knotted thread and salt to the pot.
- When the pot is full, empty it in a garbage can, saying, *Begone, tangled be, disappear into obscurity that we may be free.*

475

TO PERSUADE DIFFICULT IN-LAWS OR STEPFAMILIES TO ACCEPT YOU

You will need:

Worry dolls or featureless figures made from modeling clay, one for each person causing problems, plus one for yourself and your partner
A square-patterned scarf
A pink flower for each
A vase of water

Timing:

Friday morning

The Spell

- Wrap the figures inside the scarf one by one, saying for each, *I am stuck with you, you are stuck with me, please can we be or act as a happy family.*
- Knot the scarf and keep it hidden.
- When the people concerned are coming, put a pink flower for each one in the vase, repeating the spell words.
- Set the flowers in the room where you will socialize and, if things go badly, pretend to adjust the flowers, repeating the spell words in your mind.

476

TO OVERCOME FAVORITISM OR ADULT SIBLING RIVALRY IN A FAMILY

You will need:

Long ribbons in bright colors, one for each family member
One clothespin for each family member involved
A clothesline or piece of rope tied shoulder height at both ends, so it hangs freely

Timing:

Outdoors, Friday before sunset

The Spell

- Take one ribbon for each family member, beginning with yourself.
- Using a clothespin, put it on the line so it hangs down free, saying, *When we were small, before we were tall, we would play family favorites morning and night. But now we are older, the game it must stop, who's best, who's loved most, it just isn't right.*
- For each person, as you pin the ribbon on the line, state the unfairness.
- Tie each ribbon to the next one so all are joined, saying, *Now we are tall, no longer small. No more family favorites, but united with all.*
- Leave the ribbons outdoors and the next morning, hang them, still as one, on a tree or bush.

477

TO PREVENT FALLOUT FROM A DIVORCE OR SEPARATION AFFECTING CHILDREN AND FAMILY OCCASIONS

You will need:

A large pink wax candle
A small pink wax candle for each child or adult involved, surrounding the large candle
A heatproof metal bowl
A letter opener
A vase filled with pink flowers

Timing:
Friday, just after sunset

The Spell

- Trace on one side of the unlit large pink candle, with the index finger of your dominant hand, DISSENSION MELT and, on the other, UNITY FLOW.
- Light the central candle and say the spell words you wrote.
- Holding each small candle in turn, name who it is for and light it from the central candle, moving clockwise.
- Drip a little wax into the bowl from each candle in order of lighting, repeating the spell words for each one.
- Continue until the bowl is half full. When the wax is cool but still soft, write in the wax, LOVE CONQUERS ALL, using a letter opener.
- Let the candles burn.
- Place the dish of wax next to a vase of pink flowers in the room in which you relax.

478

A GLOVE SPELL TO STOP A FAMILY MEMBER FROM INTIMIDATING OR CONSTANTLY PUTTING YOU DOWN

You will need:

A white glove for the right hand

Timing:
Sunday morning

The Spell

- Put on the glove and say, *I hand back to you,* [name], *what you do to me, so you will see and know the pain and send not your nastiness again.*
- Hide the glove somewhere in the person's home or room, saying as you do, *Not to hurt nor to harm you is my intent, but to hand back the pain you have sent, for now your power to intimidate/criticize is spent.*

479

AN ANTIJEALOUSY RITUAL IF AN EXISTING MEMBER OF THE FAMILY HUMAN OR ANIMAL RESENTS A NEWCOMER

You will need:

A framed photo of the old family and and a framed photo of the family with the new addition, side by side

A soft pink or white cloth for polishing

Timing:

On a full moon day or night

The Spell

- With the index finger of your dominant hand, touch your heart, and then trace over the glass of the picture of the old family, ENOUGH LOVE WE HAVE TO SPARE, SUFFICIENT CARE WE HAVE TO SHARE. LOVE IS NOT A CAKE TO DIVIDE, BUT RICHNESS THAT FOR ALL WILL PROVIDE.
- Touch the figure(s) of the newcomer(s) on the second picture and say, *Welcome, you are within our kin. Enough love and more we have to spare, so welcome in.*
- Polish each glass in turn, saying the second set of spell words as you polish the first photo and the first set of spell words as you polish the second photo.
- Polish the photos weekly, repeating the spell words in this order.

480

TO DEAL WITH LAZY, MESSY CHILDREN, TEENAGERS, OR A LAZY, MESSY PARTNER

You will need:

A very big box

Timing:

When you can bear the chaos no more

The Spell

- Walk around the home and collect in the box nonbreakable items you find on the floor, under the bed, or dropped in the wrong place, chanting, *I am not your lackey, I am not your slave. That's why God/the Goddess strong hands you gave. From this day forward, room service is gone, so shape up, for nothing by me will be done.*
- Shake the box nine times so the family members have to search for their possessions, saying nine times, *No more mess to cause me stress, no more disorder, that's an order.*
- Leave the box in the hallway with this sign. PLEASE COLLECT YOUR SOON-TO-BE-LOST PROPERTY BEFORE THE GARBAGEMAN NEXT COMES. And stick to your guns.
- Put a list of chores on the kitchen wall, repeating the spell weekly until everyone gets the idea.

481

A RENEWAL OF VOWS

You will need:

A dish of salt and one of water
Two red cords
Dried rosemary, vanilla pods, or rose petals
A small fire pit, bonfire, or fire in a fireproof bucket a third filled with sand, outdoors
A large white candle and two small candles on either side of the large one, set in the middle of a circle of petals. Put the items near the candles away from the fire.
A broom on the ground, not too close to the fire
A bouquet for the bride

Timing:

Any day, outdoors in natural beauty or in a family garden, for you two, plus any guests

The Spell

- Pour salt into the dish of water, which your partner holds. Have her swirl the water and sprinkle a little on the cords, tying them together.
- Both of you say together, *So willingly do we join throughout eternity*. Then both of you cast the rosemary, vanilla pods, or rose petals on the fire, saying, *May our love always burn bright*.
- Exchange promises and rings. Then both of you light and join your separate candle flames in the larger central candle, saying, *Now we two are one*.
- Tie right hand to right hand with the cords, saying, *Those whom the God/ Goddess/the Power of Light has joined together may none set apart*.
- Kiss each other and jump over the broom as you run out of the circle, any guests scattering petals.
- Let the candles burn.

482

A SAND-MIXING CEREMONY TO JOIN TOGETHER TWO SETS OF CHILDREN AFTER A MARRIAGE OR COMMITMENT BETWEEN THEIR PARENTS

You will need:

Small pots of sand for everyone present
A large, deep dish
A spoon

Timing:

When you and your partner move in together, either formally or informally (This may be part of a wedding ceremony.)

The Spell

- Starting with the youngest child present, have the child take sand from his jar and put it in the dish, as you say, *Like grains of sand, so do we mix and blend, that none can tell us apart. For we are one unity, one family, one heart*.
- Continue with the same words and actions until you are the only one left to add sand to the dish.
- After you have added your sand, mix the dish with the spoon three times clockwise, expressing out loud a wish or a joint family dream you can all fulfill.
- Starting again with the youngest child, each participant mixes the sand, adding a wish for the new family.

483

A FAMILY TREE CEREMONY

You will need:

A white candle
Pen and ink
A large bound blank-leafed book
Photographs of deceased and living family members, set in a circle around the outside of the candle

Timing:

Friday, at sunset initially

The Spell

- Light the candle, saying, *May this family tree grow strong, nourished by memories of the past, the strength of the present, and hopes for the future.*
- By candlelight, write on the first page of the blank book the family surname(s).
- Collect research and known family links with different branches of the family, including those of current and past permanent partners, writing that information on the first set of facing pages of the book.
- When the candle burns out, close the book, saying, *May I be a wise keeper of this family tree.* Keep it with fresh flowers.
- At the next family gathering, ask family members to bring photos to paste into the book and write accompanying family memories in the book.
- Add to the book whenever there is an addition to the family, repeating both sets of spell words.

484

CREATING A LIVING FAMILY TREE

You will need:

Plants, growing herbs, flowers, and the like that remind you of different family members, living and deceased; for example, Great-grandma's favorite roses
An area of the garden or big planters
Laminated labels with the names of each of the family members, written in permanent marker pen, to be tied to their plant with a bamboo stick and a red string

Timing:

Ongoing

The Spell

- Plant and label each plant, herb, or flower, adding a separate label for any special wishes, such as that anyone who is difficult to deal with will soften her attitude or that anyone who needs healing will recover.
- Say when you have planted them, *So shall we grow as one, flourish in one soil. Our living tree brings unity, through moon, wind, rain, and sun.*
- Tend your living tree garden and show it to family members when they visit, encouraging young people to help you with the gardening.
- Allow space for additional plants when new people join the family.
- Even if someone leaves the family or dies, do not remove their plant; rather, offer the plant extra care and a blessing.

485

TO MEET A BIRTH PARENT OR CHILD FOR THE FIRST TIME OR AFTER MANY YEARS OF BEING SEPARATED

You will need:

A small gift of flowers you will take to the meeting

An identical bunch you will keep

Timing:

Before you go to the meeting

The Spell

- Hold both bunches of flowers together between your hands, saying, *Though living as strangers, yet we are kin, I part of you, you hold me within. The past is the past the future to be. Let's take the first steps to heal you and me.*
- Put your flowers in a vase after holding them to your heart, saying, *Heart to heart, sincerity, it's worth a try for unity. I ask you to accept and welcome me.*
- Hold the other bunch to your heart, repeating the spell words.
- At the meeting, touch your heart and press the flowers there before offering them.
- If it is phone contact, place a vase of flowers on either side of the phone, repeating these spell words and actions.

486

FOR MOVING INTO YOUR FIRST HOME, EITHER ALONE OR WITH A PARTNER

You will need:

A small fire pit in the garden of the new home, a barbecue, or a metal bucket, half-filled with sand or soi

A big red candle embedded in the sand or soil

A small piece of wood from your former home, plus a twig or a stick of wood from near your new home (or two flowers, if you're using a candle)

Timing:

Any day after moving in

The Spell

- Light the fire or candle and on/in it burn the wood from the old home (or burn three petals from the first flower), saying, *I kindle this fire with the good memories and happy times of my old home.*
- Light the twig (or three petals from the second flower if you're using the candle) on top of the first piece of wood, saying, *I join to the old the joys ahead in my new home (and my new relationship).*
- Let them burn and join as one flame, letting the fire/candle burn down.

487

FOR SUCCESSFUL EARLY RETIREMENT, WHETHER VOLUNTARY OR FORCED

You will need:

A straight path along a tree-covered avenue or a pedestrian underpass, leading to the light

A piece of paper and a red pen

Timing:

A sunny day

The Spell

- Walk along the pathway toward the light, saying aloud if possible, *The way from the past closes without sorrow, for joy will come in my tomorrow.*
- When you reach the light at the end of the trees/underpass, stop and look back, saying, *I need not go back there any more. My future is an open door.*
- Push away with your hands toward the direction from which you have come. Your fingers should be pointing upward and your palms facing outward from your body when doing this. Then face the sun again.
- Do not return down the path. Go home another way and write down your ten-point plan for the future, making time for leisure.

488

FOR A HAPPY RETIREMENT

You will need:

An alarm clock to represent waking time for work

Timing:

The last evening before retirement

The Spell

- Set the alarm to go off at your usual waking time for work, saying, *Tomorrow clock you will retire, your services I will need no more. Just one more day and then I say, routine you will no longer score.*
- When you wake up, put the alarm clock in a cupboard and say, *After today I will not live by work time. I will make my own day, my own way. The future now is mine.*
- The following morning, wake up naturally and say, *Today I will not live by work time. I will make my own day, my own way. The future is mine.*
- Spend the first day doing whatever you want, which, if you have had a hectic life, may be nothing.

489

CREATING A MEMORY BOX FOR A DEPARTED RELATIVE

You will need:

A wooden box with a lid

Timing:

Before the funeral

The Spell

- Hold the box and say, *Your life lives in memories, they bring you to us near. For you are here with us once more, to be forever dear.*
- In the days before the funeral, look through your deceased relative's possessions for special mementos, such as a memento from his or her earlier life, a brooch given for a milestone birthday, a wartime photograph, a medal from a sporting triumph, or a poem the deceased wrote or received.
- Ask friends and relatives to bring to the wake or funeral a small memento of the deceased or write a few lines about the deceased person in a special memory book, perhaps recalling a shared joke.
- After the funeral, fill the wooden box with the mementos and read aloud the memories from the book before putting them in the box. Say the spell words again as part of the eulogy.

490

MARKING THE ANNIVERSARY OF A FAMILY DEATH

You will need:

Six small candles in glass containers, in a circle, on the flat surface
A framed photo of the deceased
Wildflower bulbs to plant in the deceased person's favorite spot, if the home is still in the family
Birdseed
A flat rock, or take a folding picnic table and cloth
Food and drink for a picnic afterward

Timing:

The anniversary of the death or some milestone in the person's life, such as a birthday

The Spell

- The more the merrier, but you can do this alone.
- Light the candles clockwise, speaking or allowing each person to share a memory or express love and grief before you light the next candle.
- Place the framed photo of the deceased in the center of the candles.
- Blow out the candles counterclockwise with a blessing on the deceased person and thanks for his/her life by all present.
- Plant the bulbs, saying, *May you grow toward the sun, in thanks for the life of* [name of deceased] *that will go on.*
- Scatter seeds for the birds.
- Have a remembrance picnic with the deceased person's favorite foods.

491

FOR HEALING LONG-STANDING ANGER OR GUILT WITH YOUR PARENTS, WHETHER THEY ARE ALIVE OR DECEASED

You will need:

A childhood photo, showing you and your parents
A more recent picture of your parents
A separate photo of yourself
A purple ribbon tying the three photos, each face up with your personal photo on top.
Fading flowers

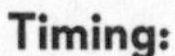

Timing:

Just before sunset

The Spell

- Hold the tied photos, saying, *Mom and Dad* [or whatever you call them], *you gave me life and in your own way, did your best with what you possessed, what seemed right and, so with hindsight, I thank you.*
- Untie the ribbon. Set the pictures side by side, saying, *From your mistakes I have learned, to those ways is no return. And so I free you and you free me with blessings.*
- Leave the photos standing side by side.
- Tie the ribbon around the flowers.
- Go to a bridge or any water source, remove the ribbon, and drop the tied flowers in the water, saying, *I set us free, free in our hearts. And so I walk forward to a new loving start.*
- Buy fresh flowers.

492

BREAKING THE CORD OF RESENTMENT WHEN A MARITAL BREAKUP IS ADVERSELY AFFECTING CHILDREN

You will need:

A deep-blue candle
A dark-blue thread
A small plastic lidded box

Timing:

The waning moon, as it gets dark

The Spell

- Light the candle and say, [Name of ex-partner], *this anger must cease. It will spread like disease. For the children and us we must fashion a peace.*
- Tie a knot in the thread, saying, *For what once was between us, though we may not be friends, for the children and us, hostility must end.*
- Extinguish the candle, saying, *Anger, hostility no more.*
- Relight the candle and let it burn, saying, *I open the door to peace.*
- Place the thread in a tiny plastic lidded box and add water to cover it, keeping it in the freezer.

493

STEPPING BACK FROM AN OVERPOSSESSIVE FAMILY RELATIONSHIP THAT IS INTERFERING WITH YOUR LIFE

You will need:

A large trailing plant, such as ivy or honeysuckle, in a pot

Another planter, or another part of the garden

Timing:

Toward the end of the waning moon cycle

The Spell

- Gently dig up the plant, saying, *You are you and I am me.* [Name], *I ask in love we move apart, that I may thrive and come alive, not clutched within your heart.*
- Separate the roots and return half to a new smaller pot, saying, *We need not sever all, but I ask you, set me free, to express my own identity, not clutched within your heart.*
- Replant the other half in another pot or in a different part of the garden, saying, *You are you and I am me, growing separately and happily, apart, not clutched within your heart.*
- Take care of both plants, repeating the third set of spell words when you water the plants.

494

TO OVERCOME A MAJOR FAMILY QUARREL IN WHICH PEOPLE ARE TAKING SIDES

You will need:

A large white candle, placed at the farthest end of the cord

A tea light for each person, set on either side of the table, according to how the family is split

A dark-blue ribbon or cord, dividing the table in half

Timing:

At sunset

The Spell

- Light the white candle and say, *May the light of reason and love prevail. Where love exists, it cannot fail.*
- Light the tea lights, first on one side of the table and then on the other, saying afterwards, *The great divide and pointless sides. This state of dissension cannot abide.*
- Remove the divider, rearranging the tea lights in a circle with the white candle in the middle. Then say, *The circle of family cannot be broken. Henceforward kind words will only be spoken.*
- Let the candles burn down. Repeat every week on the same day and time until the quarrel is mended.

495

TO MEND A RIFT BETWEEN YOU AND A FAMILY MEMBER, OR BETWEEN TWO FAMILY MEMBERS, THAT IS DAMAGING THE FAMILY

You will need:

A long piece of rope or cord in a natural fiber
A tree with a low natural cleft

Timing:

Friday morning

The Spell

- Knot one end of the rope around the left-hand branch of the cleft, saying, *Good ties that bind shall not unwind. Splits can be mended and quarreling ended.*
- Pass the cord or rope nine times counterclockwise around the two branches, saying, *Untangle the anger that makes us* [or name those who are estranged] *a stranger. Unwind the pain, restore peace again.*
- Continue to unwind and wind the rope for three cycles of nine, repeating the spell words faster and winding faster.
- Pull the rope taut, holding one end, with the other still tied, saying, *All are joined in harmony, so I ask and it shall be.*
- Wind the rope nine times clockwise around the two branches, this time repeating the second chant. Secure the other end to the right branch with a knot and leave the rope.
- If it is still there in nine days, remove it.

496

PREVENTING A VICIOUS FAMILY MEMBER FROM SPREADING LIES AND RUMORS ABOUT YOU OR ANOTHER FAMILY MEMBER

You will need:

A piece of white paper
A pencil
An eraser
A blue pen
A white cord

Timing:

Wednesday, before sunset

The Spell

- Write the name of the person spreading lies to fill the paper, faintly in pencil, then say, *Your lies do blacken my name* [or name the family victim]. *Your rumors me/him/her defame.*
- Erase the name of the person spreading lies, saying, *No more shall your lies blacken my name [or name victim] no more your rumors me/him/her defame. You stand corrected.*
- Now write first the name of the perpetrator once and then your name (and/or the name of the family member/s affected), in blue pen on the paper in a vertical row, cross out the perpetrator's name and say, *You stand corrected.*
- Tie the paper and knot the cord nine times, saying for each knot, *You stand corrected.*
- Keep the paper in a cupboard, flattened under a heavy weight.

497

IF YOU ARE BEING DENIED ACCESS TO CHILDREN OR GRANDCHILDREN BY A VINDICTIVE FAMILY MEMBER

You will need:

A piece of blue paper, folded in two
A dark-blue or black pen
Scissors
Glue or tape

Timing:
Sunday afternoon

The Spell

- Unfold the paper and on one half write your name, and on the other half the names of the children or grandchildren you are not allowed to see.
- Draw a large heart to enclose all of you and say, *I miss you from my life. I will do anything to end this strife. Though I hold you in my heart, in your life I would be part.*
- Cut the paper in half so half of the heart is on each side, saying, *Love I know cannot be severed, but absent times with tears I've weathered. Come back into my life soon.*
- Join the two halves of the heart using glue or tape the back of the paper together, saying, *What is broken can be mended. This estrangement must be ended, even if not perfectly. Bring, I ask,* [name those you are not allowed to see], *back to me.*
- Keep the paper with any photos you have of the absent children or grandchildren.

498

THAWING A FAMILY ESTRANGEMENT IF PREVIOUS ATTEMPTS TO HEAL IT HAVE FAILED

You will need:

A ring of seven long-burning tea lights set around a bowl
A metal bowl of ice cubes
A cup or mug

Timing:
At the crescent moon

The Spell

- Light the first tea light, saying, *I will not give up. Though the cup of reconciliation is empty, I have patience left aplenty. I have perseverance, too, this connection to renew.*
- Light the candles clockwise, repeating the spell words for each one.
- Let the ice melt naturally. While it is melting, write a letter or email to the estranged person, even if you do not send it. Suggest that you put the past behind you and start again.
- When the ice is melted, pour it into a cup. Use it for making tea or coffee or a cold drink in the cup, or drink some of the water. Say, *Step by step this cup is filled with love. For persevere I will, until reconciliation.*
- Refrigerate the rest of the water, using three-quarters in drinks.
- Pour the rest on thriving plants, each time repeating the second set of spell words.

499

AN IRIS ANGEL OF THE RAINBOW BLESSING TO BRING RECONCILIATION WITH A FAMILY MEMBER WHO HAS WRONGED YOU WHEN YOU CANNOT EASILY FORGIVE

You will need:

Seven candles in a circle—red, orange, yellow, green, blue, indigo or purple, and white

Seven different-colored flowers in a vase in the center of the circle of candles, ideally including irises or lilies

Timing:

Near or at the beginning of a week or month

The Spell

- Light each candle in the above order, red through to white, saying afterwards, *Iris with your rainbow wings, help me shed these bitter things. When there is a rainbow in the sky, lead me across your bridge so high, peacefully to what used to be.*
- Sprinkle water drops from the vase over the flowers one by one, saying, *Water under the bridge, Iris, lady of the rainbow, help me to let this anger go that love may once more freely flow.*
- Send flowers to the estranged person.

500

TO GAIN PEACE IF A FAMILY MEMBER DIED WITHOUT BEING RECONCILED WITH YOU OR YOU COULD NOT SAY GOOD-BYE

You will need:

The deceased person's favorite flowers

A white candle

A small bowl of soil

A small bowl of salt

Timing:

A day that was significant to both of you

The Spell

- Hold one of the flowers between your hands and express what you wish you had said to the deceased person and the love you felt was crushed by difficulties, misunderstandings, or simply lack of time.
- From the flower, take single petals and burn each in the candle flame, dropping it into the bowl of soil and saying, *Flare now and flame, as I whisper your name. Burn, burn away all sorrows at life's end, for love never dies and love I send.*
- Blow softly into the candle and whisper the name of the deceased relative.
- Add a couple of pinches of salt to the flame so it sparkles and say, *Flare, flame, the wind carries your name, and so you live on in my heart and my memory. You will always be dear to me.*
- Blow out the candle.

CHAPTER 11

ANIMAL SPELLS

The spells in this chapter include those for training or working with, healing, and helping domestic, wild, and exotic pets, as well as spells for helping pets who are lost or in distress.

501

TO FIND THE RIGHT PET FOR YOU

You will need:

An incense stick in any tree or herbal fragrance

A ceramic, glass, or wooden model of the pet you would like, or a picture taken from the Internet

Timing:

Saturday, early

The Spell

- Light the incense and, using it like a smoke pen, write in incense smoke over the animal or bird model, YOU WAIT FOR ME, FAR OR NEAR, INTO MY LIFE YOU WILL APPEAR. YOU WHO SOON WILL BE SO DEAR, GUIDE ME SOON WHERE YOU WILL BE OR SEND A SIGN THAT I CAN SEE.
- Still holding the burning incense, go outdoors. Holding the animal model your outstretched nondominant hand, turn in all four directions clockwise, saying at each direction, *I call you, beloved pet, on the four winds to find. Give me a sign wherever you be, that you are truly mine.*
- Let the incense burn. Indoors search the Internet, animal journals, rescue center notices, and local papers for the kind of pet you want (or keep an open mind).
- Within a day or so the right location will leap out at you and, when you visit, you will find your pet waiting.

502

FOR FINDING AN ANIMAL RESCUE CENTER PET OR ADOPTING AN UNWANTED ANIMAL

You will need:

An old battered treasure

Small shiny items of little value

A basket filled with the treasure and the shiny items

A dark-colored scarf

Timing:

Friday, as morning moves toward noon

The Spell

- Gently rattle the basket nine times, saying nine times, *All that glitters is not gold, this treasure is loved, though it is old. Dear pet, I will make up to you all the sorrow you've been through. Hold on, for I am coming for you.*
- Take out the treasure, hold it between your hands, and repeat the spell words three more times.
- Set it on an outward-facing window ledge, saying, *Hold on, for I am coming for you.*
- Cover the basket containing the shiny objects with a dark-colored scarf, saying, *All that glitters is not gold, my rescue pet I soon will hold. Old or injured, scared or bold, I will treasure you your whole life through.*
- Make a list of rescue centers in your area and plan a visit as soon as possible.

503

TO HELP A NEW PET SETTLE IN YOUR HOME, ESPECIALLY IF THERE ARE OTHER ANIMALS

You will need:

Four small brown or fawn-banded agate crystals, or smooth brown stones

A blanket or old garment belonging to you

Timing:

The night before the pet arrives

The Spell

- The night before the pet arrives, place the crystals at the four corners of your bed and the blanket or garment at the foot of the bed, saying six times, *You are safe here, warm and calm, protected by us from all harm.*
- The next morning, place the new pet bed or cushion where the pet will sleep with the agates underneath it and the blanket on top, repeating the spell words.
- When your pet arrives, settle it on the bed, saying the spell words three times.
- Stroke each pet, beginning with the most senior down to the newcomer, saying to each one, *Welcome your new family, you still remain beloved to me. For the love we can share, enough for all and some to spare.*

504

TO COMFORT YOUR PET IF YOU MUST BE APART FOR A WHILE

You will need:

Dried sage

Two halves of a large shell, such as oyster or mussel, or an ornamental wooden or cardboard egg that splits into two halves

Two small matching amber, smoky quartz, amethyst, or rutilated quartz crystals

Timing:

The night before you leave

The Spell

- Sprinkle a clockwise circle of sage around the shell or egg halves, set side by side near the pet's sleeping place, saying, *Within this circle of love we remain together until I/you return.*
- Place one of the crystals under your mattress and the other under the pet's bed.
- In the morning, put a crystal in each shell half, repeating the spell words.
- Join the two halves and tie them together with a ribbon.
- Leave the shell within the sage circle while you or your pet are away.

505

TO HELP A PET HAPPILY MOVE TO A NEW HOME

You will need:

Seven potted plants
Seven small brown stones found near your present home

Timing:

A week before the move

The Spell

- Place the potted plants in a semicircle around the area where the animal sleeps.
- Bury a stone in the soil of one of the plants each day, saying, *The roots are deep within you and me. Wherever we live we are family, and safe for you your new home will be.*
- On moving day, transport the plants with the animal carrier, finding a quiet corner for the pet bed as soon as you arrive and placing the plants there.

506

TO MOVE A HORSE, GOAT, SHEEP, OR CATTLE TO A NEW STABLE, PASTURE, OR PADDOCK

You will need:

A brown candle
A circle of copper wire
Hair or wool from one of the animals
Green string

Timing:

A week before the move

The Spell

- Light the candle and pass the wire ring eight times over the flame, saying as you do so, *Within this ring protection bring, from all disruption and interruption. That this move will be easy for you and you will settle in pastures new.*
- Wrap the wool or hair around and around the ring, securing it with string, repeating the spell words as you do so.
- Blow out the candle, saying, *Protection bring within this ring.*
- Hang the ring in the animal's current stable or enclosure and swing it twice, repeating both empowerments twice whenever you feed the animal(s).
- When you have transported the animal(s), hang the ring in the new stable or enclosure, swinging it four times and saying both empowerments four times. Repeat daily until the animals settle.

507

A HARIEL, ANGEL OF PETS, BLESSING ON SMALL ANIMALS OR ANY CREATURES THAT ARE TIMID AND ANXIOUS

You will need:
A small lidded container, half-filled with animal food

Timing:
When the house, coop, or garden is quiet, just before feeding time

The Spell

- Using the container like a rattle, circle the cage, pen, or pond four times clockwise, saying four times, *Hariel, bless this/these small creature(s) in my care. As you protect small creatures everywhere, keep mine safe from fear and harm, tranquil, secure, healthy, and calm.*
- Keep rattling more and more softly as you move ever more slowly until you are still and then say, *Though you are small, you are loved. Though you are small, you are protected. I thank you, Hariel, for your blessings.*
- Feed the small creatures, repeating the second set of spell words four more times.

508

A TRADITIONAL PROTECTIVE SPELL FOR ALL PETS, FROM HORSES TO HAMSTERS

You will need:
A small bell to attach to a collar, bridle, or cage
A small dish of soil
A bowl of water

Timing:
As darkness falls, late in the moon cycle, after dark

The Spell

- Dip the bell lightly in the soil three times, saying each time, *Do not stray, keep away malice and stranger, accident and danger. As this bell rings so it brings security, safety, and harmony to* [name pet].
- Shake off the soil and ring the bell, repeating the spell words.
- Sprinkle just a few drops of water over the bell, repeating the spell words three times.
- Shake it dry and ring the bell once more, saying just once, *As this bell rings so it brings security, safety, and harmony to* [name pet].
- Suspend the bell from the collar, bridle, or in the animal's cage or sleeping quarters.
- Repeat the spell monthly.

509

TO KEEP A PET FROM GETTING LOST, STRAYING, OR BEING STOLEN

You will need:

Three hairs or feathers from the pet (seven hairs for a large pet)
Red thread
A small drawstring bag

Timing:
Tuesday

The Spell

- Bind the hairs or feather with the thread in nine knots, saying nine times, *Bound are all from hurting you. Do not stray, do not roam, nor unwillingly be led from home.*
- Put the knotted feather/hairs in the bag and call your pet's name three times indoors. Then go outdoors and do the same.
- Hang the bag safely outdoors, and when it fades or rips, replace it by repeating the spell.

510

TO GUIDE OUTDOOR CATS SAFELY HOME AT NIGHT

You will need:

A cat's eye, a moonstone, a turquoise, or a dyed-blue howlite crystal
A saucer or a small plate
Soil in a garden or in a planter

Timing:
At a full moon night

The Spell

- Go outdoors and set the crystal on a saucer or small plate on top of soil, either in the garden or in a planter. Say, *Mother Moon and Mother Earth, you who give all creatures birth, guide my* [cat's name] *through dark night and stormy day. May he never lose his way.*
- Leave the crystal there until you wake up. Then set it on an indoor window ledge, facing the direction in which the cat leaves and returns home, and call the cat's name three times.
- Reempower the crystal every full moon with a new spell.

511

FOR SUCCESSFULLY TAKING A DOG TO OBEDIENCE TRAINING OR TRAINING A HORSE

You will need:

Rose hips or chamomile tea (you can use herbal tea bags, if you wish)
A leash or bridle

Timing:

The night before the training starts

The Spell

- Make and then drink a little of the tea, saying, *Together, we will learn together, through rain and wind and sun and weather. Safe in street and field and park, safe in light and safe in dark, because we walk together.*
- Hold the leash/bridle, softly call the animal's name six times even if the animal is not present, and repeat the spell words.
- Alternate drinking tea and saying the spell words with holding the leash/bridle, doing this six times.
- Sprinkle just three drops of the tea on or near the leash/bridle, saying, *Now we are together, through rain and wind and sun and weather. As you wear this, share my calm, make this leash/bridle our lucky charm.*
- Repeat the chant just before the training session, holding the leash/bridle and then having another cup of the tea.
- Always use the same leash/bridle for the training and repeat the spell words and actions beforehand.

512

TO DESENSITIZE DOGS AND HORSES TO TRAFFIC NOISE

You will need:

A picture of the animal
Seven small individual bells threaded and knotted loosely on a cord or a long ribbon (bells are often available in discount stores)

Timing:

During the waning moon

The Spell

- Hold the picture and say, *Be not afraid, be not alarmed, noise cannot hurt you, my dear one, be calm.*
- Lean over the picture and shake the bells, at first quite loudly and then more softly, as you unknot and remove one bell at a time until only one is left on the cord. Now repeat the spell words seven times.
- Then, one by one, rethread and knot the bells, except for one, shaking them softly over the picture. Say the spell words seven times.
- Leave the six bells lying on the picture overnight and, in the morning, attach the seventh bell, which you did not rethread earlier, to the collar or bridle.

513

TO CALL A PET TELEPATHICALLY FROM A DISTANCE

You will need:
A small pet treat

Timing:
When you and the pet are alone (works best for dogs, cats, and horses)

The Spell

- When the pet is in another part of the house, or outdoors, where she cannot see you, hold the pet treat in front of you.
- Say the animal's name softly in your head, followed by however you usually call the animal to you; for example, using a whistle, still all in your mind.
- Turn up the volume of the signal gradually in your head, so you are calling louder and louder in your mind, then say aloud in a whisper, *Come to me, find me, I have a treat for you.*
- When the animal arrives, praise her and offer her the treat.
- If your pet is still not tuned in after a few attempts, start to call her aloud, but softly, increasing the volume of your voice until she arrives. Persevere, reducing the volume gradually until the call is within your head. You will eventually make the psychic link.
- Gradually increase the distance between you and your pet when you psychically call her.

514

TO GUIDE HOME RACING PIGEONS, DOVES, AND BIRDS OF PREY

You will need:
A lavender, sandalwood, or fennel incense stick
Any blue crystal or bead on a pendant or one you can carry in a drawstring bag

Timing:
During the waxing moon, whenever they fly

The Spell

- Light the incense, holding it in your dominant hand and the crystal or pendant in the other hand, saying, *Fly to me, homeward bound be as I do call. Do not fall or stray or turn, but directly to your coop/perch return.*
- Over the crystal, draw in incense smoke five smoke eyes, one over the other, repeating the spell words as you do so.
- Let the incense burn away.
- Whenever the bird(s) fly, wear the pendant or hold the crystal in its bag. Touch the crystal and say the spell words, repeating them if the bird(s) take longer than expected to come home.

515

TO RETRAIN AN ANIMAL WITH BAD HABITS OR AGGRESSION, WHETHER A PERSONAL PET FROM AN ANIMAL RESCUE CENTER OR AS A PROFESSIONAL ENDEAVOR

You will need:

An old collar
Red string
A new, unworn collar

Timing:

Wednesday morning

The Spell

- Take the old collar and tie the string around the collar, making nine knots all the way around and saying, *You are bound from the old ways* [name some bad habits], *to happier days, restrained but retrained with love.*
- Cut the knots one by one, saying for each one, *I set you free from the old ways* [name some bad habits], *to happier days, unrestrained and retrained with love.*
- Throw away the old collar and the string.
- The next time you're with the animal, put on the new collar, saying, *A fresh start, and you will learn with willing heart, retrained with love.*
- Say all the spell words before beginning training.

516

TO SUCCESSFULLY TRAIN FOR AN ANIMAL CARE CAREER

You will need:

A screen saver picturing an animal on your home or work computer

Timing:

Wednesday, near noon, and whenever you use your device

The Spell

- Switch on the computer, holding your hands in front of you, palms facing the machine and fingers together, far enough away so you cannot reach it.
- Say (in your mind if you're not alone), *So far and yet near the path will appear and my future soon be clear.*
- Move closer to the screen, repeating the spell words, and print out the screen saver image small.
- Each day move closer to the screen, repeating the spell words, printing out a larger image (dispose of the previous one each time), until you can almost touch the screen and have a full-sized image.
- Repeat the spell sequence whenever you doubt that your training is succeeding.

517

FOR RUNNING YOUR OWN KENNEL, CATTERY, OR STABLES

You will need:

Seven children's plastic toy animals (the species you hope to work with) or seven small ceramic ones

A piece of paper or a flyer with your new business name written on it in boldface

A brown candle set behind the paper

Timing:

Daily for one week

The Spell

- Set the toy animals in a row, leading to the paper.
- Light the candle saying, *Come one and all and stay with me, successful will my business be:* [name it]. *Come from far, come from near, my business* [name again] *soon will manifest here. It cannot fail, it cannot fall, so come and stay, one and all.*
- Put one of the toy animals on the paper and readjust the row.
- Blow out the candle, repeating the spell words.
- Each day as you do the spell, add one more animal to the paper and on day 7 let the candle burn with all seven animals on the paper.
- Give the toy animals to a child or the ceramic ones to a charity thrift shop.

518

TO REVITALIZE AN AILING ANIMAL-BASED CAREER OR BUSINESS

You will need:

A small item you use daily in your career

Nine feathers

Timing:

Early Sunday morning

The Spell

- Place the item on a table with the nine feathers in a circle around it.
- Take feathers 1 and 2, one in each hand, and waft them over and around the item nine times, saying nine times, *Go free, revitalize, bring life back to the world I prize.*
- Repeat the words and actions with feathers 3 and 4, then 5 and 6, 7 and 8, and finally 9 and 1, then set the feathers free outdoors, one at a time, saying the same spell words for each one.
- Each time you use the item at work, repeat the spell words in your mind, and when it's not in use, keep the item where light will shine on it.

519

FOR COMPETING IN HORSE OR ANIMAL SHOWS, EVENTS, AND RACES

You will need:

A flyer or printout of a promo for the event from the Internet
A green pen
Scissors
Glue or tape

Timing:
The day before the event

The Spell

- On the flyer or printout, write your name in large letters and SUCCESS, FIRST PLACE, FIRST PRIZE, THE WINNER, BEST OF BREED, and as many winning phrases and words as you can think of.
- Cut the paper in four, saying four times, To the four corners of the world, my victory will be unfurled.
- Glue or tape the four pieces back together, saying, *It all comes together, victory will come to me.*
- Fold the paper and take it with you to the event. Look at it before you start, saying or thinking both sets of spell words fast.

520

TO ATTAIN SUCCESS IN BREEDING FINE ANIMALS

You will need:

An egg
A packet of seeds
Two identical green plants

Timing:
At a full moon

The Spell

- Dig a hole in your garden or an open space. Hold the egg in your nondominant hand, saying, *Be fertile, be healthy, may there be only the best to outshine all the rest.*
- Break open the egg and place the raw egg and broken shell in the hole, repeating the spell words.
- Open the seed packet and, holding the seeds in your dominant hand, say the same spell words and drop the seeds into the hole.
- Entwine the roots of the two plants as you set them on top of the seeds and the egg, saying, *Be joined in strength and beauty, little ones grow healthily, that I may have the Best of Breed, so this venture will succeed.*
- Whenever you tend to the plants, repeat the spell words.

521

FOR A HEALTHY AND ACTIVE PET

You will need:

A small, round green jade crystal
The pet's water bowl, half-filled with water

Timing:

At the crescent moon

The Spell

- Go outdoors and face the crescent moon, putting the jade in the water and holding the bowl up to the moon.
- Say seven times, *Be filled with vitality, be filled with activity. Moon as you glow, so will health grow in my beloved pet,* [name].
- Take the bowl indoors and remove the jade, dipping it seven times into the bowl of water before giving the water to the pet and repeating the spell words seven times.
- Each time you fill the water bowl, dip the jade in the water seven times, repeating the spell words.

522

AN ALL-PURPOSE HEALING RITUAL FOR PETS LARGE AND SMALL

You will need:

Any brown crystal, agate, jasper, or a smooth brown stone found near your home

Timing:

Early morning, when light is filling the sky, indoors or out, for as many days as needed

The Spell

- Facing the direction of the rising sun, sit, kneel, or stand beside the ailing animal, holding the crystal in your open cupped hands.
- Move the crystal to touch your heart and then touch the animal's body with it wherever is most comfortable for him, then back to your heart and to the animal again in a gentle continuous rhythm, saying softly, *Heart to heart and soul to soul, beloved one, may you be whole. Restored to health by the morning light, may the love between us make all right.*
- Gently stroke your pet with your dominant hand, holding the crystal in the other hand until the pet relaxes, saying the spell words more softly and stroking more slowly until words and movement cease.
- Leave the crystal on a plate resting on soil during the day, and at night, put it under or near the pet's sleeping place.

523

LONG-DISTANCE HEALING FOR A FRIEND OR FAMILY MEMBER'S SICK PET

You will need:

A table lamp
A photograph or the name of the pet written in green on white paper

Timing:

Wednesday, ideally at 10 p.m., in a darkened room

The Spell

- Turn on the lamp and set the photo in the light, saying, *May* [name of pet] *be healed by the light of love.*
- Hold your fingers in the lamplight and shake your fingers until they tingle. Say the spell words five times.
- Softly call the pet's name five times, then point your fingers down over the photo or name five times, shaking them, then repeating the spell words five times.
- Continue to hold your hands in the light and repeat the whole cycle, words and actions, five times in all.
- Leave the lamp shining on the picture until you go to bed.

524

TO RAISE THE ENERGY LEVELS OF A PET WHO SEEMS "OFF" FOR NO IDENTIFIABLE REASON

You will need:

A collar or small item belonging to the pet or one kept in its cage, hutch, or tank
A large plate
A large green potted plant or one in the garden

Timing:

Wednesday morning, and ongoing

The Spell

- Put the collar or item on the plate and rest the plate on the soil around the plant, saying, *May* [name pet] *be filled with new life. May my pet,* [name], *be filled with fresh energy.*
- Pass your hands around the outside of the plant, starting at the top and moving over the leaves and stems, not quite touching it, and saying afterwards, *May my pet be filled with new life. May my pet be filled with fresh vitality. So I ask and it shall be.*
- Hold the item again and say both sets of spell words.
- Leave the item on the plate a full twenty-four hours before returning it to your pet.
- Repeat the spell weekly until your pet is back in peak condition.

525

FOR SOOTHING A TIMID, FRIGHTENED, OR NERVOUS PET

You will need:

Four green candles in a square
A grooming brush, set in the center of the square of candles

Timing:
Friday, early evening

The Spell

- Light the first candle and say, *Peace*.
- Light the second candle from the first and say, *Peace and Harmony*.
- Light the third from the second, saying, Come to . . .
- Light the fourth from the third and say, *My beloved pet*.
- Pass the brush, bristles down, over each candle in turn, saying for each one, *May peace and harmony come to my beloved pet*.
- Blow out the candles in reverse order of lighting.
- Brush your pet gently and rhythmically, repeating the spell words softly as you do so.
- Repeat the spell weekly if the pet is very timid or traumatized.

526

TO HEAL AN INJURED ANIMAL, WHETHER HURT IN A FIGHT OR IN AN ACCIDENT

You will need:

A small lidded cardboard box, pink if possible, the kind used for gifts
Dried rose petals or rose potpourri
A ceramic model of the same species as your pet, or one made from children's modeling clay
Raw cotton

Timing:
Late afternoon, or when the pet is asleep

The Spell

- Line the bottom of the box with rose petals or potpourri, saying, *Safe be your bed, here rest your head, sleep will restore you to life once more. Rest now and let Mother Nature do her work.*
- Wrap the model animal in raw cotton, using two or three layers, and repeating the spell words five times.
- Place it in the box and put on the lid, saying, *Sleep tight, rest by day and heal by night, for all shall be mended and your pain will be ended. Sleep now and let Mother Nature do her work, for you are safe and protected.*
- Put the box in a drawer with soft clothes.
- Each morning hold the box, repeat both sets of spell words, and ask the angels and Mother Nature for healing blessings.

527

FOR BRINGING RELIEF TO AN OLD OR CHRONICALLY ILL PET

You will need:

A brown candle
A ball of white children's modeling clay
A jar of small golden glass nuggets or glass beads

Timing:

Saturday evening around sunset, for seven weeks

The Spell

- Light the candle and say, *Though you are no longer young and strong, yet life can be good and so I send you strength and healing.*
- Make a clay animal to represent your pet and set it where the candlelight will shine on it.
- Press a single nugget into the clay, saying, *Bless and protect, restore and heal.*
- Blow out the candle and bury the clay animal with the nugget still in it, saying, *Mother Earth restore all.*
- On week 2, repeat the spell but add two nuggets to a new clay animal and bury the second model close to the first.
- Each week, add an extra glass nugget and repeat the spell.
- On week 7, add seven nuggets, letting the candle burn with the clay animal in front of it.
- Keep the seventh clay animal until it crumbles, and then repeat the whole seven-week spell cycle.

528

TO EMPOWER A HEALING REMEDY, WHETHER PHARMACEUTICAL OR NATURAL

You will need:

Three hairs or a single small feather from your pet
A rose quartz, amethyst, or clear quartz crystal pendulum on a chain, or an old pendant or necklace you have had for a while
A bottle of the healing remedy you have been given by a vet or alternative healing practitioner or a bottle you have bought over the counter in a pet store

Timing:

Before administering the remedy

The Spell

- Attach the hairs or the feather to the pendulum/pendant.
- Hold the pendulum/pendant to the light, sun, or lamplight, turning it nine times clockwise, nine times counterclockwise, then nine times clockwise again, saying, *Make strong the connection, the healing direction that this remedy will work effectively and rapid improvement soon will be.*
- Pass the pendulum slowly over the medicine, nine times clockwise, nine times counterclockwise, and nine times clockwise, repeating the spell words nine times.
- Leave the pendulum/pendant hanging between uses, where light will shine on it and air circulate around it.

529

TO PROTECT YOUR PET AND HOME FROM ANIMAL PARASITES

You will need:

Separate dishes of any three of the following herbs: dried lavender, tansy, mint, chamomile, or basil
A deep bowl
A mixing spoon
A purple amethyst pointed crystal

Timing:

The first of every month in the warmer seasons

The Spell

- Add the herbs to the bowl one at a time. Stir steadily, saying continuously, *Far from here your irritation, far from here your infestation, from this place I banish you.*
- Sprinkle a little of the mix around the amethyst and around or under your pet's bed or cage, saying the spell words eight times.
- Carry the bowl outdoors, scattering the mix around hutches, runs, or outside a stable, and beneath exterior doors and windows of your home.
- If you live in an apartment, sprinkle the mix outside your entrance door and on a balcony. Say at each place, *Come not here, you who fly or hop or creep. Sleep outdoors.*
- Touch the inside your front door and indoor window ledges with the pointed end of the amethyst, saying the second set of spell words at each place.
- Put the amethyst in your pet's empty food bowl an hour before feeding.
- Remove the amethyst just before feeding.

530

TO HELP YOUR PET RECOVER FROM SURGERY OR OTHER INVASIVE TREATMENT

You will need:

A black candle behind the circle
A gray candle to the left of the circle and a white candle to the right, both outside the circle
A picture of your pet in good health inside the circle of crystals
A circle of nine small hematite crystals or nine round gray stones

Timing:

The day before the surgery/treatment and as many days after as you wish

The Spell

- Light the black candle, saying, *Take away pain, protected may you be, that each day is a step to recovery.*
- Light the gray candle from the black one, saying, *Slow and steady, 'til you are ready. Step by step to recovery.*
- Extinguish the black candle.
- Light the white candle from the gray one and say, *So health is restored and you will have vitality once more.*
- Extinguish the gray candle and leave the white one burning.
- Use a new white candle each time you do the spell.
- Even when the pet is better, leave the crystals enclosing the picture.

531

TO CALL HOME A LOST ANIMAL

You will need:

A table lamp with a shade
An item your pet loves

Timing:

At sunset

The Spell

- Put the lamp in a window facing the street or the back of the house, whichever route is used by or with the pet.
- Switch on the lamp and hold the item so the item and your hands are both in the lamplight. Make sure no other lights are on.
- Softly call your pet's name three times, then say three times, *Come home now,* [name pet], *to those who love you.*
- Go to the door and, holding the item, call your pet's name six times and say six times, *Stay not away, far or near hear my call, no more stray. Follow my love back here.*
- Go to the end of the garden or into the street, still holding the item. Call your pet's name nine times and say both sets of spell words nine times.
- Return indoors and hold the item in the lamplight, saying, *Three by three, come home to me.*
- Leave the lamp on all night.

532

DRAWING A LOST PET HOME, USING THE PSYCHIC LINK OF LOVE

You will need:

A flashlight

Timing:

Just before dark, or when the pet would be settling for the night

The Spell

- Facing the direction you instinctively feel the pet went, softly call the pet's name out loud seven times.
- Shine the flashlight beam directly ahead, picturing a cord of light leading from you to the pet, guiding her home.
- Spiral the beam fast seven times, saying the name of the pet seven times more and saying seven times, *Follow the light.*
- Spiral the flashlight beam in the air seven times, saying for each circuit, *Follow the light.*
- In your mind, see your pet running, trotting, or flying home.
- Close and open your eyes three times, look at the light, blink, and you may have a sudden insight as to where your pet is.
- Before going to sleep, sit in the darkness, shine the flashlight toward the window, and say seven times more, *Follow the light.*
- Repeat nightly until you have news.

533

TO KEEP A VALUABLE OR RARE PET FROM BEING STOLEN

You will need:

A turquoise or dyed-blue howlite crystal
A small piece of soft wire or strong thread to attach the crystal to a collar or cage
A dish of salt
A bowl of water

Timing:
After dark on a moonless night

The Spell

- Fasten the turquoise to the collar with wire or thread, saying, *Wind and bind protection in, still the hand of ill intention. I bind you in security, never to be taken unwillingly.*
- Add three pinches of salt to the bowl of water, stirring the salt with the index finger of your dominant hand and repeating the spell words three times.
- Using your dominant hand, sprinkle three circles of saltwater drops, moving outward from collar or looped turquoise (if it's being attached to a cage or hutch), saying for each circle, *Three by three, within this ring, protection from theft and malice bring.*
- Put the collar on the pet or suspend the looped turquoise from the cage or hutch, saying, *Stay safe with me, protected be.*
- Re-empower the turquoise monthly by leaving it in full moonlight.

TO PROTECT PETS FROM AGGRESSION FROM HUMANS AND ANIMAL PREDATORS

You will need:

Water or milk in the pet bowl
Dried mint or rosemary
An electric flashlight with a beam set to flash on and off continuously

Timing:
Late in the waning moon cycle, after dark

The Spell

- Outdoors, set the bowl of water or milk on the ground.
- Scatter a single counterclockwise circle of mint or rosemary around the bowl, saying nine times, *Cruel humans come not here, vicious people cause no fear. Aggressive creatures turn away, your claws and jaws no more have sway.*
- With the flashlight on continuous flash, move fast nine times counterclockwise around the bowl, spiraling the flashlight in counterclockwise circles nine times fast, saying nine times, *So I create this shield of light, to drive all harm from here this night.*
- Switch off the flashlight, take the bowl indoors, and put it down for your pet.
- Let the mint or rosemary blow away.

535

WHEN YOU AND YOUR PET MUST PART

You will need:

Seven strands of hair, cut from your head or taken from a brush

Seven strands of hair from the pet (if your pet's hairs are not very long strands, thread them to secure them together)

A small bag

Timing:

The night before parting

The Spell

- Tie together your hairs and your pet's hairs, making seven knotted strands and saying, *Though I know we must part, you remain precious in my heart.*
- Keep the knotted hairs in the bag under your pillow overnight.
- Take the hair out of the bag in the morning, leaving it outdoors to blow away. Say, Go *free to your new family. Happy in your new home be.*
- In the evening, face the new direction your pet is living and say, Go *free to your new family. Happy in your new home be.*

536

TO STOP YOUR PET FROM CONSTANTLY BARKING, YOWLING, PULLING OUT FUR OR FEATHERS, SPRAYING, SCREECHING, OR OTHER ANTISOCIAL BEHAVIOR

You will need:

Four drops of Dr. Bach's® flower remedies (beech, cherry, plum, or chicory, the Rescue Remedy®, or your favorite calming remedy in any other brand), diluted in a spray bottle about one-third full of water; or two drops of lavender or chamomile oil

Timing:

Initially, during the waning moon and again during the waxing moon

The Spell

- As you make the spray, say six times, *More sociable be that we may live in harmony. I no longer allow* [name worst habit(s)] *within these walls. Not anyhow, no way at all.*
- Spray any rooms the animal passes through, starting around his sleeping place or cage, around windows, inner doors, and thresholds, right to the door the animal customarily leaves through.
- Say continuously as you spray, *Loved you are and loved will be, but loved much more if sociably.*
- Open the exit door and, standing just within the doorframe, facing outward, use up the rest of the spray so it falls outside the house.
- Gently lead the creature or carry his cage on the same route. This time, as you reach the exit door, open it and say, *I no longer allow* [name worst habit(s)] *within these walls. Not anyhow, no way at all.*
- Close the front door and return the pet to his normal sleeping place.

537

EASING THE PASSING OF A BELOVED PET

You will need:

A beautiful flower or plant in a pot
A peaceful place indoors
Four dark-brown or dark-gray stones or crystals, one under each corner of the pet's sleeping place

Timing:

When you sense the end is near or the days before you take the animal to the vet

The Spell

- Set the plant near the pet in a peaceful place indoors. Put your hands around the pot, saying softly, Mother Earth will take you home when it is right to go. From love to love the angels above, the path of light will show.
- Sit close to the pet, whispering the name(s) of deceased family members who are waiting for the pet.
- Blow softly toward the pet six times, saying between each breath, With every breath comes peace. All suffering shall cease as you pass from love to love.
- Repeat the spell daily, morning and evening.
- After the pet passes, plant the flower on top of the grave or where you scatter the ashes, and bury the crystals around it.
- If you keep the ashes at home, put the plant close to the urn, surrounded by the crystals. Light a weekly candle in memory of the dear pet.

538

MOURNING THE LOSS OF A PET, IF THE PARTING WAS SUDDEN OR TRAUMATIC

You will need:

A white candle
A photograph of your pet

Timing:

Evening

The Spell

- Light the candle where you and your pet relaxed, saying, *Beloved friend, may I feel your softness and warmth one more time, until we meet again at the Rainbow Bridge at the Gates of Paradise, where you will be waiting.*
- Hold the photo in both hands, gazing at it until you have imprinted every detail on your memory, so when you close your eyes you can see your pet clearly in your mind's eye.
- Carry the photo and candle into the bedroom and say the same words while gazing at the photo once more.
- Put the photo next to the bed, repeat the spell words, and blow out the candle.
- You may be rewarded by a dream about your pet. As you fall into sleep and wake in the morning, you may feel the animal close to you in bed. Do not be surprised by a dent in the bedclothes.

539

TO SEE YOUR DECEASED PET CLAIRVOYANTLY

You will need:

A memento or photo of the pet

Timing:

The soft light of late afternoon

The Spell

- Call the pet's name softly aloud in a favorite spot, indoors or out.
- Focus on one spot of light where the pet stood or sat during life.
- Recall in your mind's eye the color of the fur, feathers, or skin in as great a detail as possible and say, *Come to me, momentarily, that I may see you safe and happy.*
- Extend your dominant hand to stroke where the fur or skin would have been.
- Continue to stroke your animal at the height he was in life, murmuring familiar words of endearment.
- Close your eyes, open them, blink, and you may see the pet in front of you just for a second, perhaps as though in mist.
- If not, you may feel her fur or just know your pet is healthy again and with you.
- Say, *I let you go in love, I would not hold you back. Until we meet again, our love always will be the same.*

540

HELPING A PHANTOM ANIMAL HAUNTING YOUR HOME OR THAT OF A FRIEND TO MOVE ON IF THAT ANIMAL IS CAUSING PROBLEMS

You will need:

A small ball

A bowl of water with three pinches of salt in it, stirred three times clockwise with a letter opener

Timing:

When the phantom creature is most active

The Spell

- Begin in the room with the most phantom animal activity.
- Sitting in the middle of the room, roll the ball slowly in the direction of the front door, saying, *This is no longer your home, do not linger, do not stay. The time has come to move away.*
- Keep rolling the ball, open the front door, and roll the ball outside.
- As you step outside, call whoever might know the animal, perhaps a deceased parent of the owner, to collect their pet.
- You may see a shimmer of light ahead or feel a breeze, for someone will come.
- Say, *Follow the ball to where those who will care for you soon will call.*
- Leave the ball and go indoors, closing the door.
- Sprinkle salt water around the entire house, saying, *Come not here again, you cannot remain. Go with those who are waiting.*

541

FOR PROTECTING ANIMALS IN THE WILD

You will need:

A green plant
Four feathers
A bowl of water

Timing:

Afternoon, especially if you hear of a danger or disaster to wildlife, locally or globally

The Spell

- Outdoors, set these three items in a triangle around you. Hold the plant between your hands and press your feet into the ground, saying, *I connect. Protect all creatures of the earth.*
- Plant the greenery near where you are standing, repeating the spell words.
- Pick up the feathers and divide them between your hands. Extend your arms upward and say, *I connect. Protect all the creatures of the air.*
- Release all the feathers except one or attach them with string to a nearby tree.
- Hold the water in your dominant hand, and, with the other, ripple it, saying, *I connect. Protect all the creatures of the waters.*
- Empty the water around the new plant and spiral the remaining feather over and around it four times, saying, *I connect. Protect all the creatures of the earth, sky, and waters.*
- Release the final feather or tie it to the tree, saying, *Fly free and send protection to all creatures of the earth, sky, and waters.*

542

TO PROTECT AN ENDANGERED SPECIES AND ITS HABITAT

You will need:

Tiny crystal chips, glass nuggets, or small stones
Dried flower petals, potpourri, or dried parsley
A smooth twig with a pointed end
A picture of the endangered creatures in their natural habitat
A green candle

Timing:

Wednesday afternoon

The Spell

- Indoors, set a square of crystals or stones and a square of flowers clockwise, enclosing the square of stones, leaving no gaps in either square. Then spiral the point of the stick over the squares, saying, *May none penetrate nor enter these walls without consent.*
- With the twig, draw a square in the air above the inner square and then over the outer square, both clockwise. Say, *Let none with ill intent or carelessness destroy this beauty, sanctity, security, safety, and sanctuary.* As you say *sanctuary*, draw in the air above the picture a diagonal cross with the twig, saying, *Security, safety, and sanctuary.* Scatter the outer square outdoors.
- Weekly, leave a green candle burning next to the crystals square, repeating, *Security, safety, and sanctuary.*

543

FOR SAVING ENDANGERED CREATURES FROM ILLEGAL HUNTING, POACHING, AND HUNTING PROGRAMS

You will need:

Small pictures of any endangered species at special risk
A red ribbon
A lidded box
Two old knives

Timing:

Monday night, during the waning moon

The Spell

- Tie all the pictures together, facedown, making nine knots with the red ribbon and saying for each knot, *Be bound you who hunt, maim, and kill. These knots restrain your evil will.*
- Put the pictures facedown in the box, saying, *Hidden be, find sanctuary from all who hunt and maim and kill, protected from their evil will.*
- Set the two knives crossed on top of the pictures (in this case, it's not unlucky to make a cross), saying, *Enter not you who hunt, maim, and kill. You are barred from your evil will.*
- Close the box and hide it.

544

A ST. FRANCIS OF ASSISI RITUAL FOR WILD CREATURES EVERYWHERE

You will need:

A clearing surrounded by a circle of trees
Natural food suitable for small animals and birds
A basket or pouch for the food

Timing:

Early on a Saturday

The Spell

- Walk around the inside of the tree circle clockwise, making smaller and smaller circles as you approach the center, scattering food and saying rhythmically, *Good St. Francis, do your part, take all creatures to your heart. The young, the old, the sick, the lame, fierce, or gentle to you are the same.*
- When you reach the center, scatter the rest of the food in all directions and stamp three times with each foot, saying, *Creatures of the ocean, creatures of the sea, creatures of the hills and plains by Francis protected be.*
- Sit in the center, naming creatures or species who need help and habitats under threat.
- Walk out in counterclockwise circles, whispering as you leave, *Good St. Francis, do your part. You hold all creatures in your heart, now and always.*

545

A ST. BLAISE RITUAL TO HELP ANIMALS IN BADLY RUN ZOOS AND IN CIRCUSES OR WHO PERFORM IN THE STREET ABROAD

You will need:

Eight small ceramic or children's miniature toy animals of ferocious or exotic species
A picture of a wild animal in its natural habitat
A picture of the same species in a cramped cage or performing
Scissors
An open pot
A handheld electric fan

Timing:

Early Friday

The Spell

- Place the toy animals in a circle, with the pictures side by side in the center, saying, *Good St. Blaise, who healed wild creatures in your cave, from cruelty and exploitation, I ask these creatures save.*
- Take the picture of the exploited creature and cut it in pieces, saying, *Good St. Blaise, you turned no creature away, release from captivity these hurt ones, I pray.*
- Name any causes dear to your heart.
- Throw the pieces into an open pot and dispose of them after the spell.
- Spiral the fan over the picture of the free creature and the model ones, repeating both sets of spell words.
- Put the picture of the free creature where you see it every day.
- Arrange the toy animals in your garden or among potted plants.

546

TO ASSIST ANIMALS AFTER A NATURAL DISASTER, SUCH AS AN OIL SPILL AT SEA

You will need:

A shallow dish
Blotting paper or an absorbent cloth
A green candle
A thriving green plant

Timing:

When you hear of the disaster

The Spell

- Put a little water in the bottom of the dish, saying, *This disaster,* [name it], *shall not hold sway. Strength and blessings I send this day to* [name creatures especially adversely affected].
- Using the cloth or blotting paper, mop up the water, saying, *May those who work to put this right be given strength by day and night, to life restore that all regrows as before.*
- Light the candle behind the dish and set the plant in its pot in the dish, saying, *New life, new light with each new dawn that after loss will come the morn.*
- Blow out the candle, sending light to where it is most needed. Each morning, relight the candle briefly and send the light to wherever it is needed.

547

A SPELL TO ABSORB THE STRENGTH OF A WILD CREATURE

You will need:

A small ceramic or wooden model of the animal whose strength you most need or a creature you regard as special to you (you could buy a whole selection for different qualities)

Timing:

When you most need the strength

The Spell

- Hold your symbol within your open, cupped hands, close to your mouth, saying, *Fill me with strength/ courage/adaptability/the power to rise high* [name the power you most need].
- Breathe in softly, then blow three times on the animal model, saying, *Let me share your power. May I absorb your strengths,* [name what is needed], *fill me at this hour as with your essence shower.*
- Close your eyes, imagining yourself merging with the creature, breathing, feeling, sensing, moving like the animal.
- Open your eyes and say, *You are within me and so shall I be* [name the power you need most].
- Gently shake the model six times in your closed hands, repeating the third set of spell words three times.
- Carry the model in a bag through the day.

548

A CHARM BAG FOR ENCOURAGING WILDLIFE TO RETURN TO AN AREA OR BODY OF WATER

You will need:

A hardy natural-fabric drawstring bag
Small natural items from the area, such as leaves, twigs, stones, or shells, to which the creatures are being called (back)
A moss or tree (dendritic) agate crystal, or a mottled stone
Dried sage

Timing:

The beginning of a week, month, or year

The Spell

- Fill the bag with the items in any order. Between each addition, shake the bag and say, *Hear my call, you creatures all. Find your way home, no longer roam, to the place you will be safe and welcome* [name any particular species you are calling, and the place].
- When you have finished filling the bag, close it and shake it as many times as there are objects or herbs, repeating the spell words.
- Take the bag to where the creatures are being encouraged to return and suspend it in a high place or under a rock.

549

FOR PROTECTING TROPICAL FISH, LIZARDS, SNAKES, AND EXOTIC PETS

You will need:
An aquamarine or fluorite crystal for fish, a snakeskin agate or turritella agate for lizards and snakes, and a sandy or brown jasper or petrified wood for exotic pets
A plate on soil or an open container in a bowl of water

Timing:
Saturday, or when you get a new pet

The Spell
- Leave the crystal outdoors on a plate on soil or floating in an open container in a bowl of water, if you're calling for protection of your own marine or pond life and for marine creatures everywhere, for a full twenty-four hours.
- Then take it and, holding it over the place where your creature is, say, *Be blessed by sun and moon and stars, by earth and sky and sea. Bring health and safety, peace and harmony, as long as your life may be.*
- Place the crystal in the tank, pond, or cage, repeating the same spell words.

550

GETTING GOOD LUCK FROM MAGPIES

You will need:
Magpies

Timing:
When you see magpie(s)

The Spell
- If you see a single magpie, traditionally regarded as unlucky, bow three times and say, *Good Morning, Mr. Magpie, and how are you today? Good luck will follow all day.*
- If you see a number of magpies together, regardless of the number, recite this adaptation of the old rhyme seven times very fast, *One's OK, two is better, three will bring a good luck letter, four for love and fertility, five and money comes to me, six brings gold in every way, and seven my secret wish, I say.*
- Turn around clockwise the same number of times as there are magpies and say, *The wish is mine and it shall be, the magpies bring good luck to me.*
- Say aloud three times what you really want, bow three times, and say, *Magpies bring my wish to me.*

CHAPTER 12

PROTECTION SPELLS

This chapter includes spells to protect you from deliberate malice and free-floating negativity, the Evil Eye and curses, paranormal influences and negative earth energies, physical attack and danger, and mind games and manipulation.

SECTION 1: PROTECTION FROM DELIBERATE MALICE AND FREE-FLOATING NEGATIVITY

551

USING FEATHERS AND KNOTS TO BIND THE TONGUE OF A REGULAR, UNAVOIDABLE VISITOR WHO CAUSES TROUBLE

You will need:

A dark-colored candle
A long red cord
Nine feathers
Red string

Timing:
Saturday, after dark

The Spell

- Light the candle and pass the cord and then each feather counterclockwise around the candle, saying for each one, *Still your tongue,* [name], *soften your words. Your unkindness shall no more be heard.*
- Secure each feather onto the cord with the red string, making a knot and saying for each one, *Bound are you from speaking nastily, barred from wounding thoughtlessly.*
- Extinguish the candle, saying, *Your power to hurt is ended, gone. Your power to harm is ended, done.*
- Hang the cord horizontally inside the front door or over an outside-facing window.
- After a month, set the feathers free outdoors, cutting the knots and saying, I release all negativity, transformed to positivity.
- If the person is set in his ways, repeat the spell monthly using new string and feathers.

552

TO KEEP AWAY THE SPITE AND VENOM OF HUMAN SNAKES

You will need:

A red candle
A wide-necked, screw-top dark glass bottle or a jar with a lid
Garlic powder
Vinegar or cheap red wine
Dried lemongrass (optional)

Timing:
Tuesday, after dark

The Spell

- Light the candle, working only by its light.
- Open the bottle and hold it between your hands, saying, *You* [do not name] *shall no longer spit your spite at me* [or name person you are protecting]. *It is not right and ends this night.*
- Fill a quarter of the bottle with the garlic powder, repeating the spell words three times.
- Add lemongrass, if you're using it, saying the spell words six times.
- Fill the bottle almost to the top with vinegar or wine, and secure the lid. Shake it nine times, saying nine times, *Hide your face in shame, you I do not name. You can no longer spit your spite at me* [or name person you are protecting]. *I am free.*
- Extinguish the candle, placing the bottle at the back of a dark cupboard or a garden shed.

553

TO DEFEND YOURSELF OR A LOVED ONE FROM UNFAIR ACCUSATIONS, LIES, AND GOSSIP

You will need:

A small bottle of vinegar with a pour spout in the lid

Timing:

When it is very dark

The Spell

- Stand outdoors, facing away from your home if the intrusion, intimidation, or gossip is a threat to you at home, even by phone or mail.
- If you are addressing workplace viciousness, face the direction of the workplace.
- If the malice is coming from a neighbor, face that neighbor's home.
- Point the index finger of your dominant hand toward the source of unpleasantness or straight ahead if it is coming from an unknown person, saying, *Desist, stop spreading lies, insinuations, defamations. All must cease.*
- Turn and drop a trail of vinegar behind you as you walk back to the house. Do not look back.
- Pour the remains of the vinegar under a cold running faucet, repeating the spell words until the bottle is empty.
- Throw away the vinegar bottle.

554

RETURNING MALICE TO THE SENDER

You will need:

Nothing

Incense stick

Timing:

After you have received a threat or experienced a nasty confrontation that has left you jittery

The Spell

- Beginning near the front door, go into every room and place your palm in the center of the window, with the palm facing the window and fingers slightly apart, and say as you do so, *This hand returns what is sent with ill intent. This hand returns to you the pain. Send it not ever again.*
- Do the same on the inside of any external doors, even if they are not glass.
- If the words or threat were particularly vicious, add at the end of each chant, *Receive back your own, that you may feel the pain, and send never again.*
- If you feel suddenly under threat at any time, draw the hand shape in incense stick smoke close to and facing each window and external doors (including balcony doors), repeating the full chant.

555

AN ALTERNATIVE WAY TO SEND BACK THE PAIN, WHETHER THE THREAT IS FROM A KNOWN SOURCE OR ANONYMOUS

You will need:

Dried tarragon or parsley
A lidded, dark-colored glass bottle
Milk that is beginning to curdle

Timing:

Toward the end of the moon cycle

The Spell

- Shake a little tarragon into the bottle and add the milk until the bottle is half full.
- Screw the lid on the bottle, shaking it, saying the person's name eight times and then saying eight times, *Bottle up the evil to me* [or name person hurt] *done. The pain is contained and all darkness gone.*
- Leave the bottle outdoors overnight.
- In the morning, dispose of the full bottle in a garbage can, if possible near the perpetrator's home or workplace, saying, *Bottled up and gone away. Returned to sender there to stay.*

556

REMOVING THE EFFECTS OF A NASTY TEXT MESSAGE, A MALICIOUS SOCIAL MEDIA POST, OR AN EMAIL

You will need:

The computer, tablet, or phone on which you received the message
A bowl of dried tarragon or parsley

Timing:

As soon as possible after receiving the message

The Spell

- Set the computer, tablet, or phone flat on a table, open to the message.
- Around it, sprinkle counterclockwise three circles of herbs, moving outward. Say as you do, *Vicious words depart from here, your malice I do hereby clear. Your nasty intent I return to source, accept back now this spiteful force.*
- Holding the phone or tablet, or putting your hands on the computer keyboard, delete the message letter by letter backwards and when the screen is empty, say, *Your nasty intent returned to source, accepted back this spiteful force.*
- Scoop up the herbs and wash them away with any leftover ones under running water.
- Block the source of the venom.

557

FOR STOPPING GOSSIP BEHIND YOUR BACK OR AN ORGANIZED SMEAR CAMPAIGN

You will need:

Two candles, one gray and one white, the gray to the left
A very long piece of dark-gray thread or dark-gray cord
A sharp knife or scissors
A bowl of soil

Timing:

When you are the victim of gossip or rumor

The Spell

- Light the gray and then the white candle, saying, *Shine light upon conspiracy, Burn away all secrecy.*
- Hold the cord in your dominant hand and cut it in thirds, saying, *Sever with steel conspiracy. Cut down to size all secrecy.*
- Take one-third of the cord and, holding an end in each hand, break the center in the white candle flame, saying as you drop it into the soil, *With flame remove conspiracy, with fire sear through all secrecy.*
- Bury the broken third in the soil, throw one third in the garbage, and hang one third on a tree or bush, saying for each one, *Let there now be clarity, an end to gossip shall there be.*

558

MAKING A PROTECTIVE BAG IF YOU HAVE TO SEE AN ANGRY EX BECAUSE OF CHILDREN, OR SOMEONE SERIOUSLY UNPLEASANT WHO UNSETTLES YOU

You will need:

A dried angelica root or rosemary
Salt and pepper mixed in a twist of silver foil
A small animal or bird bone, or seven black beads
A purple fabric drawstring bag
A few drops of brandy or barley wine

Timing:

Saturday, late evening

The Spell

- Place the angelica or rosemary, salt and pepper, bone or beads, one by one, into the bag. As you add each one, say, *Remain in secrecy. Protectors shall you be. Keep from me all fears and harm, though outside may rage, within me is calm.*
- In silence, sprinkle two or three drops of the alcohol over the contents of the bag, close the bag, and hide it at home.
- Replace the bag every two months, burying the old one under a dead tree or bush after dark.

559

TO STRONGLY REPEL NASTINESS AND BULLYING FROM SOMEONE SENIOR AT WORK

You will need:

A shiny or reflective object, such as a small hand mirror or a spare pair of glasses

Timing:

Ongoing

The Spell

- Before starting work, sit and hold your reflective shield in your closed hands, saying four times, *I charge you powerfully, let none intimidate me. Reflect back approaching negativity that none with bad intent may reach me.*
- Set your reflector between you and the route the bully takes to reach you.
- As the bully comes toward you, touch the shiny object in front of you and shout in your head, *Turn back, for me you can no longer crack. Take back what you inflict on me, for I strongly repel your negativity.*
- If she launches into a tirade, look full into her eyes, repeating the spell words in your head and refuse to react until she leaves.
- As soon as possible, splash water on the shiny or reflective object.

560

IF CERTAIN PEOPLE ARE ALWAYS BELITTLING YOU OR PUTTING YOU DOWN

You will need:

A shallow saucer or a flat dish (use an old one in case it cracks)

Tap water

Timing:

Before you encounter a particularly critical person or group, or even when you think of them

The Spell

- Put a small quantity of tap water into the saucer, setting it where the sun will shine or near a source of heat, such as a radiator.
- Say aloud or in your mind, *Sun power, at this hour, make harshness arid as the desert sands, that I may no longer feel or be helpless in their hands.*
- When all the water in the saucer has evaporated, remove it from the source of heat, saying, *Sun power at this hour, within me be the sun. For all to see against you,* [name], *I have won. I am pure gold, may all behold and treat me respectfully.*

561

TO GUARD AGAINST THE EVIL EYE

You will need:

A blue permanent marker
A small pressure-sensitive label
A double-sided small reflective mirror or an object with a shiny surface on both sides
An orange candle
A small dish of water containing a few grains of salt and a drop of olive oil

Timing:
As the sun is setting

The Spell

- Draw on the label an eye shape and stick the label onto the back of the mirror or shiny object.
- Light the candle and hold the mirror so you can see the candle in it, then flip it over so the candlelight illuminates the eye. Say, [Name], *your eye of envy, your glance of jealousy, reflected back shall be.*
- Sprinkle the unmarked side of the mirror or object with a little salt-and-oil water, and as you do, repeat the chant.
- Rub the mirror clean and keep the mirror positioned so when the person causing you problems approaches your home or workspace, the eye is facing you and the shiny surface is facing outward.
- Repeat the spell words silently when you meet the jealous person and avoid eye contact.

562

ANOTHER RITUAL TO PROTECT YOU FROM THE EYE OF ENVY IN YOUR DAILY LIFE

You will need:

A circle of six white candles
A rose or lavender incense stick
Your favorite piece of jewelry or one with a blue stone in the center of the circle
A dish of sand or soil

Timing:
Tuesday evening

The Spell

- Light each candle counterclockwise, saying for each one, *Shield me from the eye of envy by night and day, that I may live harmoniously, free from jealousy from whatever source or cause.*
- Light the incense from each candle in turn, repeating the spell words for each one.
- Holding the jewelry in your nondominant hand, draw over and over again an eye shape in incense smoke an inch or so above it, saying, *Turn away the eye from me, think not of me, speak not of me, act not against me, so is it decreed.*
- Extinguish the incense, lighted end downward, in the sand.
- Quickly blow out each candle counterclockwise, saying afterwards, *Three, two, one, envy is gone.*
- Whenever you feel under threat, touch the jewelry.

563

USING AN EGG TO BANISH CURSES, THE EVIL EYE, OR ILL INTENTIONS

You will need:
A fresh egg

Timing:
Sunday morning

The Spell

- Hold the egg so it touches the center of your brow, then the base of your throat, and finally place it against your heart, saying, *Take from me this darkness sent, its powers I now give in you. The malice is gone, it is spent and through.*
- Either leave the egg at an intersection or throw it against a tree so it breaks.

564

AN OIL BATH TO BANISH THE EFFECTS OF A NASTY PERSONAL ATTACK ON YOUR INTEGRITY OR LIFESTYLE, PROMPTED BY RESENTMENT OR JEALOUSY

You will need:
Lavender or rose essential oil or a Moroccan argan oil bath product

Timing:
The evening after the attack

The Spell

- To a bath of warm water, add six to nine drops of essential oil or your usual amount of the oil product.
- Swirl the water in both directions alternately nine times, saying nine times, *Wash from me this burden of unfairness, injustice, and iniquity, that I may once more see my worth, integrity, and beauty.*
- As you sit in the water, make crosses on the surface of the water and clear each with your hands, saying as a continuous chant, *I uncross this iniquity, that it may flow away and only blessings stay.*
- Swirl circles of the warm water all around you, saying continuously, *I have banished unjust strife and iniquity from my life. Only blessings remain and I am free again.*
- Get out of the bath, take out the plug, and afterwards rinse out the bathtub with cold water.

565

AN OLIVE OIL RITUAL TO TAKE AWAY THE EVIL EYE OF ENVY THAT CAUSES DISCRIMINATION AGAINST YOU

You will need:

A bottle of olive oil with a pour spout
A large bowl of cold water

Timing:

The end of the moon cycle

The Spell

- Add the olive oil, drop by drop, into the water until it makes a ring of oil on the surface of the water (practice this beforehand, if you wish).
- As you do this, say the Lord's Prayer or another favorite prayer or blessing, or say, *I call on the power of Light to bless this endeavor and drive away all darkness.*
- When the ring has formed, clap three times and say, The ill intention is broken.
- Throw the water out the front door, closing the door.
- Wash out the bowl, repeating, *The ill intention is broken.*

566

TO REMOVE A CURSE OR ILL INTENTIONS AGAINST YOU THAT YOU HAVE LEARNED ABOUT FROM A THIRD PARTY

You will need:

Three dark-blue candles of the same size, in a row
A jar of garlic salt

Timing:

Early Sunday morning, as dawn breaks

The Spell

- Place the candles in a row in holders, lighting them from left to right, one candle from the other.
- As the wax begins to melt, drop three grains of garlic salt into each flame. Say, *Three times as these candles burn, three times what is yours I do return. I will not accept your vicious curse, I send it back so do your worst.*
- Extinguish each candle in reverse order of lighting, saying afterwards, *The light fades, you have done your worst. Now feel the pain of your returned unwanted curse.*
- Throw away the candles and any remaining garlic salt.

567

REMOVING A CURSE WITH A SPIRIT TRAP

You will need:

Nine blackberry leaves or a thorn twig
A wide-necked, sealable bottle or jar
Three pinches of sea salt and six pinches of red (cayenne) pepper, dropped into a small jug of vinegar and swirled six times counterclockwise
Red thread
Packing tape

Timing:

Any night, at 10 p.m.

The Spell

- Add the leaves or twig to the jar. Pour in enough of the vinegar mix to cover the twig or leaves, saying, *Evil curse enter here, where you are trapped with barbs so fierce I need no longer fear.*
- Put on the lid and tie the jar all around with the red thread, making knots and saying, *Now the evil threat is bound, the curse is trapped and sealed around.*
- Seal the jar all around with packing tape, repeating the second set of spell words.
- The next morning, take the jar in a sealed bag to a garbage dump, or hide it in a dark place until the refuse is collected.

568

BLESSINGS AFTER VICIOUS WORDS WERE SPOKEN IN THE HEAT OF THE MOMENT

You will need:

A white pen or crayon and white paper
A blue pen
Rose-, sandalwood-, or lavender-based potpourri in a bowl

Timing:

The lightest part of the day

The Spell

- In white pen on the white paper, write not the nasty words but the hurt, anger, and sorrow you feel.
- Draw a blue diagonal cross over it, saying, *Let it go, for I know light is stronger than darkness, blessings are stronger than curses, and so I send blessings to you,* [name perpetrator], *that you will see the light.*
- Turn the paper over and write in blue ink, *I send blessings to* [name perpetrator], *that blessings will overcome curses and light displace the darkness that in the light revealed. All may soon be healed.*
- Fold the paper as small as possible. Bury it in the bowl of potpourri, repeating out loud the written words six times.
- Leave the potpourri in a light place in your home as long as it keeps its fragrance.

569

A CELTIC CIRCLING RITUAL TO DRIVE AWAY JEALOUSY OR ILL INTENTIONS AGAINST YOUR HOME AND FAMILY

You will need:

Photographs of any family member concerned on a table in the middle of the room

Nine white flowers in a circle around the photos (lilies are particularly effective for this spell)

An empty flower vase, also in the center of the table

Timing:

Sunday morning

The Spell

- Begin circling the table, saying, *Circle this home, Mother, Father, keep harm without, keep peace within. Circle this home, Father, Mother, keep all safe by day and night and bless them with the morning light.* Alternatively, you can dedicate this to a favorite angel.
- With each circuit, take a flower, so by the ninth circle and chant you are holding all nine flowers.
- Place the flowers one by one in the vase, saying for each one, *Blessings and protection on all.*
- Leave the flowers next to the pictures until the flowers fade.

570

A BRACELET CHARM TO GUARD CHILDREN AND OTHER LOVED ONES FROM ILL INTENTIONS AND ENVY

You will need:

A red coral or jet bracelet for adults and jade or pink coral for children; empower as many as you wish at the same time

A candle for each bracelet, with the bracelet in front of the candle in a circle

A bowl of mixed salt and pepper

Timing:

Monday morning

The Spell

- Hold each bracelet in turn, naming the recipient, saying, *May I/she/he be enclosed in this circle of love from all harm and ill intentions.*
- Light each candle in turn and hold its bracelet to the light, saying, *May I/she/he be enclosed in this circle of light from all harm and ill intentions.*
- Enclose the bracelets and candles in three counterclockwise circles of sprinkled salt and pepper, saying, *May I/she/he be enclosed in this circle of fierce protection from all harm and ill intentions.*
- Leave everything in place until the candles are burned.
- Dispose of any remaining salt and pepper under a running faucet, saying, *Wash away all harm and ill intentions.*
- Give the bracelets to the intended recipients.

PROTECTION FROM PARANORMAL INFLUENCES AND NEGATIVE EARTH ENERGIES

571

CALLING THE EARTH GUARDIANS TO KEEP AWAY ALL PARANORMAL HARM AND EVIL

You will need:

Four brown candles, one set near the corner of each internal wall in the room nearest the front door

A heatproof bowl of dried rose petals or rose potpourri, placed near the center of the room

Timing:

Sunday morning, at dusk

The Spell

- Light the first candle in the corner to the left farthest away from the door, saying, *Wise Guardians of the Earth, bless and protect my home this night. Keep us safe from bad spirits until first morning light.*
- Carry the bowl of potpourri to the lighted candle and briefly hold the potpourri above the candle, repeating the spell words.
- Return the potpourri to the center of the room and light the next candle, moving counterclockwise and repeating the spell words and actions. Do this until all four candles are lit.
- Carry and lift the potpourri in any doorway and in front of windows, moving counterclockwise, at each point repeating the spell words.
- Return the bowl to the center, letting the candles burn until bedtime.

572

A THREE-ANGEL BLESSING IF YOU LIVE ALONE AND FEEL SPOOKED OR SCARED AT NIGHT

You will need:

Three tall white candles

A mirror

A small bowl of salt

Timing:

Nightly, as darkness falls

The Spell

- Place the candles in a row, so you can see them reflected in the mirror.
- Light the candles left to right, saying for each, *Angels of light, Jeduthan, Muriel, and Natiel, turn back the phantoms of the night.*
- Put a pinch of salt into each flame, left to right, saying, *Angels of sleep, I ask you safely keep me from specters of the night, until dawn comes bright.*
- Blow out each candle in turn. As you do so, name each candle for one of the angels and add for each one, *Bless and keep me safe.*
- Replace the candles when needed, keeping the angel name order.
- Say each angel name before going to sleep.

573

TO QUIET A NOISY BUT FRIENDLY FAMILY GHOST

You will need:

A purple candle
A hand bell

Timing:
Before bed

The Spell

- Each night in the room where the ghost is felt most strongly, light the candle. If you know the identity of the ghost, name him or her, or if you just sense a benign presence, say, *Friend, you are welcome here. You keep us safe and so are dear.*
- Begin to ring the bell, first loudly and then more softly, until it can no longer be heard, and then say, *But quieter be, that we may live in harmony. Your noise can disturbing be, though I know you are helping me* (oftentimes, a noisy ghost will be tidying up or checking on children and disturbing them).
- Ring the bell softly nine times, saying once after each ring, *Let us live in harmony and share our home peacefully.*
- Blow out the candle, sending blessings to your ghost.

574

TO REMOVE A TROUBLESOME SPIRIT OR POLTERGEIST

You will need:

A white candle
A dish of salt
A bowl of water with five drops of lemon juice added
A silver-colored letter opener

Timing:
Sunday morning, early

The Spell

- Light the candle in the room where the paranormal presence is most active, saying, *By this bright flame, go now into the light, no longer linger here, by day or by night.*
- Drop three pinches of salt into the water, and with the letter opener make a cross three times on the surface of the water, mixing it nine times counterclockwise. Say, *By Water and by Earth no longer linger here. Go to those waiting to whom you are dear.*
- Carry the water to the front door, making a trail of water drops.
- Open the door and throw out the water, saying, *Go now to the light.*
- Carry the candle to the front door, step outside with it, and extinguish it, saying, *Go now to those who wait.*
- Shut the front door.

575

TO REMOVE A SPITEFUL SPIRIT OR POLTERGEIST WHO IS CAUSING TROUBLE

You will need:

A lemon-, lavender-, or pine-scented candle
A frankincense or sandalwood incense stick
A bowl of garlic powder surrounded by six six-pointed amethysts pointing outward

Timing:

Tuesday, around sunset

The Spell

- Light the candle in silence, and from the candle, the incense. Then write, around the garlic and around the amethysts in incense smoke letters, YOU MUST DEPART IN PEACE. YOUR PRESENCE I RELEASE, AND TROUBLE NOW MUST CEASE.
- With the candle in your dominant hand and the garlic in your nondominant hand, go outdoors and blow the candle out over the garlic. Empty the garlic powder bowl outside and let the candle burn.
- When the incense has burned out, place each amethyst on an indoor window ledge inside your home.
- Wash them weekly.

576

TO PREVENT GHOSTS FROM ENTERING YOUR HOME IF YOU LIVE IN A HAUNTED AREA OR NEAR A KNOWN GHOST PATH OR EARTH ENERGY LINE

You will need:

A bowl of water in which nine pinches of salt have been dissolved
Four large dark crystals, such as smoky quartz, obsidian, onyx, or jet

Timing:

The last day of the month

The Spell

- Stir the water four times with the pointed end of each of the crystals in turn, saying for each one, *Salt and water four by four, against restless spirits bar the door. All ghostly presences stay away, forbidden to enter by night or by day.*
- Immerse each crystal in the water four times, repeating for each one the spell words four times.
- Place two of the crystals, one on either side of the front door just inside the doorframe, and the same for any back door. If there is no back door, set the second two just outside the front door.
- Throw the water out of the front door, repeating the spell words.
- Wash the crystals under running water monthly and repeat the spell.

577

TO CLEAR YOUR HOME OF BLOCKED ENERGIES FLOWING BENEATH IT, WHICH MAY CAUSE LETHARGY OR MISFORTUNE AND KEEP PLANTS FROM GROWING

You will need:

Two large patchouli, pine, or lavender incense sticks

A bowl of sand or soil

Timing:

Wednesday, around 10 p.m.

The Spell

- Light the incense sticks, cross and uncross them repeatedly, moving your hands in a circle with the sticks almost upright so the smoke from each one mingles with the smoke from the other.
- Say, *May the wind's stagnation blow away; the blocked, the sour, the stagnant that may no longer stay.*
- Walk around each ground-floor room if you live in a house, or every room in an apartment, crossing and uncrossing the incense sticks and repeating the spell words softly.
- In each room or passage, start in the left-hand corner nearest the door, and move in a counterclockwise direction, pausing in front of the windows, again circling and chanting.
- Leave each room or area by facing inward through the door and crossing and uncrossing the incense sticks once, saying, *Flow free, harmoniously.*
- When you finish, stand as close to the center of the house or apartment as possible and plunge the incense sticks' lighted ends down together in the sand, saying, *Flow free, harmoniously, you energies below.*

578

USING THE NIGHT RAINBOW TO REMOVE OVERACTIVE NEGATIVE ENERGIES BENEATH YOUR HOME, IF PEOPLE ARE ALWAYS IRRITABLE AND HYPED UP

You will need:

Dark-red, silver, dark-green, dark-orange, deep-purple, midnight-blue, and burnished-gold candles, called the Night Rainbow

Seven round amethyst crystals or small crystal geodes (rocks with tiny crystals embedded inside)

Timing:

After dark

The Spell

- Start in the room where most quarrels with people or animals break out, and plants don't last long.
- Light your night rainbow candles in order, and set an amethyst in front of each one, saying, *Bring peace, let anger cease. Flow slowly, gently that there may be calm and no more harm.*
- Blow softly into each candle in order of lighting seven times, repeating the spell words once between each breath.
- Let the candles burn and then put an amethyst under the carpet or rug or behind furniture, dividing them between rooms.
- Point your index fingers down in the center of each room, repeating the spell words seven times.

579

MAKING POSITIVE ENERGIES FROM NEGATIVE TO ENHANCE THE ENERGIES IN YOUR HOME

You will need:

Nine small quartz crystals
Nine tiny bottles
A white candle (optional)
A green potted plant near the center of the home

Timing:

As the sun is rising

The Spell

- Add each quartz crystal separately to a jug with about a quart of water that has been boiled and cooled, saying, *Light flows and grows, darkness goes. Crystals work your magick and transform all.*
- Leave the crystals there until midafternoon, or until you come home. Then remove the crystals and pour the water in nine separate tiny bottles, repeating the spell words for each one as you close it.
- Pour away any excess water outdoors on either side of the front door.
- If it is dark, light a white candle next to the plant.
- Pour the first bottle of water over the plant, again saying the spell words, as you start to make a crystal circle around the plant.
- Repeat the spell whenever the plant needs watering, adding a crystal each time and saying the same words.
- When the bottles are empty, make more water for the plant in the same way.

580

USING DARK AND LIGHT CRYSTALS TO RELIEVE SICK BUILDING SYNDROME AT WORK WHERE PEOPLE ARE STRESSED AND OFTEN ABSENT BECAUSE OF MINOR ILLNESSES

You will need:

A mixture of five crystals, such as amber, amethyst, brown jasper, dark-banded agate, obsidian, or tiger's eye, untumbled if you wish
A large unpolished clear quartz crystal in the center

Timing:

Wednesday, or when you can be alone in the workplace

The Spell

- In your workspace, set the circle of crystals with the clear quartz crystal in the center.
- Hold each of the darker crystals in your hands separately, moving counterclockwise and saying for each one, *May darkness, sickness, and sorrow leave this place and be embraced by the light.*
- Return each one to the circle, holding your hands over the clear quartz crystal, fingers facing downward an inch or so above, and say, *Be filled with healing, that this workplace may be whole again and only good energies flow.*
- Turn in a circle, shaking your fingers on both hands in all four directions and repeating the second set of spell words.
- Hide the dark crystals in different parts of the workplace, perhaps in plants, and keep the clear quartz crystal in your workspace.

SECTION 4:

PROTECTION FROM PHYSICAL ATTACK AND DANGER

581

A MARS IRON PROTECTION RITUAL AGAINST INTRUDERS OR SOMEONE WHO COMES TO YOUR DOOR TO INTIMIDATE YOU

You will need:

A small quantity of soil
A small dish of salt
A ceramic lidded jar
Eighteen paper clips, each straightened out and shaped into a small horseshoe
Dried rosemary
Sour or Inexpensive red wine or vinegar

Timing:
Beginning Tuesday and for eighteen nights, consecutive if possible

The Spell

- The first Tuesday, add a sprinkling of soil and salt to the jar, saying, *The protection of Mars makes iron walls, impenetrable to those who call, with hate or malice in their heart. Depart, I say, depart.*
- Add a U-shaped paper clip to the jar, saying the same spell words.
- Place some dried rosemary in it, put on the lid, and shake it nine times, repeating the spell words nine times. Repeat this each night.
- When you have put in all 18 paper clips, add sour red wine; close the jar and shake it nine times, saying nine times, *Ferment, you are sent back by Mars's iron will. Barred from here, never again to appear.*
- When it is dark, bury the jar outside or dispose of it.

582

TO BIND A PERSON CAUSING HARM TO CHILDREN OR VULNERABLE PEOPLE

You will need:

Dark-colored modeling clay
A white candle
A myrrh, dragon's blood, or frankincense incense stick in a deep holder that will catch the ash
A dark-colored drawstring bag

Timing:
Thursday evening

The Spell

- Using the modeling clay, make a small, featureless doll to represent the dangerous person.
- Light the candle and the incense stick from the candle.
- Weave a smoke incense curtain of knots around the figure, tied with four smoke knots to form a square above the smoke curtain.
- Say as you do this, *You are bound from approaching those whom you would harm, tied until your darkness shall turn to light. Gone are your victims, gone from your sight.*
- Extinguish the candle and let the incense stick burn down.
- When the ashes are cool, sprinkle them on the doll, putting the doll in the bag out of sight in a dark cupboard, saying, *May the mists remain, you cannot harm again, for bound you are until your darkness turns to light and wrong to right.*

583

AN OLD WELSH RITE TO PROTECT YOUR HOME FROM BURGLARS OR VANDALS, ESPECIALLY IF THE HOME IS OFTEN LEFT UNATTENDED

You will need:

A key to the premises
A small metal box
A bowl of caraway, cumin, or coriander seeds
A padlock

Timing:

A cloudy night

The Spell

- Hold the key, saying, *Key of my home, of all I love, bind with iron chains my sanctuary, turn away all with ill intent. Empty-handed be you sent.*
- Place the key in the box, repeating the spell words.
- Empty the seeds into the box and say, *Turn away all with ill intent, empty-handed be you sent.*
- Close the box, fasten the padlock, and throw away the padlock key, saying, *So my treasures I secure, against this power shall none endure.*
- Bury the box in the garden or store it high on the back of an old shelf.

584

A SECOND BOX AND KEY RITE FOR RESTRAINING AN ANGRY OR VIOLENT PERSON FROM ATTACKING OR THREATENING YOU OR A LOVED ONE

You will need:

Red children's modeling clay
A wooden or metal box
Three cloves of garlic
A padlock with chain and key

Timing:

Saturday evening, late

The Spell

- Using the modeling clay, make a small featureless figure, saying, *Cut down to size, your threats and anger no more rise. From striking further fear, I restrain you here.*
- Drop the figure in the box and crumble garlic over it.
- Close and lock the box, removing the key and saying, *Your threats are empty, useless your power to prey on vulnerability, for I am strong. I bind you thus from harming me* [or name person under threat]. *I take away the key.*
- Take the box to the garbage dump and throw the box and the key into one of the deep piles, saying, *You are bound until the key be found.*

585

PROTECTIVE DRAGON POWER AGAINST ALL WHO WOULD HARM YOUR LOVED ONES, HOME, OR BUSINESS PREMISES, OR STEAL WHAT IS PRECIOUS TO YOU

You will need:

Three red candles
A small red and gold model dragon or a picture of a dragon
Dried tarragon or thyme

Timing:

Tuesday, after dark, then two more nights

The Spell

- Light a candle behind the dragon.
- Hold the dragon in your dominant hand, passing the dragon three times counterclockwise, three times clockwise, and three times counterclockwise around the flame and saying nine times, *Dragon, your fierce defense I ask, that from this hour, wrongdoers feel and fear your power. Accept this task on my behalf.*
- Add a sprinkle of tarragon to the flame, repeating the spell words.
- Let the candle burn down.
- Repeat the spell words and actions for the next two nights.
- Hide the dragon in your home or on your business premises, wrapped in red cloth.

586

DRAWING BOUNDARIES TO BANISH A STALKER, NASTY NEIGHBORS, AN UNSCRUPULOUS DEBT COLLECTOR, OR AN EX WHO HARASSES YOU

You will need:

A small bowl of salt
A small container of soil
A small jug of water

Timing:

Sunset

The Spell

- Sprinkle nine pinches of salt on top of the soil and add nine drops of water so the soil is still crumbly, then say, *By salt, earth, and water, three by three, you* [name person], *can no longer reach me. By salt, earth, and water, three by three, banished henceforward shall you be.*
- Outside your home or business, facing the sunset, scatter a straight line of the soil, salt, and water mixture in front of you.
- Take a step backwards in the direction of your home, making a second line, and step back again, making a third line.
- Stand behind the three lines, facing the fading sun, and say, *By salt, earth, and water, you can no longer reach me.*
- Go indoors and close the door, leaving the container outside to be scattered in the morning.

587

A VIKING RITUAL, USING THE HAMMER OF THOR AGAINST THREATS OF ATTACK WHEN YOU ARE IN POTENTIALLY DANGEROUS SITUATIONS OR PLACES

You will need:

An etching tool, such as a sharp screwdriver or a penknife
A small twig
A sandalwood, oakmoss, clove, or sage incense stick
A small red bag

Timing:

Thursday, the day of Thor

The hammer of Thor

The Spell

- Find a sheltered place outdoors and etch on both sides of the twig, scraping off enough bark, the rune symbol Thurisaz, the hammer of Thor. Then say, *Mighty Thunder Lord Thor, in times of threat and danger, shield me from malicious strangers and all who would do me harm.*
- Light the incense and, holding the symbol in your nondominant hand, draw nine smoke Thor symbols around it. Then say the spell words nine times.
- Carry your protective hammer symbol in its bag with you when you have to visit an unsafe location.
- If you're afraid, draw the Thurisaz sign in the air in front of you or picture it glowing red in your mind.

588

A GARLIC PROTECTION RITUAL TO GUARD YOUR HOME FROM FAMILY FRIENDS YOU DO NOT TRUST AND FROM CON MEN

You will need:

A green candle
A string of garlic bulbs
A dish of salt

Timing:

Tuesday morning, in your kitchen

The Spell

- Light the candle and set the string of garlic around it in a circle, saying, *So shall this garlic reveal those who mean not well. Garlic repel all ill intent, however sent.*
- Sprinkle a pinch of salt in the flame, saying, *So shall this light reveal those who mean not well, light repel all ill intent, however sent.*
- Touch each garlic bulb in turn, moving counterclockwise, and sprinkle salt on it, saying for each, *So shall salt and garlic reveal those who mean not well. Garlic repel all ill intent however sent.*
- Blow out the candle, saying, *I call on this garlic, I call on this light, protect me from thief and trickster by day and by night.*
- Shake off excess salt from the garlic, hanging the garlic string in the kitchen where air can circulate around it until it shrivels.
- Bury it and replace it, repeating the spell.

589

TO GUARD YOU OR FAMILY MEMBERS AGAINST ACCIDENTS, MISFORTUNE, OR ATTACK

You will need:

A bowl of salt
A feather
A bowl of water
Nine, in total, of any of the following blunt or rusty items: a knife, scissors, a razor blade, metal nails, pins, needles, or screws
A large piece of plastic protective wrapping
A large padded bag
A red pen

Timing:
At a full moon

The Spell

- Sprinkle salt around each item, except the plastic protective wrapping and the bag, moving counterclockwise, saying for each one, *Danger be blunted and lose your edge*.
- Spiral the feather nine times over each item, moving counterclockwise and repeating the same words over each one.
- Spread out the plastic wrapping, adding each item separately.
- Close the wrapping, placing the parcel in the padded bag, repeating the spell words nine times as you do so.
- On the front of the bag write in red pen, BLADE TURN YOUR SHARPNESS FROM ME/MY FAMILY. MAY THIS PROTECTION LAST FOR YEARS, THREE BY THREE.
- Put the parcel in an inaccessible place.
- Repeat the spell every nine years.

590

A TRADITIONAL SEED CHARM TO KEEP MALEVOLENT OR SPITEFUL PEOPLE FROM ENTERING YOUR HOME

You will need:

A long seed net or a fine-mesh bird feeder, the kind you hang on trees
Birdseed

Timing:
Friday, traditionally Good Friday

The Spell

- Fill the net or feeder with seeds, and, as you do so, say very fast over and over again, *Count the seeds, never the same, count the seeds or leave in shame*.
- When the net or feeder is full, seal it.
- Hold it between your hands, opening and closing your hands around it nine times, repeating the spell words nine times fast.
- Suspend it where wild birds can feed from it, and when it is empty, repeat the spell and refill it.
- Empty any leftover birdseed on the ground, repeating the spell words nine times.

591

FOR THOSE WHO LOVE TOO MUCH AND STICK WITH LOST CAUSES OR STAY WITH PARTNERS WHO WILL NEVER CHANGE OR RETURN

You will need:
Five fading flowers

Timing:
For five days, after dark

The Spell

- On day 1, take the first flower outdoors and pluck each petal, dropping it on the ground and saying afterwards, *Step by step I let you go, though my soul is heavy, it must be so. I let you go with much heartache, as this connection I now do break.*
- Each day do and say the same things.
- On the morning of day 6, buy a small fragrant plant or a crystal and set it where it will catch the light.
- Block any incoming phone numbers and cut off social media contact with the partner who you know in your heart will never change, and make plans to do new things.
- If this is too hard, repeat the five-day cycle until that new growth comes, buying a small plant or crystal each time.

592

TO LESSEN THE POWER OF RELATIVES OR FRIENDS WHO DRAIN YOUR MONEY, RESOURCES, AND TIME

You will need:
Ten coins in a circle around the jar
A clear jar with a screw-top lid
Dried bay leaves, the kind you use for cooking
An old string of beads or a chain whose links you do not mind breaking

Timing:
Wednesday evening

The Spell

- Touch each coin clockwise, saying three times, *Money is not endless, my finance is hard won. Though I dearly love you, I'm not an endless loan.*
- Drop the coins one by one in the jar, repeating the spell words three times.
- Add ten bay leaves, one at a time, saying three times, *Time is not endless, resources not limitless. Though I dearly love you, your demands do make me stress.*
- Break the links or beads, and drop them one by one into the jar, saying, *These unfair ties I do break, though not the link of love. No more advantage you shall take, enough is enough.*
- Screw on the lid, shake the jar ten times, repeating the spell words three times.
- When demanding people impose on you, shake the jar ten times before making your reply.

593

TO RESIST PRESSURE TO CONFORM TO FAMILY BELIEFS OR TO ACCEPT A SITUATION YOU KNOW IS WRONG FOR YOU

You will need:

A silver ring that fits you
A bowl of water
A small white cloth

Timing:

Full-moon night or when the moon is shining bright

The Spell

- Go outdoors and face the moon.
- Put the ring on a finger of your nondominant hand and run your other index finger around it seven times, saying seven times, *Lady Moon, none shall bind me, nor confine. Lady Moon on this ring shine, set me free, at liberty, that courage will be mine.*
- Walk in a complete circle seven times counterclockwise, repeating the spell words seven times.
- Plunge your hand, wearing the ring, in the water seven times, saying, *I will be free, at liberty. Lady Moon let this be soon.*
- Using the cloth, rub the ring dry while on your finger and empty the water on the ground, saying, *Lady Moon, take these restrictions from me, that I may be at liberty.*
- Wear the ring and touch it when you're under pressure to conform.

594

TO BLOCK EMOTIONAL VAMPIRES WITH A MIRROR

You will need:

A purple candle
A small wall mirror
A soft white cloth

Timing:

Sunday

The Spell

- Light the candle and hold the mirror in your nondominant hand so you see the reflection of the candle in the mirror. Say, *Light bright, from the sight of me, take the intensity of* [name of emotional vampire] *that no more shall I be drained by his company.*
- Still holding the mirror, use your dominant hand to polish the mirror in counterclockwise circles, saying continuously, *Mirror reflect back all you see.* [name of emotional vampire], *cease to sap your strength from me. No more shall you drain my energy.*
- Put down the cloth, look straight into the mirror, extinguish the candle, and hang or prop up the mirror so it faces the direction from which the emotional vampire will come, or above a phone or computer.

595

LEMON PROTECTION RITUAL WHEN MEETING OVERCRITICAL OR EMOTIONALLY DRAINING PEOPLE

You will need:

A small clear bottle of mineral or tap water with a lid
A bottle of lemon juice

Timing:

Before you meet the person who criticizes you or saps your energy

The Spell

- Open the bottle and add six drops of lemon juice to the water.
- Close the bottle and shake it six times, saying six times, *Protect me from hostility, shielded from* [name] *may I be. And those who come to put me down cannot reach me with their frown.*
- Keep the bottle between you and the person as she speaks, even if you put it in your bag on the floor.
- If you feel threatened, sip the water, repeating the spell words in your mind six times.
- At the end of the day, pour the water down the drain, saying as you do so, *Your negative thoughts not needed, your spiteful words unheeded, washed from the river to the sea, and so no more you trouble me.*
- If you work in a stressful environment, do this daily.

596

TO COUNTER THOSE WHO PLAY MIND GAMES WITH YOU

You will need:

Rose or lavender essential oil or a favorite fragrance

Timing:

Morning and evening

The Spell

- Each morning, rub a drop of oil or fragrance counterclockwise into the center of your brow above and between your eyes, the site of your psychic third eye center, through which most manipulators attack, saying, *I seal the entrance to my spirit against all that is not from the light.*
- Do the same for the center of your throat, saying, *I seal the entrance to my spirit against words not from the light.*
- Repeat the spell words for your two inner wrist points to protect your heart energy center, saying, *I seal the entrance to my spirit against guilt and possessiveness that comes not from the light.*
- Repeat the spell every evening and morning.

597

A DARK-OF-THE-MOON PROTECTIVE RITUAL TO COUNTER THOSE WHOM YOU SUSPECT USE BLACK MAGICK TO TRY TO CONTROL YOU

You will need:
A dark-colored candle
A dark-colored cord
A heatproof bowl of sand or soil
Water in which salt has been stirred

Timing:
One of the two nights before the crescent moon, after dark

The Spell
- Light the candle in complete darkness.
- Hold the center of the taut cord so it is in the candle flame. Say, *I break the link from you to me. No more to bewitch, twist, or reach my mind. No longer can you find me. I am gone beyond your sight, into the light.*
- When the cord breaks, let it burn in the bowl of sand or soil.
- Switch on all the lights and rub three drops of salt water clockwise in the center of your brow, saying, *I call the blessings of light and goodness to protect me from* [name any potential harmdoer].
- Blow out the candle and throw away the cord, sand/soil, and salt water.

598

TO REMOVE THE INFLUENCE OF SOMEONE CONTROLLING YOUR LIFE THROUGH FEAR OR GUILT

You will need:
A miniature bar of soap
A small letter opener or nail file (optional)

Timing:
Every time you take a bath or shower

The Spell
- Etch on the soap, THE WAY IS CLOSED.
- Draw a square around the words.
- Alternatively, write the words and draw the square invisibly with your index finger.
- Make a diagonal cross, either actual or invisible, through the square, repeating the spell words.
- Leave the soap in your bathtub or shower, even if you use a gel for washing yourself, saying, *Diminished, fading, your power melts and is no longer felt.*
- Keep the soap just for yourself.
- Next time you use the soap, etch again the words and shapes or redraw them invisibly until the soap is gone.
- If the matter is urgent, on day 1, melt the marked soap in hot water and throw water and melted soap down a drain.

599

TO LOOSEN THE GRIP OF A POSSESSIVE OR PERSISTENT WOULD-BE LOVER OR EX-LOVER WHO WILL NOT LET GO

You will need:

A long pin or strong needle
A colored candle

Timing:
Toward the end of the waning moon cycle

The Spell

- Holding the pin in your dominant hand, name the person whose power over you wish to remove.
- Light the candle, and as the wax begins to melt, stick the pin carefully about a third of the way down the candle so that it penetrates the wick within. Say, *Burn candle, burn, your gaze from me turn,* [name person].
- When the pin falls from the candle say, *Fall, pin, fall. You pierce me not at all. No longer call.*
- Let the candle burn through.

600

TO DEFEND YOURSELF FROM PEOPLE WHO HAVE A DESTRUCTIVE FASCINATION WITH YOU OR YOUR LOVED ONES

You will need:

A dark-blue candle
A pot, preferably iron or ceramic
Water
Dried parsley
Dried rosemary
Dried nettles (optional), available from health food stores or specialty food outlets
A small bowl

Timing:
Midnight

The Spell

- Light the candle and half-fill the pot with water so the light shines on the water.
- Mix the herbs in the bowl and sprinkle them, pinch by pinch, onto the surface of the water, saying as you do so, *You fascinate me* [or name family member], *and so control my mind. But when these herbs dissolve away, no longer will you bind.*
- Keep sprinkling and saying the spell words until all the herbs are in the water.
- Blow out the candle and say, *Your power to fascinate is done, your time of influence is gone. I cast away your hold on me* [or name family member], *and so your lure shall no more be.*
- Pour the herb water onto soil.
- Repeat the spell weekly, if necessary.

CHAPTER 13

SPELLS FOR FRIENDS AND NEIGHBORS

The spells in this chapter include those for making new friends and strengthening existing friendships; dealing with friendships that have gone wrong; dealing with difficult neighbors; and for living happily in the community.

MAKING NEW FRIENDS AND STRENGTHENING EXISTING FRIENDSHIPS

601

TO ATTRACT NEW FRIENDS INTO YOUR LIFE

You will need:

Two bright red candles, placed side by side
Any incense stick between the candles
A bowl of water
A long, thin strip of white paper
A bowl of soil

Timing:
Sunset

The Spell

- Light the candles, left to right, saying, *Life move and mingle, stir and shake, that I may soon new friendships make.*
- Light the incense from each candle. Holding the incense stick in your dominant hand, make large circles in both directions over the candles, repeating the words faster and faster until you can swirl and chant no faster.
- On the final word, make, plunge the incense stick's lighted end down into the water.
- Write on the paper using the end of the extinguished incense stick, BRING NEW FRIENDS SOON.
- Burn the end of the paper in the flame and drop it in the soil, saying, *Flames dance, I take a chance. New friends come to me, good friends they will be.*
- Blow out the candles,
- Bury the ashes and soil outdoors.

602

TO FIND FRIENDSHIP IN A NEW AREA TO WHICH YOU HAVE MOVED

You will need:

Seven small yellow candles
A photo of yourself in a happy social situation
Seven yellow ribbons

Timing:
Wednesday, and the following six days

The Spell

- Light a candle to begin a candle circle around the photo, saying, *I welcome new friends eagerly to increase my sociability, and soon I will find friends of like mind.*
- Tie the first ribbon to the second, saying, *I create a new circle of friendship in my life.*
- Blow out the candle, leaving the ribbons coiled on top of the picture.
- For the next five days, repeat the spell, adding an extra candle to the circle, tying one extra ribbon each time.
- On day 7, at the end of the spell, join the first and last ribbons to make a complete circle, saying, *I have created a new circle of friendship in my life.*
- Let the candles burn. Place the picture with the ribbon circle around it where natural light shines.

603

TO WIDEN YOUR CIRCLE OF FRIENDS AND SOCIAL LIFE

You will need:

Four red candles in a square, one in the middle of each side

An incense stick to the right of the square

In the center of the candles, a small item you take with you socially, such as car keys, a purse, or a favorite necklace

Timing:

Before you go out socially

The Spell

- Light the four candles, moving clockwise, starting with the one farthest from you.
- Light the incense stick from each candle in turn, and pass it in the air around the small item in the circle of candles, making four smoke squares in incense smoke about it.
- On circuit 5, hold the incense above the first candle, saying, *Four walls surround me, four walls enclose me. I take away the walls.*
- Blow out the first candle, repeating the words and actions for the other three in turn, saying after the last one, *There are no walls, friendship calls.*
- Let the incense burn.
- Take the empowered item with you to a social event.

604

FOR MAKING FRIENDS IN A NEW WORKPLACE

You will need:

A small magnet

A small deep ceramic or wooden bowl filled with either small crystals, glass nuggets, or potpourri

Timing:

Your first day at work, and then weekly

The Spell

- Hold the magnet in your close cupped hands and say in your mind three times, *Attract to me people who good friends will be. Though I am new, I offer you kindness, fun, and honesty, as you will see.*
- Put your hands around the filled bowl and say the same words three times in your mind.
- Bury the magnet, with the attracting point facing outward, in the bowl of crystals, saying in your mind, *Draw to me those who will show hospitality. But to any acting resentfully, invisible may I be.*
- At the beginning of every workweek, put your hands in the bowl, touch the magnet, and repeat both sets of spell words in your mind.

605

FOR MAKING FRIENDS THROUGH A NEW ACTIVITY OR INTEREST

You will need:

A steamed-up bathroom mirror
A small white cloth

Timing:

Before going along to the new activity for the first time

The Spell

- Write on the steamed-up mirror, POPULAR AND NOTICED I SHALL BE. MAKE FRIENDS THROUGH THIS ACTIVITY. Name the activity aloud.
- Start to slowly clear the mirror with the cloth in counterclockwise circles, so more of you gradually becomes visible.
- Once the mirror is clear, say, *Clearly accepted I will be in this shared activity. Welcome friends come now to me.*
- Smile at yourself in the mirror.
- When you reach the venue, go into the bathroom and smile in the mirror, saying all the spell words in your mind.

606

FOR MAKING FRIENDS SAFELY ONLINE

You will need:

A computer, tablet, or smartphone you use to communicate through social media or website forums online
Four green and black malachite or smoky quartz crystals
A padlock and key

Timing:

Before communicating online with people you do not know well

The Spell

- Switch on the computer, tablet, or smartphone, not yet logging onto social media.
- Hold the crystals in your closed hands, first to the center of your brow, then to the base of your throat, and finally to your heart, saying at each point, *On the information highway protect me from those with ill intent. On the information highway may only those stay with goodness sent.*
- Place a crystal at each corner of the device, saying the same spell words.
- Go to the chosen site.
- Close the padlock, saying, *Tricksters with false identity, deceivers do not trouble me.*
- Open the padlock, saying, *Welcome all with genuine heart, in my life may you long be part.*
- Make connections, but if you're unsure of someone, close the padlock, saying the words in your mind before giving out any personal information.

607

RECONNECTING WITH AN OLD FRIEND ON SOCIAL MEDIA

You will need:

A computer, tablet, or smartphone you use to communicate via social media sites online

A magnifying glass

Timing:

Before connecting live online

The Spell

- Put on the screen of your computer, tablet, or smartphone the page with the image of the person, but go offline.
- Hold the magnifying glass away from the image of the person onscreen so you can just see it through the glass, saying, *Let the years fade away, let the lost time fall. Move nearer once more and good times recall.*
- Move the glass so the image becomes closer and closer and when it blurs, put down the glass, saying, *Close are we once again and closer friends we shall remain.*
- Go online and make contact.

608

FOR A HAPPY REUNION WITH OLD FRIENDS, ESPECIALLY IF YOU HOPE TO REKINDLE A ROMANTIC CONNECTION WITH SOMEONE SPECIAL

You will need:

Any fruit-fragrance incense stick

An old photo of the class, university group, or workplace party

Timing:

The night before the reunion

The Spell

- Light the incense and, holding it like a smoke pen, swirl it around the edges of the picture, saying, *Years of pleasure I still treasure, old friends, old trends, friendship and love never end.*
- Using incense smoke above the picture, with two-way smoke lines, join you and the person or people with whom you hope to rekindle romance or friendship.
- Finally, write the name of the person or people with whom you most want to connect in smoke, then your own name above.
- Enclose any name where you hope for romance in a smoke heart, saying the spell words once more.
- Let the incense burn through.
- When you arrive at the reunion, find somewhere quiet and repeat the spell words three times.

609

TO KEEP A LONG-DISTANCE FRIENDSHIP THRIVING

You will need:

A small yellow candle
A red permanent or nonfading ink pad
A map on which you have marked the places where you and the friend live, to the right of the candle

Timing:
Wednesday, preferably on a windy day

The Spell

- Light the candle, saying, *The distance fades, miles disappear. When I think of you, I know you're here.*
- Draw a line in pen on the map from where you are to where your friend is living, saying, *Joined we are in friendship, a friendship just as strong. Across the world, across the street, our hearts and minds will always meet.*
- Leave the candle burning, go outdoors, face the direction in which your friend lives, call his name, and send a message of love.
- Follow up with a social media post, a letter, or an email before the candle is burned through.

610

FOR TURNING FRIENDSHIP INTO LOVE

You will need:

A very long yellow ribbon
A picture of you and your friend together (if necessary, crop a group photo or use an image-editing program to create a picture of the two of you together); if you don't "do" technology, cut out the two images and paste them on paper

Timing:
Any day between the crescent moon and the full moon

The Spell

- Begin to wind the ribbon around the image, saying, *Look at me through the eyes of love. Let passion flare, may closeness grow. The deep bonds are already there, but true love I would know.*
- Secure the ribbon with three knots, saying, *Three times the link between us grows. We are good friends, but true love may you show.*
- Keep the picture and ribbon under your pillow for three days.
- On day 4, undo the ribbon, saying, *Three times the link between us free; let love between us grow willingly. Look at me through the eyes of love.*
- Cut a small piece of the ribbon off and wear it in a knot next to your skin.
- Keep the rest in a drawer with the picture, wrapped in something soft belonging to you.

611

TO BANISH COLDNESS OR ESTRANGEMENT CAUSED BY A SIMPLE MISUNDERSTANDING

You will need:
A small cooking pot
Water
Dried mint
A wooden spoon

Timing:
Midday

The Spell
- Half-fill the pot with water and set it on a stove.
- Add ten pinches of mint to the water, stirring it in both directions and saying, *All can be mended and coldness be ended.*
- Heat the herb water, stirring it constantly with the spoon and saying over and over again, *All can be mended and coldness be ended. Let warmth between us be restored so we can be good friends once more.*
- When the water is boiling, turn off the heat, removing the pot from the stove.
- While it is still quite hot, empty the mixture into a hole you have dug in the ground, and fill it in, saying, *Buried is the cause of dissension. Warmth between us is restored and we will be good friends once more.*
- Make a gesture of reconciliation soon afterward.

612

TO OVERCOME A HURTFUL EXPERIENCE IN AN OTHERWISE GOOD FRIENDSHIP

You will need:
A glass bowl half-filled with water
A bottle of rose, lavender, or other floral-fragranced oil

Timing:
Friday, as light fades

The Spell
- Ripple the water with the fingers of your nondominant hand, saying, *Troubled water take away the pain of thoughtlessness, the hurt of carelessness, this undeserved distress with the ending of this day.*
- Pour six single drops of oil slowly onto the surface of the water, saying softly for each one, *Oil on troubled waters do I pour. Let go, let flow, forgive, forget; friendship can be restored once more.*
- Put down the bottle. Swirl the water very gently, this time with your dominant hand, repeating the second set of spell words six times.
- Empty the oily water under a fast-flowing faucet, saying, *Oil on troubled waters takes away all sorrows with the ending of the day.*
- Resolve to think and speak no more of the matter.

613

FOR RIDDING YOUR CIRCLE OF FRIENDS OF A TROUBLEMAKER

You will need:
A bouncy ball

Timing:
Early, when you are undisturbed

The Spell

- Bounce the ball against a wall and catch it, bounce it on the ground, or throw it up and catch it until you have established a rhythm.
- Say as you bounce, *Out you go,* [name], *for you must know: what you do just will not do; out you go. For you must know, it shall be so, go bother someone new.*
- If you drop the ball say, *Out you go, it shall be so.* Continue bouncing the ball and start the rhyme again.
- When you feel ready, kick the ball away and say, *Out you've gone, your power is done.*
- Leave the ball where a child will find it.

614

WHEN YOUR PARTNER HATES YOUR BEST FRIEND OR VICE VERSA

You will need:
Three cords or ribbons in different colors

Timing:
A few hours before you are all due to meet

The Spell

- Set the cords one below the other with the one you have chosen to represent you in the center.
- Pick up the cord for your partner, saying, *Bitch and whine, complain and whine, make an effort, love of mine. Desist, resist this bickering.*
- Do the same for your friend's cord, changing the words from *love of mine* to *friend of mine.*
- Braid the cords together with yours as the central strand, saying, *So I wind good feelings 'round, of disagreement not a sound. When together we will meet, polite and sunny will we greet. Not just you and not just me, but all three of us in harmony.*
- Knot the cord and hang it behind the front door.

615

WHEN YOUR BEST FRIEND IS POSSESSIVE OF YOU OR JEALOUS OF YOUR OTHER FRIENDS

You will need:

A box of large hooks and eyes, the kind used for fastening clothes

A small basket

Timing:

Ongoing

The Spell

- Take a hook and eye from the box and fasten them together, saying, [Name], *you are my best friend, that never will end. But you hold me far too tight. Can't you accept that I want to be free, others to see?*
- Undo the hook and place the hook and eye in the basket, close but not touching, saying, *We are still near, so you must not fear. I will not forget you, but I need freedom too, to enjoy pastures new. Jealousy is through.*
- Shake the basket vigorously three times, saying, Jealousy is through.
- Repeat the spell until all the hooks and eyes are in the basket.
- Before contact with the friend, fasten and undo a hook and eye, say the first set of spell words, and drop the hook and eye back in the basket, then shake the basket.

616

FOR RESOLVING A QUARREL WITH YOUR FRIEND WHEN YOU WERE TO BLAME

You will need:

A pink candle

Seven pink ribbons

Timing:

Starting Sunday, and continuing for eight days

The Spell

- Light the pink candle and say, [Name], *I was wrong and send you my sorrow, this Sunday, asking that friendship will regrow on the morrow.*
- Tie the first and second ribbons together, repeating the spell words, and blow out the candle.
- On days 2 through 6, repeat the spell, changing the day of the week in the chant.
- On day 7, tie the last and first ribbons together, repeating the spell words, but changing the day to Saturday.
- Let the candle burn.
- On day 8, hold the ribbon circle, quickly recite all the days of the week, and say, *Restore friendship today.*
- Attach the ribbon to a small gift and send it with an apology and a request to be friends again.

617

WHEN A FRIENDSHIP IS ONE-SIDED AND YOU ARE ALWAYS PAYING OR DOING FAVORS

You will need:

A lidded jar, half-filled with parsley or sage herbs

An empty lidded jar

Timing:

The waxing moon

The Spell

- Go outdoors with the jar of herbs and remove the lid. Turn seven times counterclockwise, holding the jar in your nondominant hand , and scatter a handful of herbs with the other hand, saying, *I give to you freely, I help you willingly. All I ask in return is that you start to learn to do things for me occasionally.*
- Take the jar indoors and add a sprinkling of herbs to the other open jar, repeating the spell words and closing it.
- Repeat the spell daily until the lidded herb jar is empty.
- Use the second jar for cooking, repeating the spell words each time you add herbs from the jar to a meal.

618

TO OVERCOME DISLOYALTY BY SOMEONE YOU THOUGHT YOU COULD TRUST

You will need:

A large piece of ice from the freezer, preferably jagged

A strong bowl

A small hammer

A small square of paper and a red pen

Timing:

Friday morning

The Spell

- Drop the ice into the bowl and carefully break it up into small pieces with the hammer, saying, Trust was shattered, *yes it mattered. You,* [offending friend], *have betrayed me. How could you behave so hurtfully?*
- Let the ice melt, either in sunlight or near a source of heat.
- When it has melted, write on the paper in red pen, [Name], BETRAY ME NOT AGAIN. EXCUSES WILL BE IN VAIN. WE CAN REBUILD, THOUGH TRUST YOU'VE KILLED. BOUND SHALL THIS ANGER REMAIN.
- Fold the paper small, put it in a container, add some melted ice, and put the container in the freezer.
- Throw any remaining water on earth where nothing grows.

619

TO END A FRIENDSHIP WHERE A FRIEND CONSTANTLY LIES TO YOU

You will need:

A dark-blue candle
Four incense sticks in separate holders
A picture of the person whose friendship you want to end

Timing:
At the end of a week or a month

The Spell

- Light the candle and say, *Love is not enough, though I deeply care. You must leave my life, for lies I can no longer bear.*
- Light the first incense stick and make a square of incense sticks around the picture and the candle, saying, *Deceit, untruths, lies, distrust, close the door on you I must.*
- Light the second incense stick, then the third and the fourth, moving counterclockwise to make the complete square of incense, repeating the spell words for each one.
- When all four sticks are in lit, let them burn.
- Extinguish the candle, saying, *No longer between me and you, sadly the friendship must be through. Between us it can be no more, and so with regret I close the door.*
- Put the picture in a drawer, and if you have doubts about whether you have done the right thing in ending the friendship, do the spell again.

620

TO BREAK AN INTERNET FRIENDSHIP WITH SOMEONE WHO SEEKS TO EXPLOIT YOU

You will need:

Scissors
A printout of a photo of the person you need to remove from your life
A padded bag
A red pen

Timing:
When you will not be disturbed

The Spell

- Begin to cut a square around the edges of the photo, continuing so it becomes smaller and smaller and less of the face can be seen as you trim the edges.
- Drop the cut pieces into the bag as they fall.
- When the picture is totally gone, seal the bag, and, on the front, write, NOT KNOWN HERE BY THIS HEART. RETURN TO SENDER, WE MUST PART.
- Delete the friend from your contacts lists and block any social media connections with this person. If you weaken in your resolve to end the friendship, repeat the spell with a new printout of the photo.

621

FOR INVITING NEW NEIGHBORS OVER FOR THE FIRST TIME

You will need:

A small cake for each person
A large plate
A knife with a slender blade

Timing:

Before the neighbors arrive

The Spell

- Set the small cakes around the edge of the plate clockwise.
- Touch each in turn gently, moving clockwise with the point of the knife, name a member of your family and then the names of the neighbors who are coming.
- Draw a clockwise circle in the air with the knife to enclose all the cakes, saying, *We are joined in the circle of neighborliness. We offer you peace and friendliness, that we side by side may live, and mutual support receive and give.*
- Move the cakes around the plate and set the plate in the center of any other food you may be offering, saying, *So we merge quite naturally, sharing hospitality, tolerance, and good harmony. Welcome, our new neighbors.*
- When the neighbors arrive, offer the cakes.

622

FOR GETTING TO KNOW YOUR NEIGHBORS BETTER, ESPECIALLY IF YOU ARE OUT AT WORK ALL DAY

You will need:

A rectangular piece of paper on which you have written your house number and name
A small candle for each of you—green for your family, blue for the neighbors—set in a horizontal row with the paper at one end of the row
A second piece of paper on which you have written your neighbors' house number and name, at the other end of the row

Timing:

Saturday, Sunday, or a public holiday

The Spell

- Touch your own house number and name and say, *Though we may not often meet, with greatest pleasure you I greet. For good neighbors are priceless treasure, and so I hope I may get to know you so much better, starting with today.*
- Light the nearest candle, saying, *I light the way to see you more, you're always welcome at my door.*
- Continue lighting the candles and saying the same spell words.
- Finally, touch your neighbors' house number and name, repeating the first set of spell words.
- Issue an invitation to meet socially, letting the candles burn.

623

IF YOU LIKE YOUR NEIGHBOR IN A ROMANTIC WAY

You will need:

A thin-bladed letter opener or screwdriver
A bright red candle
Two very small dolls made of children's red modeling clay
A scarlet ribbon

Timing:
Tuesday evening

The Spell

- Etch on one side of the candle the neighbor's name and on the other, MUCH, MUCH CLOSER I WOULD BE.
- Light the candle, saying, *You are hot, I like you a lot, come be more neighborly, for much, much closer I would be.*
- Tie the two dolls face-to-face with the ribbon and move them clockwise six times around the flame, saying, *Fix my tire, run out of tea? Come, my desire, ignite my fire, for much, much closer can we be.*
- Blow out the candle and hang the bound dolls by their waists, hidden in a tree, a bush, or a large plant on your property, close to the adjoining fence or communal entrance.

624

FOR ESTABLISHING MUTUAL HELP WITH NEIGHBORS

You will need:

Two jars of dried herbs—one sage or rosemary, the other parsley or thyme
A larger empty lidded jar or pot in the middle of the herb jars

Timing:
Friday morning

The Spell

- Name one jar of dried herbs for you and one for your neighbors.
- Add alternate sprinklings of herbs from each jar into the central jar, saying continuously, *I help you, you help me, I offer what you want, you offer what I need. On mutual support then let's be agreed.*
- When both herb jars are empty, close the middle jar and roll it on the table, nine times forward and back, saying, *Blend and mix, together we can fix anything.*
- Invite the neighbors for a meal and use the mixed herbs in cooking the meal.

625

FOR ESTABLISHING FRIENDSHIPS BETWEEN YOUR CHILDREN AND THOSE NEXT DOOR OR ON THE SAME STREET, IF THESE ARE SLOW TO DEVELOP

You will need:

Children's green modeling clay, formed into small featureless dolls, the same number as there are children you want to be friends (including your own)

Timing:

Any time during the waxing moon

The Spell

- Set the figures in a circle and touch each one, naming the person that doll represents, saying, *In and out of houses, sharing games and fun. Friendship grows in every way, uniting everyone.*
- Now roll all the figures into a big ball, repeating the spell words.
- Re-create the figures, but this time make the arms longer so each one is joining hands in the circle, saying, *Play, stay friends through the passing years, share your triumphs and your secrets, your laughter and your tears.*
- Roll all the figures into a ball again and keep it, wrapped, in a kitchen drawer until it crumbles.

626

FOR AMICABLE RELATIONS WITH NEIGHBORS WHEN RESOLVING OVERHANGING TREES, PET ISSUES, CONSTRUCTION CONCERNS, OR PARKING PROBLEMS

You will need:

Two matching vases
Seven pink roses or flowers, three in each vase and one flower set between the vases
A small basket

Timing:

When you fear there may be some fallout

The Spell

- One by one, pluck the petals of the central rose, forming a careful circle slowly counterclockwise around the two vases, saying, *Tiptoe we must go and find a compromise. The friendship between us I would not damage, and so this dilemma,* [name it], *we can manage, we'll cut it down to size.*
- When the circle is complete, one by one transfer the flowers to the right-hand vase, saying for each one, *Together we can find a way, to settle this and as good neighbors we can stay. With goodwill this will blow away.*
- Scoop up the petals into the basket and let them blow away outdoors.
- Leave the flowers on your neighbors' doorstep with a note suggesting a compromise.

627

IF A NEIGHBOR IS GETTING A BIT TOO FRIENDLY WITH YOUR PARTNER

You will need:

Paper folded in half and a green pen
Scissors

Timing:

Near the full moon

The Spell

- Fold the paper in two and draw two stick figures on one half of the paper and write the names of you and your partner underneath them.
- On the other side of the crease, draw a stick figure to represent your neighbor, and down the crease of the paper draw a thick green line. Say, *Be friendly to us and your welcome is sure, but overfriendliness I'll just not endure.*
- Cut the paper in half along the line, saying, *Groceries I'll gladly share, anything to borrow will be there. But hands off my partner and our friendship will mend, for this overfamiliarity just has to end.*
- Cut up and bury your half of the picture close to a boundary fence or in a planter on the wall adjoining your neighbor's property.
- Cut up the neighbor's half into small pieces and find an excuse to visit and drop it in her garbage.

628

FOR GETTING THE BALANCE RIGHT BETWEEN FRIENDLINESS AND PRIVACY

You will need:

A pair of kitchen scales with two balancing pans
A container of uncooked rice

Timing:

Just before a neighbor usually intrudes, when you are eating or relaxing

The Spell

- Put equal small quantities of rice in each pan, saying, [Name], *you are welcome in my home, but not 24/7. So sometimes stay on your own side, and make my life pure heaven.*
- Continue until both pans are half full and say, *Balance now I have restored, your daily intrusions will be no more. For when you do not bother me, we can live in harmony.*
- Create a line of rice from both pans along a neighboring fence, buried in earth or put in a potted plant set halfway along an adjoining wall.
- Wash out the pans.

629

FOR GETTING ON WELL WITH NEIGHBORS WHOSE LIFESTYLE IS VERY DIFFERENT FROM YOURS

You will need:

A piece of white chalk and a child's small blackboard

A small piece of cheese

Timing:

Around the crescent moon

The Spell

- Write on the chalkboard, *Cheese and chalk, chalk and cheese, our differences please us and so are no fuss.*
- Now hold the cheese and say, *Cheese and chalk, chalk and cheese, as we do talk, the more each other's lifestyles please.*
- Eat the cheese and rub out everything except the words *chalk* and *cheese*.
- Leave the board outdoors for rain to wash it or for the words fade.
- Arrange an evening at one another's homes and be sure to serve cheese.

630

FOR ATTRACTING THE RIGHT NEIGHBORS IF YOURS ARE MOVING OR THE HOUSE IS VACANT

You will need:

A blue candle

A piece of white paper

A pencil

An eraser

Pressure-sensitive gold stars

Timing:

Sunday morning

The Spell

- Light the candle, blowing into the flame, then say, *You who are good neighbors, come by land or sea. Travel from two streets away, if helpful you will be.*
- On the white paper draw a house as a box with a door, windows, roof, and chimney, or one story if it is an apartment, and draw yours adjoining it.
- Erase the dividing wall and stick stars all over the two structures, saying, *Quiet, friendly, and good company. Neighbors new, I call to you, good neighbors you will be.*
- Place the picture so it faces the front door in whatever room you put it.
- When the neighbors move in, redraw the line between the two houses, saying, *Neighbors new, I call to you, a welcome you will see, if good neighbors you will be.*
- Once you have met, dispose of the paper.

631

A FLOWER REMEDY RITUAL TO STOP A NEIGHBOR'S DOG FROM BARKING

You will need:

A Bach Flower Remedy (beech, cherry plum, chicory), or another favorite calming plant remedy
A bowl of water
A small plastic toy dog, preferably of the breed causing the trouble, one for each noisy animal
A piece of thread

Timing:
When the barking starts, and for eight days afterward

The Spell

- When the barking starts, add four drops of the remedy to the water, swirling it four times, saying, *Quieter you must be, you are too noisy, far too loud. Cease immediately.*
- Sprinkle the flower water over the toy dog, saying, *Hush, you must desist, you simply cannot resist. With all this racket, I just can't hack it, so stop barking instantly.*
- Tie the toy dog's mouth gently with the thread, knotting it four times whilst saying the second set of spell words four times.
- Sprinkle the toy dog daily with the mix for six more days, repeating all the spell words. On day 8, untie the toy dog and say, *Go free quietly, bark no more. Be not troublesome near my door.* Take the toy dog and leave it where a child will find it.

632

A CANDLE RITUAL TO QUIET NOISY NEIGHBORS AND/OR THEIR ANIMALS

You will need:

A natural beeswax or soft white candle that melts fast, on a heatproof tray or a very wide holder
A tiny jade crystal, green glass nugget, or small green bead for every offending person and animal

Timing:
Before a typically noisy time of the day or evening

The Spell

- Light the candle and say, *You are too loud with your disruptive ways, you interrupt my days, keep me awake. For everyone's sake, I bind you now with blessings.*
- As the wax melts, press the crystals around the base of the candle into the melted pool of wax, repeating the spell words.
- When there is enough melted wax to hold the crystals tight, extinguish the candle, repeating the spell words.
- Leave the candle and holder with the attached crystals on a high shelf once it has cooled.
- When the wax crumbles, retrieve and wash the crystals, disposing of the wax in a sealed paper bag.

633

TO PROTECT YOURSELF FROM THE EFFECTS OF NASTY OR THREATENING NEIGHBORS

You will need:

A bottle of lemon juice
A medium-size bowl of warm water
A long twig with a few leaves on it

Timing:

Mornings, weekly

The Spell

- Add ten drops of lemon juice to the water; stir it with the twig counterclockwise ten times, saying ten times, *Power of light, power of life, cleanse away malice, wash away strife. You are henceforward barred from hurting my life.*
- Beginning outside, and repeating the chant as you work, use the twig to sprinkle a few drops of the water onto your back gate, along boundary fences, and along adjoining internal walls. Work from back to front and top to bottom, so that you end at the front door step.
- Finally, sprinkle lemon water on any front boundary fence and your front gate.
- If you have an apartment, focus on internal adjoining walls and entrances.
- Empty any remaining water outside the front door.
- Break the twig in tiny pieces, saying, *So breaks your power from this hour. We have no fear, no longer can enter your nastiness here.*

634

ANOTHER RITUAL FOR PROTECTING YOUR PROPERTY AND FAMILY FROM ABUSIVE OR ANTISOCIAL NEIGHBORS

You will need:

A small stone or ceramic gargoyle, griffin, Chinese dog, lion, or dragon
Three small mirrors
A string of garlic cloves
A red candle

Timing:

Tuesday, after dark

The Spell

- Set everything around the candle and light the candle, saying, *This is my territory, you* [name neighbors, pointing in their direction jabbing your finger], *stay away. Do not stray by word or action beyond these boundaries, so I command and it shall be.*
- First hold the stone figure and say, *Guardian be for my property, guardian be for my family/me. As I fill you with light, assert your might.*
- Blow out the candle, setting the figure against the boundary wall (inside if you live in an apartment).
- Relight the candle and do the same for the mirrors, afterward hanging them facing the neighbors' wall or fence.
- Finally, repeat with the garlic and after blowing out the candle, string the garlic along your side of the boundary fence or in your kitchen, facing the neighbors' home.

635

TO GUARD AGAINST GRUMPY OR CONSTANTLY COMPLAINING NEIGHBORS

You will need:

A large whisky glass, brandy snifter, or wineglass, 1/4 filled with milk (lactose-free, if you are lactose-intolerant)

Timing:

Tuesday, when you wake up

The Spell

- Stand outdoors as near possible to the neighbor's fence, or in an apartment next to any adjoining wall.
- Hold the glass in both hands, raising it slowly until it is above your head and in front of you, then lower it to chest level.
- Raise it to your lips and take a sip, saying, *The milk of human kindness shall not be wasted, but flow within you,* [name neighbors], *as this is tasted.*
- Raise the glass toward the fence or interior wall and take a few sips, saying, *To your health and wealth I do drink. If you stop moaning, then I think these petty feuds now could end, and so the milk of kindness send.*
- Empty the rest of the milk into Mother Earth, or if you're indoors, pour the contents of the glass down a drain under a running faucet.

636

TO DETER A GOSSIPING OR TROUBLESOME NEIGHBOR

You will need:

Five cloves of garlic
A sharp, fine-bladed knife
An old, lidded plastic box

Timing:

On a rainy or a cloudy day

The Spell

- On each clove of garlic, etch the initials of the offender(s) (it does not matter if the initials are illegible), saying for each one, *Your gossip and your tattle rattle me, so cease your spite and let me be.*
- Chop each clove into small pieces and put it in the box, saying the same spell words just once.
- Put the lid on the box, shake it vigorously five times, and say five times, *Enough and no more, your gossip does bore. So if you have no good to say, I bid you now to stay away.*
- Throw the box of garlic away in a garbage can far from your home.

637

AN INSTANT METHOD TO PROTECT YOURSELF FROM THE FALLOUT THAT STEMS FROM AN OLD QUARREL OR AN ONGOING DISPUTE WITH NEIGHBORS

You will need:
A dust rag

Timing:
Ongoing

The Spell

- Open a window, preferably upstairs, and shake the dust rag out of the window (not on your neighbors' property).
- Say softly ten times, *Neighbors, neighbors, stay away, don't cause disruption every day. Let matters rest, let disputes lie, to pointless feuding say good-bye.*
- Tie the rag in a knot to the window catch inside the window from which you shook it, saying the spell words ten times.
- Close the window, saying, *Neighbors, neighbors, bound are you. This unpleasant business now is through.*
- Repeat daily, if necessary.

638

TO PREVENT ANTISOCIAL NEIGHBORS FROM CAUSING CHAOS IN YOUR LIFE WITH THEIR NOISE, SCREAMING CHILDREN, BROKEN-DOWN CARS, AND GARBAGE

You will need:
A piece of white paper and a red pen
Scissors
A bucket of hot water

Timing:
The waning moon

The Spell

- Write on the paper in red pen the names of your antisocial neighbors, including antisocial animals, the house or apartment name or number, and full address, and underneath write in all capital letters, CLEAN UP YOUR ACT, FOR IT'S A FACT, YOUR HOME IS AN EYESORE AND WHAT IS MORE, YOU CRASH AND YOU CLATTER, YOU CLUTTER AND SCREAM, MY PATIENCE YOU'VE CRACKED. SO CLEAN UP YOUR ACT.
- Cut up the paper into small pieces and drop them in the bucket or, if it has been raining a lot, leave the cut-up scraps of paper outside, held down with stones until the paper dissolves.
- Empty the bucket of water, if you used one, down a wide drain and flush it out well.

639

TO ENCOURAGE DIFFICULT NEIGHBORS TO MOVE

You will need:

A picture of the exterior of your neighbors' home
Pictures from a real estate advertisement or printed from a website of ideal homes, far away, that would make your neighbors happy
A box of gold and clear glass nuggets, small bright crystals, or shiny beads
Five small gold and five silver-colored candles or tea lights

Timing:
Wednesday, after dark

The Spell

- Place the picture of your neighbors' present home at one end of a straight row of alternate gold and silver candles and the picture of the ideal home at the other end.
- Light the candles, starting with the one nearest the picture of your neighbors' present home, saying for each one three times, *Find a new home where you can be secure, content, and live happily*.
- Place a nugget to the side of each candle to create a second pathway close to the first, saying for each one three times, *Follow the light that you may see, your perfect home where you will secure, content, and happy be*.
- Let the candles burn through, pick up the nuggets or crystals, and return them to the box.
- Keep the picture of your neighbors' ideal home on top of the picture of their present one.
- Weekly, light a white candle, say all the spell words three times, and blow out the candle.

640

TO REMIND A NEIGHBOR WHO KEEPS BORROWING YOUR POSSESSIONS AND NEVER RETURNS THEM TO GIVE THEM BACK

You will need:

An old-fashioned sand hourglass egg timer, used only for this spell

Timing:
As soon as the neighbor has left your house or garden with one of your possessions

The Spell

- The moment the neighbor leaves, start the sand running through the timer and say ten times very fast, *Borrow with pleasure, return it at leisure. But it is my treasure, so please bring it back.*
- Let the sand run through and put the egg timer away.
- If the item does not come back within what you would consider a reasonable period, take out the timer and repeat the spell once a day until the neighbor's memory is jogged (and the odd verbal reminder would also be a good idea).

SECTION 5: LIVING HAPPILY IN THE COMMUNITY

641

FOR SETTLING IN A NEW COMMUNITY VERY DIFFERENT FROM YOUR OLD ONE

You will need:

A selection of local produce that can be cooked
A cooking pan
Dried bay leaves or sage, if produce is savory; allspice or cinnamon, if produce is sweet
A wooden spoon

Timing:
Thursday morning

The Spell

- Chop up the produce and place it in the pan, saying, *So am I absorbed into this community, so take in its different ways. That at home here I will be and welcome feel always.*
- Add the herbs or spices and suitable liquid and stir the pot, saying, *Though I will not lose my roots, yet can I cultivate new shoots, to mix and blend and soon fit in and from my new neighbors respect win.*
- Cook the produce and invite your new neighbors to share the meal.

642

FOR CAMPAIGNING FOR BETTER FACILITIES IN THE COMMUNITY

You will need:

A campaign flyer, or if the project is not launched, write the aim and time frame on thin paper
A feathery plant, like a fern
A box of clear glass nuggets, small quartz crystals, or pure white stones

Timing:
Sunday morning, weekly

The Spell

- Fold the flyer or paper into a fan and spiral it over the plant, saying, *Winds of progress start to blow, that this campaign,* [name], *may swiftly grow.*
- Pick up a nugget and, holding it, state the cause and the desired time frame, and begin making a circle around the plant, saying, *Step by step this venture grows, winds of progress daily blow. As we strive for a better community, winds of success bring unity.*
- Each week, repeat the spell and add a new nugget to the circle.

643

FOR FINDING THE RIGHT SCHOOL FOR YOUR CHILDREN

You will need:

A piece of white paper on which you have written all possible schools faintly in pencil, except the chosen school, which will be in gold or red pen
An eraser
A gold glitter glue pen, or glitter and glue

Timing:
Before applying to the chosen school

The Spell

- Erase each of the school names except the chosen one, saying for each one, *Good you may be, but not for me. No other school,* [name of desired school], *do I see.*
- Draw a box around the chosen school in gold pen, saying, *School of gold, a place unfolds, and so I seek admission for* [name of child(ren)]. *May none deny permission, this is the school for me.*
- Draw stars in glitter glue or paste glittery stars all over the paper, leaving only the name of the chosen school free, and pin the paper where you will see it when you make the application.

644

FOR DEALING WITH ANTISOCIAL PEOPLE WHO ARE RUINING THE COMMUNITY

You will need:

A yellow candle
A large frankincense, dragon's blood, or sandalwood incense stick
A heatproof pot of sand or soil

Timing:
Wednesday

The Spell

- Light the candle and the incense from the candle, saying, [Names, if known], *your actions are not welcome here. Your antisocial deeds cause fear, anger, unrest, disharmony. I charge you stop now, live peacefully. Stop wrecking our community.*
- Draw in incense smoke large crosses in the air above and around the candle, saying nine times, *Crossed out is your power to destroy and to harm, nullified, you must not try, there is no place to hide. Desist from causing fear or get out of here.*
- Plunge the lighted end of the incense into the soil and extinguish the candle fast, saying, *Nullified, no place to hide, be civilized or go.*
- Throw away the candle.

645

FOR A SUCCESSFUL COMMUNITY PARTY OR EVENT

You will need:

Seven ribbons of equal length in red, orange, yellow, green, blue, purple, and white
A small electric handheld fan

Timing:

The day before the event

The Spell

- Tie each ribbon so that they are all joined at the top, saying for each one, *Come together, whatever the weather. For this endeavor brings joy and laughter that will endure, that's for sure.*
- Holding the ribbons at the top in your nondominant hand and the fan in your dominant hand, make the ribbons dance in the air stream, saying, *Dance, dance carefree. Bring harmony uniting our community as one, joined in friendship until day is done.*
- Take the ribbons along to the party and hang them where they will catch the breeze.

646

A TRADITIONAL WAY OF MAKING YOUR COMMUNITY SAFER, ESPECIALLY AT NIGHT

You will need:

Four tall, slender, white candles, set at the four corners of the map
A map of your community, which can be a sketched map with landmarks hand-drawn
A bowl of salt

Timing:

Before darkness falls

The Spell

- Light each candle in clockwise order, saying for each, *You Guardians of the Land, who strong and protective stand, you have been Watchers for many long years. Take away this night all dangers and all fears.*
- Sprinkle a pinch of salt in each flame in the order of lighting, repeating the spell words for each one.
- Move each candle in turn, clockwise around the map and then put each on a different window ledge, saying for each one, *Stand sentinel for me this night, repel danger with your golden light, that all with ill intent will be sent far from here, so we can sleep without fear.*
- Leave the candles burning until bedtime and then blow them out, saying for each one, *Guardians of the golden light, we entrust all in your hands this and every night.*

647

FOR FIGHTING AN EXTERNAL THREAT TO THE CHARACTER OR TRADITIONS OF THE COMMUNITY

You will need:

An old picture of the community in its heyday or showing the traditional features that still remain
Children's toy bricks
A lavender, myrrh, or patchouli incense stick
A soft, dark-colored scarf

Timing:

Saturday, especially during the waning moon

The Spell

- Begin to build a wall of toy bricks around the picture, saying, *Preserve what is of beauty, conserve what is of worth. Changes imposed unwelcome, shall not come to birth.*
- Repeat this chant until the wall is competed.
- Light the incense stick, and over the picture and wall draw nine smoke eyes in the air, saying nine times, *Turn away your eyes, look not here to spoil our heritage. Against what we do love, wage not destruction; turn away your gaze.*
- Wrap the picture in the scarf, saying, *Turn away your gaze* and put it away in a drawer where it will not be disturbed.

648

FOR RELIGIOUS AND CULTURAL HARMONY IN A MULTICULTURAL COMMUNITY

You will need:

Six small tubs of different edible nuts or seeds, such as almonds, coriander seeds, cumin seeds, hazelnuts, pine nuts, poppy seeds, sesame seeds, sunflower seeds, walnuts, or other small whole seeds
A fine-mesh sieve or strainer, with a handle, so the seeds will not fall through the mesh, or, if not, a clear container
A big ceramic or wooden bowl

Timing:

The beginning of a new week or month

The Spell

- Add some seeds or nuts from each tub to the sieve in turn, saying six times, *Though we have different views, all are one family, alike in wanting harmony. And so I offer friendship and seek your friendship too.*
- Shake the sieve six times saying six times, *United in one community, our needs are not the same. But wanting to live peacefully, that can be our aim.*
- Pour the nuts and seeds into the bowl and gently rotate it six times in both directions, saying just once, *We all have much to learn as we live side by side, for we are one community and so can share it peacefully.*
- Scatter the nuts and seeds freely outdoors *until the mix is gone*, saying, *One family, one community, in unity and harmony.*

649

FOR COMBATING INEFFICIENCY OR CORRUPTION IN LOCAL GOVERNMENT

You will need:

A medium-size, screw-top jar or tin
Dried peas or beans

Timing:

The night before you need to tackle the problem as it affects you

The Spell

- Half-fill the jar with beans and firmly screw on the lid.
- Begin shaking the jar slowly and gently, getting louder and faster as you tap your feet, slowly at first and then faster, saying all the while, *Shake them up, wake them up, for they're far too cushy. Wake them up, shake them up, we folks are getting pushy. Sort this out, or I will shout, disturb your slumber. I'm not a number, I want some action now.*
- When you can tap no longer, stamp hard with both feet and bang the jar down hard, shouting, *Now!*
- Repeat the spell before any encounter until you get satisfaction.

650

FOR CREATING OR PRESERVING GREEN SPACES AND SPORTING FACILITIES IN YOUR COMMUNITY

You will need:

Twenty, or as many as needed to allow for replacements during the spell
Ten small green plants in pots

Timing:

Any ten days starting on a Monday or during the waxing moon

The Spell

- Set ten tea lights in a circle in front of a circle of the plants.
- Light the first tea light, saying, *Grow green, bring pleasure. The joys of nature and of leisure, may* [name what is currently most needed in the area] *flourish and grow green, So good results will soon be seen.*
- Let it burn through, then plant the first greenery to begin a circle formation, either in the garden or in a large planter.
- Replace the tea light.
- On day 2, light candles 1 and 2, the second in front of the second plant, and repeat the spell.
- Replace both burned-through candles, and on day 3, light the first three candles, number 3 in front of the third plant.
- Continue the spell until all ten plants are in the earth, each night replacing the burned candles, until on day 10 all are alight.
- On day 11 move your hands in clockwise circles, palms down, ten times above the circle of plants and repeat the spell words ten times.

CHAPTER 14

JUSTICE AND PEACE SPELLS

This chapter includes spells for personal justice, for legal and financial justice, for personal peace and quiet sleep, for fighting global injustice, and for world peace.

651

TO REDRESS AN UNFAIR SITUATION WHERE YOU HAVE BEEN UNJUSTLY BLAMED

You will need:

A dark-colored candle
Six flat white stones and six black or dark-colored stones in a small bag

Timing:

Thursday or when you get home after the injustice

The Spell

- Light the candle and set the stones, alternately black and white, in a circle around it.
- As you do so, say, *So wrong, unfair, I say. Justice is not mine this day. This unfairness must now be resolved. Injustice, I demand, you must be solved.*
- Extinguish the dark candle, and return the stones to the bag, naming the injustice and saying, *I will be rid of it, every bit.*
- Go to water and skim first the six black stones, saying for each, *Banish injustice, then the six white ones rapidly, after saying, Bring justice to me.*

652

TO COUNTER BEING TREATED AS THE OUTCAST OF THE FAMILY

You will need:

Children's modeling clay in any bright color
A tea light for each member of the family, set in a circle
A large green candle outside the circle, representing you

Timing:

Thursday morning

The Spell

- Create a featureless clay figure for each member of the family, one set in front of each of the tea lights.
- Say as you make each one, *Welcome me, don't try to change me, but love me as I am.*
- Make one for yourself, setting it in front of the green candle.
- Light the green candle and from it the tea lights clockwise, saying, *Do not reject me, make me part of the family. Don't try to change me, but let me share the unity.*
- With the index finger of your dominant hand, touch the heart of each of the figures clockwise, repeating the first set of spell words for each one.
- Set your candle and figure in the center, letting the candles burn.
- Roll the clay figures, including yours, into a ball, saying, *All one family, you have accepted me.*
- Bury the ball of clay under a thriving tree or plant.

653

IF YOU ALWAYS END UP DOING THE HARD WORK IN YOUR JOB, WHILE OTHERS GET THE CREDIT OR HAVE ALL THE FUN

Note: **You can do this spell with a child if you wish and say the words in your head.**

You will need:

Ten children's plastic bowling pins
A plastic bowling ball or any soft small ball

Timing:
Saturday, early

The Spell

- Stand the ten pins in a row, aim at them, and say, *Ten unfair demands, standing in a row, I say no, down you go. Then there were nine.*
- However many pins you knock down, each time take one away before setting them up again and adjust the rhyme accordingly.
- You will next aim at nine pins, saying, *Nine unfair demands, standing in a row, I say no, down you go. Then there were eight.*
- When you have only one pin left to throw the ball at, aim at it, saying, *One unfair demand standing all alone, I say yes, you've gone. And now there are none.*
- Give the pins to a child.

654

IF YOUR FAMILY TREATS YOU LIKE A SERVANT AND ARE DISRESPECTFUL

You will need:

An old apron
A big red candle
Two pieces of paper and a red pen

Timing:
When you are home alone

The Spell

- Put on the apron and light the candle, saying, *Chores and ingratitude, you're very rude. My tolerance has hit the floor, indulgence has been shown the door.*
- Write on the first sheet of paper the things you will no longer do for your family and any inconsiderateness by them and put an X by the side of each.
- Take off the apron, extinguish the candle, and say, *Room service is done, your hotel gone. Get off your butts, you're driving me nuts.*
- Relight the candle, writing on the second sheet of paper what you expect your family to do around the home and the way you expect to be treated.
- Let the candle burn and put the apron in the recycling bin.
- Pin the lists where they will be seen by the family.

655

IF YOUR PARTNER, A RELATIVE, OR A FRIEND CONSTANTLY CRITICIZES YOU OR PUTS YOU DOWN IN PUBLIC

You will need:

Blue modeling clay
A small red crystal, such as jasper or a round red stone
A small blue bag

Timing:
Thursday initially, and then every time you go out

The Spell

- Create a featureless figure in clay and hold it in the palm of your hand, saying, *You,* [name], *you put me down constantly, criticize, and make me look small. This is unjust, not fair at all.*
- Place the crystal where the mouth would be and say, *If you can say nothing pleasant, silent be.*
- Hide the figure in a bag in the room where the person frequently sits.
- When you are going out or expecting visitors, and the culprit will be present, retrieve the figure, remove the crystal, reinsert it, and repeat the spell words.
- When the figure dries or crumbles, remove the crystal and say, *All is as it was before.* Then throw away the clay.
- Wash and carry the crystal in the bag when you go out socially with the offender.

656

IF YOU ARE PERFORMING AT A LEVEL OR TWO ABOVE YOUR PAY GRADE AT WORK, BUT CAN'T GET A PROMOTION OR A SALARY INCREASE

You will need:

A variety of coins and bills in different denominations, from nickels and dimes to a $20 bill, or the currency of your country
A big shallow dish

Timing:
Sunday night

The Spell

- Add the lowest-denomination coins to the dish, shake it three times, and say three times, *Too cheap by far, I'm a rising star. Why on earth won't you pay me what I'm worth?* [Name person/organization who should pay you more.]
- Now add coins of a higher denomination, shaking the bowl three more times and saying three times, *Pay me more or I'll walk out the door. Then where will you be? Lost without me.*
- Keep adding higher denominations of coins and bills, each time shaking the bowl three times, saying the second set of spell words three times.
- When you have finished, set the bowl where light will shine on it.
- Every morning before work, shake it once, repeating the second set of spell words.
- After a week, state your case at work.

657

IF YOU ALWAYS GET THE WORST SEAT ON THE PLANE OR THE WORST HOTEL ROOM WHILE TRAVELING

You will need:

Your plane tickets and/or hotel/travel confirmation

A small luxury item, such as a small bar of soap or a box of luxury candies

Timing:

A week before you depart

The Spell

- Hold the tickets/confirmation in your dominant hand and the luxury item in the other.
- Move your hands slowly up and down in the air, saying nine times, *First class is what I ask, luxury come to me. That is fair and it must be.*
- Swap items from one hand to the other and repeat the actions and spell words again nine times, but faster.
- Keep changing hands and repeating the spell words and actions nine times, faster and faster, until the words are unintelligible.
- Then bring both hands together over your head, still holding the items between them, and say, *Luxury for me, that is fair and it must be.*
- After the spell, use a little of the luxury item every day until departure day, repeating the first set of spell words.

658

IF LIFE SENDS YOU PARTNERS WHO ARE UNFAITHFUL OR CANNOT COMMIT

You will need:

A piece of pink paper and a red pen

Rose petals or dried lavender

A pink scarf

Timing:

Friday evening

The Spell

- On the paper, draw a large heart, within it writing your name and also within the heart, SEND HE WHO IS GENTLE, LOVING, FAITHFUL, AND COMMITTED FOREVER [add any qualities you desire in your new love].
- Scatter the rose petals or lavender over the heart, saying, *Send me the love who will never hurt me, never desert me. Wherever you this night may be, find me and love me faithfully.*
- Carefully carry the paper outside and let the petals blow away.
- Indoors, add more petals to the paper, repeating the second set of spell words, and wrap the paper in the scarf, making three knots and saying, *Fidelity and commitment may I see, and so in trust wait happily.*
- Keep the scarf under your pillow.

659

IF YOU ARE BEING KEPT FROM SEEING AN ADULT CHILD BECAUSE HER PARTNER HATES YOU

You will need:

A lemon
A citrus fruit squeezer
A small bowl
A sweet orange

Timing:

When there is a family get-together and you are not invited

The Spell

- Squeeze the lemon juice into the bowl, saying, *Don't be bitter,* [name], *don't be sour, the months rush by hour by hour. Let go the unfair rancor, release the unjust spite. Let's start again all over, and this time get it right.*
- Discard the lemon flesh and pour the juice away under running water.
- Wash out the bowl and squeezer and squeeze orange juice into the bowl, saying, *Words so sweet, let us meet, in friendship and in harmony. Mend this rift without reproach, restore joy and unity.*
- Extend an invitation to the difficult person to meet you and see if you can reach a compromise.

660

IF YOU ARE CONSTANTLY INVITING PEOPLE TO YOUR HOME OR EVENTS, BUT NEVER GET ASKED BACK

You will need:

A yellow candle
A set of party invitations
A blue pen
A box with a lid

Timing:

Ongoing

The Spell

- Light the candle and write the first invitation to yourself, signing it from THOSE WHOM I HAVE MADE WELCOME MANY TIMES [be specific and name the same or a different person for each invitation, if you wish].
- Seal and hold the invitation, saying, *I accept this invite appreciatively. Thank you for inviting me.* Put the invitation in the box and blow out the candle, saying, *This invitation to a celebration is on its way to me.*
- The next evening relight the candle and repeat the spell.
- When you have used all the invitations, open the box and let the candle burn through (or, if it's already burned through, substitute a new one), saying, *I accept these invitations appreciatively. Thank you for inviting me.*
- Keep the box in a safe place and arrange to meet the person or people concerned away from your home and suggest you meet next time at their home.

661

FOR THE RESTORATION OF WHAT HAS BEEN UNFAIRLY LOST FINANCIALLY OR TAKEN ILLEGALLY

You will need:

Seven flowering plants of the same species, growing in small pots

Timing:

Early morning

The Spell

- Set the seven pots in a circle, either on the ground or on a table for indoor planting.
- Hold your hands about an inch apart as you face the plants, palms toward each other. Move your palms slowly and rhythmically so they almost touch, then backwards seven times. As you do, say seven times, *May all be restored to my full satisfaction.*
- Put your hands on either side of each pot in turn, repeating the spell words for each one.
- Dig seven circular holes, either in a big indoor planter or in a circle in the garden, and plant the flowers, saying the spell words seven times as you cover the holes with earth.
- Walk around the outside of the circle clockwise, or, if you planted the flowers indoors, lift your hands above the center of the pot, saying, *Growing power, more and more, increase 'til loss is restored.*

662

A RITUAL TO UNMASK SOMEONE YOU KNOW WILL LIE ABOUT YOU IN COURT

You will need:

An intersection with soil; alternatively, make a symbolic three-way intersection out of sticks in a planter filled with soil, or draw one with a stick in a tray of sand

A small black crystal, such as jet, obsidian, or black tourmaline; or a small black stone

A silver-colored coin

Timing:

Around sunset

The Spell

- Go to the intersection or create one. Hold the crystal in your cupped hands and say, *I am accused unfairly. I leave all at the intersection, that justice may be done and* [name] *be unmasked as a liar.*
- Hold the crystal against the center of your brow, repeating the spell words.
- Press the crystal into the earth so it is hidden, saying the spell words as you do so for the final time.
- Leave the silver coin at the intersection or put it where it may be found as a gift.

663

WHEN YOU NEED TO GO FOR MEDIATION AND YOU KNOW THE OTHER PARTY WILL BE UNREASONABLE

You will need:
A child's remote-control car

Timing:
Three days before the mediation or preliminary hearing

The Spell

- Stand in the middle of a room and slowly drive the car in circles, saying as you do so, *Around in circles, arguing, getting nowhere fast. Better to negotiate and move ahead at last. May the matter,* [name it], *with* [name person] *be resolved amicably and to the satisfaction of all.*
- Steer the car toward the front door, avoiding any obstacles. Repeat the spell words.
- Stop the car and open the front door, saying, *May the matter,* [name it], *with* [name person] *be resolved amicably and to the satisfaction of all. I open the door.*
- Repeat the spell for two more days. Say the chants in your head before beginning any negotiations.

664

IF YOU ARE ACCUSED OF A CRIME OR OFFENSE YOU DID NOT COMMIT

You will need:
Nine unshelled nuts, hazelnuts if possible
A thin blue cord

Timing:
Tuesday night, if possible during the waning moon

The Spell

- Set the nuts in a circle, counterclockwise around yourself, and say, *May justice be done, that I am acquitted of this unfair accusation.*
- Loosely bind your hands with the cord, saying, *Unjust are these bonds, yet I know, I will be acquitted of this unfair accusation.*
- Turn around in the center of the circle nine times counterclockwise and, as you do so, untie the cord, tossing it out of the circle and saying, *I cast off this unfair accusation by the power of the hazelnut of justice.*
- If you are not allergic to them, eat the nuts, and then repeat the third set of spell words.
- Hang the cord from a bush.

665

TO CLEAR YOUR NAME WHEN AN ANONYMOUS ACCUSER HAS COMPLAINED ABOUT YOU UNFAIRLY TO SOCIAL SERVICES OR OTHER GOVERNMENT AGENCIES

You will need:

A bottle of lemon juice
A small bowl half-filled with water

Timing:
In early morning light

The Spell

- Add five drops of lemon juice to the water and swirl it five times counterclockwise, saying five times, *You without face, you without voice, cease blackening my name, at once end this game. You shall not be believed by those you deceive, your words are not feared, for I will be cleared.*
- Pour the lemon water down a drain, under a running faucet.
- Refill the bowl and repeat the spell words and actions four more times.
- Empty any remaining lemon juice, saying, *Your venom and lies, all will despise, you without face, you are a disgrace, your words are not feared, for I will be cleared.*
- Take vigorous action to defend your name.

666

TO PREVENT UNJUST ENTRY OF YOUR HOME BY PROCESS SERVERS, UNSCRUPULOUS DEBT COLLECTORS, OR AGGRESSIVE GOVERNMENT OFFICIALS

You will need:

Five copper-colored coins or disks

Timing:
Ongoing

The Spell

- Place the coins, heads up, to form a diagonal cross just outside your home, saying, *You shall not enter here, bringing intimidation. You shall not enter here, causing trepidation. Stop inflicting fear, you shall not enter here.*
- Cover the coins with earth or bury them in the same formation in a planter outside the front door, saying the spell words.
- Leave the coins in place indefinitely.

667

TO PREVENT UNPLEASANT WRITS, NASTY PHONE CALLS, OR LEGAL THREATS IF YOU HAVE RUN AFOUL OF AN EX, NEIGHBORS, OR RUTHLESS FINANCE COMPANIES

You will need:

A pot of marigolds, the anti-injustice flower, or another orange flowering plant

Timing:

Whenever you feel overwhelmed by harassing phone calls or lawyers' letters

The Spell

- Set the pot of marigolds on a window ledge facing the front of your home, and put your hands around it, saying, *My mailbox is sealed, my number is concealed, ring no more, threatening the law. Let me be, can't you see, you're harassing me?*
- Each week, on the same day, sprinkle a little of the soil from the pot on the doorstep, repeating the spell words.
- In the evening before dark, brush away any remaining soil from the step, saying, *Return no more, you and your kind. Be gone from my life, be gone from my mind.*
- Keep the marigold pot filled with soil.

668

A NAIL CHARM FOR STOPPING THREATENED LEGAL OR OFFICIAL ACTION AGAINST YOU OR A FAMILY MEMBER FROM COMING TO COURT

You will need:

Six metal nails
A sturdy post or thick plank of wood, either upright or vertical on a flat surface
Six red shoelaces

Timing:

Whenever you are being threatened with court action

The Spell

- Working from top to bottom, hammer the nails into the post in a vertical row so that an inch or so of each nail is sticking out, saying for each nail, *To this post your threats I nail, your bullying shall not prevail.*
- Tie each shoelace in a knot and hang it from a nail, top to bottom, saying, *Your threats are now securely tied. The law no longer's on your side.*
- Keep the post, standing upright, hidden near your front door, outside if possible, and say, *Invade no more my privacy. Injustice shall now banished be. Justice now will I see.*
- Once you have finished the spell, take immediate practical action to get help to resolve your problems.

669

TO GET AN UNFAIR TAX LIEN OR AN UNJUST OFFICIAL DECISION REVERSED

You will need:

A golden-brown candle
Three frankincense or sandalwood incense sticks
A brown cord

Timing:

When you receive the unfair decision or demand

The Spell

- When you wake up, light the candle and then light the first incense stick from the candle, saying three times, *I call upon the power of flame to turn my losses into gain. Let reason prevail and wisdom renew, that I recoup what I am due.*
- Write the spell words over the cord in incense smoke, using the incense stick like a smoke pen and say the spell words as you do so.
- Repeat the spell words and actions after lighting the next two incense sticks.
- Tie three knots in the center of the cord, saying, *As I wind, so I bind the taxman* [or name] *from unfair action. So I know it must be so, the taxman* [or name] *will discretion show and I recoup what I'm entitled to.*
- Blow out the candle, letting the incense burn.
- Hang the knotted cord where air will circulate around it.

670

TO BRING THE RIGHT DECISION IN ARBITRATION OR AN OFFICIAL JUDGMENT

You will need:

White paper and a red pen
Seven blue tea lights or small candles, set in a circle

Timing:

The day before the judgment is due

The Spell

- On night 1, in the center of the paper write in red pen your ideal solution and then write, MAY JUSTICE IN MY DIRECTION BE, THAT I MAY BE JUDGED MOST FAVORABLY.
- Light all seven tea lights counterclockwise, saying for each one, *May this worry melt away, and this judgment go my way.*
- Blow out the tea lights.
- On night 2, light only six tea lights, repeating the spell.
- Reduce the number of tea lights lit by one each spell night.
- Continue until on night 7, when only one tea light is alight.
- Repeat the spell but let the single light burn through.
- Replace tea lights as necessary during the seven days of the spell.

671

FOR CALMING A DISTRACTED MIND

You will need:

A children's spinning top, as small as you like
A pink or green scarf

Timing:

When you get home and can't relax

The Spell

- Start the top spinning faster and faster, saying, *Whirling and spinning, I am not winning in clearing my mind; it is unkind. Thoughts haunt and taunt me with matters unfinished and tasks undiminished.*
- Slow down the top with your hand, saying, *Slowing your spinning, at last I am winning, Slowing my mind and soon I will find the whirling will stop and I can get off.*
- When the top has stopped spinning, wrap it in the scarf, knot the scarf ends three times, and say, *Out of sight, out of mind, life unwinds and softly binds me into stillness, calm, and peace, the day has ceased.*
- Put the top away in a cupboard until you need to do the spell again.

672

TO CREATE A PERSONAL WORRY STONE TO RELIEVE TENSION

You will need:

A dark, round stone from a garden, park, seashore, or riverbank, small enough to carry with you
Eight smaller dark stones, forming a square around it
A small dark-colored bag or purse

Timing:

Monday evening, especially during the waning moon

The Spell

- Hold the central stone between your palms and gently enclose it, saying softly, *Into this stone I put all fears, doubts, anxiety,* [name specific causes of worry]. *Take them from me that I may be free.*
- Set the stone in the center of the square of stones and say, *Limited be, confined, no longer mine.*
- Put the worry stone in the bag or purse.
- Take the smaller stones outdoors and leave them there.
- Still outdoors, shake your fingers, pointing downward to the ground, and say, *Anything remaining, now is draining away.*
- Take your worry stone with you to work or any potentially anxiety-provoking situation and wash it weekly.

673

A SECOND RITUAL TO KEEP FROM WORRYING SO MUCH

You will need:

A purple and a white candle, set side by side
A dark stone in front of the purple candle and a white stone in front of the white candle

Timing:
Saturday evening

The Spell

- Light the purple candle, saying, *Worry, worry, worry, you tangle inside me, fret, fret, fret, yet I shall be free.*
- Hold the dark stone in front of the purple candle, saying, *Worry, I have no more of you, you and I, fear, now are through.*
- Extinguish the purple candle and put the dark stone just outside the door.
- Light the white candle and hold the white stone in front of it, saying, *Here is peace and harmony, happiness, and tranquillity.*
- Let the white candle burn through, afterwards putting the white stone just outside the door.
- When you return home, hold the dark stone, putting worries in it, then pick up the white stone and receive harmony.

674

FOR ALL-DAY CALM IF YOU WORK OR LIVE IN A HOSTILE OR VOLATILE ATMOSPHERE

You will need:

A silver or white candle
Rose, chamomile, or lavender essential oil, or your favorite fragrance

Timing:
Monday

The Spell

- Light the candle. Hold the unopened bottle of essential oil or fragrance in your nondominant hand so candlelight reflects within it, passing your other hand in slow counterclockwise circles, an inch or so above the bottle, three times.
- Say once, *Peace, let peace enter this bottle that I may know peace,* [name where you need it most].
- Circle your hand over the bottle three times clockwise and say just once, *Harmony, let harmony enter this bottle that I may know harmony,* [name where you need it most].
- Circle the bottle with your hand three times counterclockwise and say, *Tranquillity, let tranquillity enter this bottle, that I may experience tranquillity,* [name where you need it most].
- Leave the sealed bottle with light shining on it until the candle burns down.
- The next morning, put a few drops of oil/fragrance on your pulse points.
- Repeat the spell weekly to reempower yourself.

675

A WORRY DOLL RITUAL TO REASSURE A YOUNGER ANXIOUS CHILD

You will need:

A supply of worry dolls or small plastic dolls in a basket
A small piece of paper and a green pen
A small cloth

Timing:
Before bedtime

The Spell

- Hold the basket of worry dolls and say, *Take my beloved child's fear,* [name child and main fear], *and make his worry disappear.*
- Ask the child to choose a doll, hold it, and name his fear or worry. Then you and the child say together, *Make my worry disappear, hurry and take it far from here.*
- Write a word to represent the worry on the paper.
- Wrap the doll and the paper in a small piece of cloth, knot the cloth, and let the child place the wrapped-up doll in a drawer.
- The child can unwrap the doll and say the spell words again if problems come back.
- You can choose different dolls over the months to represent different worries.

676

A SLEEP BLESSING

You will need:

A pink or green candle

Timing:
Before bedtime or if you cannot sleep

The Spell

- Light the candle and blow softly into the flame three times, saying after the first breath, *Bring;* after the second, *Peaceful;* and after the third, *Sleep.*
- Gazing into the flame, say softly and repeatedly until you start to relax into sleep, *Sleep now peacefully, rest in true tranquillity. Weave your dreams, let all flow, into nighttime gently go, until morning's gentle sunbeams call and light shines over all.*
- Blow out the candle, saying the spell words as you drift into sleep.

677

A SECOND SLEEP BLESSING FOR YOURSELF, A CHILD, OR A LOVED ONE FAR AWAY

You will need:
A white candle
A pointed quartz crystal, if possible

Timing:
Before bedtime or when a loved one far away would be going to bed

The Spell
- Light the candle.
- Either briefly touch the flame with the point of the crystal or point the index finger of your dominant hand toward the flame, saying, *Enfold* [name person] *with blessings without ceasing this night.* (If you're doing this for a child, you may have the child present.)
- Draw a clockwise circle in the air around the candle at flame height, with the pointed quartz or the index finger of your dominant hand, saying, *Circle me* [or name] *with quiet sleep this night and banish fear until morning light.*
- Blow out the candle and place the crystal with the point facing the bedroom door (in a safe place in a young child's bedroom) or with the point facing the direction where the loved one is staying.

678

TO BANISH NIGHTMARES AND SLEEP DISTURBANCES

You will need:
A drinking glass half-filled with tap water

Timing:
Just before bedtime

The Spell
- Place a glass half-filled with water near your bedside.
- Swirl it five times counterclockwise, taking care not to spill any and saying, *Nightmares, bad dreams, and feelings of dread, enter this glass and be held there instead.*
- In the morning as soon as you wake up, whether or not you had a nightmare, pour the water down the drain.
- Rinse out the glass and leave it in the bedroom, ready to be filled before sleep the next night.

679

A DREAM CATCHER PROTECTION RITE FOR CHILDREN

You will need:

A dream catcher
A hook near the child's bed or by the window

Timing:
Weekly before the child's bedtime

The Spell

- On the first night, hold the dream catcher, allowing the child to touch it as you say, *Long ago the Wise Grandmother of the Native North American peoples wove tiny nets of thread to catch the bad dreams of little children and hung them over cradles so that the babes would sleep peacefully. Your bad dreams will be tangled in this web and only happy ones pass through. Sleep tight, little one.*
- Hang the dream catcher on the hook, or if the child is old enough, help her do it.
- When the child is asleep, swing the dream catcher, saying, *Sleep tight, little one.*
- In the morning, take the dream catcher down and shake it in the light to untangle any bad dreams caught there.
- Hang the dream catcher again the next evening and retell the story weekly.

680

FRAGRANCE MAGICK TO CREATE A BEAUTIFUL SLEEP EXPERIENCE

You will need:

A small scented candle in a glass holder
A bottle of rose or lavender essential oil

Timing:
Just before sleep

The Spell

- Light the small scented candle in a safe place in your bedroom and sit up in bed facing it.
- Hold the oil so the candlelight reflects in it, saying, *I walk through fields of fragrant flowers, to dream away the nighttime hours. I walk through blossoms to peaceful sleep and ask the angels to safe me keep.*
- Sprinkle a drop or two of oil on your pillow, repeating the spell words.
- Blow out the candle and close your eyes, saying the spell words softly and rhythmically until you drift into sleep.

FIGHTING GLOBAL INJUSTICE

681

TO BANISH INJUSTICE OR ABUSE DIRECTED AGAINST A MINORITY IN A LAND GOVERNED BY A HARSH REGIME

You will need:

A twig with dying leaves
A fast-flowing river or stream, if possible; if not, any body of water
A twig with thriving leaves

Timing:
The end of a week or the end of a month

The Spell

- Hold the dead twig between your hands, naming the injustice or abuse and the people affected by it, saying, *May all that is unjust and wrong fade like these leaves.*
- Pluck off the dying leaves, cast the twig aside, and throw the leaves one by one into the water, saying, *Flow away, go away, from the rivers to the sea. Bring I ask harmony to* [name the group suffering abuse or injustice].
- Hold the living twig between your hands, saying as you hold it, *May justice be done to* [name people] *and may they live henceforth in peace and without fear.*
- Cast the whole twig with the leaves still on it into the water, saying, *Flow to me, that I may see, justice to* [name people] *and unity.*

682

TO COUNTER TERRORISM

You will need:

A map of the world, set flat on a table
A small tree fragrance incense stick in a holder, to the right of the map
A small red candle and a taller white one, behind the map, the red one on the left

Timing:
Whenever there is a terrorist threat or attack or you must travel to a dangerous region

The Spell

- Light the red candle and from it the incense, saying, *May there be peace and safety throughout the whole world and may the innocent of every land and belief be protected.*
- Name the place where there is currently the most danger or where danger will affect you the most, then move the incense around the outside of the map, an inch or two above it, counterclockwise nine times, saying each time, *Take away harm, take away danger. Bring peace and safety to kin and to stranger.*
- Return the incense to its holder to burn.
- Light the white candle from the red one, saying, *May the light of peace and safety shine throughout the world.*
- Extinguish the red candle, but leave the white one burning.

683

FOR PEACE BETWEEN WARRING FACTIONS IN AN AREA WHERE THERE HAS BEEN ONGOING CONFLICT

You will need:

A green candle with all the spell requirements set around it
A lilac or lavender incense stick
Green children's modeling clay
A green drawstring bag or purse
Lavender, dried rose petals, or lavender potpourri
Dried sage and dried thyme
Salt

Timing:
Friday

The Spell

- Light the candle, saying, *The time has come for conflict to end, differences heal and hatred mend.*
- Light the incense from the candle and, with the clay, shape two featureless figures to represent the warring sides, then roll them together into a ball.
- Say, *May* [name factions] *be bound in new understanding, that they may learn tolerance and accept their differences.*
- Place the clay ball in the bag, together with the other ingredients in any order, one by one, repeating the first set of spell words for each one.
- Close the bag or purse, draw three knots in the air over it in incense smoke, and repeat the second set of spell words.
- Extinguish the candle, and let the incense burn.
- Keep the bag near a picture of the troubled area, printed out from the Internet.

684

TO SAVE A NATURAL HABITAT, WHETHER LOCAL OR GLOBAL, FROM THOSE WHO WOULD DESTROY IT

You will need:

A circle of seven green plants indoors or a circle of bushes and trees outdoors
Seven moss or tree (dendritic) agate or brown stones

Timing:
Seven consecutive days, starting on a Sunday

The Spell

- Name the endangered habitat represented by the circle of greenery.
- Bury a crystal in the soil of the first chosen plant, bush, or tree, saying, *Mother Earth, offerings I make. This day I ask you care to take, of* [name endangered habitat] *where danger lies, for few care if it lives or dies.*
- Hold your dominant hand over or close to each plant, palm facing the plant, repeating the spell words.
- Repeat the spell with a new crystal or stone and a different plant each day, moving clockwise around the circle.
- On day 7, repeat the whole spell, then walk three times clockwise around the circle, saying three times, *And so I trust you, Mother Earth, to give this fading place rebirth. Protect, bless, and renew* [name habitat], *keep fertile this land* [name again] *all the years through.*

685

A RITUAL TO SEND STRENGTH TO THOSE WORKING IN SWEATSHOPS TO PRODUCE CHEAP GOODS FOR THE WESTERN MARKET

You will need:

A small, clear, crystal quartz sphere or a small glass paperweight
A dark-colored scarf
A white or pale scarf
White candles (optional)

Timing:

Sunday

The Spell

- Name the place and people being exploited, saying, *May tomorrow new hope bring, against those who exploit your suffering.*
- Rub the sphere with the dark-colored scarf, and, as you do so, say seven times: *Take away the pain, take away the lust for gain, take away the profiteers who thrive on others' tears.*
- Then rub the sphere with the white scarf, and, as you do, repeat the second set of spell words seven more times.
- Set the sphere where light will shine on it or, if it's dark or there is only hazy light, place a circle of white candles around it, saying the second set of spell words seven more times and letting the candles burn through.

686

A CANDLE PEACE RITUAL FOR THOSE UNJUSTLY IMPRISONED

You will need:

A white or beeswax candle
A white lily (or a white rose) in a vase
A heatproof bowl

Timing:

Wednesday, at 10 p.m.

The Spell

- Light the candle. Place the lily or rose near the candle so light shines on it.
- Pluck a single petal and singe it in the flame, then drop it into the bowl, saying, *Open the prison gates, take away the bars. May those locked up unjustly* [name any people you have a special interest in] *once more soon be free.*
- Continue plucking the petals, and singeing them, saying the same spell words until all the petals are gone.
- Let the candle burn down.
- Add water to the bowl of burned petals and swirl it clockwise, repeating the spell words, then pour out the water outdoors, saying, *You shall be free, by water, fire, and flower, justice flows toward you, to bring freedom from this hour.*

687

TO REDRESS POVERTY IN LANDS WHERE A CORRUPT REGIME DIVERTS OVERSEAS AID SO IT DOES NOT REACH THOSE IN NEED

You will need:

A large jug of water
Two small pots or jars of equal size
A bottle or jar with a lid

Timing:

Toward the end of the waning moon, outdoors on grass or soil

The Spell

- Start pouring water from the jug into one of the pots until it overflows, saying as you do so, *Resources, money pouring in, squandered, wasted, it is a sin. That those who need it, never see it, and those in power, money for themselves do shower.*
- Start to slowly pour water from the overflowing pot into the other pot until the overfull pot has no more excess water, saying, *Carefully used and wisely spent, that is how the aid was meant. Corruption, dishonesty, they must stop, no more on the rich shall resources drop.*
- Put any spare water from the jug in a bottle or jar with a lid and close the lid, keeping the water to drink or pour on flowers.

688

TO KEEP A LARGE ORGANIZATION FROM PERPETRATING HIDDEN BUT PREVALENT PREJUDICE BASED ON RACE, RELIGION, GENDER, OR SOCIAL STATUS

You will need:

Six small, fast-melting wax candles, set in a circle
A large circular metal tray on which to stand the candle circle
Two thin blue cords or thick threads, braided and knotted at the ends
A blue cloth

Timing:

Sunday morning

The Spell

- Light the candles, one after the other, clockwise, saying continuously, *Take away the ceiling on our hopes, give us all an equal chance. Remove the favors behind closed doors, get rid of the whispered unfair laws.*
- As the wax runs together into a collective central pool, knot the cord three times and press it down into the central area of wax so the cord forms a circle in the melted wax, again saying the spell words.
- When the candles are burned through, etch the name of the organization or specific people in the circle of wax, saying the spell words once more.
- Carefully cut around the wax as it hardens and the circle of cord, so names are held firmly in the circle of wax.
- When the wax is cold, keep the cord in the wax wrapped in blue cloth.

689

TO HELP INJURED OR TRAUMATIZED MEMBERS OF THE ARMED FORCES WHO DO NOT RECEIVE THE SUPPORT THEY NEED WHEN THEY RETURN HOME

You will need:

Three blue candles in a row in ascending size, left to right

Salt

Timing:

Thursday when you wake up

The Spell

- Light the left-hand candle and sprinkle salt in the flame, saying, *May your light shine bright and all show gratitude for what you offered willingly, that you may see the care you deserve from those whom you so bravely served.*
- Light the second candle from the first, sprinkle salt into that flame, and say, *May your light still brighter shine, that all will recall how you offered your all, and you may see the care you deserve from those whom you bravely served.*
- Light the final candle from the first and second and sprinkle salt in the flame, saying, *Shine brightest of all and all will recall how you offered your all, that you will then see the care you deserve from those whom you bravely served.*
- Let the candles burn through and wash the salt under running water.

690

TO PROTECT AID WORKERS AND MEDICAL PERSONNEL IN DANGEROUS PLACES FROM ATTACK

You will need:

Eight red candles

A picture, in the center of the candles, of aid workers in a dangerous place

Timing:

Tuesday evening

The Spell

- Light the first candle and put it on the farthest corner of the picture, saying, *Be safe by day and by night, that you can unharmed spread your light. May none who bring violence, threat or danger draw near. May you save vulnerable lives without knowing fear.*
- Light the second candle in the next corner, moving clockwise, and say the same spell words repeating until four candles are burning.
- Returning to the farthest corner, light another candle halfway between the first and second candles, again repeating the spell words, then between the second and third, the third and fourth, and the fourth and first. As you light each candle, repeat the spell words.
- Let all eight candles burn and pin the picture where the morning light catches it.

691

A CANDLE WEB FOR WORLD PEACE

You will need:

A white candle

Timing:

Wednesday, at 10 p.m., in your own time zone (If you wish, you can contact people you know in different locations around the world and ask them to join in at 10 p.m. their time.)

The Spell

- Light your candle near an uncurtained window so the image of the candle is reflected in the glass. Say, *I send this beam of light to spread peace throughout the world.*
- Blow softly three times on the candle so the flame flickers and say, *I call all who light their candles in whatever land to join their light with mine, that this web of life may grow and send peace throughout the world.*
- Now say three times the World Peace Organization's prayer, *May peace prevail on Earth.*
- Blow out the candle, sending the light to wherever there is most need for peace (specify a place, if you wish, or trust the cosmos).
- Relight the candle and let it burn through.

692

A CONTINUOUS CANDLE PEACE RITUAL

You will need:

A long-burning candle in a glass or another safe holder
A small bowl of salt

Timing:

The anniversary of a tragedy, such as 9/11

The Spell

- Before the spell, email, phone, or use social media to ask people you know to do the ritual to pass the ritual on to someone *they* know.
- Ask them to light a candle two or three hours after receiving your message and request that they subsequently contact anyone else to do the same and continue passing on the ritual, with new people lighting candles for as long as possible.
- Light your candle, saying, *There is not enough darkness in the world to put out the light of a single candle.*
- Sprinkle salt into the flame, saying, *Turn away the face of hatred and division.*
- Sprinkle a second pinch of salt in the flame, saying, *I dedicate this light to* [name an act of terrorism or war where people have suffered] *that love and peace will spread throughout the world.*
- Let the candle burn through.
- Keep the salt for twenty-four hours and then pour the salt away.

693

TO BRING LASTING PEACE TO AREAS OF CONFLICT

You will need:

A sprig of evergreen in a vase
A small bowl of water
Eleven black and twelve white stones

Timing:
During the waxing moon, best of all on Sunday morning

The Spell

- Around the greenery, make a circle of the eleven black stones plus one white stone.
- Dip the sprig into the water and sprinkle each of the circle stones in turn, counterclockwise, saying, *May hatred cease, leave only peace.*
- Touch the white stone, saying, *May light and life return, and dissension turn to harmony.*
- Each day replace a black stone with a white one, touch it, and say, *May light and life return, and dissension turn to harmony.*
- Bury the black stones.
- When the greenery dies, shred it outdoors, and let it blow in the wind.

694

SO CHILDREN LIVING IN WAR ZONES MAY KNOW PEACE AND LAUGHTER ONCE MORE

You will need:

A rattle or a securely lidded tin, half-filled with dried peas or beans

Timing:
When you see or hear on the news of children suffering

The Spell

- Begin rattling quite loudly, getting louder and faster and saying as you rattle, *Noise and conflict go, attacks and warring slow, that the children may once more joy and laughter know.*
- End with a final loud rattle as you say *know.*
- Shake the rattle softly, getting softer and slower and saying continuously, *This warring is not necessary, the children crave security. May laughter once more return and playing carefree the children learn.*
- Stop rattling and say softly, *Let the only sound be children laughing, may the only noise birds once more singing. May laughter return to* [name a place that concerns you most] *and throughout the world.*

695

SO CEASE-FIRES AND TRUCES MAY TURN INTO PERMANENT PEACE

You will need:

A piece of paper and a blue pen
Nine long yellow ribbons

Timing:
When you hear of a cease-fire in a troubled area

The Spell

- Write on the paper, MAY THERE BE LASTING PEACE IN [name a specific place or say everywhere there is conflict].
- Tie the first ribbon in a loose knot around the paper, so there is an end trailing from either side of the paper, and say, *May each day cease-fires grow, and increased understanding show. So peace remains permanently, and lasting settlement there can be.*
- Knot two more ribbons and join one at each side of the first ribbon, repeating the spell words. Continue until you have knotted four ribbons to each side.
- Tie the two long loose ends of the two sides around and around the paper and secure them with a knot, saying, *Be bound in peace as truces grow and conflict flows away. Cease-fires increase to lasting peace, and harmony will stay.*
- After a week, cut all the knots and ties free, and dispose of them and the paper, saying, *So is conflict put away.*

696

TO SEND STRENGTH AND COURAGE TO INTERNATIONAL PEACE ORGANIZATIONS WHOSE LEADERS ARE HESITANT TO SPEAK OUT AND ACT AGAINST EVIL

You will need:

A red candle
A deep bowl of water
A white candle

Timing:
When leaders of international organizations hesitate to take a stand

The Spell

- Light the red candle and say, *The strength of love, the power of care are mightier than hate and fear. Do not hesitate, do not vacillate, the pleas of the desperate you must hear.*
- Blow out the candle and then relight it, saying, *Brighter still does goodness burn. Courage not expedience you must learn.*
- Extinguish the candle and plunge its wick down into the water, saying, *Invincible, undefeatable, the power of peace is strong. Kind words and deeds more powerful indeed than the cruel sword.*
- Light the white candle and let it burn, saying, *Light in the darkness, hope in despair, act against evil, show that you care.*
- Let the candle burn through.

697

SO WOMEN IN EVERY LAND WILL KNOW FREEDOM FROM FEAR

You will need:

Nine white flowers with long stems
Twine
A tall branch with long twigs attached to it, embedded in the ground
Birdseed

Timing:
Any clear morning

The Spell

- In a place where birds are flying, attach each white flower by its stem with twine to the branch so the flowers hang free, saying for each one, *Free as the birds, wild as the wind, be free. You who are oppressed* [name specific places where there is female repression, if you wish] *live openly.*
- Move around the branch nine times clockwise, stamping as you move and saying nine times, *Free from oppression, no one's possession, choosing your destiny, you shall know liberty.*
- Let the flowers blow away in their own time and scatter seeds for the birds to find.

698

SO THERE WILL BE REBUILDING AND RESTORATION IN LANDS DEVASTATED BY CONFLICT

You will need:

A jug of water
A small pot of dry soil
A variety of seeds in a basket or an open container

Timing:
After a devastating bombing raid or destruction of an area by military troops

The Spell

- Go outdoors. Pour enough water in the pot of soil to make it moist and plant seeds in it, saying, *Small beginnings, a new start, restoration shall grow to bring back the heart of* [name a specific place or, if you wish, say, *all lands devastated by war*]. *Step by step, stage by stage, may rebuilding replace destruction and rage.*
- Put down the pot and scatter additional seeds in ever-widening circles around the bowl as you move clockwise, saying, *Ever faster, ever wider, new life flowers anew. Regeneration throughout the nation, destruction must be through.*
- Sprinkle any remaining water over the seed circle, saying, *Mother Earth, grant rebirth, that all may be restored, better than before.*
- Let the seeds in the circle grow, blow away, or be eaten by birds, but take care of the pot of planted seeds indoors.

699

SO REFUGEES FROM PERSECUTION MAY BUILD NEW LIVES IN OTHER LANDS

You will need:

Dried rosemary, sage, thyme, or lavender heads
A map of the world, spread flat
A small handheld, battery-operated fan

Timing:

Friday

The Spell

- Scatter the herbs over the map, saying, *From the four corners of the earth, persecution drives you from the land of your birth. Desperation you feel as you flee, yet you shall a welcome see.*
- Using the fan, blow the herbs across the map, saying, *Seeking a new better life, free from danger, safe from strife. Blown by the winds, yet you shall see, places where you will welcome be.*
- Scoop up any remaining herbs from the map and put them in a small bowl.
- Add these to a large bowl of potpourri, dried petals, or herbs and swirl the bowl around to mix them all together.
- Each morning scatter a few flowers from the bowl onto the ground until the contents are gone.

700

SO THE HEARTS OF THOSE WHO PERPETUATE CONFLICT AND TERRORISM MAY BE SOFTENED

You will need:

A fast-burning wax or beeswax candle, in cream or white
A round tray to stand the candle on (When you light the candle, drip a little wax onto the center of the tray to secure it.)
A sharp, thin-bladed screwdriver or letter opener
A white scarf

Timing:

After an atrocity

The Spell

- Light the candle and say, *As this wax melts, soften your heart* [you can name a particular dictator or regime or say, *the heart of all who persecute others*]. *As this wax melts, soften your soul. As this wax melts, soften your mind, and become kind.*
- When the candle has melted, write in the still-soft wax, SOFTEN YOUR HEART, SOFTEN YOUR SOUL, SOFTEN YOUR MIND, AND BECOME KIND.
- When the melted wax is cool, cut out a wax circle containing the words and wrap it in the scarf, putting it on a dark shelf until it crumbles.

CHAPTER 15

SPELLS FOR ALL SEASONS

This chapter includes Halloween, Christmas, and New Year spells; seasonal celebrations; and personal celebrations throughout the year, following the old seasons and weather spells.

701

A HALLOWEEN RITUAL TO GET YOUR LIFE ON TRACK

You will need:
A sharp knife
A pumpkin
A small white candle

Timing:
October 31, before it gets dark

The Spell

- With the sharp knife, take the top off the pumpkin and scoop out the flesh. In the middle of the pumpkin in a horizontal line, make three parallel holes around the sides.
- When it gets dark, place the candle inside the pumpkin and light it. Circle the pumpkin three times counterclockwise, saying, *Time of no time, show to me, worlds long past but linked to me.*
- Gaze into the first hole, close your eyes, blink; look again to see a picture in the pumpkin or your mind from the past, your childhood, or past worlds, relevant to the present.
- Circle the pumpkin three times clockwise, saying, *Time of no time, show to me, the present world, but hidden from me to see what you need to know to understand about what is going on now.* Gaze into the second hole.
- Circle the pumpkin three times counterclockwise, saying, *Time of no time show to me, a future time but linked to me to see the best options ahead for you.* Gaze into the third hole. Let the candle burn.

702

A HALLOWEEN LOVE RITUAL TO CALL A RELUCTANT LOVER INTO YOUR DREAMS AND YOUR LIFE

You will need:
A red candle
A large round mirror
An apple
A hairbrush

Timing:
Halloween night, just before midnight

The Spell

- Light the candle and place it so it shines in the mirror. Sit facing the mirror, saying, *The fruit is sweet, so is my love, at the altar to meet. Love do not tarry, but marry me soon.*
- Take a bite of the apple and repeat the spell words.
- Put down the apple and brush your hair a hundred times, still looking into the mirror and saying, *Love I ask you walk with me, in dreams and in reality, that joined may we be eternally.*
- Put down the brush, saying, *Love show yourself within this glass to me, and walk with me in dreams that we may be, joined in love eternally.*
- Stare into the mirror, blow out the candle, blink, and in the afterglow you may see in the mirror your true love next to you. If not, close your eyes and the image will come and you can speak the words you wish to say.
- Go straight to sleep and the next morning leave the apple outdoors.

703

A TRADITIONAL, FUN HALLOWEEN RITUAL FOR A RICH, LOVING, AND ATTRACTIVE PARTNER

You will need:

A blindfold
Three plates or bowls, one empty, one filled with clean water, and one with dirty water (you need to do this with unmarried friends)

Timing:

Halloween afternoon

The Spell

- Put on the blindfold, getting a friend to place the three plates in a row.
- Turn around three times, saying, *Fortune, fortune, tell me. Am I pretty or plain? Or am I downright ugly, and ugly to remain? Shall I marry a gentleman? Shall I marry a clown? Or shall I marry old pots and pans, shouting through the town?* Adapt the words if you seeking a female partner.
- Reach out with your left hand.
- If you touch the clean water, your future spouse will be rich, attractive, successful, loving, and unmarried. If you touch the dirty water, your future spouse will have a few complications, maybe children, a difficult ex, or debts.
- If you touch the empty plate, traditionally it means you will remain unmarried until next Halloween. The quicker you reach for the right plate, the easier love will be.
- Have your friend remove the empty plate and repeat the spell with two plates and finally you will achieve the desired result.

704

A CHRISTMAS EVE LOVE RITUAL

You will need:

An open household fire or a bucket of soil with a large red candle pushed into it
Nine holly and nine ivy leaves
A prayer book open to the traditional wedding service words WITH THIS RING I THEE WED
A ring

Timing:

Late Christmas Eve

The Spell

- Light the candle if you're using one. Pull (or cut) nine hairs from your head, and drop them into the candle flame or fire, saying, *I offer this sacrifice to him most precious in my sight. May he come with wings of flame, and speak to me his own true name.*
- Either throw a holly leaf into the fire or hold it briefly in the candle flame and, as it becomes singed, drop and embed it in the sand. Continue alternating the holly and ivy leaves until all are burned.
- Put on the ring and read the wedding vows aloud.
- Extinguish the candle, close your eyes, and you may see your true love in your mind, a person known or unknown, or someone you know but had never thought of as a true love.

705

MAKING CHRISTMAS EVE LOVE CAKES, ALONE OR WITH FRIENDS

You will need:

A flapjack or oatcake mix or a traditional recipe
A sprig of holly

Timing:
Christmas Eve, 11 p.m.

The Spell

- Make the cakes in silence, marking the initials of your love if you must be apart for Christmas, or a question mark if unknown, on top of one of the small cakes and bake them.
- At midnight, hold the cake with the initials, saying, *Come to me in my dreams, find me in actuality, that we may be together as the year turns.*
- Walk upstairs (traditionally backwards), eating the initialed cake.
- Put the holly beneath the center of the headboard, saying the spell words once more.
- You may dream of your unknown love or have an unexpectedly warm connection with an absent lover.

706

A CELTIC CHRISTMAS EVE CANDLE RITUAL TO EXPERIENCE THE TRUE JOY OF CHRISTMAS

You will need:

A long-burning white candle in a safe container
A small amount of nonperishable food in a dish on the kitchen table

Timing:
Christmas Eve, as it gets dark

The Spell

- Light the candle near the food and say (if you have children, this is a nice spell to share), *Long ago on Christmas Eve, people left food and drink and lit a candle that the weary Mary might rest a while on her way to the stable.*
- Carry the candle to the kitchen windowsill indoors and blow in the flame three times, saying, *I/we send this light to all weary travelers this night, those who have no family or money at this time of joy. Blessings on them for I/we have so much to be thankful for* [say this even if you are alone or unhappy at Christmas].
- Let the candle burn, if possible all night, and make an online donation, however small, or extend a last-minute invitation to a neighbor or colleague you know is lonely.
- On Christmas morning, add the food to the Christmas festivities with blessings.

707

A NEW YEAR'S EVE CALENDAR RITUAL TO BRING A GOOD YEAR AHEAD

You will need:

A single calendar page from the current year with large squares marking the days
A red pen
A large, dark-colored candle
A ball of red yarn
A pot of soil or sand
A white candle

Timing:

New Year's Eve, fifteen minutes before midnight

The Spell

- If you're alone, write in any square of the calendar page a disaster you would rather forget.
- If family or friends are joining in, they can choose a square as well, and then share all the spell words and actions.
- Light the dark candle and tie up the calendar page using nine knots.
- Tear a corner off the calendar page, burning it in the dark candle flame.
- Drop the burned paper into the pot, saying nine times, *Old year turn, old year burn, bad luck, do not return.*
- Rip up the calendar page, throwing it unburned in the pot and put the pot outside the door before midnight.
- At two minutes to midnight, light the white candle from the dark one.
- On the first stroke of midnight, blow out the black candle and shout, *Come in New Year. You are welcome.*

708

A FIRST FOOTING RITUAL TO BRING GOOD NEW YEAR LUCK AND PROSPERITY INTO YOUR HOME

You will need:

A copper, silver, and gold-colored coin
Wrapped sweets, dried fruits, and nuts
Dried basil, juniper berries, sage, or thyme
Coal or wood
A drawstring bag
Small crystals or glass nuggets
A white candle (optional)
A large bowl of water

Timing:

New Year's Eve, before midnight

The Spell

- Five minutes before midnight, send the person chosen as First Footer (the person to first set foot in the house in the New Year in the old Scottish tradition) outside the front door with all the items, except the crystals, in the bag.
- At midnight all shout, *Come in, New Year. New Year, you are welcome, rattling pans and making welcome greetings.*
- The First Footer enters, shuts the door, and goes out the back door (if there is one) or out of the front door again, saying: *Out you go, Old Year. Your time is past.*
- The First Footer comes back in, slams the door, walks upstairs to the top of the house and down again, shouting, *Happy New Year.*
- The First Footer deposits the bag on the hearth or in front of a burning white candle.
- All toast the New Year and drop crystals into the bowl of water, making New Year's wishes.

709

A PERSONAL NEW YEAR'S DAY RITUAL TO BRING GOOD LUCK THROUGHOUT THE YEAR

You will need:

A drinking glass that's never been used before

Timing:

New Year's Eve, before you go to bed or New Year's morning, when you wake up

The Spell

- Have a drink out of a cold faucet in the glass, saying, *I welcome in the year, with joy and not with fear. May Hogmagog* [the Celtic God of the New Year] *bless this house and all that belongs to it, cattle, kin, and timbers. In food, clothes, and health of all therein, may fortune abound.*
- Go outdoors and circle the nearest tree or bush twelve times clockwise, naming a month for each circuit, saying as you name each month, *May I/ we* [name anyone close] *have happiness, luck, and prosperity all the coming year.*
- Return indoors, but do not throw any of the party garbage out, sweep, vacuum, or wash clothes until January 2, or you will jinx the New Year luck.

710

A HALLOWEEN OR NEW YEAR'S EVE RITUAL FOR KEEPING YOURSELF AND YOUR LOVED ONES SAFE

You will need:

A large red candle or hearth fire
Dried sage or rosemary

Timing:

Halloween (the end of the Celtic year) or New Year's Eve

The Spell

- Light the candle, saying, *This is the time of the year for the old fires to die and new ones be kindled that life may blaze anew.*
- Either alone or with family members or close friends, sit or kneel close to the candle or hearth fire. Sprinkle just a few grains of herbs into the flame, saying, *There are no regrets for the death of the old, for the new will return and burn bright.*
- Name a sorrow or regret you are consigning to the flame.
- Extinguish the fire or candle and then relight it, saying, *From the old comes new, from death rebirth and from decay growth.*
- Pour any remaining herbs onto the fire, or outdoors if you're using a candle, saying, *At the year's turning, past triumphs and disasters are all the same, all to be consigned to yesterday and so I/we name our future dreams.*

711

A TRADITIONAL VALENTINE'S MORNING FLOWER LOVE CHARM

You will need:
A yellow crocus or any small yellow flower

Timing:
February 14, in the morning

The Spell

- Before you go outdoors on Valentine's Day morning, fasten the yellow flower in your buttonhole or in your hair, saying three times as you do so, *St. Valentine, the lover's friend, I ask this flower true love to send.*
- If you are already in love, change the second line to, *I ask that my love will never end and if you have broken up with a partner but want him or her back,* say as the second line, *I ask that my lost love you send.*
- Greet the first three people you meet to stir up the happiness energies.
- At the end of the day, scatter the petals to the winds.

712

A ST. VALENTINE'S SEED RITUAL TO MAKE A SLOW-BURNING LOVE GROW

You will need:
A container of seeds

Timing:
February 14, in the early evening

The Spell

- Go to any open land, your garden, or, traditionally, a churchyard.
- Throw the seeds, handful by handful, over your right shoulder, for each handful, saying, *I sow this seed. This seed I sow, the one who is my true love,* [name], *your true love show, that like these seeds it will grow.*
- If your love has not contacted you on Valentine's Day, send a fun Valentine text, such as the old rhyme, I LOVE YOU, I LOVE YOU, I LOVE YOU ALMIGHTY, I WISH YOUR PAJAMAS WERE NEXT TO MY NIGHTIE. DON'T BE MISTAKEN, DON'T BE MISLED, I MEAN ON THE WASH PILE AND NOT ON THE BED.

713

A TRADITIONAL WAY TO DISCOVER WHO SENT YOU AN ANONYMOUS VALENTINE'S CARD

You will need:

A quill pen or any nibbed pen
Red ink
The anonymous Valentine's card

Timing:

The first Friday after you receive the card, just before midnight

The Spell

- Write on the back of the card, in red ink, the day, hour (if known), and year of your birth; the current year, the moon's age (i.e., the day of the current twenty-eight- or twenty-nine-day lunar cycle), and the star sign into which the sun has entered (this information is available online).
- Rest the card on or in your left shoe and put both the card and the shoe under your bed, level with your heart (the original spell suggests sleeping with the shoe under your pillow—ouch!).
- Go to bed, lying on your left side, and repeat three times, *St. Valentine, pray condescend to be this night, true love's friend. Let me now my lover see, be he or she of high or low degree. By a sign his or her station show, be it well or be it woe. Let him or her come to my bedside and my fortunes thus decide.*
- During the following week you will discover the identity of your secret Valentine-card sender, either in a dream or in everyday life.

714

AN EASTER MORNING RITUAL FOR NEW BEGINNINGS

You will need:

Three yellow candles and three green candles
A bowl of six uncooked eggs, whose shells you have decorated with a thin brush and food coloring
A basket or a large flat dish, in the center of a circle of the candles
Enough yellow flowers to half-fill the basket

Timing:

Easter morning, early

The Spell

- Light the circle of candles clockwise, saying, *Welcome is the light of new beginnings. Welcome is rebirth into my life* [name the ways you most need these] *and the ending of strife.*
- Pass the eggs one by one around the outside of the candles, saying for each egg, *Welcome is fertility* [name however you most need it, whether for a baby, a project, or finding a new home], *welcome new growth in my life will be* [name the growth you need].
- Put each egg in the basket.
- Blow out the candles, saying, *I take within the Easter light and welcome new opportunities shining bright.*
- Cook the eggs for breakfast, then scatter the flowers in a body of water where, it is said, you will see angels dancing.

715

A MOTHER'S DAY BLESSING RITUAL (MOTHERING SUNDAY IN THE UK)

You will need:

A bunch of carnations—red if your mother is still alive, white if she has passed on

A white candle

Timing:

Mother's Day in the United States and Australia, the second Sunday in May; Mothering Sunday morning, the fourth Sunday during Lent in the UK

The Spell

- Take the flowers outdoors and, holding them, say, *On this, your day, I thank you for the gift of life,* even if your mother was unloving. Add words of gratitude or regrets.
- Pluck petals from one flower and scatter them, saying, *I send you blessings, I send you love* [or *peace if things went wrong*] *on this day, your day.*
- If your mother is alive, take the flowers. If she has passed on, lives far away, or you are estranged, keep the flowers with the picture of her.
- Light a candle next to the flowers, saying, *May this light reach you, along with my blessings on this, your day.*
- Let the candle burn.

716

TO SEND LOVE ON FATHER'S DAY

You will need:

Paper, pen, and an envelope

Timing:

The third Sunday in June in the United States and the UK, the first Sunday in September in Australia

The Spell

- Sit quietly and write a letter to your father, whether you are close, estranged, or he is deceased or unknown. Express thanks for the gift of life and the guidance and care he gave you or, if things were bad between you, express peace and acceptance for what never was and perhaps never can be.
- Seal the paper in the envelope, writing whatever you call him on the front.
- Pass your hands slowly an inch or two above the envelope, the right hand moving clockwise and the left counterclockwise, palms facing down, saying continuously and softly, *On this, your day, I think of you, and send you blessings the whole day through.*
- Take the letter if you are getting together or mail it if you cannot be together. If you are estranged or your father is deceased or unknown, tear up the letter, burning the pieces on a fire or a metal bucket half-filled with sand. Bury any ashes.

717

AN INDEPENDENCE DAY FREEDOM RITUAL

You will need:

A white piece of paper and a red and blue pen

Three red, three white, and three blue candles

Timing:

July 4, early in the morning before the celebrations start

The Spell

- On the paper, write in alternating red and blue pen, WE HOLD THESE TRUTHS TO BE SELF-EVIDENT, THAT ALL MEN ARE CREATED EQUAL, THAT THEY ARE ENDOWED BY THEIR CREATOR WITH CERTAIN UNALIENABLE RIGHTS, THAT AMONG THESE ARE LIFE, LIBERTY, AND THE PURSUIT OF HAPPINESS, SAYING THE WORDS AS YOU WRITE THEM.
- Make a candle circle around the paper, saying for each as you light it, *For all the brave men, women, and children who have devoted their lives to and sometimes lost their lives for the cause of life, liberty, and happiness for all.*
- Let the candles burn until the celebrations begin.
- Blow out the candles, saying afterwards, *May the light of all the brave men, women, and children who have devoted their lives to and sometimes lost their lives for the cause of life, liberty, and happiness, never grow dim.*
- Burn the candles around your home during the evening and save the paper until next July 4.

718

A SOLITARY OR GROUP RITUAL FOR EARTH DAY OR WORLD HEALING DAY

You will need:

Seeds, dried herbs, or petals

Timing:

Earth Day or World Earth Healing Day

The Spell

- Walk around an open area in ever-increasing spirals, tracing the same path inward. As you walk, chant, *I am the rain, and the rain falls and sanctifies me.*
- If you're in a group, let individual spirals overlap as each person says the rain chant three times until all have said the spell words three times.
- Continue spiraling, and, if you're alone, when you're ready, chant, *I am the wind, and the wind blows and sanctifies me.*
- In a group, all recite the second chant three times in turn, continuing to spiral.
- If you're alone, when you're ready, change the chant to, *I am the sun, and the sun warms and sanctifies me.*
- In a group, say the new chant three times each.
- Keep walking and chanting, adding natural forces to the chant, such as the moon, the stars, and the waters.
- You or all end by scattering seeds, herbs, or petals, saying, *Heal and bless the Earth, Mother of all.*

719

A THANKSGIVING RITUAL FOR A HAPPY DAY

You will need:

Small dishes of allspice, dried bay leaves, bayberries, cinnamon, cloves, dried cranberries, ginger, powdered nutmeg, dried parsley, rosemary, sage, and thyme
A long-burning bayberry candle in a deep candle holder
A small red and white festive bag

Timing:

The fourth Thursday in November, early morning

The Spell

- Sprinkle a little of the contents of each dish around the base of the candle, saying for each one, *Herbs of luck, herbs of love, herbs of health and joy, bring to me what I do wish, that Thanksgiving I/we may enjoy.*
- Light the candle and set it in the middle of the kitchen, saying, *Candle of luck, candle of love, candle of health and joy, bring to me what I most do wish, that Thanksgiving I/we may enjoy.*
- Take sufficient berries and herbs to fill the bag, repeating the herb chant.
- Close the bag and leave it in front of the candle while you get everything ready.
- At mealtime, put the candle on the main table.
- Scatter the contents of the bag outdoors before the meal begins. You may need a new candle.

720

A SCANDINAVIAN ADVENT CANDLE RITE TO BRING JOY AND HEALTH INTO THE HOME

You will need:

Four red candles in ascending height, left to right, either in a four-candle holder or separate holders close together
Moss to put around the candles, or any festive greenery

Timing:

Beginning the Sunday nearest to St. Andrew's Day, November 30, and the next three Sundays (or the final candlelighting may be on Christmas Eve morning)

The Spell

- On Sunday nearest November 30, light the first candle at breakfast, saying, *Light the path to the star, on this day long ago the Wise Men traveled far, and on this day I/we do seek joy and health throughout the weeks, [name what is needed most]*.
- Let the candle burn until after breakfast, and then blow it out.
- On the second Sunday, light the first two candles, moving right and repeating the same spell words.
- Blow both candles out after breakfast.
- On the third Sunday, light the first, second, and third candles, repeating the same words, and blowing them out after breakfast.
- On the final Sunday (or Christmas Eve), each person makes a secret wish after you have lit all four candles. Let them burn through.

721

TO HAVE A HAPPY BIRTHDAY

You will need:

A gold candle
A picture of yourself when you were young, or younger
A current photograph of yourself
Environmentally friendly paper party streamers, the thin multicolored ones
A colorful kite
Tape

Timing:

Early on your birthday

The Spell

- Light the candle, saying, *This is my happiest birthday. So begins the best year ever and I will endeavor joyfully to make each day a treasure.*
- Place the photographs in front of the candle, with the picture of your younger self underneath the present-day one.
- Wrap birthday streamers around the two pictures, but do not secure them, saying, *I welcome the passing of the years, the best is yet to appear. And here I open the door to new adventures.*
- Unwrap and tie the birthday streamers to the tail of a kite, using tape to secure them and repeating the first set of spell words.
- Set the kite free in the first open space you come to, saying, *Happy Birthday to me, and so you can see, I welcome new adventures. Birthday fly free.*
- Alone or with others, celebrate.

722

A BIRTHDAY CAKE RITUAL FOR A CHILD'S PARTY

You will need:

The birthday cake
The correct number of candles on the cake
The same number of small white candles or tea lights circling the cake

Timing:

On the birthday morning

The Spell

- Light each of the candles around the cake clockwise, saying, *Let this day be joyous for my child, not in gifts alone but joy, may all who come together, this birthday fully the day enjoy. No tears no spills but laughing hours, that blessings on all who gather here may shower.*
- Blow out the candles fast and make a special wish for your child.
- At the party, repeat the same wish in your mind when the cake candles are blown out.
- During the evening, burn the larger candles around the home.

723

A VERY MERRY UNBIRTHDAY TO SPREAD HAPPINESS WHEN EVERYONE AROUND YOU IS GLOOMY

You will need:

Paper flowers or garlands
A circle of ten small red candles
A dish or basket of cupcakes or other small decorated cakes in the middle of the candles

Timing:

Before going to meet gloomy colleagues, or when you're expecting unenthusiastic friends or family to visit

The Spell

- Decorate the room with paper flowers.
- Light the candles one from the other, clockwise, saying, *A very merry Unbirthday to you, to me; fun and smiles and laughter on everyone I see. May gloom and doom fade and fall, as we recall this very merry Unbirthday to all.*
- Pass the dish of cakes around the outside of the candles ten times clockwise, saying faster and faster, *Unbirthdays come each day but one, and so I call my friend the sun on this delightful day to play, on this my merry Unbirthday Day.*
- Blow out the candles, shout, *Happy Unbirthday to all and take the cakes and flowers to work or give them to your guests.*

724

AN OLD FRENCH RITUAL FOR AN ENGAGEMENT CELEBRATION

You will need:

The engagement ring or use a substitute ring if you are doing the ritual for someone else
White paper and a green pen
Six red roses

Timing:

The evening before the day of the engagement party, whether yours or that of someone close to you

The Spell

- Set the ring in the center of the paper.
- Around it, draw in a circle symbols depicting clasped hands, followed by entwined hearts with your or the couple's joint initials in the center, followed by a knot, and then clasped hands again, hearts, and a knot until you have made a complete pattern around the ring.
- When you have finished, recite slowly, touching each symbol as it is mentioned, *Our/these hands and hearts with one consent have tied this knot until life is spent.*
- Touch each rose in turn, saying for each, *Let this day be joyous for us* [or name the couple]. *May this love never sever, let this love last forever.*
- Take the roses to the party.
- If the celebration is for someone close to you, fold the paper and wrap the (substitute) ring inside it, keeping it with a picture of the happy couple. If it is your engagement, place the paper beneath your pillow until the wedding.

725

FOR A JOYOUS BABY SHOWER

You will need:

A string of bells or Tibetan bells on a cord
The gift you intend to bring, or if it's your baby shower, a small item you have bought for baby
Nine yellow ribbons, or pink or blue ribbons if you know the sex of the baby
Nine paper flowers (if it is your baby shower)

Timing:

The morning of the baby shower

The Spell

- Ring the bells above the baby item nine times, saying, *One calls joy, two health, three wisdom, four wealth, five talents yet untold, six the heart and mind of gold, seven for courage, eight gentle power, nine blessings on this baby shower.*
- Tie the nine ribbons, each with a knot, around the gift (wrapped if you're taking it along), repeating a line of the chant for each one.
- If it is your baby shower, put your beribboned item in a basket decorated with nine paper flowers to hold the other gifts, saying, *Nine months to grow in your unique way, greetings baby on your shower day.*
- Alternatively, say the spell words in your mind as you hand over the gift.

726

FOR A FUN-FILLED BACHELOR OR BACHELORETTE PARTY OR WEEKEND

You will need:

A small candle or tea light for each guest, in a circle
A box of wrapped candies or sweet snacks in their box, placed within the circle of candles
A small decoration for everyone attending to wear, according to the theme of the evening, also placed within the circle of candles

Timing:

An hour or two before the event

The Spell

- Clockwise, light each candle saying, *Celebrations with those who care, sweetest is this joy to share, laughter for all and more to spare.*
- Open the box of candies and randomly scatter them around the outside of the candles, saying, *Spontaneity on this last night/weekend of liberty, will pleasure bring, many memories to treasure, then friends and kin will welcome in, the day when we/they [name] exchange their rings.*
- Eat a candy and say, *May I/you take in the fun, the laughter, and move on joyously to love hereafter.*
- Transfer the candies to a decorative box, and take them to the event.

727

A PERSONAL WEDDING OR COMMITMENT ANNIVERSARY RITUAL

You will need:

Two small matching symbols, or a charm or ring that splits in half
Two identical feathers
Two identical drawstring bags
Two identical green cords

Timing:
The night before the anniversary

The Spell

- Set the matching symbols or two halves of the charm side by side and hold them in your open cupped hands, blowing on them softly three times and saying, *Winds of the East, South, North, and West, my twin soul, I love you best and ask that many more anniversaries together in love we shall see.*
- Put them side by side once more and spiral the feathers over them, one in each hand, saying, *We are together willingly, free, yet joined in harmony and ever always may it be.*
- Put one symbol or half a charm in each bag and close each, yours first, securing the top of each with a cord in three knots, saying, *In love and caring are we bound, for lasting love we have truly found. Better and worse, sickness and health, being united is our wealth.*
- Release the feathers outdoors, saying, *Bound yet free, many more anniversaries may we see.*

728

FOR A MILESTONE WEDDING ANNIVERSARY, WHETHER SILVER, GOLD, RUBY, OR DIAMOND

You will need:

A photo in glass of yourselves on your wedding day or the happy couple in recent years
Twelve candles in the appropriate anniversary color, placed in a circle around the photo
A small white cloth
Yellow roses

Timing:
The morning of the event

The Spell

- Light each candle in turn, saying for each one, *You months of the year, you are growing, passing richly* [name the number of years the couple is married and the couple's names, if the celebrants are not you and your spouse] *our/your love did last and forever will it be.*
- Remove the photo from the circle and begin polishing the glass with the white cloth, saying, *The sorrows, worries, joys, and tears have weathered now many years, and on this happy day, so shall it be, the happiest, happiest* [name anniversary] *anniversary.*
- Return the photo to the candle circle, saying, *This anniversary* [name] *is filled with love that grows, and lasting companionship* we [or name the couple], *will we/each other show.*
- Let the candles burn until the celebration, then blow them out, saying *Happy Anniversary* and making a wish for the future.
- Keep the picture with yellow roses.

729

FOR A SPECIAL FAREWELL PARTY

You will need:

Photos of you or the person who is leaving, in different settings, some showing people who will be at the party
A bulletin board and thumbtacks or tape
A larger picture of the new location or activities relating to the next life stage
A lavender or woody incense stick

Timing:

A day or two before the event

The Spell

- Hold each picture, saying, *Golden Days, golden ways, these are the memories. But close connections never sever, for true friendship lasts forever.*
- Attach each picture to the bulletin board, leaving a space in the center for the new life picture.
- When only the larger, central picture is left, light the incense, writing over the picture in incense smoke, TRAVEL WELL TO MY/YOUR NEW WORLD. WONDERS MANY WILL BE UNFURLED. I/YOU GO WITH WISHES FOR GREATEST GOOD FORTUNE, AND KNOW WE WILL ALL MEET AGAIN SOON.
- Add the last picture, take the bulletin along to the party, and have everyone sign the back.

730

FOR A HARMONIOUS OFFICE PARTY

You will need:

A tub of brightly colored beads with holes
A long string on which to thread them

Timing:

The night before the party

The Spell

- Tie a knot in the left-hand end of the cord, saying, *I tie up all dissension, I bind in peace these I mention. List any potential troublemakers or those who will drink too much and speak or act unwisely.*
- Begin threading the beads one by one, holding each and naming anyone significant or whom you wish to impress or connect with romantically as you add it, saying, *May this connection be amicable/profitable, the occasion joyful and protect me from those who have had a skinful.*
- Tie the two ends of the cord together, saying, *Joined in harmony may we be, and if you do hope to make advantageous connections add, And may this benefit me/my career considerably.*
- Hide the beads in the room before the party.

731

AN EARLY SPRINGTIME RITUAL, CALLED IMBOLC IN THE CELTIC CALENDAR

You will need:

White candles, one for every window
A cup of ice
A cup of milk
Two small spoons

Timing:

Between January 31 and February 2 in the northern hemisphere, between July 31 to August 2 in the southern hemisphere, early evening; all dates go from early evening on the first day to early evening on the last

The Spell

- Put the candles in a circle with the ice and milk in the center.
- Light the candles clockwise, stirring the ice counterclockwise the number of times there are candles, naming obstacles in your life or people causing you unhappiness.
- Stir the milk clockwise with the second spoon, naming opportunities ahead or anyone who is helpful or whom you would like to know better.
- When the ice has melted, pour the water into a plant, saying, *Life springs anew. Old sorrows are through,*
- Afterwards, drink the milk, give it to an animal, or use it in cooking.
- Place a candle in each window, leaving them until you go to bed.
- Relight them the following evening and let them burn through.

732

A SPRINGTIME RITUAL, CALLED OSTARA IN THE OLD NORSE CALENDAR

You will need:

A broom
Water left outdoors in a bowl from dusk the night before the spell
Salt and pepper

Timing:

Between March 21 and 23 in the northern hemisphere, and between September 21 and 23 in the southern hemisphere

The Spell

- Sweep your home, sweeping all dust in counterclockwise circles out the front door.
- Chant as you work, *Dust to dust, away you must, health and luck and joy to bring. Begone winter, welcome spring.*
- Sprinkle water droplets clockwise around your home, saying, *Enter new light and life, banish strife. Welcome luck, love, money, and new beginnings.*
- Pour any remaining water out the front door.
- Finally, sprinkle salt and pepper on the doorstep threshold, saying, *Enter not here with ill intent, the power to harm me/us now is spent* [name any unwanted visitors, human or otherwise].

733

AN EARLY SUMMER RITUAL, CALLED BELTAIN IN THE CELTIC CALENDAR

You will need:

Thirteen oat cakes or biscuits; if more than thirteen people are present, add more cakes or biscuits
A bag to hold the cakes or biscuits
A sharp knife
If indoors, a large green plant; if outdoors, a tree
Colored ribbons
Different-colored flowers
Twine
Silver bells on strings

Timing:

Between April 30 and May 2 in the northern hemisphere, and between October 31 and November 2 in the southern hemisphere

The Spell

- Mark each of the cakes/biscuits except one with a cross and the last one with a star and put them in the bag.
- Say, *Welcome summer, enter now, for we honor the green tree bough.*
- Decorate the plant/tree with ribbons, flowers secured with twine, and bells, circling it thirteen times both ways, saying, *Who shall be the Summer King or Queen, who the year shall rule supreme?*
- Have each person take an oat cake from the bag. To whomever gets an oat cake with the star, supreme good luck is promised; whoever gets an oat cake with a cross makes a secret wish.
- If you're indoors, crumble the remaining biscuits on the fire or in a dish to feed the birds later, or take them outdoors to scatter the crumbs on the ground.

734

A SCANDINAVIAN MIDSUMMER RITUAL, CALLED LITHA IN THE OLD ANGLO-SAXON CALENDAR

You will need:

Seven kinds of flowers, in a basket
A small circle of wire for each person present
Red, yellow, and green threads

Timing:

Between June 21 and 23 (St. John's Eve) in the northern hemisphere, and between December 21 and 23 in the southern hemisphere

The Spell

- At dawn, preferably on the longest day of the year, set your basket of seven different kinds of flowers where they will catch first light.
- At noon, weave the flowers onto the wire, attaching them with the threads. You can do this with friends, if you wish.
- As you weave, whisper your dearest secret wish.
- When you're finished, hang the circlet(s) on a tree. Walk or dance around the tree nine times clockwise, chanting, *With seven flowers I/we meet, and when I next dance the Midsummer tree, I hope to see joy fulfilled of seven flowers sweet.*
- At sundown, take your wreath from the tree and hang it on the wall over your bed.
- Leave the wreath on the wall of your bedroom until it fades.

735

A LATE SUMMER/EARLY AUTUMN RITUAL, CALLED LUGHNASSADH, OR LAMMAS, IN THE CELTIC CALENDAR

You will need:

Long dried grasses or straw
A fire outdoors, or indoors a lighted orange candle and a bucket of soil
Red ribbon
A round loaf of bread decorated with the symbol of an ear of corn (draw this with a knife)
Red wine or dark fruit juice in a goblet

Timing:

Between July 31 and August 2 in the northern hemisphere, and between January 31 and February 2 in the southern hemisphere

The Spell

- Alone or with friends, each burn a single long grass/straw in the fire or singe the end in the candle before dropping it in the bucket.
- Name the justice or financial compensation/payment you or someone close to you needs, saying, *May justice be done and full restoration made.*
- Cast a second grass/straw into the fire, saying, *I* [or name] *free(s) myself/himself/herself of this burden.*
- Each person makes a straw knot or figure, binding it with red ribbon.
- Eat/share the bread by fire/candlelight, passing the wine/juice around, each person making a blessing for someone in need.
- Let the fire/candle burn down. Keep the straw knot/figure indoors until the twelfth night after Christmas, January 5 (the Eve of Epiphany, when the Wise Men arrived at the stable).

736

AN AUTUMN RITUAL, CALLED MABON IN THE CELTIC CALENDAR

You will need:

A deep dish filled with fallen leaves
A small bowl of berries or nuts
A deep empty bowl

Timing:

Between September 21 and 23 in the northern hemisphere, and between March 21 and 23 in the southern hemisphere

The Spell

- Take a leaf (you can do this with others if you wish, who do the same actions and say the same words, in turn), naming what is being left behind that did not work out, gently dropping the leaf into the empty bowl and saying, Go *in peace, what did not flourish in the harvest of my life.*
- Next, take a berry or nut, naming what can be taken forward from the previous months, saying, *This is the good harvest to sustain me in the months ahead until spring breaks through.*
- Continue until you have named all that is lost and gained, then scatter any remaining leaves and berries or nuts outdoors, saying, *What is lost and what is gained are now set free in equal measure. Blessings be on all.*

737

AN EARLY WINTER RITUAL, CALLED SAMHAIN IN THE CELTIC CALENDAR, A FORERUNNER OF HALLOWEEN

You will need:

A purple candle
A clove of garlic next to the candle
Photos of any deceased relatives you feel are close

Timing:

Between October 31 and November 2 in the northern hemisphere, and between April 30 and May 2 in the southern hemisphere

The Spell

- Light the candle, saying, *May only goodness and light enter here on this night of the beloved ancestors.*
- Blow softly into the candle, saying, *I call my beloved ancestors at this your special time to protect and guide me/us as winter approaches, especially* [name those in the photos].
- Hold each photo in turn, speaking words of love or regret, then saying, *As winter comes near, I carry this fear* [name your problem], *asking you to advise me or send signs to me.*
- Blow out the candle, saying, *Go in peace and blessings.*
- You may hear in your mind your deceased relative's comforting words, sense her presence, or smell her fragrance.
- The answer to your dilemma will come in a dream or an unmistakable sign in your daily life.
- Bury the garlic.

738

A WINTERTIME RITUAL, CALLED YULE IN THE OLD NORSE CALENDAR, A FORERUNNER OF CHRISTMAS

You will need:

Twelve white candles or tea lights, in a circle
A red candle in the center
Festive greenery, baubles, and the like, scattered around the candles

Timing:

Between December 21 and 23 in the northern hemisphere, and between June 21 and 23 in the southern hemisphere, in darkness

The Spell

- Light the red candle and from it the candle circle. Say, *I walk into the darkness without fear at the turning of the year, knowing the light will return. Candles no more burn.*
- Extinguish the candle circle so only the central candle flame remains.
- Say, *Let the old sun die, carrying away what must go, the illusions, the excuses, the inertia, and open the door to a new tomorrow.*
- After a few minutes relight each candle in the circle clockwise from the red one, saying, *The sun is reborn and light returns to the world. The dark times are ended.*
- Let the candles burn and use the greenery and decorations around the home.

739

AN ANGEL WET AND DRY SEASON RITUAL

You will need:

A gray candle for rain
A bowl of water
A bowl of dry soil or sand
Edible seeds such as pumpkin or sunflower seeds
A red candle for the dry season

Timing:
Just before the wet or dry season begins

The Spell

- To bring the rains, light a gray candle, saying nine times the names of the rain angels, *Mathariel, Ridya,* then adding, *Send the rains to cool the earth, bring the land back to birth. But floods hold back that the waters may lack destruction.*
- Scatter water drops over the bowl of soil or sand until it is moist, then plant seeds in it.
- To bring the dry season, light the red candle and reverse the order of the angels, saying, *Ridya, Mathariel* nine times. Add, *Send the sun to warm the earth, bring the fruit of the land to birth. But may fierceness and scorching hold back, that the sun may lack destruction.*
- Drop dry soil into a bowl of water until almost all the water is absorbed, and plant growing seedlings.
- In both rituals, let the candle burn through.

740

A WHEEL OF THE WORLD RITUAL

You will need:

Three white candles in a row, the outer ones small and the middle one larger
A small circle made from flower petals, some faded, some fresh, mixed together; or a mix of dried and fresh chopped herbs

Timing:
Any seasonal change point significant to you, wherever you live in the world

The Spell

- Light the two outer candles, saying, *The Wheel of the World is one wheel, winter and summer, fall and spring are one, as two sides of the world meet and greet the turning of the year.*
- Light the central candle by holding the two candles simultaneously in the wick, saying, *The wheel turns and the world turns, and so the world is one world and revolves in harmony.*
- Walk around your petal or herb circle, nine times clockwise then nine times counterclockwise, repeating, *The wheel turns and the world turns, I reach out to those across the seas and you reach back to me. May the circle that is open remain unbroken in our hearts and in our minds.*
- Blow out the outer candles, letting the central one burn, and scattering the petals/herbs outdoors afterward.

741

A RAINY DAY RITUAL TO BRING MONEY FLOWING INTO OR BACK INTO YOUR LIFE

You will need:

An empty bowl
Five coins of any denomination

Timing:
When it is raining

The Spell

- Set the bowl on the ground outside so rain collects in it, saying, *Rain, rain, don't go away, bring prosperity my way. Let it grow and overflow, that day by day money will grow.*
- Place the coins very closely around the bowl, repeating the spell words.
- When the coins are covered with water from the overflowing bowl, push each one into the ground, still in a circle around the bowl, saying the same spell words for each.
- Go indoors. When it stops raining, return outside and pour the water collected in the bowl onto where the coins are buried, saying, *Rain, rain, you've gone away, but come again another day, that my prosperity may flow like rain, steadily grow, and never wane.*
- Keep the bowl in place to collect rain and overflow on the same area.

742

A SECOND RAINY DAY RITUAL TO END A DESTRUCTIVE RELATIONSHIP WHEN A LOVER OR EX WON'T ACCEPT THAT IT'S OVER

You will need:

A large circle of green paper
A black pen
Pens of various colors
Scissors

Timing:
When the rain is steadily falling and looks set to continue for much of the day

The Spell

- On one half of the paper circle, draw an image to represent yourself in black pen, and on the other half, the two of you together.
- Draw a jagged line down the middle and cut the paper circle in half.
- Place the half representing the relationship from which you wish to be severed in the rain, saying, *Not to harm you, but to calm; you must let go, it shall be so. New love you'll find when you release me from your heart and mind.*
- Leave the half representing the relationship in the rain until it has dissolved.
- Color the image of yourself in bright patterns and write across it, I AM FREE.
- Pin it on a wall until you find new love and forge a new life without your ex.

743

SINGING A RAINBOW TO FILL YOUR LIFE WITH POWER AND HAPPINESS

You will need:

Nothing

Timing:

Any time you feel worried or sad, best when there's a rainbow in the sky

The Spell

- Sing the rainbow colors three times up and down the scale, then sing the seven powers listed below three times, using the same note formation up and down the scale.
- Finally, sing the colors up and down the scale three more times.
- Reverse the order for the descent, so upward would be red, orange, yellow, green, blue, indigo, violet; and downward, violet, indigo, blue, green, yellow, orange, red.
- The same applies with power names, red courage, orange joy, yellow power, green love, blue prosperity, indigo health, violet wisdom.
- Sing increasingly powerfully or hum the tune and sing the words in your mind with greater speed and intensity.
- On the last three sets, reduce the speed and intensity so the final descending color chant ends in silence.
- If there is a rainbow in the sky, cup your hands over your mouth, whisper a wish, and gently push it toward the rainbow.

744

MAKING STORMWATER FOR POWER AND POSITIVE CHANGE

You will need:

A bowl of water

Three clear quartz crystals

Timing:

When you hear the first thunderclap or see the first lightning.

The Spell

- Set the bowl of water on the ground outdoors, adding the crystals one by one and saying three times, *Power of lightning, strength of fire, mighty thunder, grant what I desire* [name the powers/changes you need].
- Cover the bowl and leave it outdoors until the storm passes.
- Filter the stormwater from the bowl into small glass bottles with lids and refrigerate.
- Splash the stormwater on your pulse points whenever you need strength or courage, repeating the spell words.
- If there is another storm before you have used it all up, pour the old stormwater away and make new.

745

SNOW MAGICK TO REMOVE OBSTACLES OR BANISH UNHELPFUL ATTITUDES FROM YOUR LIFE

You will need:

Four large white candles in a square
A large bowl, set within the four candles
Fresh snow
A wooden spoon

Timing:

Any time after the snow has fallen

The Spell

- Light each of the candles clockwise indoors, starting with the one farthest away and saying for each one, *Snow go, water flow, take from me the misery of* [name obstacles or unhelpful attitudes], *that my life may grow smoothly and harmoniously*.
- Put some snow in the bowl. Stir the snow in the bowl nine times in each direction, beginning counterclockwise and repeating the spell words nine times.
- Blow out one candle at a time, starting with the one farthest away, repeating the stirring and the spell words as before each time you blow out a candle.
- Let the last candle burn until the snow has melted, then blow it out, naming the positive results of removing obstacles/unhelpful attitudes.
- Empty the melted snow under cold running water, saying, *So power grows in me, as rivers become the sea. And I progress rapidly for all to see.*

746

AN OUTDOOR RITUAL ON A VERY SNOWY DAY TO GET LIFE MOVING IN THE DIRECTION YOU WANT

You will need:

A long pointed stick
If snow is long-lasting, a tea light or white candle

Timing:

When the snow is thick but has stopped falling

The Spell

- Draw a large circle in the snow around yourself clockwise, writing with a stick in the center, THE SNOW WILL MELT, THE SNOW WILL PASS. BRING TO ME WHAT MOST I ASK, [name the direction in which you want your life to go].
- Walk around the outline clockwise nine times, making layers of footprints and saying, *So will I make my mark.*
- If the snow is long-lasting, make a snow light in the center of the circle by creating a small circle of snowballs in the center, packed tightly one on top of the other, with a small hole in the center of the snowball circle just big enough for the light so you can easily reach inside.
- Light the candle in the snow hole and name how you wish to make your mark in the world. You can replace the light until the snow melts.

747

A DEW RITUAL FOR FERTILITY AND ABUNDANCE

You will need:

An eye dropper

A symbol of what you seek most; for example, a tiny doll to represent a baby, a silver heart for love, or a coin for money

A white cloth

A small bag or purse

Timing:

Dawn, best of all May 1 sunrise; if there is no dew, do this after rain when raindrops are still on leaves and use the raindrops in the spell

The Spell

- Collect at least twelve drops of dew/rain from flowers or green plants with the eye dropper.
- Using the eye dropper, allow a single drop at a time to fall on the symbol, saying, *Dew of the moon, dew of the dawn, bring* [name what you most want or need] *to me this morn.*
- Repeat the chant for each drop until nine drops have fallen on the symbol.
- Return the rest of the dew to the ground.
- Let the symbol dry naturally on a white cloth and place it in a small bag or purse at sunset, keeping it with you for seven days. After seven days, keep the symbol in its bag near your bed.

748

TO HARNESS THE POWERS OF THE WIND TO MAKE AN AMBITION OR DREAM COME TRUE

You will need:

Two tall white candles

A basket of green leaves

Timing:

When wind speed picks up

The Spell

- Light the first candle, saying, *From South, East, West and North, the power of this wind I summon forth. State your ambition or dream.*
- Light the second candle, repeating the spell words, and carry the two candles outdoors into the wind so their flames blow out, saying, *Carry my power at this hour, blow the changes I do desire. Carry this light higher and higher and return as the good fortune to which I aspire.*
- Go back indoors with the candles.
- Carry the leaves outdoors, setting the basket down so the leaves will blow away.
- Go back inside and relight the candles, the second from the first, saying, *Light returns and what I yearn will materialize before my eyes. I will gain the prize.*

749

TO BRING GOOD WEATHER FOR A SPECIAL OCCASION

You will need:

Five gold candles in a row
Five incense sticks in separate holders in a floral fragrance, one in front of each candle
A bowl of sand or soil

Timing:

The night before the event if the weather forecast is not good.

The Spell

- Light the left-most candle and from it the first incense stick.
- Spiral the first incense stick over the first candle, saying, *Bad weather you cannot stay. Rain/wind/fog/ice/snow, I blow you away.*
- Blow hard three times on the tip of the incense stick so it glows, saying, *Weather threaten your worst, your power I will burst.*
- Plunge the incense stick into the sand or soil, lighted end down, until it goes out, saying, *Out you go, I told you so.*
- Repeat for the other four incense sticks and let the candles burn, saying, *Sun, you will shine on this day of mine.*

750

A MISTY OR FOGGY DAY RITUAL TO CALL YOUR TWIN SOUL

You will need:

A small flashlight

Timing:

When it is misty or foggy

The Spell

- Stand outside in the mist and slowly turn around nine times clockwise, saying, *I call you my love through the mists of time, to my door I light the way. Come find me, love, that eternally together we shall stay.*
- Switch on the flashlight and cast the beam as you turn slowly nine times counterclockwise, repeating the spell words.
- Stand motionless, facing the direction of your home with the flashlight beam shining directly ahead, saying, *The mists will clear, I will be here, waiting with my love that brightly will shine through the mists of time. Come be mine.*
- Go indoors, lighting a lamp at a front-facing window, and leave the lamp on until the mist clears.

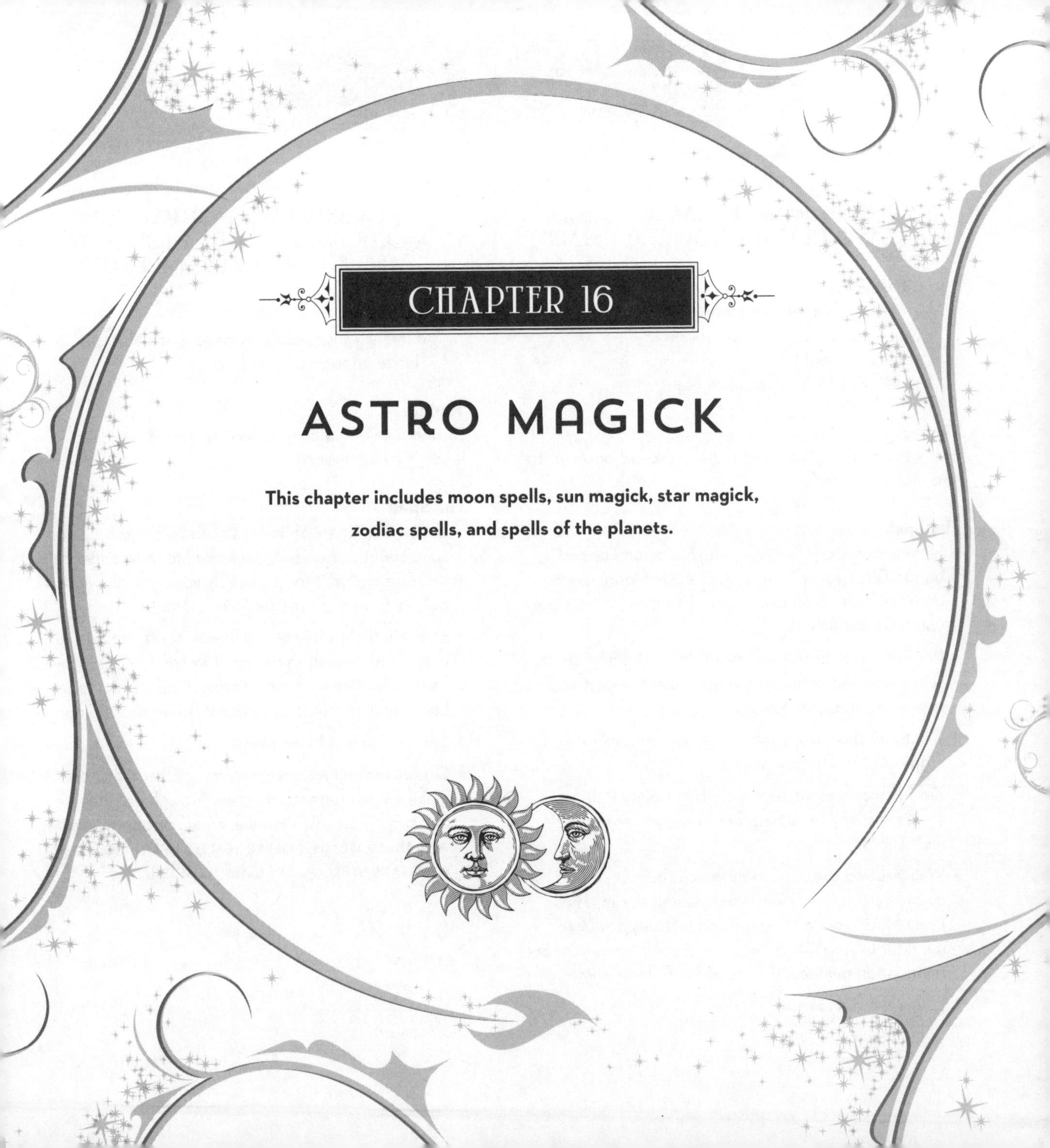

CHAPTER 16

ASTRO MAGICK

This chapter includes moon spells, sun magick, star magick, zodiac spells, and spells of the planets.

751

A CRESCENT MOON RITUAL TO RESTORE WHAT HAS BEEN TAKEN FROM YOU UNFAIRLY

You will need:

A small white stone or moonstone for each night from crescent moon to full moon night

A small white flower for each night

Timing:

Every evening outdoors from the crescent moon up to and including the full moon

The Spell

- Hold a stone/crystal between your open cupped hands. Blow softly on it, saying, *Lady Moon, as you do grow, restore all to me. Let this be so* [name what you have unfairly lost].
- Begin a circle of stones/crystals with the first stone, scattering the petals of a single flower over it and repeating the spell words.
- Continue the same spell words and actions each night until the full moon.
- On full moon night, complete the stone circle, scattering any remaining flower petals over the last stone.
- Walk around the outside of the circle counterclockwise seven times, saying seven times, *Lady Moon your night of power, restores power to me hour by hour. What was taken shall once more be mine, when next month's moon her fullness shines.*
- Leave the circle in place.

752

A WAXING MOON RITUAL FOR RECONCILIATION WITH A LOVED ONE WHO REFUSES TO COMMUNICATE

You will need:

Sufficient white petals to make a heart shape large enough to stand inside

Timing:

During a bright waxing moon, on any of the days leading to full moon

The Spell

- Make your heart of flowers outdoors, saying, *Least said, soonest mended, but Lady Moon this silence must be ended. Moon, I ask by your growing light, beloved to be in my true love's sight.*
- Stand in the center of the flower heart, facing the moon and repeating the spell words. Call your love's name aloud seven times, saying, *Call me, come to me, I offer you my heart. How can it be we are still apart?*
- Let the flowers blow away.
- On full moon night, repeat the spell and afterwards make some contact, whether through private messaging on social media, email, or phone, ending with these words: I OFFER YOU MY HEART, HOW CAN IT BE WE ARE STILL APART? CALL ME SOON.

753

MAKING A FULL MOON TREE FOR THE POWER TO COMPLETE BURDENSOME TASKS OR DISCHARGE DIFFICULT OBLIGATIONS

You will need:

A large silver candle
A leafy tree branch small enough to embed in a large pot of soil
Seven silver bells
Seven silver foil decorations or baubles
Silver thread
Seven silver ribbons

Timing:

After dark on a full moon night

The Spell

- Light the candle indoors, saying, *Moon power at this hour, this I ask, to finish these tasks that are grievously burdening me.*
- Decorate the branch with baubles and bells, using silver thread to attach them and tie the ribbons in loose bows on the branch, saying, *Mother of the Moon, with tasks undone I bind your tree that I may be free.*
- Pull the ribbons undone one after the other and shake the tree so the bells ring.
- Let the candle burn and leave the baubles and bells on the branch or plant throughout the week of the full moon.

754

A DRAWING DOWN THE FULL MOON RITUAL FOR FERTILITY OR CREATIVITY IN THE WAY MOST NEEDED

You will need:

Seven silver bells attached to a long stick with silver ribbons (about waist height)

Timing:

Outdoors, in bright moonlight, or indoors, if the moon is shining into the room

The Spell

- Hold the bells in your nondominant hand and, facing the moon, say softly and rhythmically, *Mother of the Moon, Mother of the Moon, come to me, be with me, Mother of the Moon.*
- Spin on the spot counterclockwise, continuing the chant and ringing the bells more and more loudly until you feel dizzy.
- Steady yourself and turn more slowly, chanting more quietly and ringing the bells more softly until you are motionless and silent.
- Sit on the ground again, facing the moon, and whisper, *I draw down the moon, the moon is within me. I take in with gratitude her fertility/creativity.*
- Whisper what you most want in the sphere of fertility/creativity and your time frame, then say, *I am the moon. May this, my wish, be granted soon.*
- Embed your bell stick in the ground outdoors.

755

A LUNAR ECLIPSE SPELL FOR MAKING A CHANGE THAT SCARES YOU

You will need:

A silver candle
Two pieces of white paper and a black pen
A dark-colored candle

Timing:

From just before a lunar eclipse until the moon reappears in the sky (if you have time, watch the moon disk gradually disappear until full moonlight returns)

The Spell

- Light the silver candle as the moon starts to disappear and write a list of all the things that are holding you back from success or happiness.
- When the moon is gone, light the dark candle from the silver one, saying, *Problems, obstacles flow from me, eclipsed in darkness may you be.*
- One by one, cross out the obstacles on your list, saying, *Eclipsed in darkness may you be.*
- When the moon starts to reappear, write on the second paper solutions to make change possible.
- Cut up and dispose of the first paper, saying, *Once more shine bright, you glorious light. I will succeed as darkness turns to white.*
- When full moonlight is restored, extinguish the dark candle, saying, *Eclipsed in darkness, obstacles shall be.*
- Leave the second paper where you can read it first thing the next morning.

756

A BLUE MOON RITUAL FOR BRINGING A MUCH-DESIRED OPPORTUNITY INTO YOUR LIFE

You will need:

A moonstone, preferably blue, or tumbled blue selenite
Seven blue candles, placed in a circle (if the spell is done indoors)
A large silver-colored bowl, half-filled with water

Timing:

Outdoors, full blue moon night, the second full moon in a month; if it's cloudy, indoors with seven blue candles in a circle

The Spell

- Hold the moonstone/selenite in your outstretched nondominant hand, saying as you face the moon/lighted candle circle, *Once in a blue moon has not come too soon, for I seek rare opportunity. On this blue moon may it come to be* [name the rarely occurring opportunity that would benefit you].
- Still facing the moon, toss the crystal seven times, saying seven times, *Rarely comes this opportunity, blue moon, send it soon to me.*
- Plunge the moonstone/selenite seven times into the water, repeating the crystal-tossing spell words seven times.
- Continue this cycle of tossing, chanting, and plunging until you have completed seven full cycles.
- Leave the crystal on the ground overnight (outdoors is fine) and pour the water on plants saying, *Blue moon, bring this opportunity soon.*

757

A FULL MOON RING COMMITMENT IF YOU AND YOUR LOVE ARE KEPT APART

You will need:

A silver ring to fit your wedding finger
The verses from the Songs of Solomon given below, written on white paper in black ink
A white envelope

Timing:
After dark on a full moon night, indoors

The Spell

- Put on the ring, reciting the words from the Songs of Solomon (8:6–7): *Set me as a seal upon thine heart, as a seal upon thine arm, for love is as strong as death. Many waters cannot quench love, neither can floods drown it. If a man would give all the substance of his house for love, he would be contented.*
- Fold and place the written Songs of Solomon words inside the envelope.
- Press the ring still on your finger to your heart and then your lips.
- Put the ring inside the envelope with the folded paper. Seal the envelope, repeating the Songs of Solomon verses.
- Place the envelope on an indoor window ledge overnight.
- The next morning, put it in your night-table drawer until you and your love can be together.

758

A WANING MOON RITUAL TO END AN ILLICIT AFFAIR THAT IS CAUSING TOO MUCH HURT

You will need:

An incense stick in myrrh, sandalwood, rosemary, or lemon

Timing:
After dark before the waning moon appears in the sky, outdoors

The Spell

- Find a place where no lights are shining.
- Light the incense and against the dark sky write in smoke, THIS CAN NO LONGER BE, FOR THIS LIAISON HURTS ME [or name who is most affected] GRIEVOUSLY. THE TIME FOR IT NOW IS PAST. IT CANNOT, MUST NOT LONGER LAST. AND SO WITH SADNESS I SAY GOOD-BYE, AS I CONSIGN THIS TO THE SKY.
- Say the words, then write them once more in the sky, adding, IT MUST BE GONE, IT MUST BE DONE.
- Let the incense burn away.

759

A DARK OF THE MOON BLESSING FOR YOURSELF OR A LOVED ONE WHO IS SERIOUSLY TROUBLED OR DEPRESSED

You will need:

A glass jug of water
An empty glass bowl (for performing the spell on the night of the crescent moon)

Timing:

The dark of the moon when the new moon is not visible (the first two or three days of the new moon cycle) and the first night of the crescent moon

The Spell

- Stand with the jug outdoors, saying as you look at the dark sky, *Though I cannot see you, yet your presence I do feel, cover me* [or name] *with your cloak of calm, and better days reveal.*
- Start to pour the water on the ground, saying as you do so, *Drop by drop, let sorrow fall. Drop by drop, I let go of all.*
- Repeat the spell each night until the crescent moon is visible and then slowly pour the water into the bowl, saying, *Drop by drop as you grow bright,* so *my* [or name's] *world at last turns light. Step by step, drop by drop, I walk to peace, all sorrows cease. You are welcome, Moon.*
- Wash your hands in the bowl and say, *Crescent moon, your power I seek, that I* [or name] *grow more joyous week by week.*
- Empty the water on flowers or thriving green plants.

760

A DARK OF THE MOON WATER BANISHING FOR A PHOBIA OR COMPULSION THAT DOMINATES YOUR LIFE

You will need:

Either seaweed or, if you're on an inland, green plant fronds from a pond or other water source
Sharp stone or penknife (optional)
A crystal, a silver coin, or white flowers

Timing:

New moon before the crescent moon appears, at the ebb/outflowing tide if you're working on a shore or tidal river

The Spell

- Tie or bind together enough fronds or seaweed to make a complete circle, saying, *Circle of anguish, set me free. Never does it let me be* [name the problem]. *Water/sea take now I ask, this pain from me* [name again the problem].
- Break open the circle, if necessary using a sharp stone or penknife.
- Cast the broken circle of seaweed/fronds into the water, saying, *I am captive no more. As I stand on this shore, so I am free. Moon, as you grow this I will know, though I can't see your brightness.*
- On the night of the crescent moon, face the moon, saying, *The moon I can truly see. Your light shines on me. I am free.*
- Bury a crystal or a silver coin, or leave white flowers in thanks.

761

A DAWN RITUAL FOR RELOCATION, IF IT IS PROVING HARD

You will need:

Small white stones, crystals, or clear glass nuggets to make an astrological sun disk on the ground large enough to stand in

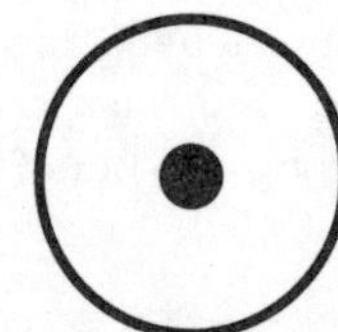

Astrological sun disk

Timing:

Beginning at or near sunrise

The Spell

- Stand in the center of your sun disk, and, looking toward the sunrise, raise your arms above your head and say, *Sunrise, flood the skies. And so my promise I renew, to live/work soon in pastures new.*
- Swing both arms down behind your back, swing them forward, and clap your hands over your head, saying, *Sun, as you climb higher, so do I aspire to reach my new location* [name desired location]. *Burn away hesitation.*
- Leave the sun disk glyph in place until noon, then walk around the outside of the glyph nine times clockwise, clapping and saying nine times, *Sun, as you near your height, I reach up for your light. Let me soar like you to pastures new, that all may now come right.*
- Go into the center of the sun disk, raise your arms, swing them behind you again, and end with a final clap over your head.
- Leave the sun glyph in place until sunset.

762

A DAWN RITUAL TO SPREAD HAPPINESS THROUGHOUT THE WORLD

You will need:

A mirror large enough to see your reflection, but sufficiently small to hold in your hands

Timing:

A bright sunrise

The Spell

- Smile into the mirror, saying, *A smile is a sunbeam, a smile a golden ray that begins with one smile to spread radiance throughout the world.*
- Pick up the mirror and, still smiling into it, turn clockwise in ever- widening circles, repeating the same spell words faster and faster, still holding the mirror.
- Then begin to slow down, making the words softer and the circles smaller, still moving clockwise until you are in the position where you began.
- Put down the mirror, face the sunrise, hold your arms upward with palms outward pushing into the air, smile, and say, *Smile, spread radiance throughout the whole world.*
- For every person you meet, smile and repeat all the spell words in your mind.

763

A MORNING RITUAL TO LOSE WEIGHT

You will need:

A bowl of seven orange or golden fruits, such as yellow apples, oranges, or peaches

Timing:

Early, as it gets light

The Spell

- Hold a piece of fruit up to the light between your open hands, saying, *I am golden, I am bright. I will not this day eat what I do not need, but only that which brings me pleasure, for my body I will treasure.*
- Throughout the day, whenever you feel tempted to overeat or binge, hold the same fruit (you can take it to work), repeating the spell words in your mind.
- After sunset, eat the fruit, saying, *This fruit I eat, my new body do I greet. I am golden, still filled with the light of dawn, to be refreshed once more at morn.*
- Repeat until all the fruit is gone, continuing the spell as long as you wish.

764

AN AFTERNOON SUN RITUAL FOR WHEN YOU NEED TO SHINE, BUT OTHERS ARE JEALOUS OR OBSTRUCTIONIST

You will need:

A gold-colored pendant or necklace, worn inside your clothes, small gold earrings you can conceal beneath your hair, or three gold-colored coins in a yellow or gold drawstring bag out of sight

Timing:

Whenever the sun is shining brightly, around 3 p.m., outdoors

The Spell

- Face the sun and, holding your jewelry in your nondominant hand, draw the sun glyph with the index finger of your dominant hand nine times, an inch or two above the jewelry in the air, saying nine times, *Let none see this powerful sun of mine, remain my secret until the time to shine.*

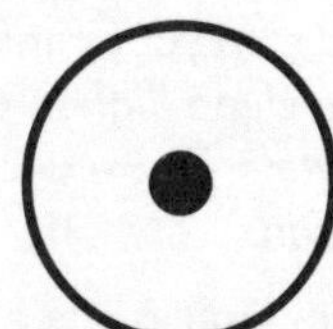

The sun glyph

- Keep the jewelry/coins out of sight.
- When the moment comes for you to shine, wear the jewelry so everyone can see it or get out your coins, saying as you touch them, *This is my time to shine. Sun power, make this moment mine.*

765

A CELTIC RETURN OF LIGHT RITUAL FOR INSPIRATION AND SUCCESS IN ALL CREATIVE VENTURES

You will need:

Three small glasses of water

The three-rayed sun symbol, the awen, drawn in earth, sand, or made out of stones, large enough to put a small glass of water in the center of each ray

A dish of sunflower or sesame seeds or cranberries or blueberries in the center of the awen symbol (which means "inspiration of the sun")

The awen

Timing:

Sunday, any time between noon and 3 p.m., outdoors

The Spell

- Facing the direction of the sun, hold the first glass from the left-hand ray, saying, *I take in the inspiration of the sun. Let this venture [name your creative plans and time frame] soon be won.*
- Take a sip from it.
- Return the glass to the ray and, holding the second glass from the central ray, repeat the same spell words and take a sip from that glass.
- Do and say the same for the third glass.
- Eat three small handfuls of the seeds/berries, repeating the spell words after eating each handful.
- Scatter the rest of the seeds/berries and pour any remaining water on the ground, saying, *May the inspiration of the sun flow within me.*

766

A SUNSET RITUAL FOR LETTING GO OF HURTFUL COMMENTS THAT YOU CANNOT GET OUT OF YOUR MIND

You will need:

Four candles in a row, the left one orange, then pink, purple, and finally yellow or gold, the colors of sunset

White paper and a pencil

An eraser

Timing:

At sunset

The Spell

- Stand so you can see the sunset through a window.
- Light the candles left to right, saying for each one, *Let it go. Words leave my mind. You, [name], were unkind. But each day I kindle your words anew. It hurts me, rather than you.*
- Write the words on the paper, then, word by word, starting at the end, erase them backwards, saying, *Word by word, gone from my mind, wiped from my heart, so peace can I find.*
- Extinguish the candles in reverse order of lighting, afterward saying, *Gone, done, I start anew. Dragging old hurts at last is through.*
- Face the darkening sky. Push your hands, palms outward toward the sunset, saying, *Sunset, take all this away, that tomorrow's dawn will be new day.*
- Fold the paper and throw it away.

767

A MIDSUMMER EVE BEESWAX RITUAL TO CONCEIVE A CHILD, IF THERE ARE FERTILITY/POTENCY ISSUES

You will need:

Seven beeswax candles, set in a circle

Timing:

Beginning at sunset the evening before Midsummer or St. John's Day (June 23) and for the six following nights

The Spell

- At sunset, light the first candle, saying, *Golden sweetness, mother bee, bring fertility/potency to me [or name partner with problems].*
- Let it burn for five minutes, then blow it out, saying, *May we be fruitful.*
- Continue lighting an extra candle each night, repeating the spell words for each one and letting them burn for five minutes (if any are burned out, replace them).
- On the seventh night, leave all the candles burning.
- Any of these nights will bring magick to lovemaking.
- Collect any remaining wax and bury it beneath a fruit tree or plant that will bear nuts or berries.

768

A MIDNIGHT RITUAL IF YOU CANNOT SLEEP BECAUSE YOU ARE WORRYING ABOUT A CONFRONTATION OR CRISIS IN THE MORNING

You will need:

A dark-blue candle
A small bowl of salt
Paper and a pen
A bowl of soil
A small, lidded plastic container
A blue pen

Timing:

Midnight, called the time of the dark sun, indoors or in the garden

The Spell

- Light the candle and, looking into the flame, say, *The dark sun across the world does shine, but let all be peaceful in this place of mine.*
- Sprinkle a few grains of salt into the flame, saying, *The sun will rise again at dawn, 'til then I consign all fear 'til morn.*
- On the paper, write over and over again the fears and the worries that are troubling you. Tear off just a corner and singe it in the candle flame. (Have a bowl of soil ready in case it catches on fire.)
- Extinguish the candle, and put the folded paper and the singed corner, burned or not, into a small plastic container in the freezer.
- Dispose of the plastic container and its contents the next morning.

769

A SOLAR ECLIPSE RITUAL FOR ANY MAJOR DREAM OR AMBITION

You will need:

A place where you can see the full or partial solar eclipse or watch it online

A sparkling yellow crystal, such as citrine or clear quartz

Timing:

Just before the eclipse until the sun reappears fully (not much more than seven minutes, often less)

The Spell

- Watching the eclipse begin as it gets darker, hold the crystal in your closed hands, saying, *Darkness from light, but soon once more to grow, the power of this eclipse I then shall know.*
- In the darkness, still holding the crystal, say, *All obstacles be carried away, lost forever in the dark. And when the light returns, on my journey I'll embark.*
- As the light returns, slowly open your hands so by the time the sun is bright, your hands are open.
- Toss the crystal high, catch it, and say, *Only light now remains, this dream of mine* [name the dream] *I shall attain.*
- Carry the crystal in a gold purse as a talisman of good fortune. Hold it whenever your dream seems elusive, saying the third set of spell words.

770

AN ALL-DAY HEALING SUN RITUAL ON THE ANNIVERSARY OF A SAD OCCASION

You will need:

Four stone fruits (e.g., peaches or plums) in a bowl, turning soft

A bowl of water left overnight outdoors to catch the first light

Timing:

At sunrise (or when you wake up), noon, sunset, and midnight (or when you go to bed)

The Spell

- Sprinkle a little light-infused water over the first fruit, saying, *I reach to new life, the past is gone. Yet on this day sad memories come.*
- Bury the first fruit, saying, *Rest in peace now.*
- Repeat the spell words and actions at noon with the second fruit, and at sunset with the third.
- At bedtime, as you bury the fourth fruit, say, *The fruit decays quite naturally, yet in spite of bad memories, good times remain. For the rest I let go what no more can be.*

771

A METEOR SHOWER/SHOOTING STAR RITUAL FOR RAPID PROGRESS IN A SLOW-MOVING MATTER OR TO RELEASE ASSETS THROUGH A FAST SALE

You will need:

A meteorite (obtainable from crystal stores or online)

A small pouch or purse

Timing:

During a meteor shower

The Spell

- Hold the meteorite in your dominant hand, and each time you see a falling star, say in the words of the old song, *Catch a falling star and put it in my pocket. Save it for a rainy day*, and make a wish, connected with the matter where you want rapid progress.
- When you have seen ten falling stars (or whatever number feels right for you), close your hands around the meteorite as you look upward and say, *This wish I make, this impasse break [name where you need fast results]. This token I take, to carry me far, on the shooting star.*
- Carry the meteorite in the pouch or put it with your official papers touching it whenever you need a burst of speed.

772

A STAR-GAZING RITUAL TO BRING OPPORTUNITY WITHIN REACH FOR A TALENT FROM WHICH YOU WANT TO MAKE MONEY

You will need:

A telescope or a pair of binoculars, even a child's one

Timing:

In bright starlight (you may need to go where there is no light pollution)

The Spell

- Choose a bright star or group of stars/a constellation, and say, *I reach out to the stars, I draw them near, that they will bring what I most hold dear:* [name desire].
- Focusing on the same star(s) through the telescope/binoculars, adjust the lens so the star(s) become clearer (it does not matter if the telescope is not powerful).
- Say, *Nearer and nearer the stars do glow, as my talent too will grow and grow.*
- When you can adjust the telescope no further, reduce the vision until you are again using your naked eye.
- Push the viewing end of the telescope/binoculars gently into your solar plexus, the upper center of your stomach, saying, *I take the power of the stars within me, that as I reach out, success comes to me.*
- Whenever you need power, touch your solar plexus, repeating the spell words.

773

A STARRY NIGHT RITUAL TO CALL A LOVER WHO IS NOT YET FREE TO BE WITH YOU

You will need:

Two small blue and gold lapis lazuli stones, two sparkling blue goldstones, or two silver or gold beads

An open box, almost filled with small, gold, pressure-sensitive stars

Paper and a blue pen

Timing:

Any starlit night, outdoors

The Spell

- Holding the stones in your dominant hand and the box of stars in your other hand, lift your hands toward the stars, saying, *The stars they shine on me and you. You see them too. Though for now we are apart, stars carry the love between our hearts.*
- Place the stones in the center of the box of stars, saying, *A hundred million stars above, and each will bring you close, my love.*
- Carry the box indoors and on the paper draw a heart with your entwined initials in the center and write, MAY WE BE TOGETHER FOREVER SOON.
- Decorate the edges of the heart with gold stars and then fill the paper with them.
- Fold the paper around the twin stones and keep it near your bed.

774

A STARLESS NIGHT RITUAL FOR LETTING GO OF GUILT, WHETHER WARRANTED OR NOT

You will need:

Candles or lamps in your home

Timing:

After dark on a cloudy night

The Spell

- Outside, look up to where the stars would be, saying, *Stars, though invisible this night, yet I know you shine your light. The clouds will clear, you will appear, and I will shed this guilt and fear.*
- Move your hands in and out slowly, palms vertical and facing each other, and create an invisible energy ball from the power in your hands. Toss the energy ball up high and say, *Guilt begone.*
- Go indoors and light candles or turn on all the lamps, saying, *Like the stars will I shine again. No guilt remains, for peace I gain.*

775

THE FIRST STAR IN THE SKY RITUAL FOR A SECRET LOVE YOU DARE NOT SPEAK OF

You will need:

A piece of tinfoil or silver paper
Scissors
Silver thread

Timing:

Just before the first star appears

The Spell

- Before the spell, make yourself a silver star about the size of the palm of your hand, cut a hole in it, and attach the thread to it.
- Go outdoors, holding it in your nondominant hand, and when the first star appears, say, *First star I see tonight, you are most precious to my sight. Though I do not speak her name, my heart is with deep love aflame.*
- Place your index finger from one hand and your middle finger from the other hand together and point them toward the star, whispering a secret message to your love and adding, *Grant this to me, when right to be.*
- Attach the star to a tree or bush, well-hidden in the branches.

776

A POLE STAR/POLARIS RITUAL FOR THOSE IN THE NORTHERN HEMISPHERE, WHEN YOU ARE LONELY AND FAR FROM YOUR ROOTS

You will need:

A lavender, lilac, or any floral incense stick
A small star charm or pendant
A photo of the people you miss

Timing:

After dark

The Spell

- Identify the Pole Star (using an online star map, if necessary) and light the incense, saying, *Star, I call you far from home, this night I feel so alone. Carry my wishes across land or sea, that I may feel my loved ones, [name], close to me.*
- Holding the star symbol in your nondominant hand, write in incense smoke in the air over it, STAR, GUIDE ME HOME WHEN RIGHT TO BE, OR LET MY LOVED ONES COME TO ME.
- Place the star symbol on top of the photo. In incense smoke, draw a star in smoke around them, an inch above, sending silent messages of love.
- Let the incense burn and take the photo and the symbol indoors.
- Make contact with your loved ones. Whenever you miss them, wear the star pendant or carry the charm.

777

A CRUX/SOUTHERN CROSS RITUAL FOR THOSE IN THE SOUTHERN HEMISPHERE, TO CHANGE CAREER OR LIFESTYLE SUCCESSFULLY WHEN YOU HAVE REACHED A CROSSROADS

You will need:

Enough white stones to make a cross so you can step between the stones, with the vertical axis longer than the horizontal axis

A flashlight

Timing:

When the Southern Cross is clear in the night sky

The Spell

- Make the stone cross outdoors, so the uppermost vertical point faces the Southern Cross in the sky.
- Walk along the vertical axis, to the center, still facing the starry Cross. Shining the flashlight on the stones, say, *I have reached the crossroads, no going back, nor sideways compromise. I walk to success, following the stars, and I will reach the skies.*
- Continue walking to the top of the stone cross, saying, *Step by step, stone by stone, this path of mine, [name it], is clearly shown.*
- When you reach the end, focus on the Southern Cross in the sky and make big crosses in the sky, using the flashlight beam and saying, *So I venture joyfully, to follow the shining path before me.*
- Leave the stone cross in place.

778

TO FOLLOW YOUR STAR IF YOU HAVE A MAJOR OPPORTUNITY THAT INVOLVES MOVING TO AN UNFAMILIAR PLACE THAT SCARES YOU

You will need:

Nothing

Timing:

A starry night

The Spell

- Turn around fast counterclockwise, then clockwise, alternately, saying faster and faster, *Starry, starry night on me cast your light, for I will follow my star to my destiny. Come now, my star, light the way for me.*
- When you are dizzy, steady yourself and point upward and directly ahead to the brightest star, saying, *I will follow my star with hope, not fear, to my great opportunity, the way is clear.*
- On a sky map online, identify the star and, the following two nights, find your star again in the sky. If it is cloudy, look where it would be according to the sky map, pointing upward and saying, *I will follow my star, be the way near or far. I will embrace this chance, without a backward glance.*
- On night 3, begin to make your arrangements. Whenever you doubt, close your eyes, picture your star, and say, *I will follow my star wherever you are.*

779

WISHING ON A STAR, FOR RECOGNITION, FAME, AND FORTUNE

You will need:

A silver helium balloon, if possible decorated with stars, or attach your own small pressure-sensitive stars

Timing:

A starry night

The Spell

- Stand, holding your balloon in your nondominant hand, and look upward to a group of bright stars above. Choose one and say, *When I wish upon a star, that wish will travel very far. Through starry skies it will rise, that all will see, fame/fortune coming rapidly to me.*
- Touch your heart with your other hand, then the center of your throat and the middle of your brow.
- Point your dominant hand toward the star, saying, *Bring me this dream, faster than it seems* [ask silently for the recognition you want].
- Touch the balloon with the same hand, then release it, saying, *I rise to the stars, I will go far. As the stars I will shine, fame/fortune will be mine.*
- Turn away and do not watch the balloon disappear.

780

A MILKY WAY RITUAL FOR BECOMING A MILLIONAIRE (OR GREATLY IMPROVING YOUR FINANCES)

You will need:

A bowl of very tiny white petals or seeds
Nine small pearls in a purse

Timing:

Whenever the Milky Way is most visible

The Spell

- Gaze upward at the Milky Way, holding the bowl of petals/seeds and saying, *Stars by the million, stars by the trillion timelessly flowing, let wealth around me be endlessly growing. A million or more and something to spare, and I will do good, my wealth I will share.*
- Scatter the petals/seeds in ever-widening circles, saying, *Increase and grow, beneath its endless glow the Milky Way flows, grows wealth for me. A million or more, open your door; limitless as the Milky Way, money's here to stay.*
- When the bowl is empty, add the pearls to it and, holding it upward, repeat the first set of spell words.
- Take the bowl indoors. Whenever the Milky Way is clear, add a pearl to the bowl, take the bowl outdoors, hold it to the sky, and repeat the first set of spell words.

781

AN ARIES DRAGON RITUAL TO OVERCOME BULLYING, WHETHER YOU ARE AN ADULT OR A CHILD

You will need:

A large sheet of paper and a red pen and a gold pen (you can help a child perform the spell)

Timing:

Between March 21 and April 20, or whenever you need the courage and strength of Aries the Ram

The Spell

- In the center of the paper, write in red letters the name(s) of the bullies and enclose it in the gold outline of a small dragon, saying, *Mighty dragon with your fierce fire, swallow up this bullying that I may no longer be afraid.*
- Draw a larger dragon outline in red around the first one, repeating the spell words, then a gold dragon around the second one, saying the same words, in alternate colors until all the dragons are enclosed in one that almost fills the paper.
- Color the innermost dragon to obscure the name(s) and hang the picture where it cannot be seen, saying, *Now you are swallowed by dragon fire. I have the power of the dragon within me.*
- When you or your child next meet the bully, say the spell words in your mind and imagine the fire flowing.

782

A TAURUS RITUAL FOR PATIENCE AND PERSEVERANCE WHEN YOU WANT TO SAY, "STUFF YOUR JOB," BUT CAN'T

You will need:

A green candle

A small silver, ceramic, or child's toy farmyard bull

Timing:

Between April 21 and May 21, or any time you need the patience of Taurus the Bull

The Spell

- The night before the first day of your workweek, light the candle and set the bull in front of it, saying, *"Stuff your job," I'd like to say, "You do not deserve me anyway." But I must be patient, watch my talk, 'til the time when I can walk. Bull, give me patience and determination not to be trampled on in the week to come.*
- Blow out the candle, saying, *I have the strength of the bull not to be trampled on, so I will remain patient in the week to come.*
- Set the bull in your workspace or keep it in a pouch inside your bag. When you are provoked, picture the bull with horns, ready to defend you, and repeat the spell words in your mind as you touch the bull.
- Repeat the spell weekly until you can change jobs.

783

A GEMINI RITUAL IF YOU NEED TO TAKE A NECESSARY SHORTCUT AND DON'T WANT TO BE DETECTED

You will need:

Five dark stones
A sleep mask, the kind worn on planes
A small bag

Timing:

Between May 22 and June 21, or whenever you need to call on the ingenuity of Gemini the Twins

The Spell

- Hold each stone in turn, saying, *Hide from the world what I must do, until this crisis is through.*
- Bring each stone close to your mouth in turn, and whisper the shortcut you must take, then put it in the bag, saying, *Hold my secret safe.*
- Set the bag in front of you and put on the sleep mask, saying, *Keep hidden from the eyes of those who'd shake their heads disapprovingly, for if I do this to survive, better times I'll see.*
- Fold the sleep mask into a small bundle and place it in the bag with the stones, close the bag, and hide it where it cannot be found, saying, *Keep my secret safe.*
- When the crisis is over, throw away the stones in water and recycle the mask.

784

A CANCERIAN RITUAL FOR RESTORING A HAPPY HOME AFTER A JEALOUS FRIEND OR RELATIVE HAS CAUSED RIFTS

You will need:

Garlic salt or garlic powder in a sealed jar

Timing:

Between June 22 and July 22, or whenever you need to restore the family unity of Cancer the Crab

The Spell

- Use a pretext to get every member of the family affected to touch/hold the jar (ask them to pass it to you in the kitchen). As they do so, say in your mind, *Take from them the hurt and negativity. Absorbed must it be so you can be free.*
- Hold the jar yourself, saying, *I am the center and the rock. Let me absorb this dreadful shock, passing it from me to the jar, and then I'll take it very far.*
- As soon as possible, go a considerable distance from your home and put the garlic jar in a garbage can after repeating the second set of spell words.

785

A LEO RITUAL FOR A CHILD OR YOURSELF PERFORMING PUBLICLY TO BANISH STAGE FRIGHT

You will need:

A gold pen and white paper
A glue stick, preferably gold
A bowl of glitter, and another of gold or glittery stars
A gold purse or drawstring bag

Timing:

July 23 through August 23, or whenever you need Leo the Lion to help you overcome stage fright

The Spell

- In the center of the paper, draw a golden lion, saying, *Power of the lion, fill me with power, that when the hour is mine I* [or name person] *will shine.*
- Spread glue around the paper, but not over the lion, and sprinkle glitter over the glue, saying, *Ever brighter, Jungle Lord, that when I* [or name] *appear, all will applaud and all will cheer.*
- Edge the paper with gold stars and, when dry, set the paper where light will shine on it.
- Put any remaining glitter and stars in the bag and carry the bag to the event.

786

A VIRGO RITUAL FOR COMPLETING BORING OFFICIAL PAPERWORK OR MANAGING OVERDUE ACCOUNTS

You will need:

A dark-green candle
An old-fashioned sand hourglass egg timer
The official paperwork or a printed sample

Timing:

August 24 through September 22, or any time you need Virgo the Maiden to help with your mountain of unfinished paperwork

The Spell

- Light the candle and set the egg timer in motion, saying, *I must endure, slow but sure. Less haste may seem boring, but success will ensure.*
- Work on the papers until the sand has run through the egg timer, blow softly into the candle, and say, *My time is spent with care, and when I am there, all will be right, my heart will be light, I trudge ever onward.*
- Continue for another three minutes. When the sand has run through the egg timer, blow again into the candle, repeating the second set of spell words.
- Repeat a third time, then blow out the candle, saying, *Nine times nine, success is mine. I will take my time.*
- Light the candle and repeat the third set of spell words before tackling the paperwork.

787

A LIBRA ANTI GUILT TRIP RITUAL FOR RESTORING BALANCE WHEN TWO FRIENDS OR FAMILY MEMBERS ARE PULLING YOU IN OPPOSITE DIRECTIONS

You will need:

A blue cord long enough to hold taut between your hands
A dish of salt

Timing:

September 23 through October 23, or whenever you need Libra the Scales to restore harmony to your life

The Spell

- Hold the cord by one end, saying, *Pulling and tugging, trying to please, these seesawing demands simply must cease.*
- Tie a loose knot in the center, saying, *You [name combatants] are bound from involving me in your conflict. No longer inflict this rivalry, which so disturbs my harmony. I shall be free.*
- Pull the knot undone and immerse the cord in the salt, saying, *Resolve it, solve it, not my business; no more stress, I will no longer witness this pettiness.*
- After twenty-four hours, dispose of the cord, still in the salt, and wash the dish well.

788

A SCORPIO SPELL TO SHIELD YOURSELF FROM SOMEONE WHO IS OBSESSED WITH YOU AND YOUR LIFE

You will need:

Strong paper, thin gray watercolor paint, and a brush or a child's gray paint stick
Scissors

Timing:

October 24 through November 22, or whenever you need the determination of Scorpio the Scorpion to get rid of a stalker

The Spell

- Paint two featureless stick figures, one representing you and one representing the stalker, on either side of the paper, and say, *Follow me no more, no longer seek me, your interest in my life does freak me.*
- Cover the whole paper, including the figures in gray paint, saying when you have finished, *Your vision of me now is obscure, your unwanted attention I will not endure. You must find a new obsession, and now shall learn this needed lesson.*
- Cut the paper jaggedly in half. When it is dry, fold the half representing yourself very small and put it in a container in the refrigerator, not in the freezer, for nine days, saying, *Your overconcern in my life I cool. No longer seek me, that's the rule.*
- Throw the other half in a garbage can.

789

A SAGITTARIUS RITUAL FOR BRINGING FUN AND ADVENTURE BACK INTO YOUR LIFE IF YOU HAVE A STICK-IN-THE MUD PARTNER

You will need:

A brown crayon or marker

A picture of your partner loosely attached with adhesive tape to the center of a sheet of white paper

Pictures of places where you would like to go, printed out from the Internet, and a photo of yourself in the center, all attached to a piece of cardboard or a bulletin board

Timing:

November 23 through December 21, or whenever you need Sagittarius the Archer to lift the restrictions

The Spell

- With the brown crayon or marker, draw mud all around your partner's photo, taking care not to mark the picture, and say, *Stick-in-the-mud, though dearly I love you, you're driving me nuts by what you won't do.*
- Carefully lift up your partner's photo from the mud picture, saying, *Dear Stick-in-the-mud, come out to play. We really could share such wonderful days, adventures, and outings, brimming with laughter. Don't stay in your mud, waiting for happy hereafter.*
- Stick your partner's photo next to yours and put the cardboard where it can be seen by your partner.
- Dispose of the mud picture.

790

A CAPRICORN RITUAL FOR CAUTION IN THE FACE OF TEMPTATION

You will need:

A fast-burning, bright-yellow wax candle on a broad flat holder or tray

A thin-bladed small screwdriver or letter opener

A small biodegradable bag

Timing:

December 22 through January 20, or whenever you need Capricorn the Goat to help you exercise wise caution

The Spell

- In the wax on the candle, lightly scratch the name of the person or situation that is tempting you.
- Light the candle, saying, *Temptation beware. Let me show care, for once the fatal steps are taken, my life will be forever shaken.*
- Blow gently into the candle flame three times and say, *Let the fire of desire melt away. Temptation you seem a glittering prize, but to stray for illusion is forever unwise.*
- Let the candle burn away, and in the melted wax, write, TEMPTATION IS NO MORE. I CLOSE THAT DOOR.
- When the wax is cool, chop it up and throw it away in the bag.

791

AN AQUARIUS RITUAL FOR AN INVENTION OR A BRILLIANT IDEA YOU KNOW WILL BE A MONEYMAKER ONCE IT IS ACCEPTED BY THE WORLD

You will need:

Five small electric candles, which change color, if possible

Your idea, or the name of your invention, written on white paper in bright purple, set in the center of the lights

Timing:

January 21 through February 18, or whenever you need the originality of Aquarius the Water Carrier to overcome a brick wall

The Spell

- Remove the paper from the circle, reading it aloud five times and saying, *This will be a hit, no doubt of it. And so I light the way, that all will say, "What an absolutely splendid, marvelous, incredible idea!"*
- Return the paper to the circle.
- Switch on the first light, clockwise, repeating the spell words.
- Light each candle five minutes after lighting the earlier one, and for each one say the spell words.
- When all are lit, say, *Original, subliminal, light the way to recognition that I will be in top position.*
- After five more minutes, switch off the lights. Say, *Light bring cooperation, and make this idea a great sensation.*
- Give your idea another push.

792

A PISCES RITUAL IF YOU WANT TO DEVELOP CLAIRVOYANT POWERS

You will need:

A red candle, the kind that drips wax

A heatproof bowl, half-filled with water

A purple candle, the kind that drips wax

Timing:

February 19 through March 20, or whenever you need Pisces the Fish to give your psychic powers a boost

The Spell

- Set the red candle to the left of the bowl and light it, saying, *Lead me to the unknown ways, that as I in this water gaze, visions will see that will show me, what most I need to know.*
- Light the second candle from the first and set it to the right of the bowl, saying, *Let me view wondrous scenes, past worlds where once my life has been, or future dreams.*
- Holding a candle in each hand, begin to drip wax from both slowly onto the water surface.
- As swirls of liquid wax mix on the water surface, you will see a picture or symbol that afterwards will become a message in the form of words or images in your mind.
- When the wax sets, empty the water, drying the solidified wax.
- Place it next to any cards you read or crystals you use.

793

A MERCURY RITUAL FOR PASSING A DRIVING TEST

You will need:

A printout of an unwritten congratulatory e-card, sent to yourself
A black pen
A yellow candle
A lavender, lilac, or lemongrass incense stick (all Mercury fragrances)

Timing:

Wednesday, Mercury's special time, the week before your driving test

The Spell

- Write in the card, CONGRATULATIONS ON PASSING MY DRIVING TEST ON [date]. Put the card in an envelope, addressing the card to yourself.
- Light the candle, saying five times, *Mercury, whizzing without rest, bring success to my driving test.*
- Light the incense stick and write the card words in incense smoke in the air around the edges of the card.
- Blow out the candle, letting the incense burn.
- Each day before the test, hold the envelope, light the candle, and repeat the spell words.
- Blow out the candle.
- On the day before the test, do the same but let the candle burn.
- On the morning of the test, open the card and read the message out loud.
- Take the card to the test. If you're using your own car, hide the card in the glove compartment.

794

A VENUS RITUAL FOR MOVING ON FROM A BROKEN HEART

You will need:

A green candle
A ring or bracelet in copper, Venus's metal
A small bag of old metal nails
An empty bowl

Timing:

Friday, the first hour after dawn, Venus's day and hour

The Spell

- Light the candle.
- Put on the copper ring or bracelet, touching it and then your heart with the index finger of your dominant hand, and say, *Lady Venus, morning star, call gentle love from near or far. Send to me a lover new, who will always to me be true.*
- Take off the ring, shake the bag of rusty nails hard, and say, *Lady Venus, fierce evening star, this old love does my future mar. Release me from my broken heart, for shattered I am that we did part.*
- Drop the nails one by one into the bowl, then say, *No more cruel love, for you I grieve. By the light of Venus, my thoughts you shall leave.*
- Put on the ring or bracelet again, saying, *Venus, star of morning, my life begins again with this new dawning.*
- Wear the ring/bracelet, dispose of the nails, and let the candles burn through.

795

A MARS RITUAL FOR VICTORY FOR A FAVORITE TEAM, IF THEY HAVE A HARD FIGHT AHEAD

You will need:

Enough dried peas, beans, or lentils to half-fill a storage jar
A stainless-steel storage jar with a tight-fitting lid
The club colors or a team picture
A small brush

Timing:

Tuesday, Mars's special day

The Spell

- Place the dried legumes in the jar, securing the lid firmly.
- Shake it nine times over the picture/colors, saying nine times, *Mars bring steel, your strength reveal. Though odds are against winning, let victory be real and sure, right from the beginning.*
- Keep shaking and begin stamping as you move clockwise around the picture/team colors, making nine clockwise stamping circuits and chanting the words nine more times.
- Take off the lid, scattering legumes over the picture/colors and shouting, *Win, win, win, it is no sin to want the best. Mars make us strong. The team's skill does the rest.*
- Sweep up the legumes with a small brush and pour them back in the jar, collecting any spilled elsewhere.
- Go outdoors and scatter the jar's contents far and wide, saying, *We shall win. Mars begin.*

796

A JUPITER RITUAL FOR PERSEVERING WITH A LONG COURSE OF STUDY OR TRAINING IF THE ROAD SEEMS ENDLESS

You will need:

A very long piece of blue cord, Jupiter's color
Scissors
A box

Timing:

Thursday, Jupiter's day

The Spell

- Tie knots along the cord to represent the stages of the course or training, including those you've completed.
- Name for each knot the stage it represents and say, *Each milestone that is passed, from first until the last, brings me closer to the end. Jupiter, perseverance send.*
- Moving left to right, cut each knot and the cord to the left of it to represent stages already passed, repeating the spell words.
- Put the cut cords into the box, saying, *When I doubt and when I fear, by Jupiter I shall know. Success does daily nearer grow.*
- Each time you reach a milestone in your training, repeat the spell, adding more cut cords to the box until you have only the knot at the end. Keep this as a talisman for your future career.

797

A SATURN RITUAL FOR REVERSING THE OUTFLOW OF MONEY THAT IS PLACING YOU SERIOUSLY IN DEBT

You will need:
A faucet in a sink
Eucalyptus or pine-scented kitchen cleaner

Timing:
Saturday after dusk, Saturn's special day

The Spell

- Turn on the cold water faucet, but leave the plug out.
- As the water constantly flows away, say, *Flowing and going, going and flowing, Saturn, stop the tide. Money continually washes away, and in my hands it does not stay.*
- Slow the flow of water and put in the plug, saying, *Slowing the flowing, slowing the going, Saturn let money stay. Reduce the debt that I may yet solvent be one day.*
- Slow the flow from the faucet until it is not much more than a drip and leave the plug in, saying: *Stay money stay, no longer flow away. Saturn, I ask, step by step ease this task.*
- When the sink is half full, turn off the faucet, leaving it for ten minutes before letting out the water for the final time.
- Pour eucalyptus or pine cleanser down the drain, saying, *Saturn help me clear my debt, that I may stable be and know security.*

798

A URANUS RITUAL TO PERSUADE FAMILY OR COLLEAGUES TO MAKE RADICAL BUT NECESSARY CHANGE

You will need:
White paper and a bright blue pen, the color of Uranus
Scissors
An electric table fan

Timing:
Saturday, Uranus's day (you can do this at home to change a work situation)

The Spell

- Partly open the windows in the room so a gentle breeze enters, saying, *Change winds do blow; inertia, you must go. Life shall alter, yet* [name those resistant to change] *still falter, always saying no.*
- Close the windows and sit near one, drawing and cutting out paper figures, and naming aloud a figure for each resistant person.
- Place the figures next to the fan, saying, *Winds of change shall blow, and forward must we go. So life can flourish in pastures new, embracing new things for me and you* [again name the resistant folk(s)].
- Switch on the fan, repeating the spell words, and let the figures blow where they will.
- Turn off the fan, pick up the figures, and partly open the window again so the breeze enters but the figures are not blown away.
- Hide the figures in a room where the people sit.

799

A NEPTUNE RITUAL FOR DEALING WITH INSENSITIVE PEOPLE

You will need:

A very large pair of old shoes from a thrift shop or discount store
Your favorite pair of shoes

Timing:

Thursday or Friday mornings, Neptune's special days

The Spell

- Put on the large shoes and stamp hard up and down, saying, *You,* [name the insensitive person or people], *trample over me, insensitively. You do not even realize, and so I cut you down to size.*
- Put on your own shoes and tiptoe over the same area, saying, *You,* [name the insensitive person or people], *shall softer be, act sensitively that we may live in harmony.*
- Hold the large shoes between your hands and say, *I have no further use for you. I have cut you,* [name], *down to size. And now you have become more wise, you tiptoe softly too.*
- Recycle the large shoes.

800

A PLUTO RITUAL FOR WHEN ENOUGH IS ENOUGH AND YOU ARE READY TO GIVE UP

You will need:

A large piece of paper and a black pen
Scissors
A computer screen

Timing:

Tuesday, Pluto's special day (when you are ready to quit your job or get out of a bad situation)

The Spell

- When you have had enough of a situation or a person, don't shout, don't yell, but steal a moment unobserved and write on the paper or onscreen over and over again in varying sized letters, THAT'S IT. I QUIT.
- Either shred the paper or cut it in tiny pieces, or delete by backspacing the words on the computer, saying, *Bide my time, so victory's mine.*
- Each time you get frustrated, repeat the ritual, making the writing larger and larger and plan your strategy for the most advantageous exit and time.
- When you finally leave, shout, *That's it. I quit!*

801

A CHIRON RITUAL FOR FIXING YOUR OWN LIFE, RATHER THAN OTHERS' LIVES

You will need:
Children's toy bricks in two different colors

Timing:
Wednesday, Chiron's day

The Spell

- Divide the bricks into two separate piles by color.
- Build the left-hand one, representing other people, into a solid structure, saying, *I always do my best for those in need, but rarely is there time for me. Always giving of myself, my life is put on the back shelf.*
- Start taking bricks from your pile to reinforce the first structure until all the bricks are gone from your side.
- Then say, *Stop. This can no longer be. I'm done with inequality. I take back what is my own. Too much generosity I have shown.*
- Create a solid structure by taking back your own bricks without destabilizing the first structure, until there are two equal-sized structures.
- Say, *Fair's fair, when we do share, both have enough and some to spare. I will still give willingly, but no more a frigging charity!*
- Leave both structures in place for a few hours and do something to make yourself happy.

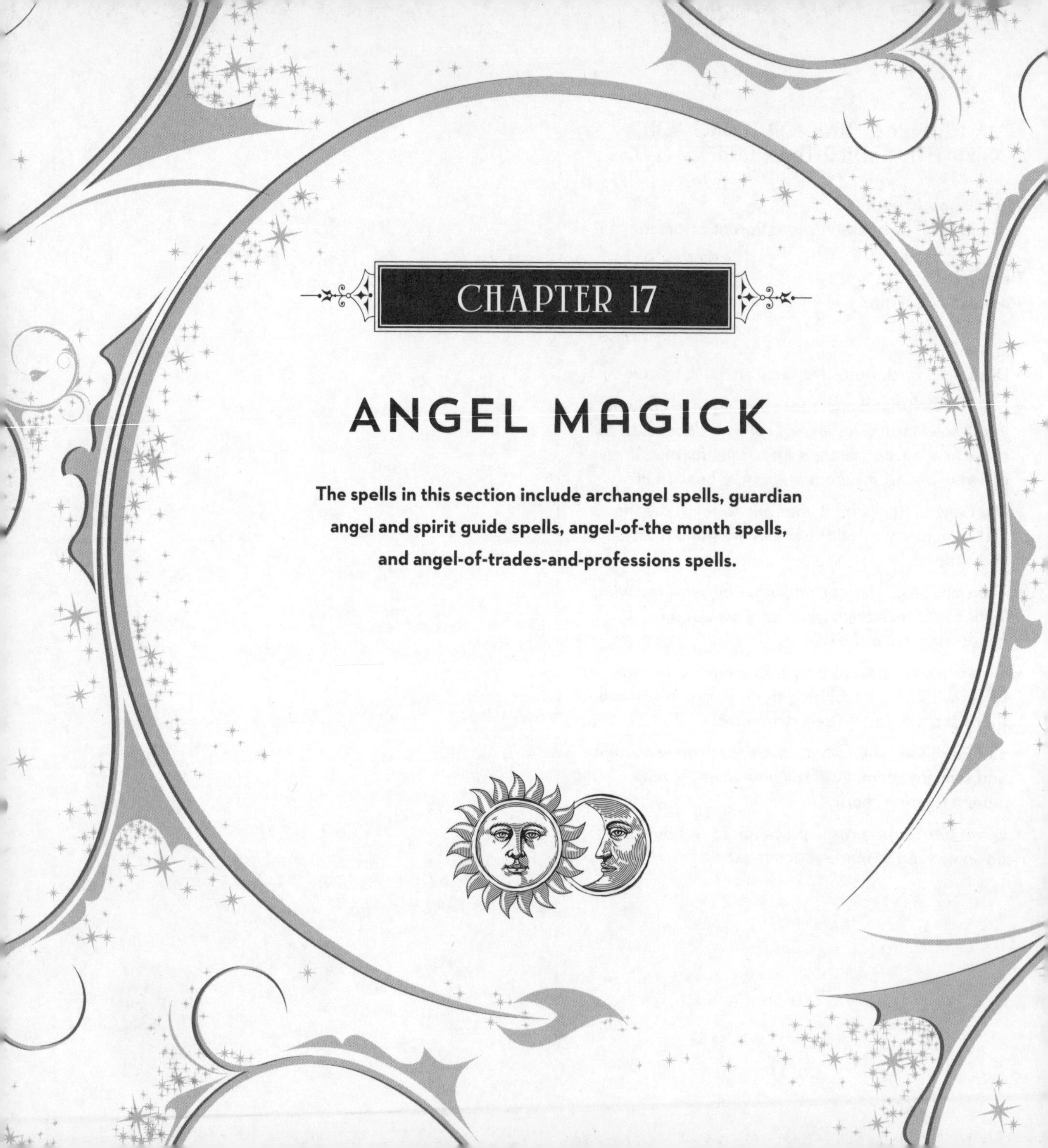

CHAPTER 17

ANGEL MAGICK

The spells in this section include archangel spells, guardian angel and spirit guide spells, angel-of-the month spells, and angel-of-trades-and-professions spells.

802

A MICHAEL, ARCHANGEL OF THE SUN, RITUAL FOR INDEPENDENCE WHEN YOUR INITIATIVE IS BEING STIFLED

You will need:

A spool of gold thread or gold string
A gold candle, Michael's color
A broad-based candleholder
Scissors

Timing:

Sunday, Michael's day

The Spell

- Wrap and knot thread around the unlit candle and holder, saying, *Mighty Michael, I cannot shine, stifled, restricted, and confined. With golden sword cut through the knots. Great Michael, you can call the shots. Bring freedom to this life/career/venture of mine.*
- Cut the threads, making sure all are removed before lighting the candle and saying as you cut, *Restraints unwinding, limits unbinding, you who tame dragons, set me free that I may live/work independently.*
- As you light the candle, say, *Michael, let my initiative shine. I thank you that independence now is mine.*

803

A GABRIEL, ARCHANGEL OF THE MOON AND UNBORN CHILDREN, RITUAL FOR FERTILITY WHEN THE ODDS ARE AGAINST YOU BECAUSE OF PREVIOUS PROBLEMS

You will need:

A silver candle
Seven eggs, Gabriel's number
A bowl and a whisk
Coriander seeds, said to make for healthy, clever babies

Timing:

Monday morning, Gabriel's day

The Spell

- Light the candle and, in turn, break each egg into the bowl, saying, *Gabriel, release fertility within me. Bring to me safe pregnancy and a child born healthily. I ask, Mother Gabriel, you let this be.*
- Whisk the eggs seven times counterclockwise, saying seven times, *Gabriel, nurturing archangel, seven by seven, you do nourish my child in heaven. Though not easy, I ask again, let my babe be born and safe remain.*
- Dig a hole outdoors and pour the beaten eggs into the hole, adding the coriander seeds and covering it, saying, *Let eggs and seeds grow together, through sun and rain, wind and shine. Gabriel, bring this babe of mine.*

804

A SAMAEL, ARCHANGEL OF CLEANSING FIRE, RITUAL FOR KICKING THE ASS OF AN IMMOVABLE PERSON OR ORGANIZATION

You will need:

Nine small red candles (Samael's color), set in a circle
Nine different spices or fiery herbs, such as cinnamon, ginger, turmeric, curry, saffron, chili, basil, tarragon, or parsley (all Samael herbs)
A bowl
A small red bag or purse

Timing:
Tuesday night

The Spell

- Light the candles clockwise, saying, *Samael, archangel of cleansing fire, I do to greater things aspire* [name them]. *All I ask is you move this block, that/who bars every door on which I knock* [name person or situation].
- Add the herbs one by one to the bowl, mixing vigorously nine times clockwise and saying nine times, *Samael, archangel of cleansing fire, grant I ask, this one desire. For I am equal to the task, so please, mighty Samael, kick his/her/their/its ass.*
- Put the herbs in the bag and pass it nine times, clockwise in both directions, around the outside of the candles, repeating the spell words nine times, faster and faster.
- On the final *ass*, blow out the candles fast.
- Carry the bag whenever encountering the problematic person or organization.

805

A RAPHAEL, ARCHANGEL OF TRAVELERS, RITUAL FOR GETTING OUT OF THE RAT RACE TO LIVE YOUR DREAM

You will need:

Five small yellow citrine (Raphael's crystals), if possible, or five yellow glass beads in a circle
A picture of your dream location/hideaway from the world, in the center of the circle of crystals or beads
A bowl of dried fennel, lavender, or lemongrass (Raphael's fragrances)

Timing:
Wednesday morning, early

The Spell

- Toss five citrine in your open cupped hands over the picture five times, saying, *Raphael, archangel, hear my plea, five citrine to bring my dream to me. Happiness and freedom my life would gain, remove an obstacle so only four remain.*
- Repeat with four citrine, adapting the rhyme each time to reflect the number of citrine being tossed, then three, two, and finally one.
- Return each one to its place.
- Scatter the herbs over the picture and carefully carry the picture outdoors.
- Shake off the herbs, saying, *Raphael, messenger, carry my golden dream. Bring it to reality, though impossible it seems.*
- Keep the picture, surrounded by citrine, indoors, where first light will catch it.

806

A ZADKIEL, ARCHANGEL OF ALTERNATIVE HEALING, RITUAL FOR FINDING RELIEF WHEN CONVENTIONAL MEDICINE HAS NO ANSWERS

You will need:

A small dish of salt
Two small bowls of water

Timing:

Thursday, Zadkiel's day

The Spell

- Add three (Zadkiel's number) pinches of salt to the first bowl of water and swirl it three times in both directions, starting clockwise. Say three times for each direction, *Wise Zadkiel, though I have looked far and wide and every remedy in vain have tried, I ask to the answer you will me guide.*
- Pour the salt water away under a running faucet, saying, *From the rivers to the sea, Zadkiel send healing swiftly to me.*
- Splash drops of the clear water on your inner wrists for your heart, the base of your throat, and the center of your brow, saying for each one, *Enter here, nature true. Zadkiel lead me to life anew.*
- Empty the rest of the water on a thriving plant. You will be guided to the right reputable alternative practitioner or a reliable health website that offers natural options, seemingly by chance, in the days after the spell.

807

AN ANAEL, ARCHANGEL OF LASTING LOVE, RITUAL IF YOU DESPAIR OF FINDING THE RIGHT PERSON

You will need:

Six small pink rose quartz crystals (the number and crystals of Anael), or six pink beads
Two white roses, two pink roses, and two yellow roses (the flowers of Anael) in a vase
A small pink bag

Timing:

Friday morning and evening for six days

The Spell

- Make a star shape from the crystals around the flowers, marking the six outer points with a crystal.
- On day 1 choose a rose. In the morning, scatter half the petals from the flower outdoors, saying, *Anael, archangel of true love, be to me a friend above. Send to me a love who will devoted be, faithful, kind, eternally. Be he near or be he far, let him follow to me sun or star.*
- Scatter the other half of the petals from the flower in the evening, saying the same spell words.
- Continue doing this for five more days.
- On day 6 after scattering the petals, bury one crystal, throw another into water, and cast a third as far as you can in the air.
- Keep the other three in a small pink bag beneath your pillow until love comes.

808

A CASSIEL, ARCHANGEL OF CONSOLATION, RITUAL IF YOU CAN'T GET OVER A SETBACK OR LOSS

You will need:

Four feathers, three black and one white, in a pouch or small purse

Timing:

A windy Saturday, Cassiel's day

The Spell

- Hold one black feather in your dominant hand and pass it in spirals, not quite touching you, around your body and head, saying, *Cassiel, archangel of consolation, take my sorrow* [name it] *as you will. Set it free that I may be, once more able joy to see.*
- Set the feather free on the wind and do the same for the other black feathers.
- Hold the white feather in both hands, touching your heart area lightly with its feathery tip, and say, *Kind archangel, who dries all tears, calming grief and banishing fears, release my heart from sorrow and pain* [name the source of that sorrow or pain], *that I may smile and live/love again.*

809

A JOPHIEL, ARCHANGEL OF JOY, RITUAL FOR BRINGING INNER SUNSHINE INTO YOUR LIFE IF YOU ARE FEELING SAD OR ANXIOUS

You will need:

A bowl of seven oranges (oranges are the fruit and color of Jophiel)

A handheld fruit juice squeezer

A glass

Timing:

Sunday, Jophiel's day, in the morning, and six more consecutive days

The Spell

- On day 1, squeeze the first orange and hold the glass of juice, saying, *Jophiel, archangel, make happiness mine, this morn I take in your sunshine. Bring laughter, pleasure, fun, and joy, that every moment I'll enjoy.*
- Drink the juice and afterwards smile at everyone you meet, saying in your mind, *I will smile this day, every mile of the way.*
- Repeat the spell for six more days.
- On day 7, having made the juice, pour it under a running faucet, saying, *Let happiness increase and never cease, and joy always be mine.*

810

AN ARIEL, ARCHANGEL OF FREEDOM, RITUAL FOR SUCCESSFULLY SETTING UP OR FOLLOWING AN UNUSUAL CAREER OR BUSINESS

You will need:

A small symbol or business card to represent the unusual career or business

A magnifying glass

Timing:

Wednesday or Friday, Ariel's special days, during daylight

The Spell

- Clap your hands above the symbol or card five times, then say five times very fast, *Applause is music to my ears; my business flourishes year by year. Originality, creativity, uniqueness, these are the keys to my success. I aim for the top and will not stop, good Ariel, aid me.*
- End with a loud single clap on the final *me.*
- Hold the magnifying glass above the symbol, slowly bringing it closer until it almost touches, then move it away and closer again, repeating the in and out movements five times in total, while saying five times, *Good Ariel, help this venture/career grow* [name it]. *Magnify it that all will know me, and so I claim victory.*
- Keep the symbol as a talisman and if things do not go as fast as planned, repeat the spell.

811

A METATRON, ARCHANGEL OF SCRIBES, RITUAL FOR GETTING A BOOK PUBLISHED

You will need:

A white or dark-red candle, Metatron's special colors

A letter opener

A sheet of white paper and a dark-red pen

A dark-red ribbon

Timing:

Saturday, Metatron's day

The Spell

- Place seven notches on the candle, equidistant from one another, scratching these lightly on the wax with a letter opener.
- On day 1, light the candle, saying, *Metatron, mighty scribe archangel, with your pen and scroll, carry my endeavors,* [name book title], *successfully to* [chosen publisher], *or if not, whoever will look favorably on my work.*
- On the paper, write the same spell words and tie the ribbon around it with three knots to form a scroll, and set it in front of the candle.
- When the candle is one-seventh burned, blow it out.
- Repeat on the next six days.
- On day 7, when the candle is burned through, send your book proposal to the publisher and each night, until you hear news, hold the scroll and say the spell words.

812

ENCOUNTERING YOUR GUARDIAN ANGEL

You will need:

An angel crystal, such as blue angelite, purple amethyst, or pink rose quartz, soaked in water for a few hours

A white, prelit candle

Timing:

When it is quiet

The Spell

- Remove the crystal from the water.
- Using your dominant hand throughout the spell, touch the crystal to the center of your hairline and say, *Above me the light.*
- Touch the center of your brow with the crystal, saying, *Within me the radiance.*
- Touch the base of your throat with the crystal, saying, *That I may hear my wise angel.*
- Touch your heart with the crystal, saying, *And feel her love in my heart.*
- Hold the crystal to the candlelight, saying, *Dear guardian angel, let your presence be known to me.*
- Close your eyes with the crystal between your hands. You may see your angel in your mind's eye, hear a melodious voice, smell flowers, or sense the presence as a light touch on your hair or brow.
- Touch your heart with the crystal, saying, *I reach out with my heart.*
- Connect with your angel any time by touching your heart with the crystal. When the presence fades, blow out the candle.

813

COMMUNICATING WITH YOUR GUARDIAN ANGEL ANYWHERE, ANY TIME

You will need:

An angel crystal (soak it in water once a week on Sunday)

A small white drawstring bag to carry it

Timing:

Whenever you need help or protection

The Spell

- Using your dominant hand throughout the spell, touch your heart with the crystal, saying, *I reach out with my heart.*
- Touch your throat with the crystal, saying, *I reach out with my words.*
- Touch the center of your brow with the crystal, saying, *I reach out with my mind and with my spirit.*
- Touch the center of your hairline with the crystal, saying, *I reach out with my soul to my guardian angel and ask that you are with me at this hour.*
- Ask your angel for the help or protection you need.
- If you need angelic help any time, but cannot be alone, subtly touch the four energy points, saying the spell words in your mind.
- Alternatively, go to the bathroom, dip the crystal in water, repeating the words and actions.
- Your angel will always respond to your call.

814

A GUARDIAN ANGEL RITUAL WHEN YOU NEED PROTECTION FOR A DIFFICULT WORKWEEK AHEAD

You will need:

A small white feather for each day of the week ahead (white feathers indicate the presence of your angel)

Timing:

Before going to work each day

The Spell

- Take the first feather outdoors, using your dominant hand to spiral it in the air five times, saying, *Guardian angel, send to me a sign that you will be with me in this week of difficulty.*
- Set the feather free, saying, *I release my fear, knowing you, my guardian angel, are forever near.*
- Take the remaining feathers in a bag to work. Keep them near you.
- Each morning before work, repeat the spell, releasing a feather each day and taking the rest to work with you.
- On the last day, after releasing your feather, say, *Guardian angel, on you I call, thanking you I did not fall. Help me through this final day, to send my troubles far away.*
- You may be rewarded by seeing a white feather in an unusual place during the week, feel feathery wings brushing against you, or sense that you have been protected.

815

A FRAGRANCE RITUAL TO BRING AN URGENTLY NEEDED MESSAGE FROM THE ANGELS

You will need:

An electric diffuser or oil burner and a tea light

Lavender, rose, mimosa, or lilac essential or fragrance oil (guardian angel fragrances)

White paper and a green pen

Timing:

When it is quiet

The Spell

- Light the burner or switch on the diffuser and add nine drops of oil (in the burner, warm a small amount of water in the bowl first), saying, *Kind angels, I know not the path to take, the way ahead's not clear. I ask you for the answer true, your wisdom I would hear.*
- Carefully waft your hands in the fragrant smoke, saying, *Speak words that through my hands you write, what I should do, what say, what know. Guide me on the road to light, show me the way to go.*
- Pick up the pen in your dominant hand and, totally without thought, allow your hand to write. When the pen slows, put it down, saying, *I thank you, wise angel, your message I will read, and follow it with every speed.*
- Read the message in answer to your dilemma.

816

AN ANGEL HARMONY RITUAL TO CALM YOU WHEN YOU ARE WORRYING ABOUT A LOVED ONE WHO IS DELIBERATELY PUTTING HERSELF IN DANGER

You will need:

A white candle
A Tibetan singing bowl and striker
A pair of Tibetan bells, a string of small bells, or a single hand bell

Timing:
When the loved one is most vulnerable

The Spell

- Light the candle, touch the base of your throat, and say, *Angels let me hear your voices, speak I ask to* [name person in danger] *this night, that she may safely see the morning light.*
- Make a single sound on the side of the singing bowl with the striker, bring the Tibetan bells together, or ring the bell(s).
- As the sound fades, touch your heart.
- Sound the bowl/bell(s) five more times, repeating the spell words after each ring.
- Then say, *On wings of song, carry danger away. Let your joyous sound guide* [name] *the right way.*
- Sit listening to Gregorian chants, choral music, or meditation music, said to call angel voices, until the candle burns down.

A GUARDIAN ANGEL SEVEN-CANDLE RITUAL TO KEEP YOU AND YOUR LOVED ONES SAFE

You will need:

Seven white candles, in a circle

Timing:
Sunset

The Spell

- Light the first candle and touch your heart with your dominant hand, saying, *Wise guardian angel, protect me from accidents, bullying, illness, or attack.*
- Light the second candle and touch your heart, saying, *Wise guardian angel, protect me from my own excesses, cravings, and unfair emotional demands of others.*
- Light the third candle and touch your heart, saying, *Wise guardian angel, protect me from those who damage my confidence and play mind games, and from envy and spite.*
- Light the fourth candle and touch your heart, saying, *Wise guardian angel, protect my loved ones, friends, and pets* [name them], *that we may be surrounded by love and protection all our days.*
- Light the fifth candle and touch your heart, saying, *Wise guardian angel, protect me from dishonesty, injustice, and gossip.*
- Light the sixth candle and touch your heart, saying, *Wise guardian angel, protect me from curses, ill intentions, and psychic attack.*
- Light the seventh candle and touch your heart, saying, *Wise guardian angel, protect me from loneliness, depression, and lack of hope.*
- Let the candles burn.

818

ASKING THE ANGELS TO BLESS YOUR WORK, TRADE, OR CRAFT

You will need:

Eight white candles, in a circle
A small item you use daily, connected with your work; for example, your electronic tablet, a computer thumb drive, keys, or a particular tool
A hand or makeup mirror

Timing:
Sunday evening

The Spell

- Light each candle, one from the other, saying for each, *I ask my wise angels and guardians to bless my endeavors. Shine your light that what I create is pure, true, and will bring love and joy to others.*
- Holding the item in your nondominant hand and tilting the mirror toward the flame in the other, pass them around and over the candle circle eight times clockwise, so light is reflected onto the item.
- Repeat the spell words over each candle and blow it out.
- Say the spell words in your mind whenever you use the item.

819

ASKING THE ANGELS FOR HEALING FOR YOURSELF OR OTHERS, WHETHER HUMANS OR PETS

You will need:

A dish of salt
A bowl of water
A crystal pendulum on a chain or a pendant
A photo of the person or animal or yourself, looking well and happy

Timing:
Wednesday

The Spell

- Add five pinches of salt to the water and swirl it around clockwise, saying, *Healing angels, salt to water, healing may you bring. Send health to* [name] *and end this suffering.*
- Plunge the pendulum/pendant five times into the water, saying, *Healing angels, light to water, healing may you bring. Send health to* [name] *and end this suffering.*
- Pass the pendulum/pendant five times counterclockwise around the picture, saying, *Healing angels, light from water, healing may you bring. Send health to [name] and end this suffering.*
- On the last *suffering*, bring the pendulum/pendant downward so the tip touches the picture where the heart would be, saying, *Healing angels, heart to heart, healing may you bring. Send health to* [name] *and end this suffering.*
- Pour out the remaining salt and water under a running faucet, leaving the pendulum/pendant on the picture for twenty-four hours.

820

FOR MEETING YOUR SPECIAL SPIRIT GUIDE

You will need:

A mirror large enough to see your head and shoulders in

Four white candles, set along the base of the mirror

Timing:

In total darkness

The Spell

- Light the candles one by one, saying, *May only goodness and light enter here. Wise guides and angels, protect me.*
- Face the mirror, saying, *May I see the spirit guide who is most with me, whether wise ancestor, teacher, healer, or protector from an old world where once I lived.*
- You are not calling up spirits, but the image of a spiritual guardian who once lived on earth.
- Slowly close your eyes, open them, blink, and stare at your reflection.
- You may see in the mirror over your shoulder a brief glimpse or sense a loving presence. Do not turn around.
- Ask if your guardian has a message for you and words will flow into your mind.
- Thank your guardian, saying, *Go in peace and in blessings until we meet again.*
- Close your eyes, and when you open them do not look into the glass but blow out the candles one by one.

821

A POWER ANIMAL RITUAL TO CONNECT WITH THE SPIRITUAL CREATURE WHO CURRENTLY IS PROTECTING YOU

You will need:

A brown or green candle

A tree fragrance incense stick

A ball of self-hardening clay

Timing:

Early morning

The Spell

- Light the candle and the incense from the candle.
- Look into the candle through the smoke, saying, *Come to me through the mists of time, from water, land or sea, protector who will be mine.*
- Still gazing at the candle, let your hands form a creature quite spontaneously from the clay.
- Close your eyes to see your creature leaping or flying toward you.
- Open your eyes slowly and, even if you are no artist, the clay creature will be recognizable as the one you saw.
- Let the light and smoke form a moving image of your creature.
- Ask if it has a message for you and words will form in your mind.
- Decorate your power creature, formed in clay, keeping it where sun will shine on it until it crumbles.
- Whenever you want to connect, light a candle and incense, and, holding your power creature, look through the smoke and you will see your creature in your mind's eye or within the flame.

822

A CAMBIEL, ANGEL OF JANUARY, RITUAL TO PROTECT YOURSELF AND YOUR LOVED ONES FROM THEFT, MUGGING, AND FRAUD

You will need:

An old bead or pearl necklace you do not mind breaking, on a tray

A necklace-length string

A box, an old padlock, and a key to the lock

Timing:

Any time in January, or whenever it's urgently needed

The Spell

- Break the necklace with a flourish so beads roll all over the tray, saying as you do so, *Possessions scattered and in danger from thieves, muggers, and fraudulent strangers, Cambiel, angel of security, you who can see all, protect me from their evil thrall.*
- One by one, rethread the beads on the new string, saying, *Tighter now and safer be, good Cambiel bring security from thieves, muggers, and fraudulent strangers; protect me and* [name any family members you want to] *from all danger.*
- When you have rethreaded the beads, knot the ends securely, saying, *So in wise Cambiel I rest secure, may this boundary of safety long endure.*
- Put the necklace in the box, close it, and lock it, then throw away the key, saying, *From theft, mugging, and fraudulent strangers, now am I safe from every danger.*
- Keep the box in a safe place.

823

A BARAKIEL, ANGEL OF FEBRUARY, RITUAL FOR FINDING WHAT YOU ARE LOOKING FOR AT THE RIGHT PRICE

You will need:

Five white candles as a pathway leading into a mirror, so the reflected pathway continues in the mirror

Timing:

Any time in February, or whenever it's urgently needed, after dark, with no other light in the room

The Spell

- Light the candle farthest from the mirror, saying, *Burn a pathway from my door, each step taken leads me more, to where what I seek most* [name it] *does wait, I follow the pathway true and straight. Barakiel, open the way soon to this good fortune.*
- Light each candle leading toward the mirror, repeating the spell words.
- When all candles are burning, stare into the mirror, saying, *Barakiel, angel of fortune, light me soon to where* [name what you are looking for] *will come into my sight.*
- Let the candles burn.
- You will be guided to a website or to a person who knows where you can obtain what you desire at the right price.

824

A MACHIDIEL, ANGEL OF MARCH, RITUAL FOR GETTING YOUR OWN WAY WHEN YOU KNOW YOU ARE RIGHT

You will need:

An email printout, official document, or judgment you know is wrong (if the judgment is verbal, write in black on white paper what is inaccurate or unfair and who says so)

A red pen (Machidiel's color)

A pair of scissors

Timing:

Any time in March, or whenever it's urgently needed

The Spell

- Write over the printout in red, MACHIDIEL, WARRIOR ANGEL, STAND FOR ME, THAT ALL MAY SEE I AM RIGHT, AND BRING THE TRUTH AT LAST TO LIGHT.
- Cut off a corner of the paper, holding it and saying, *Machidiel, warrior angel, cut these mistakes down to size, that they may be corrected and justice at last will rise.*
- Throw away the cut-off paper.
- Each day, hold the paper, say the first set of spell words, then cut off more, saying the second set of spell words before throwing that piece away.
- Continue to do this until the matter is resolved or you have cut up all the paper and disposed of it.
- If the matter is not resolved by then, write all the spell words in red on white paper and burn it.

825

AN ASMODEL, ANGEL OF APRIL, RITUAL FOR INCREASING YOUR CHARISMA GENERALLY OR WITH A PARTICULAR PERSON

You will need:

A mirror you can see your head and shoulders in

Five pink candles, placed in a row along the base of the mirror so their light reflects in the mirror

Timing:

Any time in April, or whenever it's urgently needed, for five days after dark

The Spell

- On night 1, light the candle at the far left.
- Gaze into the mirror, saying, *Asmodel, angel of radiance, let my charisma grow as this candle glows, that others* [or name that special person] *will be drawn to me. Asmodel, make this be.*
- Blow out the candle.
- On night 2, light the original candle and the next candle to its right, repeating the spell. Blow out the candles.
- On night 3, light three candles, including the original ones, repeating the spell. Blow out the candles.
- On night 4, light four candles, including the original ones, repeating the spell. Blow out the candles.
- On night 5, when all five candles are burning, say, *Asmodel, as candles glow, let my radiance likewise show, that I will shine and admiration/love be mine.*
- Blow out the candles and clap your hands, saying, *Light enter me, that all will see me radiantly.*

826

AN AMBRIEL, ANGEL OF MAY, RITUAL FOR SUCCESSFULLY DOING TWO OR MORE THINGS AT ONCE WHEN YOU ARE UNDER PRESSURE

You will need:

Two or more jars of your favorite culinary dried herbs, one for each major demand on your time, such as career, family, and social or sporting activities

A large sealable container

Timing:

Any time in May, or whenever it's urgently needed

The Spell

- Take the first jar, name one priority, and shake the jar five times, saying, *Ambriel, angel of versatility, lend dexterity to me, that I can juggle my priorities.*
- Do the same for each jar.
- Then, opening the first jar, pour its contents into the sealable container, swirling the container five times clockwise and saying, *Ambriel, angel of versatility, blend all for me in harmony.*
- Do this until you have used all the jars.
- Swirl the container five more times counterclockwise, saying, *Mix, combine, Ambriel, make versatility mine.*
- Seal the container and use the herbs in cooking.
- If things start to overwhelm you, take the container outdoors and scatter some of the herbs, repeating the second and third set of spell words.

827

A MURIEL, ANGEL OF JUNE, RITUAL FOR PREVENTING A SECRET LIAISON FROM BEING DISCOVERED

You will need:

Two sheets of paper and a green pen

A white rose

Two matching pearls (Muriel's gem)

A white scarf

Timing:

Any time in June, or whenever it's urgently needed

The Spell

- Write your full name and that of the person you love, then cross out all the consonants to reduce them to the soul names.
- Now write the numbers 1 to 9, and underneath the numbers, the letters of the alphabet in three vertical rows. Each letter according to the Greek Pythagoras had a numerological value. These numbers were said to be connected with the soul and so in this case by joining the number values of two people you are strengthening their soul connections
- On the second piece of paper, write the numerological values of the two names, joined together minus consonants, saying, *Muriel, who makes all dreams come true, this in gratitude I ask of you. Conceal our love that it may be secret 'til we can be free.*
- Pluck the rose petals and put them on the second paper (white roses are a flower of secret love), add the two pearls, and wrap them all tightly in the scarf, repeating the spell words.
- Destroy the first paper immediately, saying, *Wise Muriel, angel of secrets, keep our secret from prying eyes, 'til we can shout it to the skies.*
- Hide the scarf and its contents.

828

A VERCHIEL, ANGEL OF JULY, RITUAL FOR BEATING A RIVAL WHO USES DIRTY TRICKS AND UNFAIR ADVANTAGES

You will need:

An old glove
A jar of dried cloves
A clove of garlic
Strong gold or red thread (Verchiel's colors)

Timing:

Any time in July, or whenever it's urgently needed

The Spell

- Hold the glove, name the rival, and say, *Verchiel, fair and square, winning's there for he who does the best, but underhand I cannot stand. Verchiel, do not rest, 'til deviousness is cast away and merit rules the day.*
- Stuff the glove with the cloves and a clove of garlic, and tie it closed with gold or red thread, making three knots and saying for each knot, *Bound and tied, Verchiel I ask, be by my side, for underhand no longer stands and fair and square I can get there.*
- Write the name and the place the cheat lives and wrap this with three more knots around the glove, putting the glove in an old shed or at the back of a dark shelf until the situation/event has taken place.

829

A HAMALIEL, ANGEL OF AUGUST, RITUAL FOR BRINGING ORDER FROM CHAOS

You will need:

A jar of rice grains
An empty bowl

Timing:

Any time in August, or whenever it's urgently needed

The Spell

- Rattle the jar of rice, saying, *Too much clutter, too much chaos, overwhelm my life, unsorted and disorganized, cause me too much strife.*
- Pour the rice into the bowl and shake the bowl, saying, *Grain by grain, what does remain can be solved. Hamaliel, angel of order, let all be resolved.*
- Start sorting, writing, or calculating.
- Every time you complete a step, pour or spoon a small quantity of rice back into the jar from the bowl, saying, *Grain by grain, and step by step, moving carefully, order is getting closer, chaos shall no more be.*
- Continue until you have brought order from chaos. If any rice is left in the bowl, return it to the container, saying, *Order out of chaos, organized successfully, all now is in its place and life in harmony.*

830

A ZURIEL, ANGEL OF SEPTEMBER, RITUAL FOR STAYING OUT OF AN EXPLOSIVE SITUATION OR QUARREL WHERE YOU ARE EXPECTED TO INTERVENE

You will need:

A small drum or rattle (to make your own rattle, put dried peas or dried beans in a sealed jar)
Rose petals or rose potpourri
A large dark cloth

Timing:

Any time in September, or whenever it's urgently needed

The Spell

- Bang the rattle or drum hard and say, *It is not my battle, yet silence is hard. Zuriel, angel of reason, keep it from my backyard,*
- Start to drum or rattle more and more softly, saying continuously, *Avoid taking sides, refuse to be drawn, a time to step back, or I will be torn.*
- When the drum/rattle is silent, sprinkle rose petals over it, wrap it in the cloth, and knot it firmly three times, saying for each knot, *So are* [name people] *bound from involving me. Let me stay out of it, for hurt I will be.*
- Leave the drum/rattle in the cloth until the matter is resolved.

831

A BARIEL, ANGEL OF OCTOBER, RITUAL WHEN YOU ARE BEING PRESSURED TO MEET A SEEMINGLY IMPOSSIBLE DEADLINE

You will need:

A mint tea bag and a cup or mug of boiling water
A teaspoon

Timing:

Any time in October, or whenever it's urgent

The Spell

- When you are put under pressure, stop and make yourself a cup or mug of mint tea.
- Stir it nine times counterclockwise, saying in your mind if you are not alone, *Calm and peace, this pressure cease. You,* [name worst culprit(s)], *scramble my brain, yet quiet and focused shall I remain.*
- Stir nine times counterclockwise again, saying nine times, *This deadline I shall meet,* [name it]. *But Bariel, who defeats intensity, make them stop hounding me, so results they will see.*
- Drink some of the tea and pour the rest under a running faucet, saying, *Pressure and hassle flow away, calm I shall remain this day. And I will finish what is asked, the trouble's the people, not the task.*
- Repeat the spell whenever necessary.

832

AN ADNACHIEL, ANGEL OF NOVEMBER, RITUAL FOR TURNING AN UNWELCOME TAKEOVER OR WORKPLACE CHANGE TO YOUR ADVANTAGE

You will need:

A bright yellow candle
A picture or a hand-drawn map of your workplace, in front of the candle
A magnet and a box of straight pins

Timing:

Any time in November, or whenever it's urgent

The Spell

- Light the candle, saying, *Adnachiel, angel of adventure, assist me on this workplace venture. Let changes advantageous be, that I may survive and also thrive, and my competence all may see.*
- Spread the pins over the picture or the map, saying, *New influences they have come, bringing uncertainty. Help me Adnachiel, angel of new adventures, advantage draw to me.*
- Gather the pins using the magnet and return them to the box, saying, *Adnachiel, angel of adventure, advantage have you drawn to me, I welcome change as you arrange, to shine successfully.*
- Let the candle burn, then fold the map or picture small, put it in the box of pins, and keep the pin box and the magnet hidden in your workspace.

833

A HANIEL, ARCHANGEL OF DECEMBER, RITUAL IF YOU LOVE SPENDING MONEY AND ARE IN DIRE FINANCIAL STRAITS

You will need:

Your credit/debit/store cards, in a circle
A money box, in the center of the circle
Ten coins of any denomination, in a circle around the money box within the circle of cards

Timing:

Any time in December, or whenever it's urgent

The Spell

- Touch each card in turn, moving clockwise and saying for each, *Least spent, soonest mended, money borrowed builds up sorrow. It must slow, this I know. Haniel, cautious angel, be my guide.*
- Take the first coin from the circle and put it in the money box, repeating the spell words.
- Keep adding coins one by one, saying the same words for each until all the coins are in the money box.
- Shake the money box ten times, saying ten times fast, *Saving and not spending, the problem soon is ending. For as my expenditure does slow, so my money starts to grow.*
- Whenever you intend to use a card, repeat both sets of spell words in your mind before deciding whether to proceed with the purchase.

834

A DANIEL, ANGEL OF ACCOUNTANTS, TAXATION, AND GOVERNMENT WORKERS, RITUAL IF YOU NEED FLEXIBILITY IN YOUR DEALINGS WITH OFFICIALDOM

You will need:

A copy/printout of any official correspondence or demands

A piece of wire that will easily bend, gold-colored if possible

Timing:

Thursday, Daniel's day

The Spell

- Put the straight wire on top of the correspondence, saying, *Inflexible, immovable. Daniel, aid me in this impasse. All I ask is to see some flexibility shown to me.*
- Begin to bend the wire slowly at both ends simultaneously from the center, saying, *Bow and bend, compassion send, that my point of view, will get through.*
- Keep bending the wire until it forms a horseshoe shape, points facing down, and quickly invert it, saying, *Bend not break, wise Daniel, for my sake. My side in this please take. Grant flexibility between* [name] *and me.*
- Burn the copy or shred it and hang the horseshoe, points facing upward, where it catches the light.

835

A LAUVIAH, ANGEL OF TECHNOLOGY, RITUAL FOR AVOIDING INDUSTRIAL ESPIONAGE AND HACKERS

You will need:

The computer or tablet you work on

Timing:

Wednesday, Lauviah's day

The Spell

- Switch on the computer or tablet, passing both your hands in front of the screen so your palms are facing the screen, an inch or so away from the screen, five times counterclockwise at the same time.
- Say, *Wise Lauviah, protection be against all fraudulent activity, stealing ideas, those attacking my machine. Lauviah, for me be shield and screen.*
- Write on the screen in large capitals, BARRED YOU ARE, AT THE NEXT DESK OR AN OCEAN AWAY. LAUVIAH, STAND AS SENTINEL AGAINST CON ARTISTS, HACKERS, AND PRYING EYES. LAUVIAH, CUT THEM DOWN TO SIZE.
- Reduce the size of the letters on the screen and when you have used the smallest font possible, delete the words backwards, letter by letter, saying, *Hidden be, grant security, safety, and total privacy.*
- If you are working on something important, do this spell before starting.

836

A VASAIRIAH, ANGEL OF THE LEGAL PROFESSIONS, RITUAL FOR RESISTING CORRUPTION WHEN YOU NEED HONEST AND COURAGEOUS REPRESENTATION

You will need:

A lemon (fruit of Vasairiah)
A citrus fruit squeezer
A bowl of clear water beneath the juicer

Timing:
Thursday, Vasairiah's day

The Spell

- Hold the lemon in both hands, saying, *Incorruptibility must there be, pure in intention, free from stain, transparency from the beginning and honest you,* [name], *remain.*

- Squeeze the lemon in the citrus hand juicer so the juice falls directly into the water, saying, *Vasairiah, cast away false favor, dishonesty, impurity. Double dealings fade, not stay, into the light of clearest day.*
- Discard the lemon flesh and swirl the lemon water three times in each direction, beginning counterclockwise, then drink a few drops, saying, *Vasairiah, so truth shall grow, honesty that all will know. That openness will from this matter shine, Vasairiah, make justice mine.*

837

A KABSHIEL, ANGEL OF TEACHERS, COUNSELORS, AND PROFESSIONAL CARE WORKERS, RITUAL TO PROTECT THEM FROM BURNOUT AND ABUSE

You will need:

A deep bowl, filled with sandalwood- or vanilla-based potpourri
A small drawstring bag

Timing:
Friday, Kabshiel's day

The Spell

- Immerse your hands in the potpourri, moving your fingers around under the surface, saying, *Immersing myself, offering my all, I fear I may fail and fall. Targets I can't meet, nor a saint can I be, good Kabshiel, preserve me.*
- Lift your hands out of the potpourri, shake them over the bowl, then reimmerse your hands, saying, *Burnout without doubt, from overcapacity; people/pupils who won't listen, respond, or act respectfully; good Kabshiel, preserve me.*
- Lift your hands out of the bowl and shake them, and then immerse them a third time and say, *From attack, abusive words, answering back, unjust complaints, and the resources I lack; Kabshiel, angel, shield me.*
- Remove your hands, but this time, scoop some of the potpourri into the bag and close it, saying, *Safe, secure, positive results will be; appreciation, support, and harmony; kind Kabshiel, I thank thee.*
- Carry the bag with you and when things get fraught, hold it and say, *Good Kabshiel, preserve me.*

838

A HUMIEL, ANGEL OF CONSTRUCTION WORKERS, UTILITY WORKERS, AND MANUFACTURING PERSONNEL, RITUAL TO AVOID ACCIDENTS AND INJURY

You will need:

A mint or berry tea bag in a mug of boiling water

An orange carnelian (Humiel's crystal) or a round orange stone

Timing:

Tuesday, Humiel's day

The Spell

- When the tea has cooled, remove the bag.
- Stir the tea nine times counterclockwise, saying nine times, *Humiel, angel, I ask for your care. Keep me [or name] protected when danger is there.*
- Hold the crystal over the mug in your open hands, saying, *Angel Humiel, your stone I bring, asking with this offering, that constant guardianship of me [or name] you take, against accident, fall, or careless mistake.*
- Dip the crystal in the tea nine times, saying once, *Humiel, hazards take away, from morn to night, so safe I stay.*
- Wash the crystal under running water, saying, *Wash away all peril, hurt; keep me focused and alert. That danger I daily do avoid, good Humiel be always by my side.*
- Carry the crystal and keep it with you as you work.
- Bottle the remaining tea and empty a little outside the job site or the building where you are working, saying, *Danger enter not here.*

839

AN OCHIEL, ANGEL OF THE SECURITY FORCES AND RESCUE SERVICES, RITUAL THAT THEY MAY COME HOME SAFELY EACH NIGHT

You will need:

Ten small red candles, set in the shape of a warrior shield

A photo of yourself or the person in the forces/services, placed in the the center of the candles

A jar of powdered ginger or substitute any dried powdered spice

Silver foil

Timing:

Tuesday, Ochiel's day

The Spell

- Light the candles clockwise, saying for each one, *Angel Ochiel, fierce defender be. For me* [or name], *stand as shield, may for all danger your protection yield.*
- Shake a little ginger on the foil and wrap the foil around the spice to make a twist.
- Pass the twist of ginger around the outside of the candle circle, pausing at each candle and saying for each one, *Ochiel, for me* [or name], *act powerfully, that at each day's end, homeward you safely do me [or name] send.*
- Put the foil twist on top of the picture and let the candles burn.
- If the ritual is for you, carry the twist of ginger with you; if not, keep it with the picture of the loved one.

840

A MUMIAH, ANGEL OF THOSE IN THE MEDICAL PROFESSION, RITUAL TO HELP THEM COPE WITH OVERWORK AND UNDERFUNDING

You will need:

A wide-necked bottle or flask of water in which you have soaked small pink rose quartz or soft blue lace agate (Mumiah's crystals) overnight

A small quantity of salt

Timing:

Wednesday, Mumiah's day, in the morning

The Spell

- Remove the crystals and add to the bottle a pinch of salt, saying, *Patience within the water, compassion when mind and body can take no more. Mumiah, angel of health, uplift me to help others, my energy restore.*
- Put the lid on the bottle, and hold the bottle between your hands, saying, *Mumiah, be for me the source. Inspire me with your healing force.*
- Take the bottle to work and when you feel stressed or exhausted, shake it five times, then splash some on your brow, in the center of your throat, and on your inner wrist points, saying, *Fill me with your power, minute by minute, hour by hour, that all may see, wise Mumiah, your light in me.*
- Repeat the spell whenever necessary.

841

A YERATEL, ANGEL OF OFFICE WORKERS, MANAGERS, AND ADMINISTRATORS, RITUAL TO AVOID FEUDS, CLIQUES, AND POLITICS

You will need:

A small bowl of water

Rose, chamomile, or lavender essential oil (Yeratel's oils)

A very small empty, screw-top bottle

Timing:

Wednesday, Yeratel's day

The Spell

- Ripple the surface of the water with your dominant, saying, *Ruffled feathers, spiky words, bitching, biting, too much heard. Whispered liaisons, divisive cliques, wise Yeratel, make this cease.*
- Pour six drops of oil into the bowl and swirl it six times in both directions, beginning counterclockwise.
- Ripple your fingers on the surface of the water again, saying, *Oil on troubled waters, Yeratel I pour, no more backbiting or settling unfinished scores.*
- Add another three drops, swirl it as before, and pour a little in a small screw-top bottle.
- Take the bottle to work and put some on raw cotton on a saucer somewhere warm or in a diffuser.

842

A SALATHIEL, ANGEL OF STORE AND CALL CENTER WORKERS, RITUAL FOR RESPECT AND FAIR TREATMENT FROM CUSTOMERS AND MANAGEMENT

You will need:
A large red candle

Timing:
Saturday, Salathiel's day

The Spell

- Light the candle, saying, *Enough, no more, I know the score. Rudeness, disrespect, inconsideration, do daily stress. There must be less of no and much more yes.*
- Hold your hands so your palms face the candle and push them toward the candle (not too near), saying, *Please and thank you are magick words, seldom spoken, rarely heard. Salathiel, protector be for me, from this hassle set me free.*
- Blow out the candle fiercely and clap your hands over your head, saying, *Employers, customers, more courteous be, then I will help you willingly. Salathiel, angel, this is right; miracles won't come overnight, but make the customers at least polite.*
- Relight the candle and let it burn through.

843

A JEHOEL, ANGEL OF APPRENTICES AND STUDENTS, RITUAL FOR OBTAINING THE RIGHT TRAINING

You will need:
A feather or a paper fan
An advertisement or application for the desired apprenticeship/training program
A coin in any denomination for each year of training ahead, set in front of the application or, if the training is for a year or less, one for each month

Timing:
Wednesday, Jehoel's day

The Spell

- Spiral the fan or feather over the advertisement or application five times, saying five times, *Month by month, year by year, will I increase my skills. Year by year, month by month, my dreams shall I fulfill.*
- Holding each coin in turn in your nondominant hand, spiral the fan or feather over it five times, saying five times, *Wise angel, give to me, this much desired opportunity. Jehoel, send my way a break, for I will the chance eagerly take. I promise you I will succeed. Angel, fulfill my pressing need.*
- Give the coins to charity, and each day hold the application/advertisement, repeating all the spell words until you have landed a place in the training program.

844

A POEL, ANGEL OF REAL ESTATE AGENTS, PROPERTY, OR RENOVATION WORKERS, RITUAL FOR EXPANDING BUSINESS AT A CRUCIAL TIME

You will need:

A pile of your business cards
Your name and business name/project written in huge red letters over a large piece of white paper, with the business cards in the center
Paper glue

Timing:

Thursday, Poel's day

The Spell

- Put your hands over the business cards, saying, *Wise Poel, increase possibility, so my business/career/project expands rapidly:* [name it]. *Good Poel, grant success to me.*
- Start to cover the paper with the business cards, moving outward and repeating the spell words continuously.
- When the paper is covered with cards, pass both hands simultaneously over it from the center to all four corners in turn, moving clockwise, palms flat and down, an inch or two above the paper, saying, *May my expansion no limits know, let my reputation greater grow. Angel Poel, let results shine and shine, that I can make the future mine.*
- Each time you have success on the way to your goal, glue one of the cards to the paper, starting from the central one outward until all the cards are permanently attached and total success is yours.

845

AN ASSIEL, ANGEL OF BEAUTICIANS, MASSAGE THERAPISTS, AND HAIRDRESSERS, RITUAL FOR BRINGING OUT RADIANCE AND CONFIDENCE IN CLIENTS

You will need:

A table lamp
A small item you use daily in your work

Timing:

Friday, Assiel's day, after dark

The Spell

- Switch on the lamp and have no other light.
- Hold the small item in the lamplight, saying, *Assiel, make me an instrument of your light, that through my hands, others may shine, that they may walk in their own power, and on all they meet their radiance shower.*
- Set the item in front of the light and hold your hands so your palms face the light, moving them closer to the light and then farther away, six times for each movement, saying, *May love, light, and loveliness enter here, that through my hands others may stand, bright in their own beauty, radiantly clear.*
- Shake your fingers, still facing the lamp, directly above the item, and say, *So shall my work inspiring be, making loveliness for all to see.*
- Switch off the lamp. When you use the item with a client, say in your mind, *Assiel of beauty, enter here, that beauteousness may now appear.*

846

A HARAHEL, ANGEL OF THE MEDIA AND PUBLISHING, RITUAL FOR A FREE AND OPEN VOICE WHERE THERE IS CENSORSHIP OR FALSE INFORMATION

You will need:

A small smudge stick in cedar or sagebrush, associated in recent times with Harahel

A plant that grows tall and bushy in a small pot

Timing:

Sunday at dawn, Harahel's day and time

The Spell

- Indoors, light the smudge stick and pass it counterclockwise in spirals around the plant, saying, *Harahel, may censorship no longer reach those who are barred from freedom of speech. To read, to write, to speak true words, suppression must be ended, and the voice of liberty heard.*
- Take the plant outdoors to the garden and plant it where it has room to grow.
- Don't light the smudge stick again, but shred it, leaf by leaf, and scatter it far and wide, saying, *Harahel, grant to all a voice* [name any places of suppression and censorship that especially concern you]. *When the world is free, we shall rejoice, open the locks, remove the chains, so no corners of darkness shall remain.*
- Sign a petition or join a peaceful organization that works for freedom of speech.

847

AN ELEMIAH, ANGEL OF DRIVERS, RITUAL FOR SAFETY ON THE ROAD AND REASONABLE WORK HOURS AND CONDITIONS

You will need:

A blue candle

A turquoise crystal or a green-and-black malachite, purple-striated kunzite, or black-and-purple sugilite (all Elemiah safe-driving crystals)

A blue bag or purse

Any two of the following: dried sage, celery seeds, eucalyptus, fennel, or mint

A bowl

Timing:

Thursday

The Spell

- Light the candle and hold the crystal in cupped hands toward the light, saying, *Elemiah, drive the hard roads with me in darkness and in light. Uphold me through long hours that sap my powers and deadlines I struggle to meet.*
- Put the crystal in the bag.
- Add the herbs to the bowl and run your fingers through them, repeating the spell words.
- Pour the herbs into the bag and close it, shaking it three times and saying, *Elemiah, be my friend, from journey's start to journey's end. Wise angel, be I ask my guide, and stay always at my side.*
- Keep the closed bag in the glove compartment of the vehicle or hidden under your seat.
- Take it out and hold it before beginning a journey and whenever you are tired or hit bad weather.

848

A SOPHIEL, ANGEL OF AGRICULTURAL AND HORTICULTURAL WORKERS, RITUAL THAT WHAT YOU CREATE MAY FLOURISH

You will need:

A small leafy tree branch or a large leafy twig
A bowl of water
A gold-colored bowl, covered in gold foil and filled with fruit, berries, nuts, and grains

Timing:

Friday, Sophiel's day, outdoors

The Spell

- Dip the leafy end of the branch in the water, saying, *Sophiel, angel of thriving flowers and trees, of fruit and seeds and grain, make my endeavors,* [name them], *in right measure. Sophiel, yield the rich land's treasure.*
- Holding the bowl of fruit, seeds, and grains in your nondominant hand, make ever-widening clockwise circles, nine in all, around the bowl, using the branch to sprinkle the water.
- As you sprinkle the water, keep saying softly and continuously, *Sophiel, grow fruitful this blessed land, from width to width and length to length. Sophiel, make my hands, each day, channels of growth and strength.*
- Plant the branch outside the circle area, empty the remaining water on the ground, and carry the bowl of fruit, seeds, and grains indoors to be shared by all who enter your home over the next few days.

849

AN ARDOUSTA, ANGEL OF HOSPITALITY AND THE TRAVEL AND LEISURE INDUSTRY, RITUAL TO OFFER GOOD SERVICE EVEN TO DIFFICULT CUSTOMERS

You will need:

Grumpy-face stickers
A mini-notebook
Smiley-face stickers

Timing:

Friday, Ardousta's day

The Spell

- Stick a grumpy face in the middle of the first page of the notebook, saying, *We aim to please, we smile and smile, grumpiness is not our style. Even when you grouse and complain, the fixed smile on our face remains.*
- Put a smiley face to cover the grumpy one, saying, *Give us a break, Ardousta make the frowns and glares and hostile stares turn into praise and grateful gaze.*
- Add smiley faces in a circle around the central one, saying, *Ardousta, send some gratitude our way, and we will be sure to have cheerful stay. We give our all, so on you call, surround us with the sun.*
- Clap loudly over your head three times and give three cheers.
- Take the notebook to work, and whenever you have successfully dealt with a difficult customer, stick a grumpy-face sticker on a page, cover it with a smiley-face sticker, then surround it with smiley faces, saying, *Thank you, kind Ardousta, for turning glares to smiles, and though my feet are aching, I'll smile a few more miles.*

850

A NITHAIAH, ANGEL OF CLAIRVOYANTS, MEDIUMS, HEALERS, AND ALTERNATIVE THERAPISTS, RITUAL TO BE GIVEN DIVINE HELP AND WISDOM

You will need:

Seven silver candles in a circle
Seven hairs from your head or a hairbrush on a small, silver-colored dish, placed in the center of the candles
A silver piece of jewelry or a silver charm that can be kept with your tarot cards, crystals, and the like
Thread (optional)

Timing:

Monday, Nithaiah's day, in the evening

The Spell

- Light each candle counterclockwise, saying for each one, *Nithaiah, speak to me with celestial sound, may my work bring heavenly healing as I call wisdom down, revealing wise spirit and loved ones around.*
- Carefully lift the dish from the center of the candles and knot each hair around the charm or jewelry (using thread, if necessary), saying for each one, *With seven knots of love I bind, in truth and in true care. Nithaiah, wise angel, inspire and guide, your wisdom would I share.*
- Return the dish to the center and let the candles burn.
- Wear or carry the silver and before you begin your healing or divinatory work, touch the silver and say, *In truth and in true care, Nithaiah, wise angel, inspire and guide, your wisdom would I share.*
- Leave the silver in full moonlight every month and replace any hairs as necessary.

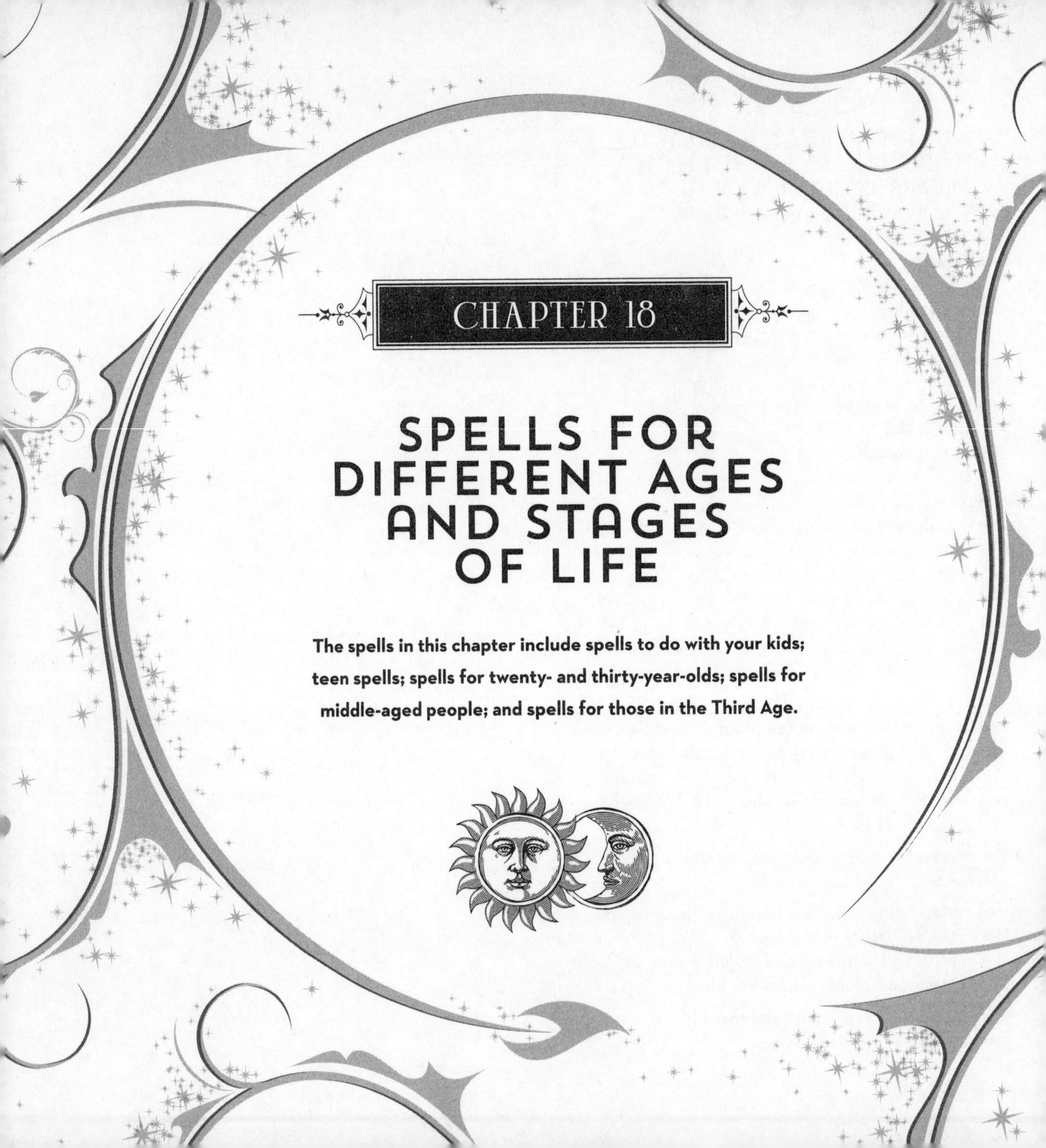

CHAPTER 18

SPELLS FOR DIFFERENT AGES AND STAGES OF LIFE

The spells in this chapter include spells to do with your kids; teen spells; spells for twenty- and thirty-year-olds; spells for middle-aged people; and spells for those in the Third Age.

SECTION 1:

SPELLS FOR YOU TO DO WITH YOUR KIDS

851

TO MAKE A MEAN TEACHER NICE

You will need:

A plastic container, half-filled with dried, uncooked pasta or rice

Timing:

Before school

The Spell

- Walk in a circle three times clockwise, shaking the container and saying three times, *Macaroni, spaghetti, ravioli, rice, please make my teacher nice.*
- Now make three circles the other way, shaking the container faster and saying the spell words faster three more times.
- Now go back the other way really fast three more times, saying the spell words so fast the words all run together.
- On the last *nice*, shake the container very loudly, stamp your feet and say really quietly as you hold the container still, *Please,* [name teacher], *be less cross, don't tell me off or make a fuss, and I will an angel stay, well nearly, all of the day.*
- Work hard all day at school and don't tell that absolutely amazingly funny joke to everyone in your class during quiet time. Adults never understand kids' jokes.

852

FOR WHEN LIFE SUCKS

You will need:

A big, round, smooth black stone
A piece of white chalk

Timing:

Saturday, the day of fixing things

The Spell

- On the stone, using the chalk, draw a picture of what is wrong, draw stick figures of people who are giving you a hard time, and/or pictures of your home or school if that's where the problems are.
- Then say, *Out go you, I say yuck. Out you go, whatever sucks.*
- Rub out the picture and throw the stone into a pond or river, or leave it outside.
- Whenever you feel fed up, draw pictures in chalk on the ground in the backyard or wherever you are allowed to draw with chalk. Jump up and down on it three times and rub it out, saying the spell words in your mind.

853

TO STOP BULLIES FROM BEING NASTY TO YOU

You will need:

A lucky coin or charm you can keep in your pocket

Timing:

Before school, or wherever and whenever you see the bullies

The Spell

Note: If you are being bullied, tell your parents or a teacher, an adult at the after-school club, or the school counselor. Nobody has the right to make other kids' lives a misery, but try this as well so you don't give off scared vibes when you see the bully or bullies heading your way.

- Hold the coin or charm between your hands and toss it up and down ten times, saying ten times, *Bully, woolly, chips for tea, pick your nose, and not on me.*
- Take the coin or charm with you, and when you see the bully or bullies approach, touch the coin or charm, then cross your fingers behind your back, saying in your mind, *I'm not scared. Don't you dare come near me or you will be really, really sorry.*
- Touch the coin or charm again, walk straight past the bully or bullies, and say hello to a nearby friend.
- Nobody heard your knees knocking, but do tell someone *now*!

854

TO MAKE NEW FRIENDS, IF YOU DON'T HAVE MANY

You will need:

A ball to bounce or kick against a wall (watch out for windows) in the playground or in your backyard

Timing:

Friday, a good time for making friends

The Spell

- Say these spell words as you kick or bounce the ball: *Lots of friends, I cannot wait, inviting me to play. Make* [say the name of someone you'd like to be friends with] *be friends with me today.*
- Name as many new friends as you wish in the spell.
- Speed up kicking or bouncing the ball, saying the words faster and faster until you can go no faster, then slow down the words and kicking and bouncing until you have stopped.
- Throw the ball high, catch it, and say, *Don't hesitate to be my friend. Come talk to me today.*
- When you see the person or people you'd like to be friends with, say *Hi*, but not during class or your teacher will be annoyed.

855

FOR MAKING FRIENDS WITH YOUR BEST FRIEND AGAIN IF YOU'VE HAD A FALLING-OUT

You will need:

A long piece of string

Timing:

After you have argued and you've both cooled down

The Spell

- Start tying knots in the string, saying, *Jumbo, mumbo, we must be insane to let something stupid block up our brains. We're tied up in knots, who's right and who's wrong. Let's just forget it, we've been friends for so long.*
- Hang the string from the branch of a tree or bush, saying, *All's forgotten, set it free. Let's be friends again, you and me.*
- As soon as you can, do something nice for your friend, like buying her a burger when it's two for the price of one.

856

IF YOU FEEL DIFFERENT FROM OTHER KIDS AND NEED EXTRA HELP AT SCHOOL OR AT HOME

You will need:

A picture of yourself or a selfie on your phone
Some salt in a little bowl
Some sugar in a little bowl

Timing:

Monday

The Spell

- Put the picture or selfie on the phone flat on a table.
- Sprinkle around the outside of your picture or phone three circles of salt (one circle on top of the other, being careful to not get salt on the phone).
- Say as you do this, *I am cool, in and out of school. If others don't get me just as I am, that's tough on them. I'll find folks who can.*
- Now sprinkle three circles of sugar outside the salt, again one circle on top of the other, saying, *I'm pretty neat, life can be sweet. If others don't get me, just as I am, that's tough on them. I'll find folks who can.*
- Clean up the mess or your mom won't be pleased.
- When people are mean or you are struggling a bit, look at the picture (not in class, though) and smile and know that you're really cool.

857

TO STOP A RUN OF BAD LUCK

You will need:

A round white shell or stone
A permanent black marker

Timing:
Sunday, the day for changing bad luck to good

The Spell

- Write GOOD LUCK all over the shell or stone.
- Toss it in your hands seven times, the number of good luck, saying, *Black cats, horseshoes, four-leaf clover, bring me good luck when I turn the stone over.*
- Keep the stone in your bedroom and every morning turn it over and say the spell words.
- When you next see the moon shining, turn your stone over three times and make a wish.
- But remember, every time you have good luck, do something nice for someone else.

858

TO KEEP AWAY FEARS OF THE DARK AND BAD DREAMS

You will need:

A flashlight

Timing:
In your bedroom, after dark

The Spell

- With the light on, walk around your bed three times clockwise, saying, *Boggits, bogey men, scaries and hairies, you don't worry me. So out of my bedroom and away with the fairies.*
- Open and shut the door, saying, *Out you go.*
- Before you get into bed, switch on the flashlight and turn off the light, swirling the flashlight all around the bedroom and saying, *Old Moon, New Moon, you're not very clear. Buy some new batteries and shine them down here.*
- Switch off the flashlight. If you get worried in the night, switch on the flashlight, swirl it around three times, and say again, *Old Moon, New Moon, you're not very clear. Buy some new batteries and shine them down here.*
- Shut your eyes and imagine the brightest moon possible.

859

IF YOUR BROTHER OR SISTER IS ALWAYS GETTING YOU INTO TROUBLE OR TAKING YOUR THINGS

You will need:

Either a toy soldier for each of your brothers and sisters who annoys you or a small doll representing each of them

A pillowcase

Timing:

Tuesday morning, a good day for standing up for yourself

The Spell

- Hold the soldier(s) or doll(s) and say, *Stop bugging me, don't you see, we are supposed to be family. Let this nastiness end.*
- Put it/them inside the pillowcase and say, *I shut your nastiness away from me, be kind and brotherly/sisterly, and when this stupid fighting ends, we can be such good friends.*
- Take the figures out of the pillowcase and leave them in the sunshine or light until nighttime, saying, *Now we are friends, the nastiness ends, we are one family, so mates let us be.*

860

IF YOUR MOM AND DAD HAVE DIFFERENT HOMES AND YOU ARE WORRIED BECAUSE THEY ARE ALWAYS ARGUING

You will need:

Something you take to both houses, like a favorite soft toy you can hug

Timing:

Anytime you feel the need

The Spell

- Try to get your mom and dad to touch the toy and, when they do, say in your mind, *We are still a family, though we live separately. I love you, you love me, so let's not fight, it's just not right, it makes me so unhappy.*
- Hug the toy and say the spell words.
- When you see your mom and dad, explain to them that you love them both and don't like the fights.
- Hug your toy each night at both houses and say the spell words.

861

TO STOP BITCHING IN ITS TRACKS

You will need:
A photo of yourself looking happy
A piece of paper with the names of the worst bitches, written in red ink
A red pen
A spool of red thread
Scissors

Timing:
Anytime you feel the need

The Spell
- Put the photo underneath the paper with the names and say, *Bitching and scratching, spitefulness and biting, you cramp my style, take away my smile. Now I will get rid of you; bitching is through.*
- Take your photo from under the paper and on the paper put a big red *X* through the names, saying, *I cross you out, bitch no more. You're nobody; that's the score.*
- Using the thread, tie nine knots around the paper, then cut it up or shred it into small pieces, and throw the pieces of thread and the paper in the garbage, saying, *Your bitching and scratching, spitefulness and biting, all are through. I have no more of you.*
- Write I AM THE BEST on the back of the photo and hang it where you can see it every day.
- Each time you pass the picture, remind yourself, *I am the best.*

862

TO AVOID BULLYING AND ABUSE FROM JEALOUS RIVALS ON SOCIAL MEDIA

You will need:
An offending social media page on your computer screen
Children's modeling clay
Small white stones, one for each of those who are perpetrating the abuse

Timing:
Thursday, the day of justice

The Spell
- Sit in front of the computer and, for each person who is responsible, make a featureless figure in modeling clay and name it.
- Into the place where each mouth would be, push a stone, saying, *You are barred and banned from slandering me, silenced from spite and jealousy. Silent will you be and silent remain. You shall not spread viciousness about me again.*
- Delete the messages and block the offenders from your social media accounts and your email account(s).
- Remove the stones and roll the figures into one ball, saying, *Lumped together now you are, your vicious words to me are barred. Hassle me you can no more, on my* [name social media platform], *to you I shut the door.*
- Give all the clay to a child to play with and throw the stones into water or dispose of them well away from your home,

863

TO PERSUADE YOUR PARENTS TO LET YOU STAY OUT LATE OR GO ON VACATION WITH YOUR FRIENDS

You will need:

A picture of yourself when you were young
A picture of yourself as you are now
A long green ribbon

Timing:
Wednesday, the day of freedom

The Spell

- Tie the two pictures face-to-face, with the photo of the younger you underneath. Tie the ribbon in three loose knots. Say, *When I was small and you were tall, you kept me safe from dangers. You protected me from every harm and shielded me from strangers.*
- Untie the ribbon and put the picture of yourself as you are now faceup on top of the younger version of yourself, saying, *Now I am tall, I will not fall. You taught me well, so I can tell right from wrong. But now I need to be more free, and you to worry less for me.*
- Tie the ribbon on the inside window latch in your room, where the breeze will blow it, and put the pictures side by side in your bedroom.
- Before talking to your parents about your plans, cut a length of the ribbon and pin or knot it inside your clothes.

864

TO TURN YOUR TOAD INTO A PRINCE OR PRINCESS

You will need:

A tiara or headband
A ceramic, wooden, or glass toad or frog
A pointed stick to act as your wand

Timing:
Whenever necessary

The Spell

- Put on your tiara or headband and tap the toad on top of the head with the pointed end of your wand. Say, *You, you do not deserve me. And yet, I observe, we still are together. But is it forever? Depends upon you and if you are true.*
- Tap the toad on the head again, saying, *You, you are not worth my undying devotion, so without commotion, if you would stay as part of my life, quit all this strife and start behaving today.*
- Tap the toad for a third time, saying, *You, you show some commitment, for if this is meant, you must give me devotion; don't faint at the notion. For know this I must, if you I can trust. If you're no longer a toad, we can take this new road, or this relationship's dust.*
- Put down the wand, kiss the toad, and contact your prince or princess for some serious talking.

865

TO TURN YOUR CHEATING BOYFRIEND OR GIRLFRIEND INTO A WOODLOUSE OR A COCKROACH OR WORSE

You will need:

A pointed stick to act as your wand
A crawling insect (make it comfortable in a box with greenery)
A picture of your soon-to-be or maybe now ex, in the bottom of the box, under the greenery

Timing:

When you have been treated badly, cheated on, or dumped

The Spell

- Point your wand at the box and say, *You are not worthy to be a toad, you are a louse, a roach, a crawling worm, so just you listen as I make you squirm.*
- Point your wand at the box again and say, *You are not worthy to be a toad, and with contempt I let you go. But you must know. You are a louse, not even equal to a mouse, of every creature you are least, the lowest squirming slimy beast.*
- Empty the box outdoors, so the picture falls onto the earth, and bury it, saying, *I set you free. Our love no longer features. So crawl away, you louse, you roach, you ugliest of creatures. New love will I find. Gone forever from my mind, you who were so unkind.*
- Watch the insect crawl away.

866

FOR A BAD HAIR DAY WHEN YOU'VE GOT TO LOOK YOUR BEST

You will need:

A long mirror so you can see your full figure in it
All your most sparkling jewelry

Timing:

When you get up and feel like a mess

The Spell

- Look at yourself in the mirror and smile, even if you feel like screaming.
- Twirl in the light so you are reflected in the mirror, saying over and over again, *So shall I shine, make this day mine. Beauty untold the world shall behold. Brighter than bling, I outsparkle everything.*
- Put on all your sparkly jewelry and, twirling faster and faster, say the spell words faster and faster.
- When you start to feel dizzy, steady yourself, raise your hands above your head, and clap six times.
- Leave on at least one bit of bling, hidden if necessary under your clothes, and as you walk out the front door, clap and repeat the spell words (in your mind, if people are around).

867

TO ATTRACT SOMEONE YOU REALLY, REALLY LIKE WHO DOESN'T NOTICE YOU

You will need:

A pink candle
Five pink roses in a vase
A bowl of soil

Timing:

Friday evening

The Spell

- Light the candle and take a petal from the first rose.
- Hold it very carefully in the flame, so just the end is singed but does not catch fire, and drop it into the soil, saying, *Burn a pathway to my door, five rose petals now are four.*
- Pluck a petal from the second rose, doing the same thing, and say, *Four to three in candle fire, bringing closer my desire.*
- Take a petal from the third rose and do the same thing, saying, *From three to two I burn the rose, love no hesitation shows.*
- Do the same with a petal from the fourth rose, saying, *From two to one 'til there is none.*
- For a petal from the fifth rose, say, *The spell is done. Come lover, come to me and stay with me eternally.*
- Blow out the candle and call your love's name. Bury the petals still in the soil.
- When the roses die, scatter their petals outdoors.

868

TO GET ASKED TO THE PROM BY THE PERSON YOU REALLY LIKE

You will need:

Rose petals or rose potpourri in a bowl
Your favorite fragrance
An item you will be wearing, such as a tiara or a cummerbund
A small drawstring bag

Timing:

The weeks before the event

The Spell

- To the bowl, add nine drops of your favorite fragrance, swirling it clockwise and saying, *By fragrance and flower I call you,* [name], *at this hour that you will think of me. Make only me your partner, and happiness we can see.*
- Put a drop of fragrance on each of your inner wrist points, saying, *May we dance together on this our special night, by fragrance and by flower, through all the hours until the morning light.*
- Surround the item and the fragrance bottle with a circle of petals or potpourri, clockwise, repeating the first set of spell words.
- Put on the item and anoint it with a single drop of fragrance.
- Scoop up the potpourri and put it in the bag to carry with you until you get invited.
- Scatter the rest outdoors, still wearing the item, and wear the fragrance daily until you get that invitation.

869

TO OBTAIN THE COLLEGE ACCEPTANCE YOU WANT WHEN THERE'S LOTS OF COMPETITION

You will need:

Five red candles in a circle
The brochure or a copy of your application, in the center of the candles
An incense stick in frankincense, sandalwood, or lavender

Timing:

Before applying or before a crucial interview or decision

The Spell

- Before lighting the candles, invisibly trace on the wax of each candle the name of the college, using the index finger of your dominant hand.
- Light each candle clockwise, saying for each one the name of the college and, *May a place/ scholarship be mine.*
- Light the incense by holding it briefly in each candle and, using it like a smoke pen, write over the brochure in smoke letters in the air, being careful not to drop ash, the name of the college and, THE PLACE/SCHOLARSHIP IS MINE.
- Return the incense to its holder and let the candles and incense burn.
- Each night when you can, light a candle next to the brochure, saying, *The place/scholarship is mine* five times. After five minutes, blow the candle out, repeating the spell words.
- Continue until the candle is burned away or will no longer light.

870

TO PASS A REALLY IMPORTANT EXAM WHEN YOU KNOW YOU HAVEN'T STUDIED AS HARD AS YOU SHOULD HAVE

You will need:

A jar of one of the following herbs: dried rosemary, sage, or thyme
A small drawstring bag or purse

Timing:

For three days before the exam

The Spell

- On day 1, wash away a little of the herb under a running faucet, put a little on your tongue, bury a little, scatter some in the air, and put some in the bag or purse.
- As you do each action, say, *Earth, Water, and Sky, I do not know why I did not study more, but I will do my best. By winds North, South, East, and West, so powers that be, come help me, that I may see success, no less.*
- Repeat the actions and the spell words on days 2 and 3, and if any herbs are left, scatter them on the ground.
- Take the bag to the exam and hold it before starting, repeating the spell words.

871

TO OBTAIN THE CREDENTIALS YOU NEED FOR YOUR DREAM JOB, IF YOU HAVE TO WORK AS WELL AS STUDY

You will need:

A shiny gray hematite crystal
An incense stick in any tree fragrance
A business card you have designed for yourself (either with software or drawn freehand), giving your name and dream title

Timing:

Every Tuesday

The Spell

- Hold the crystal between your open cupped hands, blow on it softly three times, and say, *This is my dream:* [name your dream title]. As you continue to hold the stone, name any current worries and frustrations, fears, and doubts.
- Pass the lighted incense around and over the stone, saying nine times, *Take my worries right away; my dream can stay.*
- Return the incense to its holder.
- Now, holding the stone in your dominant hand, pick up the business card with the other hand, read the business card aloud, and say, *This is my dream.*
- Put the hematite on top of the business card and leave it there until the following Tuesday.
- Let the incense burn away.
- Repeat the spell each Tuesday.

872

FOR A MAJOR TRAVEL EXPERIENCE BEFORE SETTLING INTO YOUR CHOSEN CAREER

You will need:

A green candle
A small green jade (the traveler's crystal) or a pearl
An empty bivalve shell (oyster, mussel, or other shellfish—washed out)
Green string

Timing:

When you are planning the trip of a lifetime, but there are lots of obstacles or people who do not want you to go

The Spell

- Light the candle and say, *The world is my oyster and this the time. I seek the world to make it mine.*
- Put the crystal in one half of the shell and cover it with the other, saying, *The world is my oyster. This is the place from which to launch my great escape.*
- Tie string around the shell halves, making three loose knots and saying, *The world is not big enough, South, East, West, and North, for the adventure I have planned. I shall go by sea, air, land. I will venture forth.*
- Take the tied shell to water, preferably flowing, untie the knots, and, holding the shell closed, cast it into the water, saying, *The world is my oyster.*
- Keep the unknotted string with your plans, brochures, and the like.

873

FOR FINDING YOUR PRINCE OR PRINCESS AMONG THE FROGS

You will need:

A pink or green candle
A small ceramic frog

Timing:
Anytime

The Spell

- Light the candle, saying, *Some day my prince or princess will find me, but will you hurry please. Find me soon and quickly, I'm getting cobwebby.*
- Hold the frog to the light and kiss it, saying, *Turn into my ideal mate, I simply can no longer wait. Enrapture me, capture me, and seal my loving fate.*
- Leave the frog in front of the candle until the candle burns down, and then put the frog next to your bed. Whenever you are going out socially or engaging in online dating, kiss your frog and repeat the second set of spell words.

874

WHEN YOUR FAMILY WON'T LET YOU LIVE YOUR OWN LIFE

You will need:

A lemon
A knife
A deep bowl of salt
A lemon squeezer
A bowl of water

Timing:
Saturday

The Spell

- Cut the lemon in half and press one half down in the salt so it is covered, saying, *Beloved family, you are stifling me, I need to follow my own way. And so I say as this lemon dries, so your interference dies.*
- Squeeze the other half so the juice falls in the bowl of water, saying, *But love lives on, don't you see? When I can equal be and you accept the real me, then can there be true family harmony. Blessings on you all.*
- Swirl the bowl of lemon water, repeating the second set of spell words, and then drink a little of the juice, pouring the rest under a running faucet and saying, *Love flow free, that we may equal be, and so I call, blessings on you all.*
- When the salted lemon is dry, dispose of it.

875

TO MOVE IN WITH YOUR PARTNER FOR THE FIRST TIME

You will need:
Two matching white candles, in broad deep holders

Timing:
The night before moving in

The Spell
- Near the center of the home you are leaving, light the first candle, saying, *My last night alone, tomorrow we shall be as one.*
- Carry the candle from room to room, saying, *I take with me the happiness, the memories and pleasure. And with me in this light I keep the moments I have treasured.*
- Blow out the candle.
- Take both candles to your new home.
- Relight the first candle and from it light the second, as near to the center of your new home as you can.
- Walk around your new home with a candle in each hand, saying, *Now we are two, two hearts, two lights, two minds. May we hold the best of the past and leave the rest behind.*
- Let the candles burn in the center of the home.

876

TO BUY YOUR OWN HOME, IF YOU ARE STRUGGLING TO GET A FOOTHOLD IN THE MARKET

You will need:
Children's toy bricks
Twelve gold-colored coins
A blue candle

Timing:
For twelve days

The Spell
- On day 1 build a house from toy bricks, saying, *Up the ladder, stage by stage; borrow, save, or loan. I/we'll soon buy a home of my/our own, starting life's new page.*
- Then put a coin directly in front of the toy house to start a straight pathway from the house, saying, *Money grows slowly, seems so far away, but my/our home I/we will move toward, before too many days.*
- On days 2 to 12, add a coin to the path until you have placed twelve coins, saying the same spell words each day.
- On day 12, light the candle at the end of the path (next to the twelfth coin), saying, *The road is hard, yet I/we do know, though progress sometimes seems so slow, money will grow, it shall be so, and I/we will realize our dream.*
- When the candle is burned, pick up the coins, moving along the money path toward the house, and buy something small for your new home.

877

FOR DEALING WITH INTERFERING IN-LAWS OR FAMILY WHO MAKE YOUR RELATIONSHIP AND YOUR LIFE STRESSFUL

You will need:

A purple or dark-blue candle
A small, unglazed pot
A red permanent marker or glass paint pen
Dried basil and sage

Timing:

When interference gets too hard to bear

The Spell

- Light the candle, saying, *This interference now must end* [name in-laws or family member(s) who interfere], *though no harm to you I send. You constantly poke, make trouble, pry, to your intrusion I say good-bye.*
- Write around the center of the pot and say as you write it, *You,* [names], *are barred from causing stress, standing in the way of our happiness* [name you and your partner]. *With blessings ends here your duress.*
- Fill the pot with basil and sage, saying, *Be wise and restrained, so friendship remains. I wish only peace, but disruptions must cease.*
- Hold the pot up to the candle and blow the candle out, saying, *Enter here light, there will be no more fight.*
- Keep the pot out of sight, where it will not be damaged or used by anyone.

878

WHEN TWO BECOME THREE

You will need:

Three long strong strands of yarn or ribbon, one yellow, one green, and one blue
Three small silver bells
Thread to attach the bells to the ribbon

Timing:

During the weeks before the baby is due

The Spell

- Braid the three strands of yarn or the ribbons, saying softly and continuously, *Two becomes three, you and me will soon be a family. Entwined together in love and care, we count the days 'til you are here.*
- When the braid is finished, knot each end, saying, *Bound in devotion happily, a loving family shall we be.*
- Attach the bells to the yarn/ribbon with thread at equal distances along the braided yarn/ribbon and hang it where the breeze will catch the bells in the baby's room.
- Each morning until the baby arrives, ring each bell in turn and say, *Little one, soon to see, welcome to our family.*

879

FOR CHANGING A WORKPLACE WHERE THERE IS A LOT OF PREJUDICE, SEXISM, OR OUTDATED ATTITUDES

You will need:

A toy dinosaur
A piece of paper divided into four squares, labeled in red, left to right, top to bottom, respectively, Eighteenth Century, Nineteenth Century, Twentieth Century, and Twenty-First Century

Timing:
Tuesday morning

The Spell

- Put the dinosaur in the eighteenth-century square and say, *Mr./Ms. Dinosaur, Mr./Ms. Dinosaur, hop forward a century or two. You're clearly behind the times and so I find your attitude totally askew.*
- Jump the dinosaur into the nineteenth century, saying, *Mr./Ms. Dinosaur, Mr./Ms. Dinosaur, more modern by the day, but you've got so far to go, in the past you cannot stay.*
- Jump the dinosaur into the twentieth century, saying, *Mr./Ms. Dinosaur, you're making some progress, just a hundred years to go. Try it, no stress, then you I'll like to know.*
- Now move the dinosaur into the twenty-first century, saying, *Made it to reality, now you are up-to-date. Trying out the modern ways, don't hesitate. Twenty-first century, it's a date.*
- Take the dinosaur to work, shaking it five times each morning.

880

FOR OVERCOMING PREJUDICE WITHIN YOUR FAMILY IF YOU ARE IN A SAME-SEX RELATIONSHIP OR ARE TRANSGENDER AND YOUR FAMILY MEMBERS JUST DON'T GET IT

You will need:

A jug of water
A green plant for each family member, in a circle
A single flowering plant for you, in the center of the circle
A small pink rose quartz or amethyst

Timing:
Before a family event where you know there will be coldness or nastiness

The Spell

- Water each of the plants in the circle clockwise, yours last, saying for each, *We all are nourished from one source, through the years we've been together. I ask you now accept my course, I am just the same as ever.*
- Hold the rose quartz/amethyst over each plant in turn, in the same order, saying for each one, *The peace of love and the family, I am as I was and always will be. Welcome the choices I have made, respect and value me this day.*
- Go outdoors and plant the greenery in a circle around the flowering plant.
- Push the rose quartz/amethyst into the soil beneath the flowering plant, saying, *All one family, can we still be. Please be happy and loving to me.*

881

TO CURE MIDDLE-AGED BLUES AND LOST LIBIDO

You will need:

Six whole red chili peppers
A bowl
A long, strong string

Timing:

When you feel like a wet dish rag

The Spell

- Put the chiles in the bowl and shake the bowl vigorously six times, saying six times, *May I burn again with desire and with fire. May I be filled with the passion for life's bright flame, that I may live and love again, ecstatically, wildly, and wantonly.*
- Hang the chiles, knotted on the string, from a small hook on the kitchen wall and each evening touch each one and repeat the spell words for each.
- Replace the chiles with new ones using the same spell words, when they dry out or start to decay, burying them under a red tree, flower, or plant.

882

TO DETER A PARTNER FROM STRAYING TO RECAPTURE LOST YOUTH, RATHER THAN REGAINING IT WITH YOU

You will need:

Red, yellow, and blue strong, long threads or yarns
Nine hairs from your partner's hairbrush or comb and nine from your own head
Thin red thread
A very small mirror

Timing:

Friday evening

The Spell

- Braid the three long threads, adding in the hairs, one from each person alternately, into the braid, using extra thread to secure the hair, if necessary. Say softly and continuously, *Thread and wind, secure and bind, the love between us willingly, as we are joined soul, mind, and heart. Let none try our love to part.*
- When it is finished, knot each end and join the ends, saying, *Two as one, through good and bad, united we remain, 'til time is run. Let none break the knots of unity, the thread of love, long may it be.*
- Hide the braid under the mattress.

883

TO GET SOME PRIVACY FOR YOURSELF IF YOUR HOUSE IS OVERRUN BY TEENAGE CHILDREN OR OLDER RELATIVES WHO LIVE WITH YOU

You will need:

A small smudge stick or a lavender incense stick
A deep bowl of soil
Rosewater, either store-bought or make your own (place a tablespoon of rose petals in a cup of boiling water, leave it for for fifteen minutes and strain it just before the spell)

Timing:

Monday evening

The Spell

- Go to a chosen family-free room, such as the bedroom.
- Light the smudge/incense stick and make counterclockwise spirals over the threshold and around the doorframe, saying, *May this be my/our sanctuary, a haven of my/our privacy. I/We love you all, but though I'm/we're patient, it's like living in a railway station.*
- Continue making counterclockwise spirals around the edges of the room and over window ledges, repeating the spell words until you have made a complete circuit.
- Extinguish the smudge/incense stick, lighted end down, in the soil, saying, *Intrusion begone, though love goes on.*
- Repeat the spell words and actions, sprinkling the rosewater and saying, *So do I seal the way, may none over this threshold stray.*

884

TO DEAL WITH KNOW-IT-ALL YOUNGSTERS IN THE WORKPLACE IF YOU ARE WORRIED ABOUT YOUR JOB SECURITY

You will need:

A small tub of whole cloves
An orange
Skewer (optional)
A drawstring bag

Timing:

Thursday, just before sunset

The Spell

- At home, stick ten cloves into the skin of the orange, being careful not to pierce the flesh (use a skewer, if necessary, to make the holes), saying for each as you jab the cloves in, *I am sharp, I am smart, experience and wisdom are success's true art. I have nothing to fear from know-it-all kids. Of me no way can they get rid.*
- Bury the orange with the cloves still in it, repeating the spell words.
- Add the rest of the cloves to the drawstring bag and keep the bag in your workspace, holding the bag each morning and saying the spell words in your mind.
- Replace monthly.

885

FOR INVESTING IN LAND OR PROPERTY TO SECURE YOUR FUTURE AND MAYBE BUILD YOUR DREAM HOME

You will need:

A yellow candle
Jars of three different spices, such as allspice, chili powder, ginger, saffron, or turmeric
A brown bag or purse
A very small dish of clean soil
A packet of sunflower or other flower seeds
A gold-colored coin

Timing:

Wednesday, around sunset

The Spell

- Light the candle and say, *May my investments multiply, may my land/property deals intensify, so I will gain prosperity, security, and stability that will stay. With this endeavor I light the way.*
- Add a little of each spice to the bag, shaking it five times and saying five times, *Increase and multiply, speculate, don't wait or hesitate, secure and sure, that profit will expand and fall into my hands.*
- Add a little soil, saying, *Secure and sure that profit will expand and fall into my hands.*
- Add the seeds and then the coin, saying the second set of spell words.
- Close the bag and bury it as close as possible to the land/property you wish to acquire or build on.

886

FOR STARTING A DIFFERENT KIND OF WORK/ BUSINESS WHEN YOU WANT TO MAKE A COMPLETE CAREER CHANGE IN MIDLIFE

You will need:

A small symbol or item to represent your past or current career
A small symbol or item to represent the new venture
An old sock
A new sock

Timing:

Sunday, just before noon

The Spell

- Put both items in the old sock and shake them three times, saying three times, *The path is outworn, I have walked it so far. But now I seek to follow my star.*
- Transfer both items to the new sock and shake that three times, saying three times, *The path is not yet walked, the words are not yet talked, yet I can successfully forward go, that I may grow and know fulfillment.*
- Remove the items from the new sock and hold the old one in your nondominant hand and the new one in the other hand, saying, *Old life to new, not without stress, but unless I take this opportunity, achievement will not come to me.*
- Leave the old and new items side by side in the light of the sun from noon until 3 p.m.; if it's raining, leave them on an indoor window ledge.

887

FOR PLANNING THE GREAT ESCAPE THAT MAY INVOLVE TOTALLY UPROOTING THE FAMILY

You will need:

A large picture of your planned location
Paste
Small passport-sized photos of each of you who will be sharing the adventure
Messages, such as HERE WE GO, BON VOYAGE, JOURNEY OF A LIFETIME, all written on different-colored papers in different-colored inks

Timing:

If other people are raising objections to the move

The Spell

- Hold the location picture between your hands and say, *Our happy future is awaiting, no time for doubts or hesitating. Just needs us to seize the dream. Only lacks us to complete the scene.*
- As fast as you can, paste the family photos on top of the location, saying, *Step into the picture, leap into the future; any day, every way, we'll be there, no time to spare. We'll not wait, the great escape, take the leap, not too steep. After all, freedom calls.*
- Read aloud the messages you've written and add one every day, writing more each day.
- Keep the picture near the front door and take it on the great escape.

888

FOR PERSUADING OVERSIZED BABY BIRDS TO LEAVE THE NEST IF THEY ARE TOO COMFORTABLE

You will need:

A long feather duster

Timing:

Early Tuesdays, for as often as necessary until they take the hint

The Spell

- Go to an upstairs window (if you do not have one, use a downstairs window at the front of the house) and open it.
- Shake the duster out the window, saying three times, *Overgrown birds, please fly and flee. Find your own nests away from me.*
- Keep shaking the duster while saying three more times, *My love for you is deep, my care for you sincere, but daily I fall over you, so please move on from here.*
- Continue shaking and saying three times, *The nest is small, you've grown so tall, you do not fit in it at all, so out of it, fly and flit. Shoo.*
- Go in the center of the home downstairs and turn around three times clockwise, three times counterclockwise, and three times clockwise again, saying three times, *Visit me, I'll visit you, but time to move on somewhere new. Baby birds, please leave the tree. I love you but I must be free.*

889

FOR REINVENTING YOURSELF IF YOU'VE BEEN DUMPED FOR A YOUNGER MODEL

You will need:

A photo of the two of you in happier times
Scissors
An envelope
A large blank piece of card
A green pen

Timing:

Sunday morning

The Spell

- Hold the picture and say, *One day you will regret this folly. Sacrificing true love for a plaything dolly, throwing away years for vanity; at least I've kept my sanity.*
- Cut the figure of your partner from the photo and put it in the envelope, writing on the front of the envelope, NO MORE OF YOU, YOU AND I ARE THROUGH. SCREW YOU!
- Stick your picture in the middle of the card. Write all over the card compliments to yourself in big letters, I AM FABULOUS, I AM AMAZING, I AM DESIRABLE, and the like.
- Then say, *The future is all about me, free to do anything, off with the ring.* (If you have a ring take it off and put it in the envelope; if not, put in a cheap ring.)
- Place the envelope in a drawer and focus on doing exciting things and taking selfies of them to fill the card.

890

FOR LOVE IN MIDLIFE, WHEN YOU'VE BOTH GOT KIDS, INTERFERING EXES, AND ALIMONY CLAIMS

You will need:

A green candle
Two small boxes, filled with old buttons and beads and lots of knots of black thread
A large empty box with a lid
Two spools of green thread

Timing:

Thursday evening

The Spell

- Light the candle, saying, *Love's not easy, commitments piled high, baggage reaching to the sky. But we will win through, me and you, our hearts are willing, our love is true.*
- Start emptying the small boxes alternately into the bigger one, saying, *Loose ends, tangled threads, we both our luggage haul, need a carriage for a marriage, but better encumbered, sooner lumbered, than not together at all.*
- When everything is in the large box, put or cram on the lid and start wrapping it, first with the one spool of thread going around the big box in one direction, then the second spool going around the box in the other direction, securing them together with big knots. Then say, *Tied together, just about, we'll muddle through, not a doubt. If things spill out, we'll laugh, not shout.*
- Blow out the candle, saying, *Together forever.*
- Find somewhere safe to keep your *togetherness* box.

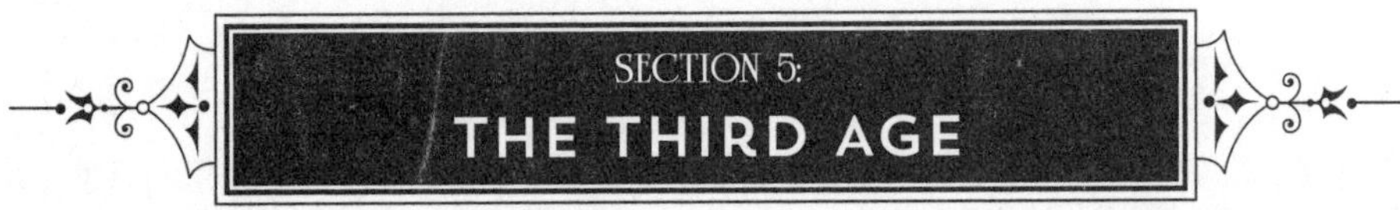

891

FOR LIVING YOUR OWN WAY IF ADULT CHILDREN CONSTANTLY INTERFERE

You will need:
A light-colored feather
A small box without a lid
A net large enough to fit over the box, such as an old-fashioned hair net or a shower cap
A spool of red thread
A sharp knife

Timing:
Wednesday morning

The Spell
- Put the feather in the box, with the net over the box, and secure the net with tight knots of red thread, saying, *You think you know better than me, what I should do and where I should be. I know you mean well, but frankly it's hell. I've still got a brain behind this old face, so back off my case.*
- Cut the knots, take off the net, and go outdoors with the box.
- Release the feather and, indoors, fill the box with potpourri or crystals.
- Whenever you feel pressured, shake the box and repeat the spell words.

892

FOR THE RETIREMENT RELOCATION MOVE FOR WHICH YOU HAVE WAITED SO LONG

You will need:
A jar of dried rosemary
Four yellow candles, set in a square
A picture of where you want to be, placed in the center of the candles

Timing:
Sunday

The Spell
- Scatter rosemary over the picture, saying, *Rosemary, rosemary, carry me/us, to where I/we most want to be:* [name the location].
- Light the first candle and then each candle from the other, saying for each one as you light it, *Light the way to my/our new home, let restrictions melt away. Remove all barriers to my/our dream, that I/we move closer every day.*
- Extinguish the candle farthest from you and remove it from the square, saying, *I/we take the first step to freedom, opening the door, on the road to my/our new tomorrow, and it will open more and more.*
- Do the same with the other three candles, repeating the same spell words.
- Carry the picture carefully outdoors and spill the herb off it in an open space, saying, *Rosemary, rosemary, carry me/us, to where I/we most want to be* [name the location again].
- Take four definite steps toward the move and then repeat the spell.

893

IF YOUR NEST EGG AND INVESTMENTS FALL SHORT OF WHAT YOU HAD HOPED AND YOU HAVE TO POSTPONE RETIREMENT

You will need:

A gold candle
A gold-colored coin for each month/year you fear you may have to wait to retire
A small pot with a lid, set in front of the gold candle
A mixture of ginger and cinnamon in a small dish with a spoon

Timing:

Thursday, before sunset

The Spell

- Light the candle and place the first coin in the pot, saying, *Money incubate, bringing new prosperity, for we cannot forever wait. Our happy future we would see, soon and sooner may it be.*
- Add a spoon of spice to the pot, saying, *Speeding up, adding money that will last, accumulating, speculating, to make our fortune fast.*
- Repeat the spell words and actions until all the coins and spice are in the pot.
- Put on the lid and, holding the pot, say, *Miracles we do not seek, but fast financial growth each week. With spice and gold, may wealth unfold; enough in the pot and a little more, our fortune is an open door.*
- Each Thursday, hold the pot and repeat all three sets of spell words.

894

FOR PURSUING A CREATIVE, SPIRITUAL, OR PEOPLE-BASED BUSINESS AFTER RETIREMENT

You will need:

A large piece of gray paper
Bright-colored children's paints and a big brush
Scissors
Green thread
A long thick piece of ribbon

Timing:

Sunday morning

The Spell

- On the paper, paint brightly colored figures of yourself, plus anyone you are sharing your retirement with, flowers, birds, butterflies, and symbols of your creative or spiritual venture, such as a potter's wheel, crystals, or a computer, if you are writing a novel.
- Say as you paint, *Life ahead is bright, colors fill my sight, no more gray, not any day.*
- When the painting is dry, cut it into long strips; make holes in each strip of paper and attach them using thread to the ribbon.
- Hang the ribbon where you will be working creatively, saying, *I shall create beauty, from desire and not from duty. The future waits for none, I claim my place in the sun.*

895

IF YOU HAVE TO LEAVE A BELOVED LIFETIME HOME

You will need:

A small item that is filled with good memories of your years in your home

A pot of growing lavender, rosemary, sage, or thyme

A small drawstring bag

Timing:

Sunset

The Spell

- Hold the item in your closed hands, saying, *Memories you fill my heart, sad it is that we must part. And yet I carry away with me, the essence of love that will always be.*
- Pluck five leaves from the plant and put them in the bag, along with the memento, saying, *Herbs of fond remembrance, I leave with regretful backward glance. But for me you do remind that memories new I still can find.*
- Leave the plant as a gift for the new owners/tenants.
- Set the memento in the center of your new home as soon as you arrive and release the leaves from the bag outdoors.

896

IF YOU HAVE LOST YOUR PARTNER AND DON'T WANT TO GO ON ALONE

You will need:

A candle marked with seven equidistant notches

A vase of seven white carnations or roses (symbols of love that survive death), placed in front of the candle

A bowl of soil

A photo of the two of you, placed in front of the candle

Timing:

For seven days at sunset

The Spell

- Light the candle, saying, *You are with me, I am with you, and so I promise to live for two.*
- Burn a petal from the first flower in the flame and drop it into the soil, saying, *Flower of memory, through my eyes you shall see the places we said we would go, for I know it is so, still you and me.*
- When the candle is burned to the first notch, blow it out and say, *I send you light, for you are near to me every night, just out of sight.*
- Repeat the spell for the next six nights and, when the flowers fade, release the faded petals into flowing water, saying, *I will go on 'til my life is done, and we can be together once more as one.*

897

TO TAKE UP THE UNIVERSITY OF THE THIRD AGE LEARNING

You will need:

A set of sharpened pencils in a pencil case, even if you are taking an online course

A few pages of course material (a printout, if the course is online)

Timing:

Before your first lecture or assignment

The Spell

- Shake the pencil case five times so the pencils rattle, saying five times, *Sharpened pencils, ready for school, I am sharper than ever, twice as clever. I will succeed at this endeavor.*
- Open the pencil case and write your name on the front page of the material or on the inside cover of the book in pencil, saying, *My name, and claim to fame. Ready to learn, eager to discover, I'll whiz through this material/book, cover to cover.*
- Put the pencil back in the case, close it, and shake the case five times, repeating both sets of spell words.
- Whenever you get disheartened, write your name at the top of the page you are currently working on in pencil (print your name, even on the computer, since you can delete it later), shake the pencil case five times, and repeat the spell words five times.

898

IF YOUR RETIREMENT IS SEEN AS FREE BABYSITTING 24/7 BY ADULT CHILDREN

You will need:

A piece of white paper, divided into squares, a square for every day of the month ahead

A white-leaded pencil

A blue candle

A pot of soil

A black pen

Timing:

The first day of the month

The Spell

- In each square, write in white pencil so it is virtually invisible on the paper, ON CALL 24/7.
- Light the candle and tear off a corner of the paper, saying, *Babysitting* [or whatever you are expected to do], *always on call, all about them* [name offending adult children] *and not me at all. No gratitude, taken for granted, dropped when not wanted, it's really so rude.*
- Hold the torn-off corner of the paper near the flame so it is just singed and drop it in the soil, repeating the spell words.
- Now write in every square in black pen, WHATEVER I CHOOSE TO DO.
- Keep the paper where you can get it out and remind yourself when the next demand comes.

899

FOR MEETING A PARTNER LATER IN LIFE

You will need:

A beeswax or fast melting wax candle secured on a metal tray (light the candle and pour a little melted wax to hold it in place)
A letter opener
Parchment paper
A pink scarf or cloth

Timing:
Friday, just before sunset

The Spell

- Light the candle, saying, *Love in later years is twice as sweet. My love through candle fire I ask we meet.*
- Breathe into the candle softly six times.
- When the wax is melted and still warm, draw a heart shape in the melted wax using the letter opener, gently lifting it onto parchment paper before it hardens.
- With the remaining wax, make two small figures, holding hands, and gently press them into the heart, saying, *Heart to heart and soul to mind, come kindred spirit and me find. Our true love in this wax I bind.*
- Wrap the figures and the heart in the cloth when the wax is cold.
- Knot them in the scarf and keep it in a drawer in your bedroom.

900

FOR REDISCOVERING WHY YOU MARRIED YOUR PARTNER, IF YOU SEEM LIKE STRANGERS

You will need:

Six red candles in a row
Two small figures made from children's modeling clay or self-hardening clay, or worry dolls, one set in front of the candle at each end of the row
ribbon

Timing:
Tuesday, after dark

The Spell

- Light the candles at either end of the row, saying for each, *Candle fire, bring back desire, friendship, and affection. For these past years, I do fear, we've gone in different directions.*
- Now light candles 2 and 5, saying, *Candle fire, bring back desire, kinship, and affection, so we can move back once more in the same direction.*
- Move the figures in front of the central candles and light those candles.
- Bind the figures together with the ribbon in six knots, saying, *I reach out to you and you reach out to me, so are we joined once more willingly, and forever may this be.*
- Let the candles burn.
- Hide the bound figures in the bedroom.

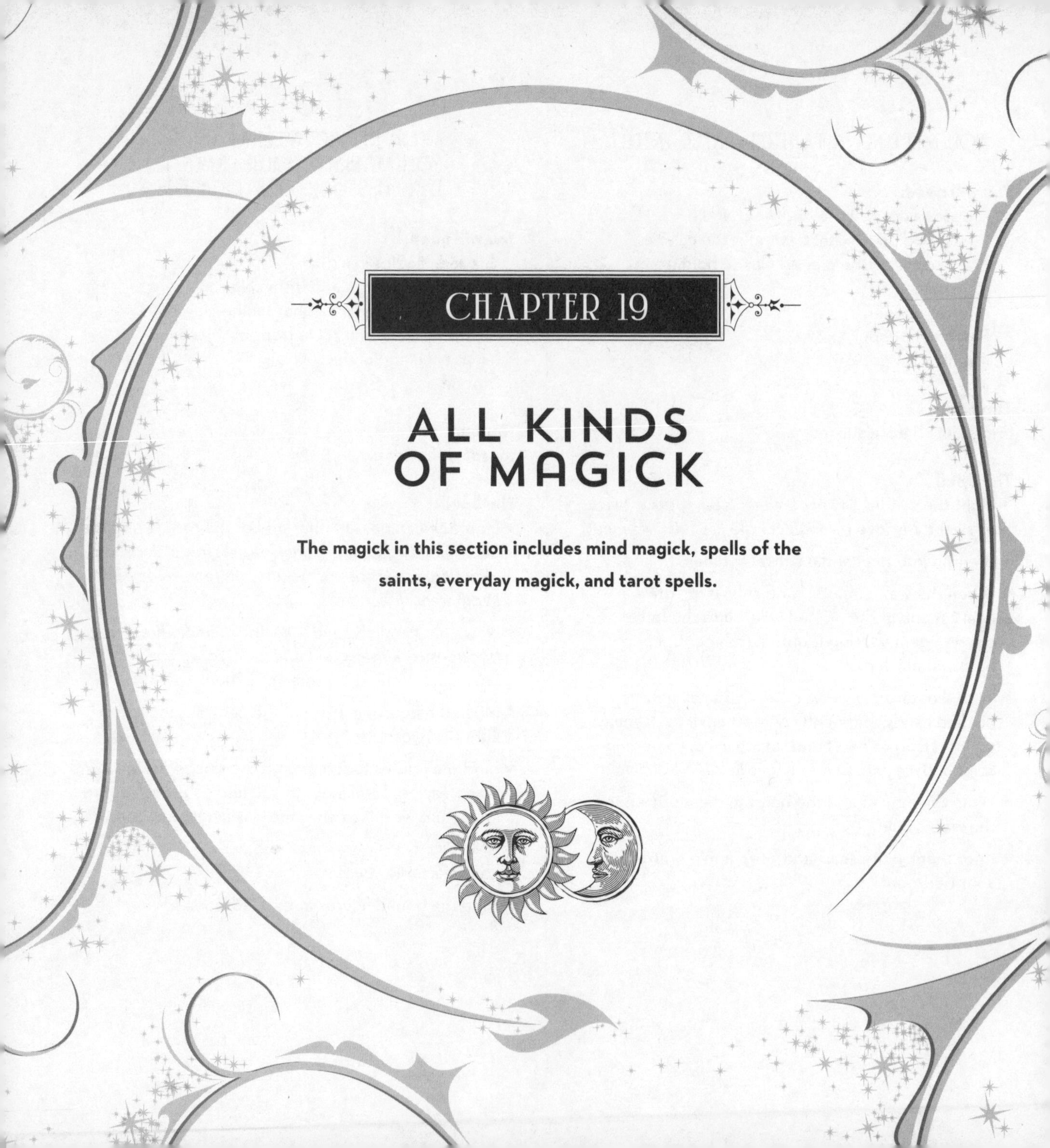

CHAPTER 19

ALL KINDS OF MAGICK

The magick in this section includes mind magick, spells of the saints, everyday magick, and tarot spells.

901

TO CALL A LOVE TELEPATHICALLY IF YOU ARE BOTH INVOLVED IN OTHER RELATIONSHIPS AND CAN'T MEET

You will need:
A body of water, whether inland, still, or flowing, or the ocean

Timing:
When you know your love will be quiet and not distracted

The Spell
- Touch the water with your hands or, if it's shallow, stand in it and move your feet, saying your love's name in your mind, softly but persistently.
- Keep saying the name and rippling your hands or feet until you feel a warm connection, as if you were being hugged by your love.
- Extend your hands outward, as if reaching out and holding hands across the water. Say in your mind, *Winds from the waters, winds from the sea, across the land, as we join hands, [name], hard though it be, reach out, my love, now to me.*
- Now speak the words in your heart you cannot say aloud and lower your hands.
- Cast a stone, shell, flower, or crystal in the water in thanks.
- Try to make actual contact in the next twenty-four hours and you may find normal obstacles no longer stand in the way.

902

TO CREATE A PSYCHIC ELECTRIC FENCE TO STOP A POTENTIAL ATTACKER, PHYSICAL OR PSYCHOLOGICAL, IN HIS TRACKS

You will need:
A gold candle

Timing:
Sunday morning

The Spell
- Vigorously shake your fingertips on both hands until you can feel energy flowing.
- Hold your hands about six inches (15cm) apart, fingers spread wide open, and palms facing each other.
- Keep bringing your hands together so that they nearly touch, move them apart, then move them back together, continuing this for five or six cycles, faster and faster.
- As you move your hands, picture the light becoming brighter and clearer, and creating sparks or rays.
- Shake these sparks from your left hand so that they move clockwise upward, until they join with your right hand, and continue traveling downward around your body to join with those rising from your left hand in a sealed sphere.
- Picture the sparks as a golden zigzag in yellows and orange, not in any way harmful, but firmly repelling any negativity.
- When in a hazardous situation or with a nasty person, shake your hands subtly to activate the shield.

903

TO INFLUENCE A DECISION AT AN IMPORTANT MEETING IF NO ONE EVER LISTENS TO YOU

You will need:
A pen or a small item you can touch at a meeting without attracting attention

Timing:
Thursday morning, in bright light, or in the beams of a bright lamp if it's a dark day

The Spell

- Hold the pen or your chosen item in your nondominant hand and stroke it gently with the index finger of the other hand, saying in your mind over and over again, *Brighter and brighter, lighter and lighter, listen to me. You talk and you talk, argue and squawk, the solution you just cannot see.*
- After two or three minutes, the pen will be filled with light and power.
- Take it to any meetings and, when you are talked over or ignored, point the pen outward, saying the spell words louder and louder in your mind.
- When you feel ready, say aloud, *Please listen to me. I don't agree* [or something similar] and you'll find that your coworkers will listen.
- Re-empower the pen monthly with the spell.

904

TO GET A PARKING SPACE

You will need:
Nothing

Timing:
Before going out in the car

The Spell

- Before setting off, gently tap the center of your brow three times with the index finger of your dominant hand and say three times in your mind, *I will find a parking space.*
- Just before arriving at the location, repeat the words in your mind three more times.
- As you draw into the parking lot or the street where you need to park, be guided by your inner radar, your psychic GPS.
- Begin a soft, regular, rhythmic chant in your mind, *My parking space is waiting. I park, no hesitating.*
- Keep saying the spell words in your mind, allowing yourself to be drawn as if a magnet were attached to the front of your car along the correct lanes of access to the waiting space.
- Relax into the experience, confident of success. In a multistory car park, ask, *Which floor?* and let your psychic knowing guide you.

905

TO REASSURE A PET WHEN YOU ARE GOING TO BE HOME LATE OR ARE STAYING AWAY

You will need:

Nine hairs from the animal (can be taken from a grooming brush), placed inside a locket or a tiny purse

Timing:

Ten or fifteen minutes before you would normally be home

The Spell

- Start thinking of your pet about ten minutes before you normally get home and, holding the locket or purse in your nondominant hand, picture yourself stroking the animal or move your hand in a stroking movement at animal height, saying in your mind four or five times the pet's name and soothing words.
- Visualize the texture of the fur as you mentally stroke your pet.
- Call the animal again in your mind several times five minutes before you actually reach home and again picture yourself stroking the pet.
- If you're staying away, use any gentle reassuring phrases you usually say when you are fussing over the pet.
- You can be sure when you do arrive home that the pet will be happily waiting in the hall.

906

TO FIND A LOST FELLOW TRAVELER, FAMILY MEMBER, OR FRIEND IN A CROWDED AIRPORT OR SHOPPING MALL IF YOUR PHONE OR THEIRS HAS NO SIGNAL

You will need:

The camera on your phone or tablet

Timing:

When you realize you have lost each other

The Spell

- Take a phone image of where *you* are.
- Focusing on the image, rather than the external scene, call in your mind the name of the lost person, saying, *Stop and I will find you.*
- Picture in your mind what she is wearing and expand on your inner camera from the figure outward on all sides, noting any landmarks.
- Picture a series of lights leading you to the location and start walking slowly, still holding the phone, saying her name in your mind and the phrase *Stop and I will find you* continuously.
- Follow your feet and not your mind and, if you doubt or start to panic, pause, look at the image, repeat her name in your mind, and continue thinking, *Stop and I will find you* until you find your friend or the phone kicks in.

907

TO GET YOURSELF CHOSEN AT AN INTERVIEW OR AUDITION

You will need:

A gold candle
A box of gold glitter
A drawstring bag or a purse

Timing:

The day before the interview or audition

The Spell

- Light the candle and take the lid off the box of glitter, saying in your mind ten times as you scatter glitter around the candle, *More dazzling do I become hour by hour, my talents on the world will I shower.*
- Continue to say the spell words in your mind ten more times, seeing the light of the golden candle surrounding you like golden rays of sunshine, filled with glittering light.
- Blow out the candle and repeat the spell every hour on the hour for three consecutive hours, if possible.
- Put a little glitter in the bag or purse.
- On the morning of the interview or audition, say the spell words in your mind ten times as you get ready and take the bag of glitter with you.
- When you arrive, try to sprinkle a little glitter (in the bathroom, if necessary), and say the words ten times more in your mind as you sit waiting.
- Picture that gold glittering energy around you, spreading its rays so you appear to the interviewing panel exactly as the candidate they want.

908

TO PERSUADE A PARTNER TO BUY YOU THE GIFT YOU REALLY WANT IF YOU ALWAYS GET SOMETHING BORING FOR BIRTHDAYS AND CHRISTMAS

You will need:

To take your partner shopping where the desired item is on sale, as well as boring items

Timing:

Saturday, any time between noon and 3 p.m.

The Spell

- Hold the desired item and hand it to your partner, saying aloud, *This is so beautiful* and adding in your mind, *And if you are dutiful, in my Christmas stocking/on my birthday this I will find.*
- Put it back without overtly hinting, but linger a moment, picturing your partner handing over the money/credit card and the present being beautifully gift-wrapped (or left in the bag as usual).
- Now pick up a boring item and put it down again, walking off and saying in your mind, *This is so boring and so I'm ignoring this horrible gift.* [Name your partner], *take this as a warning, buy that and there'll be a huge rift.*
- Picture your partner picking it up and putting it straight down as it sets his teeth on edge.
- The week before the gift buying, picture both scenes and say both sets of spell words daily.

909

TO STOP SNIDE REMARKS OR SOMEONE BEING CONSTANTLY SPITEFUL TO YOU IN FRONT OF A GROUP OR IN THE WORKPLACE

You will need:
A long piece of string or a bootlace

Timing:
Tuesday evening

The Spell

- Tie the string/lace in as many knots as possible, left to right, saying in your mind for each knot, *Tongue tie, bid malice good-bye. You* [name the worst perpetrator], *hence shall silenced be about me, and I shall be free.*
- Touch each knot in turn, right to left, and repeat the spell words for each one, picturing the perpetrator red-faced or shunned by the others and her tongue in knots.
- Take the string to work and touch each knot left to right when the nasty person starts to make you the butt of jokes.

910

IF YOU KNOW SOMEONE IS WISHING YOU ILL, BUT YOU HAVE TO SEE HIM EVERY DAY

You will need:
A shiny metallic pendant, totally unmarked on one side

Timing:
Sunday, at the brightest time of the day, or light a white candle if it's dark

The Spell

- Swirl the pendant at your eye height, clockwise and counterclockwise alternately, nine times in each direction.
- Say continuously in your mind as you watch it turning, *Eye bright, protect me from the sight of* [name assailant], *repelling his malice with three times the might.*
- Wear the pendant when you must meet the malicious person, avoiding direct eye contact, and turn the pendant so the blank side is facing out.
- Repeat the words in your mind until you feel the force of the attack lessening.
- Wash the pendant under running water in the bathroom, dry it, and put it on, decorated side out, until the next attack, saying the spell words in your mind nine times as you wash it.

911

A ST. MARTHA DRAGON-SLAYING RITUAL FOR BANISHING A DISRUPTIVE PERSON WITH WHOM A FAMILY MEMBER IS OBSESSED

You will need:

A red candle
A small dish of salt
A bowl of water
A silver letter opener
Nine shiny beads from a broken necklace or from a cheap one you break
A red scarf or cloth

Timing:

Nine consecutive Tuesdays, after dusk

The Spell

- Light the candle.
- Add three pinches of salt to the water and make a cross in the water with the letter opener, saying, *Mother Martha, who slew your dragon with magical sacred water, protect with this blessed water* [name person needing protection] *from* [name disruptive person] *who fascinates, harms, and disrupts with dazzling destructive fire what was once a united family.*
- Set the beads on the scarf where candlelight will shine on them.
- Using your dominant hand, scatter around the scarf a single circle of water droplets, repeat the spell words, wrap the beads in the scarf, and blow out the candle. Hide the scarf near possessions of the affected family member.
- Repeat for eight Tuesdays, and, on the ninth Tuesday, let the candle burn, knot the scarf, and tie it to a tree with the beads inside.

912

A ST. JOSEPH, THE CARPENTER, RITUAL IF YOU OR A LOVED ONE CANNOT FIND WORK

You will need:

Seven small cards, business-card size
A black pen
Seven small candles, set in a circle

Timing:

Beginning Thursday, first thing in the morning, and continuing for six more days

The Spell

- On day 1, write these words on a card, using both sides, DEAR ST. JOSEPH, YOU PROVIDED FOR YOUR FAMILY WITH YOUR OWN HANDS. PLEASE HELP ME TO FIND GAINFUL EMPLOYMENT VERY SOON, THAT I AM SOON ABLE TO PROVIDE FOR MYSELF/THOSE ENTRUSTED TO MY CARE.
- Light the first candle, read the spell words aloud seven times, and put the card in the middle of the candle circle.
- Blow out the candle.
- Repeat the spell each morning, lighting an extra candle each day as well as relighting the original one(s), writing the words on a new card each day and adding it to the growing pile of cards in the center of the candles each day.
- On day 7, leave all the candles burning, then pin each card in seven different places indoors where the light shines on them, reading each as you attach it.

913

A ST. JUDE, PATRON SAINT OF HOPELESS CAUSES, RITUAL TO BRING RELIEF IF YOU ARE BEING THREATENED LEGALLY OR ARE THE VICTIM OF BULLYING TACTICS

You will need:

An upright wooden post, wide enough to write vertically on
A thick blue permanent marker
A hammer
Six old metal nails
Six new metal nails

Timing:
When you need breathing room to get assistance and advice in a seemingly impossible situation

The Spell

- Write on both sides of the post, top to bottom, THANK YOU, ST. JUDE, FOR BLESSINGS SOON TO BE RECEIVED.
- Working downward, hammer the old nails into the back of the post in a vertical row, saying continuously, *Good St. Jude, I trust the most. Nail these threats to the post.*
- Now hammer the new nails from bottom to top on the front of the post, saying, *Good St. Jude of hopeless causes, work a miracle so hardship pauses.*
- Once you have finished, take immediate practical action to get advice.
- Embed the post in soil where it will not be noticed.

914

A ST. ANTHONY OF PADUA RITUAL FOR FINDING LOST ITEMS OR DOCUMENTS

You will need:

Nothing

Timing:
When you realize something precious or essential to you is missing

The Spell

- Begin clapping softly and after each clap say one of the lines below.
- As you do so, picture the missing object, the last time you remember seeing it, and, as you speak the set of spell words, imagine your pleasure at getting it back.
- For clap 1, say, *St. Anthony, St. Anthony, please come down. Something is lost and can't be found.*
- For clap 2, *Good St. Anthony, this I pray. Bring [name item] back today.*
- For clap 3, *Anthony, good saint, I pray return, this [name item] to me, for which I yearn.*
- For clap 4, *Dear St. Anthony, this I lack, [name item]. Haste I pray and bring it back.*
- For clap 5, *Good St. Anthony, this is gone [name item]. Look around and it return.*
- Repeat the clapping cycle five times.
- An image may come into your head where you left or dropped the item. If not, within a few days the missing item should turn up.

915

A ST. AGNES LOVE RITUAL FOR A LASTING LOVE, IF YOU DESPAIR OF FINDING THE RIGHT PERSON IF YOU HAVE BEEN MARRIED BEFORE

You will need:

A pincushion or a square of folded cloth
Twelve straight pins stuck in the pincushion
A pajama top or a nightdress (not worn for the spell)

Timing:

St. Agnes Eve, January 20, at 10 p.m.

The Spell

- Working by a dim light, pull out from the pincushion the pins, one by one, fastening each, one at a time, to the sleeve of the nightgown or pajama top so that they form horizontal rows.
- Each time you transfer a pin, say, *Fair St. Agnes, play the part, and send to me my own sweetheart, that when I see my love, I will know. Our love will eternally and joyfully grow.*
- When all the pins are in the sleeve, recite the months of the year, starting with January and ending with December, adding, *Good St. Agnes, do not tarry, but send the one I shall marry.*
- Place the garment close to your bed for three nights.

916

A TRADITIONAL ST. ANDREW OF SCOTLAND EVE RITUAL FOR CALLING A FUTURE PARTNER, IF HE IS PROVING RELUCTANT OR SLOW TO COMMIT

You will need:

Scissors
A piece of natural fabric
Dried rosemary

Timing:

Midnight, St. Andrew's Eve, November 29

The Spell

- Sit at the table, cutting one hair at a time from your head for as many years you are old. Over-twenty-fives could perhaps take one hair for each five years. Place each hair on the fabric.
- Say for each hair, *I offer this my sacrifice to him most precious in my sight; I charge thee now, come forth to me, that you my lover true will be.*
- When you have finished, sprinkle a little of the rosemary on the corners of the cloth.
- At one o'clock, turn every hair on your cloth, one at a time, as you do so saying for each hair the same spell words.
- Open the front door, casting out the hairs one by one.
- Afterwards, say the words one more time and call your would-be love's name three times out of the door before closing it.

917

A ST. PATRICK OF IRELAND PROTECTION RITUAL WHILE TRAVELING

You will need:

Two lavender incense sticks

Timing:

The day before you or a family member travel

The Spell:

- Light both incense sticks and, with one in each hand, spiral them in both directions at the same time around the luggage, or if you're taking a day trip, around an item that will be taken along.
- Say this modern adaptation of the ancient St. Patrick prayer: *I arise today through the light of the sun, the radiance of the moon, the splendor of fire, the fierceness of lightning, the swiftness of wind, the depths of the sea, and the hardness of rock. May the mists enclose me/us [or name], that I/we* [or name] *may travel in security and be within your care, wise Patrick, everywhere.*
- Let the incense burn.

918

A MODERN VERSION OF AN OLD ST. BRIDGET, THE MIDWIFE SAINT, SAFE CHILDBIRTH RITUAL

You will need:

A dish of sea salt
A small glass bowl of water
A small silver-colored knife
A clear, lidded glass bottle

Timing:

The week before baby is due

The Spell

- Add three pinches of salt to the water and stir it with the knife three times clockwise, saying three times, *Bridget, midwife to Mary, midwife to all, with these precious water drops, on you I do call. Be with me, fair Bridget, at my infant's birth. Keep us both safe as my child enters this earth.*
- Make either the Celtic Christian equal-armed cross or the Earth Mother's diagonal cross three times in the water with the knife, and as you do so repeat the chant.
- Pour the water into the bottle and keep it cool, each day putting three drops in the center of your brow and repeating the spell words.
- When you go into labor, take the water and ask your birth partner to put three drops on your brow whenever you feel it will help.
- In the hours after birth, put three drops on your baby's head, repeating the spell words.

919

A ST. JOAN OF ARC RITUAL FOR COURAGE WHEN FACED WITH ADVERSITY OR INJUSTICE

You will need:

A silver letter opener

Timing:

Tuesday, at sunset

The Spell

- Facing the sunset, hold the letter opener about half an arm's length away from you, level with your forehead (carefully), saying, *St. Joan, give me courage for this fight, that I may show nobility as day turns into night.*
- Bring the letter opener down to knee level at the same distance, saying, *St. Joan, give me strength for this fight, that I may show nobility as day turns into night.*
- Bring the letter opener diagonally toward your left shoulder, holding it horizontally to the left of your shoulder, saying, *St. Joan, give me justice in this fight, that I may show nobility as day turns into night.*
- Bring the letter opener horizontally to just beyond your right shoulder, saying, *St. Joan, give me power for this fight, that I may show nobility as day turns into night.*
- Put the letter opener down, name your cause, and say, *St. Joan, give me victory, for my cause is right. Be with me now and always, as day turns into night.*
- Wash the letter opener under running water.

920

A ST. BERNADETTE OF LOURDES CIRCLING RITUAL FOR SOMEONE WHO HAS BEEN DIAGNOSED WITH A TERMINAL ILLNESS

You will need:

A circle of eleven small yellow candles
Rose petals in a basket or bowl

Timing:

Wednesday, in the dawn light

The Spell

- Light the first candle, saying, *St. Bernadette, who brings miracles to those whose hope has gone, bring life and healing to* [name] *that this battle may be won.*
- Repeat the spell words as you light each candle from the one before, circling the candle ring slowly and clockwise.
- When all are burning, circle the candle ring three times, scattering rose petals while saying, *Whether life is short or long, bring quality and peace and song, that* [name] *may know joy and peace and Bernadette may you not cease, 'til you have offered your loving healing. For miracles they do come true, and this, wise saint, I ask of you.*
- Let the candles burn, then scoop up the petals and scatter them in flowing water.

921

A BEAN LOVE RITUAL TO GET THE GUY OR GAL NEXT DOOR TO BECOME MORE ROMANTIC

You will need:
Six dried beans

Timing:
A few minutes before he or she arrives at your home

The Spell

- Shake the beans in your closed hands and say six times, *Jump beans, my love inspire, that his or her heart may leap with fire. Six, five, four, three, two, one—hop beans, let romance come.*
- Put the beans one at a time under the doormat where your neighbor has to walk over them, saying for each one, *Pass over these beans, fulfill my dreams.*
- Leave the beans in place until he or she has passed over them ten times, then bury them, saying, *Love grow fast not slow, that you at last will know, love must be so.*
- Replace the beans under the mat.

922

A FIRST LOVE OR LOVE AFTER BETRAYAL CUCUMBER RITUAL

You will need:
A cucumber
A knife

Timing:
Monday or Friday morning

The Spell

- Cut off a chunk of cucumber the length of your hand and on the skin score, MAY OUR LOVE BE BEAUTIFUL. It does not matter if it is not clear.
- Cut the cucumber chunk in half, and on one side of the flesh, score your name and on the other side your love's name.
- Put the two haves of the cucumber together, chop it in small pieces, and add it to the filling of a pita, a wrap, or a sandwich, saying, *May our love be beautiful.*
- Eat the bread and, if possible, share it with your love.

923

AN AEROBICS, FITNESS, OR DANCE CLASS RITUAL TO BUILD UP THE COURAGE TO DO SOMETHING SCARY

You will need:
Light weights, if you normally use them.

Timing:
During an exercise class or a private exercise session

The Spell

- Set up a rhythm involving a sequence of six movements (adapt if you're in a class).
- Create a six-word chant, with one word for each movement, such as *I dare no longer scared—there!*
- Continue with the chant (in your head if you're in a class) and the movement sequence until you feel confident and powerful, then say, *I dare* for each movement and end by bringing the weights or your arms up and down once fast, saying, *Got there!*

924

A STONE-SKIMMING RITUAL FOR A SPECIAL WISH

You will need:
A pile of flat white or gray stones suitable for skimming
A black marker pen
A body of water, anything from a pond to the ocean

Timing:
Any morning

The Spell

- Write on each stone one word or a symbol to represent your wish.
- Decide how many skims you will need to release the wish (minimum of three, but if you are an experienced skimmer, go up to six skims across the water to send the wish flying).
- Skim the first stone, saying the word representing your wish, and repeat it each time the stone skims.
- If the stone does not skim enough times, repeat with the second stone and keep skimming stones until you achieve the arranged number of skims.
- When you have succeeded, clap your hands high in the air and say, *The wish flies, across water, through the skies, wish come true, free are you.*
- Throw the rest of the stones one by one into the water without skimming.

925

TO MAKE A VISIT FROM A CROTCHETY OLD RELATIVE OR DIFFICULT IN-LAWS GO WELL

You will need:

A teapot
A sugar bowl, even if the visitors do not take sugar
Cups for each person, including yourself
Teaspoons

Timing:

Ten or fifteen minutes before arrival

The Spell

- Around the middle of the teapot, write invisibly with the index finger of your dominant hand, saying as you write, *May this visit be peaceful, may all words be tranquil, and sharp tongues be still.*
- Do the same around the center of each cup.
- Stir the sugar in the bowl with a spoon six times counterclockwise, saying, *May all be sweet, that we may meet and part in harmony.*
- When the visitors arrive, as you pour the hot water in the pot, say in your mind and again as you stir the tea counterclockwise, *May this visit flow, I ask it shall be so.*
- Strain the tea into the cups, repeating in your mind for each cup as you hand it over the first set of spell words.
- If no one takes sugar, hold the sugar and stir it counterclockwise once, saying the set of second words.

926

A SEVEN-BY-SEVEN CAKE OR COOKIE RITUAL FOR YOUR HAPPY FUTURE MARRIAGE OR MOVING IN TOGETHER

You will need:

Six friends or relatives of the same sex living at different addresses so you make the seventh
Seven ingredients to make cookies or a large cake
A sharp knife
A mixing bowl and a mixing spoon

Timing:

Friday evening

The Spell

- Add the ingredients, then each of you, in turn, starting with yourself, stirs the mix seven times clockwise, saying, *May I be happy, live in harmony, seven by seven years and more, let this love match be.*
- Then each person, in the same order, draws on the surface of the mix with the knife a word or symbol of love or happiness.
- When cooked and cool, on the individual cookies or on top of the cake, each person in the same order invisibly draws or writes the same symbol with the tip of the knife, being careful to not break or mark the surface.
- Cut the cake into seven slices and eat it, or eat the individual cookies.
- You can do this ritual if someone else is being betrothed, then they take the lead.

927

A HONEY, JAM, OR CHOCOLATE SPREAD RITUAL TO HELP A RELUCTANT CHILD OR TEENAGER TO GO TO SCHOOL OR A FIRST JOB

You will need:

Honey, jam, or chocolate spread
Two slices of bread or a crepe
A knife

Timing:

Monday morning

The Spell

- If the child wishes she can do the spell; otherwise you do it on her behalf.
- Spread the honey or chosen topping on one slice of bread or in the crepe, and with the knife write on the surface of the spread, SCHOOL WILL BE BRILLIANT or TODAY WILL BE COOL AT SCHOOL/JOB.
- Cover the sandwich with the second slice of bread or roll the crepe and give it to the child or teenager to eat.
- Repeat the spell daily, if necessary.

928

A BEESWAX CANDLE SPELL IF YOU CAN'T MEMORIZE ESSENTIAL MATERIAL OR DATA AND A TEST OR YOUR JOB DEPENDS ON IT

You will need:

A natural beeswax candle
Dried sage and thyme
A flat-based candleholder or small tray
A knife
A spatula
Parchment paper
A small bag or purse
The material you need to memorize

Timing:

A week before you need to use the learning

The Spell

- Roll the candle to and fro nine times on the table, saying softly nine times, *Sage and thyme, make memory mine, as this candle flows, so my blocks do go. I will recall what I need, achievement indeed.*
- Light the candle and scatter sage and thyme around the base of the candle on the candleholder, saying the spell words.
- When the wax has melted, enclosing the herbs, say, *Easy will learning be. Knowledge flows into me.*
- As the candle is cooling, cut out a small herb and wax disk with the knife, lifting it with the spatula onto parchment paper. Dispose of the remaining wax.
- When cooled, put the disk in a small bag and keep it near the material you need to memorize.
- Carry it with you on the day you need to use the knowledge.

929

TO GROW HEALTHY POTTED PLANTS IF YOU KILL OFF EVERY ONE YOU BUY

You will need:

A ball of red string
A strong thick stick to put in the potted plant (bamboo is especially powerful)

Timing:
When you bring a new plant home

The Spell

- Knot a piece of red string around the stick three times, saying, *You will grow, you will thrive, this time next week you'll be alive.*
- Push the stick into the soil of the plant, repeating the spell words.
- Hold your hands around the pot and say the spell words once more.
- Each week, repeat the whole spell, removing the stick from the pot, knotting a new piece of string around the stick, and replacing it.
- Continue weekly until the stick is covered with red string and the plant is flourishing.

930

TO GAIN CONFIDENCE IF YOU OR A FAMILY MEMBER ARE VERY SHY

You will need:

A strip of paper
A blue pen
An empty flowerpot
A pot of marigolds or another yellow flowering plant, just starting to bloom

Timing:
Three days before the full moon, in daylight

The Spell

- On one side of the paper, write the name of yourself or the family member, and on the other, I GROW IN CONFIDENCE DAY BY DAY, SHYNESS DISAPPEARS AWAY.
- Walk over a patch of earth or get the family member to do so (make an excuse), scoop up some of the soil, and put it in the bottom of an empty flowerpot.
- Either dig a hole in the garden and drop in the hole the walked-over soil, followed by the piece of paper, or add the paper to the new plant pot and in both cases add more soil to cover the paper.
- In either case, plant the marigolds over the paper and soil and fill in the hole, saying, *I* [or name] *grow in confidence every day, shyness disappears away.*
- When you water the flowers, repeat the spell words.

931

A PROTECTIVE DILL RITUAL IF YOU ARE BESIEGED BY UNFAIR TAX RETURNS OR DEMANDS

You will need:
A jar of dried dill herbs

Timing:
Thursday after dusk

The Spell
- Hold the jar between your hands and, making sure the lid is on firmly, alternately shake it vigorously and bang it down on the table three times, saying three times, *Tax commands, tax demands, I implore you, dill, drive off taxmen at your will. Of this matter I've had my fill.*
- Walk up and down your path or the pavement outside your home three times, scattering (subtly if you're doing this in the street) a trail of dill, saying (in your mind if you're in the street), *Send no more to my door, unfair demands, hostile commands. By the power of dill, I drive off taxmen at my will—taxmen, bother me no more, I've not broken any law!*
- Go on the offensive officially, and before sending a letter or phoning, scatter dill around the computer or on the letter.

932

A STAMPING SPELL IF YOU'RE TIRED OF GIVING IN TO OTHERS' DEMANDS

You will need:
Nothing if you do the spell at home
In the office, you can press your feet into the floor rhythmically and circle your pen slowly in the air clockwise while you say the spell words in your mind

Timing:
When you have said yes one too many times

The Spell
- Stamp hard nine times, saying nine times, once after each stamp, *I insist.*
- Name the change you insist on and stamp nine times more.
- Now stamp hard nine more times and clap nine times at the same time, saying, *I want* nine times, once after each stamp.
- Then name what *you* want and stamp nine more times.
- Stamp nine more times, saying nine times, once after each stamp, *I will have.*
- Name what you will have and stamp and clap nine more times.
- End by naming what you insist, what you want, and what you will have, and make a last stamp and clap, saying, *Now!*

933

A DEFENSIVE RITUAL AGAINST A BITTER RELATIVE WHO ALWAYS PICKS ON YOU OR ONE OF YOUR CHILDREN

You will need:
A small, unpeeled onion
A deep dish of vinegar
A teaspoon of sugar
A stone

Timing:
Tuesday morning

The Spell

- Using the index finger of your dominant hand, trace around the onion peel the name of the person who is nasty and the words, I STRIP YOUR POWER TO HURT AWAY.
- Immerse the onion in the vinegar, saying, *Your sourness, your spite, I strip away; your sharp tongue must be still. Your vicious words are not right, and so I strip away your power to hurt when you will.*
- Let the onion soak for twenty-four hours, add a teaspoon of sugar, and mix it in, saying, *Sweeter be, permanently*, then empty the onion and the vinegar and sugar mix into a hole in the earth.
- Cover the hole, put a stone on top, and say, *Your nastiness is buried deep, venom in the earth does sleep.* [Name], *on you I call, if you can't be nice don't come at all.*

934

A SQUASH OR TENNIS BALL BACK-OFF-BULLY RITUAL WHEN YOU CAN'T DIRECTLY RETALIATE AGAINST INTIMIDATION

You will need:
A squash or tennis racquet and a ball

Timing:
Tuesday, any time

The Spell

- Go to a squash court by yourself or find a wall and hit the tennis ball with a racquet against a wall.
- Establish a steady rhythm, saying every time you hit the ball, *You* [name person], *you must stop bugging me.*
- And as the ball bounces back say, *You,* [name], *you make me mad; enough I've had.*
- Build up the speed and intensity of the hitting, speeding up how fast you say the words and increasing their intensity until you can go no faster.
- Then slow down, saying as you hit the wall, *Calm, calmer shall I be* and as the ball returns, *So listen you,* [name], *the game of bugging me is through.*
- When the ball returns very slowly, catch it and say, *I can't, I won't hit out, not scream or shout. But I have won, your power to upset me is done.*

935

A SIXTY-SECOND KICK-ASS RITUAL IF YOUR TEENAGER'S ROOM IS A DUMP

You will need:

A large garbage bag
Any device with a timer

Timing:

When your teenager absolutely refuses to clean up, the day before garbage collection

The Spell

- Stand outside your teen's room with your bag open and say, *Sixty seconds, just one minute, tidy up, or all goes in it.*
- Set your timer, knock, enter the room, and start putting items and dirty clothes in the bag, saying the spell words.
- When the timer beeps or your child's protests act as the spell energy release, stop, empty the items on the floor, and say, *Just one more hour, sort it or I will and can deliver it to the garbage truck.*
- Leave your teenager to sort out the mess and, after an hour, stand in the doorway with your bag as a reminder until action begins or continues.

936

A GET-YOUR-NOSE-OUT-OF-MY-BUSINESS RITUAL

You will need:

Children's modeling clay
A small lidded box

Timing:

Wednesday morning, or before you see the nosy person

The Spell

- Make a short fat nose out of modeling clay and, as you are shaping it, say, *Out of my business keep your nose, daily it longer and longer grows.*
- Make the nose longer and longer, saying, *Each day your interfering seems to me a lot more wearing. Yet friends we could be, I suppose, if you'd just not poke in my business your nose.*
- Break off the long end of the nose and roll all the clay into a ball, saying, *No harm I would do you, let's start anew, no more intrude, it's really rude. And so, I stress, please, please mind your own business.*
- Make another small nose from the clay and keep it in a little box with a lid until it crumbles naturally or dries out.

937

A SECRET KICK-ASS RITUAL WHEN SOMEONE IS CONSTANTLY BOASTING, UNTIL YOU WANT TO SCREAM, BUT YOU CAN'T BE OPENLY RUDE

You will need:
Nothing

Timing:
When you know you have to meet the boaster

The Spell

- Create a polite outward response you will always use when the person starts showing off. But in your mind decide what you would *really like* to say, but can't.
- The only requirement is you must always make the same outwardly spoken response and in your mind make the same response that you decided you would *really* like to say.
- So, for example, when you answer, *Wish I was you* or *How nice* to the latest acquisition or achievement of the boaster, in your mind you could be saying, *Go play in traffic* or something milder but dismissive, according to how unpleasant the boasting is.
- When you see the person and he starts his self-serving boasts, smile, cross your fingers behind your back, and say aloud your chosen phrase (in your mind substituting the secret words).
- After a few days, the person gets the subliminal message and does not bother you anymore.

938

A KICK-ASS RITUAL TO TAME A THOUGHTLESS PARTNER WHO DELIGHTS IN MAKING YOU LOOK DUMB IN PUBLIC

You will need:
Modeling clay
A back-view photo of your partner (enlarge or print it out so the backside is clearly in view)
Another photo with a head and shoulders view of your partner

Timing:
Before leaving for a social event

The Spell

- Make a series of small clay footprints, enough to cover your partner's backside on the back-view photo and stick them on, saying, [Name], *I love you, but hate what you do, making me look dumb and small, just won't do, won't do at all. A kick up the ass is what you need, and that is overdue indeed.*
- Now put a clay smile over your partner's mouth in the second photo, saying, *Speak thoughtfully, respectfully to me, whenever we're in company, and we can loving be. Your mouth I stop from belittling me.*
- Hide the photos and, just before going out, say all the spell words.

939

A MOVE-YOUR-ASS RITUAL FOR A LAZY BOSS OR COLLEAGUE WHOSE WORK YOU HAVE TO DO

You will need:

Two large red candles

Timing:

Monday morning before work, and thereafter every morning

The Spell

- Write the name of the lazy person invisibly on the first candle, top to bottom on one side. On the other side trace invisibly, MOVE YOUR ASS, using your dominant hand's index finger.
- Light the candle, blow into the flame vigorously three times without putting it out and, between each blow, say, *Move your ass, this cannot pass; lazy bones always moans. No more shirking I do say, move your ass and I mean today!*
- Blow out the candle.
- Each morning before work, relight the candle and repeat the spell.
- When the candle is almost burned through, light it, light another red candle from it, and blow out the first candle, using the new candle for the spell until the situation drastically improves (maybe in an unexpected but good way).

WHEN YOU KNOW SOMEONE IS WISHING YOU ILL, BUT YOU HAVE TO SEE THAT PERSON REGULARLY

You will need:

A pair of glasses, even if you don't wear them, or a shiny item with a lid (like a makeup mirror) that will not attract attention

A small white cloth

A pair of chopsticks to use as magick wands

Timing:

Saturday, just before sunset

The Spell

- Polish the glasses or the closed shiny item counterclockwise, saying nine times, *[Name], returning to you what is yours, sent to me with malicious force, I do not wish to receive this pain, you are barred from inflicting it on me again.*
- Pass the chopsticks simultaneously over the glasses/shiny item in spirals, saying nine times, *Your ill intent is taken away, banned from my life by night and day. Be gone spite by day or night.*
- Cross the chopsticks above the glasses/shiny item and keep it facing outward toward your front door, the shiny item with the lid up as a shield or if the ill intentions are at work, set the glasses/shiny item in front of you in your workspace.

941

A WHEEL OF FORTUNE CARD RITUAL FOR MAKING MONEY IN REAL ESTATE

You will need:

The Wheel of Fortune card in the center of a vertical row with the Ace of Pentacles at the bottom and the Ten of Pentacles at the top
Ten golden-colored coins

Timing:
Saturday

The Spell

- No tarot knowledge is needed, but use a pack with illustrated minor cards Ace to Ten.
- Touch the Ace, saying, *From small beginnings do great things grow, I move toward wealth though it may be slow.*
- Put the first coin down to start a circle around the Wheel of Fortune, saying, *Year by year will my properties increase, more acquisitions without cease.*
- Touch the Ten of Pentacles, saying, *Within ten years I will attain, prosperity through property as more I gain.*
- Repeat the spell cycle, touching the Ace again, saying the first set of spell words, then add another coin clockwise, repeating the second set of spell words. Touch the Ten and say the third set of spell words once more. Continue the spell until you have ten coins in the circle.
- Set the Ace and the Ten on either side of the Wheel. Finally, bury the coins in front of your first property acquisition.

942

A WORLD CARD RITUAL TO BRING TRAVEL INTO YOUR LIFE IF YOU HAVE ITCHY FEET

You will need:

The World card
The Eight of Wands, the swift movement card
The Six of Wands, the riding home in victory card
A feather and a lavender or frankincense incense cone on a heatproof dish

Timing:
Wednesday afternoon

The Spell

- Make a triangle with the World at the top, the Eight of Wands at the bottom left, and the Six of Wands at the bottom right.
- Light the incense cone and, holding it in your dominant hand, waft the smoke using the feather over the Eight of Wands, saying, *I would go, I have itchy feet, up and flying, adventures to greet.*
- Wave the smoke over the World card with the feather, saying, *The world awaits, I cannot be late. No delay, I'm on my way.*
- Move the incense to the Six of Wands, again wafting the incense over it, saying, *Home in victory, but not to stay. The World it calls me, come out and play.*
- Leave the incense in the center of the triangle and plan your first or next trip.

943

A SUN, MOON, AND STAR CARD RITUAL TO GET A PLACE ON A REALITY TV OR TALENT SHOW

You will need:

The Moon card, for dreams fulfilled and that extra ingredient of talent, to the left in a horizontal row

The Sun card, for success and getting noticed positively, in the center

The Star Card, for fame and fortune, to the right.

A diamond stud earring on top of the Star card

A gold earring on top of the Sun

A silver earring on top of the Moon

A little gold bag

Timing:

Before you send in your audition tape

The Spell

- Hold the diamond, saying, *Star of Fortune make me shine.*
- Put it in the bag.
- Hold the gold earring, saying, *Sun of Success, make success mine.*
- Put it in the bag.
- Hold the silver earring, saying, *Moon of Dreams, make this dream mine that I may shine.*
- Put it in the bag, close the bag, and shake it three times, repeating all the spell words in order three times.
- Put the cards and the bag on top of your audition tape and take the bag along with you to auditions.

944

TO START A SUCCESSFUL BUSINESS FROM SCRATCH

You will need:

The Magician, for the successful entrepreneur, at the top of a visualized square

The Ace of Wands, for beginning a venture, on the left side

The Eight of Pentacles, for making your own gold, at the bottom

The Nine of Pentacles, for financial independence businesswise, on the right side

Timing:

Thursday around noon

The Spell

- Move your hands, the left clockwise, the right counter-clockwise, over the Magician, a few centimeters above, saying, *Business grow rapidly, spread influence instantly, that I will succeed beyond all expectations.*
- Put the Magician under the Ace of Wands. Move your hands over the Ace card, saying, *That this will bring gold from every direction.*
- Put the Ace of Wands and the Magician under the Eight of Pentacles.
- Move your hands as before over the Eight, saying, *That my business will grow without hesitation.*
- Put the first three cards under the Nine of Pentacles, then move your hands over the Nine of Pentacles, saying, *Three by three, prosperity comes to me. I have removed all barriers, success will be.*
- Keep the four cards with business papers for forty-eight hours.

945

TAROT LOVE CARDS FOR RESTORING TRUST AND REBUILDING A SHATTERED RELATIONSHIP

You will need:

A green candle
The King and Queen of Cups, for lasting love
The Prince and Princess of Cups (even for a same-sex relationship), love cards for rebuilding trust
Rose petals or rose potpourri

Timing:

Friday around sunset

The Spell

- Light the candle and place the Queen card behind it to the left and the King behind it to the right.
- Put the Princess card in front of the candle to the left and the Prince card to the right, parallel with the King and Queen.
- Begin scattering the petals as a pathway from the Princess to the Queen, saying, *Step by step, our love remains. We will learn to trust again.*
- Repeat the spell words and actions, scattering petals from the Prince to the King.
- Scatter a circle of petals to enclose the four cards and the candle, counterclockwise, starting at the Princess, saying, *'Round us grows the circle of trust. The future waits golden, the past is dust.*
- Remove the Prince and Princess cards and let the candle burn.

946

A CUPS AND SWORDS RITUAL TO REMOVE THE DESTRUCTIVE EFFECTS OF A LOVE RIVAL WHO IS TRYING TO BREAK UP THE RELATIONSHIP BETWEEN YOU AND YOUR PARTNER

You will need:

The Lovers Card, representing united love
A Prince or Princess of Swords, representing a destructive rival, set horizontally across the Lovers card
A letter opener

Timing:

Tuesday at sunset

The Spell

- Put the letter opener, diagonally, blade down, over the Princess card, saying, *Though you,* [name], *intrude upon our lives, your efforts to split us will not thrive. Our love is strong and will survive.*
- Remove the letter opener and the Princess card and put the Princess card well away from the Lovers card.
- Make a diagonal cross in the air over the Princess card with the letter opener, saying, *Removed forever from our lives, we two are one. Your interference now is done, be gone.*
- Put the Princess card facedown with the letter opener across it diagonally, blade pointing up, and leave it there for twenty-four hours. Put the Lovers card where light will shine on it.

947

AN EMPEROR AND EMPRESS CARD FERTILITY RITUAL

You will need:

Emperor and Empress cards, representing parents, the Empress to the left and the Emperor to the right

The Prince or Princess of Pentacles, to represent a healthy child, in the center, according to whether you want a boy or a girl

Two small green candles, one behind the Empress card and the other behind the Emperor

A larger green candle, in the center of the two candles, behind the Prince or Princess card

Timing:

Early Sunday morning

The Spell

- Light the Empress candle, saying, *Two hearts, two souls, two minds as one. We ask that to us a babe may come.*
- Light the Emperor candle from the Empress candle, saying the same spell words.
- Hold both flames in the central candle, saying, *Baby, we call you in this light. Join our family, bring us delight.*
- Move the Emperor and Empress cards so they are side by side in front of the middle candle.
- Put the Princess card on top, so it overlaps both.
- Blow out the outer candles, saying, *No more two but three shall we be. Dear baby, join our family.*
- Let the central candle burn.

948

A QUEEN OF CUPS AND KING OF WANDS TWIN SOUL HOLY GRAIL LOVE DEDICATION

You will need:

A Queen of Cups, to represent the female Grail cup symbol in the traditional Grail ceremony, set to the left

A King of Wands, to represent the traditional male lance or wand symbol in the Grail ceremony, set to the right

A smooth stick pointed at one end to act as a wand or lance

A glass goblet or large wineglass, half-filled with wine or dark fruit juice

Timing:

Saturday at midnight

The Spell

- Touch the Queen card with the wand, saying, *As cup to wand, so our love stands. Twin soul, I greet you, forever will our love be true.*
- Hold the goblet above the King card, saying the same spell words.
- Plunge the wand into the goblet, saying, *As Grail to lance, twin soul, I greet you. Forever will our love be true.*
- Remove the wand and drink a little of the wine/juice, pouring the rest on the ground outdoors.
- Sleep with both cards under your pillow.

949

A TOWER OF FREEDOM CARD RITUAL IF YOU CAN'T LET GO OF A LOVE WHO HAS DESERTED OR BETRAYED YOU

You will need:

The Tower of Freedom card, representing freedom from restrictions but not without pain
A dark candle behind the Tower
The four Aces, two on either side of the Tower: Pentacles, for a new practical start; Cups, for a new love; Wands, for new ventures; and Swords, to cut free
Four white candles behind the four Aces

Timing:
Wednesday, at 10 p.m.

The Spell

- Light the dark candle, saying, *No more of you, lover untrue.*
- Blow out the candle, saying, *Gone from my heart, old love depart.*
- Light the Pentacles candle, saying, *Just one step at a time, to a life that's truly mine.*
- Light the Cups candle, saying, *New love when my heart is whole, who will cherish me, mind, body, soul.*
- Light the Wands candle, saying, *New adventures, exciting ventures.*
- Light the Swords candle, saying, *Hardest of all, but I walk tall. I cut the ties to you, good-bye.*
- Clap your hands fast over each of the four candles and let them burn.

950

A JUSTICE CARD RITUAL TO RID YOU OF THE PAIN OF A LONG-AGO ABUSE OR INJUSTICE

You will need:

The Justice card, for resolving what is unfair, even many years later, to the left
Sand in a small bowl
A filter funnel
An empty bowl
The Judgment card, for freeing yourself of old anger and resentment, to the right
The Temperance card, for restoring balance to your life, in the middle

Timing:
Saturday, in fading light

The Spell

- Touch Justice, saying, *What was done was so unjust, but let it go I must. For Justice will one day be done, to the wicked one.*
- Pour some sand into the filter.
- When the sand has filtered through to the bowl below, touch Judgment, repeating the spell words.
- Pour more sand into the filter.
- When that sand is gone, touch Temperance, saying, *This injustice has been eating me, but Justice will one day be done to the wicked one.*
- Pour the remaining sand in the filter. When it has trickled into the bowl, take the sand and empty it where nothing grows, repeating, *One day justice will be done, to the wicked one.*

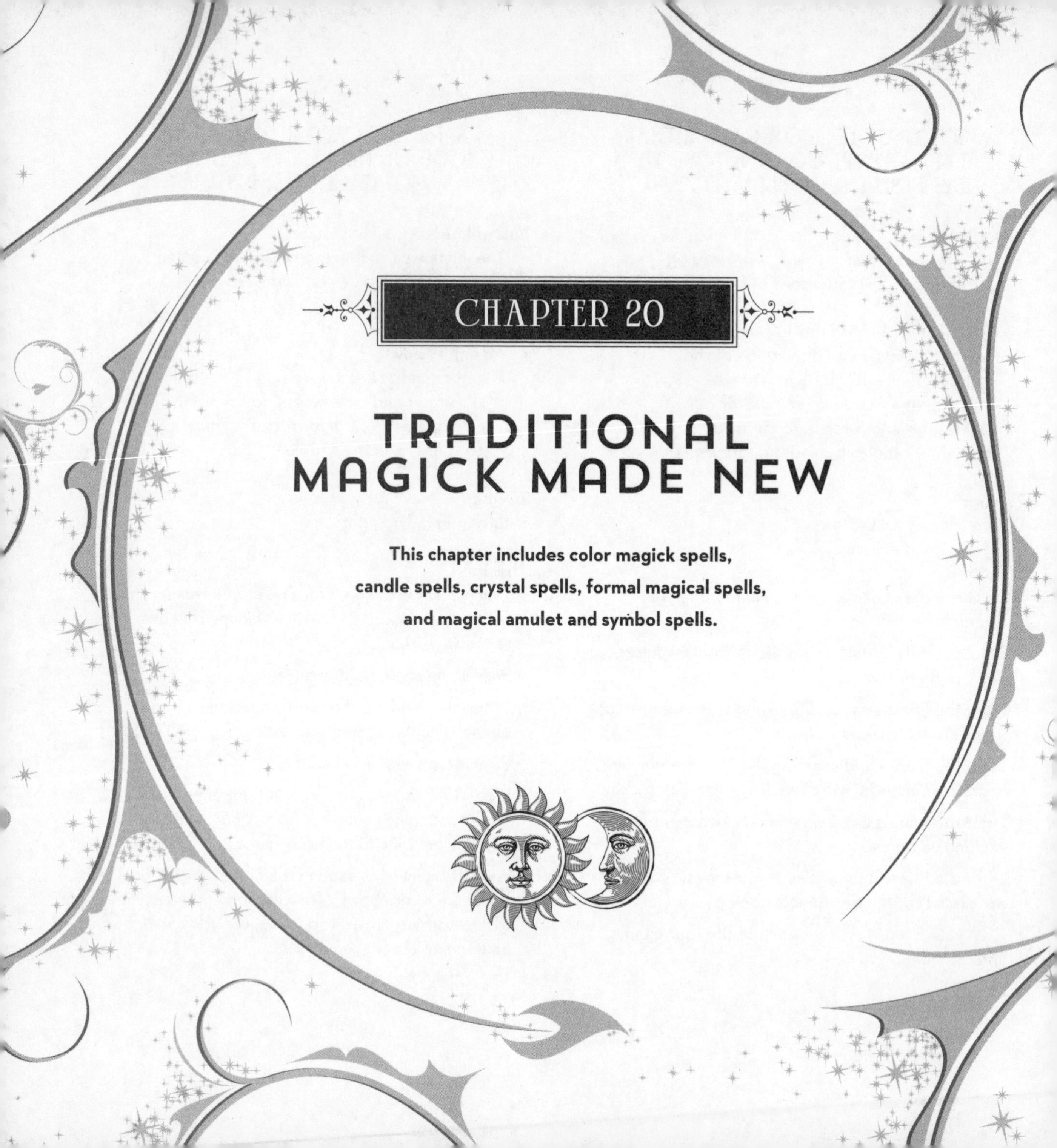

CHAPTER 20

TRADITIONAL MAGICK MADE NEW

This chapter includes color magick spells, candle spells, crystal spells, formal magical spells, and magical amulet and symbol spells.

951

A RED AND GREEN RITUAL FOR CALMING DOWN A PERSON WHO IS ALWAYS ANGRY

You will need:

A red scarf, the color of anger
A small item belonging to the angry person that he will not miss or something he has used, like a teaspoon
A green scarf, the color of gentleness

Timing:
Friday, early

The Spell

- Spread out the red scarf and on it put the item belonging to the angry person, saying, *Red rag to a bull, why must you,* [name], *always pull an angry face? It's a disgrace when you rant and rave. When I tie up your anger, you'll not be so brave.*
- Tie the scarf in nine knots and shake the scarf nine times, saying, *Always, always shouting loud, really nothing to be proud; of your yelling and bombast, this anger really cannot last.*
- Wrap the green scarf around the red one to enclose it, and knot it six times, saying, *Fury cease, be at peace, this has been fixed on the count of six: 1, 2, 3, 4, 5, 6.*
- Gently shake the scarves six times and put them away in a drawer.

952

A BLUE BACKGROUND COLOR SPELL FOR A HARMONIOUS AND SAFE PARTY FOR TEENAGERS AT YOUR HOME

You will need:

Six soft-blue candles, set around the main party room
Six pale-blue ribbons, one in front of each candle

Timing:
An hour or two before the party begins

The Spell

- Light each candle in turn, saying, *Bring harmony, may this party pass happily, safely, and joyfully. May* [name teenager(s)] *and my home be enfolded in security.*
- Let the candles burn until just before the party, then blow them out, saying the spell words for each.
- Tie the ribbons together, repeating the spell words five times, and hang them as a decoration in the party room.

953

AN ORANGE FLOWER AND SPICE RITUAL TO SPICE UP A DATE AT HOME IF YOUR WOULD-BE PARTNER LACKS PASSION

You will need:

Four small orange flowers
A bowl
An orange-colored spice, such as saffron, cinnamon, turmeric, or curry powder
An orange pepper, chopped small and deseeded
Four small orange paper or cloth bags

Timing:

An hour before your date arrives

The Spell

- Pluck the petals one by one and put them in the bowl, saying, *Lover, do not be so slow, passion's fun, don't you know. Warmer be, filled with spice, then this date will be twice as nice.*
- Add some spice and chopped pepper to the bowl, repeating the spell words.
- Swirl the bowl four times, twice in each direction, saying, *Liven up, loosen up, don't be so sedate. Spice is nice, let's heat the mood, a spicy date is passion's food.*
- Divide the mix among the four bags, tie, and shake each one, then hide them in the four corners of the room where you will eat or relax.
- Add the remaining spice and pepper to the meal.

954

A SPEEDY YELLOW RITUAL FOR GETTING MOVING ON A DAY YOU DON'T WANT TO GET OUT OF BED

You will need:

Five yellow candles in a row
A yellow garment or scarf

Timing:

When you get out of bed

The Spell

- Light the first candle, saying as fast as you can, *Feeling gloomy, doom, and grumps; just can't face life's humps and bumps.*
- Light the second candle, saying even faster, *Come on, sun, come creeping through, if I can get up, so can you.*
- Light the third candle, saying faster still, *Crack my face with a smile, so folks don't see me and run a mile.*
- Light the fourth candle, saying very fast, *Good cheer, nearly here, in my life, stuff the strife.*
- Light the fifth candle, saying fastest of all, *Good day ahead, so much to see. Hello world, welcome me.*
- Blow out the candles, saying, *Five, four, three, two, one; watch out, life, here I come.*
- Toss the garment in the air five times, repeating the final spell words five times.
- Get ready for your day at top speed and wear the yellow item.
- As you leave home, say, *And a very good morning to you all.*

955

A BLACK AND WHITE RITUAL TO GET YOUR POINT ACROSS ONCE AND FOR ALL TO A STUBBORN COLLEAGUE, BOSS, FAMILY MEMBER, OR FRIEND

You will need:

Ten small round black stones
Ten small pointed white stones
A sieve or a colander
A drawstring bag or purse

Timing:

The evening before the confrontation

The Spell

- Toss all the stones in the sieve, saying, *Black and white, clear as day, you simply cannot have your way.*
- Remove the black stones from the sieve, saying, *Black and white, I am right. Just you, [name], listen to what I say. I'll get through to you, come what may.*
- Leave the black stones on the way to work or outside the house and carry the white ones in a bag or purse, touching them before making your statement.

956

A PINK RITUAL TO HELP A CHILD OR TEENAGER RESOLVE THE HURT OF A BITTER DIVORCE WHEN THE OTHER PARENT HAS GONE AWAY

You will need:

A ball of pink modeling clay, pink representing reconciliation
A pink scarf
A small basket
A body of water

Timing:

When the child is grieving

The Spell

- Make two figures out of modeling clay, representing the parents, plus one for each child.
- Set the parent figure who has gone away apart from the others, saying as you hold it, *You are angry, you are cold, yet we send love as you I hold. A parent always you will be, don't cut off your family.*
- Bring the figures together and wrap them together in the scarf with a loose knot, saying, *Grow warm again, the link regain, your child(ren) miss you in their life. Let go of bitterness and strife.*
- Leave the wrapped figures for twenty-four hours in a warm place, then untie the scarf, place the figures in the basket, and let it sail away on water, saying, *I set you free from obligations due to me, but return to see your family.*
- Leave the scarf in a drawer near the front door.

957

A SILVER MOON RITUAL TO BRING GOOD LUCK FOR AN ADULT CHILD'S FIRST JOB, FIRST MAJOR JOURNEY, OR FIRST DAY AT COLLEGE

You will need:

A small branch of a tree, spray-painted silver, the color of the moon and good fortune

A small silver-colored bell, placed in front of the tree

Three silver candles in a triangle around the tree, with the bell in the middle of the triangle

Small silver paper lucky horseshoes, or other small silver paper or foil decorations, hung from the tree branches, plus one real silver horseshoe or other lucky charm.

Timing:

Full moon before the big event, after dark indoors or out

The Spell

- Ring the bell softly three times, saying three times, *Silver bells bring luck to you,* [name], *now and for your whole life through.*
- Light each candle, starting from the top and moving counterclockwise while repeating the spell words for each one.
- Touch each horseshoe, saying, *Silvery fortune follow you,* [name], *now and for your whole life through.*
- Blow out the candles, saying, [Name], *I send good luck to you as you begin your new journey.*
- Ring the bell three times.
- Leave everything in place until morning and give the adult child the real horseshoe charm on the morning of the big adventure.

958

A COLOR-MIXING RITUAL SO EVERYONE WILL GET ALONG WELL AT AN IMPORTANT FAMILY CELEBRATION

You will need:

Child's poster paints in red, yellow, and blue (primary colors) and a paintbrush

A sheet of white paper

A small palette

Timing:

A few hours before the event

The Spell

- Paint stick people in a circle, one for each significant person coming to the celebration, using the three colors alternately—red, yellow, and blue—around the circle, naming each person and saying, *Mix and blend from day's beginning to day's end. Be cheerful, considerate and polite, that this party/wedding/occasion* [name it] *will bring delight, and not a single fight!*
- Around the outside of the circle, paint a small circle, level with each person, first in orange by mixing on the palette red and yellow, then green by mixing yellow and blue, and finally purple by mixing blue and red. Continue painting the outer circle in alternating orange, green, and purple until you have completed it.
- Now say, *All are harmonized beautifully, that bright and peaceful all shall be.*
- Let the paper dry and pin it where it cannot be seen behind some furniture or in a closed bag at the venue.

959

A GREEN TWIN SOUL COLOR RITUAL FOR LINKING ONLINE LOVERS SO YOU CAN BE TOGETHER IN REAL LIFE BEFORE TOO LONG

You will need:

Two pictures, one of each of you printed from the Internet
A blue ribbon, for fidelity
A yellow ribbon, for happiness
A green ribbon (blue and yellow mixed), for twin soul love

Timing:
Friday, before sunset

The Spell

- Put the two pictures face-to-face, saying, *Blue for love, fidelity, love I pledge eternally; soon together may we be.*
- Place the blue ribbon across the picture and then the yellow one next to it, saying, *Yellow brings joy, for our tomorrow, long days together without sorrow.*
- Finally, put the green ribbon across the other two, saying, *Yellow and blue together green does make. Twin soul, never shall we forsake the other; forever true, green, yellow, and faithful blue.*
- Braid the three ribbons around the picture and keep it next to your computer whenever you speak.

960

A GRAY RITUAL FOR KEEPING A SECRET WHEN YOU WANT TO TELL THE WORLD

You will need:

A piece of gray paper
A gray-colored pen
A deep, fireproof dish, filled with sand or soil

Timing:
Saturday, as twilight falls

The Spell

- On the paper, write the secret with the gray pen so it cannot be seen.
- Set fire to it (carefully) in the dish, saying, *A secret never to be spoken, words that must not be told. Hard to keep this secret, but now gray ash enfolds.*
- Bury the ash, still in the soil, after dark in silence where nothing grows.

961

MAKING A MAGICAL CANDLE SO YOUR WISHES COME TRUE

You will need:

A sheet of beeswax (approximately 16 x 8 inches), available at craft stores or online
A palette knife or letter opener
A square, braided wick
A hair dryer

Timing:
Friday

The Spell

- Score a ditch toward the horizontal end of the beeswax sheet, about an eighth of an inch from the edge of the wax. Lay the wick in the ditch so its end is level with the bottom of the candle and the wick extends about a thumb's length past the top. Cut the wick when the candle is finished to a thumbnail height. Gently warm but do not melt the wax.
- Crease the edge of the beeswax sheet over the wick and press firmly so that it is well sealed, making the first roll very tight. When finished rolling, press the outer edge of the candle gently but firmly to seal the candle, warming the wax gently, if necessary. Do the same with the bottom.
- Continuously voice your dearest wish as you make the candle. As you seal the candle, say, *So is this wish sealed within the wax*. Light the candle, saying, *As this candle burns, so melt all obstacles in the way of the fulfillment of my dearest wish.*
- Bury the melted wax beneath a thriving plant.

962

A BEESWAX CANDLE RITUAL FOR CONCEIVING A CHILD IF YOU HAVE TRIED MANY TIMES AND HAD NO SUCCESS

You will need:

Two beeswax candles on a small, round, heatproof tray with a space between them, store-bought if you wish (secure the candles by dropping melted wax from another candle where they will stand on the tray)
A thin screwdriver or letter opener

Timing:
At night, according to when conception is most likely in your hormonal cycle.

The Spell

- Light the left-hand candle, saying, *May fertility flow between us that this night we may know the joy of conceiving our beloved child.*
- Light the second candle, repeating the spell words.
- As the candles melt, in the cooling pool of wax draw an image of a baby or write, BABY, YOU ARE WELCOME.
- Blow out the candles, and when the wax is cool, carefully extract the wax containing the words or image and wrap it in a white cloth.
- Make love.
- Burn the other two candles the next morning and dispose of the wax.

963

A SECRET LOVE RITUAL TO RESTORE HAPPINESS TO A FAILING RELATIONSHIP

You will need:

A hand-rolled beeswax candle, as described in spell 962
Dried rosemary or thyme

Timing:

Saturday, at twilight

The Spell

- Before you roll your candle, scatter a few pieces of rosemary or thyme, herbs for love restored, on the wax, starting an inch or two from the wick and saying, *Bring back the loving joy, the closeness we once shared. For I know, though you never show, the love that is buried there.*
- When the candle is burned through, hold it and repeat the spell words.
- Light the candle in your lover's presence or, if she has gone away, next to a photo of her.

Note: **When doing a candle spell, never leave candles unattended. Put handmade candles in a deep bowl of sand or soil, or if you are using their wax as part of the spell, on a large flat slate or heatproof tray as they can occasionally spit a bit. There are many good candlemaking sites on the Internet.**

964

A TWELVE-CANDLE RITUAL TO RESTORE PROSPERITY TO YOUR LIFE AFTER A STOCK MARKET CRASH OR OTHER MAJOR FINANCIAL SETBACK

You will need:

Twelve small white candles in a circle, positioned like the twelve hours of a clock
Three gold candles in the center
Twelve gold-colored coins, placed around the gold candles in a circle

Timing:

Three days, at dusk

The Spell

- On day 1, light the first gold candle, saying twelve times, *Prosperity grow, it shall be so.*
- Beginning with the white candle in the twelve o'clock position, light all twelve white candles clockwise, saying once very slowly as you light them, *One for joy; two for gladness; three and four to banish sadness; five and six prosperity; seven, eight, nine, come soon to me; ten for increase; eleven the same; abundance returns as it I name.*
- Blow out all the candles, saying as you do so: *12, 11, 10, 9, 8, 7, 6, 5, 4, 3, 2, 1, bad times be gone.*
- On day 2, light two gold candles and repeat the spell exactly.
- On day 3, light all three gold candles and again repeat the spell words and actions but let all the candles burn through.
- Save the coins.

965

A TWENTY-FOUR-HOUR CANDLE VIGIL IF SOMEONE IS VERY ILL AND YOU ARE AWAKE, WAITING FOR NEWS

Note: You can also adapt this spell for a twelve-hour vigil and share it with others.

You will need:

Twenty-four long-burning tea lights in a circle (have a supple of spares for those that burn through)

A photo of the person or the person's name written in green ink on white paper

Timing:

Every hour on the hour

The Spell

- Light the first tea light, name the person, and say, *I send you blessings at this hour, that your illness/affliction/danger may pass and you be restored to health or safety or know a peaceful passing.*
- Call on God/the Goddess/your personal focus of worship or any angels.
- Let the light burn while you pray, meditate in the flame, or keep yourself busy.
- On the second hour, light the second tea light and say the same spell words, each hour lighting a new tea light.
- Replace any that are burned with new ones, so after twenty-four or twelve hours all are alight.
- Let them burn. When the last one goes out, say, *The light of hope burns still in my/our hearts, never to be dimmed. Blessings to you at this hour.*

966

A SEVEN-WICK CANDLE RITUAL FOR INCREASING YOUR CHANCES OF BEING OFFERED THE PROMOTION YOU DESERVE, WHEN THERE IS BEHIND-THE-SCENES FAVORITISM

You will need:

A blue or white candle with seven wicks

Timing:

Every evening for seven days, starting on Thursday

The Spell

- On evening 1, light the first wick and blow into it softly three times, saying between each breath, *I deserve advancement, I merit promotion. Secret utterings, unfair mutterings, private commotions shall not bar my way.*
- Blow out the wick, saying, *Promotion shall be mine. I blow away unfair favoritism, hidden appeals, nepotism, and dodgy deals. My true worth I do reveal.*
- On evening 2, light two wicks, repeating the same spell words and actions for each wick lighting and extinguishing.
- Continue lighting an extra wick each evening, saying the spell words and doing the actions as you light and blow out each wick in turn.
- On evening 7, leave all the wicks alight until the candle is burned.
- When it is burned through, say, *Favoritism, nepotism, are melted away. I will get this promotion, come what may.*

967

A ROSE-SCENTED CANDLE RITUAL FOR TOLERANCE AND PATIENCE IF YOU HAVE TO CARE FOR A DIFFICULT, SICK, OR FRAIL ELDERLY RELATIVE

You will need:

A rose-scented candle
A bottle of rose essential oil

Timing:
Friday, as dawn breaks

The Spell

- Hold the candle and say, *Rose of gentle love and kindness, release patience in me, that I may speak and act to* [name] *tolerantly.*
- Light the candle and lift the oil so light shines through it, repeating the spell words.
- Let the candle burn and leave the oil where the light will reflect into it (but not too near the flame).
- When the candle is burned through, put a drop of oil on your brow, at the center of your throat, and on your two inner wrists points for your heart, repeating the spell words each time.
- When you get stressed or impatient with the difficult person, anoint yourself with the oil on your brow, throat, and inner wrist pulse points, saying the spell words.
- Once a week, repeat the spell to re-empower the oil.

968

A LEMON-SCENTED CANDLE RITUAL TO CLEANSE A HOME AFTER A BAD QUARREL THAT KEEPS RE-ERUPTING

You will need:

A lemon-scented candle in a deep heatproof holder that can be carried, set in the middle of the home
A letter opener, a small screwdriver, or a palette knife

Timing:
Seven days, starting on a Friday

The Spell

- Score the candle in seven places, an equal distance apart.
- Light the candle and raise it, saying, *Lemon, take away harsh words and anger, let this quarrel no longer linger. Within these walls, cleanse and purify all.*
- Walk around the whole house from back to front, upstairs and then downstairs, and return to the center of the house, repeating the spell words continuously.
- Let the first seventh of the candle burn away, then blow out the candle, saying, *Peace, anger cease. Happiness restore as it was before.*
- Repeat the spell exactly for six more nights until the candle is burned away.
- If you still feel negativity, leave half a lemon in the center of the home, until it dries out, then throw it away.

969

A SAGE BEESWAX CANDLE RITUAL IF A FAMILY MEMBER OR PARTNER IS BEHAVING BADLY, BUT YOU DON'T WANT TO GIVE UP ON THAT PERSON

You will need:

A beeswax candle, either store-bought or handmade
A hair dryer
Dried sage or rosemary
A heatproof bowl, filled with sand or soil

Timing:

Thursday evening

The Spell

- Warm the candle very gently with the hair dryer to soften the wax before lighting and then roll it in the plate of dried herbs, saying, [Name], *be wise, cautious be, stop this stupidity. By the power of sage, act your age.*
- Put the candle in a heatproof bowl of sand or soil, as it can spit a bit toward the burning end, and light it, saying, [Name], *so melts away your thoughtlessness, your carelessness and recklessness. Return to the fold. To act the fool, you're far too old. Common sense you lack, get it back. Consider yourself told!*
- Blow out the candle, relight it, and when it is three-quarters burned, blow it out and bury it along with any melted wax still in the sand or soil, saying, *Enough, the candle's snuffed. Before too late, embrace your fate by the power of sage. Please act your age!*

970

A LEAVE-US-ALONE SPELL IF YOUR PARTNER'S BEST FRIEND OR YOURS ALWAYS TAGS ALONG

You will need:

An red or white entwined lovers' candle, if possible (available online and from candle stores), or two matching red candles in matching holders, side by side
A small brown or gray candle, placed either close to the right of the entwined lovers' candle or squeezed between the matching candles

Timing:

Just after the best friend has left you

The Spell

- Light the entwined or twin candles, saying, *Two's company, three's a crowd. Please give us space,* [name], *because that's allowed.*
- Light the friend's candle, name the friend, and say, *Welcome you are, but not 24/7. Give us a break, that would be heaven.*
- Now move the friend's candle as far as possible away from yours, blow it out, and relight it, saying, *Your light is too bright, it dazzles our sight. So sometimes keep your distance, can't you feel our resistance? See you again, but not too soon. That way good friends we can remain, no more strain.*
- Let the candles burn through.

971

A CLEAR QUARTZ CRYSTAL RITUAL TO ATTRACT GOOD CUSTOMERS AND KEEP AWAY THIEVES AND TROUBLEMAKERS

You will need:

Two pointed gray smoky quartz crystals
Eight quartz crystals, pointed at one end and a sparkling yellow citrine

Timing:

Monday morning, on the business or company premises before anyone is around

The Spell

- Hold a gray crystal, point facing out, in each hand, face the door, and say, *Keep away all with ill intent, barred shall you be. Crystals be guardians of this place, drive away negativity.*
- Set the two gray crystal points just inside the main door, about two feet apart, points facing outward to the street.
- Hold the clear crystals and the citrine in your open cupped hands, saying, *Enter all with good intent, welcome shall you be. Follow the crystal path and bring in prosperity.*
- Set the clear crystals in pairs at regular intervals, one on either side of the path that customers take to the cash registers or point of service.
- If you have a shop window, hide an extra crystal point on each side of the display, facing inward.
- Put the citrine in the cash register or near the computer where you process orders.
- Wash the crystals weekly, except the citrine, which does not need cleansing.

972

A SEVEN OBSIDIAN ARROWS CRYSTAL RITUAL TO DRAW TO YOU THE RIGHT EMPLOYMENT OPPORTUNITIES IF YOU HAVE BEEN UNEMPLOYED FOR A LONG TIME

You will need:

Seven obsidian arrows, placed in a circle with points facing outward
A piece of white paper on which you have written in black the job you want or a printout of a post of one for which you have applied

Timing:

Thursday, around noon, and any time for the next seven days

The Spell

- Read the job specifications aloud and then put the paper, facing up, inside the obsidian circle.
- Gently touch the point of each arrow, moving clockwise and starting with the one farthest away, saying seven times for each one, *Arrows fly swift and swift return.*
- After three days, turn the arrows to face inward, again repeating seven times as you touch each arrow, *Arrows fly swift and swift return.*
- On the seventh day, go around the circle, alternately placing four arrows pointing outward and three inward.
- On day 8, burn the paper. Keep the seven arrows in a bag and take the bag to interviews.

973

AN AMETRINE RITUAL FOR HELPING A PROSPECTIVE NEW PARTNER TO WARM TO YOUR CHILDREN FROM A PREVIOUS RELATIONSHIP

You will need:

A yellow candle, to the left
A yellow citrine, in front of the yellow candle
A purple candle, to the right
A purple amethyst, in front of the purple candle
An ametrine, combining yellow citrine with gentle amethyst, set between the other two

Timing:

Before a meeting between your prospective partner and your children

The Spell

- Light the yellow candle and hold the citrine to it, saying, *Warmed be, melt away any hostility, that you,* [name prospective partner], *will become good friends with my family.*
- Light the purple candle from the yellow one.
- Pick up the citrine and the amethyst and hold them to the light of the purple candle, repeating the spell words.
- Add the ametrine to your hands and pass all three in front of, first, the yellow candle, then the purple candle, saying, *Purple and yellow, yes, opposites can blend, and you and my family will become friends.*
- Blow out both candles together.
- Arrange a meeting at your home. Relight the two candles and set the three crystals in a triangle around them with the ametrine at the top.

974

A LEMON CHRYSOPRASE RITUAL TO BREAK A HEX PUT ON YOU IN ANGER THAT HAS MADE YOU JITTERY

You will need:

A lemon or green chrysoprase crystal
A small plastic container
Fresh lemon juice
A red permanent marker

Timing:

Saturday, after dark

The Spell

- Hold the lemon chrysoprase in your dominant hand and move your other hand to enclose the crystal, saying, *Hex, you shall no more be free.* [Name perpetrator], *in your power shall I no longer be.*
- In the container, pour a little lemon juice and add the crystal, saying, *Cleansed may I be from your hexing, you shall longer me be vexing. Frozen in activity, suspended for perpetuity.*
- Add more lemon juice and some water until the container is full. Seal it, draw a red diagonal cross over the lid, and put it in the coldest part of the freezer.
- Shut the door, saying, *Hex, locked away shall you be, no more shall I your malice see. The hex is broken.*
- Bury the container with the crystal after three months.

975

A RED GARNET RITUAL TO PROTECT YOURSELF FROM EMOTIONAL VAMPIRES

You will need:

A dark-red candle
A red garnet on a chain long enough to be at heart level (it does not need to be gem quality)
Garlic powder (open the windows, as burning garlic smells foul)

Timing:

Tuesday, after dark

The Spell

- Light the candle and, holding the garnet on the chain above the candle, swing the garnet all around the candle in nine counterclockwise spirals, saying, *No more do I give my energies away, no more shall vampires* [name the current one] *into my mind stray. No longer intrude through my sympathies, be gone with you and your miseries.*
- Sprinkle just a grain or two of garlic in the candle and swing the garnet nine more times counterclockwise while repeating the spell words.
- Extinguish the candle and hold the garnet over your heart, saying the spell words again.
- Dispose of the candle and put on the garnet.
- When you feel under attack, touch the garnet and say the spell words in your mind.
- Spiral the garnet around a dark-red candle nine times counterclockwise monthly.

976

A GOLDSTONE RITUAL FOR WINNING COMPETITIONS INVOLVING SKILL

You will need:

A goldstone
A small deep bowl, almost filled with gold-colored coins of any denomination, mixed with small gold-foil stars
A small gold-colored purse or bag

Timing:

The night before the day of entering or going to a competition

The Spell

- Hold the goldstone in your dominant hand, saying, *Goldstone, grow luckier by the hour, increase in power, that my skill will rich rewards on me shower.*
- Immerse the goldstone in the coins and stars, repeat the spell words, and leave the goldstone in the bowl overnight.
- Before entering or going to the competition, pull the goldstone out of the bowl. Take a small handful of coins and stars and put them in the bag with the goldstone, shake the bag nine times, and say the spell words very fast nine times.
- After the competition, return the goldstone, coins, and stars to the bowl.
- Always use the same goldstone, as its powers will accumulate over the weeks and months.

977

A WHITE AND BLUE HOWLITE RITUAL FOR SELLING A HOUSE FAST IN A BUYER'S MARKET

You will need:

A small ceramic bowl
Six small pieces of blue howlite
One piece of white howlite
A rose or frankincense incense stick

Timing:

Before an open house

The Spell

- Shake the bowl seven times fast, saying seven times, *Fast will this sale be, folks will flock to this property. Right price, right location, it will sell, no hesitation.*
- Add the crystals to the bowl, hold it high, and repeat the spell words seven times even faster.
- Light the incense stick and, over the bowl, write in incense smoke as fast as you can the address of the property and SOON IT WILL BE SOLD WITH NO HESITATION.
- Put the white howlite over the lintel of the door to the main living area or, if it won't fit, on the highest object in the room.
- Put the blue howlites on downstairs window ledges (if you have a really small apartment, arrange them along the inside of the largest window ledge). For each, as you set it, say the words, *Soon it will be sold with no hesitation* fast.
- Let the incense burn through.

978

AN OLIVINE RITUAL TO KEEP PEOPLE AT WORK OR AT HOME FROM BORROWING YOUR THINGS WITHOUT PERMISSION

You will need:

Five small green olivines (the cheaper version of sparkling peridot)
A small green bag
A green candle

Timing:

Wednesday, after dark

The Spell

- Hold the olivines in the open hand you do not write with and pass the other hand in clockwise circles an inch or two above the olivines, saying, *Keep safe against those who borrow and never ask. Olivines, this is your task.*
- Put the olivines one after the other into the bag, repeating the spell words for each and close the bag and shake it five times.
- Carry the bag to work, and each morning pass it around your workspace five times clockwise and again five times over any items that are at risk of going missing, saying the spell words five times in your mind.
- Before a "*borrower*" visits your home, pass the bag five times clockwise over any items you know he will want to borrow and say just once for each one, *Attached remain and do not stray. In my home, untouched stay.*

979

A PETRIFIED OR FOSSILIZED WOOD RITUAL IF YOU BUY OR LIVE IN AN OLDER BUILDING

You will need:

Four petrified or fossilized wood stones
A wooden cutting board or slab
A mug of cool peppermint tea (this can be made with a peppermint tea bag, but remove the tea bag after the tea has brewed)

Timing:

Saturday afternoon

The Spell

- Set the four stones in a square on the cutting board and sprinkle around them four clockwise circles of peppermint tea, moving outward and saying four times, *Stand firm, beloved home, remain secure, that many more years you will endure. Structure be safe and lasting sound, so no structural harm is found.*
- Place the four stones indoors in the four corners of your home, downstairs behind furniture or under carpets, saying as you set each one, *From highest roof to beneath the ground, beloved home, stand safe and sound.*
- Throw the rest of the peppermint tea out the front door.

980

A PUMICE STONE RITUAL TO END BITCHING ONCE AND FOR ALL

You will need:

A piece of pumice stone (available at pharmacies and beauty-supply stores)

Timing:

Before the beginning of the workweek or before the social situation where you encounter the bitches

The Spell

- Hold the pumice stone to your lips and into the main hole whisper the name of a bitch, one after the other, until you have named all the bitches.
- Hold the pumice stone and say, *Bitch no more, you know the score.*
- Float the pumice stone (it's the only stone that floats) on a body of water and repeat the spell words until the stone becomes water-logged or disappears from view.

981

AN ALL-PURPOSE FOUR ELEMENTS RITUAL TO CALL WHATEVER YOU MOST NEED IN YOUR LIFE

You will need:

A dish of salt, for Earth

A symbol of what you need, for example a silver key charm for a new home or a silver heart for love

An incense stick for Air, to get things moving in the East

A red candle for Fire power, to fuel the magick in the South

A bowl of water in the West, to blend the other elements

Timing:

During a waxing moon

The Spell

- If you live in the southern hemisphere, cast circles counterclockwise and designate Earth as the direction of the largest landmass as you face it, Air as the nearest mountains or windy plain, Fire as the direction of the equator, and Water the nearest ocean.
- Sprinkle clockwise a circle of salt around the symbol, saying three times, *I call* [name your need] *with the power of Earth.*
- Light the incense and spiral it clockwise around the symbol, saying three times, *I call* [name] *with the power of Air.*
- Light the candle, passing the candle around the symbol and saying three times, *I call* [name] *with the power of Fire.*

982

A PROTECTIVE CIRCLE RITUAL WHENEVER YOU FEEL AFRAID OR ANXIOUS

You will need:

A long pointed quartz crystal, a massage wand, a letter opener, or a pointed smooth stick, held in your dominant hand

Timing:

Before going to a potentially hazardous place or into a toxic situation; thereafter, you can visualize the ritual wherever you are

The Spell

- Hold the wand or blade in an outstretched arm, at a forty-five-degree angle, pointing down, and slowly turn clockwise until you have made a complete circle, picturing light streaming from the blade or wand and creating a circle of light around you.
- As you do so, say, *May the circle be open to all that is from the light, but remain unbroken against harm, day and night.*
- Reverse directions and picture the light returning to the blade or crystal, saying the same spell words.
- Whenever you need protection, subtly circle both index fingers three times clockwise and picture the light circle enclosing you, saying the spell words in your mind. The light will fade when it's no longer needed.

983

A TRIPLE ELEMENTAL CIRCLE TO SHIELD YOURSELF, YOUR HOME, AND LOVED ONES IF LOCAL GANGS ARE THREATENING YOU

You will need:

A photo of you/the family, taken outside your home

Four candles in a circle around the photo—green for North (Earth), yellow for East (Air), red for South (Fire), and blue for West (Water)

A bowl of water in which nine pinches of salt have been mixed, to the left of the picture

A frankincense incense stick, to the right of the picture

Timing:

Tuesday

The Spell

- Light each candle clockwise, green first, saying, *Earth, Air, Fire, and Water, protect my home and family, that we will no more harassed be, within or outside our own front door. I ask no more.*
- Make a clockwise circle of saltwater drops around the outside of the candles, repeating the spell words.
- Light the incense from the green candle, making a smoke circle outside the saltwater circle, saying the spell words again.
- Pass the red candle around the outside the smoke circle, saying, *Three by three, the power I raise, for tranquil nights and secure days. Protect us.*
- Leave the candles burning.

984

A FAIRY GODMOTHER MAGICK WAND RITUAL BEFORE A PARTY OR ANOTHER SOCIAL EVENT WHERE YOU DESPERATELY WANT TO MEET SOMEONE SPECIAL

You will need:

A smooth pointed stick, a long pointed crystal, a crystal massage wand, or a child's play wand

Timing:

When you're all dressed up and ready to go

The Spell

- Hold the wand, pointed end upward, in front of your face in your dominant hand, saying, *Against creeps and freaks, Good Fairy, protect me, that I may see the one who will be everything to me.*
- Turning clockwise on the spot, make five clockwise circles around yourself, one over the other, with your wand at a forty-five-degree angle, point up and facing outward. Say, *Make me scintillating, totally dazzling, kind fairy. Bring the one who will be everything to me, that there will be love everlastingly.*
- Finally, raise your wand in the air vertically and bring it down behind you in a slashing movement and back up again, waist high, to release the power.
- Say, *No horse and carriage, but maybe marriage, off I go.*

985

A SACRED WATER RITUAL IF YOU ARE OVERSENSITIVE TO GHOSTS AT NIGHT

You will need:

Four white candles, arranged in a square
A small bowl of salt to the left and a small bowl of water to the right, within the square of candles
A silver-colored letter opener in the center of the bowls

Timing:

An hour before bed in your bedroom

The Spell

- Light the four candles clockwise and, taking the letter opener in your dominant hand, touch first the surface of the salt and then the surface of the water with the blade, saying for each one, *May you be blessed and purified, empowered and sanctified.*
- Add nine pinches of salt to the water bowl.
- Swirl the water bowl clockwise nine times and make a cross on the surface repeating the spell words.
- Pass the water bowl clockwise four times over each candle, saying, *Protect me against all specters of the night, that safe I may sleep until morning light.*
- Put water drops either side of the bedroom doorframe, along window ledges, at the four corners of the bed, and at the center of your brow.
- Let the candles burn until you are ready to sleep.

986

A DOUBLE KNIFE UNCROSSING RITUAL FOR PROTECTION BEFORE AN IMPORTANT OFFICIAL MEETING OR COURT CASE WHEN THE KNIVES ARE OUT TO GET YOU

You will need:

A dark-colored candle
Two black-handled kitchen knives (not too sharp)
A piece of paper on which you have written in red the names of those who are out to get you, set in front of the candle
A piece of dark-colored cloth

Timing:

Thursday, after dark

The Spell

- Light the candle and cross the knives over the paper, saying, *Dark deeds indeed, crossed knives bode ill, yet can I remove them and triumph still.*
- Take away one knife and repeat the spell words.
- Remove the remaining knife, wash the knives separately, and put them away.
- Fold the paper in the cloth, extinguish the candle, and, when it is cool, add it to the cloth, knot the cloth, and dispose of the cloth and its contents.

987

A LIFE CHAIN KNOT RITUAL TO KEEP LOVE ALIVE IN THE YEAR AHEAD

You will need:

A thin red ribbon or any strong red cord, about eighteen inches long

Twelve hairs from your head and twelve hairs from your lover's head, one of each entwinedwith the other for each month (you can get these from a brush or a comb)

Thread (optional)

A soft bag to keep your knot cord safe between spells

Timing:

Saturday midnight by a dim lamp, the first day of any month continuing once a month for a year

The Spell

- Tie a knot at the right-hand end of the cord, and hold it in the air, saying, *May the four winds enter this knot and hold the love within.*
- Blow over the knot three times.
- Add the two hairs entwined together to the knot, if necessary using thread, and repeat the spell words.
- Put the knot cord safely in the bag and extinguish the lamp, saying, *Safe are we in love. United shall we be when next we this cord remove.*
- Continue tying knots and performing the spell for the next eleven months and if any hairs become detached, replace them.
- After the year and a day, cast the cord in running water.

988

AN ALCHEMICAL SALT RITUAL FOR ONGOING HEALTH, WEALTH, AND HAPPINESS IN YOUR LIFE

You will need:

A large white or natural beeswax candle

A letter opener or a thin palette knife for marking the wax

A small bowl of salt

A small white bag

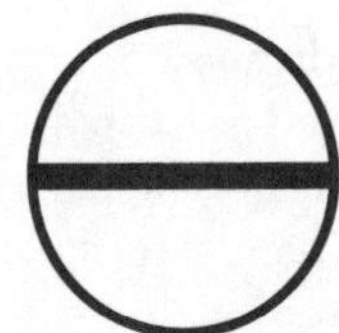

The alchemical sign for salt

Timing:

Beginning Sunday evening, around sunset

The Spell

- Etch the alchemical symbol for salt on the side of the candle.
- Set the candle in the center of your home with the bowl of salt in front of it.
- Light the candle, saying, *Health, wealth, and happiness, gifts I seek these three. Magical salt, I ask you, draw them to me.*
- Draw the symbol on the surface of the salt.
- Sprinkle a few grains of salt into the flame so it sparkles, saying the spell words again. Blow out the candle.
- Repeat the spell exactly each night until the candle is burned through.
- Put some salt in the bag, and on the bag trace with the index finger of your dominant hand the alchemical salt symbol.
- Hide the bag in the room nearest the center of the home.
- Wash away the rest of the salt under a faucet, repeating the spell words.

989

A HYSSOP INFUSION RITUAL FOR CLEANSING ITEMS YOU BUY FROM MARKETS OR GARAGE SALES OR WITH SAD MEMORIES AFTER A DEATH OR DIVORCE

You will need:

Dried or fresh hyssop, the ultimate magical cleansing herb (Note: substitute nettle or dandelion if you're pregnant)
A teacup
A tea strainer and small bottle for the infusion

Timing:
Sunday morning

The Spell

- Place one teaspoon of dried hyssop or three teaspoons of the fresh herb in a boiling cup of water.
- Stir nine times clockwise and nine times counterclockwise, saying, *Hyssop, hyssop, with every drop you make* [name item] *my own. Take away sadness, return gladness. Remove the energies before, and new its energies restore.*
- Cover and leave for five to ten minutes, then strain off the herbs and discard them.
- Stir the strained liquid again nine times clockwise and nine times counterclockwise, saying the spell words again and adding any special influences you want removed, for example, things bought for you by an ex.
- Sprinkle hyssop drops in three circles counterclockwise round the items you want to cleanse (put them together if you wish), saying, *Hyssop, hyssop, with every drop you make* [name item/s] *my own. Take away sadness, return gladness. Remove the energies before and new its energies restore.*
- Pour the remainder of the infusion down a faucet.

990

A FOUR GUARDIANS OF THE WATCHTOWERS RITUAL ON BEHALF OF SOMEONE GOING TO WAR OR WHO HAS A DANGEROUS JOB

You will need:

Four white candles, each at a compass point on an imaginary circle, called, in magick, the Watchtowers
Inside the circle, a photo of the person who is facing danger

Timing:
Tuesday, after dark

The Spell

- Light the candle at the approximate North, saying, *Lady of the Earth, enfold* [name] *in your security, that she will wake and live and sleep, while you unwearyingly watch do keep.*
- Moving clockwise, light the candle in the East from the North one, saying, *Lord of the Skies, enfold* [name] *in your security, that she will wake and live and sleep, while you unwearyingly watch do keep.*
- Light the South candle from the East one, saying, *Lord of the Sun, enfold* [name] *in your security, that she will wake and live and sleep, while you unwearyingly watch do keep.*
- Light the final candle from the South candle, saying, *Lady of the Moon, enfold* [name] *in your security that she will wake and live and sleep, while you unwearyingly watch do keep.*
- Let the candles burn. Repeat weekly with new candles.

991

A PENTACLE CLAY TALISMAN FOR STABILIZING YOUR FINANCES AT A CRITICAL TIME

You will need:

Self-hardening clay
A rolling pin or bottle
Tracing paper
Scissors
A broad-tipped pencil
A palette knife or spatula

A pentacle

Timing:
Saturday, as it gets light

The Spell

- Roll out a circle of soft clay the size you need for your pentacle (a pentagram in a circle) on a wooden cutting board, using a rolling pin or bottle.
- Draw an invoking or attracting pentagram on the tracing paper, cut to precisely the same size as your clay, saying continuously, *Bring stability, restore security, let my finances be contained and no more drained.* Let the five points touch the edges of the paper circle.
- Place the tracing paper over the clay and press down hard with the pencil. Then redraw over the outline so it presses through and appears on the clay, saying continuously, *Bring stability, restore security, let prosperity slowly grow/regrow. By the power of the pentacle, let it be so.* Loosen the clay pentacle with a palette knife or spatula and let the clay harden.
- Keep the amulet with your financial papers.

INVOKING

1, 6
4 3
2, 7 5

992

AN ARCHANGEL PENTAGRAM RITUAL FOR KEEPING AWAY EVIL SPIRITS AND EVIL PEOPLE

You will need:

Nothing

Timing:
Whenever you are afraid

The Spell

- Face approximate East and draw in the air in front of you with your elbow bent, a banishing pentagram (see diagram) using your index and second fingers together of your dominant the hand, and say, *Archangel Raphael, protect me.*
- Start at the bottom left-hand point, level with your left hip, and move your hand upward in a single stroke to draw the top point level with your head.
- Draw the downward point level with your right hip. Go diagonally halfway across to draw the middle point level with your left elbow, straight across horizontally to the right, and down again to the point where you started.
- Turn to the South and draw another banishing pentagram in the air in front of you, saying, *Archangel Michael, protect me.*
- Face West and draw another pentagram in front of you, as before, saying, *Archangel Gabriel, protect me.*
- Face North to create your final pentagram, saying, *Archangel Uriel, protect me.*
- Raise your hands, looking upward, saying, *And above me is the radiant star.*

993

A VIKING BIND OR COMBINED RUNE AMULET FOR COURAGE AND STRENGTH IF YOU NEED TO GET OUT OF A DESTRUCTIVE OR ABUSIVE RELATIONSHIP

You will need:

A small rectangular piece of wood
An etching tool, like an awl or
a sharp screwdriver
Red paint and a thin paintbrush
A red bag to hold the finished bind rune

Timing:

Thursday, the day of the thunder god Thor

The Spell

- Practice drawing *Thurisaz*, Thor's hammer rune, and *Uruz*, the strength of the wild cattle rune separately and then as one bind rune, as shown.

At left, Thurisaz; in the middle, Uruz. The combined rune is at right.

- Smooth a horizontal area in the piece of wood and etch deeply the combined runes to make the bind rune, saying nine times, *By the hammer of Thor and the power of the wild beasts, I shall be free of* [name person or situation that is hurting you].
- Paint the bind rune red, repeating the spell words nine more times.
- Keep the bind rune in a bag and each night and morning open the bag, trace the shape of the bind rune left to right nine times on the wood, and repeat the spell words nine times.

994

A CELTIC TREE STAVE RITUAL TO RESTORE PASSION AND EXCITEMENT TO A MUNDANE RELATIONSHIP OR TO LIFE

The tree stave symbol Ur, which represents Heather

You will need:

A large twig
An etching tool, like an awl or
a sharp screwdriver
A black permanent marker (optional)

Timing:

Friday

The Spell

- Smooth away the bark from one side of the twig and etch on the smooth part of the twig the tree stave symbol Ur (Heather), saying, *Lady Heather, passionate queen, long it seems since passion I have seen. Restore in me the ecstasy, the joy that now is lost within me.*
- Hold the finished stave and repeat the words. If the symbol is not clear, you can enhance it with a black permanent marker.
- Place the stave in soil outside your front door (in a planter, if necessary), facing inward, and each morning, touch the stave and repeat the spell words.

995

AN EGYPTIAN ANKH HIEROGLYPH AMULET RITUAL FOR TWIN SOUL LOVE, WHETHER OR NOT THE LOVER HAS COME INTO YOUR LIFE

You will need:

Red fabric paint and a thin brush or a very thin red waterproof marker
A small square of white linen
A very small clear glass bottle with a stopper

The ankh

Timing:
Friday, during daylight on a full moon night

The Spell

- Draw or paint the ankh symbol on the linen, saying, *Isis and Osiris, twin souls through eternity, within your ankh I call my twin soul to me, the key and symbol of eternal love.*
- Let the paint dry and, as it gets dark and you can see the moon in the sky (even a glimpse), fold the linen into the bottle, symbol facing outward, put on the lid, and hold it up to the moon, saying seven times, *Isis restored Osiris to life, promised immortality. Twin soul come, be with me, and stay throughout eternity.*
- Leave the sealed bottle on an indoor window ledge or outdoors if the weather is fine until the next morning.
- Keep it close to your bed and kiss it every evening.

996

AN EGYPTIAN SCARAB AMULET RITUAL FOR A TOTALLY NEW BEGINNING

You will need:

A bright blue permanent marker or a ceramic scarab (widely available online)
High-quality white paper
A lavender or musk incense stick
A flat stone or a small piece of slate

Timing:
Sunday morning, at dawn

The Spell

- Draw and color in a scarab about as big as your thumb, or if you have a model, set it on the rock, saying in either case, *Scarab of rebirth, scarab of better times on earth, who rolls the sun and gives it birth? You, whose symbol releases power, I ask you on me, opportunities shower.*
- Light the incense and, using it like a smoke pen, draw a smoke scarab outline above the drawing/model over and over again, repeating the spell words, speaking more slowly and quietly and drawing more slowly until words and movements cease.
- Let the incense burn.
- Affix your drawing or set your scarab on the stone in a place indoors that will catch the morning sun, until you feel the energies change around you.
- Then bury your scarab under a plant that loves the sun.

The scarab

997

MAKING A CLAY SALUS RING FOR HEALING A CHRONIC CONDITION THAT IS GETTING WORSE

You will need:

A ball of self-hardening clay
A white or beeswax candle
A thin paper or palette knife for marking the clay
Salt
A white scarf
Silver foil

Timing:

Wednesday, at first light, in the waning moon period

The Spell

- Make a flat round clay disk about the size of your palm. Set it in front of the candle.
- In the center of the disk, draw the Hermes healing caduceus symbol and enclose it in the ouroboros symbol, the coiled snake of long and healthy life (see diagrams). Name who needs healing (it may be yourself) and say, *Healing, health, long life may I* [or name] *know, as long as the sun does shine and the waters flow.*

The ouroboros

- Light the candle and sprinkle a circle of salt clockwise, followed by one counterclockwise on top of the other, repeating the spell words.
- Let the candle burn, and when the clay is hard, wrap the symbol in a three-times knotted scarf with three twists of salt in foil.
- Keep it close to the bed or close to a picture of the sick person.

The caduceus of Hermes

998

MAKING A COPPER AMULET FOR FERTILITY IF YOU TAKE DIFFERENT FERTILITY TREATMENTS OR HAVE TRIED SEVERAL UNSUCCESSFUL IVF TREATMENTS

You will need:

Six small green candles
A copper ring or bracelet (copper should be worn on the left side of the body by right-handed people and on the right by left-handed people)
Rose or lavender essential oil

Timing:

Friday, at sunset

The Spell

- Light each of the candles in turn clockwise, saying for each one, *I charge you with fertility, I charge you with this fire. I will persist, will not desist, until my babe is with me.*
- Pass the ring or bracelet six times around the outside of the candle circle clockwise, saying six times, *Let all that is not beautiful, let all that is not fruitful leave this ring, and I will sing at the conception of my baby.*
- Put on the ring/bracelet and, on your wrist or finger just outside the copper, rub in a few drops of oil clockwise, saying, *I charge you with fertility, I charge you with this water, I will persist, will not desist 'til I have a son or daughter.*
- Blow out the candles and wear the copper until you conceive.

999

MAKING A MAGICAL HEALING POPPET DOLL

You will need:

A rectangle of pink or green fabric, large enough for the two sides of the poppet to be cut from the one piece (the doll need only be tiny)
Scissors
White thread for physical ills and purple for a troubled mind
A needle
A selection of dried healing herbs, for example, lavender, chamomile, mint, rose, and rosemary
Vanilla essence
A white linen cloth

Timing:
Just before sunset

The Spell

- Cut out the front and back of the doll as shown below, saying three times as you cut, *I create this image of* [name] *in love and in healing. May he be healed by the angels and kind Mother Earth,*
- As you sew the doll, visualize each stitch filled with healing light.
- Before you sew up the feet, fill the poppet with the herbs, saying three times, *Herbs of healing, herbs of gentleness, fill* [name] *with your life-giving and restorative light.* Now sew the feet, repeating the first set of spell words.
- Finally, sprinkle over the poppet a few drops of water mixed with one or two drops of vanilla essence, and keep the doll wrapped in white linen until recovery.

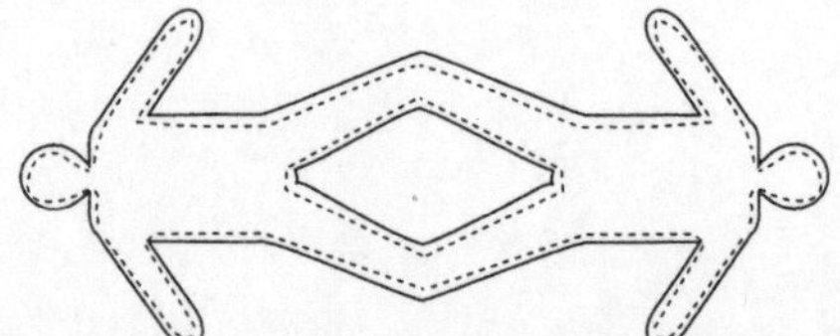

1000

A SEAL OF SOLOMON RITUAL FOR THE PERFECT WEDDING OR SPECIAL OCCASION WHEN NOTHING MUST GO WRONG

You will need:

A blue candle
A piece of white paper divided into six equal squares
A blue pen
A small bowl of water left outdoors from dawn to noon
Adhesive

Timing:
Noon, the day before the event

The Spell

- Light the candle and hold the paper so you can see light through it, saying, *Mystical seal, your power reveal, make this occasion* [name it] *perfect be, for it means so much to me.*
- Place the paper in front of the candle and draw a Solomon's seal in each square, left to right, bottom to top, saying once for each one, *Water descending, Fire ascending, in these elements perfection blending.* When finished, sprinkle water clockwise around the paper.
- Cut the seals out and, before the special occasion, affix each in a different place in the main room where they will not be seen.

The Triangle of Water

The Triangle of Fire

Solomon's Seal

1001

A BE-ALL-END-ALL SPELL TO REMIND YOURSELF THAT YOU ARE THE BEST AND CAN DO ANYTHING

You will need:

A bowl of water
A hand mirror

Timing:
Sunday morning

The Spell

- Stand outdoors facing the sun or the brightest part of the sky.
- Say, *I am as I am and I like what I am and the Earth supports me.*
- Press your feet into the ground and repeat the words.
- Say, *I am as I am and I like what I am and the Air uplifts me.*
- Raise both hands to the sky and repeat the Air words.
- Say, *I am as I am and I like what I am and the Water supports me.* Ripple your hands in a bowl of water and repeat the Water words.
- Say, *I am as I am and I like what I am and the Fire inspires me.*
- Pick up the mirror, smile into it, and say the Fire words again.
- Now turn clockwise in all four directions and, as you do so, say, *Earth supports me, Air uplifts me, Water flows through me, and Fire inspires me.*
- Now do something amazing that you have always wanted to do but never dared. The spell is done.

INDEX

ABOUT THE AUTHOR

During a writing career spanning over forty years, Cassandra Eason has written in excess of 100 books, many of which have been serialized around the world and translated into 13 different languages, including Russian, Japanese, Hebrew, Portuguese, German, Dutch, Spanish, and Chinese. Among her many titles are *The Mammoth Book of Ancient Wisdom, A Little Bit of Crystals, A Little Bit of Tarot, The Psychic Power of Children, The Complete Book of Women's Wisdom*, and *A Spell A Day*.

In addition to her writing, Cassandra had her own weekly mini-series, *Sixth Sense*, on UK cable television for many years. More recently, she worked as the dream analyst for Britain's *Big Brother* for three seasons. She has appeared many times on television and radio on ITV's *Strange But True*, BBC 1's *Heaven and Earth*, and *Richard & Judy* on NBC and Paramount.

Cassandra originally trained as a teacher and, while bringing up her five children, took a psychology Honors degree with the intention of training as an educational psychologist. However, a seemingly inexplicable psychic experience involving her two-year-old son Jack led to extensive research and the publication of a book on psychic children published by Random House in 1990. Over the twenty years since this experience, Cassandra has become one of the UK's most prolific authors, and is now recognized as a world expert on parent/child intuitive links.

For some years, Cassandra worked in Sweden writing directly for the Swedish market, holding regular lecture tours, healing workshops, and training courses for mediums. She presently spends a few months each year touring Australia, running workshops and acting as a psychic consultant throughout major regional centers in Queensland and the Northern Territory.

In the United States, Cassandra has had her work featured in the *National Enquirer* and *Woman's World*.

Cassandra is a regular contributor to such publications as *Spirit and Destiny, Fate & Fortune, Prediction, Homes & Gardens*, and *Good Housekeeping*, and to *Woman's Day* and *New Idea* in Australia. She had her own psychic column in the national women's magazine *Best* and in *Writer's News* and has also written for *Beyond* magazine. Cassandra has also been a regular contributor to *Guardian Woman* and *The Sunday Telegraph*.

ABOUT THE AUTHOR

During a writing career spanning over forty years, Cassandra Eason has written in excess of 100 books, many of which have been serialized around the world and translated into 13 different languages, including Russian, Japanese, Hebrew, Portuguese, German, Dutch, Spanish, and Chinese. Among her many titles are *The Mammoth Book of Ancient Wisdom, A Little Bit of Crystals, A Little Bit of Tarot, The Psychic Power of Children, The Complete Book of Women's Wisdom*, and *A Spell A Day*.

In addition to her writing, Cassandra had her own weekly mini-series, *Sixth Sense*, on UK cable television for many years. More recently, she worked as the dream analyst for Britain's *Big Brother* for three seasons. She has appeared many times on television and radio on ITV's *Strange But True*, BBC 1's *Heaven and Earth*, and *Richard & Judy* on NBC and Paramount.

Cassandra originally trained as a teacher and, while bringing up her five children, took a psychology Honors degree with the intention of training as an educational psychologist. However, a seemingly inexplicable psychic experience involving her two-year-old son Jack led to extensive research and the publication of a book on psychic children published by Random House in 1990. Over the twenty years since this experience, Cassandra has become one of the UK's most prolific authors, and is now recognized as a world expert on parent/child intuitive links.

For some years, Cassandra worked in Sweden writing directly for the Swedish market, holding regular lecture tours, healing workshops, and training courses for mediums. She presently spends a few months each year touring Australia, running workshops and acting as a psychic consultant throughout major regional centers in Queensland and the Northern Territory.

In the United States, Cassandra has had her work featured in the *National Enquirer* and *Woman's World*.

Cassandra is a regular contributor to such publications as *Spirit and Destiny*, *Fate & Fortune*, *Prediction*, *Homes & Gardens*, and *Good Housekeeping*, and to *Woman's Day* and *New Idea* in Australia. She had her own psychic column in the national women's magazine *Best* and in *Writer's News* and has also written for *Beyond* magazine. Cassandra has also been a regular contributor to *Guardian Woman* and *The Sunday Telegraph*.